A DIRECT PATH TO THE BUDDHA WITHIN

Studies in Indian and Tibetan Buddhism

This series was conceived to provide a forum for publishing outstanding new contributions to scholarship on Indian and Tibetan Buddhism and also to make accessible seminal research not widely known outside a narrow specialist audience, including translations of appropriate monographs and collections of articles from other languages. The series strives to shed light on the Indic Buddhist traditions by exposing them to historical-critical inquiry, illuminating through contextualization and analysis these traditions' unique heritage and the signifcance of their contribution to the world's religious and philosophical achievements.

STUDIES IN INDIAN AND TIBETAN BUDDHISM

A DIRECT PATH TO THE BUDDHA WITHIN

Gö Lotsāwa's Mahāmudrā Interpretation of the Ratnagotravibhāga

Klaus-Dieter Mathes

Wisdom Publications • Boston

Wisdom Publications, Inc.
199 Elm Street
Somerville MA 02144 USA
www.wisdompubs.org

Library of Congress Cataloging-in-Publication Data
Mathes, Klaus-Dieter.
A direct path to the Buddha within : Go Lotsāwa's mahāmudrā interpretation of the Ratnagotravibhāga / Klaus-Dieter Mathes.
p. cm.
Includes bibliographical references and index.
ISBN 0-86171-528-4 (pbk. : alk. paper)
1. 'Gos Lo-tsā-ba Gzon-nu-dpal, 1392-1481. Theg pa chen po rgyud bla ma'i bstan bcos kyi 'grel bśad de kho na ñid rab ru gsal ba'i me loṅ. 2. Ratnagotravibhāga—Criticism, interpretation, etc. 3. Mahāmudrā (Tantric rite) I. Title.
BQ3025.G673M37 2008
294.3'420423—dc22

2007036423

12 11 10 09 08
5 4 3 2 1

Cover and interior design by Gopa & Ted2, Inc.
Set in Diacritical Adobe Garamond 10.5/13.

Wisdom Publications' books are printed on acid-free paper and meet the guidelines for permanence and durability of the Production Guidelines for Book Longevity of the Council on Library Resources.

Printed in the United States of America

This book was produced with environmental mindfulness. We have elected to print this title on 50% PCW recycled paper. As a result, we have saved the following resources: 35 trees, 24 million BTUs of energy, 3,074 lbs. of greenhouse gases, 12,758 gallons of water, and 1,638 lbs. of solid waste. For more information, please visit our website, www.wisdompubs.org.

Contents

Abbreviations

BHSD	Edgerton: *Buddhist Hybrid Sanskrit, Dictionary*
BHSG	Edgerton: *Buddhist Hybrid Sanskrit, Grammar*
DRSM	Gos Lo tsā ba Gzhon nu dpal: *Theg pa chen po rgyud bla ma'i bstan bcos kyi 'grel bshad de kho na nyid rab tu gsal ba'i me long*
J	Johnston (with reference to his *Ratnagotravibhāgavyākhyā* edition)
LC	Lokesh Chandra: *Tibetan-Sanskrit Dictionary*
MVY	*Mahāvyutpatti*
MW	Monier Williams: *A Sanskrit-English Dictionary*
NGMPP	Nepal-German Manuscript Preservation Project
Skt.	Sanskrit
Tib.	Tibetan

For the abbreviations of Sanskrit sūtras and śāstras, see the bibliography.

Preface

This mind, O monks, is luminous!
But it is defiled by adventitious defilements.

—The Buddha: *Aṅguttara Nikāya* I.5, 9

Like cloth purified by fire,
[That is,] when one puts [a cloth]
Sullied with various stains over a fire,
The stains are burnt
But not the cloth,
Similarly, with the luminous mind,
Sullied with stains arisen from desire,
The stains are burnt by wisdom
But not the luminous [mind].
Those sūtras taught by the victorious ones
In order to reveal emptiness—
All eliminate defilements
But do not diminish the [buddha] element.

—Nāgārjuna: *Dharmadhātustotra,* stanzas 20–22

NUMEROUS PASSAGES in the sūtras and śāstras distinguish the adventitious stains of a suffering mind from its coexisting natural purity, which is at times called *luminosity, buddha nature,* or *dharmadhātu.* This natural purity is a kind of true nature of mind endowed with innumerable buddha qualities since beginningless time, even during our wildest excesses of attachment or hatred. Put another way, buddha nature (Skt. *tathāgatagarbha*) is empty of adventitious stains but not of its own qualities. If we take the above-quoted passage from the *Dharmadhātustotra* seriously (and all Mahāyāna exegetes accept that this *stotra* was composed by Nāgārjuna), we have to restrict the validity of Madhyamaka logic to the adventitious defilements—anything else cannot be the object of a conceptualizing mind. Some Tibetan interpreters have distinguished two modes of emptiness: being "empty of an own-being" (Tib. *rang stong*), and being "empty of other" (Tib. *gzhan stong*). The former *rangtong* view is that buddha nature means simply that the mind, like all phenomena, lacks an own-being or self. The latter *zhentong* view is that buddha nature is an ultimate nature of mind that is endowed with all buddha qualities and that is empty only of adventitious defilements (the "other"), which do not reflect its true nature.

The old Tibetan discussion of whether the teachings of a luminous mind or buddha nature in the so-called third turning of the wheel of Dharma *(dharmacakra),* such as in the passage above, should be taken more literally or whether the third dharmacakra should be interpreted via the rangtong analysis became a contemporary issue when my Tibetan teachers Khenpo Tsultrim Gyamtsho and Thrangu Rinpoche began to propagate the controversial zhentong interpretation of the *Rgyud bla ma* (the *Uttaratantra* or *Ratnagotravibhāga*) in the 1970s and 80s. Up until then the Tibetan reception of the *Ratnagotravibhāga* had mainly been known of in the West through David Seyfort Ruegg's publications, which were to some extent influenced by the prevailing Gelug (Dge lugs) hermeneutics. The Gelug school follows Candrakīrti's (seventh-century) lead in taking the teaching in the second dharmacakra of the lack of an independent nature or own-being as the underlying intention of any positive statement about the ultimate.

Against this background, it would of course be useful to investigate how other Tibetan schools have interpreted the theory of buddha nature, and when I was appointed director of the Nepal-German Manuscript Preservation Project in Kathmandu in October 1993, I had great hopes of collecting new material for a future research project on this subject. But it was only when I went through the Tibetan texts kept at Chetsang Rinpoche's library in Dehra Dun in March 1997 that I finally discovered something interesting, namely Gö Lotsāwa Zhönu Pal's ('Gos Lo tsā ba Gzhon nu dpal) (1392–1481) *Ratnagotravibhāgavyākhyā* commentary, which is said to belong to the meditation tradition (Tib. *sgom lugs*) of the Maitreya works. A first reading revealed two important points: Zhönu Pal was not at all concerned with propagating *zhentong* (at least not the Jonangpa (Jo nang pa) variety), but he did see in the *Ratnagotravibhāga* and the other Maitreya works doctrinal support for his mahāmudrā tradition.

Having realized the importance of this work, I decided to edit it, and on the basis of an old blockprint of the same text, I was able to publish a critical edition of Zhönu Pal's *Theg pa chen po rgyud bla ma'i bstan bcos kyi 'grel bshad de kho na nyid rab tu gsal ba'i me long* ["A Commentary on the Treatise *Mahāyānottaratantraśāstra (i.e., Ratnagotravibhāga)*—The Mirror Showing

Reality Very Clearly"] at the beginning of 2003. This commentary is the main source for the present study, which was accepted as my habilitation thesis by the University of Hamburg in April 2004.

It is my pleasure to acknowledge the various forms of help I have received from others in preparing this work. First of all, I wish to express my sincere gratitude to the Venerable Thrangu Rinpoche, who assisted me in my research continuously, whether in Kathmandu, Sarnath, or the West, by patiently going through long lists of questions and discussing the subtle points of my research on buddha nature, emptiness, and mahāmudrā. Similar thanks go to Khenpo Lobsang from the Vajra Vidya Institute in Sarnath, who helped me to understand difficult passages in the Tibetan and who, thanks to his having memorized many treatises, was able to identify some of the unattributed quotations. Even though I was able to meet the Venerable Dzogchen Ponlop Rinpoche only once—in the summer of 2002 in Hamburg—I gratefully recall his clear and precise explanations of certain aspects of tantric zhentong, sūtra-mahāmudrā, and essence mahāmudrā at an important stage in my writing.

I also express my gratitude to professors Lambert Schmithausen and David Jackson, who carefully read important parts of my study and offered most welcome solutions to a number of difficult points. Having only joined the Indian and Tibetan Department in Hamburg in the summer of 2001, I nevertheless feel sufficiently qualified to praise the collegial, "bodhisattva-like" atmosphere in which scholarly problems are addressed. This is true in particular of Dr. Diwakar Acharya, who provided repeated assistance in deciphering all the nearly unreadable *akṣaras* of the *Ratnagotravibhāgavyākhyā* manuscripts and in working with the numerous *Laṅkāvatārasūtra* manuscripts from Nepal.

Many thanks also to Philip Pierce (Nepal Research Centre, Kathmandu) and David Kittelstrom (Wisdom Publications) for carefully reading through the entire manuscript and improving my English. Furthermore, I profited from the very fruitful exchanges I had during regular meetings with Kazuo Kano (Kyoto, currently University of Hamburg), whose doctoral thesis on Ngog Loden Sherab's (Rngog Blo ldan shes rab) *Ratnagotravibhāga* commentary (the *Theg chen rgyud bla'i don bsdus pa*) I have been supervising for the past two years.

Finally I would like to thank the German Research Council (Deutsche Forschungsgemeinschaft) for enabling me to conduct the present study in the first place by financially supporting me for three years with a scholarship.

Introduction

General Remarks

THE DOCTRINE of "buddha nature" (Tib. *de bzhin gshegs pa'i snying po*),[1] or the teaching that all sentient beings are already buddhas or have the ability to attain buddhahood (depending on which interpretation you prefer), became an important issue in the fourteenth and fifteenth centuries in Tibet. It was not only much discussed among masters, such as Dölpopa Sherab Gyaltsen (Dol po pa Shes rab rgyal mtshan) (1292–1361), who were intimately involved in the practice of the *Kālacakratantra*, but also came to form an important doctrinal foundation for the dzogchen (rdzogs chen) teachings of Longchen Rabjampa (Klong chen rab 'byams pa) (1308–63) and the mahāmudrā instructions of the Kagyüpas (Bka' brgyud pa). Thus, Rangjung Dorjé (Rang byung rdo rje) (1284–1339) equated buddha nature with the central mahāmudrā term *natural mind* (Tib. *tha mal gyi shes pa*), and Gö Lotsāwa Zhönu Pal ('Gos Lo tsā ba Gzhon nu dpal) (1392–1481) composed an extensive commentary of the standard Indian work on buddha nature, the *Ratnagotravibhāga*, from within the mahāmudrā tradition of Maitrīpa (ca. 1007–ca. 1085)[2] and Gampopa (Sgam po pa) (1079–1153). Zhönu Pal and his mahāmudrā interpretation of the *Ratnagotravibhāga* are the main subject of the present study.

One of the main goals of Zhönu Pal's *Ratnagotravibhāga* commentary is to show that the Kagyü path of mahāmudrā is already taught in the Maitreya works and the *Laṅkāvatārasūtra*. This approach involves resting your mind in a nonconceptual experience of luminosity or the *dharmadhātu* (the expanse or nature of all phenomena) with the help of special "pith instructions" (Tib. *man ngag*) on how to become mentally disengaged.[3] A path of directly realizing buddha nature is thus distinguished from a Madhyamaka path of logical inference[4] and it is with this in mind that Zhönu Pal's commentary can be called a "direct path to the buddha within."

The *Ratnagotravibhāga Mahāyānottaratantra* belongs, if we follow the Tibetan tradition, to the "five treatises of Maitreya,"[5] though its oldest layers had probably already been composed by Sāramati in the third or fourth century. It was not quoted in India until centuries later, and the only safe *terminus ante quem* for it is 508 C.E., the year in which Ratnamati, who translated the *Ratnagotravibhāgavyākhyā* into Chinese, arrived in China from Madhyadeśa (India).[6]

According to Tibetan tradition, the future Buddha Maitreya taught the *Ratnagotravibhāga* to Asaṅga in the Tuṣita heaven. Asaṅga is also said to have composed the *Ratnagotravibhāgavyākhyā*. This commentary on the *Ratnagotravibhāga* quotes a number of sūtras that teach that all sentient beings possess the nature of a buddha, doubtlessly in the sense that they are already complete buddhas but do not know and actualize their true being because of their adventitious stains or spiritual defilements. But the *Ratnagotravibhāga* and its *vyākhyā* also contain passages that try to embed the teaching of buddha nature within mainstream Mahāyāna and relate it, for example, with suchness, and thus only with the cause or seed of buddhahood.

Such a form of the *tathāgatagarbha* theory can be discerned in the Yogācāra works among the Maitreya texts,[7] and in his *Madhyamakāloka*, Kamalaśīla (ca. 740–95) brings the *tathāgatagarbha* theory in line with Madhyamaka thought in order to establish the teaching of a single path *(ekayāna)*.[8] But the Indian reaction on the whole was simply to ignore the *Ratnagotravibhāga* and its teaching of buddha nature for six centuries. Things changed, however, in the eleventh century. During this period scholars such as Jñānakīrti (tenth/eleventh century)[9] or Maitrīpa started to use tantric terms more freely. Their works reflect the latest developments in Indian Buddhism, which may be characterized as a genuine attempt to incorporate certain elements of the originally tantric teachings of the mahāsiddhas into the more traditional mainstream Mahāyāna, though they still maintained the superiority of tantra. In this undertaking, the teaching of buddha nature proved to provide good doctrinal support, and thus, not surprisingly, the *Ratnagotravibhāga* became a highly esteemed treatise in these circles. Tradition has it that the *Dharmadharmatāvibhāga* and the *Ratnagotravibhāga* were rediscovered and taught by Maitrīpa, but Maitrīpa's teacher at Vikramaśīla, Jñānaśrīmitra (ca. 980–1040),[10] must have already known these two works when he composed his *Sākārasiddhiśāstra*[11] and *Sākārasaṃgraha*.[12] Ratnākaraśānti, another teacher of Maitrīpa, also quotes the *Ratnagotravibhāga* in the *Sūtrasamuccayabhāṣya*.[13] Maitrīpa passed the *Dharmadharmatāvibhāga* and the *Ratnagotravibhāga* on to *Ānandakīrti and Sajjana. With the help of Sajjana, the Tibetan scholar Ngog Loden Sherab (Rngog Loden Sherab) (1059–1109) translated the *Ratnagotravibhāga* and its *vyākhyā* into Tibetan. For Loden Sherab (Blo ldan shes rab) buddha nature was a synonym of emptiness, which could be realized by means of nonaffirming negations. He thus founded what is known as the *analytical tradition (mtshan nyid lugs)* of interpreting the Maitreya works.

The corresponding *meditation tradition (sgom lugs)* was founded by Tsen Kawoché (Btsan Kha bo che) (b. 1021), who received explanations of the *Ratnagotravibhāga* from Sajjana with the help of the translator Zu Gawai Dorjé (Gzu Dga' ba'i rdo rje).[14]

This set the stage for the different interpretations of the *Ratnagotravibhāga* in Tibet. The main issues at stake were whether the teaching that all sentient beings are already buddhas within themselves has a provisional or a definitive meaning—in other words, whether the doctrine of buddha nature was taught with the intention of furthering beings who would otherwise be afraid of the true doctrine of emptiness, or whether the Buddha truly meant that sentient beings are buddhas within. Among those who accepted the teaching of buddha nature as definitive, it was further discussed whether all or only some qualities already exist in sentient beings, and whether they exist in a fully developed or only a subtle way. Apart from these issues, the *Ratnagotravibhāga* and its related sūtras were also used in different ways to doctrinally support disputed traditions, such as the zhentong *(gzhan stong)* ("empty of other") of the Jonangpas (Jo nang pa) or sūtra-based mahāmudrā.

Delimitation of the Subject and Methods Employed

To determine Gö Lotsāwa Zhönu Pal's position on buddha nature, which is the main goal of the present study, we are forced to rely completely on his extensive commentary on the *Ratnagotravibhāgavyākhyā,* for the simple reason that it is his only philosophical work available to date. Fortunately, his work is far more than a simple commentary. It not only quotes and discusses nearly all Mahāyāna treatises and a number of sūtras, but also explains a few passages of the *Ratnagotravibhāga* in the light of the (sūtra-based) mahāmudrā tradition of Maitrīpa and Gampopa. Still, the result of our analysis must remain preliminary, since it is difficult to say whether Zhönu Pal's commentary on the *Ratnagotravibhāga* reveals his true opinion on the subject of buddha nature. It may well be that, like others, his statements as a commentator merely reflect an ordinary explanation in line with general Mahāyāna, the final view on the buddha qualities and so forth being revealed only in a tantric context. Dölpopa (Dol po pa), for one, refrains as a commentator from presenting his extraordinary zhentong understanding in his *Ratnagotravibhāga* commentary. If we only had Dölpopa's *Ratnagotravibhāga* commentary, then we would have remained ignorant of his full-fledged zhentong interpretation.[15]

Zhönu Pal subdivides his commentary into three explanations for disciples with sharp, average, and inferior faculties.[16] Besides his introductory remarks, it is the explanation for those with average faculties which is of particular interest. Technically, it is a commentary on the first three stanzas of the first chapter of the *Ratnagotravibhāga*. The mahāmudrā-based explanations Zhönu Pal offers in his commentary on the threefold purification of a *vaiḍūrya* gem and the three dharmacakras[17] in RGVV I.2 are especially helpful in assessing his hermeneutic strategy of fully endorsing the *Saṁdhinirmocanasūtra,* which only assigns definitive meaning to the teachings of the last dharmacakra. The superiority of the last dharmacakra derives, according to Zhönu Pal, from the particularly efficient, direct approach to the natural mind that the mahāmudrā pith instructions allow. An annotated translation of this explanation for disciples with average faculties thus forms, together with the translation of the introduction and the explanation for those with sharp faculties, the basis of our analysis of Zhönu Pal's *Ratnagotravibhāga* commentary.

Because Zhönu Pal deals in the main part of his commentary with almost every aspect of the Buddhist doctrine, it is necessary to delimit the scope of our inquiry and define methodological principles that will enable us to structure this vast material and evaluate it in terms of a history of ideas. In other words, it is first necessary to identify and describe the specific points Zhönu Pal makes with regard to buddha nature in order to be able to systematically compare his position with those of other exegetes.[18] An initial study of Zhönu Pal's *Ratnagotravibhāgavyākhyā* commentary suggests three promising lines of inquiry:

1. What does Zhönu Pal mean by the presence of "subtle" buddha qualities in sentient beings?
2. How does Zhönu Pal tie the teaching of buddha nature in with the *prajñāpāramitā* literature by distinguishing two types of emptiness?
3. In what way does Zhönu Pal read his mahāmudrā pith instructions into certain passages of the *Ratnagotravibhāga,* the other Maitreya works, and the *Laṅkāvatārasūtra?*

Given Zhönu Pal's broad educational background,[19] a systematic comparison of his views with all other major commentarial traditions of his time would seem called for, but such a wide-ranging study would go beyond the scope of a single monograph. Since it is Zhönu Pal's main concern to explain the *Ratnagotravibhāga* and the other Maitreya works from within his mahāmudrā tradition, which is closely related to the meditation tradition of Tsen Kawoché,[20] Zhönu Pal's position will be mainly evaluated against the background of a carefully chosen selection of interpretations by masters of the Kagyü, Nyingma (Rnying ma), and Jonang (Jo nang) schools who figure within or are close to his tradition. The fourteenth century, which experienced some of the most important developments of the above-mentioned traditions, together with the fifteenth century, Zhönu Pal's own century, will form the time frame for the present study.

The earliest exegete I have chosen is the Third Karmapa Rangjung Dorjé (1284–1339), who not only stands in the tradition of Tsen Kawoché,[21] but also combines mahāmudrā and dzogchen with Asaṅga's Yogācāra, whose strict distinction between an impure *ālayavijñāna* (basic consciousness) and the pure dharmadhātu (expanse of phenomena) served as a basis for later zhentong traditions. The next two are Dölpopa (1292–1361) and his disciple Sabzang Mati Panchen (Sa bzang Mati paṇ chen) (1294–1376), both of whom contributed considerably to the spiritual history of Tibet by their extraordinary zhentong interpretation of buddha nature. Since Rangjung Dorjé assimilated dzogchen ideas, it is also of great interest to determine Longchen Rabjampa's view on buddha nature,[22] which may have influenced Zhönu Pal's theory of beginningless subtle qualities. In fact, Zhönu Pal's teacher Lhakhang Tengpa Sangyé Rinchen (Lha khang steng pa Sangs rgyas rin chen) (1339–1434)[23] belonged, together with Longchenpa, to the circle of disciples of the Sakya (Sa skya) master Lama Dampa Sönam Gyaltsen (Bla ma Dam pa Bsod nams rgyal mtshan) (1312–75).[24] Of great interest is also a *Ratnagotravibhāga* commentary by Sangpupa Lodrö Tsungmé (Gsang phu pa Blo gros mtshungs med) (thirteenth/fourteenth century) who, as an assistant professor under Jamyang Shākzhön ('Jam dbyangs Shāk gzhon),[25] must have had some exchange of views with the Third Karmapa Rangjung Dorjé about the *Ratnagotravibhāga*.[26] Finally I have selected the Drugpa ('Brug pa) Kagyü master Barawa Gyaltsen Palzang ('Ba' ra ba Rgyal mtshan dpal bzang) (1310–91), whose mahāmudrā interpretation of buddha nature is nearly identical with that of Zhönu Pal.

The differences between the various *Ratnagotravibhāga* commentaries, while numerous, are often a matter of minor technical detail, and in order to avoid a mere collection of subsidiary material, we will concentrate in each case on a few major philosophical issues that can be directly compared or related with the three above-mentioned questions regarding Zhönu Pal's position. Toward this goal it is not enough to simply compare how a few crucial stanzas of the *Ratnagotravibhāga* are explained. Especially since *Ratnagotravibhāga* commentaries do not survive for each chosen exegete, and furthermore, in some cases only the independent works of the master clearly reveal his philosophical views. To give an example, when reading Dölpopa's commentary on RGV I.152–53 (J I.149–50),[27] we could get the impression that the fortified potential, from which the qualities of the form kāyas arise, is something newly acquired by effort, and based on this passage alone we are not able to correctly describe the Jonang position that in reality all buddha qualities exist throughout beginningless time. The explanation of this *prima facie* contradiction is that the latter is the extraordinary explanation, which is not given in an ordinary commentary. But we only come to know this by consulting Dölpopa's *Ri chos nges don rgya mtsho*. Longchenpa, on the other hand, comments on these stanzas (RGV I.152–53) in the nontantric part of his *Grub mtha' mdzod* fully in line with the dzogchen notion that qualities are not produced but spontaneously present. Thus the ascertainment of a given exegete's philosophical position not only involves a critical assessment of the sources used, be it his *Ratnagotravibhāga* commentary or any other text, but also requires a thorough knowledge of the hermeneutical principles to which an exegete adheres.

Still, while our limited selection of texts by these fourteenth-century masters does not provide scope for a comprehensive description of the traditions related to Zhönu Pal's position in this period, it does provide a basis for depicting a few first prominent spots on an otherwise empty map, and so serves as a preliminary guide for understanding the development of ideas during this interesting period. To sum up, my study of Rangjung Dorjé, Longchenpa, Lodrö Tsungmé (Blo gros mtshungs med), Barawa, and the Jonang position remains a first step and is only meant to better contextualize some of Zhönu Pal's important views on the buddha nature.

The "analytic" interpretations of the *Ratnagotravibhāga* in the Gelug and Sakya traditions have been accurately dealt with by Seyfort Ruegg.[28] Zhamar Chödrag Yeshé (Zhva dmar Chos grags ye shes) (1453–1524) mentions in his biography of Zhönu Pal the interesting detail that the latter was fond of Tsongkhapa (Tsong kha pa) (1357–1419) for having taught a possible distinction between provisional and definitive meaning according to the *Ratnagotravibhāga*.[29] On the other hand, Zhönu Pal is reported to have had an argument with Tsongkhapa's student Gyaltsab Jé (Rgyal tshab rje) (1364–1432) over great bliss in highest yoga tantra (Tib. *rnal 'byor bla na med pa'i rgyud*). While Gyaltsab Jé explained that such bliss cannot be ascertained as anything, Zhönu Pal insisted that there is a way of ascertaining it in his (Zhönu Pal's) own tradition.[30] It would thus be interesting to find out if Tsongkhapa really did uphold, contrary to his disciple Gyaltsab Jé, a tradition embracing a positive direct approach to the ultimate—one that met with the approval of Zhönu Pal—but this would go beyond the scope of this study.

The Ratnagotravibhāga *and Its* Vyākhyā

The *Ratnagotravibhāgavyākhyā* was translated from the Tibetan by Obermiller in 1931. After Johnston (1950) had edited the original Sanskrit on the basis of two manuscripts brought by Sāṅkṛtyāyana from Tibet, the *vyākhyā* was translated for a second time, from the Sanskrit, by Takasaki (1966). Both Johnston's edition and Takasaki's translation are pioneering works,[31] yet they contain a number of serious mistakes, as can be seen from de Jong's (1979) and Schmithausen's (1971) extensive reviews. Unfortunately, the latter two did not correct the entire edition and translation, so each time I quote and translate or refer to a passage from the *Ratnagotravibhāgavyākhyā,* I have had to check the original manuscript. Even though Seyfort Ruegg's (1969) French paraphrases of the most important parts of the latter are also very valuable, they are sometimes too influenced by the prevailing Gelug interpretation of the *Ratnagotravibhāga.*[32] In RGVV I.1, for example, the buddha qualities are characterized, based on a quotation from the *Anūnatvāpūrṇatvanirdeśa,* as being inseparable:

> "Śāriputra, the dharmakāya taught by the tathāgata possesses inseparable *(avinirbhāga)* properties and qualities impossible to recognize as something disconnected *(avinirmuktajñāna-),* in the form of properties of the tathāgata, which surpass in number the grains of sand of the river Gaṅgā." Thus the sixth vajra point should be understood according to the *Anūnatvāpūrṇatvanirdeśa.*[33]

Seyfort Ruegg (1969:360) regards the compound members *avinirbhāga*— and *avinirmuktajñāna*—as qualifications of the dharmakāya and translates: "...le dharmakāya...a pour qualité d'être inséparable, et il a la propriété du savoir non séparé—[inséparable] des dharma de *tathāgata* dépassant [en leur nombre] les sables de la Gaṅgā." In the *Śrīmālādevīsūtra,* however, both compounds are used to mark the buddha qualities,[34] which is also the most natural grammatical construction here.[35] The difference is significant. If the qualities themselves are inseparable, it is much more difficult to read the Gelug understanding that the qualities are produced by the fortified potential[36] into the *Ratnagotravibhāga.* Still, Seyfort Ruegg's work was groundbreaking in having accurately described the *Ratnagotravibhāga* interpretation of the later dominant school of Tibetan Buddhism, the Gelug, whose lines of scholastic thought sometimes influenced the other schools.

The *Ratnagotravibhāgavyākhyā* quotes a group of sūtras which clearly state that all sentient beings possess a buddha nature that is inseparably endowed with innumerable buddha qualities. This doctrine is clearly expounded in the nine examples from the *Tathāgatagarbhasūtra,* which are also presented and discussed in detail in the *Ratnagotravibhāga.* According to Michael Zimmermann, all nine examples convey the idea of a full-fledged tathāgata in living beings throughout beginningless time. The authors of the *Tathāgatagarbhasūtra* were obviously somewhat uncautious, attributing as they did substantialist notions to buddha nature and fitting them out with philosophically ambiguous terminology.[37] It could be argued, as Zhönu Pal does,[38] that the examples of a tree grown from a seed and the future monarch *(cakravartin)* in the womb indicate a growth of the buddha qualities, but in support of the original purport of the sūtra, we can say that the main focus of the example of the tree lies not on the growing tree, but on the imperishability of its seed and that the result *(kārya),* namely the tree, is already contained in the seed. Again, in the second example adduced, that the *cakravartin* is still an embryo does not seem crucial for understanding it. His nature of being a *cakravartin* will not change, for his future role is already preordained, and his poor mother already protected.[39]

The *Śrīmālādevīsūtra,* too, conveys the idea that the inconceivable buddha qualities are inseparable from buddha nature. In other words, sentient beings already possess the buddha qualities, and only differ from an actual buddha in that they have not yet purified themselves from their adventitious stains. This is also supported by the *Anūnatvāpūrṇatvanirdeśaparivarta* which is quoted in RGVV I.1 as canonical support for the fourth vajra point, namely buddha nature:

> "Śāriputra, *ultimate* is an expression for the [buddha] element in sentient beings. The *[buddha] element in sentient beings,* Śāriputra, is an expression for buddha nature. *Buddha nature,* Śāriputra, is an expression for the dharmakāya."[40] Thus the fourth vajra point should be understood according to the *Anūnatvāpūrṇatvanirdeśaparivarta.*[41]

The crucial stanzas on emptiness in the *Ratnagotravibhāga* and its *vyākhyā* (RGV I.157–58, (J I.154–55)) are also clear in this respect: they fully endorse the inseparable connection of the qualities with buddha nature:

> There is nothing to be removed from it and nothing to be added.
> The real should be seen as real, and seeing the real, you
> become liberated.[42]

> The [buddha] element is empty of adventitious [stains], which have the defining characteristic of being separable; but it is not empty of unsurpassable qualities, which have the defining characteristic of not being separable.[43]

The *vyākhyā* is:

> What is taught by that? There is no characteristic sign of any of the defilements *(saṁkleśa)* whatsoever to be removed from this naturally pure buddha element, because it is naturally devoid of adventitious stains. Nor does anything need to be added to it as the characteristic sign *(nimitta)* of purification, because its nature is to have pure properties that are inseparable [from it].[44] Therefore it is said [in the *Śrīmālādevīsūtra*]: "Buddha nature is empty of the sheath of all defilements, which are separable and recognized as something disconnected. It is not empty[, however,] of inconceivable buddha qualities, which are inseparable [in that it is impossible] to recognize [them] as something disconnected, and which surpass in number the grains of sand of the river Gaṅgā." Thus we truly see that something is empty of that which does not exist in it, and we truly realize that that which remains there is present, [and] hence exists there. Having [thus] abandoned the extremes of [wrong] assertion and denial, these two stanzas correctly elucidate the defining characteristic of emptiness.[45]

This passage clearly states, in the sense of the *Śrīmālādevīsūtra,* that buddha nature is not empty of inseparable qualities, and the traditional formula on being empty as found in the *Cūḷasuññatasutta*[46] confirms that these inseparable qualities are left in emptiness.[47] The quotation from the *Śrīmālādevīsūtra* that immediately follows in the *vyākhyā* ("The tathāgatas' wisdom [that knows] emptiness is the wisdom [that knows] the buddha nature"[48]) must be understood in the same context. The sūtra does not simply here equate the buddha nature with Madhyamaka emptiness, but takes emptiness as an aspect of the buddha nature, namely its being empty of adventitious stains. Seyfort Ruegg remarks on this point that the *Ratnagotravibhāgavyākhyā* tries to integrate the theory of emptiness into a particular doctrine of an absolute that is inseparable from buddha qualities.[49] Schmithausen here identifies a form of "inclusivism" under which emptiness is understood as buddha nature empty of adventitious stains.[50]

On the other hand, there are some passages in the *Ratnagotravibhāga* and its *vyākhyā* that try to avoid a too substantialist notion of buddha nature and its qualities. Thus, RGV I.29 introduces the ten aspects of buddha nature in the first chapter with the remark that the latter are taught with the underlying intention of the ultimate buddha element:

> [The ten aspects are:] [its] own-being, cause, fruit, function, connection, manifestation, phases, all-pervasiveness, unchangeability, and inseparable qualities. With regard to them we should know that the intended meaning [is that] of the ultimate [buddha] element.[51]

In other words, RGV I.29 would have us understand the unchangeability of the element and inseparability of its qualities in terms of the ultimate aspect of buddha nature—this, after all, is also implied in the above-quoted passage from the *Anūnatvāpūrṇatvanirdeśa,* which equates buddha nature not only with the dharmakāya, but also with the ultimate. Now two different sets of qualities can be taken as pertaining to the ultimate. First, an ultimate kāya *(paramārthakāya)* is said to be endowed with the "thirty-two qualities of the dharmakāya"[52] (i.e., the ten strengths, the four fearlessnesses, and the eighteen exclusive features);[53] and secondly, an ultimate aspect is referred to in the introduction of the *Ratnagotravibhāgavyākhyā* to the stanzas II.29–37,[54] in the following way:

> The explanation that the Buddha has the defining characteristics of space was taught with the underlying intention of the ultimate and exclusive buddha characteristic of the tathāgatas.[55]

In RGV II.46c–47d it is further specified how the endowment of immeasurable qualities is to be understood:

> Since its nature is [that of] the dharmadhātu, [the svābhāvikakāya] is luminous and pure.
>
> The svābhāvikakāya is endowed with qualities that are immeasurable, innumerable, inconceivable, and incomparable, and that have reached the [state of] final purity.[56]

In other words, the svābhāvikakāya is here said to possess largely space-like qualities, which are not at variance with the concept of emptiness in mainstream Mahāyāna. Various Tibetan exegetes such as Barawa saw in this ultimate aspect of the qualities the inseparable qualities of the *Śrīmālādevīsūtra* and the *Anūnatvāpūrṇatvanirdeśa.* Following this line of thought, Gö Lotsāwa Zhönu Pal, for example, took the sixth and the eighth examples of the *Tathāgatagarbhasūtra* as an indication that the qualities exhibit aspects of growth, notwithstanding the clear intention of the sūtra, which becomes evident in its explanation of the fifth example (a treasure buried under a poor man's house), where buddha nature is fully equated with the thirty-two qualities of the dharmakāya.[57] The *Ratnagotravibhāga* (I.117 (J I.114)), which otherwise faithfully renders the nine examples of the *Tathāgatagarbhasūtra,* only speaks of the *treasure of properties (dharmanidhi).*[58] That this is not only an unintentional inaccuracy is clear from RGV I.152–55 (J I.149–52), where the treasure illustrates the naturally present potential, from which the svābhāvikakāya (i.e., the thirty-two qualities of the dharmakāya) is said to be obtained (see below). In other words, the treasure of buddha nature no longer stands for the thirty-two qualities of the dharmakāya, but rather for their cause. Given these somewhat unbalanced strands of the *Ratnagotravibhāga,* we can either follow the *Tathāgatagarbhasūtra* and fully equate the qualities of buddha nature with the thirty-two qualities of the dharmakāya, or elaborate on a difference between a buddha nature that consists of merely space-like qualities, on the one hand, and a buddha endowed with all qualities, on the other.

Such a strategy of distinguishing buddha nature from the dharmakāya finds support from one of the oldest building blocks of the *Ratnagotravibhāga,* stanza I.27,[59] which implies a subtle distinction between buddha nature, or potential, and an actual buddha:

> By virtue of the presence of buddha wisdom in [all] kinds of
> sentient beings,
> The fact that its (i.e., buddha nature's) stainlessness is by nature
> without duality
> And the fact that its (i.e., buddha nature's) fruit has been
> "metaphorically" applied (Skt. *upacāra*) to the buddha potential,
> All sentient beings are said to possess the essence of a buddha.[60]

Zhönu Pal here explains *upacāra* by citing the example of a Brahmin boy who is called a lion because he is a hero and fearless.[61] Whereas a real lion is an animal, the word *lion* is applied to the brave boy only metaphorically. It may be the case, however, that *upacāra* simply stands for a "custom or manner of speech," the buddha potential being vaguely called a buddha, even though the buddha element, which already possesses its inseparable qualities, has not yet been purified from its separable stains.[62] But Dölpopa, for whom the only difference between an actual buddha and buddha nature is whether one has purified all stains or not, ignores this stanza, while his disciple Sabzang Mati Panchen has great difficulty in making it fit the Jonang position.

Further support for a distinction between different sets of qualities is offered in the first three stanzas of the third chapter of the *Ratnagotravibhāga,* which distinguish between the qualities of the dharmakāya (i.e., the ultimate kāya) and those of the form kāyas:

> Benefit for oneself and others is [equivalent respectively to] the state of having the ultimate kāya and the kāyas of apparent [truth], which are based on it. Representing the state of dissociation and maturation, the fruit possesses a variety of sixty-four qualities.
>
> The body partaking of the ultimate is the support for accomplishing one's own benefit, while the support for accomplishing the benefit of others is the embodiment *(vapuḥ)* of the Sage on the level of conventional [truth].
>
> The first body is endowed with the qualities of dissociation, such as the [ten] strengths, and the second with those of maturation, the [thirty-two] marks of a great being.[63]

The major (and minor) marks of a buddha, or the thirty-two qualities of the form kāyas, are called qualities of maturation and belong to the conventional level of truth. This distinction between two sets of qualities is also clearly stated in RGV I.152–55 (J I.149–52):

> One should know that the potential is twofold in being like a treasure and a tree [grown] from a fruit. It is the primordial naturally present [potential] and the acquired (=fortified)[64] supreme [potential].
>
> It is maintained that the three kāyas of the Buddha are obtained [by starting] from these two potentials: the first kāya from the first, and the latter two from the second.
>
> One should know that the beautiful svābhāvikakāya is like a precious image, since it is nonartificial by nature and since it is the source[65] of precious qualities.
>
> The saṁbhoga[kāya] is like the *cakravartin,* since it possesses the great kingdom of Dharma. The nirmāṇa[kāya] is like the golden statue, since its nature is that of being a reflection.[66]

In other words, the form kāyas and thus their qualities are obtained from the acquired or fortified potential, which is normally explained as the accumulation of merit. It should be noted that it is only the svābhāvikakāya that is described as "nonartificial." Given that in RGV III.3 the ultimate kāya is said to be endowed with the ten strengths, etc. (i.e., the thirty-two qualities of the dharmakāya), the latter cannot be taken as something artificially produced either.

Another important issue among Tibetan scholars was the question whether the *Ratnagotravibhāga* comments on sūtras that have definitive or provisional meanings, namely whether the teaching of buddha nature is to be taken literally or interpreted in line with the emptiness taught in the *prajñāpāramitā* sūtras. Immediately after the stanzas on emptiness (RGV I.157–58 (J I.154–55)), the relation between the teachings of the *prajñāpāramitā* sūtras and the *tathāgatagarbha* sūtras, together with the aim of the latter, is spelled out:

> [Somebody] says: If the [buddha] element is thus so difficult to see, given that it is not a fully experiential object for even the highest saints who abide on the final level of nonattachment, what is gained then by teaching it [even] to foolish (i.e., ordinary) people? [Thus] the [following] two stanzas [are dedicated] to a summary of the aim/motive *(prayojana)* of the teaching. One is the question, and in the second the explanation [is given]:
>
> > Why did the buddhas teach here that a buddha element exists in all sentient beings, after they taught everywhere[67] that everything should be known to be empty in every respect, like clouds, [visions in a] dream and illusions.
> >
> > One may have the five faults of being discouraged, contempt for inferior persons, clinging to the unreal [adventitious stains], denying real [buddha] properties, and excessive self-love. [A buddha element] has been [already] taught [at this stage] in order that those who have these [faults] abandon them.[68]

According to Madhyamaka hermeneutics, you have to fulfill three requirements in order to show that a teaching has a provisional meaning *(neyārtha)*, that is, that it has been given with a hidden intention (Skt. *ābhiprāyika*, Tib. *dgongs pa can*).[69] You have to be able to name the basis of such an intention, or the intentional ground (Tib. *dgongs gzhi*), namely the hidden truth; the motive (Skt. *prayojana,* Tib. *dgos pa*) behind the provisional statement; and a contradiction that results from taking the provisional statement literally (Tib. *dngos la gnod byed*).[70] Seyfort Ruegg has shown that the exegetical principles of the Madhyamaka school were already applied in Dharmamitra's subcommentary on Haribhadra's (ca. 800) *Abhisamayālaṁkāravṛtti,* the *Prasphuṭapadā,*[71] and it is not entirely impossible that early forms of these principles were already being used at the time stanzas I.159–60 (J I.156–57) of the *Ratnagotravibhāga* were written. Nor is it impossible to see in the *Ratnagotravibhāga* a formal proof that the teaching of buddha nature has a hidden intention and thus a provisional meaning. The intentional ground would be emptiness as taught in the *prajñāpāramitā,* and the motive of teaching buddha nature the removal of the five faults; while the contradiction between the teachings of the *prajñāpāramitā* sūtras and the *tathāgatagarbha* sūtras is clearly formulated in RGV I.159 (J I.156).[72]

The first three introductory stanzas (RGV I.1–3), on the other hand, suggest that the final editor of the *Ratnagotravibhāga* and its *vyākhyā* was more familiar with the five principles of Yogācāra hermeneutics.[73] In the *Vyākhyāyukti* these five principles, which must be addressed when explaining the meaning of a sūtra, are: (1) the aim/motive *(prayojana),* (2) the concise meaning, (3) the meaning of the words, (4) the connections [between its different topics], and (5) the objections [urged by opponents] together with rebuttals [of them].[74] It is obvious that the concise meaning of the treatise (point 2) can be presented by listing the seven vajra points (Buddha, Dharma, Saṅgha, buddha nature, enlightenment, buddha qualities, and activity) in RGV I.1, while the connections between them (point 4) are clearly explained in RGV I.3. We could further argue that the meaning of the words *(padārtha) buddha,* etc. (point 3), is explained by the term *vajra point* (or *-word*) *(vajrapada),* which conveys the notion that these seven points are difficult to realize by listening and thinking.[75] The seven main topics of the treatise (vajra points) thus hint at a reality that is beyond the reach of the intellect, and the aim (point 1) of the treatise would then be to realize this reality.[76] Whether the aim called for by the *Vyākhyāyukti* is hinted at in RGV I.1 or not,[77] the way it is described in RGV I.160 (J I.157) accords with Vasubandhu's list of possible aims in the *Vyākhyāyukti.*[78] If it is thus the hermeneutics of the Yogācāra school that is being followed in this passage of the *Ratnagotravibhāga* and its *vyākhyā,* the mentioning of an aim in the RGV does not imply that the latter is *neyārtha.*[79] Moreover, stanzas I.159–60 (J I.156–57) would seem to present a contradiction urged by opponents and a rebuttal of it (point no. 5 of the *Vyākhyāyukti*).

In this case, however, it is the *prajñāpāramitā* sūtras that are *neyārtha* and whose intention *(abhiprāya)*[80] must be clarified in the light of the tathāgatagarbha doctrine, precisely the way it has been done in the preceding stanzas I.157–58 (J I.154–55). This is, at least, the hermeneutic strategy of the *Vyākhyāyukti,* in which Vasubandhu tries to show that the *prajñāpāramitā* sūtras can only be protected against criticism on the part of the Hīnayāna schools (which assert that the "nihilistic" teaching of the *prajñāpāramitā* harms people)[81] by demonstrating that the teaching of emptiness possesses a thought content *(ābhiprāyika)* of what is really true. Therefore it must be interpreted in the light of this truth, which is the *trisvabhāva* theory.[82] While Vasubandhu refers to the *Saṁdhinirmocanasūtra,*[83] the *Ratnagotravibhāgavyākhyā* adduces the *Dhāraṇīśvararājasūtra,* in which the three dharmacakras are explained as in the *Saṁdhinirmocanasūtra,* except that the second dharmacakra, with the *prajñāpāramita* sūtras, is not explicitly called *neyārtha.* Still, the ambiguous term *leading principle of the tathāgata (tathāgatanetrī)* doubtlessly hints in this direction.[84] To sum up this possible interpretation, for the reasons described in stanza I.160 (J I.157) it is necessary to clarify already at an early stage the provisional teaching of emptiness in the *prajñāpāramitā* sūtras with the help of the *nītārtha* teaching of buddha nature, even though the latter is difficult to grasp even for advanced bodhisattvas.

The uncertainty of the *Dhāraṇīśvararājasūtra* with regard to the status of the second dharmacakra leaves room for a third interpretation, namely that both the second and third dharmacakras are *nītārtha.* Following this line of thought, we could argue that since buddha nature is taught as being as inconceivable as emptiness, stanza I.159 (J I.156) does not simply express a contradiction between the teachings of the *prajñāpāramitā* sūtras and *tathāgatagarbha* sūtras, but rather objects that either the two dharmacakras contradict each other or the teaching of an inexpressible buddha nature (third dharmacakra) is a redundant repetition of the teaching of an inexpressible emptiness (second dharmacakra). Stanza I.160 (J I.157) would then explain why the third dharmacakra is not redundant, even though it is in accordance with the second dharmacakra.[85]

What goes against the first possibility, that is, the theory that the author of the final *Ratnagotravibhāga* views his own treatise as *neyārtha,* is its entire fifth chapter, which explains the advantages of experiencing faith in buddha nature, enlightenment, the buddha qualities, and activity. In stanza V.5 it is said, for example, that only hearing one word of these teachings on buddha nature yields much more merit then anything else.[86] This reminds us very much of *Saṁdhinirmocanasūtra* VII.31–32, which describes in a similar way the advantage of hearing the teachings of definitive meaning *(nītārtha),* namely those of the third dharmacakra.[87] Stanza RGV V.20, which refers to the means of avoiding becoming deprived of the teaching, also warns against violating the sūtras of definitive meaning:

> There is nobody anywhere in this world who is more learned than the Victorious One,
> No other who is omniscient and knows completely the highest truth in the right way.
> Therefore, the sūtra[s] of definitive meaning put forth[88] by the Sage (i.e., the Buddha) himself should not be violated;
> Otherwise the correct doctrine *(dharma)* will be harmed, since they will fall away from the way of the Buddha.[89]

If this stanza is by the same author as the one who penned stanzas I.159–60 (J I.156–57), it is difficult to see how one and the same person could have composed an extensive treatise on the *Tathāgatagarbhasūtra* in which he takes the latter to have provisional meaning, and then issue a warning not to violate the sūtras of definitive meaning. It is also not the case that the *Ratnagotravibhāgavyākhyā* refers to the *Laṅkāvatārasūtra,* which explains that the teaching of buddha nature has a provisional meaning.[90] To summarize, the similarities between RGV V.5 and the *Saṁdhinirmocanasūtra* do indeed suggest that the latter sūtra is being followed and that the third dharmacakra (and thus the *Tathāgatagarbhasūtra*) is taken to have definitive meaning.

With regard to the later discussion of the zhentong and mahāmudrā interpretations of the *Ratnagotravibhāga,* the question whether the latter propounds a form of monism or not remains to be addressed. Whereas the Jonangpas assert a substantial identity between the dharmakāya and buddha nature, in that the true nature is the real dharmakāya of enlightenment, some mahāmudrā traditions identify buddha nature with the natural unfabricated mind, which naturally manifests as dharmakāya after the purification process has been completed. According to Thrangu Rinpoche, a modern proponent of mahāmudrā, every sentient being manifests, then, its own dharmakāya. Lambert Schmithausen has pointed out that the latter explanation is supported by a passage from the *Avataṁsakasūtra* quoted in RGVV I.25. Its teaching that the wisdom of the Buddha is contained in all sentient beings, which is an early stage of the doctrine of buddha nature, does not vindicate monism, since enlightenment is described as being equal to but not identical with the already existing tathāgata.[91] The following statement comes after the example of the huge silk cloth with a painting of the universe inside an atom (which illustrates the immeasurable buddha qualities inside the ordinary mindstream):

> I will try to remove in sentient beings all bonds of conceptions, through the teaching of the noble path, so that they themselves cast off by themselves the big knot of conceptions by attaining the strength of the noble path, recognize the wisdom of the tathāgata [within themselves] and become equal to a tathāgata.[92]

The Reaction of Mainstream Mahāyāna to the Theory of Buddha Nature

The earliest Indian reaction to the theory of buddha nature is found in the *Laṅkāvatārasūtra,* which is of an extremely heterogeneous structure. It is safe to say, though, that it mainly upholds the Yogācāra doctrine of the three natures *(trisvabhāva),* mind-only, and basic consciousness *(ālayavijñāna).* In this Yogācāra sūtra buddha nature is said to be the purity of natural luminosity and to abide in the body of all sentient beings as the bearer of the thirty-two marks [of a great being].[93] In reply to Mahāmati's objection that this comes close to the heretical teaching of a personal self, the Buddha is reported to have said:

> Mahāmati, my teaching of buddha nature does not resemble the heretical doctrine of a self *(ātman).* Rather, O Mahāmati,[94] the tathāgatas teach as buddha nature what [really] is emptiness, the limit of reality, nirvāṇa, nonorigination, signlessness, wishlessness, and similar categories, and then the tathāgatas, the arhats, the perfect buddhas, in order to avoid [giving] fools a reason for becoming afraid of the lack of essence, teach the nonconceptual experiential object without characteristic signs by means of instructions that make use [of the term] *buddha nature.*[95]

Based on that, we could argue that the notion of buddha nature is simply a provisional teaching *(neyārtha)* for those who do not grasp emptiness. The *Laṅkāvatārasūtra* also equates buddha nature with the *ālayavijñāna:*

> The illustrious one then said this to him: "Buddha nature, Mahāmati, which contains the cause of wholesome and unwholesome [factors], and which is the agent of all [re]birth and of [all] going [to this and that state of existence], moves on to the distress of [various] states of existence, like an actor [assuming different roles]. Yet it is devoid of an *I* and *mine*. Not understanding [this], [buddha nature, which] is endowed with the impulse of the condition of the three meeting [factors], moves on. But the non-Buddhists who adhere to a persistent belief in [metaphysical] principles do not understand this. Being permeated throughout beginningless time by the various imprints of baseness left by mental fabrication, [buddha nature is also] called *ālayavijñāna*. Together with [the other] seven forms of consciousness which arise on the level of dwelling in ignorance, it moves on in such a way that its body is never interrupted, just as the ocean and the waves."[96]

This raises the question whether the *Laṅkāvatārasūtra* then considers the *ālayavijñāna* to be a provisional expression for emptiness, too. Based on the *Laṅkāvatāra*'s equation of buddha nature with emptiness, Candrakīrti (seventh century) in his *Madhyamakāvatāra* indeed infers that the Yogācāra notions of *ālayavijñāna*, mind-only, and *trisvabhāva* are *neyārtha:*

> Having shown with the help of this canonical passage [from the *Laṅkāvatārasūtra*][97] that all parts of sūtras with a similar content, of which the Vijñānavādins claim that they are *nītārtha*, are [really] *neyārtha*.... [98]

That Candrakīrti holds the teaching of an *ālayavijñāna* to be *neyārtha* becomes clear in his autocommentary on MA VI.42, which asserts that only emptiness is implied by the term *ālayavijñāna*.[99] It is doubtful, however, whether we can go as far as to affirm that other parts of the Yogācāra doctrine, such as that everything is only mind *(cittamātra)*, is taken by the *Laṅkāvatārasūtra* as being *neyārtha* too. But this is precisely what Candrakīrti does with reference to LAS II.123:

> Just as a physician provides medicine for each patient,
> So the buddhas teach mind-only *(cittamātra)* to sentient beings.[100]

This stanza taken on its own suggests indeed that the *cittamātra* teaching is of provisional character *(neyārtha)* in that it is compared to a healing agent for a particular disease. But the following stanza (LAS II.124), which has not been quoted by Candrakīrti, sheds a different light on the issue:

> [This *cittamātra* teaching] is neither an object of philosophers
> nor one of śrāvakas.
> The masters (i.e., the buddhas) teach [it] by drawing on their
> own experience.[101]

In other words, the *Laṅkāvatārasūtra* takes the main point of the Yogācāra teaching as something that can be only experienced by the buddhas, being beyond the reach of an analytical intellect. But while most parts of the Yogācāra doctrine (e.g., *cittamātra, trisvabhāva*) are presented as a definitive teaching in the *Laṅkāvatārasūtra,* it could be argued that the notion of buddha nature (and implicitly that of *ālayavijñāna*?) is not accepted according to its literal meaning, and is thus *neyārtha.*

The argument could be given further, however, that this only refers to a too-substantialist definition of buddha nature, namely as possessing the thirty-two marks of a supreme being, and that a more moderate understanding of it (namely as suchness mingled with stains, as in the *Ratnagotravibhāga*) would be accepted at least by some Yogācāras. This is indeed implied by the equation of buddha nature with suchness in *Mahāyānasūtrālaṁkāra* IX.37:

> Even though suchness is undifferentiated in all [living beings],
> in its purified form it is the state of the tathāgata. Therefore all
> living beings have the seed/nature *(garbha)* of the [tathāgata].[102]

In the *Madhyāntavibhāga,* too, the influence of buddha nature (taken as suchness) can be noticed. Whereas in the *Ratnagotravibhāga* suchness can be accompanied by stains (buddha nature) or not (enlightenment), a positively understood emptiness may be taken to be either defiled or not in MAV I.22:

> [Emptiness is] **neither defiled nor undefiled, neither pure nor impure** (MAV I.22ab). How is it that it is neither defiled nor impure? It is because of the natural **luminosity of mind** (MAV I.22c). How is it that it is neither undefiled nor pure? It is **because of the adventitious nature of defilements** (MAV I.22d).[103]

In the same way as in the *Ratnagotravibhāga,* mind's luminosity is compared to the natural purity of water, gold, and space, which can coexist with adventitious stains. This becomes clear in *Madhyāntavibhāgabhāṣya* I.16:

> How should the differentiation of emptiness be understood? **As being defiled as well as pure** (MAV I.16a). Thus is its differentiation. In what state is it defiled and in what is it pure? **It is accompanied as well as not accompanied by stains** (MAV I.16b). When it occurs together with stains it is defiled, and when its stains are abandoned it is pure. If, after being accompanied by stains it becomes stainless, how is it then not impermanent, given that it has the property of change? This is because **its purity is considered to be like that of water, gold, and space** (MAV I.16cd). [A change is admitted] in view of the removal of adventitious stains, but there is no change in terms of its own-being.[104]

It should be noted how the terms "defiled" and "pure" of the first section are explicitly equated with the imported terminology "accompanied by stains" and "stainless." The latter doubtlessly stem from the *Ratnagotravibhāga* and its *vyākhyā,* where buddha nature is defined as suchness accompanied by stains *(samalā tathatā)* and the transformation of the basis as stainless suchness *(nirmalā tathatā).* Such an understanding of the transformation of basis is also found in the *Dharmadharmatāvibhāga.*[105] Even though the term *tathāgatagarbha* is not found in the *Dharmadharmatāvibhāga,* it is clearly implied by the comparison of natural luminosity with the original purity of space, gold, and water, which can coexist with adventitious stains.[106] To sum up, we can discern an influence of the *Ratnagotravibhāga* on the Yogācāra texts among the Maitreya works, while the way buddha nature or its equivalent of an original purity is referred to in them, namely as emptiness, suchness, or natural luminosity, accords well with the interpretation of buddha nature as emptiness, etc., in the *Laṅkāvatārasūtra.*

Judging from his critique of Yogācāra in the *Madhyamakāvatāra,* it is hard to imagine that Candrakīrti accepted such an interpretation of buddha nature. There must, however, have been some other currents within Madhyamaka that more readily accepted the new developments in Mahāyāna. Thus, the *Sūtrasamuccaya* (attributed to Nāgārjuna by tradition) quotes and discusses certain Mahāyāna sūtras, such as the *Śrīmālādevīsūtra,* that restrict the dictum that all phenomena lack an own-being (i.e., their emptiness) to the level of the phenenomenal world. In order to show that there is ultimately only one single *yāna,* the compilers of the *Sūtrasamuccaya* even quote from the *Dhāraṇīśvararājasūtra* the example of the threefold purification of a *vaiḍūrya* stone, which illustrates the successive teachings of the three dharmacakras.[107] This passage plays an important role in the hermeneutics of the *Ratnagotravibhāgavyākhyā,*[108] implying that the second dharmacakra, which teaches the emptiness of the *prajñāpāramitā* sūtras, is outshone by a final dharmacakra, which describes the ultimate in positive terms. The question thus arises how some Mādhyamikas could selectively pick certain passages from the above-mentioned sūtras instead of endorsing the entire *Śrīmālādevīsūtra* literally, and thus claim, for example, that buddha nature is empty of all defilements, which are separable, but not of inseparable buddha qualities.

Part I
The Tibetan Historical Context

1. The Development of Various Traditions of Interpreting Buddha Nature

In the first part of my study, I will present the Tibetan historical background necessary for understanding Zhönu Pal's enterprise of commenting on the *Ratnagotravibhāga* toward his specific ends. The first chapter of this part is dedicated to an analysis of the dramatic changes Indo-Tibetan Buddhism went through in the eleventh and twelfth centuries with particular emphasis on the analytical and meditation schools of interpreting the *Ratnagotravibhāga.* It is followed by a chapter on the stances of our selected masters from the fourteenth century and a comparison of their positions.

As we have already seen in the introduction, there were basically two main approaches to interpreting the *Ratnagotravibhāga* and its doctrine of buddha nature. The first is to follow the *Laṅkāvatārasūtra* and see in buddha nature (equated with *ālayavijñāna*) a term connoting emptiness. Following this line of thought, we can either take the *Ratnagotravibhāga* to be *neyārtha,* or, if we see in buddha nature a synonym of emptiness, even *nītārtha.* The second possibility is to take the *Ratnagotravibhāga* and the sūtras upon which it comments more literally, as is done by the proponents of an "empti[ness] of other" (Tib. *gzhan stong*). Further, a tradition espousing an analytical approach, in describing buddha nature as a nonaffirming negation, must be distinguished from a *meditation school,* which takes positive descriptions of the ultimate, such as buddha nature, to be experiential in content. It should be noted that the latter school may still accept buddha nature as a synonym of emptiness.

Ngog Loden Sherab's Analytical Interpretation of the Ratnagotravibhāga

Loden Sherab (1059–1109) played a crucial role in the transmission of the *Ratnagotravibhāga* in Tibet. Not only were his translations of the

Ratnagotravibhāga and its *vyākhyā* the ones included in the Tengyur, but he also composed a "summarized meaning" or commentary of the *Ratnagotravibhāga,* in which he tries to bring the teaching of buddha nature into line with his Madhyamaka position. The latter is usually identified as being Svātantrika.[109] Since this summary, which is of great significance for the understanding of Zhönu Pal's mahāmudrā interpretation of the *Ratnagotravibhāga,* has received little attention by Western scholars up till now,[110] the main points of Loden Sherab's strategy will be presented in this section.

Some ten years ago, the text of the summarized meaning was reproduced from blockprints of the edition by Geshé Sherab Gyatso (Dge bshes Shes rab rgya mtsho) (1884–1968) and published with an extensive introduction by David Jackson (1993).[111] Seyfort Ruegg, who must have had access to the blockprint in the possession of Dagpo Rinpoché (Dvags po Rin po che) in Paris, only briefly refers to Loden Sherab's commentary when discussing the ineffable and inconceivable nature of ultimate truth.[112] Contrary to the Gelug position, Loden Sherab radically rejects the possibility that the ultimate can be grasped by conceptual thought:

> This is because the ultimate [truth] is not an object amenable to speech; for the ultimate [truth] is not an object of thought, since conceptual thought is apparent [truth]. The intended meaning of not being able to be expressed by speech is here [because the ultimate is] not a basis for any verbal or conceptual ascertainment. This does not [mean] that [the ultimate] merely does not appear directly[113] to the verbal consciousness. For if it were so, then it would follow that [objects] of apparent [truth], such as a vase, would also be such (i.e., not a basis for verbal ascertainment[114]).[115]

This position is in accordance with the interpretations of Sakya Paṇḍita (Sa skya Paṇḍita) (1182–1251) but greatly at variance with the position maintained by Chapa Chökyi Sengé (Phya pa Chos kyi Seng ge) (1109–69) and many later Gelug scholars.[116] Loden Sherab differs from Sakya Paṇḍita, however, in taking the *Ratnagotravibhāga* to be a commentary on the discourses with definitive meaning:

> When the illustrious Maitreya clarified in an unmistaken way the intention of the discourses of the Sugata, he presented reality, which is the true meaning of Mahāyāna, by composing the

> treatise of the *Mahāyānottaratantra [Ratnagotravibhāga],* which[117] teaches the precious sūtras of definitive meaning, [namely] the irreversible dharmacakra, the dharmadhātu as a single path;[118] and which precisely teaches the meaning of all the very pure and certain discourses.[119]

It should be noted, however, that the remaining four Maitreya works, namely the *Abhisamayālaṁkāra* and the three Yogācāra works, are taken to be commentaries on sūtras with provisional meaning.[120]

Zhönu Pal informs us in his *Blue Annals* that Loden Sherab equated buddha nature with the inconceivable ultimate, whereas Chapa took the latter (and thus buddha nature) to be a nonaffirming negation, bringing it within reach of logical analysis:

> The great translator (i.e., Loden Sherab) and Master Tsangnagpa (Gtsang nag pa) take the so-called buddha nature to be the ultimate truth, but say, on the other hand: "Do not regard the ultimate truth as being an actual object corresponding to words and thoughts." They say that it is by no means a conceptualized object. Master Chapa for his part maintains that nonaffirming negation (which means that entities are empty of a true being) is the ultimate truth, and that it is a conceptualized object corresponding to words and thoughts.[121]

The way in which Loden Sherab equates buddha nature with the ultimate becomes clear in his commentary on the third vajra point of the Noble Saṅgha, where he explains the awareness of how reality is *(yathāvadbhāvikatā)* and the awareness of its extent *(yāvadbhāvikatā)* in the following way:

> Awareness of the extent refers to the "vision that a perfect buddha is present in all [sentient beings]." The awareness that the common defining characteristics—the very selflessness of phenomena and persons—are the nature of a tathāgata, [namely] buddha nature, and that [this reality] completely pervades [its] support, [i.e.,] the entire element of sentient beings, is the [awareness of] the extent. Furthermore, the unmistaken awareness of mere selflessness, which exists in all sentient beings, is the awareness of how [reality] is. The apprehension that every support is pervaded by it is the awareness of its extent. Both are

> supramundane types of insight, [and so] ultimate objects, not a perceiving subject bound to the apparent [truth].[122]

This passage not only shows that awareness of emptiness is an ultimate object, but also that buddha nature is taken as the mere lack of a self in sentient beings. How buddha nature is defined becomes clearer in the commentary on the first and third reasons for the presence of a buddha nature in sentient beings, in RGV I.28:

> Pure suchness is the kāya of the perfect buddha. [Its] radiation *(spharaṇa)* means being pervaded by it (the kāya)—pervaded inasmuch as all sentient beings are fit to attain it (i.e., a kāya of their own). In this respect, the tathāgata [in the compound *tathāgata-nature*[123]] is the real one, while sentient beings' possession of his [i.e., the tathāgata's] *nature* is nominal,[124] because "being pervaded by it" has been metaphorically applied to the opportunity to attain it (i.e., such a kāya).... With regard to the [reason] "because of the existence of a potential," *tathāgata* is nominal, because the [tathāgata-nature] is the cause for attaining suchness in the [resultant] state of purity—[is, in other words,] the seeds of knowledge and compassion, the mental imprints of virtue, and [thus only] the cause of a tathāgata. The only real [in *tathāgata-nature* here] is the "nature" of sentient beings (and not that the latter consists of an actual tathāgata).[125]

Buddha nature is thus not only taken as emptiness (namely the lack of self in sentient beings) but also as the seed or cause of buddhahood. We wonder, then, how Loden Sherab explains similes such as the huge silk cloth from the *Avataṁsakasūtra,*[126] which illustrates the presence of immeasurable buddha qualities in sentient beings. Against the purport of the sūtra, according to which each sentient being has its own buddha wisdom, Loden Sherab claims that this buddha wisdom is the one of the illustrious one himself:

> As the picture on a silk cloth exists in an atom, just so the wisdom of the Buddha exists in the [mind]stream of sentient beings. If you ask what [this wisdom] is, [the answer is] the dharmadhātu. If you ask how this [can] be wisdom, [the answer is:] Since the illustrious one came to know that all phenomena lack defining characteristics thanks to the insight that encompasses

> [everything] in a single moment, this insight is inseparable from its objects. Therefore the ultimate, the very dharmadhātu itself, is [in this respect also] the wisdom that is aware of this [dharmadhātu]. Since [the dharmadhātu] abides in all sentient beings without exception, the example and the illustrated meaning are fully acceptable.[127]

The question arises whether this contradicts Loden Sherab's presentation of the first reason for sentient beings having buddha nature in RGV I.28. In his explanation of the nine examples from the *Tathāgatagarbhasūtra,* Loden Sherab specifies exactly how sentient beings are pervaded by the dharmakāya:

> As to the phrase "[the dharmakāya that] pervades the entire sphere of sentient beings": The Dharma of realization of previous tathāgatas was accomplished on the basis of immeasurable accumulation [of merit and wisdom]. [The resulting dharmakāya, i.e.,] the very pure suchness and the wisdom apprehending it, namely that which by nature is separate [from sentient beings], pervades all sentient beings, for this dharmakāya is emptiness, and it is emptiness, too, that exists in sentient beings.[128]

In other words, even though the buddha nature of sentient beings is different from the wisdom of the buddhas, the former is still pervaded by the latter since the buddha wisdom realizes the emptiness of sentient beings' minds. The space-like buddha qualities of RGV II.29–37, which Loden Sherab, in accordance with the *vyākhyā,* also subsumes under the ultimate truth,[129] must be taken in the same way. They pertain to the ordinary mind only insofar as it, too, is emptiness. Equally inconceivable as the ultimate is natural luminosity, as this must be actualized through wisdom without any objective support, so that luminosity is actually taken to be wisdom.[130] To review, the emptiness of the ultimate cannot become the object of ordinary perception. But being the object of a buddha, it is pervaded by the wisdom or luminosity of the Buddha, this insight being no different from its object.

The buddha nature or element, which is repeatedly said to be the emptiness of each mindstream,[131] can become the objective support of inferential cognitions that negate without affirming anything. As such it becomes the substantial cause for the attainment of buddha qualities:

> As to the [buddha] element that has become the conventional object of a nonaffirming negation, it is called the substantial cause that has become the conventional object of a nonaffirming negation; but something that amounts to human effort [as a substantial cause of buddhahood] does not actually exist. As to the conventional object, it has the meaning of a nonaffirming negation—namely that anything that is established as an own-being does not exist in reality.[132]

This leads to the question whether the qualities are for Loden Sherab something newly produced. In his introduction to the second chapter of the *Ratnagotravibhāga*—a commentary on stanza RGV II.3—the notion of nothing being newly produced is brought up in the presentation of the essence of enlightenment (compared to natural luminosity, the sun, and the sky in RGV II.3a). But with the unchangeability of buddha nature restricted to its true nature, the possibility of development with nonconceptual wisdom as a cause remains untouched:

> [Verse RGV II.3c:] "Buddhahood is endowed with all stainless buddha qualities; it is permanent, stable, and eternal"[133] expresses wisdom, abandonment, and the qualities based on them. [It further states] that it is not the case that these [qualities] have arisen as something that did not exist before, and that they existed in previous state[s] [still] accompanied by hindrances. In all this the essence [of enlightenment] is taught. As for the cause, here [in this stanza] it is the wisdom of not conceptualizing phenomena, and the distinguishing wisdom attained after that.[134]

In other words, in terms of the essence of enlightenment nothing is newly produced, which means that emptiness is present throughout beginningless time and nothing needs to be added to it (see below).

Of particular interest is, in this respect, Loden Sherab's commentary on RGV I.51,[135] in which he restricts the statement of being naturally endowed with qualities to the very pure state in which these qualities are not experienced as something disconnected. In the same way as they are experienced as something inseparable from the pure state, their cause, or the dharmadhātu, can be apprehended in impure states:

> [The verse RGV I.51b] "being naturally endowed[136] with qualities" shows that the immutability of the properties of qualities

> (i.e., the buddha qualities) in the very pure state is acceptable. This means that the true nature is not tarnished when qualities suddenly manifest, nor is [this nature] experienced as being separate from any natural[ly endowed] qualities, in the same way as it [cannot] be established as something that possesses a particular qualitative feature that did not exist before in the impure state, for example. For the meaning of naturally established qualities lies in their being naturally[137] established as an objective support without superimposition; or rather as the objective support that is the cause of [these very] qualities. This is because the correct apparent [truth] abides without superimposition, or because the ultimate abides in such a way, respectively. The realization of the ultimate is the cause of all qualities, because all buddha qualities are summoned as if called when you realize the dharmadhātu.[138]

In other words, the naturally established (or endowed) qualities are nothing else than the cause of these qualities, which is mind's emptiness. To put it another way, to perceive your mind as it is, without superimposing an ultimately existing own-being, is the buddha nature that causes qualities.

The crucial stanzas RGV I.157–58 (J I.154–55) on emptiness, which state that nothing needs to be added and that buddha nature is not empty of inseparable qualities, are explained in the following way:

> Neither superimposing the ultimate existence of an objective support for all defilements nor denying the relative[139] existence of an objective support for the mind and the mental factors of purification, one abides in the two truths as they are. With regard to this it has been said: "The meaning of emptiness is unmistaken." This has been expressed [in the following verses RGV I.157ab (J I.154ab)]: "In it[140] nothing is to be removed [and nothing to be added]." [That is,] in this reality, nothing is to be removed—[namely,] an objective support for all defilements—because [no such thing] has ever been established. [Likewise,] in this reality nothing need to be added—[namely,] characteristic signs of purification, such as the strengths and clairvoyance, because the objective support for [the attainment of the ten] strengths, etc., and purification, which exists on the level of apparent [truth], abides throughout beginningless time....[141]

> The phrase "possessing the defining characteristic of being inseparable" means that the nonapprehended unsurpassable qualities exist on the level of apparent [truth], and since reality and existence on [the level of] apparent [truth] do not contradict each other, they are said to exist as mere nature. If you therefore directly realize illusion-like apparent [truth], you [automatically] establish the qualities, because the nature of qualities is simply such that one has them (i.e., the illusory phenomena of the apparent) as an objective support.[142]

The quoted passages clearly show that Loden Sherab avoids defining what exactly the qualities of which buddha nature is not empty are, or rather, instead of accepting the literal meaning of RGV I.158 (J I.155) that the buddha element is not empty of unsurpassable properties, Loden Sherab suggests replacing the *unsurpassable properties* by the conditioned phenomena of apparent truth. In fact, qualities are circumscribed by "having the illusory phenomena of the apparent as an objective support." Such phenomena are conducive to purification, if an ultimate own-being is not wrongly superimposed. As we have seen above, this is the correct apparent truth. What it comes down to is the objective support that is the mere cause of qualities, the dharmadhātu, or rather to the ability to meditate on emptiness by taking buddha nature as the conventional object of a nonaffirming negation. This observation is also shared by Śākya Chogden (Śākya mchog ldan) (1428–1507), who asserts that Loden Sherab sees buddha nature as a "nonaffirming negation that is not qualified by qualities such as the [ten] strengths."[143]

Finally, it should be noted that Loden Sherab brings the buddha element into relation with the *ālayavijñāna* when he explains, on the basis of the *Mahāyānābhidharmasūtra,*[144] that the buddha element is the seed of the buddha qualities, and that all sentient beings, too, arise from it. Sentient beings are, however, affected through additional conditions.[145]

Ratnogotravibhāga *Commentaries in the Meditation Tradition*

In the introduction to his *Ratnagotravibhāga* commentary, Zhönu Pal informs us that during a visit to Kashmir, Tsen Kawoché, who was a disciple of Drapa Ngönshé (Grva pa Mngon shes), requested Sajjana to bestow on him the works of the illustrious Maitreya along with special instructions, since he wanted to make these works his "practice [of preparing] for death" *('chi chos).* Sajjana taught all five Maitreya works, with Lotsāwa Zu

Gawa Dorjé (Lo tsā ba Gzu Dga' ba rdo rje) functioning as a translator. In addition, he gave special instructions with regard to the *Ratnagotravibhāga.*[146] Until now only little has been known about Tsen Kawoché's "meditation tradition" of the five Maitreya works. In his *Blue Annals,* Zhönu Pal informs us that whereas Ngog Loden Sherab takes buddha nature to be the inconceivable ultimate, Tsen Kawoché emphasizes it under the aspect of natural luminosity:

> The followers of the tradition of Tsen (Btsan) maintain that since the luminous nature of mind is the buddha nature, the cause of buddha[hood] is fertile.[147]

According to Kongtrül Lodrö Tayé's (Kong sprul Blo gros mtha' yas) (1813–99) introduction to his *Ratnagotravibhāga* commentary, Tsen Kawoché and his translator Zu Gawa Dorjé became well known as followers of the meditation tradition of the Maitreya works, which was unique in terms of both explanations and practice. Zu Gawa Dorjé wrote his own commentary on the *Ratnagotravibhāga* in accordance with the teaching of Sajjana.[148] Based on this commentary, the Third Karmapa Rangjung Dorjé composed a summary of the contents of the *Ratnagotravibhāga,* and Karma Könzhön (Karma Dkon gzhon) (b. 1333) commented at length on it. Karma Trinlepa (Karma Phrin las pa) (1456–1539) composed a commentary of his own by inserting corrections into Karma Könzhön's commentary.[149] None of these works has turned up to date; but since in Kongtrül's presentation of the Tsen tradition Zhönu Pal's *Ratnagotravibhāga* commentary is mentioned next to Karma Trinlepa's commentary, a study of Zhönu Pal promises to shed the first light on this meditation tradition. In the colophon of his *Ratnagotravibhāga* commentary, Zhönu Pal tells us that he used notes written by Chöjé Drigungpa Jigten Sumgön (Chos rje 'Bri gung pa 'Jig rten gsum mgon) (1143–1217) as the basis for spelling out his own Mahāyāna hermeneutics, which attempt to demonstrate the superiority of the last dharmacakra mainly on the basis of mahāmudrā pith instructions.[150] He further says that Drigungpa's explanations both of the three dharmacakras and the *Ratnagotravibhāga,* and the explanations deriving from Sajjana's heart disciple Tsen Kawoché, are all in accordance with mahāmudrā.[151] On the other hand, Zhönu Pal tells us that he also consulted in-depth explanations that follow along the lines of Ngog Loden Sherab.

In this respect it is of interest how Śākya Chogden summarizes the views of Pagmo Drupa (Phag mo gru pa) (1110–70) and many other Dagpo Kagyüpas on buddha nature. Whereas Loden Sherab is said to define the latter as a nonaffirming negation that is not qualified by qualities such as the ten strengths, Śākya Chogden says about mainstream Dagpo Kagyü:

> As to the definition of [buddha] nature, it is either taken to be the part made up of natural purity only, or as [also including] the accumulation of qualities that are inseparable from it (i.e., this purity). With regard to the second, [buddha nature] is either taken as that which enables the realization of these qualities, [namely,] the qualities of the dharmakāya, or it is taken to be, as natural [purity], the qualities of the dharmakāya.... [The latter is claimed by] upholders of the Dagpo Kagyü such as Pagmo Drupa.[152]

By combining Loden Sherab's nonaffirming negation with the qualities of the dharmakāya as natural purity, Zhönu Pal developed his theory of the subtle qualities of the dharmakāya in sentient beings. These subtle qualities are described as resembling the space-like qualities of the svābhāvikakāya. They evolve in their own sphere, without depending on artificial conditions, as the hindrances are gradually removed.

The Mahāmudrā Interpretation of the Ratnagotravibhāga

At least two of the masters who are mentioned in the context of the meditation tradition of Tsen are known to have given mahāmudrā explanations on the basis of nontantric Mahāyāna works. Besides Zhönu Pal, this can be also confirmed now for the Third Karmapa Rangjung Dorjé, who in his newly discovered *Dharmadhātustotra* commentary equates *prajñāpāramitā* with mahāmudrā, both being for him a defining characteristic of the dharmadhātu.[153] It is therefore reasonable to assume that Rangjung Dorjé also composed his summarized meaning of the *Ratnagotravibhāga* from a mahāmudrā perspective. It is all the more reasonable since Gampopa had once said to Pagmo Drupa that the *Ratnagotravibhāga* was the basic text of their mahāmudrā. Zhönu Pal explains this background in his *Blue Annals:*

> Moreover, Dagpo Rinpoché (Gampopa) said to Pagmo Drupa: "The basic text of this mahāmudrā of ours is the *Mahāyānottaratantraśāstra (Ratnagotravibhāga)* by Venerable Maitreya." Pagmo Drupa in turn said the same thing to Jé Drigungpa (Rje 'Bri gung pa), and for this reason many explanations of the

> *Mahāyānottaratantraśāstra* are found in the works of Jé Drigungpa and his disciples. In this connection, the Dharma master from Sakya (i.e., Sakya Paṇḍita) maintains that there is no conventional expression for mahāmudrā in the *pāramitā* tradition, and that the wisdom of mahāmudrā is only the wisdom arisen from initiation. But in the *Tattvāvatāra* composed by the Master Jñānakīrti it is said: "As for someone with sharp faculties who practices the *pāramitās* diligently, by performing the meditations of calm abiding and deep insight, he [becomes] truly endowed with the mahāmudrā[154] [already] in the state of an ordinary being; [and this] is the sign of the irreversible [state attained] through correct realization." The *Tattvadaśakaṭīkā* composed by Sahajavajra clearly explains wisdom that realizes suchness as possessing the following three particular [features]: in essence it is the *pāramitās*, it is in accordance with the *mantra[yāna]* and its name is *mahāmudrā*. Therefore Götsangpa (Rgod tshang pa), too, explains that Jé Gampopa's *pāramitā-mahāmudrā* is [in line with] the assertions of the master Maitrīpa.[155]

This passage from the *Blue Annals* clearly shows that Zhönu Pal defends the *pāramitā*-based mahāmudrā tradition against the critique of Sakya Paṇḍita by pointing out that it had Indian origins, namely in the persons of Jñānakīrti and Maitrīpa (together with Maitrīpa's disciple Sahajavajra). Even though Zhönu Pal agrees with Sakya Paṇḍita that during the time of Marpa (Mar pa) (1012–97) and Milarepa (Mi la ras pa) (1040–1123) the realization of mahāmudrā was understood as implying that first the wisdom of inner heat has to be produced before it can occur,[156] he argues against any attempt to disqualify Gampopa's nontantric mahāmudrā teachings for showing signs of Sino-Tibetan influence.[157] Zhönu Pal reports in his *Blue Annals* (namely in the chapter on Dagpo Kagyü) that Marpa received from Maitrīpa not only tantric teachings, but that Maitrīpa's mahāmudrā pith instructions also contributed to Marpa's direct realization of the true nature of mind.[158]

In his *Ratnagotravibhāga* commentary, Zhönu Pal further informs us that, according to Götsangpa, Maitrīpa's mahāmudrā teachings go back even further, to Saraha and Śavaripa.[159] This opinion is also shared by Mikyö Dorjé (Mi bskyod rdo rje), who explains in his commentary on the *Madhyamakāvatāra* that Maitrīpa realized that his doctrine of not becoming mentally engaged (i.e., mahāmudrā) has the same meaning as the Madhyamaka taught by Saraha the elder, Saraha the younger (i.e., Śavaripa), Nāgārjuna, and Candrakīrti.[160] Dagpo Tashi Namgyal (Dvags po Bkra shis rnam rgyal) (1512–87) claims in his *Zla ba'i 'od zer* that Maitrīpa received from Śavaripa essence mahāmudrā teachings that were not based on tantras.[161] Moreover, Zhönu Pal refers to Dampa Sangyé (Dam pa sangs rgyas) (d. 1105), who maintained that everybody—men and women, old and young, [even] lepers—can see reality if they possess the skillful means of a lama. In this context, Zhönu Pal also claims that the meditation tradition of Tsen was closely connected with the mahāmudrā pith instructions of Maitrīpa's circle:

> The followers of the tradition of Tsen also believe that these states (of being old or even a leper) are made into the path by pith instructions.[162]

During the time of Maitrīpa and his disciples, Indian Buddhism went through dramatic changes, with the tantric teachings of the mahāsiddhas being not only accepted on their own terms but also integrated into more general Mahāyāna expositions.

This can be observed in Jñānakīrti's *Tattvāvatāra,*[163] in which three approaches to reality are distinguished, namely those of Mantrayāna, Pāramitāyāna, and "the path of freeing oneself from attachment" (i.e., Śrāvakayāna). Each of these three has again three distinct forms, for adepts with sharp, average, and inferior capacities. Zhönu Pal's point in the above-quoted passage from the *Blue Annals* is that the practice of Pāramitāyāna among adepts with sharp faculties (not, that is, only the practice of Mantrayāna) is referred to as mahāmudrā. Jñānakīrti also uses the term *mahāmudrā* as a synonym of *prajñāpāramitā* in the third chapter of the *Tattvāvatāra:*

> Another name for the very great mother *prajñāpāramitā* is mahāmudrā, for [mahāmudrā] has the nature of nondual wisdom.[164]

Further down in his *Tattvāvatāra,* Jñānakīrti also finds a place for mahāmudrā within the traditional fourfold Mahāyāna meditation by equating *Mahāyāna* in *Laṅkāvatārasūtra* X.257d with mahāmudrā. The *pādas* X.257cd "A yogin who is established in a state without appearances sees Mahāyāna"[165] thus mean that the yogin finally sees or realizes mahāmudrā.[166] Zhönu Pal must have had such Indian sources in mind when he read the four mahāmudrā yogas into the *Laṅkāvatārasūtra*[167] and the *Dharmadharmatāvibhāga.*[168]

A study of the *Tattvadaśaka* and its commentary shows that tantric concepts are used freely in the more general Mahāyāna context as well. Thus, a direct mahāmudrā approach to reality is presented without tantric initiation and related practice. Still, the yogin of the *Tattvadaśaka* is said to have adopted a "yogic conduct" *(unmattavrata)* and to be "blessed from within" *(svādhiṣṭhāna)*.[169] We could argue that the very use of these terms supplied a tantric context, but from the *Kudṛṣṭinirghātana* it becomes clear that Maitrīpa takes *unmattavrata* as an extreme form of Mahāyāna conduct that results from having perfected the six *pāramitās*.[170] Moreover, Sahaja-vajra's explanations of the terms *unmattavrata* and *svādhiṣṭhāna* are not tantric either.[171] To be sure, the term *svādhiṣṭhāna* does not refer here to the third stage in the *Pañcakrama*, for example, where an initiated yogin who has already practiced the creation stage solicits his tantric master's pith instructions on the *svādhiṣṭhāna* level[172] in order to attain the luminous state.[173] Moreover, (the tantric) Āryadeva (ninth century)[174] is said to have started a tradition of reading the five stages of the *Pañcakrama* into the *Laṅkāvatārasūtra*, thus presenting the tantric stage of *svādhiṣṭhāna* in the context and on the basis of a Mahāyāna sūtra.[175]

In the *Tattvadaśaka* the yogin is described as being "adorned with the blessing from within *(svādhiṣṭhāna)*" as a result of having generated an enlightened attitude (bodhicitta) and experiencing the reality of all phenomena as luminosity. This becomes clear in stanzas TD 5–6:

> Thus phenomena, which are [all] of one taste, are unobstructed, and without an abode.
> They are all [realized as being] luminous through the samādhi [of realizing] reality as it is.
> This samādhi occurs because of engaged [bodhi]citta,
> For reality arises without interruption for those acquainted with its abode.[176]

To sum up, the *Tattvadaśaka* propagates a direct approach to reality that is in accordance with Vajrayāna, but is mainly made possible by pith instructions. In other words, reality is not only understood to be neither existent nor nonexistent, but also directly realized as "[natural] luminosity" (Skt. *prabhāsvaratā*). Traditionally, this direct realization is only possible from the first bodhisattva level onward, or made possible through tantric practice.[177] But in the *Tattvadaśaka* such a direct realization is said to be brought about by engaged bodhicitta, and the *Tattvadaśakaṭīkā* confirms that the required practice is a Mahāyāna sequence of calm abiding and deep insight. Still, Sahajavajra points out a major difference with Kamalaśīla's approach:

> The differentiations made with respect to engaged [bodhi]citta within the tradition of *pāramitā* are presented both in short and [also] extensively in the *Bhāvanākrama* and other works of Kamalaśīla. You should look them up there; they are not written here for reasons of space. No such engaged [bodhi]citta [as implied] here is intended [by them],[178] [however,] since in this *[Bhāvanākrama]* it is not pure, having been produced on the basis of analysis, whereas here [in the *Tattvadaśaka*] it must be directly meditated upon with a nonanalytical mind.[179, 180]

And a little further down Sahajavajra quotes *Mahāyānaviṁśikā* 12:

> [The quintessence] to be realized in the thousands of collections of teachings is emptiness.
> [Emptiness] is not realized through analysis. The meaning of destruction (i.e., emptiness) [is rather attained] from the guru.[181]

Of particular interest is the following commentary on *Tattvadaśaka* 7, in which the pith instructions of a guru and the reality they reveal are called mahāmudrā. Sahajavajra starts by defining nonduality in terms of his so-called Yuganaddha-Madhyamaka as being "bodhicitta, or the reality of nondual knowledge, whose nature is skillful means and insight."[182] As an introduction to his explanation on the second part of the verse (TD 7cd), the following objection is addressed. To define reality in the above-mentioned way has the fault of bearing the characteristic sign *(nimitta)* of an interpretative imagination of reality, in the same way as the practice of *yathābhūtasamādhi* is accompanied by the characteristic sign of an interpretative imagination of the remedy, and such characteristic signs must be abandoned by not becoming mentally engaged, as preached in the *Nirvikalpapraveśadhāraṇī*. TD 7cd is then taken as Maitrīpa's answer to such a possible objection. It says that nothing, not even the characteristic signs of attainment and the like, is really abandoned, but every state of mind is simply realized as natural luminosity:

> And [even] the vain adherence to a state free of duality is taken,
> in like manner, to be luminous [as well].[183] (TD 7cd)

Sahajavajra comments:

> The underlying intention here is as follows. In order that those who do not know reality thoroughly realize [that] reality, it was taught that you must give up the three interpretative [imaginations] as in the case of the complete abandonment of the four extremes. This is because it is stated [in Maitrīpa's *Sekanirdeśa,* stanza 36]:
>
> > He who does not abide in the domain of the remedy and is not attached to reality,
> > And who has even no desire for the fruit, knows mahāmudrā.[184]
>
> Here mahāmudrā [refers to] the pith instruction on the reality of mahāmudrā.[185]

In other words, both the pith instructions and the revealed reality are here called mahāmudrā. Sahajavajra further points out that the vain adherence to nonduality, that is, the interpretative imagination of reality, does not exist as anything other than its luminous nature. Abandoning the characteristic signs of these imaginations by not becoming mentally engaged thus leads to the realization of their luminous nature, which is achieved by not focusing on a supposed own-being of phenomena. The latter practice is performed on the basis of either precise analysis or the pith instructions of a guru.[186] To sum up, nothing is really abandoned, but phenomena are ascertained for what they are: in the light of analysis they lack an own-being, and in *yathābhūtasamādhi* they are experienced as luminosity.

Even though Sahajavajra introduces the term mahāmudrā by quoting from a tantric work (i.e., the *Sekanirdeśa*), the pith instructions on reality are referred to as mahāmudrā in a purely nontantric context, since the yoga tradition of directly realizing reality through pith instructions is clearly distinguished from both Pāramitāyāna and Mantrayāna. This is obvious from Sahajavajra's commentary on *Tattvadaśaka* 8. The root stanza is:

> By the power of having realized this reality, the yogin whose eyes are wide open, moves everywhere like a lion by any means[187] in whatever manner.[188, 189]

Sahajavajra immediately adds concerning this stanza:

> The yogin,[190] who accurately realized previously taught nondual reality with the help of pith instructions of the right guru.[191]

Further down Sahajavajra then distinguishes such an approach from the Mantrayāna and Pāramitāyāna:

> If you are wondering "In that case, what are the differences [between that yogin and] a yogin of the way of Mantrayāna?" [The answer is:] There are great differences with regard to what is to be accomplished and that which accomplishes, given that [the yogin's practice] is without the sequence of the four *mudrās*, and given that complete enlightenment by way of equanimity, [that is,] without the taste of the great bliss resulting from the pride of being a deity, takes a long time. On the other hand, it differs from the yogin of the way of Pāramitāyāna, it being especially superior in terms of accurately realizing the suchness of the union into a pair, [that is,] emptiness analyzed on the basis of the instructions of the right guru. Therefore, there is no engaging in austerities. Those who ascertain very well the reality of one taste to be emptiness are like [skillful] village people grasping a snake. Even though they touch the snake, they are not bitten. Some call this the wisdom of reality [or] mahāmudrā.[192]

Gampopa distinguishes in a similar way a third path of direct perceptions set apart from a general Mahāyāna path of inferences and a Vajrayāna path of blessing:

> As to taking inference as [your] path, having examined all phenomena by arguments, [such as] being beyond one and many,[193] you say that there is no other [ontological] possibility and posit that everything is empty. [This is the path of] inference.
>
> [The practice of] inner channels, energies, and drops, the recitation of *mantras*, and so forth, based on the stage consisting of the generation of the deity's body, is the path of blessing.
>
> As to taking direct perception for [your] path, the right guru teaches that coemergent nature of mind is the dharmakāya in terms of its luminosity. Having thus been given an accurate pith instruction of definitive meaning, you take, with regard to this "coemergent mind" *(shes pa lhan cig skyes pa)* that has been ascertained in yourself, the natural mind as the path, without being

> separated from any of the three [aspects of the mahāmudrā teaching]: view, conduct, and meditation.[194]

For Gampopa, this direct approach is supreme and of definitive meaning, in that it is based on direct perception as opposed to inferences, as on the general Mahāyāna path. Sometimes Gampopa even criticizes ordinary Vajrayāna for descending to the level of conceptualization,[195] and in so doing goes one step further than Sahajavajra, who unreservedly accepts the superiority of Vajrayāna over mahāmudrā pith instructions. It is noteworthy that Gampopa distinguishes two types of individuals, namely the gradualist *(rim gyis pa)* and simultaneist[196] *(cig car pa)* as similarly propounded in the *Bsam gtan mig sgron,* which is ascribed to the dzogchen master Nub Sangyé Yeshé (Gnubs Sangs rgyas ye shes) (tenth century).[197] The latter considers that the simultaneist system originates in the sūtras of definitive meaning *(nītārthasūtra)* while the gradualist system is based on the sūtras of provisional meaning *(neyārthasūtra).*[198] For Gampopa, too, the gradualist teaching among the pith instructions has provisional meaning, whereas the simultaneist ones are of definitive meaning. Beginners, however, can only enter the paths of *pāramitā* and *mantra.*[199] Further research will be required in order to determine to what extent Gampopa's path of direct perception is really a continuation of the tradition of Maitrīpa and what part of it goes back to Sino-Tibetan influences.[200]

Drigungpa Jigten Sumgön, who, as a disciple of Pagmo Drupa, stands in the tradition of Gampopa, explains that his mahāmudrā practice is in accordance with the *Ratnagotravibhāga.* Thus, it is reported in the *Chos kyi 'khor lo legs par gtan la phab pa:*

> Mahāmudrā is [taught on the basis of] the *Mahāyānottaratantra [Ratnagotravibhāga].* Great effort was taken to explain the latter, and I listened again and again to [such explanations] from Jigten [Sum]gön.[201]

In the commentary on this passage it is explained:

> The mahāmudrā practiced by the venerable Great Drigungpa (i.e., Jigten Sumgön) himself is in accordance with this *Mahāyānottaratantra [Ratnagotravibhāga],* the qualities [of] mahāmudrā being taught with exactly this meaning in the latter.[202]

The seven vajra points of the *Ratnagotravibhāga* are stated to be a commentary on the meaning of the third dharmacakra,[203] earlier in the text described as the dharmacakra of definitive meaning.[204] In his *Dgongs gcig* I.4–6 Jigten Sumgön[205] further explains that the three dharmacakras differ in conformity with the concepts typical of the different groups of disciples, that all three dharmacakras are contained in each individual one, and that the seed of the following dharmacakra is already present in the previous one.[206] This means that the Buddha himself did not teach anything provisional *(neyārtha)* in the sense of being intentionally wrong; it is only due to the differing faculties of the disciples that the contents of a teaching acquire provisional or definitive status.

Thus the seed of the three dharmacakras is the dharmacakra of definitive meaning, just as all *yāna*s are ultimately identical and ascertainable as a single *yāna.*[207] In this sense all dharmacakras have definitive meaning, but the third dharmacakra is still considered superior in its effectiveness.[208]

In his *Chos 'khor gtan phab,* Jigten Sumgön defines a simultaneist as someone who attains enlightenment at the time of the fruit. It is essential that he have already accumulated merit previously; in other words, when on the path, he is still a gradualist. Thus, even Śākyamuni was a gradualist when he generated bodhicitta and traversed the path:

> [Practitioners] are called simultaneists and gradualists. The [buddha] element in sentient beings makes enlightenment attainable. This enlightenment is attained gradually and not instantaneously.... Having generated a mind that is directed toward supreme enlightenment, [the Buddha] traversed [the bodhisattva levels] gradually, [in accordance with] the three dharmacakras.[209]

In the autocommentary, this passage is explained as follows:

> Instantaneous [enlightenment] is not at all possible. If one wonders who is then called a simultaneist, [the answer is:] He who attains in this life the fruit of having accumulated merit previously is called a simultaneist. Likewise, our teacher, the illustrious Buddha, is also a simultaneist. It was in virtue of the fruit of having previously accumulated merit throughout innumerable eons that he awakened during his life. But without the previous accumulation of merit, the fruit would not have been attained during his life. Therefore he was a gradualist along the entire path.[210]

> Even our teacher, the illustrious Buddha, first generated a mind that is directed toward unsurpassable enlightenment, and during an incalculable eon traversed the path up to the first [bodhisattva] level in accordance with the first dharmacakra. During [another] incalculable [eon] he traversed the path up to the seventh level in accordance with the second dharmacakra, and during a [third] incalculable [eon] he traversed the three pure levels in accordance with the third dharmacakra.[211]

Again in *Dgongs gcig* I.13–14 it is said that all paths traverse the ten levels, and that these levels are entered gradually.[212] In his commentary on *Dgongs gcig* I.14, Rigdzin Chökyi Dragpa (Rig 'dzin Chos kyi grags pa) (1595–1659) quotes Pagmo Drupa, who said that a simultaneist (lit. "a person who enters all of a sudden") is somebody whose accumulations are gathered, whose mindstream is purified, whose mind is trained, and in whom experience has arisen.[213]

On the other hand, it is stated in *Dgongs gcig* I.15 that "the hindrances of knowable objects have been abandoned throughout beginningless time,"[214] while *Dgongs gcig* IV.18 has it that "all levels and paths are traversed by the same realization."[215] According to the sixth chapter of the *Dgongs gcig*, "the sole means of giving rise to realization is devotion" (VI.6).[216] Now "to possess realization is considered to be the supreme view" (VI.7),[217] and "to make yourself familiar with such a realization is taken to be meditation" (VI.10).[218] In other words, since the supreme view or realization can, or rather must, be attained by devotion, a practitioner can start at a relatively early stage to work with the one realization of the true nature of his mind that leads him through all the levels to buddhahood.[219] In this sense there is no difference between view and meditation, meditation simply being the cultivation of realization (namely the supreme view). This is definitely a continuation of Sahajavajra's Yuganaddhavāda and Gampopa's path of direct perceptions.

Zhang Tsalpa Tsöndrü Drag (Zhang Tshal pa Brtson 'grus grags) (1123–93) is more radical when he claims in his *Phyag rgya chen po lam zab mthar thug* that mahāmudrā is attained in one go and that the confused err when they reckon it in terms of levels and paths.[220] Zhönu Pal tries to defend such an extreme position in his *Ratnagotravibhāgavyākhyā* commentary by quoting a *Laṅkāvatārasūtra* passage on the gradual and instantaneous purification of the mindstream, and explaining that on the pure bodhisattva levels all objects of knowledge appear instantaneously, while the gradual purification of stains through the three dharmacakras goes up only to the seventh level. Referring to the *Vairocanābhisambodhitantra,* he argues that this seventh level may be also a provisional one already found on the path of accumulation,[221] one that brings the sudden realization within the reach of more ordinary practitioners.

Besides these attempts to justify the simultaneist mahāmudrā teachings of his tradition, Zhönu Pal is also concerned with reading the gradual teachings of the four mahāmudrā yogas into the Maitreya works and the *Laṅkāvatārasūtra.* Given that Gampopa claims that the *Ratnagotravibhāga* is the basic text for his mahāmudrā, it is very likely that the explanations of mahāmudrā that we find in Zhönu Pal's *Ratnagotravibhāga* commentary were already known at Gampopa's time. Moreover, such a mahāmudrā interpretation must have already existed in India, as can be seen from Jñānakīrti's *Tattvāvatāra,* in which mahāmudrā practice is related with the traditional fourfold Mahāyāna meditation by equating *Mahāyāna* in LAS X.257d with mahāmudrā. Further research may even show that at least some of these explanations had already been transmitted by Tsen Kawoché. Zhönu Pal also once refers to Dampa Sangyé as a source for his reading the four mahāmudrā yogas into RGV I.31.[222] It is thus reasonable to assume that besides the traditional tantric mahāmudrā, Gampopa propounded both a mahāmudrā beyond sūtra and tantra and something that was later called sūtra-based mahāmudrā.

But only later doxographers, such as Kongtrül Lodrö Tayé, identify and classify these different approaches as (1) sūtra mahāmudrā, (2) mantra mahāmudrā, and (3) essence mahāmudrā. Sūtra mahāmudrā is connected with the Pāramitāyāna but is also in accordance with tantra, and mainly consists of resting the mind in the state of nonconceptual wisdom. The method of this approach is hidden in the sūtras, wherefore sūtra mahāmudrā is also called the hidden or secret path of the sūtras *(mdo'i gsang lam).* Mantra mahāmudrā is transmitted through the Vajrayāna path of method, which involves tantric initiation. Essence mahāmudrā leads to the sudden or instantaneous realization of the natural mind *(tha mal gyi shes pa).* It requires a realized master who bestows a particular type of blessing called the *empowerment of vajra wisdom* on a receptive and qualified disciple.[223] In the Kamtsang (Kaṁ tshaṅg) transmission, the traditional sūtra mahāmudrā work is considered to be Dagpo Tashi Namgyal's *Zla ba'i 'od zer,* and that of essence mahāmudrā the *Nges don rgya mtsho* by the Ninth Karmapa Wangchug Dorjé (Dbang phyug rdo rje) (1556–1603).[224]

As will be shown later, we can also distinguish sūtra and essence mahāmudrā explanations in Zhönu Pal's *Ratnagotravibhāga* commentary, even though the technical terms are not used in it. Sūtra mahāmudrā would be Zhönu Pal's attempt to read the gradual path of the four mahāmudrā yogas into various passages of the *Ratnagotravibhāga* and the *Laṅkāvatārasūtra*. Essence mahāmudrā explanations are mainly quoted from various mahāmudrā masters in order to justify the superiority of the third dharmacakra at the beginning of the commentary. Zhönu Pal leaves no doubt that the gradual approach of the four yogas is provisional and outshone by the instructions on how to realize the natural mind suddenly or in "one go."[225] For Zhönu Pal this sudden realization of mahāmudrā does not mean, however, that a practitioner can reach full enlightenment in one moment. It simply refers to the possibility of having moments of direct insight,[226] even though the subtle qualities still have to keep on growing.[227]

The Zhentong Interpretation of the Ratnagotravibhāga

The Jonang tradition of zhentong Madhyamaka asserts a truly existing ultimate that is endowed with all buddha qualities and thus not "empty of an own-being" *(rang stong)*, but "empty of other" *(gzhan stong)* nonexisting adventitious stains. The validity of the common Madhyamaka assertion that "all phenomena are empty of an own-being" is thus restricted to the level of apparent truth. Such a stance is mainly based on the Tathagatagarbhasūtras, but also Yogācāra works are adduced, since their theory of *trisvabhāva (three natures,* i.e., the *imagined, dependent,* and *perfect natures)*[228] allow such a distinction between rangtong and zhentong.[229] In his *Ri chos nges don rgya mtsho,* Dölpopa defines zhentong in the following way:

> Since it has been said that the dharmatā [or] perfect [nature], which is empty of the imagined and dependent, ultimately exists, the ultimate is well established as being zhentong only.[230]

"Ultimate" or "true" existence should not be taken in an ontological sense,[231] however, as becomes clear from the following passage:

> The dharmakāya is free from mental fabrications throughout beginningless time. Because of recognizing it as being free from mental fabrications, it is truly established.[232]

The definition of the dharmakāya, or the ultimate, as being free from mental fabrications excludes the extreme of an ontological existence. "Being truly established" rather means that the experience of the dharmakāya is really true.[233]

It is said that such an insight dawned in Dölpopa's mind during a Kālacakra retreat at Jonang,[234] but later proponents of zhentong such as Tāranātha (1575–1634) claim the continuity of the meditation tradition of Tsen Kawoché with the zhentong of the Jonangpa.[235] Thus, Tsen Kawoché points out that his Kashmiri teacher Sajjana already adhered to a distinction between the real and imputed in the last dharmacakra, which was taken to have definitive meaning. According to an important collection of one hundred instructions *(khrid)* preserved by Jonang Künga Drölchog (Jo nang Kun dga' grol mchog) (1507–66), Tsen Kawoché said with regard to the "instruction" of zhentong:[236]

> Sajjana, the *paṇḍita* from Kashmir, made the very significant statement that the Victorious One turned the dharmacakra three times. The first [dharma]cakra concerned the four [noble] truths, the middle one the lack of defining characteristics, and the final one careful distinctions. Of them, the first two did not distinguish between the real and the imputed. During the ultimate ascertainment of the final one, he taught by distinguishing between the middle and the extremes[237] and by distinguishing between phenomena and their true nature.[238]

Even though Sajjana's statement does not prove that zhentong was already being taught in India, as Künga Drölchog (Kun dga' grol mchog) would have us believe, it does suggest that at least one of the hermeneutical traditions that strictly follow the *Saṁdhinirmocanasūtra* already existed in Kashmir.

In his *Zab mo gzhan stong dbu ma'i brgyud 'debs,* Tāranātha surprisingly lists in a zhentong transmission—besides Sajjana, Zu Gawa Dorjé, and Tsen Kawoché—Ngog Loden Sherab and Chomden Rigpai Raldri (Bcom ldan rig pa'i ral gri),[239] whose *Ratnagotravibhāga* commentaries are, to say the least, not exactly in line with Dölpopa's zhentong position as it is described in his *Ri chos nges don rgya mtsho,* but this must be seen against the background of Dölpopa's distinction between an extraordinary zhentong explanation with primordially existing ultimate qualities and an ordinary Mahāyāna explanation.[240] In other words, in the eyes of the Jonangpas both Ngog Loden Sherab and Tsen Kawoché explain the *Ratnagotravibhāga* on an ordinary Mahāyāna level in such a way that they do not exclude the ultimate existence of qualities in a Vajrayāna context.[241]

In his description of the diffusion of zhentong, Kongtrül Lodrö Tayé claims that it goes back to Nāgārjuna's and Maitreya's commentaries of the final dharmacakra (i.e., Nāgārjuna's collection of hymns and the Maitreya works except the *Abhisamayālaṁkāra*),[242] which were further commented upon by Asaṅga, Vasubandhu, Candragomin, Śāntipa, and Sajjana. Both Ngog Loden Sherab and Tsen Kawoché are mentioned as having received these teachings from Sajjana, which shows that for Kongtrül, too, Ngog Loden Sherab figures significantly in the zhentong transmission. Whereas these commentaries were interpreted along the lines of both the Cittamātra and Madhyamaka views, Tsangnagpa, the Third Karmapa Rangjung Dorjé, Dölpopa, and Longchen Rabjampa, among others, explained them according to the great Madhyamaka tradition of definitive meaning that goes beyond Cittamātra.[243]

In other words, both the mahāmudrā and zhentong traditions refer to the transmission of the Maitreya works of Ngog Loden Sherab and Tsen Kawoché. Besides Dölpopa and his disciples, it is especially Rangjung Dorjé and Longchen Rabjampa who are of particular interest, since they are mentioned as proponents of zhentong and, at the same time, interpret the *Ratnagotravibhāga* from their respective mahāmudrā and dzogchen traditions. As will be shown further down, both Rangjung Dorjé's and Longchenpa's positions differ considerably from the zhentong of the Jonangpas, with Rangjung Dorjé's works containing explanations that can be described as a prototype of what I propose to provisionally call "Kagyü zhentong."

Karma Trinlepa had already described a major difference between the zhentong views of Rangjung Dorjé and a position that accords with the Jonangpa, a difference that can be confirmed by a comparison of Dölpopa's, Sabzang Mati Panchen's, and Kongtrül Lodrö Tayé's *Ratna-gotravibhāga* commentaries. Whereas for Kongtrül buddhahood is unconditioned only inasmuch as its dharmakāya does not appear to disciples,[244] Dölpopa claims that buddhahood is free from moments, while Mati Panchen (Mati paṇ chen) in his commentary on RGV I.6 quotes the *Mahāparinirvāṇasūtra* according to which unconditioned buddhahood means that it does not belong to the three times. Dölpopa criticizes Kagyü mahāmudrā for claiming that the mind or thoughts are the dharmakāya, because the ultimate (taken by the Jonangpas as something that is beyond the three times) cannot be the nature of something adventitious and impermanent.

This same difference is also addressed by Tāranātha in his *Zab don nyer gcig pa,* in which he compares, among other things, the *trisvabhāva* interpretations of Dölpopa and Serdog Panchen (Gser mdog paṇ chen) Śākya Chogden. Dölpopa claims that the ultimate is exclusively the unchangeable perfect nature,[245] which is empty of the dependent and imagined natures, Śākya Chogden restricting the negandum to the imagined nature alone. The basis of emptiness is the dependent, the entire mind, which takes on various forms of a perceived object and perceiving subject. Tāranātha concludes his comparison by pointing out one fundamental difference: Śākya Chogden takes nondual wisdom to be something multiple and momentary, whereas Dölpopa explains it as permanent in the sense of being beyond permanence and impermanence and transcending one and many.[246]

In a similar way to Śākya Chogden, both Rangjung Dorjé and, on this point, Zhönu Pal take the momentary natural mind as the basis of negation and the adventitious stains as the negandum. If we decide to follow Śākya Chogden and call this zhentong, we need to distinguish at least two main types of zhentong that differ in defining the basis of negation as being either completely transcendent (Jonangpa) or at least to a certain extent immanent (Śākya Chogden).

Finally, it should be noted that the opposition between zhentong and mahāmudrā can be traced back to a different understanding of the *ālaya-vijñāna* in Asaṅga's *Mahāyānasaṁgraha* and the *Laṅkāvatārasūtra*. In the *Mahāyānasaṁgraha* (MS I.45–48) Asaṅga maintains a clear-cut distinction between an *ālayavijñāna* and a supramundane mind that arises from the seeds of the dharmadhātu (or its outflow).[247] The line between pure and impure mind is so clearly drawn that ordinary beings are implicitly not included in the dharmakāya and only have the *ālayavijñāna* as a basis. It was in view of this that Paramārtha (500–69) developed his theory of a ninth consciousness, the so-called *amalavijñāna*.[248] The *Laṅkāvatārasūtra*, on the other hand, equates the *ālayavijñāna* (i.e., the eighth *vijñāna*) with buddha nature, so much so that the latter is taken to be permeated by mental imprints and to move on under the other seven consciousnesses like the ocean and its waves. For certain proponents of mahāmudrā who take the nature of thoughts to be the dharmakāya this equation is essential, and it is not surprising that Zhönu Pal heavily relies in his *Ratnagotravibhāga-vyākhyā* commentary on the *Laṅkāvatārasūtra*, even though the latter is not quoted even once in the *Ratnagotravibhāgavyākhyā*.

2. Various Positions Related to Zhönu Pal's Interpretation

IN ORDER to assess Zhönu Pal's way of explaining and using the *Ratnagotravibhāga,* it is helpful to compare it with the positions of exegetes who are close to him, both in terms of philosophical view and time. As already explained in the introduction, it is not possible to do this by simply comparing the commentaries on certain stanzas of the root text or using some similar approach, given that each master reveals his particular view in a different context, and sometimes not at all in his *Ratnagotravibhāga* commentary. The method I shall use here is rather to find answers to the questions of how each exegete presents the buddha qualities and emptiness,[249] and how he uses the *Ratnagotravibhāga* or the teaching of buddha nature in his own hermeneutical tradition. Textual passages from the respective *Ratnagotravibhāga* commentaries and other works dealing with buddha nature will be selected and evaluated against the backdrop of these hermeneutical traditions.

It would go beyond the scope of this work to take all major scholars of the fourteenth and fifteenth centuries into account here. We could argue, for example, that the positions of Rongtön Sheja Künrig (Rong ston Shes bya kun rig) (1367–1449) or Tsongkhapa (1357–1419) should be considered, since Zhönu Pal was a disciple of both of them.[250] But judging from the way Rongtön (Rong ston) comments RGV I.26 or RGV I.157–58 (J I.154–55), it is likely that Zhönu Pal did not adopt anything specific from Rongtön for his own interpretation of the *Ratnagotravibhāga.*[251] To be sure, I do not wish to suggest that it is useless to compare Zhönu Pal with Rongtön, but this would require a careful study of other works by Rongtön and of his hermeneutical principles as well. Suffice it to say that Zhönu Pal must have been influenced by Rongtön in his adherence to Loden Sherab's distinction between a buddha nature and a fully matured buddha.[252]

It is difficult to say the extent to which Zhönu Pal was influenced by Tsongkhapa. Zhamar Chödrag Yeshé claims in his biography of Zhönu Pal that the latter was fond of Tsongkhapa's distinction between the provisional and definitive meanings on the basis of the *Ratnagotravibhāga*,[253] but unfortunately we are not further informed how this distinction was made and if it was in line with how Zhönu Pal makes it in his commentary. Of further interest is the information from the same biography that Zhönu Pal was told by his teacher Rimibabpa Sönam Rinchen (Ri mi 'babs pa Bsod nams rin chen) (1362–1453)[254] in 1440, after teachings at the Dagpo pass, to abandon neither the mahāmudrā view nor the tradition of the Gelugpas;[255] and the Eighth Karmapa Mikyö Dorjé somewhat pointedly remarks that Zhönu Pal took Tsongkhapa's view as a guideline and at the same time upheld the tradition of the Dagpo Kagyü.[256] Even though it cannot be ruled out with certainty that Tsongkhapa gave Zhönu Pal teachings that accord with the latter's *Ratnagotravibhāga* commentary, it should be noted that some passages in the description by Zhamarpa (Zhva dmar pa)'s of Zhönu Pal's life also suggest substantial differences with the Gelugpas. Thus, we are informed that Zhönu Pal criticized the Gelugpas for being expert in the gradual path to enlightenment without knowing Atiśa's *Bodhipathapradīpa*,[257] and Zhönu Pal is further reported to have had a low opinion of Tsongkhapa's student Gyaltsab Jé.[258] Most importantly, Zhönu Pal does not mention Tsongkhapa in his *Ratnagotravibhāga* commentary even once.

Whatever instructions Zhönu Pal received from Tsongkhapa, from a doctrinal point of view it is easier to combine the nonconceptual mahāmudrā approach with Loden Sherab's definition of ultimate truth as being completely beyond the reach of conceptual mind. In fact, Zhönu Pal does declare that he followed Loden Sherab, and this can be observed, among other places, in Zhönu Pal's commentary on RGV I.26, in which the buddha element is explained as a cause. The root text (I.26) lists the last four vajra points, namely the buddha element (i.e., buddha nature), enlightenment, qualities, and activity, and takes the first to be the cause and the remaining three to be conditions of purification. In the *Ratnagotravibhāgavyākhyā*, the buddha element is explained in the following way:

> Here, of these four [vajra] points, the first one should be understood as the cause that brings forth the Three Jewels, after you come to rely on its [natural] purity on the basis of your own correct mental engagement, given that it is the seed of the supramundane properties.[259]

In his *Ratnagotravibhāga* commentary Zhönu Pal strictly follows Loden Sherab and takes the buddha element to be a substantial cause *(nye bar len pa'i rgyu).*[260] Earlier, however, in his Kālacakra commentary called *Rgyud gsum gsang ba*[261] he seems to have advocated a more sophisticated explanation in distinguishing the buddha element (or buddha nature) from a substantial cause and attending conditions, a distinction that allows buddha nature to be only a necessary cause of enlightenment.[262] This would be similar to Gyaltsab Jé's explanation of the buddha nature as "cause without which enlightenment would not occur" *(med na mi 'byung ba'i rgyu mtshan),* which means that the buddha nature does not function as a fortified potential[263] or a substantial cause.[264] Indeed, Mikyö Dorjé states in his review of Zhönu Pal's *Rgyud gsum gsang ba* that the latter was influenced by Tsongkhapa in his presentation of the natural and fortified potentials.[265] Zhönu Pal is further criticized by Mikyö Dorjé for citing the Third Karmapa Rangjung Dorjé in support of his claim that the buddha nature in sentient beings is merely their six sense fields *(āyatanas),* which resemble a buddha.[266] But even though such an interpretation is found in Zhönu Pal's *Ratnagotravibhāga* commentary, in the context of elucidating DhS 66–68, it is clearly ruled out as a possible explanation of buddha nature in his commentary on RGV I.25.[267] Still, it is an interesting question for future research: what exactly did Zhönu Pal, and thus a part of the later Kagyü tradition, inherit from Tsongkhapa?

It is evident, on the other hand, that Zhönu Pal's main concern in his *Ratnagotravibhāga* commentary is to demonstrate that the *Ratnagotravibhāga* offers doctrinal support for the direct mahāmudrā path of the Dagpo Kagyü. This is what he repeatedly claims, basing himself as he does on Gampopa,[268] Jigten Sumgön,[269] and various other mahāmudrā masters. Moreover, his theory of subtle buddha qualities hints at a synthesis of Loden Sherab's position with commentarial traditions other than those of the Gelugpas. For these reasons, the background against which Zhönu Pal's position will be evaluated is restricted (apart from Loden Sherab's summary of the *Ratnagotravibhāga*) to a narrow selection of masters of the Kagyü, Nyingma, and Jonang schools who were active in the fourteenth century, a time of dramatic intellectual change in Tibet.

The Position of the Third Karmapa Rangjung Dorjé

Rangjung Dorjé is said to have composed a summary of the *Ratnagotravibhāga,* on the basis of which his disciple Karma Könzhön (b. 1333) and then later Karma Trinlepa wrote commentaries of their own.[270] Unfortunately none of these three works has come down to us, so that we have to rely on other sources if we wish to assess Rangjung Dorjé's contribution to the exegesis of the *Ratnagotravibhāga* and buddha nature—for instance, his recently discovered commentary on the *Dharmadhātustotra* or his *Snying po bstan pa* and autocommentary on the *Zab mo nang gi don*. The latter work shows how the doctrine of buddha nature can be blended with mahāmudrā and dzogchen in a tantric context.

The introduction of Rangjung Dorjé's *Dharmadhātustotra* commentary contains the interesting remark that the *Ratnagotravibhāga* and the *Madhyamakāvatāra* teach in detail how the form kāyas and the dharmakāya arise from the accumulations of merit and wisdom respectively.[271] That this should not be understood in the sense that the kāyas are produced from scratch can be seen from the way Rangjung Dorjé explains the seven examples of how the dharmadhātu (equated by him with the buddha nature or even the Buddha)[272] abides in all sentient beings. The first example, of the essence of butter in milk and manifest butter, is taken as signifying that the Buddha appears through the causal act of removing all hindrances on the path, but it is not that he arises on his own, through another, a combination of both or from no cause.[273] The second example of the *Dharmadhātustotra* (DhS 5–6), namely the lamp inside a vase, illustrates for Rangjung Dorjé that the dharmadhātu does not mean that things are merely empty. In order to show that it refers to the two types of wisdom (the one that knows what reality is like, and the one that knows its extent), Rangjung Dorjé quotes and explains RGV I.87–88 (J I.85–86):

> That this is certainly the case can be seen from the *Uttaratantra* (i.e., the *Ratnagotravibhāga*), in which it has been said:
>
> > In brief, it should be known that there are four synonyms,
> > The dharmakāya and so forth,
> > Reflecting four aspects of meaning
> > With regard to the immaculate sphere (i.e., dharmadhātu).
> >
> > [The four are:] [It contains] inseparable buddha properties,
> > Its potential is attained as it is (i.e., as dharmatā),
> > It is not of a false, deceptive nature,
> > And it is quiescent by nature throughout beginningless time.[274]

> Under the aspect of [it as] fruit, [the sphere] is taught as being inseparable from the buddha properties; under the aspect of [it as] cause, [it is taught] as the naturally present and fortified potentials; under the aspect of [it as] the two truths, as a correct and nondeceptive valid cognition; and under the aspect of [it as] abandonment, as being naturally quiescent and quiescent in terms of [having abandoned] adventitious [stains]. To be sure, [these aspects] are not essentially separate. This is explained in detail in the *Anūnatvāpūrṇatvanirdeśasūtra*.[275]

In other words, both the naturally present and the fortified potentials are simply an aspect of the dharmadhātu and thus not different from the dharmakāya. This becomes particularly clear in Rangjung Dorjé's commentary on the seventh example (DhS 14–15), which illustrates that something with no essence (namely the banana tree) has a fruit with an essence. Rangjung Dorjé explains:

> When you split a banana tree, no essence is found; nevertheless first a fruit ripens and then it is eaten. Likewise, when you analyze saṁsāra, no essence whatever is found. [For] even saṁsāra is [only] thoughts.... Thoughts have no essence and are like an illusion and a mirage. Still, from the transformation of the basis of these very [thoughts], form kāyas emerge that benefit all sentient beings. Therefore, a consciousness that is caught in the net of defilements is called saṁsāra. By becoming free from defilements, it turned into the all-accomplishing wisdom, which is nectar for sentient beings.[276]

It is noteworthy that for Rangjung Dorjé the notion of growth is restricted to the form kāyas.[277] The hollow banana tree serves to point out that you do not find an essence upon analysis, which does not rule out that qualities of the dharmakāya are present (the dharmakāya being beyond the reach of the intellect). Contrary to such an understanding, Śākya Chogden (1428–1507) cautions in his commentary on DhS 15–16 that in the example the sweet fruits (bananas) are not taught as being the essence of the banana tree. This means that even though sentient beings possess a buddha element, it is not exactly the case that the essence of sentient beings is a buddha.[278] Rangjung Dorjé's view on the relation between the buddha nature and the dharmakāya can best be seen from his summary of the seven examples in the *Dharmadhātustotra:*

> Thus the stages of teaching the natural purity of the element by way of examples [are:] The example of butter illustrates the essence. At the time of [existing as] a sentient being a mere sentient being appears and not a buddha, just as in milk a mixture of water and butter appears [and not pure butter]. When you have become a buddha, you are not mingled with stains; this is like the appearance of butter which is not in the least mixed with liquid. The example of the lamp illustrates the noncontradictory inherent qualities. Even though the light of qualities does not differ at all, regardless of whether you are purified, it appears to become stronger and weaker depending on the extent to which you are enveloped by hindrances. The example of the gem illustrates that the proper qualities of the dharmakāya are free from all hindrances and that the [latter] possesses the quality of engaging in nonconceptual activity. The example of gold illustrates cause and effect, namely the unfabricated and the sambhogakāya, which latter is of the nature of virtue and of the pure mental faculty *(yid)*. The example of the rice and its husk illustrates that the intellect does not see until it is liberated from the imprints of ignorance. The example of the banana tree is an example of the fruit of the nirmāṇakāya, namely the transformation of the basis of [your] clinging and thoughts.[279]

To sum up, Rangjung Dorjé fully equates the dharmakāya with the dharmadhātu, which is thus inseparably endowed with buddha qualities. The latter are simply hindered by adventitious stains and unfold fully at the time of purification. In other words, the accumulations of merit and wisdom only cause the kāyas indirectly, in that the accumulations enable the removal of all hindrances and the manifestation of what has always existed. It is noteworthy, though, that the only example implying real growth (namely the fruit of a banana tree) concerns the nirmāṇakāya, but the way Rangjung Dorjé interprets it, we could infer that the hollow banana tree only stands for not finding any essence in the thoughts of the impure mind, and that these empty thoughts coexist with all buddha qualities. Further down, we will see that in tantric contexts Rangjung Dorjé indeed claims that the qualities of the form kāyas exist primordially.

Some Tibetan sources[280] speak of Rangjung Dorjé as an adherent of zhentong and even of his possibly having influenced Dölpopa. Kongtrül Lodrö Tayé, whose *Ratnagotravibhāga* commentary is generally referred to as representing the "zhentong tradition" of the Karma Kagyü school, says in the colophon of his commentary that he has presented the seven essential vajra points of the *Ratnagotravibhāga* in terms of phenomena and their true nature *(dharmatā)* following Rangjung Dorjé's lead.[281] In his description of how zhentong spread,[282] Kongtrül mentions, after Tsangnagpa, the second Buddha Rangjung Dorjé, suggesting that the latter stood in a "zhentong tradition"[283] that came down to him through Tsangnagpa.[284] Karma Trinlepa explicitly calls Rangjung Dorjé a zhentongpa (i.e., a follower of the "empty-of-other [view]"):

> My lama, Omniscient [Seventh Karmapa Chödrag Gyatso (Chos grags rgya mtsho) (1454–1506)][285] says: "Nowadays, some who are proud of being proponents of zhentong [claim that] a permanent, stable, steadfast, unchangeable ultimate truly exists, and since it is empty of the adventitious [stains resulting from] clinging to an object and a subject, [they claim that] it is profound zhentong. Since they thus rejoice in an eternalist view, this is [but] the deceiving words of propounding a profound emptiness—the clinging to an extreme—and not the pure zhentong taught in the sūtras. Being confused about Jina Maitreya's teaching [according to which] the true nature of mind *(sems nyid)* is not empty of unsurpassable qualities, they say that the sixty-four qualities that are [already] present at [the level of the] ground are empty of adventitious stains and call this zhentong. [Thus] they demean the Victorious One by saying that he wanders in saṁsāra, inasmuch as a perfect buddha whose hindrances are exhausted and whose wisdom is fully blossomed [would then] experience the suffering of the six realms—hell and the like.[286] What has been taught in accordance with the tantras, the *Bodhisattva Trilogy (sems 'grel [skor gsum]),*[287] many sūtras, and the Maitreya works is the zhentong professed by Rangjung Dorjé." Thus I have heard in the discourses of the Jinendra (i.e., the Seventh Karmapa).[288]

The Eighth Karmapa Mikyö Dorjé, who claims to follow Rangjung Dorjé, also takes buddha nature in the sense that sentient beings do not possess their own qualities. These qualities, rather, are possessed by the Tathāgata, who is a buddha endowed with both purities; and *nature (garbha)* refers to the fact that all sentient beings are pervaded by the Tathāgata's tantric form kāyas,[289] and that his dharmakāya of luminosity is inseparable from the suchness of sentient beings.[290]

In the above-quoted passage, Karma Trinlepa obviously distinguishes Rangjung Dorjé's zhentong from an "eternalist" version of it, and thus also from the zhentong upheld by Dölpopa and Sabzang Mati Panchen. My comparison of their *Ratnagotravibhāga* commentaries with the one of Kongtrül Lodrö Tayé has shown that the latter differs considerably with regard to the explanation of unconditioned buddhahood in RGV I.6. Kongtrül quotes Rongtön's classification of four types of being unconditioned *(asaṁskṛta)* and explains that even though the dharmakāya has, among other things, an unconditioned quality to it (because it does not appear to disciples), it is not the case that it is unconditioned; for if it were it would contradict that it possesses knowledge, compassion, and power.[291] Dölpopa claims with reference to RGV I.6 in his *Ri chos nges don rgya mtsho,* on the other hand, that the "unconditioned nature of buddhahood" refers to the fact that this is free from momentariness, while Mati Panchen in his commentary on RGV I.6 quotes the *Mahāparinirvāṇasūtra* according to which *unconditioned* means not being subject to the three times.[292] Dölpopa's critique of the Kagyü mahāmudrā position that realization is attained by recognizing that the nature of mind or thoughts is the dharmakāya must also be seen in the light of this different conception of the ultimate and its relation to the apparent truth, for the dharmakāya cannot be the nature of something adventitious if it is taken as wholly stable and permanent.[293]

Given these differences, some scholars have assumed up to now that Situ Panchen Chökyi Jungné (Situ paṇ chen Chos kyi byung gnas) (1699/1700–1774) blended the seemingly irreconcilable zhentong and mahāmudrā positions and spread them throughout all the Kagyü traditions of Kham *(khams),*[294] and that followers of the nonsectarian movement *(ris med),* such as Kongtrül Lodrö Tayé, described Rangjung Dorjé and others as zhentongpas in a biased way.[295] Karma Trinlepa's remark and its conformity with Kongtrül's different understanding of RGV I.6 suggest rather that Kongtrül's description of Rangjung Dorjé should be taken more seriously—namely that the latter actually upheld a Kagyü version of zhentong, even though he himself did not call it that. Based on the autocommentary on the *Zab mo nang gi don,* I will show that Rangjung Dorjé's so-called zhentong is mainly based on Asaṅga's distinction between the *ālayavijñāna* and a supramundane mind in the *Mahāyānasaṁgraha* and on a combination of this Yogācāra explanation with mahāmudrā and dzogchen.

It is an important concern of zhentong to clearly distinguish that which is empty from that *of which* it is empty. In attempting to do so, Dölpopa contrasted a *kun gzhi rnam shes (ālayavijñāna),* which is the basis of saṁsāra, from the pure basis of buddha qualities, which he called *kun gzhi'i ye shes* ("wisdom of the [primordial] ground").[296] Even though Rangjung Dorjé does not make use of Dölpopa's terminology (i.e., *kun gzhi'i ye shes*), he distinguishes in his autocommentary on the *Zab mo nang gi don* a *ground (kun gzhi),* which can also mean suchness,[297] from a *kun gzhi rnam shes,* namely the normal "ground consciousness"[298] *(ālayavijñāna):*

> In this regard, if *ground (kun gzhi)* is not mentioned [together with] the word *consciousness, ground* may refer to suchness. Therefore, consciousness is mentioned [together with it].[299]

This distinction is made in the context of explaining the pure and impure aspects of mind that function as a cause of everything, the topic of the first chapter in the *Zab mo nang gi don.* The first three *pāda*s of the first chapter are:

> As to the cause, it is the beginningless true nature of mind
> *(sems nyid);*
> Even though it has no dimension and does not fall into any possible
> [conceptual, ontological, or metaphysical] category,
> it unfolds [as] unimpeded play.... [300]

The commentary starts by pointing out that in the common language of all *yāna*s the "true nature of mind" *(sems nyid)* is known under two aspects, namely *possessing purity* and *being impure.* Mind in its purity is illustrated by recourse to the simile of the element space in the *Ratnagotravibhāga,* in which the purity of mind is compared to space, which is without support, and the defiled mind to the supported elements (earth being supported by water, water by air, and air by space):

> In the *Uttaratantra* [*Ratnagotravibhāga* I.55–57] it has been said: "Earth is supported by water, water by air, and air by space. But space has no support [among] the elements of air, water, and earth. Similarly, the skandhas, elements, and sense faculties are supported by *karman* and defilements, *karman* and defilements by [constantly][301] uncalled-for mental engagement, and uncalled-for mental engagement is supported by the purity of mind. The nature of mind, however, has no support in any phenomena."[302] These [stanzas] express the buddha nature[303] *(sangs rgyas kyi snying po)* as mind, which means that it is the basis of saṁsāra and nirvāṇa in their entirety.[304]

This explanation of buddha nature as a basis of saṁsāra and nirvāṇa is further reinforced by quoting a stanza from Saraha's *Dohākośagīti,* stanza 43:

> The true nature of mind *(sems nyid)* alone is the seed of everything;
> I prostrate to [this] mind,
> In which worldly existence and nirvāṇa spreads,
> And which is like a wish-fulfilling jewel in bestowing the desired fruit.[305]

As we shall see, for Rangjung Dorjé the true nature of mind *(sems nyid)* (as buddha nature) functions as the basis of saṁsāra, in that it contains the stainlessness of the eight consciousnesses, which must be taken as mere appearances empty of duality. With such a mahāmudrā interpretation of buddha nature, Rangjung Dorjé can still draw a clear line between the pure and impure mind, while following Asaṅga's restriction of the *ālayavijñāna*[306] to that which merely consists of all seeds or mental imprints of skandhas, elements, and *āyatanas*, which are said to be "embraced by false imagining" and to be the root of all hindrances.[307] In conformity with the *Abhidharmasamuccaya* and the *Mahāyānasaṁgraha,* the *ālayavijñāna* is not considered to be the cause of buddha wisdom; the properties of purification arise rather from the dharmakāya. This becomes clear from an answer to a rhetorical question in the autocommentary of the *Zab mo nang gi don:*

> Question: How are the properties of purification produced? They are supported by buddha nature, [inasmuch as] it is the dharmakāya of the above-mentioned purity of mind.[308]

In support of this, Rangjung Dorjé refers to RGV I.152 (J I.149), in which the natural and fortified potentials are compared respectively to the "underground treasure" and the "fruit from the tree." By further quoting the *Mahāyānasaṁgraha* (I.45–48), Rangjung Dorjé indicates his predilection for Asaṅga's clear distinction between the *ālayavijñāna* and that which serves as a basis for the fortified potential (in the following called the "Yogācāra portion"):

> If that which contains all seeds, [namely] the consciousness of maturation (i.e., the *ālayavijñāna*), is the cause of all defilements, how can it be the seed of the supramundane mind, which is the

remedy for this *[ālayavijñāna]?* The supramundane mind is unfamiliar *(ma 'dris pa);* thus there is no [mental] imprint from it [in the *ālayavijñāna*]. Question: "If [its] mental imprint does not exist [there], from which seed must it be said to arise?" Answer: It arises from the seed [or][309] mental imprint of studying,[310] which is the outflow of the very pure dharmadhātu.[311]

Objection: "Is the mental imprint of studying identical with *(ngo bo nyid)*[312] the *ālayavijñāna* or not? If it were identical[313] with the *ālayavijñāna,* how would it be suitable as the seed of the remedy for it? If you say that it is not identical with it, you [must] see what the basis for this seed of the mental imprint of studying is." [Answer:] The mental imprint of studying [occurs] based on the enlightenment of the buddhas.[314] Even though it enters into the consciousness of maturation (i.e., *ālayavijñāna*) in the same way as water [into] milk, arising together with the basis into which it enters, it is not [this] *ālayavijñāna,* given that it is the seed of the remedy for [the *ālayavijñāna*]. From a small mental imprint it [gradually] turns into an average one and then a big one, since you will [eventually] be endowed with [the fruits of] having studied, reflected, and meditated many times. It [must be] regarded as the seed of the dharmakāya. Being the remedy for the *ālayavijñāna,* it is not identical with[315] the *ālayavijñāna.* Even though [this seed] belongs to this world, it is the outflow of the very pure supramundane dharmadhātu, and thus the seed of the supramundane mind. [And] even though the supramundane mind may not have arisen [yet], it is [still] the remedy for entanglement in all defilements and migration to lower realms, and [the remedy that] suppresses all faults. It supports the connection with buddhas and bodhisattvas.[316]

Although it (i.e., this seed) is [still] of a mundane nature for beginner bodhisattvas, it is regarded as being included in the dharmakāya, and for śrāvakas and pratyekabuddhas as being included in the "body of liberation."[317] It is not the *ālayavijñāna,* but included in the dharmakāya and the "body of liberation." As it gradually increases,[318] turning from being small into being average and then big, the consciousness of maturation wanes and becomes completely transformed, [so that] the [*ālayavijñāna,* which] comprises all seeds, even does not exist [any more], having been abandoned in every respect.[319]

Rangjung Dorjé adds to this *Mahāyānasaṁgraha* passage the following remark:

> If some think that the fortified potential has newly arisen, it is not so. The naturally present potential is the dharmadhātu. As to the array of eight (the *ālayavijñāna* and so on) in it, they have been placed [there] and are characterized by false imagining. Likewise, the true nature, namely the stainlessness, of the eight accumulations [of consciousness] exists as the nature *(rang bzhin)* of the four wisdoms.[320] Thanks to the virtuous elements that have been placed [in the mind] by proper thought and that are supported by the enlightenment of the buddhas, previous stains are destroyed, and the delusion of the eight accumulations [of consciousness] ceases to exist. This, then, has been called the "wisdom of the transformation of the basis." ...Stainlessness [of mind] is regarded as wisdom, and the [state of] being mingled with stains [is regarded] as consciousness.[321]

Nothing is newly produced, since the nature of the four wisdoms already exists as the true nature or stainlessness of the eight consciousnesses. In other words, the four wisdoms, or the part of the naturally pure ultimate that is temporarily covered by the adventitious stains of the eight consciousnesses, already exist. It is this part that is revealed by the virtuous elements that have been placed in the mind (and that are supported by the enlightenment of the buddhas rather than the *ālayavijñāna*). It should be noted that this stainlessness of the eight consciousnesses is thus not included in the *ālayavijñāna.* To return to the example used in the *Mahāyānasaṁgraha,* even though water and milk are mixed, they are still "unfamiliar" *(ma 'dris pa).* The sentence "Although it (i.e., this seed) is [still] of a mundane nature for beginner bodhisattvas, it is regarded as being included in the dharmakāya" (MS I.48) suggests that ordinary beings are not included in the dharmakāya, having as they do the *ālayavijñāna* as their only basis. Rangjung Dorjé follows Asaṅga in drawing a clear-cut distinction between the impure and pure mind, implicitly equating ordinary sentient beings with the *ālayavijñāna* (including its active forms of consciousness) and excluding them from the dharmakāya. The positive factors of the path are but the outflow of the pure dharmadhātu, with an increasingly larger part of it manifesting itself as the hindering defilements of the impure mind are removed.

To review, even though Rangjung Dorjé only distinguishes an *ālayavijñāna (kun gzhi rnam shes)* that is the impure mind from a *kun gzhi* (which may also refer to suchness), he in fact distinguishes the *ālayavijñāna* from the pure dharmadhātu in such a way that it would be an easy play on words to call the latter *kun gzhi ye shes,* inasmuch as the manifestation of the pure dharmadhātu (or suchness) is called the "wisdom of the transformation of the basis."

The Eighth Karmapa Mikyö Dorjé includes the same passage from the *Mahāyānasaṁgraha* in his commentary on the *Abhisamayālaṁkāra,* weaving it into a general outline or introductory presentation in the second paragraph of the first chapter, which deals with the "foundation of accomplishment," or, for him, buddha nature.[322] Indeed it represents an essential part of his "zhentong interpretation" of buddha nature, which again centers on a similar distinction between a *kun gzhi rnam shes* and a *kun gzhi,* with the only difference that Mikyö Dorjé uses the term *kun gzhi ye shes* instead of *kun gzhi.*[323] *Kun gzhi* is equated then with the transformation of the basis in the *Dharmadharmatāvibhāga,*[324] the naturally present potential, and the synonyms for emptiness (including suchness) in the *Madhyānta-vibhāga.*[325]

It is probably in view of this interpretation of Mikyö Dorjé that Kongtrül Lodrö Tayé writes in his own commentary on the *Zab mo nang gi don* with reference to Rangjung Dorjé's autocommentary:

> Having in this regard designated in [his] autocommentary the dharmatā or suchness, viewed as the ground of all of saṁsāra and nirvāṇa, by the term *kun gzhi (ground),* he [taught] within this [part of the commentary] that the [mind that] is endowed with purity is the "wisdom of the ground of everything," while under the aspect of [it as the mind] containing all seeds he taught that it is the "consciousness of the ground of everything" *(ālaya-vijñāna).* This is a twofold division of the mind into pure and impure.[326]

As can be easily seen from the above-quoted passages, Kongtrül presents the contents of Rangjung Dorjé's autocommentary in line with Mikyö Dorjé's zhentong understanding, and in using the term *kun gzhi ye shes,* Kongtrül wanted to imply exactly that, and not that Rangjung Dorjé had the same zhentong view as Dölpopa.[327] The fact that the autocommentary on the *Zab mo nang gi don* was already written in 1325,[328] eight years before Dölpopa became a zhentongpa in 1333,[329] could be thus easily explained by seeing in Rangjung Dorjé's sharp distinction between the impure and pure (i.e., the *kun gzhi rnam shes* and *kun gzhi*) an older layer or a predecessor of a "zhentong position," which was not necessarily called that and was nothing other than a particular interpretation of Asaṅga's Yogācāra. If we follow Kongtrül or the Sakya master Mangtö Ludrub (Mang thos Klu sgrub), who claims that Rangjung Dorjé held a zhentong view before Dölpopa,[330] we have to add for clarity's sake that it was a different one.

But as already mentioned above, the term *zhentong* is not found in Rangjung Dorjé's works. A little further down, though, in his elucidation of the term *beginningless nature of mind (sems nyid thog med)* in the first *pāda* of the first chapter in the *Zab mo nang gi don,* Rangjung Dorjé uses the term *liberated from other,* which resembles zhentong:

> As to the "beginningless [mind]," since a beginning and end of time is a [mere] conceptual superimposition, [the cause of everything][331] is here [taken as] the true nature *(rang gi ngo bo)* of both the stainless [mind] and the [mind] mingled with stains, it is precisely this dependent arising; and it is completely liberated (i.e., free) from [all] else. Since there is no other beginning than it, one speaks of beginningless time.[332]

Now it would have been just as easy to say "empty of other" *(gzhan gyis stong pa)* as "completely liberated from [all] else" *(gzhan las rnam par grol ba).* But as we shall see further down, Rangjung Dorjé may have had other reasons for not using the term.[333] Karma Trinlepa must have had this passage in mind when he called Rangjung Dorjé a zhentongpa. A permanent and stable ultimate is clearly excluded here. The basis of emptiness is the true nature of mind *(sems nyid),* which is also the buddha nature endowed with inseparable qualities. If Dölpopa's more transcendent zhentong view had already gained prevalence at the time Rangjung Dorjé wrote these lines, the inclusion of "dependent arising" would have been a very clever move to set off his position from it.

It is also for this reason that Rangjung Dorjé wants us to understand Asaṅga's sharp distinction between the *ālayavijñāna* and the supramundane mind as being in harmony with Saraha's famous stanza stating that the mind is the seed of both saṁsāra and nirvāṇa. With the help of the latter, Rangjung Dorjé introduces into his commentary a mahāmudrā interpretation of buddha nature. This synthesis of Yogācāra and mahāmudrā led to some misinterpretations of Rangjung Dorjé, which Mikyö Dorjé addresses in his *Abhisamayālaṁkāra* commentary (Mikyö Dorjé adheres to a similar synthesis, equating as he does the actual wisdom of the ground *(kun gzhi ye shes)* with buddha nature:

> Some fools say that the omniscient Karmapa, the glorious Rangjung [Dorjé], asserts that the purport of the *Mahāyānottaratantra [Ratnagotravibhāga]* is: "Buddha nature exists in an inseparable way in the dharmadhātu of the mind of sentient beings." This noble being did not put it that way. In [his] autocommentary on the *Zab mo nang gi don,* he makes a twofold classification in calling both—the pure and the impure—"mind." Having explained that possessing impure mental impulses [means] to "possess mind" *(sems can)* (i.e., to be a sentient being), he says that such sentient beings do not possess the dharmadhātu. Moreover, he takes these sentient beings themselves to be the adventitious stains, which occur because of the false imagining that deviates from the dharmadhātu. Having called the pure mind *natural mind, original protector, original Buddha,* and so on, he says that [this mind] is the one that possesses the mode of being inseparable from the buddha qualities.[334]

If this assessment of Rangjung Dorjé's view is correct (and we have to admit that it is so with regard to the distinction between a pure and impure mind, as based on the *Mahāyānasaṁgraha*), we wonder how well it reflects Rangjung Dorjé's mahāmudrā teachings. In the *Rang byung rdo rje'i mgur rnams,* the following mahāmudrā definition of the term *ground (kun gzhi)* is given:[335]

> The *ground* is the basis of all saṁsāra and nirvāṇa. When not realized, it is saṁsāra, and when realized it is the "heart of the Tathāgata" (i.e., buddha nature). [This is how] the nature *(ngo bo)* of the "ground" has been expressed. For example, just as reflections appear in a polished mirror, the consciousness of the manifold [world] occurs and ceases in the stainless sphere of your own mind, because the clinging to the duality of an object and subject appears and occurs naturally in the sphere [of your own mind]. Saṁsāra and nirvāṇa are not two but one in essence *(ngo bo).* When you do not realize this, you are confused; when you realize it, you are liberated. Neither what must be realized nor the one who realizes it exists. Nevertheless, clinging to them as though they were two is the basis of saṁsāra. If you see the nature of nonduality, buddha nature *(rgyal ba'i snying po)* is actualized.[336]

The "Yogācāra portion" of the autocommentary (see above) requires distinguishing between the mirror of the stainless sphere of the mind, which displays the various reflections of the world, and the impure dualistic clinging to these appearances. Still, the ground can function as the basis of both, nirvāṇa and saṁsāra, depending on whether the reflections in the mirror of stainless mind are or are not recognized for what they are. It is in this sense that Rangjung Dorjé takes saṁsāra and nirvāṇa as one in essence, while adhering at the same time to the distinction between a pure and impure mind.

But things get even more complex: the following three *pādas* of the *Zab mo nang gi don* introduce a description of mind on the basis of the dzogchen categories *essence (ngo bo), nature (rang bzhin),* and *compassionate responsiveness (thugs rje).* The first five *pādas* (repeating the first three) of the first chapter in the *Zab mo nang gi don* are:

> As to the cause, it is the beginningless true nature of mind *(sems nyid);*
> Even though it has no dimension and does not fall into any possible [conceptual, ontological, or metaphysical] category,
> It unfolds [as] unimpeded play.
> Therefore [its] essence[337] is empty, [its] nature clear,
> [And its compassionate responsiveness][338] is unimpeded, [able to] appear as anything.[339]

Rangjung Dorjé's autocommentary on *pādas* 3–5 is:

> This very mind presents the aspect of an unfolding play that, in its momentary consciousness, is unimpeded in itself.[340] In view of this, [its] nature *(rang bzhin)* is present as emptiness and as natural luminosity. These two are the ground, given that from it the individual forms of the accumulation of mental factors and the seven accumulations of consciousness appear unimpeded and in one moment. In the impure state it has been taught as being the "mind," "mental faculty," and "consciousness." When pure, it is expressed by the terms *three kāyas* and *wisdom.*[341]

The true nature of mind *(sems nyid),* which is again referred to as the "ground," is called mind in an impure state and wisdom in a pure state. It should be noted that the appearances of the impure consciousness (mental factors, etc.) are said to appear from the ground, whose nature is taken to be emptiness and natural luminosity. It should be further noted that Rangjung Dorjé introduces the correct dzogchen terminology, according to which the *essence (ngo bo)* is normally defined as emptiness. But in his commentary he uses *nature (rang bzhin)* instead of *ngo bo* for emptiness, having undoubtedly been aware of the possible confusion that results from the quoted Yogācāra passage, in which it is said that the "essence" *(ngo bo)* of the *ālayavijñāna*[342] is not the seed of the dharmakāya. Having already used the term *rang bzhin* for emptiness, he could not use it again for clarity *(gsal)*. But in order to solidify the impression that he is still commenting on the three dzogchen categories, the term *rang bzhin* is skillfully repeated in the explanation of the term *gsal,* namely in the expression *rang bzhin gyis 'od gsal ba* ("natural luminosity").

To sum up, in his explanation of buddha nature, Rangjung Dorjé combines three different strands of interpretations:

1. The mahāmudrā interpretation stemming from Saraha
2. The interpretation according to Asaṅga's *Mahāyānasaṁgraha*
3. The dzogchen interpretation

In other words, for Rangjung Dorjé, well-founded mahāmudrā and dzogchen explanations need be combined with Asaṅga's Yogācāra distinction. Mikyö Dorjé for his part criticizes in his *Abhisamayālaṁkāra* commentary those followers of mahāmudrā among his contemporaries whose confusion, he says, is a hundred thousand times greater than the assertion: "The *ālayavijñāna,* by being purified, becomes the fruit, [namely] the mirror-like wisdom."[343] In the introduction to his *Madhyamakāvatāra* commentary we find an interesting explanation of the mahāmudrā approach. It is said that statements in mahāmudrā teachings to the effect that thoughts can appear as dharmakāya (given that saṁsāra and nirvāṇa are the same in essence) simply reflect the realization that thoughts do not exist as anything other than their dharmatā, not that thoughts can appear as the real dharmakāya:

> When the Madhyamaka view of this [mahāmudrā system] has arisen in the mindstream, the natural mind is said to have been actualized and the dharmakāya to have been made directly [manifest].[344] When you realize that phenomena *(dharmin),* such as sprouts and thoughts, are nothing other than their [respective] true nature *(dharmatā),* you use the verbal convention "thoughts appear as dharmakāya."[345]

We do not know if Rangjung Dorjé was of the same opinion, but given his attempt to combine mahāmudrā with Yogācāra, we should be at least careful not to define his position one-sidedly on the sole basis of his mahāmudrā teachings.[346]

Directly related to the question of how Rangjung Dorjé could blend the mahāmudrā- and Yogācāra-based explanations of buddha nature is how he defines the two truths. In the first seven *pāda*s of the ninth chapter of the *Zab mo nang gi don*, the chapter on purification and its basis, the two truths are both explained as being contained in the stainless buddha nature. The root text of the *Zab mo nang gi don* is:

> As for the [buddha] element in sentient beings, it is the stainless buddha nature *(sangs rgyas kyi snying po),*
> Endowed with the two truths.
> This [is stated] in the *Vajrajñāna[samuccayatantra]:*
> *Apparent* means to appear as a perceived and a perceiver.
> [This] truth is like [a reflection of] the moon in water.
> *Ultimate* refers to the eighteen [types of] emptiness.
> [This] truth is called *nondual wisdom.*[347]

Rangjung Dorjé explains in his autocommentary:

> What exists ultimately? It is the mind beyond every net of thought, the naturally pure element of sentient beings, [and] the buddha nature (*sangs rgyas kyi snying po*[348]).[349] These two exist, and so are expressed by these [terms]. Therefore it is stated: "As for the...[buddha] element of sentient beings, it is the stainless buddha nature endowed with the two truths." In this regard, the buddha nature is simply the nonexistence of the stains [or] delusion of the above-mentioned eight accumulations of consciousness,[350] but those who have not actualized the meaning of the two truths are deluded with regard to the mode of dependent arising, cling to two different views,[351] and fall into saṁsāra.[352]

From this it is not possible to infer that the two truths are one in essence but different isolates *(ngo bo gcig la ldog pa tha dad),*[353] for it is not the ordinary apparent truth which is included in buddha nature here, but only the stainlessness of the eight forms of consciousness. Indeed, this part of the commentary shows how Rangjung Dorjé blends the above-mentioned mahāmudrā and Yogācāra strands of thought. Once apparent truth is defined as the stainless forms of consciousness or mere appearance (see below), both truths can be taken as being inseparable and included in buddha nature (and clinging to them as being separate results in saṁsāra). This is what enables Rangjung Dorjé to accommodate his mahāmudrā teachings. But it does not mean that buddha nature is equated with the *ālayavijñāna*, as in the *Laṅkāvatārasūtra*. The inclusion of only a restricted apparent truth within buddha nature still allows Rangjung Dorjé to uphold a more moderate "zhentong," or rather *zhendröl (gzhan grol)*, distinction between the level of "normal" deluded appearances and buddha nature. This becomes clearer in a further definition[354] of the ultimate truth, on the basis of a passage from the second chapter of the *Guhyasamājatantra*, according to which the nonarisen mind is free from all entities, skandhas, and so on.[355] The apparent truth is further elucidated along the lines of Yogācāra philosophy, namely the tenet that apparent truth implies that no dualistic appearances are true:

> What has been imagined as the duality of a perceived and a perceiver does not exist at all, given the pronouncement [in MAV I.3] by Venerable Maitreya: "A consciousness arises that produces the appearances of objects, sentient beings, a self, and perceptions. There is no [corresponding outer] object, and since [such] an object does not exist, that [other, i.e., a perceiving subject] does not exist either."[356] Thus it has been said that no perceived [objects] and perceiving [subjects] of the imagined [nature] exist at all. Well then, how can this be presented as a truth? [The answer is:] Even though it does not exist, [something] appears. That is why it is called apparent truth, since its nature *(rang gi ngo bo nyid)* is that of not being deceptive.[357]

In response to the objection that these mere appearances would then be the ultimate truth, since the ultimate truth is defined as not being deceptive in the treatises on logic, Rangjung Dorjé further clarifies his understanding of the ultimate truth:

> These [mere appearances] are presented as the expressible ultimate *(paryāyaparamārtha)*, whereas the ultimate truth [here] is that which is related to the principle of true nature *(dharmatāyukti)*, [namely] the natural emptiness previously mentioned when presenting the eighteen great [types of] emptiness.[358]

In other words, buddha nature or the pure mind includes "mere appearances" in the form of the expressible ultimate truth, and it is only the expressible ultimate truth that is taken as apparent truth here. That it is different from what is ordinarily meant by apparent truth is clear from Rangjung Dorjé's *Dharmadhātustotra* commentary, where the two aspects *(nirvikāra* and *aviparyāsa)* of the perfect nature in MAV III.11cd are explained in the following way:

> The two [aspects of the perfect], the unchangeable and unmistaken, are taken [respectively] as the defining characteristics of the two truths. Acceptance by common consent *(lokaprasiddha)* and acceptance by reason *(yuktiprasiddha)* are varieties of the apparent truth.[359]

This means that the unchangeable perfect is taken as the ultimate, while the perfect in terms of being unmistaken is taken as a restricted form of apparent truth, which does not include acceptance by common consent or the like.

The relation between the two truths is then defined as being neither identical nor different:

> The two truths, which have been explained in such a way, are suchness and that which is liberated from other, in the same way as they are phenomena *(dharma)* and their true nature *(dharmatā)*. They can be expressed as being neither identical nor different. This is how the buddhas realized it, and it is also the meaning of the entire Dharma that has been taught.[360]

In other words, the apparent truth is dharmas understood as mere appearances, or suchness; and the ultimate truth is the dharmatā or that which is "liberated from other." As noted above, Rangjung Dorjé prefers the term *liberated from other (gzhan las grol ba)* to the term *empty of other (gzhan gyis stong pa)*. His term, probably newly created, bespeaks his inclination to dzogchen teachings, as evident from his usage of the three dzogchen categories in his commentary on the initial stanzas of the first chapter in the *Zab mo nang gi don*. In fact, "being liberated" could refer to the dzogchen notion of *rang grol*, a term that describes the mind having already been liberated on its own—without effort, so to speak.

Rangjung Dorjé's term *gzhan las grol ba*, then, could combine the aforementioned Yogācāra-based zhentong distinction with the dzogchen line of thought. The mind, which is already naturally liberated, is at the same time empty of or free from something other than its nature, namely the adventitious stains. Emptiness in the Maitreya works is defined according to the canonical formula for *being empty*[361] as the absence of something (namely duality) in something else that exists (false imagining and emptiness).[362] In this context, emptiness is taken as a "state of being free from [something] *(bral ba nyid)*. Thus it has been stated in the *Madhyāntavibhāgabhāṣya:*

> Emptiness refers to this false imagining *(abhūtaparikalpa)* that is free from the relation between a perceived and a perceiver.[363]

Contrary to the notion of mere appearance (apparent truth), the notion, namely, that appearances are perceived just as they are (not, that is, as a dualistic appearance), the state of "being liberated from other" also has a positive connotation. Being the ultimate truth, it is equated with natural emptiness *(svabhāvaśūnyatā,* at times also called *prakṛtiśūnyatā)* in line with the Yogācāra view that the absence of duality is considered an all-pervasive positive quality.[364] "That which is liberated from other" refers to this natural emptiness. As we have seen above, it is also equated with the true nature of mind *(sems nyid)* or buddha nature, and given the similar meaning of *grol ba* (liberated) and *bral ba* (being free) in this context, and the equation of *emptiness (stong pa nyid)* with the *fact of being free (bral ba nyid)* in the *Madhyāntavibhāgabhāṣya,* it is understandable that Karma Trinlepa and Kongtrül Lodrö Tayé should have come to the conclusion that Rangjung Dorjé is a zhentongpa.

But here again there is a major difference from Dölpopa's zhentong. For Dölpopa, the Yogācāra definition of the two truths as being neither identical nor different does not exclude their difference as long as it is not in terms of essence. This is not possible since it is only the ultimate that exists in terms of its essence, and we need at least a second ontological category in order to speak of an essential difference.[365] In other words, Dölpopa draws the line between the two truths more strictly; by no means would he include "mere appearance" within buddha nature. Dölpopa defines the two truths in such a way that he is forced to accept the consequence that the ordinary world does not appear to a buddha any more.[366]

In this context it should be also noted that the Jonangpas usually reject the notion that the wisdom of the path (i.e., the unmistaken perfect nature) is included in the perfect nature and thus the ultimate truth, while they include the dependent in the imagined nature.[367] But such a sharp distinction between the two truths, which is premised by denying the dependent nature altogether, is hardly compatible with the Yogācāra works.[368]

According to them, a pure aspect of the dependent nature is left over in the ultimate—namely the nonconceptual cognition of suchness.[369] Precisely this is what is connoted by Rangjung Dorjé's term *mere appearance.* Thus it comes as no surprise that, unlike Dölpopa, Rangjung Dorjé does not take the basis of emptiness or negation to be a permanent stable state of being, but rather dependent arising, or the continuous flow of the true nature of mind *(sems nyid).* It is obvious that such an understanding of zhentong is much more compatible with Rangjung Dorjé's mahāmudrā instructions.

When we take a closer look at Rangjung Dorjé's initial definition of mind, namely that the true nature *(rang gi ngo bo)* of the stainless mind and the mind mingled with stains is "precisely this dependent arising and the liberation from [anything] other,"[370] we notice that it appears to be the result of blending together the three different traditions we have already identified in his commentary on the first *pāda.* "Dependent arising" refers to the continuous flow of the natural mind as described in mahāmudrā, "from other" stands for the emptiness within this natural mind continuum of other, namely adventitious stains (the *zhentong* view), and "liberation" *(rnam par grol ba)* refers to the fact that this mind is liberated throughout beginningless time (the *rdzogs chen* view).

Rangjung Dorjé describes the fortified potential simply as the manifestation of the pure dharmadhātu, or the naturally present potential, and thus claims that all buddha qualities exist throughout beginningless time. Quoting Nāgārjuna's *Dharmadhātustotra* in order to prove that the presentation of buddha nature as the ultimate was also the intended meaning of the Mādhyamikas, he further points out that the buddha element is synonymous with the dharmakāya, suchness, and the potential, and that this is illustrated by the nine examples of the *Tathāgatagarbhasūtra:*

> "...Those sūtras taught by the victorious ones in order to reveal emptiness all eliminate defilements and do not diminish the [buddha] element."[371] And so on. Thus it has been taught extensively [in the *Dharmadhātustotra*]. As for synonyms of it (i.e., the buddha element), they have been taught in detail in the *Uttaratantra [Ratnagotravibhāga]:* "The nature of the element of the very pure mind is the dharmakāya, suchness, and the potential"[372] and so on. Through the nine examples it has been taught that the sixty-four stainless buddha qualities are made to appear by purifying [all] defilements, however many there are, in short, there are sixty-four.[373]

This clearly shows that Rangjung Dorjé identifies the main purport of the *Ratnagotravibhāga* as being contained in the nine examples, and not in other passages which suggest that at least the thirty-two qualities of the form kāyas do evolve. But is Rangjung Dorjé of the opinion that the thirty-two marks of a buddha already exist in the mindstream of an ordinary being?[374] Unfortunately his *Ratnagotravibhāga* commentary has yet to be discovered, but in his commentary on the *Dharmadhātustotra* Rangjung Dorjé presents the arising of the buddha qualities in an ordinary way, and it is reasonable to assume that he explains the appearance of apparent form kāyas, like Dölpopa, in line with the various passages of the *Ratnagotravibhāga* and mainstream Mahāyāna. In any case, it is not possible to simply transfer a presentation of buddha nature such as the one given above to a nontantric context and conclude that the ordinary marks of a buddha can thereby automatically be taken to exist in sentient beings. That Rangjung Dorjé distinguishes an ordinary presentation of the kāyas from an extraordinary one becomes clear in his commentary on the first two lines of the second introductory stanza of the *Zab mo nang gi don*, which is:

> Homage to the single coemergent [wisdom], which is real,
> That which consists of the two, which possesses the three kāyas,
>   [namely] the *nāḍīs*, *prāṇa*, and *bindus*,
> The four states [of daily life, which] are properly the four kāyas,
> And the nature of the five kāyas.[375]

Rangjung Dorjé comments:

> "The single coemergent [wisdom], which is real" abides, mingled indistinguishably with stains, in all sentient beings. It is the dharmakāya of all buddhas together with [their] qualities and activity. "That which consists of the two" [refers to the possession of] skillful means and insight, the nature *(rang bzhin)* of the apparent and ultimate, [and] the fruit, [namely] the two kāyas of the truly stainless dharmadhātu and its truly profound outflow (i.e., of Dharma teachings and so on).
>
> "Which possesses the three kāyas, [namely] *nāḍīs*, *prāṇa*, and *bindus*" means: The ultimate dharmadhātu [of] great bliss is the dharmakāya. With respect to the kāya of the truly profound outflow [of teachings], which depends on the apparent truth, the sambhogakāya and nirmāṇakāya arise. [The sambhogakāya arises through] the purification of dreams and the transformation of the

> basis of the mental faculty and the life wind, both of which are based on the *ālaya[vijñāna]*. [The nirmāṇakāya arises] through the purification of the [accumulations of] consciousness, which are engaged in [the projection of] entities, [or] ordinary appearances. These [three] are, moreover, the *nāḍīs*, [or] [vajra] body; *prāṇa* [or] [vajra] speech; and *bindu*, [or] vajra mind. It has been taught that these three are obtained by purifying them. Therefore they have been taught as being the body, speech, and mind of all buddhas.[376]

In his commentary on the first line, Rangjung Dorjé says in accordance with RGV I.27–28 that only the dharmakāya of all buddhas truly abides in sentient beings. The form kāyas are then explained as the outflow of the Dharma teachings on the level of the fruit, which corresponds to the pertinent passages in the first and third chapters of the *Ratnagotravibhāga*.[377] In other words, this is what Dölpopa calls the ordinary presentation in his *Ri chos nges don rgya mtsho*. The dharmakāya is ultimate, and the form kāyas appear in dependence on the disciples and apparent truth after the purification of hindrances.

Contrary to this ordinary presentation, the "tantric" sambhogakāya and nirmāṇakāya exist primordially in ordinary beings in the form of the vajra body and vajra speech, or, to use the technical terms, *nāḍīs* and *prāṇa*. That the tantric kāyas also exist in states that are mingled with stains becomes even more clear in the commentary on the third line, which says that the four states of daily life (i.e., the states of deep sleep, dream, waking, and sexual union) are the dharmakāya, sambhogakāya, nirmāṇakāya, and *jñānakāya*, and it is explicitly said that these four kāyas are mingled with the hindrances of sentient beings.[378]

To sum up, the tension in the *Ratnagotravibhāga* between explanations that center around the *Tathāgatagarbhasūtra* or the *Anūnatvāpūrṇatvanirdeśa* on the one hand and the parts that suggest a growth of at least some of the buddha qualities on the other simply reflect two different levels of teachings for Rangjung Dorjé, and for Dölpopa too. The ordinary presentation of the kāyas was given in a general context explaining buddha nature as seen from the perspective of a beginner, whereas teachings such as "nothing needs to be removed from or added to the buddha element" (RGV I.157ab (J I.154ab)) point to the ultimate level of interpretation, or the extraordinary Vajrayāna teachings. A beginner sees his qualities grow to the same extent as he removes his hindrances, but from an ultimate point of view, he has been a buddha throughout beginningless time without knowing it.

Rangjung Dorjé's *Snying po bstan pa* reveals the same findings. By carefully choosing in the beginning three stanzas from different sources, Rangjung Dorjé skillfully demonstrates his particular understanding of buddha nature.[379] By starting with the simile of a gold statue, he leaves no doubt that it is the original purport of the *Tathāgatagarbhasūtra* that must be followed:

> Though beginningless, [saṁsāra] has an end.
> Pure by nature, [the element] is endowed with the property of being eternal.
> Being covered from outside by a beginningless sheath, it is not seen,
> Like a gold statue covered [by clay].[380]

By saying that the element only has the property (among others) of being eternal is not the same as saying that it is eternal. (Kongtrül Lodrö Tayé notes in his commentary on the *Ratnagotravibhāga*[381] that the dharmakāya is only eternal in the sense that it does not appear to sentient beings.) Next, in order to counteract the impression that the buddha element and the adventitious stains are distinct entities, a stanza from the *Mahāyānābhidharmasūtra* is quoted:

> The beginningless sphere (i.e., the buddha element) is the basis of all phenomena.
> Due to its existence, [it can assume] all forms of life [as well as] the attainment of nirvāṇa.[382]

Thus it is made clear that buddha nature is the basis of all phenomena including saṁsāra. The third stanza (HT 2, IV.69)[383] is from a passage of the *Hevajratantra*, in which the three kāyas, namely the dharmakāya and the two form kāyas, are said to be located in the yoginī's body in the form of cakras, which indicates Rangjung Dorjé's ultimate tantric interpretation of buddha nature, all ultimate buddha qualities being already ever complete.[384]

Rangjung Dorjé dedicates a relatively long part of his short text to an explanation of the sixty-four buddha qualities, and it deserves our attention. Having equated buddha nature with the mahāmudrā term *natural mind (tha mal gyi shes pa)*, he says that there are sixty-four qualities to its uninterrupted play.[385] After a detailed presentation of the first thirty-two, namely those of the dharmakāya, he states that these are not seen as they really are, and are thus fabricated as something they are not.[386] This is then illustrated by the famous two stanzas on emptiness (RGV I.157–58 (J I.154– 55)). In other words, Rangjung Dorjé applies only the thirty-two qualities of the dharmakāya to the classical formula of what the buddha element is empty of and what not. This shows that the original purport of the *Ratnagotravibhāga* is followed, namely that the thirty-two marks of the Buddha are acquired and not present throughout beginningless time. After the quotation of RGV I.157–58 the *Snying po bstan pa* continues:

> Furthermore, the nature of the two form kāyas
> Are the thirty-two major and [eighty] minor marks.
> [These] attained qualities are your own body.
> This body is not created by a self, [the creator Gampa (Sgam pa)]
> Cha (phyva),[387] [or] Śiva,
> By Brahman, real external atoms,
> Or hidden [matter].
> Because the impure modifications of the perceived and the perceiver
> [Of] the five [sense] gates were purified,
> They were labeled with the conventional expression *attained.*
> Therefore the pure *nāḍīs*, *prāṇa*, and *bindus*
> Are the pure form kāyas.
> When not purified, they are the impure form kāyas.[388]

This shows clearly that Rangjung Dorjé respects the *Ratnagotravibhāga.* He says, in accordance with mainstream Mahāyāna, that the form kāyas are attained. But at the same time he argues that they cannot be newly created. His solution of the seeming contradiction is the same tantric interpretation that we have already observed in Rangjung Dorjé's autocommentary on the initial stanzas of the *Zab mo nang gi don:* the primordial form kāyas are the *nāḍīs*, *prāṇa,* and *bindus* of the subtle body.[389] To make sure that this point is really taken in the sense he intends, he illustrates this purification of the impure form kāyas by way of the simile of the threefold cleansing of a *vaiḍūrya* gem in the *Dhāraṇīśvararājasūtra.*[390]

Finally I point out that Rangjung Dorjé excludes a too eternalist interpretation of buddha nature by rejecting the extreme position that buddha qualities have no causes at all. Thus, it is said in the *Snying po bstan pa:*

> Some who have adopted negative views realize that
> The buddha qualities are without cause
> Or that they are not [contained] in the [mind]
> Or produced by external causes and conditions.

What is the difference between [such views] and the [extremes of] eternalism and nihilism?
It is clear that conditioned[391] [buddha qualities] arise and stop every moment,
Just like impure conditioned [factors].
If this were not the case,
The activity of the form kāyas would be interrupted.
Still, [these qualities] are not referred to by the term *conditioned*.[392]

The description of the buddha qualities in terms of a momentary continuum or dependent arising reflects Rangjung Dorjé's mahāmudrā background and constitutes the main difference between his interpretation of buddha nature and Dölpopa's zhentong.

The Position of Dölpopa Sherab Gyaltsen

Dölpopa's exegesis of buddha nature was remarkable and controversial at the same time. Not only did he formulate a "transcendent" version of zhentong that strictly distinguishes a completely unchangeable buddha nature from the external and nonexistent stains of worldly constituents, but he also used terminology in an unorthodox way. Hookham and Stearns[393] have already described Dölpopa's system of interpretation at length. Stearns has given a detailed account of Dölpopa's life based on two early biographies written by his disciples Lhai Gyaltsen (Lha'i rgyal mtshan) (1319–1401) and Künpang Chödrag Palzang (Kun spangs Chos grags dpal bzang) (1283–1363?).[394] In the following I shall offer a brief survey of the main points before presenting my own observations.

According to traditional Tibetan accounts, the revolutionary theory that the ultimate is not "empty of an own-being" *(rang stong)* but "empty of other" *(gzhan stong)* arose in Dölpopa's mind during a Kālacakra retreat at Jonang.[395] Lhai Gyaltsen informs us that Dölpopa's realization was connected with the *Kālacakratantra* and the construction of the great *stūpa* in Jonang, which was consecrated in 1333. One of the first works in which Dölpopa expressed his new zhentong understanding of the Buddhist doctrine was his famous *Ri chos nges don rgya mtsho.*[396] His last major work was the *Bka' bsdu bzhi pa (Bka' bsdu bzhi pa'i don bstan rtsis chen po, The Great Reckoning of the Doctrine That Has the Significance of a Fourth Council),*[397] which can be seen as a final summary of Dölpopa's views.[398]

The hermeneutical principles according to which Dölpopa interprets the Buddhist teachings along the lines of his zhentong are laid out in the

Bka' bsdu bzhi pa, in which the entire Buddhist doctrine is "reckoned" by dividing the Buddhist teaching into four epochs. Besides the four epochs of varying quality that make up a cosmic age, Dölpopa also uses a lesser set of four epochs to refer to the qualitatively different periods of the teaching. He thus allocates philosophical doctrines to epochs *(yuga)* according to purely dogmatic criteria. As a support, Dölpopa refers to the *Kālacakratantra,* but in the relevant passage in the *Vimalaprabhāṭīkā*[399] it is only the irreligion of the *cakravartin*, the spreading of the religion of the barbarians, and the religions of others who are being converted that are related with the four *yuga*s.[400]

Important for our study here is Dölpopa's description that not only the teachings transmitted by Śākyamuni but also the Maitreya works belong to the Kṛtayuga of doctrine, whereas the works of Ārya Vimuktisena and Haribhadra represent the teachings of the inferior Tretāyuga. The common interpretation of the Yogācāra works of Maitreya, Asaṅga, and Vasubandhu as mere *cittamātra* itself reflects the historical degeneration of the Dharma.[401] I have shown elsewhere that Dölpopa's zhentong owes much to a particular explanation of these Yogācāra works along the lines of the Great Mahyamaka teaching *(dbu ma chen po),* and that the *Ratnagotravibhāga* thereby plays a crucial role.[402] As we shall see below, the *Ratnagotravibhāga* can be explained in both an ordinary and extraordinary way, and it is the latter that serves as the proper guideline for gaining a correct "Kṛtayuga understanding" of the Yogācāra works. Still, the *Ratnagotravibhāga* does not fully endorse, for example, Dölpopa's strict distinction between the two levels of truth (so strict that there are even two sets of form kāya qualities, one belonging to the apparent level of truth and an ultimate one that exists throughout beginningless time); and it was rather the new Jonang translation of the *Kālacakratantra* that became the ultimate scriptural basis for Dölpopa's innovative teaching.[403]

For those interested in the characteristic points of Dölpopa's view on buddha nature, his commentary on the *Ratnagotravibhāga*, namely the *Theg pa chen po rgyud bla ma'i bstan bcos legs bshad nyi ma'i 'od zer*,[404] poses the problem that the ultimate zhentong understanding is only hinted at in a subtle way. To give an example, in the commentary on the crucial stanza I.158 (J I.155), it is not clear to what the "ultimate unsurpassable buddha qualities, such as the ten strengths," namely those qualities of which the dharmadhātu is not empty, exactly refers.[405] Is it only the thirty-two qualities of the dharmakāya that are ultimate, as opposed to the thirty-two qualities of the form kāyas, which are explained as appearing to the disciples as a result of the accumulation of merit?[406] Are the form kāyas, as a consequence of this, something newly produced on the path? In order to clarify such questions, we have first to consult the *Ri chos nges don rgya mtsho*, in which the *Ratnagotravibhāga* is often quoted and also commented upon. The differences between the *Ri chos nges don rgya mtsho* and the *Nyi ma'i 'od zer* are so fundamental that Hookham wonders if the *Nyi ma'i 'od zer* is by Dölpopa at all and not rather by the Third Karmapa Rangjung Dorjé.[407] But as we shall see further down, the doctrinal differences between the *Nyi ma'i 'od zer* and the *Ri chos nges don rgya mtsho* must be viewed against the backdrop of two different hermeneutic strategies, the aforementioned ordinary and extraordinary explanations, pursued by Dölpopa.[408]

That this was Dölpopa's strategy becomes clear in a discussion of the three kāyas and the two potentials at the beginning of the third chapter ("The State of the Result") in his *Ri chos nges don rgya mtsho*. First, Dölpopa explains the ultimate dharmakāya and apparent *(kun rdzob)* form kāyas in largely general and conservative terms, and then proceeds to "the extraordinary [presentation of] the *vajrakāya* or *mantrakāya* according to the *mantra[yāna]*."

Dölpopa starts his ordinary presentation of the ultimate dharmakāya and the apparent form kāyas in the *Ri chos nges don rgya mtsho* by quoting RGV III.1–3[409] and then comments:

> The fruit of dissociation, [or] the dharmakāya, is the kāya of the unchangeable perfect [nature], and [thus] suchness. In it the qualities of dissociation, [namely] the [ten] strengths and so on, are complete. The generated fruit, [or] the form kāyas, are that which is endowed with the unmistaken perfect [nature], and [thus] correct wisdom. In them the generated qualities, such as the [thirty-two] marks, exist. Thus it is said.[410] These [three stanzas] rule out the [view of] some who claim that even the dharmakāya is a generated fruit [on the level of] apparent [truth], and some [others who] claim that even the form kāyas are the fruit of dissociation [on the level of] ultimate [truth]...Likewise [the view of] some [who] claim that even the dharmakāya does not exist in sentient beings from the beginning is extremely confused, [as is that of] some [others who] claim that even the form kāyas exist in sentient beings from the beginning, inasmuch as it has been said in great detail [in RGV I.152 (J I.149)]: "[You should know that the potential is twofold in being] like a treasure and a tree [grown] from a fruit..." and so on.[411]

As we will see below, Dölpopa explains the two potentials in a way common to exegetes like Lodrö Tsungmé, claiming as he does that the fortified potential must be newly produced. In his ordinary exposition Dölpopa quotes the *Mahāyānasūtrālaṁkāra* and the *Abhisamayālaṁkāra*, and even includes the view of Ārya Vimuktisena. Based on these texts he concludes that the two form kāyas come under the apparent truth, in line with the common Mahāyāna presentation of the kāyas.[412] It is interesting that Ārya Vimuktisena, whose teachings are described by Dölpopa elsewhere as belonging to the Tretāyuga of doctrine, should be mentioned here.[413] In other words, Dölpopa's distinction between an ordinary and extraordinary interpretation could be compared to what is described by him as the Kṛtayuga and Tretāyuga of doctrine.

In his paragraph on "the extraordinary [presentation of] the *vajrakāya* or *mantrakāya* according to the *mantra[yāna]*" Dölpopa explains:

> Here, there are two types of form kāyas. [First,] the commonly known sambhogakāya and nirmāṇakāya of the apparent [truth]; and [second,] the ultimate sambhogakāya and nirmāṇakāya; [the latter] are completely [contained] in the dharmatā, perfect [nature], and suchness.... Therefore the ultimate sambhogakāya and nirmāṇakāya are known by way of the extraordinary *mantra[yāna]*.[414]

In other words, Dölpopa distinguishes two ways of explaining the three kāyas that do not really contradict each other, it being simply the case that in an ordinary presentation, as in his *Ratnagotravibhāga* commentary, the ultimate sambhogakāya and nirmāṇakāya are not explicitly mentioned. The extraordinary or "tantric" explanation of the buddha kāyas in the *Ri chos nges don rgya mtsho* involves a distinction between ultimate and apparent kāyas and qualities. In the same way as ultimate form kāyas are distinguished from their normal ones, the thirty-two qualities of the ultimate dharmakāya are explained as existing on the level of apparent truth as well. But whereas the latter are conditioned, the ultimate ones are not.[415] To put it another way, even though the ultimate buddha qualities of both the dharmakāya and the form kāyas exist in all sentient beings throughout beginningless time, the apparent (or "normal") form kāyas must be generated on the path.[416] Likewise an ultimate abandonment and realization are distinguished from apparent ones, in that the ultimate ones are already complete in your own dharmatā, while the apparent ones must be attained on the path, as becomes evident in the following passage of the *Ri chos nges don rgya mtsho:*

> Also with regard to abandonment there are two: the abandonment that is [due to the fact] that no stains are established in their own right throughout beginningless time; and the destruction and extinction of adventitious stains with the help of the remedy.... Likewise there are also two realizations of a buddha: the realization of [your] dharmatā that is aware of itself by itself throughout beginningless time, [namely] self-arisen wisdom; and the realization that has come from meditating on the profound path, [namely] wisdom arisen from other.[417]

The question thus arises, what is the exact relation between these two types of abandonment and realization, or the ultimate and apparent truths? Rather than use the definition that they are "one in essence, but different isolates" *(ngo bo gcig la ldog pa tha dad),* Dölpopa follows the *Saṁdhinirmocanasūtra* and defines the relation between the two truths with the phrase "different in that their identity is negated" *(gcig pa bkag pa'i tha dad pa),* in the same way as dharmas and dharmatā are defined in the *Dharmadharmatāvibhāga* as being neither different nor identical. From this it does not follow that the two truths are different entities,[418] but simply that the ultimate *(dharmatā)* exists and the apparent *(dharmas)* does not (negation of identity). On the other hand, dharmatā is defined as the absence of duality (equated with dharmas) and as such in a sense is not different from the nonexistent dharmas (negation of difference).[419] It is only because mainstream Tibetan Buddhism emphasizes the essential identity of the two truths that Dölpopa stresses the aspect of the negation of identity in the *Ri chos nges don rgya mtsho:*

> Therefore there is a big difference [in saying] "empty of everything" and "empty of all phenomena," given that on the level of the fundamental state [there is] empti[ness] of phenomena *(dharmas),* but not of their true nature *(dharmatā).* This excludes [the views of those who] claim that phenomena and their true nature are one in essence, but different isolates, or that a difference does not exist at all, for the two are different, their identity being negated.
>
> If you ask: Well then, in the *Saṁdhinirmocana[sūtra]* [III.6]—"The defining characteristics of the conditioned realm and of the ultimate are the [one] defining characteristic of being free from identity and difference. Those who conceptualize sameness and identity are improperly oriented."[420]—it has been said that the

> two truths are neither identical nor different, [has it not]? This canonical passage negates both identity and difference in terms of essence, for even though the essence of the ultimate exists in the fundamental state, the essence of the apparent does not. As for all other explanations, if you claim that the two truths do not have these two [different] modes of truth, two modes of appearance, or two modes of being empty, [you adhere to] a nihilistic view; you are [reflecting] the simple carelessness of being intoxicated with the poison of mixing [the two truths] together without distinguishing any difference between [their] two modes at all.[421]

In other words, if there is only one essence, namely that of the ultimate, it does not make sense to speak of an essential difference, since this would require the existence of another essence from which it differs. But apart from the ultimate, nothing else really exists, the apparent truth not being established in terms of an essence of its own. This also means that Dölpopa's distinction between ultimate and apparent kāyas does not entail the absurd ontological view that there really are two different sets of kāyas.[422] Rather, only the ultimate kāyas really exist. The kāyas of apparent truth do not really exist, any more than the apparent world. Still, on the level of apparent truth they are produced to the same extent as the accidental stains of the apparent truth are removed, and in this sense there are accumulations of merit and wisdom.

In order to back up his view on ultimate truth, Dölpopa adduces the following sentence from the *Śrīmālādevīsūtra* quoted in RGVV I.12:

> And this dharmakāya of the Tathāgata, O illustrious one, is called *buddha nature* when not liberated from the sheaths of defilements.[423]

Dölpopa further points out that even though the ultimate has been given different names according to the impure state of ordinary persons, the partly pure and partly impure state of bodhisattvas, and the perfectly pure state of a tathāgata, it is not different in reality.[424] To be sure, Dölpopa takes this unchangeability or permanence of the ultimate as a continuous unending flow of moments not (as most of the exegetes explain it) as though the buddha kāyas remained in the endless world as long as sentient beings are in need of their buddha activity, but rather as being free of moments. The ultimate is thus understood as transcending the three times (i.e., the past, present, and future), and all kāyas have an ultimate aspect that is beyond the three times:

> That the permanent Buddha and the liberation of the Buddha are form, that even space is a form of the Buddha, and so forth—the meaning of such statements must be understood in the context of forms, etc., being explained [on the level] of suchness or as forms, etc., that are beyond the three times and the threefold world.[425]

Thus Dölpopa comments on RGV I.5a in his *Ri chos nges don rgya mtsho* in the following way:

> Even though [the verse RGV I.5a states that]: "[Buddhahood] is unconditioned and spontaneously present,"[426] and other [passages] teach that the ultimate buddha is not conditioned, the underlying intention is that he is free of moments.[427]

It should be noted that Dölpopa does not make this explicit statement, which is crucial to the zhentong distinction between the two truths, in his commentary on the *Ratnagotravibhāga*. With only Dölpopa's *Nyi ma'i 'od zer* (i.e., his *Ratnagotravibhāga* commentary) at hand, we would be hard put to define his view as precisely as above.

It is nevertheless possible to identify in the *Nyi ma'i 'od zer* a subtle allusion to the above-mentioned apparent and ultimate qualities. Dölpopa explains the third inconceivable point of RGV I.23 (i.e., the "stainless buddha qualities") in the following way:

> As to the stainless buddha qualities, they are any property of the Buddha whatsoever, including the fruit of dissociation, [namely] the ten strengths, the four fearlessnesses, and the eighteen exclusive features, and so on, all connected with precisely this dharmakāya, and the fruit of maturation, [namely] the thirty-two [major and minor] marks, and so on.[428]

In the next sentence of the commentary, the fourth inconceivable point, that of activity, is defined:

> As to the deeds of a victorious one, they are the...performance of effortless and uninterrupted activity for the sake of sentient

> beings by the attained power [of] the qualities—the ten strengths and the like.[429]

In other words, Dölpopa states here that the power of qualities is somehow attained or brought about, and it goes without saying that the "[ten] strengths and so on" *(stobs la sogs pa)* include the qualities of maturation as well, because, if anything at all, it is these qualities of maturation that are attained.

In his commentary on RGV I.25, Dölpopa explains again the term *stainless buddha qualities,* which is used in the same context as in RGV I.23.[430]

> As to the meaning of the stainless buddha qualities, the ultimate qualities, such as the ten strengths, also exist as inseparable properties even in defiled ordinary persons (i.e., those who are not yet on the path). But since they have not [yet] been actualized, this seems to be contradictory and thus inconceivable.[431]

It should be noted that the reader has already been forced to include the qualities of maturation under the abbreviated list of the "[ten] strengths and so on" just one page above in the commentary, and the same thing may be happening here. In other words, Dölpopa indirectly hints at the ultimate qualities of the form kāyas or the fruit of maturation. This skillful allusion is then repeated each time Dölpopa adds the genitive attribute *don dam pa'i* to the buddha nature or qualities, but he is otherwise at ease in commenting on the *Ratnagotravibhāga* in a more common way. The crucial stanza I.27, in which the three reasons for the presence of a buddha nature in sentient beings are presented, is thus explained in the following way:

> Since the dharmakāya of the perfect buddha embraces and pervades all phenomena, since there is no differentiation [to be made] within the dharmatā concerning all saṁsāra and nirvāṇa, and since the potential of the tathāgata exists in all sentient beings as the natural purity of the dharmadhātu, which can be purified of hindrances, truly every being possesses, always, continuously, and throughout beginningless time, the ultimate essence of the Buddha.[432]

Apart from the qualification of the "essence of the Buddha" as being "ultimate," the explanation is pretty standard. The potential of a tathāgata is simply taken as the purity of the dharmadhātu, which is indicative of the usual process of acquiring qualities on the level of apparent truth, as explained in the definition of buddha activity in RGV I.23 above. The attentive reader will understand that "ultimate essence of a buddha" includes all ultimate qualities (themselves including the qualities of the form kāyas), in the same way as the term "ultimate qualities, such as the [ten] strengths" *(stobs la sogs pa don dam pa'i yon tan)* does in Dölpopa's explanation (RGV I.157 (J I.154)) of the primordial qualities to which nothing needs to be added.[433]

Having thus indirectly hinted at the extraordinary zhentong understanding that suchness, dharmatā, or dharmadhātu contain all ultimate buddha qualities throughout beginningless time, Dölpopa has no trouble commenting on passages in the *Ratnagotravibhāga* that clearly suggest a generation and growth of at least the form kāyas, since it is automatically understood that such explanations refer only to the apparent level of truth. To put it another way, there is no contradiction in explaining a stanza, according to its original purport, in the common way, since to do so is a legitimate part of the extraordinary zhentong interpretation, one that can be seized upon in each case (without even being hinted at). As an example, I present here Dölpopa's full commentary on RGV I.152–53 (J I.149–50). It should be noted that no attempt at all is made to interpret the generation of the form kāyas as only appearing to arise.[434]

> For example, in the same way as the inexhaustible treasure underground is naturally present, not newly brought about by effort, and the tree with its fruits gradually grows in the garden by having brought about [the necessary conditions] with effort, the buddha potential, which has the ability to bring forth the three kāyas, should be known to be twofold as well. It is both the natural potential, [namely] the pure dharmadhātu, which is closely present as the nature of mind throughout beginningless time, and the fortified potential, [which is] supreme in terms of virtues and conducive to liberation). [The fortified potential] arises from [virtuous deeds] being newly acquired with effort, [namely by] something being done, such as focusing on [the naturally present potential] and studying.[435]
>
> As to how the three kāyas are attained, it is [here] maintained that the fruit, [namely] the three kāyas of a perfect buddha, are attained owing to a cause, [namely] these two naturally present and fortified potentials. First, the naturally present potential is

> perfected through many accumulations of wisdom, and becomes free from all adventitious stains, and the Ārst kāya, [namely] the svābhāvikakāya, the dharmatā endowed with both purities, is thereby attained. Second, the accumulation of merit is perfected by increasing the fortiĀed potential, and the latter kāyas, [namely] both the sambhogakāya and the nirmāṇakāya, which appear to disciples near and far, are thereby attained.436

To summarize, since Dölpopa acknowledges the existence of produced and conditioned qualities on the level of apparent truth, he obviously does not feel urged to read his ultimate zhentong view into such passages that pass as ordinary presentations. All a reader sharing the extraordinary zhentong view has to do is to remember that all ultimate qualities are fully contained in the ultimate nature of the defiled dharmadhātu. Having enjoyed a full-fledged Sakya education,[437] Dölpopa may have still felt obliged even in his later life to clearly distinguish between the sūtras and tantras, and not to read a "tantric view" (a dharmadhātu that possesses the ultimate qualities of the form kāyas) too insistently into the *Ratnagotravibhāga* (which is a sūtra text), at least not within his commentary on it. Thus he formally fulfills the scholarly rules of explaining an Indian treatise, and is still able to point out to the careful reader his zhentong understanding indirectly and to repeat this allusion by skillfully adding an attribute ("ultimate") to a few technical terms at the right place. It should be noted that on this point, Dölpopa's method was obviously not satisfactory enough for Kongtrül Lodrö Tayé, whose *Ratnagotravibhāga* commentary follows Dölpopa's for the most part verbatim. Thus, Kongtrül felt obliged to quote Karma Trinlepa and the Third Karmapa Rangjung Dorjé, who both reject the widespread notion that the fortified potential in the Maitreya works is taken to be conditioned.[438]

The Position of Sabzang Mati Panchen

The *Ratnagotravibhāga* commentary by Sabzang Mati Panchen Jamyang Lodrö Gyaltsen ('Jam dbyangs Blo gros rgyal mtshan) (1294–1376), the *Theg pa chen po'i rgyud bla ma'i bstan bcos kyi rnam par bshad pa nges don rab gsal snang ba* (in the following called the *Nges don rab gsal*), has been included by Khenpo Abbey in his collection of works of ancient Sakya scholars.[439] In the colophon, the commentary is ascribed to the Tibetan *paṇḍita* Jamyang Lodrö writing at the great Sakya college.[440] According to Stearns, his full name is Mati Panchen Jamyang Lodrö Gyaltsen, and he is thus also called Lodrö Gyaltsen.[441] Having enjoyed a full-fledged Sakya education,[442] he proceeded to Jonang, received Dölpopa's teachings, and became his supreme "heart disciple." Later Mati Panchen was given the monastery Sabzang Ganden Gön (Sa bzang Dga' ldan dgon) by Lama Dawa Gyaltsen (Bla ma Zla ba rgyal mtshan).[443]

Sabzang Mati Panchen follows Dölpopa's *Ratnagotravibhāga* commentary faithfully, usually quoting his master verbatim and adding further clarifications and sometimes justifications of Dölpopa's zhentong as well. He also places an interesting introduction in front of his commentary. In it, his hermeneutical classification of the five Maitreya works is of particular interest. According to Mati Panchen, the *Abhisamayālaṁkāra* elucidates the view of the second dharmacakra, the *Mahāyānasūtrālaṁkāra* the view and conduct of the third dharmacakra, and the remaining three, namely the *Madhyāntavibhāga*, *Dharmadharmatāvibhāga*, and the *Ratnagotravibhāga*, elucidate the view of the third dharmacakra by way of analyzing the dharmadhātu. It is further pointed out that the teachings of the third dharmacakra, including those propounded in the *Saṁdhinirmocanasūtra*, go well beyond *cittamātra*. If, as Mati Panchen stated, we claim that the notion of a "natural luminosity of mind" in the Maitreya works does not hold up against Madhyamaka reasoning, we could subject the tantras to the same Madhyamaka critique as well, since they propound the same "natural luminosity."[444]

As in Dölpopa's *Nyi ma'i 'od zer*, buddha nature is referred to as the ultimate buddha. The *Kālacakratantra* is adduced first in support of this assertion, which is not surprising, given that Mati Panchen's new translation of this tantra became the main foundation of Jonang hermeneutics. But in quoting the *Dharmadhātustotra*, he shows at the same time that his zhentong view is still in line with Nāgārjuna's Madhyamaka:

> That which must be attained, namely this ultimate buddha, dharmakāya [or] self-arisen, coemergent wisdom, is [already] present [now] by virtue of its pervading the nature of mind of all sentient beings. Thus it is not difficult to accomplish it, for it is actualized by simply abandoning [all] hindrances, as has been stated in detail in the *Śrīlaghukālacakratantrarāja*: "Sentient beings are simply buddhas. Another buddha of the great (?) does not exist in this world..."; in the *Hevajratantra* [Part 2, IV.69] as well: "Sentient beings are simply buddhas, save for being hindered by adventitious stains. After these are removed, there is [no uncertainty that sentient beings are] simply buddhas;"[445] and in passages such as *Dharmadhātustotra* [37]: "When covered by the

net of defilements, it is called *sentient being;* the very same thing is called *buddha* when freed from defilements."[446]

Mati Panchen seems to follow Dölpopa's strategy in commenting on the *Ratnagotravibhāga* according to the ordinary presentation of the *Ri chos nges don rgya mtsho* while at the same time not failing to indicate the extraordinary zhentong explanation of the Mantrayāna. Thus, the above-quoted stanza from the *Hevajratantra* is from a passage in which the three kāyas, namely the dharmakāya and the two form kāyas, are said to be located in the yoginī's body in the form of cakras.[447] But at the beginning of his commentary (on RGV I.3), Mati Panchen has an opponent ask if the tantric practice of viewing your own body as a deity could not serve as a basis for taking the form kāyas to be ultimate truth, and answers that such teachings only refer to the dharmatā of the body. In any case, Mati Panchen deals in his *Ratnagotravibhāga* commentary, like Dölpopa, only with the "normal" form kāyas of the sūtras:

> In case you should cling to the idea: "If, from explanations[448] in the tantras, namely teachings in the *Vairocanābhisambodhi-[tantra]* and so forth, this body is known to be a deity, [it therefore follows that] it is the buddha kāya," [the following should be realized]. The Buddha gave thought to the dharmatā of this and that [body], but this impure body, being a "phenomenon possessing dharmatā" *(dharmin),* is not exactly a buddha, given that it is conditioned and without essence, whereas a buddha is an unconditioned, self-arisen kāya.... As to the abandoning of the claim that the ultimate is the form kāyas: Again, if you think that the ultimate buddha is the form kāyas (for it has been taught that the twelve deeds spread out and so on), you [should] not think that way either, because form kāyas are taught as being established as appearances for others in dependence on [others'] fortune, [namely] as conditioned entities, but not as possessing ultimate qualities, which are not conditioned and so forth.... As to the ultimate buddha, it is simply the dharmakāya.[449]

That the ordinary presentation of the kāyas clearly excludes the form kāyas from the ultimate becomes clear in Mati Panchen's commentary on RGV I.148 (J I.145), in which only the stainless dharmadhātu, equated with natural luminosity, is taken to be the real dharmakāya, but not its outflow.[450]

Still, the following sentence, which elucidates RGV I.25 (namely the third inconceivable point, which Dölpopa used for his indirect inclusion of the ultimate qualities of the form kāyas), could be an allusion to the extraordinary explanation of buddha nature:

> The tathāgata knows that even all ultimate qualities are present in all sentient beings—not one of them is missing....[451]

Of great interest are Mati Panchen's occasional additions to Dölpopa's commentary. They not only ensure a clearer zhentong understanding, but also defend some problematic notions entertained by his master. In his commentary on RGV I.6ab (which explains why buddhahood is not conditioned) Mati Panchen quotes the *Mahāparinirvāṇasūtra* to the effect that "not being conditioned" also implies "being beyond time." As we have seen above, Dölpopa refrains from such an inference in his commentary, though he does explain in his *Ri chos nges don rgya mtsho* that RGV I.6ab means that buddhahood is free from momentariness (and thus beyond time). Mati Panchen's *Nges don rab gsal* on RGV I.6ab is:

> Buddhahood is unconditioned since in the beginning, middle, and end it has the nature of being free from conditioned phenonema that arise, abide, and pass out of existence; as has been said in the *[Mahāpari]nirvāṇasūtra:* "A phenomenon that abides in permanence does not belong to the three times. Likewise, the tathāgata does not belong to the three times either, and is therefore permanent."[452]

It should be noted that Kongtrül Lodrö Tayé, who otherwise strictly follows Dölpopa's commentary, deviates from this zhentong understanding of the term *unconditioned (asaṁskṛta).* Referring to Rongtön's explanation of four types of understanding *unconditioned,* Kongtrül states that the dharma-kāya only shares this quality of being unconditioned to a certain extent, namely inasmuch as it does not appear to disciples. If we claimed that it is completely unconditioned, it would contradict that it possesses knowledge, compassion, and power.[453]

Mati Panchen's commentary on RGV I.26 contains a few interesting and noteworthy remarks. Stanza I.26 lists the last four vajra points, namely the buddha element (i.e., buddha nature), enlightenment, qualities, and activity, and takes the first to be the cause and the remaining three to be conditions of purification. In the *Ratnagotravibhāgavyākhyā* the buddha element as a cause is explained in the following way:

> Here, of these four [vajra] points, the first one should be understood as the cause that brings forth the Three Jewels, after you come to rely on its [natural] purity on the basis of your own correct mental engagement, given that it is the seed of the supramundane properties.[454]

Like Dölpopa, Mati Panchen merely paraphrases this explanation from the *Ratnagotravibhāgavyākhyā* (both of them having good reasons not to quote it), thus tacitly passing over the possibly intended meaning of a real growth by omitting the causal clause with the word *seed:*

> One [vajra] point is the suchness mingled with stains. It is the cause that must be purified, for the Three Jewels come forth from that which is completely pure of stains.[455]

A little further down, though, and still within his general explanation of this vajra point in RGV I.26, Mati Panchen directly rules out the equation of the buddha element with a seed from which a fruit really grows:

> It is not acceptable to say either that [buddha nature] in the state of ordinary beings does not [yet] exist as the buddha endowed with all ultimate qualities, [and that the Buddha] thought [buddha nature] to be only a seed [in this state] when he taught that it exists [in sentient beings as a buddha]. A fruit produced from a seed that grows and fully matures is conditioned [and thus not a buddha quality].[456]

What is also interesting in this passage are the remarks on the fortified potential. Even though Mati Panchen follows Dölpopa's rather traditional presentation of the fortified potential as something newly acquired as a result of effort (RGV I.152 (J I.149)), he qualifies such an understanding by saying that the different potentials of the three *yānas* (i.e., the fortified potentials) are ultimately one, since the natural luminosity of mind pervades all sentient beings,[457] and concludes the discussion with the following statement:

> Therefore, the ultimate buddha, being regarded as the direct manifestation of something that exists, should never be taken as the new product of something that [previously] did not exist. As for [its] synonyms, [apart] from [being] the very dharmadhātu,

> it has also been called "potential," "uncontaminated seed," "element of sentient beings," and "the nature of everything."[458]

In other words, the notion of real growth is invalidated by equating the *seed* with the dharmadhātu and by denying a real difference between various potentials. In fact, the theory of a newly acquired individual potential that is the cause of the form kāyas is somewhat disturbing in a zhentong interpretation that takes the ultimate as an unchanging absolute in which all qualities are present throughout beginningless time. It is thus not surprising that Mati Panchen remarks in his conclusion of the paragraph on the three aspects of buddha nature (dharmakāya, suchness, and potential) in relation to the nine examples from the *Tathāgatagarbhasūtra* (I.147–55 (J I.144–52)):

> Moreover, what has been taught in distinguishing the nine meanings (i.e., of the nine examples) with regard to the three natures (i.e., aspects of buddha nature), [namely] the two [types of] dharmakāya, the potential that arises from adopting [virtuous deeds], and the form kāyas is for the sake of [becoming] skilled in distinctions, but it is not the case that [the clause] "because it pervades every [sentient being]" [applies to these distinctions]. It is rather their support, the uncontaminated sphere, that is all-pervading.[459]

In other words, for Mati Panchen the notions of form kāyas, acquired or fortified potential, and so on are things alien to, and not in line with, the real purport of the *Ratnagotravibhāga*, which he obviously interprets on the basis of the *Tathāgatagarbhasūtra*. Like Dölpopa, he accepts that the ordinary explanations of a fortified potential and form kāyas do not really support the zhentong view, apart from being valid descriptions of the apparent truth in their system.

Dölpopa would not accept any notion of real growth with regard to the ultimate qualities. For this reason, as we have seen above, both Dölpopa and Mati Panchen ignore in their commentaries the clause "because [the element] is the seed of the supramundane properties" of RGVV I.26. Similarly, Dölpopa does not comment on what is RGV I.27 in the Sanskrit edition (a stanza not included in the root text of the *Ratnagotravibhāga* by most Tibetan traditions) and thus does not have to deal with another problematic passage that suggests a real difference between the potential and a buddha, namely the third reason for the presence of buddha nature in all sentient beings:

> ...because its fruit has been "metaphorically" applied[460] to the buddha potential....[461]

If the potential is called a buddha only in a metaphorical sense, there must be a difference that is more substantial than the existence or nonexistence of adventitious stains. Mati Panchen first informs us that he has chosen not to ignore this passage given that it is found in some Indian texts, which means that he still doubts its authenticity, even though it is found in the Tibetan translation of the *Ratnagotravibhāgavyākhyā* (according to all available Tengyur editions). The root text Mati Panchen quotes (and which he corrected based on the Sanskrit[462]) has Tib. *nye bar spyod pa* ("to enjoy") instead of Tib. *nye bar btags pa* ("to apply metaphorically") for Skt. *upacāra.* With the help of this "skillful translation," Mati Panchen arrives at the following zhentong interpretation:

> All beings possess the ultimate buddha nature...because the potential [or] buddha element, which will be established as buddhahood, [can be] enjoyed as something that is not different from the dharmakāya, [or] the fruit free of stains, even in a state when [the potential] is mingled with hindrances.[463]

This strict denial of any change in buddha nature led a number of scholars to the conclusion that the zhentongpas would then claim the existence of a permanent entity,[464] which is a paradox according to Buddhist philosophy. An entity *per definitionem* fulfills a function and by virtue of this it must be impermanent. But Mati Panchen explains:

> As to abandoning the undesired consequence that [buddha nature] is a permanent entity, if you contend that since it is without any difference before and after, and since it is also, in view of [its] causes and conditions, an attained fruit, the sphere (i.e., the buddha element) is a permanent entity, [the counterargument is as follows]. It is permanent in view of its not being conditioned. Where [will you find] the view that something is a conditioned entity on the grounds that it is free from the defining characteristics of production, cessation, and abiding? ...If you contend that something is an entity in view of its fulfilling a function, [the counterargument is as follows]. It possesses the ability to bring the two needs (i.e., for yourself and others) to perfection in every respect. Therefore, it is not an

> ephemeral conditioned entity, since everything conditioned is false, deceptive, and without essence. Still, there is no contradiction in saying that [buddha nature] is permanent and at the same time a nonconditioned entity.[465]

Nobody would have denied that the kāyas unfold buddha activity, but it must have seemed outrageous to hear someone calling them an "entity."[466] A considerable part of the problem with the Jonang position is therefore not so much philosophical but the unorthodoxically free use of terminology, which must have caused a hermeneutical shock to many contemporary scholars.[467] Still, the zhentong view raises the question of how an ultimate dharmakāya that is really permanent and beyond the three times can function as a basis of buddha activity in this world, or how something entirely transcendent can be at the same time the nature of a mindstream and thus something immanent.

To conclude, a few passages in Sabzang Mati Panchen's commentary suggest that he endorses Dölpopa's ultimate zhentong view as described in the *Ri chos nges don rgya mtsho*, even though the commentary neither makes a distinction between ultimate and apparent buddha qualities nor mentions ultimate form kāyas. Unfortunately there are no other works by Mati Panchen available to substantiate the hypothesis that he followed Dölpopa's hermeneutic strategy of only expounding the ordinary presentation of buddha nature in the *Ratnagotravibhāga* commentary.

The Position of Lodrö Tsungmé

Even though a handwritten copy reproduced from an ancient manuscript of Lodrö Tsungmé's (thirteenth/fourteenth century) *Ratnagotravibhāga* commentary from the library of Riwoché Jedrung Rinpoché (Ri bo che Rje drung Rin po che) of Pema Kö (Padma bkod) was published under the Library of Congress program some three decades ago, the commentary has hardly been used by Western scholarship before now.[468] The Nyingma lama Paldan Sherab, who for a long time lived in Varanasi but now lives in New York, thought that this commentary was what was long thought to be a merely legendary *Ratnagotravibhāga* commentary by Longchen Rabjampa. Paldan Sherab probably removed the introductory page from one of the Indian reproductions of Lodrö Tsungmé's commentary[469] and added three prefatory pages: on the first is Paldan Sherab's newly created title *Kun mkhyen Klong chen pa'i rgyud bla ma'i 'grel pa bzhugs;* on the second a picture of Longchenpa; and on the third the same picture again together with the *ye dharmā hetuprabhavā* formula in Lantsha script and a stanza by Terdag Lingpa (Gter bdag gling pa) (1646–1714) in which Longchenpa is praised under the name of Lodrö Tsungmé.[470] Paldan Sherab added two further pages along with a colophon of his own at the end, in which he explains why this commentary is by Longchenpa.[471] The only other reason Paldan Sherab came up with this (besides the fact that Longchenpa was also called Lodrö Tsungmé) is that his tradition has it that there is a general outline of the five Maitreya works and a *Ratnagotravibhāga* commentary by Longchenpa.[472] The former is mentioned in the biography of Longchenpa, which contains an extensive list of his works, but a *Ratnagotravibhāga* commentary by him is not listed there.[473]

From Zhönu Pal's *Deb ther sngon po* we know that a certain Dragpa Sengé (Grags pa Seng ge) (b. 1283) went to Sangpu Neutog (Gsang phu Sne'u thog) in order to study under the "senior teacher" *(bla chos pa)* Jamyang Shākzhön and the "assistant teacher" *(zur chos pa)* Lodrö Tsungmé.[474] Unfortunately we are not told in which year this was, but before going to Sangpu (Gsang phu), Dragpa Sengé received teachings in Tsurpu (Tshur phu), where he arrived in 1308. Zhönu Pal further informs us that Dragpa Sengé left Sangpu to meet the Third Karmapa Rangjung Dorjé after the latter returned from Kongpo.[475] According to the biography of Rangjung Dorjé written by Situ Panchen Chökyi Jungné and Belo Tsewang Künkhyab ('Be lo Tshe dbang kun khyab), the Third Karmapa left for Kongpo in 1310 and returned to Ü in 1313.[476] From this we can infer that Dragpa Sengé must have studied under Shākzhön and Lodrö Tsungmé sometime between 1308 and 1313. Since Longchen Rabjampa was born in 1308, it is impossible that he could have been this Lodrö Tsungmé who was teaching at Sangpu. It is also known that Yagdé Panchen (G.yag sde paṇ chen) (1299–1378), who was a teacher of Longchenpa, was a disciple of Lodrö Tsungmé.[477]

Now it is still possible that Longchenpa composed a *Ratnagotravibhāga* commentary under the name Lodrö Tsungmé at Sangpu Neutog.[478] In other words, we may assume that there were two persons with the name Lodrö Tsungmé there. This is not very likely, though. It is not so much that Longchenpa was only a student at Sangpu Neutog,[479] as the way Lodrö Tsungmé explains the *Ratnagotravibhāga*. The latter's view on buddha nature, as we will see, differs considerably from Longchenpa's.[480]

According to Khenpo Abbey (Kathmandu), to whom I presented a copy of the text published in India, Lodrö Tsungmé, the teacher at Sangpu and author of the *Ratnagotravibhāga* commentary, was from Nedrug (Gnas drug) in Kham[481] and thus a close disciple of Lama Dampa Sönam Gyaltsen (1312–75).[482] But in his forthcoming thesis, Kano claims that the

Lodrö Tsungmé from Sangpu is not the same person as the one from Nedrug.

Kongtrül Lodrö Tayé says of the *Ratnagotravibhāga* commentary by a certain Lodrö Tsungmé that the latter follows, together with Pagdru Gyaltsen Zangpo (Phag gru Rgyal mtshan bzang po) and Rongtön Sheja Künrig, the commentarial tradition of Chapa Chökyi Sengé's disciples, such as Tsangnagpa Tsöndrü Sengé (Brtson 'grus seng ge) and Darbagpa Mawai Sengé (Dar 'bags pa Smra ba'i seng ge).[483] They are "all [said] to follow the great translator Ngog [Loden Sherab] [in spite of] many unimportant discrepancies in the Dharma language."[484] But the differences between Ngog Loden Sherab and Lodrö Tsungmé seem to be more substantial than that, for Lodrö Tsungmé was criticized by Butön Rinchen Drub (Bu ston Rin chen grub) (1290–1364) for ascribing definitive meaning to the teaching of a real buddha nature within the mindstream of sentient beings.[485]

In the introduction to his *Ratnagotravibhāga* commentary, Lodrö Tsungmé states that the first and the last of the five Maitreya works, namely the *Abhisamayālaṁkāra* and the *Ratnagotravibhāga*, comment on the intention of the Buddha's words, which literally have definitive meaning, and should thus truly be considered to be *nītārtha*.[486] Hence the three reasons for the presence of a buddha nature in RGV I.28 ((1) because you are embraced and pervaded *(spharaṇa)*[487] by the embodiment of the perfect buddha, (2) because suchness cannot be differentiated, (3) because of the potential)[488] are taken in a strict sense.

Lodrö Tsungmé does not comment on what in the Sanskrit edition[489] is RGV I.27 (not included in the root text of the *Ratnagotravibhāga* by most Tibetan traditions) and does not have to deal with its slightly different third reason, according to which "its (i.e., buddha nature's) fruit has been metaphorically applied to the buddha potential."[490] He argues rather that there is nothing metaphorical with regard to the above-mentioned three reasons. In particular, Lodrö Tsungmé does not accept the notion that the pervasion of sentient beings by the embodiment of the perfect buddha (reason 1) only refers to their ability to obtain the dharmakāya; that the presence of a potential (reason 3) merely means possessing suchness; or that a tathāgata is caused by the mental imprints of virtue and the seeds of insight and compassion.[491] In his commentary on RGV I.28, Lodrö Tsungmé explains:

> The dharmakāya is the dharmadhātu inseparable from qualities. It is real in that it exists as something pervading all sentient beings by virtue of being identical [with them]. Since there is no

> disproof against such a claim, it is not acceptable to say that it is [merely] nominal. All the more so, because if the pervasive nature of the dharmakāya meant that it can be attained [as a matter of course] it would not be necessary to [present this first reason] separately from the [third reason,] [namely,] "[because of] the existence of a potential." If you object that [the reason] "[because of] the existence of a potential" [refers to] what has arisen from practice,[492] [then the following should be considered:] In that case [it would follow that the fortified potential] would exist as something pervading all sentient beings,[493] given that it is because [the dharmakāya] exists as something pervasive that [the proposition] "All sentient beings possess a buddha nature" can be proven...It is [only] the naturally present potential among the two [potentials] that pervades sentient beings. Therefore, to abandon buddha nature, which [after all] has actually been taught, and to teach a nature of sentient beings is not the intention of the Buddha's words with definitive meaning.[494]

Even though the third reason is taken at face value, namely that a buddha nature or potential really exists as something pervading all sentient beings, Lodrö Tsungmé restricts the validity of this statement to the naturally present potential. The fortified or acquired potential is something produced when virtue is striven for and thus has a different beginning in each individual mindstream.[495] From the commentary on passages such as RGV I.51cd ("[Buddha nature] is of an unchangeable nature—as it was before, so it is after")[496] and RGV I.157 (J I.154) ("There is nothing to be removed from it and absolutely nothing to be added"),[497] it becomes clear that the naturally present primordial qualities are taken as the thirty-two qualities of the dharmakāya (the ten strengths and so forth).[498] They are what is referred to as the ultimate truth with regard to qualities in Lodrö Tsungmé's introduction. Lodrö Tsungmé thus loosely relates them with the ultimate aspects of the remaining vajra points, namely the pure dharmatā of mind, which is the ultimate aspect of the buddha element *(dhātu),* and the dharmakāya, or the ultimate aspect of enlightenment *(bodhi).* The corresponding aspects of apparent truth are the thirty-two marks of the Buddha, the ability to generate undefiled buddha properties (i.e., the potential acquired through practice), and the form kāyas (sambhogakāya and nirmāṇakāya).[499] In other words, ultimate truth is equated with the qualities of the dharmakāya, the dharmakāya itself, and the true nature of mind. The ultimate then is not taken as a mere nothingness or void, but described in positive terms. The ontological status of this positive ultimate becomes clear in a discussion about the naturally present potential functioning as a real cause:

> Objection: If the naturally present potential were an actual cause, would it [not then] be an entity? Answer: The naturally present potential abides as the beginningless dharmatā, [or] emptiness mingled with stains [and] inseparable from immeasurable qualities. Even though the aspect of dharmatā (or emptiness) is what causes the transformation of the basis into the stainless dharmakāya, it is not an efficient cause and thus not an entity. [But] the aspect of wisdom is [such] an entity in view of being the efficient cause of the future [ten] strengths, etc., of the Buddha, which resemble [those of] the potential, and there is nothing invalid in such a position.[500]

Here it would be difficult to draw the line between ultimate and apparent truth. The introduction of Lodrö Tsungmé's commentary clearly states that the thirty-two qualities of the dharmakāya belong to the ultimate aspect of the buddha element, apparent [truth] being what has the ability to generate undefiled [buddha] properties, namely that aspect of wisdom that is an efficient cause and thus an entity. On the other hand, Lodrö Tsungmé equates a *naturally present wisdom* with natural luminosity,[501] which is usually taken as a synonym of emptiness and the ultimate. But claiming that an entity (wisdom as an efficient cause) partakes of the ultimate is philosophically problematic and would expose Lodrö Tsungmé to the same critique the Jonangpas had to face.

Whatever truth they belong to, it is remarkable that Lodrö Tsungmé distinguishes the thirty-two qualities (the ten strengths, etc.) of the potential and those of a buddha, notwithstanding that he fully endorses stanza I.157 (J I.154) and explains that the ten strengths, etc., exist throughout beginningless time and that nothing that did not exist before needs to be newly created. In the introductory remarks to the explanation of stanza I.23, it becomes clear that Lodrö Tsungmé resolves the tension by distinguishing an aspect of sphere from an aspect of wisdom:

> As to the [buddha] nature, if ascertained under the aspect of sphere, it is the dharmatā of mind mingled with stains and inseparable from the inconceivable buddha qualities. It is the dharmakāya that exists since beginningless time.[502]

But under the aspect of wisdom, as we have seen above, some kind of production is maintained. It is true that wisdom is taken to be an aspect of the naturally present potential, and as such to be primordially existent,[503] but in terms of wisdom a fruit can clearly be distinguished from a cause:

> [Question:] Is the fruit present in the cause? [Answer:] No, for even though the wisdom that is purified from all stains is the fruit, it does not exist in sentient beings; and even though wisdom mingled with stains exists in the continuum of sentient beings, this is not the fruit.[504]

Lodrö Tsungmé's position on the relationship between buddha nature as a cause and the three kāyas as a fruit becomes particularly clear in his commentarial remarks on RGV I.152–55 (J I.149–52),[505] which explain how the last five of the nine examples from the *Tathāgatagarbhasūtra* (those of the treasure, the tree, the precious image, the future *cakravartin*, and the golden statue) illustrate the nature of the buddha potential, out of which the three kāyas arise. First of all, Lodrö Tsungmé points out that the naturally present potential is a cause of the buddha kāyas in the real sense of the word, and not only metaphorically, in that wisdom arises by acts of correct mental engagement, namely by focusing on emptiness (which is taken to be the naturally present potential by the proponents of a metaphorical understanding):

> Since the fruit, the three pure bodies of the perfect buddha, are attained from these two potentials, [namely] the naturally present potential and the one arisen through practice, [these] are taken to be their cause. Therefore the element or potential is the cause. [Question:] Which fruit [or] kāya is attained through which cause? [Answer:] First, as to the kāya [attained] through the naturally present [potential], it is the actual svābhāvikakāya[506] which is attained, since previously suchness existed mingled with stains, and the transformation of the basis into the purified dharmakāya is attained by virtue of having purified its stains. Some very intelligent people say that nonconceptual knowledge arises by becoming familiar with the correct mental engagement of focusing on emptiness; thus it was taught that [emptiness] was [only] metaphorically called a *cause of wisdom.* This is not acceptable, given that it [has been said] in the *[Ratnagotravibhāga]vyākhyā:* "Tathāgatahood is the state of being con-

stituted by the threefold buddhakāya. Therefore, since[507] the element of the tathāgata is a cause of its being attained, the meaning of element here is 'cause.'"[508]

It is interesting that no attempt at all is made to downplay the element of causation in the relationship between buddha nature and the buddha kāyas. This becomes even more evident in the explanation of the nirmāṇakāya, where its property of being something really produced is underlined by ascribing to it an artificial character:

> Second, the latter, [namely] the two form kāyas, are attained through the fortified potential. Having [previously] accomplished virtues that are a cause of liberation and having taken vows, he appears, at the time of becoming a buddha, as the two form kāyas for disciples near and far.... The nirmāṇakāya is like an artificial image made of gold, since its nature is to appear as the reflection [of the sambhogakāya] to the mind of disciples through the power of the sambhogakāya.[509]

From this it is clear that the form kāyas are something artificially created and thus do not exist since beginningless time, all the more so as their cause, the fortified potential, has been said to have a beginning in time (see above). The way the three kāyas emerge from buddha nature is then summarized in the following way:

> ...the dharmakāya, suchness, and the naturally present potential, [all] three [of them][510] literally pervade all sentient beings. The outflow of the dharmakāya, [namely] the two[fold] teaching of the profound and the vast, and the fruit of the potential, [namely] the three kāyas, are taught as existing on the level of the fruit. Even though these "somehow exist" *(yod pa dang yod kyang)* in sentient beings, they are obstructed by hindrances. This is taught as such because the two[fold] wisdom of what [reality] is like and how far [it reaches], [namely] the dominant condition of the two[fold] discourses, exists, as do the four wisdoms that govern the arising of the two [form] kāyas. When these wisdoms are purified of adventitious stains, they arise by virtue of this as the appearance of the two[fold] discourses and the two [form] kāyas. Svābhāvikakāya has the same meaning as dharmakāya, and since the fortified potential is a potential that

> is newly achieved through conditions, it does not pervade all sentient beings.[511]

In other words, we loosely speak of the presence of the three kāyas in sentient beings only in the sense that the causes of the form kāyas, namely the twofold wisdom of what reality is like and how far it reaches together with the four wisdoms (mirror-like wisdom, etc.), exist in sentient beings since beginningless time. The fortified potential not only removes hindrances, but also, by way of the purification process, causes the primordial wisdoms to unfold as form kāyas, and as we have seen above, even the thirty-two qualities of the dharmakāya (the ten strengths, etc.) undergo a change, since it has been said that the qualities of the fruit resemble those of the potential (see above).

To recap, Lodrö Tsungmé's commentary resembles Dölpopa's ordinary or "nontantric" presentation of buddha nature. Another similarity with Dölpopa, and also Sabzang Mati Panchen, is the way unconditioned buddhahood is explained. In his commentary on RGV I.5 Lodrö Tsungmé takes the dharmakāya to lack any conditioned phenomenon whatsoever.[512] In other words, the way Lodrö Tsungmé comments on the *Ratnagotravibhāga* does not exclude the possibility that he adhered to a similar extraordinary view as Dölpopa. This is indicated by Lodrö Tsungmé's statement that the three kāyas somehow exist in sentient beings and that they manifest from the primordial wisdom when the hindrances are removed.

The Position of Longchen Rabjampa

Longchenpa's interpretation of buddha nature in his *Treasure of Tenets (Grub mtha' mdzod)* deserves our interest for several reasons. First, most of the stanzas dealing with the fourth vajra point (on buddha nature) in the *Ratnagotravibhāga* are quoted and commented upon in thirty continuous pages in the *Treasure of Tenets.*[513] Second, this work's theory of buddha nature plays a central role in linking the dzogchen teachings with older strands of Indian Buddhism.[514] Third is the *Grub mtha' mdzod*'s positive interpretation of the *Ratnagotravibhāga,* maintaining that emptiness needs to be understood in the sense of buddha nature's luminosity, and that such a positive assessment of the ultimate has definitive meaning.[515] This and texts such as the *Rdzogs chen sems nyid ngal gso'i grel pa shing rta chen po,* in which an "empti[ness] of an own-being" *(rang stong)* is distinguished from an "empti[ness] of other" *(gzhan stong),*[516] probably led Kongtrül Lodrö Tayé to list Longchenpa among the masters who figured in the diffusion of zhentong.[517] Most modern Nyingma scholars think, however, that such a stance is naive, in that Longchenpa did not endorse a zhentong view in any of his other works, especially his more mature ones including the *Chos dbyings rin po che'i mdzod* or the *Gnas lugs rin po che'i mdzod.* The latter rather show that Longchenpa was perfectly in line with Prāsaṅgika Madhyamaka.

It would go beyond the scope of this study to establish what the final view of Longchenpa was and whether it is reflected in the *Grub mtha' mdzod* or the *Shing rta chen po.* Still, we should keep in mind the possibility that there were already different ways of defining zhentong at the time of Dölpopa.[518] This said, we will now investigate Longchenpa's interesting dzogchen interpretation of the *Ratnagotravibhāga* in the *Grub mtha' mdzod.*

The short title *Treasure of Tenets* is a little misleading, since more than one third of the text (namely the last four chapters) is on Vajrayāna and dzogchen, which are not, strictly speaking, contained in the traditional system of four tenets (Vaibhāṣika, Sautrāntika, Cittamātra, and Madhyamaka). But the full title shows that the *Treasure of the Jewels of Tenets* "elucidates the meaning of all *yāna*s." In other words, it is the system of nine—or in this text, sixteen—*yāna*s of the Nyingma school that are presented.[519] The sixteen *yāna*s are listed at the beginning of the third chapter,[520] which introduces an explanation of both the Buddhist and other tenets. It is, of course, the explanation of the last of these sixteen *yāna*s that reflects Longchenpa's ultimate view.[521] The nature of the fundamental state, which is repeatedly equated with the *primordial ground, self-arisen wisdom,* or *awareness,* is described in line with the dzogchen categories *essence (ngo bo), nature (rang bzhin),* and *compassionate responsiveness (thugs rje).* The essence of the primordial ground is taken to be empty (like space), its nature is luminosity (like that of the sun and the moon), and its compassionate responsiveness is all-pervasive (like the rays of light). These three categories are further equated with, respectively, the dharmakāya, sambhogakāya, and nirmāṇakāya. Inseparable in essence, the three kāyas abide throughout beginningless time as the nature of wisdom in an ever-unchangeable sphere.[522]

As doctrinal support for a sphere with ever-existing qualities, Longchenpa cites the stanza from the *Mahāyānābhidharmasūtra* ("the beginningless sphere is the basis of all phenomena") quoted in RGVV I.155 (J I.152)[523] and stanza 43 from Saraha's *Dohākośagīti,* which also plays an important role in the mahāmudrā interpretation of buddha nature:[524]

> Mind alone is the seed of everything.
> I prostrate[525] to [this] mind

> In which worldly existence and nirvāṇa spread,
> And which is like a wish-fulfilling jewel, bestowing the desired fruit.[526]

Of particular interest is the following description of how buddha wisdom (in all its aspects of body, speech, and mind) exists throughout beginningless time even in confused states of mind.[527] A little further down, Longchenpa describes this state in detail:

> [Primordial] awareness *(rig pa)*[528] is empty in essence, exists by its own nature in the form of five lights, and its compassionate responsiveness pervades [everything] in the form of rays. Even though it is present as the great source of the kāyas and wisdom, it is hindered [in three ways]: The aspect where it is in essence the empty dharmakāya, [namely] the pure vision of wisdom, is hindered by the eight accumulations [of consciousness] together with the ground *(kun gzhi)*.[529] [Its] nature, the luminosity of the five lights, is hindered by the tangible skandha of flesh and blood. [Its] compassionate responsiveness, [which] abides [in a state of] manifesting [light] rays and awareness, is hindered by *karman* and mental imprints. Even though [this *rig pa*] is [only] present in a state that is very difficult to perceive, it is not the case that it does not exist. It pervades all sentient beings and exists in the body together with a support.[530]

Longchenpa, thus, adduces the crucial stanza I.28 from the *Ratnagotravibhāga*, which lists the three reasons for the presence of buddha nature in sentient beings. In his explanation of the third reason ("because of the potential"), Longchenpa equates *potential* with the dzogchen term *awareness*, adopting as he does the reading *rig* instead of *rigs (potential)*, and glossing buddha nature as *rig pa* in the following paraphrase. In other words, all sentient beings possess buddha nature because of their intrinsic primordial awareness.

At the beginning of his presentation of the secret Mantrayāna,[531] Longchenpa defines both the basis of purification *(sbyang gzhi)* and that which must be purified *(sbyang bya)* in line with the *Ratnagotravibhāga* and its terminology:

> The subject being characterized *(mtshan gzhi)* is the naturally pure sphere, which is inseparably united[532] with the luminous

> kāyas and wisdom, together with what is based on that [sphere], namely the phenomena to be purified and the purifying factors.... The naturally pure dharmatā of the sphere [and] luminosity is the basis of purification. The adventitious hindrances, [which are] *karman*, defilements, the phenomena of saṁsāra, and the eight accumulations [of consciousness] including the "ground" (i.e., the *ālayavijñāna*)[533] are the stains to be purified. The ground, which consists of the various mental imprints, is repelled, given that it is the root of saṁsāra. Even though the real object of the real ground, [namely] the fundamental state, is not repelled, that aspect of it that is conventionally given the name *ground* is turned back and becomes what is called *dharmadhātu wisdom.*[534]

As in RGV I.157–58 (J I.154–55), adventitious stains that must be removed are distinguished from a *dhātu*[535] that is inseparable from the buddha qualities, which here are all the kāyas and wisdom. It should be noted, too, that Longchenpa was aware of the two different meanings of *kun gzhi:* the real ground, which is the fundamental state; and that which is conventionally given the name *kun gzhi.* Thus an impure *ālayavijñāna* (the conventional "ground") is distinguished from a *kun gzhi* that signifies the fundamental state, which in dzogchen is inseparable from primordial awareness or self-arisen wisdom. Similar to a zhentong interpretation, the *kun gzhi* is equated with the fundamental state. This is like Rangjung Dorjé's *pure mind,* which becomes manifest simply when the impure *kun gzhi rnam shes (ālayavijñāna)* is removed.[536] This distinction between an impure *ālayavijñāna* and a pure *kun gzhi* could have been the forerunner of what later became known as zhentong. In fact, Longchenpa once in his *Rdzogs chen sems nyid ngal gso'i grel pa shing rta chen po* draws the distinction between "empty of other" *(gzhan gyis stong pa)* and "empty of an own-being" *(rang gyis stong pa)* in the context of discussing the Yogācāra theory of the three natures.[537] Longchenpa explains:

> The empti[ness] of an own-being [has] two [aspects]: the non-existent appearances, which are devoid of a specific characteristic of their own like a [reflection of the] moon in water; and the empti[ness] of an own-being, [which is the emptiness of] the imagined [only], where spontaneously present phenomena are not abandoned, even though elements that can be labeled in terms of self and other do not exist. "Empti[ness] of other"

> [means] to be empty of what is other, or uncontained and empty of [what is referred to by] any other synonym [of the ultimate].[538] "Empty of both" also includes two [parts]: being empty of [what is referred to by] synonyms[539] and being empty of what is specifically characterized in terms of words [and] things. In this regard, the dharmatā of the mind, [that is] luminosity or the natural element of buddha nature, is empty of all flawed entities. It has the defining characteristics of qualities. The aspect of it which is the purity of [its] own essence is beyond the accomplishment of qualities and the discarding of faults.... [False] imagining or the eight accumulations of consciousness do not exist in the ground, and are thus also empty of an own-being.... In sum, *empty of an own-being* means that no phenomena truly exist in terms of an own-being. As to *empty of other*, this phenomenon (or, nature of phenomena?) has been designated under its aspect of not possessing other phenomena.[540]

In other words, the nature of the buddha element, or the dharmatā of the mind, which has been equated with the unchangeable perfect nature,[541] is not empty of qualities, but empty of the eight accumulations of consciousness (including the *ālayavijñāna*). The last definition of *empty of other* (zhentong) is unclear, specifically whether to read *dharma (chos)* or *dharmatā (chos nyid)*. Furthermore, the demonstrative pronoun *de* in *chos de la* found here is also problematic; to which phenomenon spoken of before does it precisely refer? Further up it was said that the dharmatā *(chos nyid)* is empty of flawed entities, in particular what is other. Thus speaking of dharmatā *(chos nyid)* here in the context of zhentong would make logical sense. This omission of the single syllable *tā (nyid)* (perhaps by a later redactor) changes the meaning of the whole passage, since that which is empty of something else (i.e., buddha nature) is then subsumed under phenomena, which do not truly exist in terms of an own-being. Philosophically, the interpretation based on reading dharma *(chos)* holds water. It could be argued that even though the dharmatā of the mind is empty of other, it still lacks a true own-being. Longchenpa may have preferred such a zhentong definition because it does not conflict with his dzogchen view that the essence of primordial awareness is emptiness.

Even though a later emendation seems likely, it is difficult to conclude from this passage alone that Longchenpa is a zhentongpa who denies, like the Jonangpas, that dharmatā lacks an own-being. Still, Longchenpa clearly states in his *Grub mtha' mdzod* (in his commentary on a stanza quoted in RGVV I.158 (J I.155)) that the ultimate is not merely emptiness in which nothing exists at all:

> The sphere is the ultimate truth. It is said that by seeing its nature you see ultimate truth. But again, it is not the case that an emptiness in which nothing exists at all is the ultimate truth. To fools, ordinary beings, and beginners, the teachings on selflessness and so forth were given as a remedy for being attached to a self. But [this selflessness or emptiness], it should be known, [is] in reality the sphere [or] luminosity, [which is] unconditioned and exists as something spontaneously present.[542]

Nowhere in the entire *Grub mtha' mdzod* does Longchenpa distinguish between the thirty-two qualities of the dharmakāya and the qualities of the form kāyas. Both types of qualities exist throughout beginningless time. This is made clear in the following passage, in which Longchenpa addresses the question of the exact relationship between the buddha element and buddhahood in the *Ratnagotravibhāga* by letting a fictive opponent ask why a buddha is not taken to be the result of purifying the stains of the [buddha] element *(khams)* on the path of adopting and abandoning.[543] Longchenpa answers:

> Since self-arisen wisdom, great perfection *(rdzog chen)* itself, exists throughout beginningless time as the spontaneously present qualities of the Buddha's vast abundance [of treasures], the three kāyas are [already] complete as his own possession. Therefore, they do not need to be searched for once [the *ālayavijñāna*] has been turned back.[544]

Nevertheless, the *Ratnagotravibhāga*, in which the form kāyas are explained to be a product of the path and caused by the fortified potential, is adduced in support of dzogchen. The beginning of the paragraph on dzogchen in the seventh chapter shows the importance of the *Ratnagotravibhāga* as a canonical underpinning for the great perfection, even though it is, technically, part of the Sūtrayāna. In listing the flaws of inferior vehicles, Longchenpa blames the sūtras for obstructing the great bliss of atiyoga (i.e., dzogchen) by trying to conceptualize and analyze dzogchen, which is beyond concepts and analysis.[545] Having ridiculed the remaining inferior vehicles, Longchenpa describes dzogchen in the following way:

> In terms of its nature [the great bliss of atiyoga] is great perfection (dzogchen), luminosity, the essence of the sphere, [and] self-arisen wisdom. Since it has neither cause nor fruit accompanied by conditions (as if there were something to be produced and something that produced), it has, like space, naturally existed throughout beginningless time.[546]

In support of this, Longchenpa refers to RGV I.51cd—two *pāda*s that have been quoted in the *Kun byed rgyal po*:[547]

> [The buddha element is of] an unchangeable nature—as it was before, so it is after.[548]

And in the same line and sentence—that is to say, on an equal footing with the *Kun byed rgyal po*—Longchenpa quotes RGV I.5a, once again in support of the above-mentioned description of dzogchen:[549]

> [Buddhahood] is unconditioned and spontaneously present.[550]

It is noteworthy that the *Ratnagotravibhāga*, which belongs to the sūtra rather than tantra category, is quoted in support of dzogchen immediately after the sūtras and all other inferior vehicles have been ridiculed. Probably aware of this inconsistency, Longchenpa simply quotes this *pāda* without mentioning the source.

In the presentation of the higher *yāna*s in the *Grub mtha' mdzod*, it is mainly the *Ratnagotravibhāga* (along with two closely related sūtras) that is adduced from a category of texts that normally belong to the *yāna*s of the inferior sūtras. One of the most obvious reasons for this is that the *tathāgatagarbha* theory, with its concepts of natural luminosity and inseparable buddha qualities, displays a high degree of similarity with dzogchen, and given that the dzogchen tradition is otherwise at a loss to cite identifiable Indian Buddhist sources, it is no surprise that the *Ratnagotravibhāga* would have become a central focus.

Such an approach requires a particular interpretation of the *Ratnagotravibhāga*, one that Dölpopa calls the extraordinary interpretation of the Vajrayāna. While Dölpopa and Rangjung Dorjé clearly distinguish a regular explanation of the *Ratnagotravibhāga*, in which the two potentials and the three kāyas are presented in an ordinary Mahāyāna context separate from an extraordinary tantric interpretation, it is not so clear whether Longchenpa follows the same strategy. Those who adhere to the thesis that

Lodrö Tsungmé was Longchenpa would, of course, say that the differences between Lodrö Tsungmé's *Ratnagotravibhāga* commentary and the dzogchen interpretation of buddha nature in the *Grub mtha' mdzod* result precisely from such a distinction between an ordinary Mahāyāna interpretation and an extraordinary Vajrayāna one. In order to discuss this reasonable point, we need to turn to Longchenpa's presentation of the lower *yānas* in the *Grub mtha' mdzod.*

First of all, it is interesting to note that the *Ratnagotravibhāga* and the *tathāgatagarbha* theory do not figure significantly in the definition of the tenets in the third chapter of the *Grub mtha' mdzod.*[551] One exception is the Cittamātra section, where RGV I.51cd (see above) is quoted to illustrate the unchangeable aspect of the perfect nature *(pariniṣpannasvabhāva),* with which buddha nature is implicitly equated. This equation is further substantiated on the basis of *Mahāyānasūtrālaṁkāra* IX.37.[552] In his definition of the unchangeable perfect nature, Longchenpa introduces two new synonyms for it, the *fundamental state (gnas lugs)* and the *real ground (don gyi kun gzhi),* neither of which is found in the traditional Yogācāra works.[553] By weaving these terms into the presentation of a lower vehicle, he establishes a connection between the Yogācāra and the primordial or real ground, and thus shows that already the Cittamātra presentation of the ground is itself compatible with the highest view of dzogchen.

Apart from this, the presentation of the philosophical tenets is quite conservative. Neither the *Ratnagotravibhāga* nor its *tathāgatagarbha* theory is mentioned even once in the explanation of the Madhyamaka systems. Other exegetes did not stay so strict. For example, Tāranātha (1575–1634), in his own presentation of the four tenets, the *Gzhan stong snying po,* divides the fourth tenet (Madhyamaka) into ordinary and Great Madhyamaka *(dbu ma chen po).*[554] In this work, he based his Great Madhyamaka on a zhentong interpretation through a particular understanding of the Yogācāra combined with the *Ratnagotravibhāga.*[555] In contrast, Longchenpa speaks of a *Great Madhyamaka* only in the sense of "being free from mental fabrication" *(spros bral).*[556]

It is noteworthy, however, that Longchenpa defines ultimate truth in the Prāsaṅgika (Madhyamaka) as the *essence (ngo bo),* which is free from the mental fabrication of a perceived object and a perceiving subject.[557] It is true that the concept of the emptiness of perceived and perceiver originally comes from the *prajñāpāramitā* literature, but it is first and foremost a concept favored by Yogācāra works,[558] in which restricting the object of negation to the duality of subject and object does not negate nondual wisdom and other buddha qualities. In the context of explaining the transformation of the basis[559] in chapter 4, Longchenpa shows how his notion of a primordially existing wisdom can be explained from a Prāsaṅgika view, without any allusion to the *Ratnagotravibhāga:*

> Some who consider themselves to be Mādhyamikas [say]: Since a buddha does not have wisdom, he does not have the knowledge of wisdom either, because knowable objects are mental fabrications, and he is free from mental fabrications.... As has been said in the *[Madhyamaka]-Avatāra* [XI.17d]: "The mind being suppressed, the [dharma]kāya makes [the state of nonarising and nonobstruction] directly manifest."[560] [Answer:] This is not acceptable for the following reasons. Since in terms of empti[ness], from the view of the dharmakāya, neither the existence nor nonexistence of wisdom is established, you may present it as "existent," [and] this [can be] negated; and, similarly, you may claim [its] "nonexistence," [and] this, too, [can be] negated. Therefore nonexistence is not defensible either. In terms of appearance, from the view of the form kāyas, after disciples manifest, wisdom, too, must appear, since [the visible kāyas] necessarily appear in order to work for the benefit [of others]. Although the tenets concerning knowable objects, knowers, and so forth, [in short,] anything imputed, are mental fabrications, objects *(yul)* belonging to the system[561] of that which manifests without being imputed by anyone should not be taken as mental fabrications.[562]

This view of the ontological status of buddha wisdom matches the view of Sakya Paṇḍita (1182–1251), who says in his *Thub pa dgongs gsal:*

> If [you claimed that] wisdom is truly established in his own (i.e., the Buddha's) continuum, you would be like the non-Buddhists who maintain the permanence [of the absolute].... [But] if wisdom were a [mere] appearance for others, without existing in his own continuum, the Buddha would be without qualities.[563]

Similarly, the Eighth Karmapa Mikyö Dorjé and Śākya Chogden claim, according to Kongtrül Lodrö Tayé:

> Wisdom is beyond existence and nonexistence on the level of a buddha; on a conventional level, though, wisdom exists.[564]

Coming back to Longchenpa: with regard to philosophical theory or views, the Prāsaṅgika occupies a privileged place where the *Ratnagotravibhāga* has no bearing at all for him.

The situation is different in the fourth chapter, which explains how to proceed on the paths of these tenets.[565] The presentation of the bodhisattva path starts with an explanation of how bodhicitta is generated, by pointing out that everyone possesses a natural [buddha] potential *(rigs)*. This subchapter is basically a commentary on the main passages of the first chapter of the *Ratnagotravibhāga* (on buddha nature). It should be remembered in the following passage that the discussion of buddha nature in this fourth chapter still formally belongs to the nontantric part of the *Grub mtha' mdzod.*

Based on RGV I.62ab ("The luminous nature of mind, like space, never undergoes change"[566]), Longchenpa defines *potential* as follows:

> The naturally pure sphere, which is the ultimate truth or self-arisen wisdom, is called the *potential* or *[buddha] element* when mingled with stains. When stainless, it is called *enlightenment* or *tathāgata.*[567]

This definition is fully in line with the *Ratnagotravibhāgavyākhyā* (on I.23–24) except that the [buddha] element (Skt. *dhātu*, Tib. *khams*) is replaced with Longchenpa's own dzogchen terms, *naturally pure sphere* and *self-arisen wisdom.* Quoting RGV I.157 (J I.154) ("There is nothing to be removed from it and absolutely nothing to be added. The real should be seen as real; and seeing the real, you become liberated"),[568] Longchenpa defines the nature of the potential:

> With regard to the essence of this sphere, which is [buddha] nature, stains that must be abandoned have never existed, because [in terms of their true being,] they are natural luminosity and stainlessness. Qualities that previously did not exist will not be newly produced, since qualities are spontaneously present.[569]

But according to RGVV I.25, it is the uninterrupted and effortless buddha activity that is "spontaneously present" *(lhun grub)*, and not the qualities.[570] In the entire *Ratnagotravibhāga* and its *vyākhyā*, qualities are not even once called *spontaneously present (lhun grub)*. In dzogchen, the nature *(rang bzhin)* of awareness *(rig pa)* (equated with buddha nature) is *spontaneously present (lhun grub),* which is understood to imply that the qualities have been spontaneously present throughout beginningless time. Even though there are no "spontaneously present qualities" in the *Ratnagotravibhāga,* it is not entirely impossible to read them into it, given that the qualities are inseparable from the primordial buddha nature and the basis on which spontaneous buddha activity unfolds. It should be noted that a normal Mahāyāna text is here not simply being quoted and commented on according to its original purport, but it is being brought into line with a dzogchen view.

Of particular interest is how Longchenpa also claims in this "nontantric" portion of the *Grub mtha' mdzod* that all the three kāyas exist throughout beginningless time. His agenda is therefore to prove that the buddha qualities already exist in both the naturally present and fortified potentials, that is, that these two potentials are only liberating causes and not efficient causes. He starts by presenting the following etymology of *potential (gotra):*

> *Go-* in *gotra* (Longchenpa: *gautra*) [stands for] *guṇa,* which translates as *quality,* and *-tra* for *tara,* which translates as "to liberate" *(sgrol ba).*[571] The qualities, regarded as the support, liberate [by bringing you] beyond saṁsāra. [As] has been said in [*Mahāyānasūtrālaṁkāra* III.4cd]:
>
> > As for the qualities, you should know
> > That they have the meaning of "to liberate."[572]

Two lines further down Longchenpa quotes the entire stanza (MSA III.4) which not surprisingly, judging from the way he quotes the second half of the third *pāda* and the fourth *pāda* above, he understands in the following way:

> [The potential] should be known as the naturally [present] and the fortified. They are the support and the supported, exist [as cause] but do not exist [as fruit], and as for the qualities, you should know that they have the meaning of "to liberate."[573]

Longchenpa explains how the all-pervading luminosity of buddha nature (as established by the three reasons in RGV I.27) can be divided into the two aspects of emptiness and appearance, so as to accord with both types of potential:

> As to the sphere, [or] empti[ness], it is the liberating cause with regard to the dharmakāya[574] and the svābhāvikakāya, [which are] the support *(=prakṛtisthagotra);* and as to wisdom, [or] appearance, including your own luminous major and minor marks [of a buddha], they abide as the supported *(=paripuṣṭagotra),* [which is] the liberating cause with regard to the two form kāyas.[575, 576]

In other words, for Longchenpa neither potential is an efficient cause, in the sense of really producing qualities, but is only a liberating cause, which means that each is already imbued with all qualities that bring about liberation from what hinders them, namely adventitious defilements and the like. The two potentials are further equated with the sphere and wisdom, or emptiness and appearance, and from what has been said till now about the sphere and wisdom, it follows that both potentials are inseparable and exist throughout beginningless time.

Contrary to this line of thought, Lodrö Tsungmé takes the fortified potential as something newly accomplished (and consequently, as something with a beginning in time):

> As to the [potential] arisen from practice,[577] it has been newly accomplished thanks to conditions of the various potentials of the noble ones. In this regard, the naturally present one is the support, and the one arisen from practice (i.e., the fortified potential), the supported. As for the defining characteristic of the potential, it is a property of the state mingled with stains, and it is effective in generating the abandonment and realization of the noble ones. As for [its] etymology, up to *go* in *gotra*, it is derived from *gu*, [which stands for] *guṇa* ("quality"). By separating *ta* and *ra* [in *tra*], you obtain *tara* ("to liberate").[578] [So it is] *guṇa-tara.* Since it is the qualities that it liberates[579] and generates, it is a potential.[580]

Next, Lodrö Tsungmé quotes MSA III.4. But this time the stanza must be understood in the light of Vasubandhu's commentary, since the last sentence of Lodrö Tsungmé's explanation is an abbreviation of Vasubandhu's analysis of the compound *guṇottāraṇatā-,* which is:

> It should be known that the potential has the meaning of the "coming out of the qualities"—the qualities come out[581] in the sense that they arise from it (i.e. the potential).[582]

A "natural reading" of the Tibetan translation of MSA III.4 supports Longchenpa, but Vasubandhu's commentary and also the general context of the third chapter of the *Mahāyānasūtrālaṁkāra* suggest that Lodrö Tsungmé's interpretation is more accurate. Still, the main point here is not to settle the question who is right; it is rather that one and the same author cannot be expected to quote and interpret an important stanza from the *Mahāyānasūtrālaṁkāra* in such fundamentally different ways. It is inconceivable that the "Lodrö Tsungmé" who composed a *Ratnagotravibhāga* commentary could have ignored the original purport of the *Mahāyānasūtrālaṁkāra* and the *bhāṣya* on it when writing the *Grub mtha' mdzod*, if he were the author of both works.

It seems to me that Longchenpa's interpretation of MSA III.4 would not be different in another context, such as a simple commentary on the *Mahāyānasūtrālaṁkāra*. Longchenpa's way of presenting buddha nature in this passage of the *Grub mtha' mdzod* cannot be following a strategy of distinguishing an ordinary from an extraordinary interpretation. Dölpopa would have simply accepted the purport of MSA III.4 and the *bhāṣya* on it, because it is in accordance with the level of apparent truth on which form kāyas and qualities are actually produced, or to use Lodrö Tsungmé's terminology, the potentials are efficient causes.

For those who claim that Longchenpa was the Lodrö Tsungmé who composed a *Ratnagotravibhāga* commentary in Sangpu Neutog there is still one possible argument left, which is that Longchenpa changed tack after he left the university of Sangpu, adopting a full-fledged dzogchen view only after his years of study.[583] Future researchers investigating the works of Longchenpa will have to keep this question in mind.

Based on his particular understanding of MSA III.4, Longchenpa comments on the last five of the nine examples from the *Tathāgatagarbhasūtra* (the treasure, the tree, the precious image, the future monarch, and the golden statue), which illustrate the nature of the buddha potential out of which the three kāyas arise (RGV I.152–55, J I.149–52):[584]

> There is a twofold division into a naturally present potential and an acquired potential corresponding to the division of ground and path. During the time [the potential] abides in the nature of the sphere, the ground, as something all-pervading, it resembles, as an aspect of the sphere, [which is] the primordial ground of manifestation,[585] a treasure of precious jewels. In the same way as the abode, which is the ground that gives rise to anything one may wish, is not determinable as something manifest, [the

> potential] is the sphere of the dharmakāya, [or] the svābhāvikakāya. It is presented [as such] because it enables the manifestation of the kāyas and wisdom. As to awareness and the kāyas under [the] aspect of appearance, [both of which are then] the manifested wisdom, they are actualized qualities that exist in yourself. This comes about by their power to free from hindrances. It is merely with respect to this ascertainment that the [acquired or fortified] potential has been illustrated previously by the example of a mature tree with fruits. The pure cause is labeled as the pure fruit. This is elucidated in the examples of the gold mine and the [mine of] supreme jewels in the *Mahāyānasūtrālaṁkāra.*[586]
>
> Moreover, when it is explained what [the potential] is like when on the path of learning, both potentials of the sphere are called natural potential abiding as the support, given that they exist as something spontaneously present by nature. The roots of virtue, beginning from the initial generation of bodhicitta all the way up to the tenth level, [that is] everything included in the two accumulations of merit and wisdom, which is all based on that [natural potential], are called acquired or fortified potential. These virtues are taught as if the qualities that exist in yourself newly arise on the strength of having removed the stains of the natural potential, which is endowed with a newly acquired remedy. Nowadays the [natural potential] is [often] taken as the suchness of the ground, and the path as the fortified potential, the two potentials not being counted as part of the ground. This obviously implies a misunderstanding of the sphere, since [such a view] contradicts the spontaneous presence of appearance and emptiness in the [primordial] ground.[587]

In other words, there is no real production of anything for Longchenpa. What happens simply is that the purification process makes the primordial qualities of the three kāyas apparent:

> In view of the apparent production of the three kāyas by the strength of training on the path and the removal of stains, it is said to have the nature of a potential. This is illustrated by the five similes of the treasure [under the ground], the tree, the precious Buddha statue [wrapped in a garment], the *cakravartin,* and the golden statue [in the earthen mold].[588]

To conclude, Longchenpa interprets buddha nature in the fourth chapter of the *Grub mtha' mdzod* from a dzogchen perspective, the implication being that the qualities of the primordial form kāyas do not refer to the real thirty-two marks of the Buddha in the body but to the thirty-two "luminous marks."[589] At the expense of reinterpreting MSA III.4 and the meaning of *spontaneously present (lhun grub)* in RGV I.25, he tries to establish that theories of the two potentials in the *Mahāyānasūtrālaṁkāra* and the *Ratnagotravibhāga* do not present the primordial ground differently from dzogchen.

Among philosophical tenets, Longchenpa takes Prāsaṅgika to be the highest. It still belongs to the analytical approach of the lower Sūtrayāna, however, and so is outshone by the unsurpassable *yāna* of dzogchen. But if we understand the teaching of an ultimate buddha nature to mean that the qualities of a buddha have been spontaneously present throughout beginningless time, and if we take the final passage of the first chapter literally, and thus accept that the teaching of emptiness has five defects that can only be removed by the definitive teaching of buddha nature (which Longchenpa sets forth), the *Ratnagotravibhāga* must indeed be said to outshine Prāsaṅgika. The superiority of Prāsaṅgika is accepted within the lower analytical approach of the sūtras, but the *Ratnagotravibhāga*, a text whose doctrine is so closely associated with dzogchen, has definitive meaning, counteracting the defects of the analytical approach in a way similar to dzogchen.[590]

The kind of relation between the *tathāgatagarbha* theory of the *Ratnagotravibhāga* and dzogchen, which is necessary for such an approach, is first of all established by what Dölpopa would call an extraordinary Vajrayāna explanation of the *Ratnagotravibhāga*. This implies, for example, that not only the thirty-two qualities of the dharmakāya but also the thirty-two qualities of the form kāyas exist throughout beginningless time (which is, in view of the nine examples from the *Tathāgatagarbhasūtra*, not entirely impossible). Second, dzogchen notions such as *spontaneous presence (lhun grub), sphere (dbyings),* and *[primordial] ground of manifestation ('char gzhi)* are systematically introduced as synonyms of key philosophical terms in the *Ratnagotravibhāga*. The technical terms do not need to be entirely new: *spontaneously present (lhun grub),* for example, is repeatedly found in the *Ratnagotravibhāga*, where it denotes effortless buddha activity, but in a dzogchen context it is necessarily associated with the buddha qualities, and so has a slightly different connotation.

Having thus been introduced to the *tathāgatagarbha* theory from a dzogchen perspective, we are prepared to accept the *Ratnagotravibhāga* as a canonical basis for dzogchen when the latter is presented as the final *yāna*. Such a twofold strategy not only offers a way to proceed smoothly, and without too many contradictions, to the higher vehicles when studying texts like the *Ratnagotravibhāga*, but also reflects a hermeneutic attempt to set dzogchen on a firmer canonical foundation.

The Position of Barawa Gyaltsen Palzang

Four texts from Barawa's collected works prove to be very helpful in determining his view on the *Ratnagotravibhāga*. In all four of them Barawa establishes his mahāmudrā understanding of buddha nature over other views, particularly the zhentong of the Jonangpas. In the first work, *The Sunbeam of Explaining the Intention of Two Dharma Masters*,[591] which Barawa composed after hearing that two omniscient masters, namely Künkhyen Sherab Gyaltsen (Kun mkhyen Shes rab rgyal mtshan) (Dölpopa) and Khenchen Tamché Khyenpa Butön Rinpoché (Mkhan chen thams cad mkhyen pa Bu ston Rin po che), upheld seemingly incompatible views:

> [Barawa] heard the [following]: "The Omniscient Butön (Bu ston) claims that buddha nature does not exist in sentient beings," while "the Omniscient [Dölpopa] claims the existence of both a pure ground of wisdom and an impure ground of consciousness; he [further] claims that these two are not identical in essence, and he [finally] claims that the reflections of emptiness are properly buddha nature [in the form of] firmness of mind."[592]

In other words, whereas Butön denies the presence of buddha nature in sentient beings altogether, Dölpopa accepts its existence even in terms of distinct images, such as the reflections of emptiness that are experienced during the six-branch yoga *(ṣaḍaṅgayoga)* of the *Kālacakratantra*.[593] Barawa argues that both masters, Butön and Dölpopa, must have made their respective statements with a hidden intention, and so he assumes that they have provisional meaning. In order to establish that a statement has a hidden intention *(dgongs pa can)* you have to be able to indicate the basis of such a hidden intention *(dgongs gzhi)*[594] through demonstrating what the author really believed to be true, the motive *(dgos pa)* of the provisional statement, and a contradiction that results from taking the provisional statement literally *(dngos la gnod byed)*.[595] Thus, Barawa tries to show that it is his own mahāmudrā understanding of buddha nature—not only emptiness but also clarity and awareness—that is the sole basis on which the ultimate purport of both Dölpopa and Butön rests. In short, Barawa presents his interpretation of buddha nature as the only possibility left for explaining the contradictory positions of Butön and Dölpopa (provided that both are omniscient and so see the same ultimate reality). Through these hermeneutics we can see Barawa's own view in a concise way. In three other texts, Barawa criticizes the Jonang position even more directly. They are two long letters addressed to Dükhorwa Dorjé Nyingpo (Dus 'khor ba rdo rje snying po), a follower of Dölpopa, and a reply to eight other disciples of Dölpopa. Even though much is repetition, some points are more elaborated on than in the *Dgongs bshad nyi ma'i 'od zer* (the first text mentioned).

In his study of Butön's *De bzhin gshegs pa'i snying po gsal zhing mdzes par byed pa'i rgyan*, Seyfort Ruegg comes to the conclusion that it is mainly the equation of buddha nature with the real dharmakāya of a buddha that led Butön to the conclusion that the teaching of buddha nature has only provisional meaning.[596] Butön's disciple Dratsepa Rinchen Namgyal (Sgra tshad pa Rin chen rnam rgyal) (1318–88) in his commentary on the *Mdzes rgyan* (i.e., the *Yang rgyan*) takes this further, stating that even on a tantric level the teaching of buddha nature has only provisional meaning.[597] In other words, Butön and Dratsepa deny that a buddha nature that is fully adorned with all qualities exists in sentient beings. Dratsepa explains in his *Yang rgyan:*

> If you say that the buddha nature which somebody possesses is the suchness *(tathatā)* of the Buddha, we also accept that it exists in sentient beings, but as for your thesis that it is the dharmakāya of a buddha, it has already been explained before that it is not established that the latter exists in sentient beings.[598]

But Dratsepa leaves no doubt that this suchness is nothing other than emptiness, which he takes, in accordance with Sakya Paṇḍita, as the basis of the ultimate purport *(dgongs gzhi)* with regard to all sūtras that proclaim a buddha nature.[599]

Barawa contrasts such a description of Butön's view with the common opinion that Dölpopa shares, namely that buddha nature possesses all qualities throughout beginningless time, and concludes that both are extreme positions and inadequate formulations of their ultimate views; otherwise both would be contradicting all sūtras and tantras of the third dharmacakra, which say that buddha nature exists in the sheath of defilements, but as the true nature of phenomena (though not as something possessing all qualities).[600] Barawa here quotes a passage from the *Śrīmālādevīsūtra* that was transmitted in two different versions. The way it is quoted by Barawa, the Sanskrit manuscripts and the Derge Tengyur of the *Ratnagotravibhāga-vyākhyā* is:

> And this dharmakāya of the tathāgata, illustrious one, is called *buddha nature* when not liberated from the sheath of defilements.[601]

Butön for his part followed the reading of the *Śrīmālādevīsūtra* in the Kangyur, which does not have the negative particle *ma* and thus conveys an entirely different meaning:[602]

> And this dharmakāya of the tathāgata, illustrious one, which is liberated from the sheath of defilements, is called *buddha nature.*

According to Seyfort Ruegg, it was owing to this direct equation of the real dharmakāya free from stains (and not only its dharmatā) with buddha nature that Butön disqualified the teachings of buddha nature from having more than provisional meaning.[603] Indeed on this point, Barawa explains that there is no contradiction between his understanding of buddha nature and that of Butön:

> As to the Omniscient Butön Rinpoché's statement that sentient beings do not possess buddha nature, he asserts that it is [only] buddha nature [understood as] the dharmakāya that does not exist in sentient beings—namely a buddha nature that would be free from the sheath of adventitious stains and endowed with the two purities that possess the ten strengths, the four types of fearlessness, the Buddha's eighteen exclusive features, and so forth.[604]

And this would be impossible, since the ten strengths would immediately destroy ignorance[605] and the dharmakāya would unfold the form kāyas. Barawa points out that Butön explains in his *Mdzes rgyan* that sentient beings possess buddha nature by virtue of the potential they have to bring forth the three kāyas. Moreover, Butön refers in his *Sbyor drug gi ngo sprod* to sentient beings as not having realized their natural luminosity, which is free from mental fabrication.[606] Repeating that Butön cannot have meant that all teachings of buddha nature in the third dharmacakra have a hidden intention, Barawa sums up:

> [When Butön] taught that [buddha nature] exists, he thought of its existence as dharmatā [or] luminosity. [When] he taught it as being empty, he thought of it as having neither shape nor color.[607]

Against the backdrop of Seyfort Ruegg's findings, Barawa's assertion that Butön does not mean that a correctly understood buddha nature has only provisional meaning could have a basis as long as he does not see in the existing luminous aspect of mind anything that goes against the constraints of emptiness.[608] Still, Barawa's attempt to show that Butön's view accords with his own could have been to some extent merely a way to avoid expressing disagreement. But it seems that Barawa was more in need of help against Dölpopa's position, which he not only tries to reinterpret but also opposes more directly, especially in his letters.

Barawa's *Dgongs bshad nyi ma'i 'od zer* is thus not so much a reliable analysis of Butön's and Dölpopa's true intentions as a presentation of his own views on buddha nature. Right at the beginning of the *Nyi ma'i 'od zer* he gives the following definition:

> This ground, [or] bodhicitta, is clear in that it is not covered by [any] substantial hindering stains. This is clarity. Not having turned into [dead] matter, it knows, as explained above, happiness and suffering, and is thus awareness. [Finally,] it is empty, because it lacks shape and color. These three are inseparable. If you distinguish [different states] mingled with adventitious stains, [these three] are the buddha nature of sentient beings.[609]

This definition of buddha nature is quite interesting, for it combines the typical mahāmudrā description of directly experiencing the true nature of mind as inseparable clarity, awareness, and emptiness with the analytical definition of a buddha nature as being mingled with adventitious stains.[610] These adventitious stains, then, are explained as resulting from not recognizing this true nature of mind, which is always present, whether recognized or not:

> This buddha nature that exists in sentient beings is mingled with the stains of defilements. The confusion of not recognizing [your own] true nature by yourself is ignorance. [This] ignorance has been taught as being defilements and adventitious stains. For this reason the dharmatā or luminosity that

> abides within the sheath of defilements is buddha nature. It is said to be hindered by adventitious stains. The clarity of not being hindered by anything other than that—for example, a substantial impurity with shape and color—this [fundamental] clear state is called luminosity or the naturally pure state. [When] it does not recognize itself by itself, this is ignorance. Under these conditions [the fundamental clear state] appears as the multiformity of a perceived object and a perceiving subject, [and] you wander in saṁsāra. The consequence of this is the seed of the phenomena of saṁsāra, [that is,] the buddha nature of sentient beings.... By practicing [meditation on] the dharmatā, that which abides in the sheath of *karman* and defilements, is purified of its *karman* and defilements, along with [all] mental imprints, and therefore the dharmatā or luminosity is actualized. This is the dharmakāya, or buddha nature, on the level of a buddha.[611]

This short explanation demonstrates the main points of Barawa's mahāmudrā position. The difference between saṁsāra and enlightenment is simply defined by whether you recognize your own true nature of mind or not. This point is repeated several times in the four works of Barawa that deal with the position of the Jonangpas, and is not only backed up by quotes from Saraha, but also elaborated with the help of the *Laṅkāvatārasūtra* and the *Ghanavyūhasūtra*, in both of which buddha nature is equated with the *ālayavijñāna*.[612] Contrary to Asaṅga's *Mahāyānasaṁgraha*, the distinction between an impure and pure aspect of the mind (or, translated into the terminology of the *Ratnagotravibhāga*, of impure adventitious stains and a pure buddha element) is thus downplayed.[613] Barawa even accepts the consequence that buddha nature experiences suffering, and reads his interpretation of the buddha element's perception of suffering into the *Ratnagotravibhāga* (stanzas I.40–41):[614]

> If there were no buddha element, there would not be aversion to suffering either,
> Nor would there be desire or earnest wish for or the intention [to attain] nirvāṇa.
> The perception of worldly existence as suffering and fault, and of nirvāṇa as bliss and quality,
> Only occurs in the presence of a potential, and not in beings without one.[615]

For Barawa, buddha nature thus transforms into saṁsāra when it does not recognize that it is inseparable clarity and emptiness. When it does come to that recognition, buddha nature then transforms into the real dharmakāya of a buddha. Consequently, Barawa distinguishes two types of buddha nature: one of sentient beings and one of a buddha.[616] This bespeaks a particular understanding of buddha qualities, one according to which they are brought forth in the real sense of the word:

> Under the condition of the [presence of] disciples, the fruit of liberation, [namely] the ten strengths, the four types of fearlessness, the eighteen exclusive features, and so forth appear in the dharmatā, [or] luminosity; and as a result of that, [buddha] nature and the fruit of maturation appear as the two form kāyas and so forth. Therefore [we speak of] the seed of [buddha] nature.[617]

It is interesting that Barawa includes the qualities of liberation among those that are caused by the presence of needful disciples—normally only said of the qualities of the form kāyas. His understanding of the production of qualities becomes clear from how he takes the common simile of separating butter from milk:

> You collect butter by churning milk. By whipping a lump of butter [already] freed from the buttermilk, it [will become] free of buttermilk, hair, and so forth. This is called the *essence of butter*. As this essence becomes manifest, [the qualities of] good color and taste, great richness, and the ability to make a lamp burn arise automatically. Likewise, as the dharmatā, [or] luminosity, manifests it becomes free from everything that must be abandoned, and is thus the [buddha] nature from which all qualities pertaining to the level of a buddha come forth.[618]

In other words, the buddha qualities on the level of the fruit are compared to the good color and taste of butter and its ability to feed the flame of a lamp—qualities that do not exist in milk. They manifest spontaneously, however, when the process of churning is completed. Thus buddha nature, or the dharmatā that abides in the sheath of defilements, is taken to be a seed that brings forth a buddha.[619] Barawa not only claims that this understanding is the ultimate purport of Butön's teachings, but also that of Dölpopa's:

> As to this assertion of the Omniscient Chöjé Rinpoché (Chos rje Rin po che) (i.e., Dölpopa) that the buddha nature of a sentient being is a buddha, and that the qualities of a buddha exist [in it]: when he taught that the buddha nature that exists in a sentient being is a buddha, he was thinking of the fact that buddha nature is [in reality] dharmatā, or luminosity, and not different in essence whether it exists in a sentient being or a buddha. His intention was to seal the cause by means of the fruit, and he [metaphorically] applied the name of fruit to the cause. [He thought that] the buddha nature of sentient beings possesses the ability to make the qualities of the level of a buddha come forth.[620]

But if this had been the true intention of Dölpopa, he would not have ignored the crucial stanza RGV I.27, in which it is said that the "fruit [of buddha nature] has been metaphorically applied to the buddha potential."[621] Indeed, Dölpopa's disciple Sabzang Mati Panchen had great difficulty in interpreting this phrase and bringing it in line with zhentong. The immediately following passage is nevertheless of great interest, because that which Barawa claims to be Dölpopa's intention is in fact Barawa's own view; the buddha nature of sentient beings already possesses the five qualities of the svābhāvika[kāya] but is only in partial concordance with the four perfections of the dharmakāya (being clean, the self, permanent, and blissful). Referring to the *Bodhisattvabhūmi*, Barawa rules out that ordinary beings possess the ten strengths and so forth.[622] This is also clear from Barawa's own statements:

> ...then the [ten] strengths and so forth would not be a fruit, since they would not be a fruit that has arisen from causes and conditions. The [ten] strengths and so forth do not exist throughout beginningless time. [Their] cause is buddha nature, and the condition [for their arising] is meditation [on this buddha nature] along the path. From [these two] the [ten] strengths and so forth arise later, when you are free from adventitious stains. Therefore [the ten strengths and so forth] are the fruit of liberation. Likewise it has been said that buddha nature is not a real buddha, but the cause or seed of a buddha.... Thus it has been said in [Saraha's] *Dohā[kośagīti*, stanza 43]: "Mind alone is the seed of everything...."[623]

Barawa justifies his interpretation by pointing out that in RGV I.51[624] it is not said that buddha nature is endowed with the ten strengths and the like, but only that it is naturally endowed with qualities.[625] This means either that the qualities referred to are not necessarily the ten strengths, etc., or that Barawa understands the compound *yon tan rang bzhin nyid* in the sense of "the true nature of qualities." In his letter to eight disciples of Dölpopa, Barawa is more precise:

> It is not said [in RGV I.51] that buddha nature exists as a [real] buddha. It is obvious that [this stanza] teaches the major and minor marks of buddha nature as the defining characteristics of the ultimate, or the dharmakāya. This has been explained in the *Ratnagotravibhāgavyākhyā:*[626] The assertion that the Buddha has the defining characteristics of space was made with the ultimate and exclusive characteristics of the tathāgatas in mind.[627]

These are the fifteen defining characteristics of the ultimate, as explained in RGV II.29–37.[628] Barawa warns that it does not follow from this that there are fifteen distinct factors, since they have been taught as being the ultimate characteristics of a buddha in particular. Now, what is never changing according to Barawa are the defining characteristics of the ultimate:

> As to the defining characteristics of the ultimate, there is not the slightest difference between the defining characteristics of the ultimate of an ordinary being and those of a tathāgata. But since there is a difference with regard to the characteristics of the ultimate major and minor marks, he taught [the defining characteristics of the ultimate] with the ultimate and exclusive [space-like] characteristics of the Buddha in mind. Thus [it has been said].[629] Therefore, as a force [or] capacity, these defining characteristics of the ultimate exist in buddha nature with [only] partial concordance. In the dharmakāya of a buddha, however, they exist in a completely perfect way.[630]

With regard to the various statements that the buddha qualities are inseparable, Barawa explains in his *Dgongs bshad nyi ma'i 'od zer* that such statements can be referring only to the ultimate qualities. This, he says, is clearly stated in RGV I.29, which lists ten aspects of buddha nature, among which the inseparability of the qualities is the last one:

...and the inseparability [of the qualities]. With regard to them you should know that the intended meaning [is that] of the ultimate [buddha] element.[631]

A little further down, according to Barawa, it is made clear to which inseparable qualities exactly this stanza refers. He says that buddha nature possesses in full the five qualities of the svābhāvikakāya, which are enumerated in RGV II.46c–47d:[632]

[The svābhāvikakāya] is luminous, since as the nature of the dharmadhātu it is pure.[633] The svābhāvikakāya is endowed with qualities that are immeasurable, innumerable, inconceivable, incomparable, and that have reached [the state of] final purity.[634]

In other words, it is only the natural quality of unconditioned luminosity that is inseparable—the dharmatā that cannot be differentiated in terms of shape, color, and quantifiable numbers.[635] Now, Barawa argues that the major and minor marks (i.e., the qualities of the form kāyas) are separable because they have shape and color, and the ten strengths and so forth are separable for being multiple:

The pure dharmadhātu is said to be the qualities of the dharmakāya. They are inseparable and have neither shape nor color nor number. The major and minor marks have shape and color, and the [ten] strengths and so forth are multiple. Therefore they are [all] separable.[636]

In Barawa's "Presentation of the Basic Consciousness and Wisdom," which is a refutation of Dükhorwa Dorjé Nyingpo's reply to his questions, the crucial stanza on emptiness in the *Ratnagotravibhāga* (I.158 (J I.155): "The buddha element is empty of adventitious stains, which have the defining characteristic of being separable; and it is not empty of unsurpassable qualities, which have the defining characteristic of not being separable") is explained along the same line of thought:

That which has perceptible attributes in terms of the particulars of forms, [namely] various shapes and colors, is not established as it appears, and is thus empty. [This refers] to the adventitious phenomena of apparent truth. Buddha nature has the defining characteristic of lacking anything that can be separated in terms

> of the particulars of forms—various shapes and colors—and lacks characteristic signs. It is the wisdom of self-realization, free from all mental fabrications. It has been taught that the unsurpassable dharmatā is not nonexistent.[637]

From this it is clear that for Barawa the inseparable qualities in RGV I.158 (J I.155) refer to the dharmatā and thus to the qualities of the ultimate, as described above. In other words, since the thirty-two qualities of liberation (namely the ten strengths and so forth) and the thirty-two qualities of maturation or the form kāyas are separable, they are implicitly taken to be empty, just like the phenomena of apparent truth. Thus it is clear why Barawa cannot accept Dölpopa's stance that the reflections of emptiness, such as the appearance of smoke during the practice of the six-branch yoga, amount to seeing a part of your buddha nature, namely an aspect of the major and minor marks.[638] Barawa "interprets" Dölpopa in the following way:

> Even though sunlight is not the real solar disk, its unobstructed radiance shines in the form of light. Therefore light is not different from the solar disk; and when you see sunlight you say that you see the sun. Similarly, even though the reflections of emptiness are not the real buddha nature, the unobstructed radiance of buddha nature shines forth in the form of the ten signs, such as smoke. Therefore [Dölpopa] thought that the reflections of emptiness are not different from buddha nature and called them buddha nature.[639]

In discussing the reflections of emptiness, Barawa insists that the buddha nature of ordinary beings is simply luminosity endowed with the five qualities of the svābhāvikakāya but not with the major and minor marks of the form kāyas.[640] This excludes the possibility that Barawa would have accepted the primordial existence of the qualities of the form kāyas on an extraordinary tantric level of interpretation, all the more so since he reinterprets Dölpopa on this very point.

The differences between Barawa's mahāmudrā interpretation and Dölpopa's zhentong become most evident in how Barawa explains the relation between the impure "ground of consciousness" (i.e., the *ālayavijñāna*) and the pure "ground of wisdom" *(ye shes kyi kun gzhi)*.[641] Already in his introduction to the *Dgongs bshad nyi ma'i 'od zer* he equates the terms *ground (kun gzhi)* and *consciousness of the ground (kun gzhi'i rnam shes),*[642] and defines their pseudo-difference, in line with mahāmudrā, as depending upon whether you have recognized the true nature of mind. Barawa reads his understanding into Dölpopa's zhentong distinction between an impure and pure ground in the following way:

> [The *ālayavijñāna*] is the awareness of buddha nature [in the aspect of it] as the impure ground. Confusion arises when [buddha nature] does not recognize itself. Various extroverted thoughts thereby occur.... Inasmuch as [buddha nature] forms the ground of the phenomena of saṁsāra, it is the impure *ālayavijñāna*. Inasmuch as it does not possess such qualities as the [ten] strengths, it is [what is called] sentient being.[643]
>
> When buddha nature recognizes itself by itself, [when it is] without confusion and left in its original state, it is the dharmakāya of a buddha. Given that it functions as a support of the kāyas, wisdom, deeds, activity, and so forth that pertain to the level of a buddha, it is the pure ground of wisdom, namely a buddha.[644]
>
> The impure *ālayavijñāna* does not form the ground of properties pertaining to the level of a buddha because it does not possess such qualities as the [ten] strengths. The pure ground of wisdom does not form the ground of saṁsāra, since it is without adventitious stains and thus does not experience saṁsāra's happiness, suffering, and so forth. Therefore, if you distinguish them as isolates, it can be said that they are two opposing kingdoms. But since the nature of both grounds is buddha nature, they are one in essence.[645]

In other words, Barawa defines the relationship between the two as "being one in essence, but different isolates," the standard formula for defining the two truths in mainstream Madhyamaka.[646] But this is exactly what Dölpopa opposes, favoring the competing formula: "different in that their identity is negated" *(gcig pa bkag pa'i tha dad pa).* In support of this Dölpopa refers to the definition of the relationship between dharmas and dharmatā[647] in the *Dharmadharmatāvibhāga*,[648] which Barawa counterexplains in his letter to Dükhorwa Dorjé Nyingpo:

> [In the *Dharmadharmatāvibhāgavṛtti*, ll. 143–145] it has been said:
>
> > You may ask: "How is it possible that they (i.e., dharmas and dharmatā) are not different?" [The answer is that] the

> dharmatā is characterized by the mere nonexistence of dharmas, because the [dharmatā] does not exist in terms of the particulars of forms and so forth.

> The pure dharmatā and the impure consciousness (or dharmas) are inseparable by nature. On the other hand, since [mind] has arisen as two impure dharmas [in the form of] isolates, [namely ones capable] of recognizing dharmatā and [ones that can]not, [the dharmas and dharmatā] are [also] different. This is what I think.[649]

In other words, Barawa has shifted the emphasis from the ontological difference between an existing dharmatā and nonexisting dharmas to the epistemological one between recognizing the true nature or not. The phenomenal world is a form that buddha nature assumes when it fails to recognize itself. Ontologically the two are not different, any more than the existence of ocean water is not affected when the flat surface of the ocean is churned into waves, to use an oftquoted example from the *Laṅkāvatārasūtra*.[650] Dölpopa, however, criticized precisely this view in his *Bka' bsdu bzhi pa*.[651]

Even though Barawa follows mainstream Madhyamaka and avoids a strict division between two grounds (or apparent and ultimate truths), he still adheres to a definition of the ultimate in positive terms. Thus the common intersection of saṁsāra and enlightenment is not only a buddha nature that is emptiness, but also clarity and awareness. How these two, clarity and emptiness, belong to the ultimate is made clear in the following explanation of the ground and path:

> Such a clarity, awareness, and empti[ness], are, [all] three [of them], inseparably the ultimate truth. They do not change at all either in ground, path, or fruit. Their manifestation is not obstructed, and owing to mental imprints they appear as the variety of a perceived and a perceiver. This is apparent truth. When you meditate on the path, the three: clarity, awareness, and empti[ness] are experienced—just like the clear autumn sky—as being vivid *(sal le)*, vibrant *(sing ge)*, and sharp *(hrig ge)*.[652] This is ultimate truth.[653]

In other words, the phenomenal world of saṁsāra is simply one particular way that clarity, awareness, and emptiness subsist. It is clear that such a view favors the *Laṅkāvatārasūtra*'s equation of buddha nature with the *ālayavijñāna* and ignores, for example, Asaṅga's distinction between the *ālayavijñāna* and a pure supramundane mind in the *Mahāyānasaṁgraha*. In the latter, it is emphasized that the remedy for the *ālayavijñāna* (namely the outflow of the pure dharmadhātu) is necessarily something different from the *ālayavijñāna*. Whereas Rangjung Dorjé manages to bridge the opposing strands of the *Laṅkāvatārasūtra* and the *Mahāyānasaṁgraha*, Barawa clearly argues against Asaṅga when he writes to Dükhorwa Dorjé Nyingpo that the remedy does not need to be different:

> Since nothing other than not recognizing yourself as being dharmatā needs to be abandoned, wisdom, the remedy for abandoning, arises, when you recognize yourself as being dharmatā. [That which must be abandoned] disappears, for [it was nothing but] not having recognized yourself as being dharmatā. Therefore, even though that which must be abandoned disappears, the self-recognition does not disappear, and thus the remedy does not either.[654]

In the same letter Barawa illustrates this with the following example:

> Water freezes into ice under cold conditions such as wind. Even though it has become like a stone, the two, ice and water, are identical by nature, and under conditions of fire and so forth, the ice melts. Even though the ice has disappeared, the water has not—has it?[655]

A Comparison of the Positions

With regard to the presentation of buddha qualities, we can distinguish two groups. The first consists of Rangjung Dorjé, Dölpopa, Mati Panchen, and Longchenpa. These share the opinion that all buddha qualities, including the thirty-two marks of the form kāyas, exist throughout beginningless time. Whereas the first three members of this group make it clear that the claim of primordial buddha qualities reflects a tantric understanding (ordinary beings do not possess the common thirty-two marks of a buddha but only the thirty-two tantric marks of the form kāyas contained in their vajra body), it is not clear whether Longchenpa follows along the same lines. Even though Longchenpa calls the qualities of the form kāyas "luminous major and minor marks" *('od kyi mtshan dpe)* which shows that he does not mean the actual marks of a buddha, their primordial existence is claimed in a strict Mahāyāna context of explaining the fortified potential on the basis of MSA III.4. In other words, Longchenpa obviously does not refrain from reading his dzogchen view into ordinary Mahāyāna explanations. It is precisely this commentary on MSA III.4 that differs from the corresponding one of Lodrö Tsungmé in such a way that the latter cannot be confused with Longchenpa.

In fact, Lodrö Tsungmé forms together with Barawa the second group, which explains, in accordance with Ngog Loden Sherab, that the qualities of the form kāyas are produced. But while Lodrö Tsungmé takes the qualities of the dharmakāya (the ten strengths and so on) to be the ultimate qualities, Barawa here again follows Ngog Loden Sherab, and accepts only the space-like defining characteristics of RGV II.29–37 as ultimate qualities. Still, Lodrö Tsungmé distinguishes between the ten strengths and so forth of an ordinary sentient being and those of enlightenment. Tāranātha included Ngog Loden Sherab in his eulogy of the zhentong transmission,[656] which means that he considers Loden Sherab's *Ratnagotravibhāga* commentary as an ordinary Mahāyāna explanation that admits of an extraordinary tantric interpretation. In other words, when Lodrö Tsungmé explains the *Ratnagotravibhāga* in line with Ngog Loden Sherab, it may be that he did not exclude a tantric zhentong interpretation either, but in order to settle this question it is necessary to consult his respective tantric works, which have not been available to me.

A comparison of how emptiness is defined yields first of all the already familiar position of the Jonangpas (Dölpopa and Mati Panchen) that a permanent ultimate is empty of everything conditioned. The ultimate buddha nature, which is inseparable from all buddha qualities, is taken as being beyond the three times in the same way as the tathāgata. Longchenpa defines in his *Rdzogs chen sems nyid ngal gso'i 'grel pa* (219–21) the nature of the buddha element in a similar way, as being the changeless perfect nature (or the *dharmatā*) of the mind, which is empty of other *(zhentong),* namely all the faults (false imagining or the eight accumulations of consciousness) that by nature do not belong to the buddha element. On the other hand, buddha nature, or primordial awareness, is also explained in terms of the traditional dzogchen categories of being empty in essence,[657] spontaneously present by nature, and compassionately responsive. Lodrö Tsungmé equates the ultimate buddha nature with the dharmatā of the mind, and explains the ultimate aspect of enlightenment, or the dharmakāya, as being unconditioned, in view of its being empty of all conditioned phenomena.[658]

For Rangjung Dorjé and Barawa, too, buddha nature is empty of adventitious stains, but contrary to Dölpopa's and Mati Panchen's positions, buddha nature is taken as consisting of moments. Thus Rangjung Dorjé equates buddha nature with the natural mind and dependent arising, both of which contain mere appearances empty of duality or the stainlessness of the eight accumulations of consciousness, but not the impure part of consciousness that is clearly distinguished from it. Here, however, Barawa follows the *Laṅkāvatārasūtra* and equates buddha nature with the *ālayavijñāna* (the impure part of the mind is thus included in buddha nature). For him buddha nature is emptiness, clarity, and awareness, emptiness here meaning that the mind lacks color and shape.

Related to these different presentations of emptiness is the question of how the relationship between the two truths is defined. While the zhentong tradition of the Jonangpas defines them as being different in that their identity is negated *(gcig pa bkag ba'i tha dad pa),* Barawa's mahāmudrā equation of buddha nature with the *ālayavijñāna* requires the two truths to be one in essence, but different isolates *(ngo bo gcig la ldog pa tha dad).* It is clear that Dölpopa could not adopt the formula of their being one in essence, since he defines zhentong as the existing eternal ultimate that is empty of the conditioned apparent truth. His distinction between the two truths is so clear-cut that he is at pains to explain how his understanding does not contradict the *Saṁdhinirmocanasūtra,* which excludes not only the identity of the two truths, but also their difference. His explanation is that since only the ultimate really exists he would need a second truly existing ontological category for the relationship *difference in essence.*[659]

We wonder how Rangjung Dorjé, who combines a strict Yogācāra distinction between the *ālayavijñāna* and the supramundane pure mind (similar to zhentong) with Saraha's mahāmudrā explanation (the mind is the basis of saṁsāra and nirvāṇa), defines the relationship between the two truths. As we have seen above, Rangjung Dorjé faithfully follows the Yogācāra definition of emptiness by endorsing the *Madhyāntavibhāga* formula that the perfect nature is the dependent empty of the imagined. This is contrary to Dölpopa, who reinterprets the *Madhyāntavibhāga* to be saying that the unchangeable perfect nature is empty of both the dependent and the imagined. To put it another way, both the unchangeable perfect nature and the unmistaken one (the latter consisting of the dependent factors of the path) are empty of duality, namely that which does not exist and so is different from them. If we choose to call that *zhentong,* we need to point out that not only the unchangeable perfect nature is left in this emptiness, but also a "pure dependent nature," or as Rangjung Dorjé puts it, mere appearances (or the stainlessness of the eight accumulations of consciousness). Rangjung Dorjé restricts apparent truth to these mere appearances or pure dependent nature, which means that both truths are left over in emptiness, or that both the ultimate and the apparent truths are empty of duality. With what is normally the expressible ultimate *(paryāyaparamārtha)* being called apparent truth and the ordinary world of dualistic appearances being excluded from this apparent truth, Rangjung Dorjé's strict distinction between the pure and impure mind simply does not address the relationship between the two truths. In other words, when we read in Rangjung Dorjé's mahāmudrā works that both truths are one in essence and included in buddha nature, we have to keep the above-mentioned restriction relating to apparent truth in mind. (Be it added that I have not been able to locate the formula "one in essence but different isolates" in Rangjung Dorjé's works to date.)

Reservations against the formula "one in essence but different isolates" can also be sensed in the works of later Kamtsang (Kaṁ tshang) Kagyüpa. In his *Shes bya kun khyab mdzod*, Kongtrül Lodrö Tayé explains that

> ...without [further] analysis and only conventionally are the two truths taken as one by nature, but different isolates; ultimately they cannot be said to be either identical or different in essence.[660]

Kongtrül quotes Rangjung Dorjé in support:

> Since both truths are free[661] from being identical and different, just like phenomena and their true nature, their [relation] cannot be expressed in terms of anything, being [neither] one [nor] different.[662]

In his *Madhyamakāvatāra* commentary,[663] the Eighth Karmapa Mikyö Dorjé argues that even conventionally the two truths are neither one nor different, on the grounds that they mutually depend on each other.[664] With regard to the mahāmudrā teachings, Mikyö Dorjé explains that statements of Kagyü masters to the effect that "thoughts are the dharmakāya" or that "saṁsāra is nirvāṇa" were meant to imply that ultimately the two truths do not exist as something different; this does not mean, however, that thoughts and the dharmakāya (which stand for the respective two truths) are one in essence.[665] What is being said is simply that both lack an own-being and are thus bound to the same mode of being, as explained in the *prajñāpāramitā* sūtras.[666] Mahāmudrā teachings that the two truths (i.e., thoughts and the dharmakāya) are of the same nature may be misunderstood as implying that they share the single nature of an ultimately existing entity. But once fully qualified recipients realize the real meaning of mahāmudrā teachings, they are liberated from such wrong conception about the two truths.[667]

To sum up, we need to distinguish two mahāmudrā views: the one held by Barawa, which defines the two truths as being one in essence, but different isolates; and the one held by Rangjung Dorjé who, like the Jonangpas, negates both identity and difference, but differs from them in taking buddha nature to consist of moments.

3. A Short Account of the Most Important Events in Zhönu Pal's Life

THE COMPARATIVE DESCRIPTION of the six positions in the previous chapter puts us in a position to determine Zhönu Pal's views on buddha nature against the backdrop of ideas that are close to his, both in terms of doctrine and time. Before we embark on that investigation, a brief account of his life on the basis of Zhamar Chödrag Yeshé's (1453–1524) biography will set the historical context and describe the broad education of this nonsectarian scholar. This background information will help us to understand the development of his views. One fact that will emerge, for example, is the connection between Zhönu Pal's close relations with Pagdru rulers and his preference for Gampopa's and Drigung Jigten Sumgön's mahāmudrā interpretation of the *Ratnagotravibhāga*.

The following account of Gö Lotsāwa Zhönu Pal's life is mainly based on his extensive biography, which was written by his disciple the Fourth Zhamarpa Chödrag Yeshé.[668] Other than the short account by Künga Gyaltsen (Kun dga' rgyal mtshan) (b. 1440)—another disciple of Zhönu Pal—of the teaching convent in Tsetang (Rtses[669] thang), Zhamarpa's biography is the second oldest to my knowledge that survives.[670] Not only is it by far the longest, but it is also the most convincing one, containing as it does many details of day-to-day life, such as Zhönu Pal being attacked by a drunken robber from Kham (Khams) with a sword—things only personal acquaintances would normally know about.[671] The first half of the biography is the most important one for us, since it describes in detail Zhönu Pal's education and his various masters. The remaining half is a presentation of various events in Zhönu Pal's life, which are loosely arranged according to different topics, such as how he kept his *samayas*, or how he was spiritually supported by his teachers. There are also paragraphs on Zhönu Pal's qualities, translations, dreams, and visions, how he entered the gate of the Dharma and attained realization, his teaching activity, and finally his literary output. It would go beyond the scope of this work to present all this material in detail. Thus the following account is based on a selection of events, mainly ones enabling a better understanding of the formation of Zhönu Pal's views on buddha nature, emptiness, and mahāmudrā.

Before beginning the actual life story, Zhamar Chödrag Yeshé reviews possible previous incarnations of Zhönu Pal. Thus, Zhönu Pal was once told by his personal deity in a dream that he had been a disciple of the mahāsiddha Orgyenpa Sengé Pal (O rgyan pa Seng ge dpal) (1229/30–1309).[672] Moreover, it was believed that one of his previous incarnations had been present when the Buddhist doctrine was introduced in Samyé (Bsam yas), since the story of the construction of Samyé and the arrival of Khenpo (Mkhan po) Bodhisattva and Padmasambhava once brought tears to his eyes.[673] Zhamar Chödrag Yeshé's teacher and Zhönu Pal's disciple Namkha Lodrö (Nam mkha' blo gros) (1403–77) claims that Zhönu Pal must have also been among the disciples of Pagmo Drupa (1110–70),[674] while Lochen Sönam Gyatso (Lo chen Bsod nams rgya mtsho) (1424–82), another important disciple of Zhönu Pal, repeatedly told Zhamar Chödrag Yeshé that in his eyes Zhönu Pal was the reincarnation of the famous Rongzom Chökyi Zangpo (Rong zom Chos kyi bzang po) (1042–1136), in view of the former's extraordinary knowledge of the doctrine and his capability as a translator:

> The precious Dharma master Lochen obviously rejoiced in [Zhönu Pal's] complete knowledge of all sūtras and tantras, [his] perfection as a translator, and his own compositions. For this reason he repeatedly told me: "Surely he is a reincarnation of Rongzom Chökyi Zangpo."[675]

We are further informed that Zhönu Pal himself claimed to possess special qualities from previous lives. Thus he asserts that he had to read the *Ratnagotravibhāga* only once to get it down by heart.[676] That he had access to an original Sanskrit version of the *Ratnagotravibhāgavyākhyā* is clear from his commentary on it, in which he sometimes quotes the Sanskrit original of the *vyākhyā* and reviews Ngog Loden Sherab's translation.[677]

Zhönu Pal was born as the third son of Tönpa Jungné Dorjé (Ston pa 'Byung gnas rdo rje) and Śrī Tarkyi (Sri thar skyid) in a water monkey year (1392) in a lay village in the lower part of the Chongyé ('Phyong rgyas)[678] valley, below the Gyamen (Rgya sman) temple.[679] This must be Gyamen Yangpo (Rgya sman yang po), a place to which his family moved from Gö ('Gos). His ancestors descended from Trisong Detsen's (Khri srong lde btsan) minister Gögen ('Gos rgan).[680] Tönpa Jungné Dorjé was very fond of his son Zhönu Pal, but he was murdered, and his wife, the young mother Śrī Tarkyi, had to bring up their eight children alone.[681] Lechen (Las chen) Künga Gyaltsen informs us that at the age of nine Zhönu Pal entered the Kadam monastery of Chenyé (Spyan g.yas) in the upper part of the Chongyé valley[682] and renounced worldly life in the presence of Khenchen Rinpoché Sangyé Tenpa (Mkhan chen Rin po che Sangs rgyas bstan pa). It was during this ceremony that he was given the name Zhönu Pal.[683] Zhamar Chödrag Yeshé offers the additional information that Zhönu Pal was fully ordained at the age of nineteen under the Tsetang Khenpo Samten Zangpo (Rtses thang mkhan po Bsam btan bzang po).[684] At this point in the biography we are also told about some further later events, such as Zhönu Pal taking bodhisattva vows in the presence of the Fifth Karmapa Dezhin Shegpa (De bzhin gshegs pa) (1384–1415) and later again in the presence of the Chittagong yogin and great paṇḍita Vanaratna (1384–1468),[685] and then at another time receiving a Cakrasaṁvara empowerment from Tsongkhapa's teacher Gungnang Chöjé Dzepa Pal (Gung snang Chos rje Mdzes pa dpal).[686] This completes the three vows in Zhönu Pal's mindstream, at which point he can activate his former potential to clearly distinguish the provisional and definitive meanings of the sūtras:

> The great being, who activated his potential with the help of positive imprints stemming from former virtues...penetrated the vast expanse of the Dharma language of definitive meaning and [his ability to] distinguish the provisional and definitive meanings of the profound sūtras became unobstructed.[687]

Chödrag Yeshé (Chos grags ye shes) then starts a long chapter on how Zhönu Pal studied under sixty-six learned and realized masters without taking sides.[688] Following his "renunciation of worldly life" *(rab tu byung ba),* that is, from his ninth to twelfth year, he used his summer vacation in Chenyé, in spite of having to do work for his mother, to study the *Bodhicaryāvatāra* under his uncle Sangyé Dragpa (Sangs rgyas grags pa) and Lobpön Sherab (Slob dpon Shes rab). At this time the fifth Pagdru (Phag gru) ruler Dragpa Gyaltsen (Grags pa rgyal mtshan) (1373–1432) fell sick, and when monks of Chenyé recited Medicine Buddha sādhanas for their king, Zhönu Pal quickly learned them by heart.[689] At the age of twelve he participated in the summer teachings at Tsetang and studied the *Pramāṇavārttika* under Samdrub Zangpo (Bsam grub bzang po), who is described as having bloodshot eyes and a black face, and as being so very aggressive that Zhönu Pal was afraid of being beaten.[690]

During the teaching break of the wood monkey year (1404) Zhönu Pal studied at Chöding Monastery, and in the following years (1405–7) received *prajñāpāramitā* teachings from Tön Śākpa (Ston Śāk pa) (1355–1432).[691] Under Tön Śākpa, he studied *pramāṇa* works along with the commentaries by Norzang (Nor bzang). Tön Śākpa repeatedly beat Zhönu Pal, who at one point ran away from Chöding.[692] In the winter of the preceding dog year (1406) Zhönu Pal participated in discussions and explanations of the doctrine in Tsetang.[693] After he had left Tön Śākpa's community of monks, he together with the Tsetang Khenpo Samzangpa (Rtses thang mkhan po Bsam bzang pa) was given to Kyangchenpa (Rkyang chen pa) Śākya Śrī.[694] In the summer of the year 1407, when Zhönu Pal visited Chenyé Monastery after the summer examinations,[695] the teacher Sherab Darwa (Shes rab dar ba) served him tea and presented a golden statue of Mañjughoṣa to him, praising his studies and good performance during the examinations.[696]

In the autumn of the ox year (1409), Zhönu Pal again served Tön Śākpa on his trip to Rutsam (Ru mtshams) in Nyemo (Snye mo), but having been repeatedly reprimanded by the Tsetang Khenpo, he returned to Chenyé.[697] In the iron tiger year (1410), the year Zhönu Pal received full ordination under the Tsetang Khenpo (see above), he left for Lhasa and Tangsag (Thang sag), where he studied the *Madhyamakāvatāra*, *Mūlamadhyamakakārikā*, *Prasannapadā*, and *Catuḥśataka* (the *Catuḥśataka* with the help of a commentary by Rendawa [Red mda' ba]) under Martön Zhöngyalwa (Dmar ston Gzhon rgyal ba) (who was a disciple of Rendawa).[698] Of particular interest is the following account of Zhönu Pal's attempt to obtain teachings from the zhentong master Lötang Nyagpo (Blos btang nyag po):

> [Zhönu Pal] told me: "Once, on the ridge of Sé (Sras) [Peak] (?), Lötang Nyagpo, who had attained the realization of zhentong, was seated on a Dharma throne. He was surrounded by many monks and lay persons and gave Dharma teachings. Both of us went closer in order to find out what he had to say. As we were approaching him, somebody was quickly sent to us. He told us not to go any further—we were not allowed to do so. He (i.e., Lötang Nyagpo) must have had supernatural perception."[699]

While Tön Śākpa was explaining the *Ratnagotravibhāga* together with Asaṅga's *vyākhyā*, Zhönu Pal managed to obtain the transmission of Dölpopa's (1292–1361) *Ratnagotravibhāga* commentary as well.[700] In order to receive teachings from various masters, Zhönu Pal traveled even without the consent of the Tsetang Khenpo, as can be seen from the passage in

Zhamarpa's biography that immediately follows the story of the unsuccessful approach made to Lötang Nyagpo:

> Then, when I went to the master Samzangpa [i.e., the Tsetang Khenpo], he asked: "Why did you go to Penyül ('Phan yul) without permission?"[701]

A little further down we are informed that he left Chenyé secretly in order to receive guruyoga teachings from Khenchen Sanglowa (Mkhan chen Sangs blo ba) in Yöl Rinchen Ling (Yol Rin chen gling). Just when Zhönu Pal was starting to study the six-branch yoga, Tönpa Wangö (Ston pa dbang 'od) and Tenpa Bum (Brtan pa 'bum) arrived to take him back to Chenyé Monastery.[702] Back in Chenyé he received various teachings from Khenchen Sangyé Tenpa (Mkhan chen Sangs rgyas brtan pa).[703] Later, in Tsetang, he took part in the examinations on the *prajñāpāramitā, Madhyamakāvatāra, Bodhicaryāvatāra,* and *Ratnagotravibhāga*, and the Tsetang Khenpo scolded him for having fallen behind.[704]

In 1413, at the age of twenty-two, he took the examinations held at Kyishö (Skyid shod) and went on to study, under Samten Döndrub (Bsam gtan don grub) in Kyormolung (Skyor mo lung) (in the Tölung (Stod lung) valley), the Vinaya, sūtras, and the *Abhidharmakośa.*[705] In Tölung (probably at Tsurpu) he went to see the Fifth Karmapa to obtain his blessings,[706] and then, under Tsalminpa Sönam Zangpo (Mtshal min pa Bsod nams bzang po) (1341–1453) (who had come there from Tsalmin (Mtshal min) Monastery for a visit), he studied the *blo sbyong* and *sems pa'i rim pa* by Sumpa Lotsāwa (Sum pa Lo tsā ba).[707] Sönam Zangpo (Bsod nams bzang po), who had been installed as the abbot of the monastery of Tsalmin by the Fifth Karmapa in 1403, was one of the main disciples of the Jonang abbot Choglé Namgyal (Phyogs las rnam rgyal).[708] Later that year (1413) Zhönu Pal received *zhi byed* instructions from Lobpön Yabpa Chöjé (Slob dpon Yab pa Chos rje),[709] and under Śākya Zangpo (Śākya bzang po) he studied the *Skyes mchog ka dag gsal ba* and the Jātakas.[710] Back in Tsetang, he obtained various teachings including the six Dharma [Practices] of Nāropa *(nāro chos drug)* from the Fifth Karmapa.[711]

In the following year (1414) Zhönu Pal developed an interest in astrology, which he had first studied under Kyangchenpa (Rkyang chen pa) in Tsetang, and in the following year he continued to reflect on the subject during a teaching break in Tangpoché (Thang po che) (located in the Chongyé valley).[712] Later on, in the spring of the year 1418, he visited Chenpo (Chen po) Saṅghaśrī in Nartang (Snar thang) and went through the entire "astrological calculations of Śāmbhala" with him.[713] Zhönu Pal's Kālacakra-based calculations would eventually lead to some important corrections, which he published in a work called *Rtsis la 'khrul sel*.[714]

In the autumn of the year 1414, Zhönu Pal received teachings (*lam rim*, the *nāro chos drug* empowerment, etc.) from Tsongkhapa at the court of the Pagdru ruler Dragpa Gyaltsen.[715] On this occasion he also served the king.[716] A little further down in the biography we are told that Zhönu Pal became particularly fond of Tsongkhapa's analytical approach, and also of the distinction he makes between the provisional and definitive meanings on the basis of the *Ratnagotravibhāga*. Tsongkhapa is reported to have said in Nyal (Gnyal) in 1415:

> One way of distinguishing the provisional and definitive [meanings] which does not contradict what has been explained here is to expound according to the *Mahāyānottaratantra* (=*Ratnagotravibhāga*).[717]

Zhamar Chödrag Yeshé does not inform us how exactly this distinction is made. It is thus difficult to say whether Tsongkhapa influenced Zhönu Pal's Kagyü-oriented *Ratnagotravibhāga* commentary at all, and if so, in what way. It should be noted that some passages in Zhamarpa's description of Zhönu Pal's life suggest substantial differences from the Gelugpas. Thus, we are informed that Zhönu Pal criticizes the Gelugpas for being expert in the gradual path to enlightenment without knowing Atiśa's *Bodhipathapradīpa*.[718] We are further told that his own understanding of great bliss in Vajrayāna differs from Tsongkhapa's student and successor at Ganden (Dga' ldan), Gyaltsab Jé (1364–1432).[719]

In the winter of the sheep year (1415) Zhönu Pal approached Kyangchenpa for explanations on the Kālacakra (i.e., *ṣaḍaṅgayoga*). He had thought that having been given previously with the Tsetang Khenpo to Kyangchenpa (see above) would prove helpful in obtaining Kālacakra teachings at this time,[720] but instead Kyangchenpa told him to ask in Ju Lhakhang Teng ('Ju Lha khang stengs), where Zhönu Pal indeed received a Kālacakra empowerment and six-branch yoga instructions from Lhakhang Tengpa Sangyé Rinchen (Lha khang stengs pa Sangs rgyas rin chen).[721] Later, in the summer of the same year, he went again to Lhakhang Teng (Lha khang stengs), this time in the company of Kyangchenpa. Sangyé Rinchen (Sangs rgyas rin chen), who was one of the main disciples of the great Jonang abbot Choglé Namgyal,[722] conferred on both of them seven empowerments relating to a sand maṇḍala of the Kālacakra.[723] Zhönu

Pal also received at Lhakhang Teng the reading transmission of Dölpopa's *Ri chos nges don rgya mtsho.*[724] A little further down in Zhamarpa's biography of Zhönu Pal we are told how highly Zhönu Pal esteemed his teacher Lhakhang Tengpa Sangyé Rinchen:

> Out of natural compassion the Dharma master Lhakhang Tengpa delighted in everyone. In general, [Zhönu Pal] was grateful to all [his] lamas, but he was particularly grateful to this Dharma master. That [Zhönu Pal] has had a long life until now is probably due to a "long-life practice" he gave [to him]. The precious Dharma master [Lhakhang Tengpa] had a broad knowledge of both the Kama *(bka' ma)* and Terma *(gter ma)* [traditions] of the Nyingmapa. He [also] knew many tantras, maṇḍalas, etc., of the Sarma *(gsar ma)* [tradition],[725] including the Kālacakra. He relied on many noble beings, [namely] the great omniscient one from Jomonang (Jo mo nang) [i.e., Dölpopa], the [Sakya] Dharma master Lama Dampa [Sönam Gyaltsen] (Bla ma dam pa [Bsod nams rgyal mtshan])....[726]

Although this is not mentioned in particular, Zhönu Pal must have known through his teacher Sangyé Rinchen the extraordinary zhentong interpretation of the Kālacakra as propounded by the Jonangpas. According to Lechen Künga Gyaltsen, Zhönu Pal received the six-branch yoga of the Jonangpas from Lhakhang Tengpa.[727] In the following year (1416), while again in Lhakhang Teng, Zhönu Pal also studied the *Bodhisattva Trilogy,*[728] the three tantric commentaries that are the main textual basis for the Jonang exegesis of zhentong.[729]

In the same year (1416), Zhönu Pal traveled to Riwo Gepel (Ri bo dge 'phel) in Tsang, where he spent five months receiving detailed explanations of the *Kālacakratantra* from Shangpa Künkhyen Sherab Palzang (Shangs pa Kun mkhyen Shes rab dpal bzang). Zhamarpa's biography of Zhönu Pal notes that the explanations were based on the topical outline *(sa bcad)* and notes by Butön, and that Zhönu Pal was told to use them from then on when explaining the *Kālacakratantra* himself.[730] From Künkhyen Shangpa (Kun mkhyen Shangs pa) he also obtained, among numerous other tantric teachings and empowerments, the Kālacakra empowerment in the tradition of Butön.[731]

Much later, in the year 1436, when Vanaratna was teaching at the court of the sixth Pagdru ruler Dragpa Jungné (Grags pa 'byung gnas) (1414–45), Zhönu Pal was also initiated into the *Kālacakratantra* by that great paṇḍita.[732] When giving his disciple Lochen Sönam Gyatso Kālacakra teachings at Yizangtsé (Yid bzang rtse) in 1447, Zhönu Pal remarked that it would be best to seek the related six-branch yoga explanations from Vanaratna,[733] whose transmission lineage of the *Kālacakratantra* belonged to the "cycle of *upadeśa* tradition of Śavaripa" *(sha ba ri dbang phyug gi man ngag lugs kyi skor).* The initial representatives of this lineage were Vibhūticandra (twelfth/thirteenth century) and his disciple Kodragpa Sönam Gyaltsen (Ko brag pa Bsod nams rgyal mtshan) (1170–1249).[734]

Zhönu Pal showed such a great interest in Kālacakra that one of his teachers, Densapa Sangyé Gyaltsen (Gdan sa pa Sangs rgyas rgyal mtshan), wondered in a discussion with Lhakhang Tengpa Sangyé Rinchen whether he ought to be included among the Kālacakra masters. Sangyé Rinchen brushed this idea aside, pointing out that he had also mastered other tantras, such as the *Guhyasamāja,* without any difficulty and offered the explanation that he had studied these tantras in former lives.[735]

In 1420, when Zhönu Pal was only twenty-nine years old, he composed a commentary on the first chapter of the *Kālacakratantra,*[736] and in the same year he had to return to his Chenyé Monastery in order to teach the extensive Kālacakra commentary *Vimalaprabhā* at the request of Tönpa Rinchen Palzang (Ston pa Rin chen dpal bzang).[737] Lechen Künga Gyaltsen mentions in his biography a Kālacakra commentary among the ten important works composed by Zhönu Pal.[738] Zhönu Pal's position among the transmission lineages of the Kālacakra is within both the so-called "Rva [Lotsāwa] system" *(rva lugs)* and the "Bro [Lotsāwa] system" *('bro lugs).* The transmission of the former he received from Shangpa Künkhyen Sherab Palzang in the years 1416 and 1417 in Riwo Gepel, and the latter from Sangyé Rinchen in the year 1415 in Lhakhang Teng.[739]

In the spring of the pig year (1419), Zhönu Pal went to the famous Nyingma teacher Drölmawa Sangyé Rinchen Palzangpo (Sgrol ma ba Sangs rgyas rin chen dpal bzang po)[740] (1350–1430) at Tanag (Rta nag) in Tsang and obtained numerous Nyingma teachings[741] along with the Vajrakīlaya cycle according to the tradition of the Sakya Khön (Sa skya 'khon) family. In the historiographical literature of the Nyingma school, he is thus counted within the *mahāyoga* transmission going back to Dropugpa Śākya Sengé (Sgro phug pa Śākya seng ge) (1074–1135) of the Zur family.[742] Khetsun Sangpo, too, considers Zhönu Pal a Nyingma lineage holder.[743] Zhönu Pal also entertained close relations with Götrugpa (Rgod phrug pa) (1363–1447), who was a propounder of the Orgyen Nyendrub (O rgyan bsnyen grub) teachings.[744] From Götrugpa he received prophecies, and later also a Tsering Chenga (Tshe rings mched lnga) empowerment, and instructions on the cycle of the six Dorjé Pagmo (Rdo rje phag mo) works.[745] Lechen Künga Gyaltsen reports that Zhönu Pal also obtained teaching cycles of the Drugpa Kagyüpa at the feet of Götrugpa and the Pagdru ruler Dragpa Jungné.[746]

Given his nonsectarian attitude, Zhönu Pal sought out teachings from masters of other traditions as well, such as the famous Rongtön. Further down in Zhamarpa's biography, in a chapter on how Zhönu Pal finds the marvelous door of the Dharma, we are told that he went to hear the Dharma teachings of Rongtön,[747] and that during a teaching break he gained a crucial insight into the meaning of buddha nature and the two truths:

> [Zhönu Pal] went to the garden outside for a break and while sitting in the shadow of an apricot tree, he gained a genuine certainty about the meaning [of the sentence] "The buddha nature is the natural luminosity of mind," and instantly understood the subtle and precise Dharma terminology of it.... [Moreover,] even though he [at first] did not appreciate the explanation that the two truths can [be taken as] isolates, from then on he rejoiced in it (i.e., such an approach).[748]

It is not clear to what extent Rongtön's teachings influenced this insight, but in the first part of Zhamarpa's biography we are told that in the summer of the ox year (1421) Zhönu Pal heard Rongtön's explanations of the entire treatise of the *Ratnagotravibhāga*, the *Pramāṇaviniścaya,* and the five stages of the *Guhyasamājatantra.*[749] In the wood dragon year (1424) he also listened to Rongtön's *Madhyamakāvatāra* teachings.[750] According to Lechen Künga Gyaltsen's biography, Zhönu Pal also studied the *prajñāpāramitā* and the *Bodhicaryāvatāra* under Rongtön.[751]

Enjoying as he did very close relations with the Pagmo Drupa rulers and their monastic seats (see below), Zhönu Pal must have naturally felt inclined toward the various Kagyü transmissions that he received from such famous teachers as the Fifth Karmapa Dezhin Shegpa (see above) or Ngog Jangchub Pal (Rngog Byang chub dpal) of Dreuzhing (Spre'u zhing).[752] In the same wood dragon year Zhönu Pal obtained from Ngog Jangchub Pal, in Dreuzhing, numerous important Kagyü teachings, such as special instructions on the *Nāro chos drug* or the Oral Transmission of Cakrasaṃvara *(bde mchog snyan rgyud).*[753] Before the year was out he returned to Tsetang and received teachings from the abbot of Densatel, Chöjé Nyernyi Rinpoché Sönam Gyaltsen Palzang (Gdan sa thel, Chos rje Nyer gnyis rin po che Bsod nams rgyal mtshan dpal bzang) (1386–1434).[754] Zhamar Chödrag Yeshé notes that Zhönu Pal expressed preference for the Dharma terminology of this abbot during a discussion of the doctrine with numerous scholars in Tsetang.[755]

The next six years (1425–30) were spent at the monastic seat of Densatel, where Zhönu Pal composed a *prajñāpāramitā* commentary up to the third chapter. In between he visited Rabtenling (Rab brtan gling) in order to obtain meditation instructions from Tsültrim Gyaltsen (Tshul khrims rgyal mtshan),[756] and Dreuzhing, where he studied, under Khenchen Sengé Pal (Mkhan chen Seng ge dpal), the great Hevajra commentary of Nāropa and the *Mkha' 'gro rgya mtsho* tantra.[757] In the iron dog year (1430) Zhönu Pal was offered a chair in Gyadur (Rgya dur). He reluctantly accepted, but ran away shortly afterward, saying that Gyadur meant *cemetery of [this] trap.*[758]

In the iron pig year (1431) he studied Sempa Chenpo's (Sems dpa' chen po) commentary on the *Guhyasamājapradīpoddyotana* with the author himself.[759] Afterward he returned to Dreuzhing in order to receive various teachings from Ngog Jangchub Pal (Rngog Byang chub dpal).[760]

The water rat year (1432) he spent at Tsetang teaching extensively.[761] For the next five years, Zhönu Pal attended the sixth Pagdru ruler Dragpa Jungné (who was enthroned in 1432) at his secular seat Neudong (Sne'u gdong), and spent most of his time in conversation with other geshes. Occasionally he taught at Tsetang, but was repeatedly ordered back to Neudong. It is not clear to what extent Zhönu Pal was affected by the internal revolt of the Pagmo Drupa in 1434, which marked the beginning of the decline of the dynasty's power,[762] but Zhamar Chödrag Yeshé informs us at this point in the biography that Zhönu Pal wished to escape the same way he did at Gyadur before, thinking that it would not serve his own ends in the long run to stay with the king.[763]

Still, Zhönu Pal would eventually be known as the preceptor of the Lhazig Lang (Lha gzigs rlangs) family, in other words, the Pagdru dynasty. It was the first ruler of this dynasty, Tai Situ Jangchub Gyaltsen (Ta'i Situ Byang chub rgyal mtshan) (1302–64)[764] that founded, in the immediate vicinity of his palace Neudong in the lower Yarlung (Yar klung) valley, the monastery of Tsetang, in which Zhönu Pal received many teachings and where he was ordained.[765] (The seventh king, Künga Legpa (Kun dga' legs pa) (r. 1448–81), would later also serve as the abbot of Tsetang.) Zhönu Pal entertained good relations with the chief religious authority of the Pagdru family, namely the nephew of Künga Legpa and son of Dragpa Jungné, Chennga Ngagi Wangpo (Spyan snga Ngagi dbang po) (1439–90), who was enthroned on the seat of Densatel in 1454.[766] According to the colophon of Zhönu Pal's *Ratnagotravibhāgavyākhyā* commentary it was this same abbot Chennga Ngagi Wangpo who in 1479 ordered the wood blocks for the commentary to be carved.[767]

In the ox year (1433), still during his stay with Dragpa Jungné at Neudong, Zhönu Pal went to Gyalzang (Rgyal bzangs) in the Yön (Yon) valley in order to supervise the corrections of a new Kangyur,[768] which was being compiled in honor of the late Pagdru ruler (Dragpa Gyaltsen).[769] It was in the spring of this same year that Vanaratna for the first time arrived in Tibet. At the court, Dragpa Jungné asked him many questions, and together with the king, Zhönu Pal studied not only a host of tantras, but also the Maitreya works *Abhisamayālaṁkāra*, *Mahāyānasūtrālaṁkāra*, and *Madhyāntavibhāga* (together with the commentaries), a commentary on the first chapter of the *Pramāṇavārttika*, and the *Prasannapadā*, to name only a few. They read the Sanskrit texts of these works, asked questions, and listened to the numerous explanations. Moreover, they received a Cakrasaṁvara empowerment. During all this, Zhönu Pal offered much assistance (probably translating).[770]

At the end of the rabbit year (1435) Vanaratna returned to Tsetang from a visit to Paro in Bhutan.[771] Together with many geshes Zhönu Pal listened to special instructions on the six-branch yoga and received an Acala empowerment.[772] In the summer of the following dragon year (1436) Zhönu Pal served Vanaratna during his trip to the sacred sites of Samyé and Chimpu (Mchims phu). All along the way he took the opportunity to ask many questions of and to have long discussions with the realized Indian paṇḍita. Thereafter he frequently translated for Vanaratna at Neudong, and while doing so received numerous teachings.[773] Before leaving Tibet, Vanaratna said of Zhönu Pal:

> I have traveled through two-thirds of Jambudvīpa and seen the great scholars with great knowledge—like suns for men. Among them I have not seen [one whose] knowledge is greater than Zhönu Pal's.[774]

During Vanaratna's third visit to Tibet, which lasted from 1452 to 1454,[775] Zhönu Pal translated Vanaratna's *Śabarapādastotra* and acted as interpreter during his teachings and empowerments at Dingri (Ding ri) until the main translator, Lotsāwa (Lo tsā ba) Mañjuśrī,[776] arrived.[777] But later on, when Vanaratna was teaching again at the court of Neudong, the Pagdru ruler Künga Legpa felt so uneasy in the presence of Zhönu Pal that the king forced him to leave for one month to Kyamchepa Teng (Skyam 'chad pa stengs).[778] Further down in the biography, Zhamarpa tells us that at one point Zhönu Pal had to calm down Künga Legpa with the power of his samādhi after the ruler had become angry for no reason—so much so that he almost expelled him from his kingdom. This happened in a pig year (probably 1467).[779]

Zhönu Pal had already felt uncomfortable in 1438 at the court of Neudong under Künga Legpa's predecessor Dragpa Jungné, and repeatedly requested in vain, over a period of half a year, to be allowed to leave for Dagpo, where a certain Drudawa ('Bru mda' ba) had agreed to pay for his livelihood.[780] Then, the king ordered everybody to take empowerments from the Sakya master Martön Gyaltsen Özer (Dmar ston Rgyal mtshan 'od zer)[781] at Tsentang (Btsan thang)[782] near Tsetang. On this occasion Zhönu Pal received a *Krīyasamuccaya* empowerment and many other teachings and empowerments.[783] According to the biography of Lochen Sönam Gyatso (Lo chen Bsod nams rgya mtsho), Gyaltsen Özer (Rgyal mtshan 'od zer) on this occasion also conferred the empowerments of the Hevajra and Yamāntaka cycles of the Sakya school.[784] Zhönu Pal then followed Martönpa to Chöding, where both of them received teachings from Götrugpa (Rgod phrug pa), whose actual name, Dragpa Jungné, is also mentioned here. On several previous occasions in Gyalzang (Rgyal bzangs), Zhönu Pal had obtained many instructions from Götrugpa, reports Zhamarpa's biography.[785] According to Lechen Künga Gyaltsen, Zhönu Pal also studied Drugpa Kagyü texts under Götrugpa.[786]

In the seventh month of the same year (1438), several people were intending to travel to Kongpo (Kong po), and Zhönu Pal approached the king again, firmly set on leaving that month. Having made offerings to the king, he was finally freed from his duties for good.[787] In Dagpo, Zhönu Pal discussed various points of the doctrine (such as the differences between the *lam rim* of the Gelugpas and Atiśa's *Bodhipathapradīpa*)[788] with Khenchen Tashi Jangwa (Mkhan chen Bkra shis byang ba).[789] In the winter of the horse year (1438), he was invited by the local governor Paljor Zangpo (Dpal 'byor bzang po) to teach at Kurab (Sku rab), the administrative center of Dagpo.[790] In the autumn of the sheep year (1439) the Third Zhamarpa Chöpal Yeshé (Zhva dmar pa Chos dpal ye shes) (1406–52) came from Kongpo to Druda ('Bru mda') (Dagpo), and Zhönu Pal obtained from him the reading transmissions of the *Mkha' spyod dbang po'i chos drug*, the *Karma pakṣi'i dam tshig gi bshad pa,* and the Third Karmapa's *Dam tshig rgya mtsho*,[791] and, according to the biography of Situ and Belo, the six Dharma [practices] of Nāropa.[792]

In the spring of the monkey year (1440) Zhönu Pal visited Gampo (Sgam po),[793] and later he received teachings on numerous Kagyü works—by the Second Zhamarpa Khachö Wangpo (Zhva dmar pa Mkha' spyod dbang po) (1350–1405), the Third Karmapa Rangjung Dorjé, and Minyag Sherab Zangpo (Mi nyag Shes rab bzang po)—from Rimibabpa Sönam Rinchen (1362–1453) at Dagpo pass.[794] Before parting, much to Zhönu Pal's astonishment, he was advised by Rimibabpa to abandon neither the mahāmudrā view nor the independence of the Gelugpas:

> Later, [to Zhönu Pal's] astonishment [Rimibabpa] said: "Just as I do not reject the mahāmudrā view, don't you reject it either. Just as I do not reject the tradition(?) of the Gandenpas (Dge ldan pa) (i.e., Gelugpas), don't you reject it either." [Zhönu Pal] replied: "I will surely hold [this] tradition sacred" and showed great respect.[795]

The way Zhamar Chödrag Yeshé reports this event we get the impression that Zhönu Pal was surprised and politely showed respect but did not fully take this advice. This view is not met with total agreement. In a review of the *Rgyud gsum gsang ba*,[796] which Zhönu Pal composed only two years later in 1442,[797] the Eighth Karmapa Mikyö Dorjé somewhat pointedly remarks that Zhönu Pal takes Tsongkhapa's view as a guideline while at the same time upholding the tradition of the Dagpo Kagyü.[798] This suggests that Zhönu Pal may have taken Rimibabpa's words more seriously than Zhamarpa suggests.

In the summer of the monkey year (1440), Zhönu Pal wanted to attend the teachings of the Third Zhamarpa in Kongpo, but his sponsor Drudar ('Bru mdar) would not allow him to go. Thus he abandoned his trip to Kongpo and gave a *gshed dmar* empowerment in Drudar instead, but he refused to stay any longer with his sponsor and returned to the Yarlung valley in the winter of the same year.[799]

In the spring of the bird year (1441) he participated in the prayer festival *(smon lam)* at Densatel, where many geshes gathered on the orders of the ruler Dragpa Jungné. During this time he daily sat at the feet of Götrugpa. After that he spent some time at Tingnamo Dzong (Rting sna mo rdzong) instructing numerous Dharma masters, such as Namkha Lodrö from Tsetang and Lochen Sönam Gyatso.[800] From 1448 onward Zhönu Pal considered these two as jewel disciples and at a residence called Jangpo Drang (Ljang pho brang) offered them more explanation on the definitive meaning than he offered to anyone else after that.[801]

In the summer of the bird year (1441) Zhönu Pal received, among many other teachings, special instructions on the *Rdo rje gsum gyi bsnyen sgrub* from Götrugpa at Chöding in the On ('On) valley (to the east of Densatel).[802] Again in the following dog year (1442) he sat at the feet of this great master.[803]

Under the sponsorship of a high official from Neudong called Drung Sönam Gyaltsen (Drung Bsod nams rgyal mtshan) (1417–87),[804] Zhönu Pal stayed at Neudong in the autumn of the year 1441, giving various empowerments, such as the *phur pa man ngag drug pa.*[805] With the help of Namkha Paljor (Nam mkha' dpal 'byor) he then moved to his residence Yizangtsé and spent the winter of the bird year (1441) there.[806] At Yizangtsé Zhönu Pal instructed Sönam Gyaltsen in the six-branch yoga practice.[807] From Zhamarpa's biography of Lochen Sönam Rinchen we know that from then on he regularly visited Zhönu Pal at Yizangtsé.[808]

The remaining first part of Zhamarpa's biography of Zhönu Pal does not give much detailed information of the remaining years. From the water dog year (1442) until the water monkey year (1452) we are told that Zhönu Pal was mainly teaching, as described further down in a separate chapter.[809] After the narration of the events relating to Vanaratna's third visit to Tibet (see above), we are told that in the fire rat year (1456) Zhönu Pal received from Sherab Zangpo in Menchig (Sman gcig) *zhi byed* teachings that he promised to practice for six months.[810] After obtaining various other teachings from Sherab Zangpo, he returned to Yarlung.[811] Up to the water horse year (1462) Zhönu Pal is said to have devoted most of his time to conversations with geshes and to have stayed in retreat only for one month during this period.[812]

Even in his eighties Zhönu Pal remained quite active. In the wood sheep year (1475) he traveled to eastern Tibet,[813] and in the following fire monkey year (1476), the king Künga Legpa offered him a hundred gold coins and requested Dharma teachings. Zhönu Pal complied and over a period of two years, up into the earth dog year (1478), gave teachings such as an explanation of the five levels in the *Guhyasamājatantra* (based on notes of the Second Zhamarpa Khachö Wangpo). During this time Zhönu Pal also granted the king a Bernagchen (Ber nag can) Mahākāla empowerment.[814] This then concluded the first part of Zhamarpa's biography.

Of particular interest in the remaining part of the biography are some details about the composition of Zhönu Pal's commentary on the *Ratnagotravibhāgavyākhyā.* As for the date of its composition, Zhamar Chödrag Yeshé only mentions a snake year, but this must be Zhönu Pal's last snake year (1473) for the following reasons. First, Zhönu Pal's mental presence is described as not having deteriorated, his understanding at the time of death being as good as when he composed the *Ratnagotravibhāgavyākhyā* commentary,[815] and second, he is said to have been nearly blind, dictating the commentary to his assistant Mönlam Dragpa (Smon lam grags pa)[816] over a period of four months entirely from memory. Zhamar Chödrag Yeshé further informs us that the editors only found a few mistakes when checking the numerous quotations from the Kangyur and Tengyur.[817] That Zhönu Pal was capable of such a work is corroborated by the fact that he completed his *Blue Annals* in the earth dog year (1478).[818] Third, according to the colophon the commentary was composed in Möndang (Smon ldang), an area where Zhönu Pal was teaching and writing in the early 1470s (see below).

To sum up, thanks to his nonsectarian attitude, Zhönu Pal was able to receive instructions and tantric empowerments from the most important masters of his time. On top of that, he also had direct access to the Indian origins of Tibetan Buddhism, studying and translating a number of Sanskrit texts with Vanaratna. The way Zhönu Pal combines all these traditions is seen especially in a chapter on how he discovered the marvelous door of the Dharma. In it, Zhamar Chödrag Yeshé reports how Zhönu Pal gains the strength of faith by visiting the place where Pagmo Drupa saw the true nature of phenomena:[819]

> [Zhönu Pal realized that] buddha nature, or the natural luminosity of mind, is the basis of all saṁsāra and nirvāṇa. Just as the abiding nature of this [luminosity] is present in [his] mind, so are similar abiding natures [in the minds of all from] buddhas down to [each] sentient being. "Being beyond the experiential sphere of the mind, it is beyond expression." All Madhyamaka explanations of this kind apply here....[820]
>
> This great expression *union into a pair,* from the tradition of the unsurpassable secret [Mantrayāna], he now ascertained as the true nature of all phenomena, [that is,] not with regard to the fruit [anymore], and with the help of the Buddha's teachings he proclaimed widely that this [union into a pair] can be experienced even by fools and ordinary persons. Even those who had only little experience he properly introduced [to the true nature of their minds] on the basis of precisely this [little experience they had]. He did not utter this like a talking parrot pronouncing empty words but taught properly, as properly based on his own experience.... The entire superiority of qualities contained in the buddha mind arose through the power of his having realized the ultimate view of the *union into a pair.*[821]

In other words, Zhönu Pal is described as having realized, in confirmation of the insight of Pagmo Drupa, that buddha nature, or the natural luminosity of mind, is the basis of both saṁsāra and nirvāṇa. This, and the following explanation that the true nature of phenomena can even be experienced by ordinary practitioners, is typical of Kagyü mahāmudrā, and, as we shall see in the following chapters, fully in line with Zhönu Pal's *Ratnagotravibhāgavyākhyā* commentary.

Also of great interest is Zhönu Pal's summary and critique of Dölpopa's view that immediately follows in this paragraph of the biography:

> [Zhönu Pal] said that the omniscient Jomonangpa (i.e. Dölpopa) posited that an appearance [produced by] *karman* and the appearance of wisdom are two separate individual things that have been mixed together. [It is] precisely this appearance [produced by] *karman* that is designated as "ice, which is the appearance of wisdom" and pointed out as being the appearance of wisdom...[this] being illustrated by the example of water and ice. As long as distinctions are made between a self and other, a material world and living beings, corresponding conventions will be used. Otherwise, in terms of the appearance of wisdom, they are of one taste.[822]

In other words, for Zhönu Pal the realms of ordinary experience and wisdom are not two distinct things mixed together, but of one nature, in the same way as ice is not really different from water.

His thoughts on the "reflections of emptiness" *(śūnyatābimba),* however, seem to be more in line with zhentong:

> Some wish to analyze even in the unsurpassable secret Mantra[yāna] in the following way: "Given the reflections of emptiness, they do not truly exist." But [for Zhönu Pal] a vision [consisting in the] reflections of emptiness is a vision of the true nature of mind.[823]

This valuable description of Zhönu Pal's position concludes with the following statement:

> He taught perfectly, without contradiction, the teachings of the spiritual friends gone before him, such as those of the mahāsiddha Yumo[wa Mikyö Dorjé] (Yu mo [ba Mi bskyod ro rje])

> (eleventh century)[824] and Gampopa and his disciples; the teachings of the master of siddhas, Vanaratna; the *Bodhisattva Trilogy;* the *[Guhya]samājapradīpoddyotana;* the instructions of [the translator] Mañjuśrī;[825] numerous profound sūtras; and many cycles of the "old" (i.e., Nyingma) secret Mantra[yāna].[826]

Thus Zhönu Pal must have brought the tenet of Yumowa, whom Tuken Lozang Chökyi Nyima (Thu'u bkwan Blo bzang chos kyi nyi ma) (1737–1802) considers to have been the originator of the zhentong teachings (Stearns 1999:44), in line with the teachings of Gampopa. This suggests that Zhönu Pal was yet another master who blended zhentong with mahāmudrā. It should be noted again, however, that Zhönu Pal never uses the expression zhentong in his entire *Ratnagotravibhāgavyākhyā* commentary.

Part II
Translation

4. Zhönu Pal's *Ratnagotravibhāgavyākhyā* Commentary

Translator's Introduction

THE PRESENT STUDY of Zhönu Pal's *Ratnagotravibhāgavyākhyā* commentary is based on my edition of a handwritten *dbu med* text and a blockprint (Mathes 2003).[827] Common throughout the *dbu med* manuscript are features that are generally considered to be old, such as *bstsags* for *bsags*, or *ngo ti* for *ngo bo*. The entire manuscript has 698 folios[828] with seven lines on each page. Unfortunately the backside of folio 483 and the last page are missing. The headings of the five chapters of the commentary (Zhönu Pal follows the Indian *vyākhyā*) are listed together with the folio numbers on a cover page, which bears the seal of the Zhamarpa and assigns the letter *ha* to the volume containing Zhönu Pal's commentary. It is thus reasonable to assume that the original was kept in the library of the Zhamarpas in Yangpachen (Yangs pa can), which was seized by the Gelug government after the war with the Nepalese king Raṇa Bahādur Śāha in 1792. But the *dbu med* text of Zhönu Pal's commentary, which is now in the library of the Potala Palace, has only 691 folios,[829] and it is thus doubtful whether our text was still at Zhamarpa's seat when his seat was sacked and the booty brought to Lhasa. The blockprint has 463 folios with seven lines on each page, and could be the text described by Akhu Ching Sherab Gyatso (A khu ching Shes rab rgya mtsho) as having 461 folios.[830]

Both texts have significant common mistakes.[831] Unlike the blockprint (B), though, the *dbu med* text (A) has a few serious copying mistakes of its own, such as the one on p. 161.5 where the scribe jumped from the second *gcig* back to the first one, repeating the syllables in between.[832] A also has the peculiarity, contrary to B, of consistently writing some words with the superscript *sa* instead of *ra (sdzu 'phrul* instead of *rdzu 'phrul, sdzogs* instead of *rdzogs,* and *sdzob* instead of *rdzob).* This and the fact that the colophon of B, which is missing in A, does not fit on one folio the size of our *dbu med* manuscript A (it is known from the prefatory page that only the last folio is missing in A) make it unlikely that the *dbu med* manuscript (A) is a copy of the blockprint (B). In the case of B being a copy of A, the blocks would have been carved on the basis of a handwritten text that already contained significant copying mistakes; the text would have had to have been emended by the editors. Moreover, the probability that the original was no longer available at the time the blocks were carved, only six years after Zhönu Pal had composed his work, is very low. This leaves us with the probable case that A and B share a common source. In fact, as a close disciple of Zhönu Pal, Zhamar Chödrag Yeshé (text A has the seal of the Zhamarpas on its prefatory page) may well have obtained a handwritten copy of the commentary before the blocks were carved.

The colophon of the actual text simply states that the Buddhist monk Zhönu Pal composed his commentary in the mountain solitude called Möndang.[833] In the biography of Lochen Sönam Gyatso we find the location "castle of Möndang" *(smon ldang mkhar),* where Lochen is said to have received explanations relating to the *pāramitās* at the feet of Zhönu Pal in the winter of the year 1472,[834] and according to Zhamarpa's biography, Zhönu Pal had already stayed at the same castle in 1469 or 1470, composing a commentary on *Pradīpoddyotana* up to the tenth chapter.[835] The colophon of the *Ratnagotravibhāgavyākhyā* commentary does not give any further details, but Zhamar Chödrag Yeshé informs us in his biography of Zhönu Pal that the commentary was composed in a snake year (1473).[836]

According to the colophon of the printing press, the blocks of the *Ratnagotravibhāgavyākhyā* commentary were carved only six years after Zhönu Pal completed his work, which means that he lived to see his "publication." The relevant passage of the colophon is:

> All the [material for] wood blocks and sheets of paper from the thick forest [collected by] the faithful who follow the orders of the glorious and supreme Lochen [Sönam Gyatso], and all the [material] from the glorious, everywhere victorious, and mighty southern chief[837] eventually arrived in the vicinity of Künzang Nag (Kun bzang nags). In the courtyard of both [worldly and religious] traditions, [the one called] "Glorious Yangpachen," which resembles a fine abode of immortality within the sphere of the earth, to be served by many scholars—in this palace where many glorious ones gather—[the abbot of Densatel] enjoyed to

> the full a handful of the lama's (i.e., Zhönu Pal's) kindness, [namely,] the nectar of all the tantras' profound meaning and the perfection of the ocean of text traditions, which are directly[838] known by [the lama], while his heart was filled with the nondual supreme bliss of profound luminosity. Since the order was given by this universal monarch of "awareness holders," the powerful chief of the retinue of the maṇḍala, the supreme chief who is the head of all practice lineages, the glorious Ngagi Wangchug Dragpa (Ngagi dbang phyug grags pa) (1439–90),[839] the everywhere-victorious god, the Dharma king, and "attendant of the Dharma" *(chos kyi spyan snga),*[840] all necessary material was obtained in great splendor [and] was in no way incomplete. With regard to the supervision of Dharma [activity] and [requisite] worldly activity, the necessary arrangements were properly made, thanks to the efforts of the learned[841] Samdrub Dragpa (Bsam 'grub grags pa). Gyalwai Trinlé Lhündrub Namrin (Rgyal ba'i phrin las lhun grub nam rin) and Palden Zangpo Ngödrub (Dpal ldan bzang po dngos grub), two miraculously learned scribes, [together with] six ([and later even] more—ten) specialists in the craft of carving, Gönpopal (Mgon po dpal) and so forth, gathered and finished the [wood] blocks at the beginning[842] of summer in the earth pig year (i.e., 1479).[843]

Künzang Nag, where the various materials for carving the blocks arrived, is the place where the monastic seat of the Pagmo Drupas, Densatel, is located. The courtyard called Yangpachen, in which Ngagi Wangpo (Ngagi dbang po) (who became the eighth Pagdru ruler in Neudong in 1481)[844] heard teachings from Zhönu Pal and gave orders to carve the blocks, is probably located at Künzang Nag as well.

A cursory glance makes it clear that Zhönu Pal's work differs in its format from an ordinary Tibetan commentary. He hardly uses the typical Tibetan system of analyzing topical divisions and subdivisions *(sa bcad)* but rather follows the Indian commentarial tradition of first quoting a portion of the root text and then commenting upon it. The actual commentary is divided into three parts: (1) a relatively short one with an explanation of the title—that is, the terms *mahāyāna, uttara, tantra,* and *śāstra*—for those with sharp faculties (DRSM, 8.3–13.2), (2) an explanation of the first three stanzas of the first chapter for those with average faculties (DRSM, 13.2.–80.11), and (3) the longest part, the entire remaining commentary, for those with lesser capacities (DRSM, 80.11–576.17).

In the section below, I have translated the introduction and the first two commentaries, that is, the ones for sharp and average faculties. The introduction starts with a long quotation from the *Vairocanābhisambodhitantra* that describes eight levels attained by ordinary persons without proper guidance, and then praises the qualities of the Buddha and his teaching. After a short historical survey of the transmission of the *Ratnagotravibhāga* the relatively short introduction concludes with a discussion of how buddha nature can be explained either as a nonaffirming negation, natural luminosity, *ālayavijñāna,* or all bodhisattvas and sentient beings. The explanation of the title targets various connotations of the terms used in it, especially the compound member *tantra,* which is elucidated by several quotations that reveal Zhönu Pal's understanding of what the underlying intention of the *Ratnagotravibhāga* is. It is also noteworthy that Zhönu Pal follows Maitrīpa and the mahāsiddha Saroruha in listing the Sautrāntrika among the Mahāyāna schools. The commentary for those with average faculties contains an extensive analysis of the seven vajra points. It demonstrates how Zhönu Pal weaves in his mahāmudrā pith instructions and presents his mahāmudrā hermeneutics of viewing the last dharmacakra as the peak of Buddhist teachings.

Technical Notes

The following translation and study of Zhönu Pal's *Ratnagotravibhāgavyākhyā* commentary is based on my edition of this text.[845] When quoting it, I refer to the abbreviation DRSM, followed by page and line numbers. The numbers in brackets at the beginning of each paragraph of the translation again refer to page and line numbers of my edition of the DRSM (i.e., the *Theg pa chen po rgyud bla ma'i bstan bcos kyi 'grel bshad de kho na nyid rab tu gsal ba'i me long*).

Zhönu Pal's *Ratnagotravibhāga* commentary contains numerous quotations of the sūtras and śāstras. These quotations will be identified and compared, as far as possible, with the original Sanskrit.[846] In addition, the pertinent manuscripts were consulted when available. This was especially important in the case of the *Ratnagotravibhāgavyākhyā,* which Johnston edited on the basis of two manuscripts. This edition was sometimes improved by referring to the same two manuscripts Johnston used. In the footnotes, the letters A and B are employed in the same way as in Johnston's edition, namely to denote the manuscript with the old Śāradā script (A) and the Nepalese manuscript (B).[847] The negatives of the photographs that Rāhula Sāṁkṛtyāyana made of these manuscripts are now preserved by the Bihar Research Society, Patna. Positive copies of a number of these negatives were made in the sixties and seventies and brought to Germany. Currently they are kept at the Niedersächsische Staats- und Universitätsbibliothek, Göttingen,[848] where both *Ratnagotravibhāgavyākhyā* manuscripts have the shelf-mark Xc 14/1.[849] I thank Dr. Gustav Roth for providing me reader-printer copies from these photographs.

Equally important are the numerous quotations from the *Laṅkāvatārasūtra.* A first comparison of the twenty-two manuscripts microfilmed by the Nepal-German Manuscript Preservation Project (NGMPP) with Nanjio's (1923) edition allowed a selection of ten manuscripts on the basis of which the Sanskrit edition could be cross-checked. The variant readings I noticed are far too few to establish a stemma of the twenty-two Nepalese manuscripts, and given that a critical text edition of this important sūtra is not yet available, I simply attempt in the present work to establish a tentative Sanskrit text so as to enable a better understanding and translation of the Tibetan. The quoted passages are not critically edited and not all variant readings have been listed. Here are some of my observations and present reasons for having selected the ten manuscripts I used.

Based on the joint variant reading *śraddhā-* of six manuscripts[850] against *sarvva-* or *sattvaṁ* (the *akṣaras* *rvva* and *ttva* can be easily confounded), I selected from these six what appears to be the oldest manuscript (reel no. C 13/7, dated 1753 A.D.[851]), which is from Kesar Library.[852] Ms. H 45/6 is selected because it is probably the oldest of all twenty-two, containing as it does the name of King Śrījayasiddhinarasiṁhamalla, who reigned from 1619 to 1661 A.D.[853] D 58/6 was selected on the grounds that it once contradicts H 45/6[854] and has an older Newari script.

Ms. A 112/8 is dropped for using a later script, displaying some scribal errors and being closely related to H 45/6 (both share common mistakes). Ms. A 112/10 shares common mistakes with D 58/6 but is retained for contradicting the latter once.[855] E 406/2 and H 45/6 have the same handwriting and do not differ in the checked passages. E 1200/8 shares a significant common variant reading with D 58/6[856] but was retained for being comparatively old (dated 1698 A.D.).[857] D 58/4 is incomplete (it lacks required passages). D 52/5 was selected for once opposing most of the remaining manuscripts.[858] A 917/6 has a common variant reading with ms. C 13/7[859] and was a private copy of Hemraj Shakya, whose library was later incorporated into the collection of the National Archives. B 88/1 is a copy of A 917/6.

Ms. E 1725/5 is a retake of D 16/2, E 406/2 of H 45/6, and E 1308/4 of E 3/3 (which is a copy of E 625/14). A 112/9 is kept for playing an important role in the eighth chapter of the *Laṅkāvatārasūtra* that is at the moment critically edited by Lambert Schmithausen.

The manuscripts of the *Laṅkāvatārasūtra* selected are referred to by the following letters:

A Reel no. A 112/9
B Reel no. A 112/10
C Reel no. C 13/7
D Reel no. D 52/5
E Reel no. D 58/6
F Reel no. D 73/8
G Reel no. E 625/14
H Reel no. E 1200/8
I Reel no. E 1725/5
K Reel no. H 45/6

The Commentary on the Treatise "Mahāyāna-Uttaratantra": The Mirror Showing Reality Very Clearly

(Introduction and Initial Commentaries)

Introduction

[2.2] I prostrate to all buddhas and bodhisattvas.

[2.2–4] I bow down to the lamas who, in human form, are expert in the loving skillful means of listening to and reflecting on [the Dharma];
[Their forms have been molded] from the substance of the *mantras* of compassion of the victorious ones and the perfection of insight.[860]
[In the form of] marvelous illusory troops they defeat the troops of [different] groups of demons,
And they serve as guides for those who conform to the purposes of the wise.

[2.4–6] I bow entirely to the most excellent among the sons of the Victorious One,
[To him] who completely pervades the [buddha] element of sentient beings with his clouds of love,[861]
Who completely moistens the limitless fields[862] with the rainwater of Dharma,
And who ensures that they are completely filled with the supreme fruits of virtue and goodness.

[2.6–7] I bow to Maitrīpa, in whom the treatise of the
[Ratnagotravibhāga Mahāyāna-]Uttaratantra [began to] blaze
As a consequence of his having found [the realization of] mahāmudrā
Through the kindness of the venerable Śabaripa.

> [2.7–8] I bow to Dampa Sangyé,[863]
> Who carried the lion-sound of emptiness
> Into [every] side valley of the Snowland,
> And is thus the unconquered protector victorious over all.
>
> [2.9–10] I bow to the feet of Lama Rinchen (Rin chen) (i.e., Gampopa),[864]
> Who fulfilled a prophecy by the Victorious One,
> Because the "youthful moonlight" (i.e., the ever young Candraprabha)[865]
> Has shone on the mountain peak of the fortunate ones.
>
> [2.10–11] I bow to [all] sentient beings,
> Who possess the treasure of the essence[866] of all buddhas,[867]
> Who have obtained from it a mind of jewels,
> And who [can] therefore generate the supreme joy of bodhisattvas [or] heroes.
>
> [2.11–12] I prostrate also to the great treatise of the *Uttara[tantra]*,
> Which without exception is included among the utterances of the great ones,
> for [among] all the extensive and limitless teachings of the victorious ones
> It is the most excellent of measures in the world.

[2.12–15] Here[868] the *[Ratnagotravibhāga] Mahāyānottaratantraśāstra* taught by the Illustrious Ajita (i.e., Maitreya) and the commentary on it composed by the master Ārya Asaṅga are the Dharma to be explained. [The *Uttaratantra* and its commentary] should be explained[, however, only] after they have been accepted in the sense of taking the unsurpassable teacher and his entire teaching as a standard of authenticity.

[2.15–16] Concerning these [two points], it is first stated how the teacher is unsurpassable. Various teachers come into being in the world. In this regard, it has been said in the **Āryavairocanābhisambodhitantra:*[869]

> [2.16–24] Also, Guhyakādhipati,[870] with regard to[871] fools—ordinary persons, who are like cattle; to some [of them][872] the notion of Dharma occurs by chance. It is as follows. Keeping something merely on the order of, "I must fast" in mind generates enthusiasm and makes you cultivate the same [conduct] over and over

again. Guhyakādhipati, this is like a seed that brings forth virtuous deeds; it is the first [level of enhanced] mind. As a result of[873] this [fasting] you are led to give presents[874] to your parents, son and daughter, relatives, and kinsmen on this or that day marked by a good configuration [of stars].[875] This is like a sprout; it is the second [level of enhanced mind]. Furthermore, such generosity also makes you give to unknown persons. This is like a trunk; it is the third [level of enhanced mind]. Furthermore, such [extended] generosity makes you look hard for suitable recipients and give [alms to them]. This is like a leaf; it is the fourth [level of enhanced mind]. Furthermore, such generosity makes you rejoice in gurus and musicians and give [to them as well]. This is like a flower; it is the fifth [level of enhanced mind]. Furthermore, this [type of] generosity makes you give to aged persons. This is like a fruit; it is the sixth [level of enhanced mind].

[2.24–3.7] Also, Guhyakādhipati, you remain disciplined in order to be born in the higher realms. This is like nourishment; it is the seventh [level of enhanced mind]. Also, Guhyakādhipati, thanks to a mind like this, you hear from individual spiritual friends the following words while wandering in saṁsāra: "These gods are great gods. They bestow bliss on everyone. Make respectful offerings and [so] become somebody who has accomplished[876] everything. They are: Īśvara (i.e., Śiva),[877] Brahman, then Viṣṇu, Śaṁkara, Rudra,[878] Skanda,[879] then the sun [god], the moon [god], Varuṇa, Kubera Dhanada,[880] Indra, Virūpākṣa, Viśvākara, Yama, Kālarātrī,[881] Nirṛti,[882] the so-called Chiefs of the Eight Directions,[883] Agni, the sons of Vinatā,[884] then Devī,[885] Tapastakṣa,[886] Padma,[887] the Nāga [called] Takṣaka, Vāsuki,[888] the so-called Śaṁkha, Karkoṭaka, Mahāpadma, Kulika, Śeṣa,[889] Sadā (?), Ananta,[890] Ādideva,[891] the most excellent gods and *ṛṣis*, Veda[puruṣa],[892] and the sons of Draupadī.[893] May the wise make offerings [to them]."

[3.7–9] After you hear such[894] words from [spiritual friends], [your] mind becomes enthused. Then, being full of devotion, you hasten to make offerings to the [gods]. Guhyakādhipati, this is the best of relief for fools or ordinary persons wandering in saṁsāra. It is [the state of] having become strong; and the victorious ones have declared it to be the eighth [level of enhanced] mind.

[3.9–11] Accordingly, people rely on their own individual teachers when on the eighth [level of enhanced] mind. But these teachers cannot liberate [sentient beings] from [cyclic] existence, and they have defects. The Buddha, the illustrious one, alone is free from defects. As [Udbhaṭasiddhasvāmin] has explained in [his] *Viśeṣastava* [1–2]:

> [3.11–12] Having given up other teachers,
> I have taken refuge in you, illustrious one.
> If somebody asks why I [do] this, [I answer:]
> You are without defect and endowed with qualities.
>
> [3.12–14] Because the world rejoices in defects
> And is too weak to perceive the qualities,
> It sees even defects as being like qualities
> And takes refuge in other [teachers].[895]

[3.14–15] Likewise, since [the gods]—Īśvara and the others—are not omniscient, their assertions, too, destroy [people's] minds. Therefore it is difficult for them to develop devotion toward the Buddha. In the same text (*Viśeṣastava* 72) it has been said:

> [3.15–16] Fools[896] whose mind is destroyed
> By the defects of the tenets
> Of those who are not omniscient in the sense [taught above]
> Have not seen you, the teacher who is without defect.

[3.16–17] Likewise, when investigating whether a teacher is of highest quality or not, it has been said in [Dharmakīrti's] *Pramāṇavārttika* [I.219[897]]:

> [3.17–18] [As for] the defects of others or a state without defects,
> To say: This [person has] such [defects] or not—
> Others know that this[898] is something difficult to determine
> Because it is difficult to arrive at a valid cognition [about it].[899]

[3.18–19] Thus it is difficult to know whether another [being] is omniscient. On the other hand, it has been said in the *Devātiśayastotra* [17]:[900]

> [3.19–20] I have not taken the side of the Buddha,[901]
> Nor am I hostile to [people] like Kapila;

Indeed, I regard as teachers [all those]
[Whose] words are suitable.[902]

[3.20–23] Likewise, discourses that are not vitiated by either direct or inferential valid cognitions, and that do not contradict each other when setting forth what is completely hidden,[903] are perfect discourses. Therefore, the Buddha who delivered [such discourses] is a perfect being of authority. The discourses of the Buddha do not contradict each other. As has been said in the *Viśeṣastava* [19]:

[3.23–24] It is heard that the many words spoken by Vyāsa
Contradicted each other in the beginning and the end
Because his memory was weak.
This, O wise one, is not the case with any of your [words].[904]

[3.24–4.2] Likewise, the great masters who uphold the Buddhist tenets not only ascertain that [these] are the teaching of the Buddha, but also take the discourses as a measure. On the other hand, here in the [Land] of Snow those who [maintain] that [our] teacher [also] taught, out of his very great compassion, things that are not correct[905] very much predominate; and very few [maintain] that he taught straightforwardly. Because of such [arguments], the teacher and the teaching are greatly despised and harmed. Therefore it has been said here [in the *Ratnagotravibhāga* V.20]:

[4.2–4] Nobody anywhere in this world is more learned than the Victorious One,
No other who is omniscient and knows completely the highest truth the way he does.
Therefore, the sūtra[s][906] of definitive meaning put forward[907] by the Sage [i.e., the Buddha] himself should not be violated;
Otherwise the correct doctrine *(dharma)* will be subverted, since you will fall away from the way of the Buddha.[908]

[4.5–6] Therefore, the treatise *[Ratnagotravibhāga Mahāyāna-]Uttara-[tantra]* teaches all words of the Buddha in a "correct way."[909] It has also shown the difference between the provisional and definitive meaning of these [Buddha words].[910]

[4.6–11] With regard to the [Maitreya works], three among the works of the Illustrious Maitreya, [namely] the *Abhisamayālaṁkāra*, the *Mahāyānasūtrālaṁkāra*, and the *Madhyāntavibhāga*, were translated by the translators

Paltseg (Dpal brtsegs), Yeshé Dé (Ye shes sde), and others[911] during the first period of the spread of the doctrine [in Tibet]. As for the [remaining] two, the *[Ratnagotravibhāga Mahāyāna-]Uttaratantra[śāstra]* and the *Dharmadharmatāvibhāga* together with its commentary, Lord Maitrīpa saw light shining from a crack in a *stūpa* and, wondering what the source of the light was, tried to determine it. As a consequence, he obtained the texts of the two treatises. He rejoiced [in them] and prayed to the venerable [Maitreya], whereupon he arrived—directly visible in an opening between clouds—and duly bestowed [on Maitrīpa] the "oral transmission" *(lung)* [of both texts]. Thus it is known.[912]

[4.11–14] Then he who is called Paṇḍita Ānandakīrti heard [the teaching of both texts] from Lord Maitrīpa and carried the texts to Kashmir disguised as a beggar. Upon his arrival, the great paṇḍita Sajjana recognized him as a scholar and invited him to his home. [Sajjana] listened to [the teaching of] both treatises and copied the texts.[913] The great translator Loden Sherab heard them[914] [from Sajjana], translated them in Śrīnagar in Kashmir, and composed an extensive explanation in Tibet.[915]

[4.14–20] Also, the [well-]known Tsen Kawoché, a disciple of Drapa Ngönshé, came with the great translator (i.e., Ngog Loden Sherab) to Kashmir. He requested Sajjana to bestow on him[916] [the Maitreya works] along with special instructions, since he wanted to make the works of the Illustrious Maitreya his "practice [of preparing] for death" *('chi chos)*. Thereupon [Sajjana] taught all five works, with Lotsāwa Zu Gawa Dorjé serving as translator. He also gave special instructions with regard to the *Uttaratantra* in the due way, and back in Tibet, Tsen explained it to numerous [spiritual friends] in Ü and Tsang.[917] The translator Zu Gawa Dorjé wrote a commentary on the *Uttaratantra* in accordance with the teaching of Sajjana,[918] and translated the *[Dharma]dharmatāvibhāga*, both root-text and commentary. Thus neither the *Uttara[tantra]* nor the *[Dharma]dharmatāvibhāga* was spread in India before the time of Lord Maitrīpa. Neither is found in the great treatises such as the *Abhisamayālaṁkārāloka*,[919] not even "a single phrase of them" *(zur tsam)*.

[4.20–24] The translation by Jowo (Jo bo) [Atiśa] Dīpaṁkara (982–1054) and Nagtso (Nag tsho) (b. 1011)[920] was well done before the one by the great translator (i.e., Ngog Loden Sherab).[921] It is clear that the great Sharawapa (Sha ra ba pa) (1070–1141) explained [the *Uttaratantra*] on the basis of [Nagtso's] translation.[922] Given that later [his] disciples on the whole preferred Ngog's translation, he explained it a second time on the basis of that translation.[923] He also wrote a small *ṭīkā* on the *Uttaratantra* commentary by Ngog, and Drolungpa (Gro lung pa)[924] and Zhangtsé (Zhang tshes)[925] wrote a *ṭīkā* based on it [also]. Based on these two, Nyangdren (Nyang bran) wrote [another] *ṭīkā.* Later, many masters, such as Chapa [Chökyi Sengé] (Phya pa [Chos kyi seng ge]) (1109–69),[926] Tsangnagpa [Tsöndrü Sengé (Brtson 'grus seng ge)], and Denbagpa [Mawai Sengé] (Dan bag pa [Smra ba'i seng ge]),[927] wrote *ṭīkās*, and [so] this tradition spread widely.

[4.24–5.4] In this regard, all explanations of this treatise (i.e., the *Uttaratantra*) put forward their own assertions on how the so-called buddha nature [should be understood] and then established a basis for these [assertions]. In the canonical scriptures I have seen that buddha nature is expressed in four ways: as (1) emptiness with the defining characteristics of a nonaffirming negation; (2) the natural luminosity of mind; (3) the basic consciousness *(ālayavijñāna);* and (4) as all bodhisattvas or sentient beings. In this treatise it is explained with a fourfold meaning: with the three specific defining characteristics: dharmakāya, suchness, and potential, and the general defining characteristic—nonconceptual.

[5.4–10] The great translator (i.e., Ngog Loden Sherab) together with his followers postulate that the ultimate, or emptiness with the defining characteristics of a nonaffirming negation, as explained in the analytical corpus [of Madhyamaka works],[928] is buddha nature and call it *naturally endowed*,[929] since when you apprehend that which is naturally endowed with qualities, [that is,] that emptiness,[930] all qualities are gathered together as if called. Having taken the characteristic sign of purification[931] to be the objective support of wisdom [conducive to] purification, they explain that there is nothing to be added. Having taken the characteristic sign of all defilements to be the self of a person and that of phenomena, which are [wrongly] superimposed by [a mind consisting of] all the defilements, they explain that nothing that existed before need be removed, since these [two] objective supports of the defilements are not established as anything at all. *Being pervaded by the dharmakāya* they explain as meaning that all sentient beings are fit to attain the dharmakāya.

[5.10–12] In this regard,[932] the Master Gampopa said:

> The basic text of this mahāmudrā of ours is the *[Ratnagotravibhāga] Mahāyānottaratantraśāstra* by the illustrious Maitreya.

[5.12–13] It is clear that those who correctly understand the pith instructions of the [Three] Masters from Kham and others[933] follow and assert this. [And] with regard to that, the Dharma Master Götsangpa (1189–1258) said:

> [5.13–15] Generally speaking, the one who was [most] adept at supporting [sentient beings] on the marvelous path called

> mahāmudrā within the teaching of the victorious Śākyamuni was the great Brahmin Saraha. The holders of his tradition in India were Master Śabarapāda, the father[, and his spiritual] son. That even a stupid cowherd in Tibet was enabled to understand[934] the word *mahāmudrā* goes to the credit of Master Gampopa.

[5.15–16] The son in the expression "father and son" is the Great Lord Maitrīpa.

[5.16–21] [This] is very clear from the *Tattvadaśaka*, a work [among] the many small ones of [Maitrīpa] that have been transmitted, and [even more] so in a commentary on it by Sahajavajra. Moreover, the *paṇḍita* Vajrapāṇi, Maitrīpa's direct disciple, explained this tradition extensively to many learned ones in Tibet. [Another] direct disciple of Maitrīpa, Dampa Sangyé, called the mahāmudrā teachings—which are in essence the *pāramitās* and in accordance with the secret *mantra[yāna]*—the "Calming of Suffering," and taught them extensively to innumerable disciples in Tibet. Furthermore, the words of pith instructions and the explanations of treatises deriving from Tsen Kawoché are considered to be only in accordance with Maitrīpa.

[5.21–22] When you are asked to describe here how [exactly] buddha nature is [to be taken] in terms of these eight stages,[935] a description must be given:

[5.22] In the *Ldog pa bsdus pa [bstan pa'i tshig le'ur byas pa]* it has been explained:

> However many negations may be enumerated, they boil down to two, nonaffirming and affirming [negation].[936]

[5.22–23] Of these, the nonaffirming negation has been explained in the *Ldog pa bsdus pa* in the following way:

> There is no object to be taught in the case of the nonaffirming [negation].[937]

[5.23–24] As for the affirming negation, it has been said:

> As for the affirming [negation], there is an object [to be taught].[938]

[5.24–6.1] The commentary [i.e., the *Ldog pa bsdus pa bstan pa'i rnam 'grel*] says:[939]

Question: How is it that there is no object to be taught in the case of the nonaffirming negation? [Answer:] There is no reality to the thing (i.e., object) [it refers to], since making someone understand that [something] does not exist in a particular way, and nothing more, is not to assert any existence of a thing. As for the affirming negation, there is [such a reality to the thing it refers to]. In any case, because the perception of an existence, or [in other words, of] the existence of nonexistence,[940] is postulated, an apprehended thing exists, and thus exists as an objective support.

[6.1–2] In the same [text] it is said:

Likewise, the nonaffirming [negation] applies directly, the affirming one indirectly.[941]

[6.2–6] In the commentary on this it has been explained:

As to the nonaffirming negation, the way the [negating] expression applies is that it applies directly. For example, when you tell blind persons, in order to teach [them], that a hare has no horns: "Because something harsh and sharp has not grown on a [hare's] head, a hare's horn does not exist," you make [them] understand only the nonexistence of a hare's horn, not [the existence of] something else. As to the affirming negation, it applies indirectly. For example, if you describe a Kṣatriya with the words "is not a Brahmin," that which is to be understood by negating Brahmin is something else, [namely] the Kṣatriya. Therefore, it is an indirect way.[942]

[6.6–7] In accordance with the present treatise (i.e., the *Ldog pa bsdus pa*), [Bhavya[943] (490–570)[944]] had stated in the *Tarkajvālā* (i.e., *Madhyamakahṛdaya* III.26ab):

Here, earth and the like [are] not something that has the own-being of the elements on the ultimate level.[945]

[6.7–15] In the commentary on this *[pratīka]* it is said [in the *Tarkajvālā*]:[946]

The [negative particle] *not*[947] is a word indicating negation and must be taken to mean "are not." [Question:] What is not what?

[Answer:] It must be taken to mean that "earth and the like are not something that has the own-being of elements on the ultimate level." Here the negation *not* (Skt. *na*) is a word used for a nonaffirming negation, and not for an affirming negation.

[Question:] What is the difference between the two, affirming and nonaffirming negations? [Answer:] Affirming negation is negating the own-being of a [certain] entity [at the same time] establishing the own-being of another [categorically] similar entity. For example, the negation "he is not a Brahmin" implies [that he is] somebody other than a Brahmin, a non-Brahmin, [that is,] people who are lower in terms of asceticism, studying, and the like. The nonaffirming negation does no more than rule out the own-being of an entity, and so does not affirm another [categorically] similar entity. For example, saying "Brahmins shall not drink alcohol" repudiates only that, and so does not say that they shall drink or not drink some other liquid.

[6.15–18] All proponents of tenets, non-Buddhist and Buddhist [alike], commonly accept that a nonaffirming negation negates whatever is to be negated, and that apart from that nothing else is established, as in the statement "There is no horn on a hare's head." As to the negation "the earth and the like are not something that has the own-being of elements on the ultimate level," [that is,] the ultimate that has been made into a [cognitive] object,[948] it does not refer to the sublime wisdom of self-realization that is free from mental fabrications. [This ultimate,] rather, is pure worldly wisdom endowed with mental fabrications.

[6.18–23] Again from the *Tarkajvālā:*[949]

You may wonder if the ultimate is beyond all [forms of] speech and intellect.[950] Is it therefore not the case that the [the ultimate equated with] the negation of an own-being of an entity is [in reality] not a negation (i.e., not a negation proper), since it is an object [expressed in] words?[951] [Answer:] There are two aspects of the ultimate: One is "having entered into nonactivity *(anabhisaṁskāra)*"[952]—[this is] beyond the world and without stains and mental fabrications. The second [aspect is when] you are engaged in activity—this is in accordance with the accumulation of merit and wisdom; it is pure worldly wisdom endowed with mental fabrications. Here (in the *Madhyamakahṛdaya*) the [second ultimate] is taken as the qualification of the thesis ("does not ultimately exist").[953] Therefore there is no mistake.[954]

[6.23–7.1] Further Candrakīrti said in [his] commentary on [the thirteenth stanza of] the sixteenth chapter of the *[Catuḥ]śataka* (i.e., the *Bodhisattvayogācāraśāstracatuḥśatakaṭīkā*):[955]

> With regard to the nonexistence of all entities
> A differentiation does not make sense.
> What is seen in all things
> Is undifferentiable. (CŚ XVI.13)[956]

> This is because they have arisen from causes and conditions, and because it would follow that [their] own-being consisted of something produced. [On the other hand,] any [possible] own-being of all entities [could] only consist of something without a cause, and since something without a cause cannot have any existence, the own-being is a mere nonexistent *(dngos po med)* based on a nonaffirming negation. This is because it is not an entity *(dngos po)*.

[7.1–4] Therefore it is obvious that only a nonaffirming negation can be taken as the basis for defining[957] the nature [of things], emptiness, and the like. Such an emptiness was called buddha nature by Bhavya, because in the *Tarkajvālā* it has been explained as a reply to the criticism of some śrāvakas that in the Mahāyāna buddha nature is taught as having the defining characteristic of being [all-]pervasive, in contradiction to the seal of nonself:[958]

> [7.4–8] This is because even [the expression] "being endowed with buddha nature" [means that] there is emptiness, signlessness, wishlessness, and the like in the mindstream of all sentient beings. It is not the case that a permanent "personal self"[959] pervades everything. This is because we find [passages] like: "All phenomena [have] the nature of emptiness, signlessness, and wishlessness. Emptiness, signlessness, and wishlessness are the tathāgata, and so on."

[7.8–9] Also, the master Candrakīrti said in [his auto]commentary on the *[Madhyamaka] Avatāra* [VI.42]:[960]

> Since [basic consciousness] follows the nature of all phenomena,[961] it should be understood that mere emptiness is taught in terms of basic consciousness *(ālayavijñāna).*

[7.9–13] Since it is not possible that this master [Candrakīrti] did not see that buddha nature was proclaimed to be the basic consciousness—in the *Laṅkāvatārasūtra* this has been stated in many [passages]—[buddha] nature was accepted [by him] as being emptiness that has the defining characteristics of a nonaffirming negation.[962] It is said that [Candrakīrti] saw the explanation that sentient beings are, [in terms of] this emptiness, buddhas ornamented with the major and minor marks, [that is,] the explanation that [a buddha nature of this kind is ascribed] provisional meaning with reference to the *Laṅkāvatārasūtra,*[963] and thus explained [only in this respect] in [his] *Madhyamakāvatāra* that buddha nature has provisional meaning. It is clear that not the smallest part [of buddha nature] is distinguished [in terms of provisional and definitive meaning].[964]

[7.13–16] The masters Ārya Vimuktisena and Haribhadra have explained the emptiness of a nonaffirming negation as potential *(gotra)* and svābhāvikakāya. The master Jñānagarbha even explained it as dharmakāya, and thus he implicitly asserts that it is [buddha] nature. In this present treatise (RGV I.63ab) it is said:[965]

> The luminous nature of mind, like space, never undergoes change.

[7.16–17] Thus, [buddha nature] is explained [as] suchness *(tathatā).* In the *[Mahāyāna]sūtrālaṁkāra* (XIII.19cd) it is said:

> Luminosity is not another mind *(cetas),* [one] different from the mind as true nature.
> It is taught as being the nature [of mind].[966]

[7.17–20] This and other [passages] explain the true nature of mind, [or] the element of awareness, as [buddha] nature. This explanation is given in many textual traditions of the master Nāgārjuna, such as the *Dharmadhātustotra,* the *Cittavajrastava,* and the *Bodhicittavivaraṇaṭīkā.* Many sūtras of the last [dharma]cakra, too, explain it [thus].

[7.20–22] The explanation of basic consciousness as buddha nature has been taught many times in the *Laṅkāvatāra* and the *Ghanavyūha.* The *Śrīmālādevīsūtra,*[967] the Vajra Songs, and the like have also explained it [as such].

[7.22–23] As for the explanation of sentient beings as buddha nature, in the *Pradīpoddyotana[nāmaṭīkā]*[968] it has been said:

> All sentient beings are buddha natures.

[7.23–24] [Here] in this [text, the *Ratnagotravibhāga*], too, this is explained in [passages] such as:

> The [buddha] element in [its] three states is known under three names.[969] [RGV I.48cd]

The fourfold division of [buddha] nature as explained in this treatise (i.e., the *Ratnagotravibhāga*)[970] will be elucidated later many times and not [further] elaborated here.

[7.24–8.1] Thus I have shortly explained who the author of the *[Ratnagotravibhāga] Mahāyānottaratantraśāstra* was, which master found it, and how it has been transmitted together with two levels of explanation, namely an explanation [of it] in terms of the path of logical inference, based on Madhyamaka works, and the path of directly realizing the meaning of [buddha] nature.

The Commentary for Those with Sharp Faculties

[8.1–3] Now the treatise itself will be explained. There are three levels. For those with sharp faculties who understand as soon as the main points are mentioned, [merely its] name (i.e., title) is explained.[971] For those with average faculties [the treatise] is explained by way of a summary,[972] and for those with dull faculties it is explained by elaborating [each stanza] extensively.[973]

[8.3–4] The title [of the treatise] is:

> **In Sanskrit:** ***Mahāyāna Uttaratantra Śāstra***[974]
> **In Tibetan:** ***Theg pa chen po rgyud bla ma'i bstan bcos***
> **[In English:** ***A Treatise on the Unsurpassable Continuum of the Great Vehicle*****]**[975]

[8.4–6] Those with sharp faculties can usually understand the principal meaning by hearing this title only. How is that? The [term] *treatise* furnishes a general name for the text of the subject matter, and the remaining [terms] a title for the particular [subject matter]. In this regard, Sthiramati has said in [his] *Madhyāntavibhāgaṭīkā:*

[8.6–12] Now it should be explained what the nature of a treatise is, and why it is [called] a treatise. Perceptions that display [the mental forms][976] of an aggregate of names, words, and letters are [what constitutes] a treatise. Or rather, the perceptions that display [the mental form] of specific terms leading to the attainment of supramundane wisdom [make up] a treatise. [Objection:] How are [these acoustic] perceptions produced and expressed? [Answer:] There is nothing wrong [here], since the hearer's perceptions arise from the perceptions of the author and expounder.[977] Since it chastises *(śās)* the disciples, it is a treatise *(śāstra)*. In chastising disciples, it gives rise to a distinctive form of discipline, meditative stabilization, and insight, and thus they abstain from the base deeds of body, speech, and mind, and instead perform suitable deeds.[978]

[8.12–18] Alternatively, it is a treatise because it is in accordance with the defining characteristics of a treatise. These are: that [teaching] which [causes] you to eventually abandon defilements together with [their] imprints by making you familiar with the received teachings, and that protects [you] from [cyclic] existence and the lower realms, which are frightening owing to various incessant and long-lasting violent sufferings. Therefore, since it chastises *(śās)* [your] enemies the defilements, and because it protects *(trai)* [you] from the lower realms and [cyclic] existence, it possesses the defining characteristics of a treatise *(śāstra)*. These two [features] are found in the whole Mahāyāna and in the whole explanation thereof, and nowhere else. Therefore it is a *śās-tra*. Thus it has been said: "That which chastises all [your] enemies, the defilements, and protects you from the lower realms and [cyclic] existence is, owing to these qualities of chastising and protecting, a treatise. These two are not found in other traditions."[979]

[8.18–23] The explanation of the term *treatise* should be taken as it has been taught by this master, [Sthiramati]. The [phrase] "and nowhere else" refers only to outsiders (i.e., non-Buddhists). Since the Śrāvakayāna protects from both the lower realms and [cyclic] existence, it is not included within what is referred to by "else." As to taking "perceptions that display the [mental forms] of names, words, and letters" as [a definition for] a treatise, this follows from having distinguished and explained the analyzed and investigated meanings [of a treatise]. Those who follow what is generally accepted in the world will necessarily take the essence of a treatise to reside in the grand vocalizations whose nature is [mere] sound. [As to] "to chastise and to protect," the verbal root of "to chastise" in Sanskrit is *śās*, and [the Sanskrit root] *trai* is in Tibetan *skyob pa* ("to protect"). The primary [meaning] of the derivatives of these [verbal roots] is taken according to the Sanskrit.

[8.24–9.1] All the Dharma teachings of the teacher are explained on the basis of the insight [which consists of] the ten strengths, the patience of fearlessness, and the quick-wittedness of detailed knowledge. Among [these explanations] is the following [in the *Ratnagotravibhāgavyākhyā*, on I.1]:

> [They (i.e., the seven topics of the *Ratnagotravibhāga*) are "vajra bases"[980]] in that they are the basis or support of vajra-like meaning, [that is, the object] of realization.[981]

Therefore [the teachings] are based on the ability to distinguish right from wrong,[982] on the fearlessness of omniscience, and on the detailed knowledge of word and meaning.

[9.1–4] [Next comes an explanation of the term] *Mahāyāna* [in the title]. With regard to the discourses of the illustrious one, there are teachings whose subject matter is Hīnayāna properly speaking. Among them are the *[Avadāna]śataka*,[983] the *Udānavarga*, the two sets of the four categories of scriptures [of the Vinaya and the sūtras],[984] and the *Bimbisārapratyudgamana[nāma]mahāsūtra.* They are called Hīnayāna, because they express the meaning of the Hīnayāna. The *prajñāpāramitā* sūtras, the presentations of the five perfections, and so forth are called Mahāyāna because they express Mahāyāna.

[9.4–8] When all [the teachings] are summarized, they [can] be presented as the three "wheels of the Dharma" *(dharmacakra)* along the lines of the *Saṁdhinirmocanasūtra.* In this regard, the basket of Hīnayāna [teachings] is the first dharmacakra, while the basket of Mahāyāna is the [teachings of] the middle and last dharmacakras. Belonging as it does to the last of these three [dharmacakras], [the treatise being commented here] is called the "highest continuum" *(Rgyud bla ma).* The term *uttara* (i.e., the Sanskrit equivalent for *bla ma*) means, in terms of direction, *north;* in terms of quality, *supreme;* in terms of substance, *excellence;* and in terms of time, *subsequent.* Of these [its meaning] here is *subsequent,* and *bla ma* is also a synonym of *subsequent.*

[9.8–13] As to *rgyud,* since it means *continuum,* it must be applied, according to circumstances, in the sense of temporary strength. For example, just as the term *gaṇḍi* (trunk of a tree) expresses [one of] the three "[parts of a] continuum" (i.e., the trunk) and the single top, and just as the [phrase] "sound of the melody" expresses the "continuum" of first praising [the Three Jewels], that of [reciting] the sūtra in the middle, and that of finally dedicating [the merit acquired during the ritual,] which consists of the three "[parts of a] continuum" *(rgyud)*,[985] in the same way the three dharmacakras are a continuous [process] of gradually guiding a person, and thus called "[parts of a] continuum." Among them [the *Rgyud bla ma* (i.e., the *Ratnagotravibhāga*)] is called the *subsequent*, the *highest (bla ma)* or *supreme* [continuum *(rgyud)*, that is, the final dharmacakra]. This meaning has been expounded in the following lines (II.73cd) of this *[Ratnagotravibhāga]:*

> Therefore this final stage of the Buddha[986] is unknown
> Even to the great sages who have obtained empowerment.[987]

[9.13–14] If somebody requests: "When the Mahāyāna is explained in the discourses [of the Buddha], express [its] meaning, [namely] Mahāyāna itself!" it must be expressed. The opposite of great *(mahā-)* is inferior *(hīna)*, and this is the vehicle *(yāna)* of the śrāvakas and pratyeka[buddhas]. In the *Mahāyānasūtrālaṁkāra* [I.9–10] and the *bhāṣya* on it, it is stated:

> [9.14–15] For the following reasons Śrāvakayāna is not called Dharma of Mahāyāna: it is incomplete, contradictory, without skillful means, and not taught in such a way.[988]
>
> [9.15–25] [The *bhāṣya* on this stanza is:] "It is incomplete" with respect to teaching the benefit of others. In Śrāvakayāna, benefit for others has not been taught at all, the śrāvakas being taught the skillful means of aversion, detachment, and liberation for themselves only. Merely teaching others [the need] to benefit themselves does not deserve to be [called] benefit for others. "It is contradictory": the other being used for your own benefit, [your mind] is bent exclusively on your own benefit. That somebody whose [mind] is bent on nirvāṇa[989] for himself alone should fully awaken to unsurpassable perfect enlightenment is contradictory. Even though he has been intently occupied with the means of enlightenment according to Śrāvakayāna for a long time, [a śrāvaka] is not fit to become a buddha. "It is without skillful means" means Śrāvakayāna has no skillful means for attaining[990] buddhahood. He who has striven for [enlightenment] without skillful means, for however long a time,[991] does

not attain the desired goal. It is like milking horns and the like.[992] Well then, is the way a bodhisattva should train taught any differently here? It is not taught in such a way. Śrāvakayāna by itself is not worthy of Mahāyāna. You do not find in it such a teaching. Since Śrāvakayāna and Mahāyāna only contradict each other, there is [here] a stanza on [their] mutual contradiction:[993]

> [9.25–26] Because [the two *yānas*] contradict [each other] in terms of intention, teaching, practice,
> Reliance, and time, the inferior *(hīna)[yāna]* really *is* inferior.[994] (MSA I.10)

> [9.26–10.5] [The *bhāṣya* on this stanza is:] How do they contradict [each other]? They contradict each other through a fivefold contradiction, namely a contradiction in terms of aspiration, teaching, practice, reliance, and time. In the Śrāvakayāna the aspiration is nirvāṇa[995] for yourself alone. The teaching is for the sake of this [goal] alone, as is the practice. Reliance, which consists of the accumulation of merit and wisdom, is limited.[996] The time is also shorter.[997] Their goal is attained within only three lifetimes. In Mahāyāna everything is opposite to that. Thus they contradict each other, and as a consequence the inferior *yāna* really is inferior. It is not worthy of Mahāyāna.[998]

[10.5–9] To attain the desired goal within three lifetimes—this [possibility] exists for bodhisattvas, too. Thus, we may wonder why in the *[Yogācārabhūmi]viniścayasaṁgrahaṇī* it has been stated that some arhats who turned toward [full] enlightenment [did so by] hiding in an isolated place in their physical body, while completely perfecting the accumulation of enlightenment with an emanation body that is qualitatively similar, and attaining buddha[hood] together with it. [Answer:] Even though something like that may be possible, how could [you reckon with only] one lifetime, [compared to] this emanation body undergoing birth and death many times? It would be necessary, then, for [such arhats] to complete [the accumulations] in innumerable [lifetimes] three [times over].

[10.9–15] The vehicle that is wholly great is called Mahāyāna because these five points—aspiration, practice, and so forth,[999] are not inferior. The term *yāna*, or vehicle, refers to *going*. *[Yāna]* in the instrumental [refers to] that upon which[1000] you go, [namely,] the paths of being in partial concordance with liberation[1001] up to the tenth level.[1002] Used in the locative, it [refers to] the place where you go, [namely,] the level of a buddha itself. Even though the way the two terms (i.e., *yāna* in the instrumental and locative) are understood is therefore different, according to such great treatises[1003] the level of a buddha may also be referred to by using the term in the instrumental. This has been said, among other places, in the *[Prajñāpāramitāratnaguṇa]saṁcayagāthā* [I.21]:

> "Why is it called the vehicle *(yāna)* of enlightenment?"
> Riding on it takes all sentient beings beyond misery.
> This vehicle is a mansion, like [limitless] space;
> It is the great vehicle that lets you attain direct happiness and joy.[1004]

[10.15–20] Accordingly, the term *vehicle* is also a synonym of *mount,* and carrying as it does all sentient beings to the mansion of unsurpassable enlightenment, it is called the *great vehicle.* Since such load-bearing is not found among the śrāvakas and pratyekabuddhas, [their vehicle] is called an inferior mount. Yogācāras are generally subsumed strictly under the Mahāyāna, but they take the teachings to the effect that [some] sentient beings definitely do not pass into nirvāṇa in the sense that [those] beings do not have a chance to pass into nirvāṇa at all, not that they do not have [such] a chance only temporarily. Moreover, they maintain that the arhats of the other two *yānas* will definitely not be able to become [practitioners of] the Mahāyāna after they have entered [nirvāṇa] without remainder.

[10.20–25] In the *Tattvaratnāvalī,* composed by Lord Maitrīpa, it is said:

> Here there are three *yānas*, the so-called Śrāvakayāna, Pratyeka[buddha]yāna, and Mahāyāna. There are four positions, according to the division into Vaibhāṣika, Sautrāntika, Yogācāra, and Mādhyamika.[1005] In this regard, it is according to the position of the Vaibhāṣikas that the Śrāvakayāna and Pratyeka[buddha]yāna are explained.[1006] Mahāyāna is twofold, the so- called tradition of pāramitās and the one of mantras. With regard to Pāramitāyāna, there are three [divisions], explained[1007] [respectively] according to the positions of the Sautrāntikas, Yogācāras, and Mādhyamikas.[1008]

[10.25–11.1] Therefore the Sautrāntikas are taken to be followers of Mahāyāna. Likewise in accordance with Maitrīpa, the mahāsiddha Saroruha explains in his commentary on the eighth chapter of the appendix to the *Hevajratantra* [that]:

The so-called Sautrāntikas are Mahāyāna-Sautrāntikas.

[11.1–4] Moreover, Nāgārjuna has stated in his *Ratnāvalī* [V.85–87]:

As long as any sentient being
Anywhere has not been liberated[, even a single one],[1009]
May I remain [in this world] for the sake of [that being],
Even after attaining unsurpassable enlightenment.[1010]

If the merit of he who says this
Had form,
It would not fit into [all] the world's realms,
As numerous as the [grains of] sand of the Gaṅgā.[1011]

This is what the illustrious one said,
And the reason for it is apparent:
[The merit] should be known[1012] to be of the same extent
[As the wish] to benefit the limitless realm of sentient beings.[1013]

[11.4–11] Thus the limitless realm of sentient beings has been taken as the reason for the limitless merit dedicated to sentient beings. The Yogācāras generate [bodhi]citta [out of a] wish to bring all sentient beings possessing [the corresponding] potential to enlightenment, even though [the latter] are limitless inasmuch they cannot be counted. Similarly those without the potential are likewise innumerable and limitless in the tradition of these [Yogācāras]. Also those who abide in the extreme state of quiescence are innumerable and limitless as well. Therefore, since [the Yogācāras also] lack the mental strength to resolutely bring those [arhats] to buddha[hood], it is quite evident that [their] mental strength is inferior to [that of] the Mādhyamikas. As to the wish on the part of the Yogācāras being [limited] in such a way, this is very clearly explained in the *Madhyamakāloka*, where it sets forth [the position of] the Yogācāras as the opponent[s'] view. I [can] only claim or think that the Sautrāntikas are similar [to the Yogācāras].

[11.11–13] As to *great (mahā-)*, in the *Mahāyānasūtrālaṁkāra* [XIX.59–60] it has been taught [as referring to] the seven[fold] greatness:

The greatness of the focus, [the greatness] of the two
accomplishments,
Of wisdom, of initiating effort, of skill in means,

> The greatness of final achievement,[1014] and the greatness of buddha activity—
> Since it has this [sevenfold] greatness, it is called Mahāyāna.[1015]

[II.13–15] All these seven are also taught in this *[Ratnagotravibhāga]*. In [RGV V.15cd] the greater focus is taught:[1016]

> Insight is supreme [among the *pāramitās*], and its source is studying. Therefore studying is supreme.[1017]

[II.15–16] In [RGV I.39ab] the greatness of accomplishment is taught:

> Having cut off all affection for himself by means of insight,
> [The bodhisattva,] being full of mercy, does not attain[1018] quiescence, out of [his] affection for sentient beings.[1019]

[II.16–17] In [RGV I.13b] the greatness of the wisdom of realizing both [types of] selflessness is taught:

> [...and, as a consequence, have completely realized] the extreme limit of the selflessness of all [sentient beings and] the world as quiescent....[1020]

[II.17–18] In [RGV II.62ab] the [twofold] greatness of effort and skill in means is taught:

> Having limitless causes, having [as a focus of his activity] an inexhaustible [number of buddha] elements in sentient beings,[1021] possessing mercy, powers, wisdom, and perfection, [...the protector of the world is eternal].[1022]

[II.18–19] As to the greatness of final achievement, it is taught in the chapter on qualities, and as to great activity, it is extensively taught in the fourth chapter.

[II.19–20] The "greatness of the Mahāyāna" [as exemplified] in the *prajñāpāramitā* is explained [in *Abhisamayālaṁkāra* I.43ab]:

> The mind [that takes each sentient being as] the supreme among all sentient beings,[1023] abandoning, and realization—with regard to these three....[1024]

[11.20–22] It is also explained very well in this [treatise here]. As to the "taking of each sentient being as supreme among all sentient beings," it is taught [in RGV IV.2c]:

> Having seen that buddhahood is indistinguishable in all sentient beings, whose treasure is the stainless qualities....[1025]

[11.22–23] and the greatness of abandoning is taught [in RGV IV.2d]:

> The compassion of the victorious ones, like wind, blows away the net of the cloud[-like hindrances of] defilements and the intellect.[1026]

[11.23–24] The greatness of realization is taught in passages such as [RGV I.26a]:

> That which must be realized, realization (i.e., enlightenment)....[1027]

[11.24–12.1] Somebody may ask: As for the uninterrupted discourses of the three dharmacakras, they [present] a continuum *(rgyud)* of [different types of] subject matter, [but] if so, how is the continuum of the [actual] objects of [these types of] subject matter [referred to]? In this treatise [of RGV I.132] it is said:

> [In the previous stanzas] it was stated that the natural purity of the mind, which has no beginning, lies within sentient beings' sheaths of defilements, similarly beginningless, which have no connection [with the mind's natural purity].[1028]

[12.1–3] Thus we have two continua with regard to what is without beginning, while [according to RGV I.79b and so forth:]

> [Buddha nature]...is the refuge in the world, because it has no limit in the future....[1029]

there are two continua with regard to what has no limit [in the future]. Thus four continua are taught.

[12.3–5] In the appendix[1030] of the *[Guhya]samājatantra* [XVIII.33–34] it has been said:

A continuum *(rgyud)* is called a continuous [flow].
The continuous [flow] may be threefold,
Corresponding to the classification into basis,
Nature, and the irresistible.

[Its] nature is the cause of well-formed appearance *(ākṛti),*
[Its] basis the "[skillful] means,"
And [its] irresistibility the fruit.[1031]
The meaning of *continuum* includes these three.[1032]

[12.5–6] It has also been taught here [in RGV I.48cd]:

The buddha element is, corresponding to [its] three states, taught under three names.[1033]

[12.6–10] This has also been taught in the *Vajraśikhara[mahāguhya]tantra:*[1034]

Why is this [called] subsequent continuum?

Continuum [means] "continuous [flow]."
Saṁsāra is taken to be a continuum,
[Your continuum is] a "subsequent one" when you have gone beyond [saṁsāra];
It is called a subsequent continuum.

Continuum [means] "continuous [flow]."
The subsequent [one] is the suchness arisen from the former [one];
It is known for being secret and hidden.
It is called the subsequent continuum.

Why is it a continuum and subsequent?

It is the supreme victorious one of the perfected level:
[His continuum] has broken out from the prison of [cyclic] existence.
In other words, whatever has broken free
Is termed the subsequent of the continuum.

[12.10–17] When [attempting to] briefly clarify this and the question before, we are here [faced with] what the terms of [the question] "Why is it a continuum and subsequent?" mean. The meaning of *continuum* is to be a continuous [flow]. As long as you have not reached [the first bodhisattva] level [called] Very Joyful, [your existence in] saṁsāra is in a continuous [flow]. Thus it is called a continuum. From the level [called] Very Joyful onward, you perform buddha activity for as long as space exists, and this is a continuum [as well]. Once it has gone beyond saṁsāra, [your continuum] is called subsequent. Even if you condense this down to saṁsāra and purification, it is [still] a single continuum, given the continuous connection resulting from its having arisen from a [previous state], that is, given that the subsequent [continuum], [or] purification, has arisen from a previous [one], [or] saṁsāra. What has been so condensed into a single [continuum] is reality, the luminous nature of mind. Having been hindered by ignorance in the previous state of saṁsāra, it was like a secret treasure. As a result of knowledge it has [now] become the continuum of purification. Thus [the questions] are explained.[1035]

[12.17–21] In the explanation of the subsequent [continuum] above, [it was taken to be] simply the [state of] having gone beyond [saṁsāra]. [Then] it was asked, "Why is it a continuum and subsequent?" The answer [is:] [Sanskrit] *tara* [has] the meaning of "having broken free/out" or "having liberated yourself." [The Sanskrit prefix] *ud*[1036] has the meaning of "very" *(lhag pa)*, "on" *(steng)*, "subsequent" *(phyi ma)*, or "superior" *(rab)*, and so forth. Thus a great bodhisattva of the final level [first] went beyond saṁsāra [to reach] the level [called] Very Joyful. As to the clause "having reached the ultimate level[s] after crossing over *(brgal)* the ocean-like level of mental imprints caused by ignorance" in the *Daśabhūmika[sūtra]*, it needs to be taught in exact words: "because you have crossed over *(brgal)* the [ocean...], you have become somebody who has 'broken out/free' *(brgal)*...."[1037]

[12.21–23] To sum up these explanations, it has been said in the *Dharmadhātustotra* (stanza 2):

> Whatever the cause of saṁsāra is—this very thing has been purified.
> Thus nirvāṇa is this purity, and the dharmakāya, too, is precisely this.

[12.23–26] This method [of teaching] is truly fantastic! Throughout beginningless time—that long—you have repeatedly experienced immeasurable suffering in the cities of the six realms. Through all that[, however,] your buddha nature has not rotted, and by its power your potential is awakened, resulting in an even stronger aversion toward saṁsāra. When you have [finally] found enlightenment, for as long as space lasts, you will abide as the [buddha] element of sentient beings, which are [but a] continuous flow of defilements and suffering.

[12.26–13.1] Also with regard to the continuum of [different types of] subject matter: although this treatise teaches the meaning of all the *yānas*, still its main subject is the subsequent or unsurpassable [dharma]cakra.

[13.1] Homage to all buddhas and bodhisattvas.[1038]

[13.1–2] This [homage] has been inserted by the translators in order to mitigate obstacles and render [their work] auspicious.

The Commentary for Those with Average Faculties

[13.2–6] The explanation that [elucidates] the concise meaning for those with average faculties[1039] has three [points]: an explanation of the meaning together with the aim [of the treatise], the canonical texts *(lung)* with which [the treatise] is associated, and the explanation of [how] the former topics are related to the subsequent ones.[1040] As to the first [point], Master Vasubandhu said in [a text called] "What Has Been Obtained [as] an *Upadeśa* of the Venerable [Maitreya]":[1041]

> To those whose intellect is inferior to mine
> And who wish to explain the sūtras,
> I will give a minor instruction:[1042]
> You must state the aim [of the sūtra], together with its concise meaning,
> The meaning of the words, the sequence [of] or connections [between its different topics],
> And the contradictions [pointed out by opponents] together with their rebuttals.[1043]

[13.6–10] Clever disciples [who need to be guided by] the treatise wonder what the subject matter of this treatise is, what the aim and the ultimate aim (i.e., the attainable aim) of the subject matter are, and what the nature of the connection between the subject matter *(abhidheya)* and the text *(abhidhāna)* is. To those who have become engaged in an investigation marked by such initial doubts, I will address these [points[1044]] by [elucidating] the concise meaning [of the treatise]. With regard to those who are both faithful und clever, I will explain it in the form [of a full-fledged commentary on] the five chapters.

The Explanation of RGV I.1

[13.10–11] As to the subject matter, it is taught in [the following points]:

> **The Buddha, [his] teaching and community, [his] element, enlightenment, [and] qualities, and finally the activity of the Buddha.**[1045] [RGV I.1ab]

[13.12–18] As for the aim of the subject matter, it is not the aim of merely [explaining the motive of] the subject matter, but also the realization of the subject matter.[1046] Here, [in the *pāda*] "is the seven vajra points,"[1047] the seven points of the subject matter are [each] called a *vajra* because they are very difficult to realize by hearing and thinking about. As for the treatise, it has been taught as a basis [for understanding] these [points], and so the connection between the defining characteristics of the subject matter *(abhidheya)* and the text *(abhidhāna)* is clarified. As for what makes you realize the individual subject matter, it is not proper [to think of this as] a particular aim, given all the common phraseology [used in the treatise]. The aim is[, however,] once you know that [the subject matter] has a meaning that, like a vajra, is difficult to analyze,[1048] you [come to] know that it is a discourse on the essence (i.e., buddha nature), which has definitive meaning. The ultimate (i.e., attainable) aim is the direct actualization [of the subject matter] as the result of cultivating meditation in stages, which has been grounded in an initial faith because this meaning of [buddha] nature (as has been stated) is difficult to determine by hearing and thinking about.[1049]

[13.18–23] With regard to the explanation of the seven points: once this treatise, [this] great discourse, has explained one principal point and connected [it] with the others as with its branches, the aim of teaching [their] connection will be thoroughly understood. If somebody therefore asks which of these seven points is the principal one, [the answer is that] the Buddha is the principal one, because the other six points are defined by describing his qualities. This has been taught in the words [of RGV I.3], which show the successive interconnections of the seven [points]:

> From the Buddha [comes] the teaching and from the teaching the noble community.
> Within [the setting of] the community, [buddha] nature leads to the attainment of the [buddha] element of wisdom.[1050]
> And the attainment of this wisdom is the highest enlightenment,

> Which is endowed with properties, such as the [ten] strengths, that benefit all sentient beings.[1051] [RGV I.3]

[13.23–25] Now, these seven points will be explained. As for the stages of the seven [points]: since on the path of the supreme vehicle the engendering of a mind committed to enlightenment is like a caravan leader, they are in accordance with the stages of correctly arousing [such] a mind, as has been explained in detail in the *Mañjuśrīvikrīḍitasūtra* in the following passage:[1052]

> [13.25–14.7] Mañjuśrī decked [his] body out with ornaments and put on bright clothes [from which light shone].[1053] He positioned himself along the way the [noble] prostitute *Suvarṇaprabhāśrī[1054] was coming, and [when she reached him,] she got down from her chariot and clutched the clothes Mañjuśrī had on. Mañjuśrī told her: "I will give you [my] clothes if you enter [the path] to enlightenment."[1055] So the young woman asked what enlightenment was like. When Mañjuśrī elucidated the meaning of enlightenment in broad terms, starting with emptiness, she opened up to the Dharma,[1056] became very joyful, and touched both feet of the youthful Mañjuśrī. She took refuge in the Buddha, Dharma, and Saṅgha, fully embraced abstinence *(brahmacarya)* and the [other] moral commandments,[1057] generated with strong determination a mind committed to unsurpassable perfect enlightenment (i.e., bodhicitta) and spoke the following words: "Mañjuśrī, I too will generate a mind committed to the unsurpassable perfect enlightenment, as taught by you, so that, based on what you have taught, [namely,] love and compassion for all sentient beings, the lineage of the Buddha will not be disrupted, the lineage of the Dharma will not be disrupted, and the lineage of the Saṅgha will not be disrupted." And so forth.

[14.8–11] Taking refuge in the Three Jewels has been explicitly taught in this [treatise,] too. The objective support for arousing [bodhi]citta is the welfare of others and enlightenment [for yourself]. As for the others from among [these two: other and self], the [others] are the sentient beings for whose sake [bodhi]citta is cultivated. So it has been taught here [in this treatise], in [the chapter] "Suchness Mingled with Stains." [This also] because the impure [buddha] element has been called a sentient being in [RGV I.47]:

> [Depending on whether the buddha element is] impure, [partly] impure and [partly] pure, or perfectly pure, it is called a sentient being,[1058] bodhisattva, or tathāgata respectively.[1059]

[14.11–15] The welfare of others has been taught in [the chapter on] activity. As to enlightenment, which is the cause of the activity, it has been taught in the chapter on enlightenment. The qualities are the instruments or tools with the help of which enlightenment works for the sake of others. All seven must be understood in terms of the two truths. In this regard, the Three Jewels in terms of the ultimate [truth] has been explained in [RGV I.21]:[1060]

> Ultimately, buddhahood is the only refuge for the world, because the Sage has the Dharma as his body, and the Community "sets it (i.e., buddhahood) as its ultimate goal."[1061]

[14.15–17] What follows (i.e., RGV I.22) is buddhahood on the level of apparent [truth], the bodies in terms of the apparent [truth] being explained as being for the sake of others. The Dharma and Saṅgha on the level of apparent truth are taught in [RGV I.20]:

> [The Dharma] will be abandoned [and] is of a deceptive nature and nonexistent, and [the Saṅgha] is fearful.
> Therefore, the two kinds of Dharma and the Noble Community are ultimately not the supreme refuge.[1062]

[14.17–19] The teaching of buddha nature explained in terms of emptiness [leads to] ultimate suchness mingled with stains, while in [passages] like:

> If there is no buddha element, there will be no aversion even to suffering[1063] (RGV I.40ab)

the appropriated potential is explained. Thus this is [the buddha element] on the level of apparent [truth].

[14.19–22] To explain the function of enlightenment, ultimate enlightenment is explained in terms of the svābhāvikakāya, and enlightenment on the level of apparent [truth] in terms of the two form kāyas. The thirty-two qualities of dissociation [from hindrances] are the ultimate ones, and the thirty-two qualities of maturation are those of apparent [truth]. The dharmakāya, the master of activity, belongs to the ultimate, and the form kāyas belong to the apparent [truth]. Thus explaining [the seven vajra points] with two aspects each results in fourteen categories.

[14.22–15.1] Among these [seven vajra points] I shall first explain the [buddha] element. If it be asked why, it is because the [buddha] element is called emptiness or suchness, and therefore known as suchness pure and simple, while every explanation of the seven [vajra points] in their ultimate aspects differs only with regard to [whether they] are purified from stains or not. In this regard, emptiness as explained in the middle [dharma]cakra is taught as being a nonaffirming negation, in the sense of being empty of an own-being that is not mixed with other own-beings; and it needs to be realized by the perceiving subject *(yul can)* [on the basis of] an inferential valid cognition. It is also described as not having arisen from any causes and conditions at all, as explained in the *Satyadvayavibhāgavṛtti* (4ab):

> [15.1–3] An understanding[1064] arisen through a logical proof [that fulfills] the three criteria [of a syllogism] is the ultimate *(paramārtha),* because it is the aim *(artha)* plus the supreme *(parama).* Also, the object that is determined by it is described as the ultimate [object] *(paramārtha),* just as a direct perception [can be either a cognition or an object].[1065]

[15.3–8] As it is said in the *Prasannapadā:*

> "How can an own-being be [artificially] created?"[1066] To be both created and [have] an own-being—this has no coherent meaning, [the two] contradicting each other. Here, own-being means being in itself, and according to this etymology, a created thing is nowhere in the world called an own-being, just like the heat of hot water, for example, or the creation[1067] of rubies and the like from such things as quartz crystals through the efforts of an alchemist. That which is not created is an own-being,[1068] for example, the hotness of fire or the own-being of such things as the "rubiness" of genuine rubies. This is called their own-being because it has not arisen from contact with other things.[1069]

[15.8–10] Here, in the last dharmacakra, you ascribe such an emptiness to the outer husk and then determine the emptiness that is [buddha] nature.[1070] This is not a nonaffirming negation of an own-being but the [buddha] element of awareness, for it has been said in [RGV 106b]:

> Having seen the [buddha] element of awareness, which is like honey.[1071]

[15.10–12] [This element] is not an object concretized by inferential [cognition] but rather an object of direct [cognition]. Even though it has not arisen from causes and conditions, it is not the case that it has not arisen at all. In the same way as the element of space evolves within its own sphere, [the buddha element] does rather not, in [its natural] flow, undergo change because of contact with other phenomena.

[15.12–18] Also, the great Madhyamaka masters assert that the sūtras of the last dharmacakra are authoritative, and it is not the case that they do not accept the emptiness of [buddha] nature. For in [Bhavya's] *Prajñāpradīpa* it has been said:

> Since it is [mainly] dependent arising qualified as nonorigination and so forth that has been taught [by the illustrious one], the subject matter of [this] treatise [here is accordingly].[1072] The nonconceptual wisdom[, namely,] the ultimate [state] of not conceptualizing this nectar[-like] reality [of dependent arising], apprehends an object, which is like the stainless autumn sky. [This,] the complete pacification of all mental fabrications, the freedom from difference and identity, and the quiescence, which must be realized by oneself, have been pointed out [in this treatise]. The way of the illustrious one [corresponds to this] reality, but somebody with base thoughts may not believe [in it]. Therefore, it (i.e., reality) is [basically] apprehended because of the preeminence of mainly inferential cognitions.[1073]

[15.18–20] Here again, in the last dharmacakra, the hotness of fire and so forth is used as an example, it having been said in the *Bodhicittavivaraṇa* (stanza 57):[1074]

> I claim that the nature *(prakṛti)* of all phenomena is emptiness, in the same way as sweetness is the nature of sugar and hotness that of fire.[1075]

[15.20–16.2] The negandum, too, that of which something is empty, is [here] a little different from [how it is defined in] the middle [dharma]cakra. From sentient beings up to the Buddha [something] exists [that is] established as the nature of mind because of being neither impaired by, nor fabricated under, other conditions. It is thus called *empty of fabricated adventitious phenomena.* The adventitious, again, [consists of] mind insofar as it is:

a. The direct cognition of blue, yellow, and so forth, as long as it is colored into various objective mental forms *(ākāra).*[1076]
b. The mental form of the perceiving subject *(grāhakākāra)* of this.
c. The mental form of an object appearing to the conceptual [faculty,] which (form and concept) have arisen by the power of mental imprints left by the appearances of direct cognition.
d. The mental form of perceiving, which is the subject of this [object].
e. The appearances of inferential cognitions, as explained in the Madhyamaka, together with the mental forms of [their] perception.
f. The mental forms of such appearances as falling strands of hair or yellow conch shells created by impaired sense faculties.
g. The mental forms of perceiving these [things].
h. The appearances in clear dreams.
i. That which has arisen from meditation, such as on a skeleton or [involving] the total [fixation of the mind].[1077]
j. The appearances of defiled clairvoyance.
k. The appearances of concentration and the formless [absorptions].
l. The appearances of objects during śrāvakas' and pratyekabuddhas' realization of the selflessness of persons.
m. The mental forms of perceiving these [appearances] (i.e., h–l).

[16.2–7] Depending on the circumstances, all these are fabricated from [cognitive] objects, [mental] imprints, or impaired sense faculties, and thus not what the original mind is like. Therefore the original mind is said to be empty of them. On the other hand, they do not arise as something entirely different from the nature of mind. It is like space, for example: even though it does not turn into phenomena like clouds and mountains, and is thus termed empty, it would not be appropriate to say that these clouds and so forth abide somewhere else than in space. Moreover, in view of their being produced out of ignorance, even the outer material world and the bodies of sentient beings are artificial [or fabricated], and thus [themselves] neganda, things of which [the buddha element] is empty.

[16.7–12] The Buddha does not see this element of awareness as [having] any of the mental forms of [characteristic] signs, for it has been said in the *Bodhicittavivaraṇa* (stanzas 43–46):[1078]

In short, buddhas did not see[, do not see,] and will not see.[1079]
How could they see what has the nature of lacking an own-being?[1080]

An entity is a concept; [whereas] the nonconceptual is emptiness.
Where concepts have appeared, how can there be emptiness?[1081]

A mind that [manifests] the mental forms of a cognitive object and subject is not seen by the tathāgatas.
Wherever there is a cognitive object and subject, there is no enlightenment.[1082]

That which is without defining characteristics and origination, without abiding and beyond words—
Space, bodhicitta, and enlightenment—[all share] the defining characteristics of nonduality.[1083]

[16.12–16] In the *Madhyāntavibhāga* [I.14–15] it has been said:

In short, the synonyms of emptiness are: suchness, the limit of existence,
Being without characteristic signs, the ultimate, and the dharmadhātu.

The meaning of the synonyms follows respectively from the fact that [emptiness is] unchangeable, not mistaken,
Their [i.e., the characteristic signs'] cessation, the object of the noble ones, and the cause (in the sense of *sphere*)[1084] of the qualities of the noble ones.[1085]

Also, the synonyms taught here should be applied to both forms of emptiness, those of nonaffirming negation and of awareness.

[16.16–17] The lord of this doctrine (i.e., the *Ratnagotravibhāga*), the father, the venerable Maitrīpa, and his son [Sahajavajra] assert that the emptiness taught in the *Madhyamakāvatāra* is middling Madhyamaka, the emptiness of awareness being the tradition of supreme Madhyamaka.

[16.17–21] You may ask if Mādhyamikas first determine emptiness by logical inference and then get used to it, [and] if you accept that [the process of] getting used to what logical inference has revealed counteracts conceptual [effort], and that [as a consequence of this] a direct cognition arises, in the same way as a fire kindled from rubbing pieces of wood burns these very same pieces, does then an unobstructed direct cognition arise within this "awareness-emptiness" *(rig pa stong pa nyid)* of the last dharmacakra? Is there an investigative valid cognition or not? If there is one, what is it like?

[16.21–17.3] In the tradition of the followers of pith instructions this has been taught to some: "Investigate thoroughly day and night what your mind is like." Thus the notion of investigation is given first. Some are then instructed: "Having given up [unnecessary] thinking[1086] about past, present, and future, settle[1087] [your mind] in an unwavering state. As a result, what is called *one-pointedness* will arise. It has the defining characteristics of a direct cognition. Once it has arisen, watch the mind, which will meditate in such a way that this direct cognition itself is turned inward." Then [the guru] will cause [the disciple to remain in this state of] mere gazing. He causes [the disciple to remain in such a state of] mere gazing after having made him wonder, for example, whether there are sentient beings in [a particular body of] water, and [so made him] focus his eyes. This is a way of investigating by means of nonconceptual direct cognition. From this arises the direct perception that all phenomena lack a [truly existent] self. The sense faculty associated with the eyes, which sees the water in the above [example], stands for devotion to, and respect for, the lama who sees the truth. The eye consciousness stands for the direct cognition that is turned inward.

[17.3–9] This mode [of this investigative cognition is taught in the following *pāda*s] of this *[Ratnagotravibhāga]:*

> ...who see that—in view of the natural luminosity of that mind—defilements lack an own-being.... [RGV I.13a]

This teaches one-pointedness, while [the *pāda*]:

> ...and, as a consequence, have completely realized the extreme limit of the selflessness of all sentient beings and the world as quiescent.... [RGV I.13b][1088]

teaches the direct realization of selflessness, and this is also given the name *yoga of freedom from mental fabrication.* Freedom from mental fabrication is not merely a nonaffirming negation, but [also] a quality of awareness that cannot be established as any[thing with] characteristic signs. The finger of mahāmudrā points to the momentary awareness, which does not come down on either of the [two] sides, appearance or emptiness. Thus say those versed in the pith instructions. Even though this tradition belongs to the Pāramitāyāna, it is labeled mahāmudrā. Thus it is explained in the *Tattvadaśakaṭīkā* by Sahajavajra. It is also explained in the *Tattvāvatāra* by Jñānakīrti in the root text and its commentary.[1089]

[17.9–11] Likewise in the teaching of Pagmo Drupa:

> The actual "path of liberation"[1090] is the mahāmudrā yoga of awareness and emptiness. It is not [successfully traversed] by a mere analytical meditation on emptiness. Even though you may have meditated on an intellectually understood emptiness for eons,[1091] there is no possibility of throwing off the bonds of [this] golden chain.[1092]

[17.11–19] In this regard, his outstanding disciples said at length, among other things:

> The right guru, [that is, one who embodies] a condition different [from yourself],
> Brings about [your] maturation;
> Still, the causal connection of devotion and respect is wonderful,
> Since [maturation] will be accomplished by a profound causal connection,
> As in the case of the sun and its rays of light
> Or a seed and its fruit.
> If [your] devotion and respect is developed properly,
> [Your] realization will follow accordingly.
> And the emptiness that you analyze
> With the insight *(shes rab)* of listening and reflection
> Without proper devotion and respect
> Is taken by the guru to be an intellectually understood empti[ness].
> Likewise the preliminary realizations *(nyams)* and experiences—
> Those realizations put in the mind
> By the profound teaching of the victorious one,
> The songs of the previous mahāsiddhas,
> And the words of the four yogas—
> May arise very easily
> In a person who has no devotion or respect,
> But [your] defilements and concepts are not [easily] abandoned.
> How will you cross the ocean of saṁsāra then?

Without knowing what it is to be free from mental fabrication,
How will you abandon the characteristic signs of mental
fabrication?
Without realizing the luminosity of nonorigination,
How will you cut the stream of origination?[1093]

[17.19–24] In the same way as you know, by drinking a random handful of ocean water, the taste of all [the rest of it] which you have not drunk, a yogin who knows the reality of his own mind will know the seven [vajra] points as they really are, [that is,] the reality of the mind of sentient beings from the Avīci [hell] up to the dharmakāya of a buddha. For it is said in the *Śrīmālādevīsūtra:*

> Illustrious one, whoever has no doubts that that which is covered by the extremity of the sheath of all defilements is [still] buddha nature has also no doubts about the dharmakāya of the tathāgata, who is liberated from the sheath of all defilements.[1094]

[17.24–18.2] As for the [first vajra point,] the Buddha, we must take as a measure what earlier scholars say in the *Sgra sbyor bam po gnyis pa:*

> With regard to the synonyms of the name of Buddha—if you [attempt to] derive [etymologic meaning] from the word *buddhaḥ*—one is [as follows]: *mohanidrāpramardanāt(?)*[1095] *prabuddhapuruṣavat,* [which means]: "[he is] like a person awakened from sleep *(gnyid sangs pa)* having awakened from the sleep of delusion"; [thus] you strive for awakening. Another synonym *(rnam=rnam grangs?)* is explained [as follows]: *buddher vikāsanād buddha[ḥ //]*[1096] *vibuddhapadmavat,* [which means]: "[he is] like an open *(vi-?),* blossomed *(-buddha?)*[1097] lotus, since his intellect has opened and blossomed *(bye zhing rgyas pas).*" [To sum up,] he is called "[the one whose intellect] has awakened *(sangs)* and blossomed *(rgyas).*" The general meaning of the word is that he thoroughly knows all phenomena and is [thus] completely enlightened.

[18.2–7] As for the actual usage of the word Buddha, whether (depending on circumstances) truly or metaphorically, it has been said in the *Āryadharmasaṁgītisūtra:*[1098]

Son of a noble family, a bodhisattva should thoroughly know [the meaning of the word] Buddha on the basis of the ten [forms of] entering the way of the Dharma. If you ask which ten, they are: the Buddha of the natural outflow, the Buddha arisen from maturation, the Buddha of samādhi, the Buddha of aspiration, the Buddha of the mind, the Buddha of the true nature, the Buddha of enjoyment, the Buddha of emanation, the metaphorical Buddha, and the Buddha (i.e., statues, etc.) that you place in front of yourself.

[18.7–9] Here, if you ask what the Buddha of the natural outflow is, [the answer is:] That which is established from both the natural outflow of the *pāramitās* and the achievement of the qualities of the *pāramitās* is the Buddha of achievement. Therefore he is called the *Buddha of the natural outflow.*

[18.9–12] If you ask what the Buddha arisen from maturation is, he is the maturation of the natural outflow [of] the *pāramitās*. It is what arises from this maturation in the form of the Buddha of maturation. He blesses sentient beings and comes into being by the blessing of the Dharma. This is what is referred to as the *Buddha arisen from maturation.*

[18.12–14] If you ask what the Buddha of samādhi is, [he is] the samādhi into which the tathāgata is absorbed and [from which,] once absorbed, a hundred thousand buddhas arise spontaneously, without the tathāgata making [any] effort. It is by the blessing of [this] samādhi that [buddhas] have arisen from [this] samādhi; therefore they are called *buddhas of samādhi.* This is what is referred to as the *Buddha of samādhi.*

[18.14–18] If you ask what the Buddha of aspiration is, [he is] the bodhisattva who prays: "By means of whatever forms, colors, and paths of conduct[1099] sentient beings are disciplined, may I be disciplined by means of these same forms, colors, and paths of conduct."[1100] They are [bodhisattvas] disciplined by the Buddha, being disciplined by the form of the Buddha. You should know that this is the Buddha of aspiration, since he has arisen from this aspiration. This is what is referred to as the *Buddha of aspiration.*

[18.18–22] If you ask what the Buddha of the mind is, it is a bodhisattva who has gained full control over the mind, and can, in virtue of this control, turn into whatever he thinks about. Having seen sentient beings being disciplined by the buddhas, he wishes: "May I assume the form of a buddha." Since he has arisen from the mind, he is a buddha of the mind. Moreover, these disciplined ones see and know the Buddha because they have purified their mind. This is what is referred to as the *Buddha of the mind.*

[18.22–25] If you ask, what is the Buddha of the true nature?[1101] The Buddha of the true nature is the transformation of the basis, [the basis that is responsible for] the assumption of bad states; the inconceivable; the stainless; that which has various forms; the dharmadhātu in its different aspects; the variety of form, beauty, and shape; and the appearance of a buddha form endowed with the thirty-two marks of a great being—[all] this is called the *Buddha of the true nature.*

[18.25–19.1] If you ask what the Buddha of enjoyment is, it is bodhisattvas, [their] enjoyment, a corresponding manner of conduct,[1102] form, food, speaking, rules (or rituals?),[1103] and the corresponding activity—[all] this is called the *Buddha of enjoyment.*

[19.1–4] If you ask what the Buddha of emanation is, it is this: once they have obtained the samādhi of [being able to] display all forms, buddhas and bodhisattvas remain absorbed in samādhi. Having obtained [this] power and being moved by compassion, they emanate as buddha forms and discipline sentient beings. This is called the *Buddha of emanation.*

[19.4–7] If you ask what is the metaphorical Buddha? It is when some regard [their] teacher or preceptor as a buddha and respect him as they would a buddha. Regarding and respecting him in this way, they take [his instructions as] the teachings of the Buddha and fully enjoy and follow through on them. This is called the *metaphorical Buddha.*

[19.7–10] If you ask, what the Buddha you place in front of yourself is, it is when some make a statue of the Buddha (or have one made), make offerings to it, honor it by all acts of worship, treat it with respect, adore it, and take it as [embodying] the teachings of the Buddha and fully enjoy and follow through on those teachings.[1104] This is called the *Buddha you place in front of yourself.* Son of a noble family, a bodhisattva should thoroughly know [the meaning of the word] Buddha on the basis of these ten [forms of] entering the way of the Dharma.

[19.10–17] Among these, the natural outflow *(niṣyanda)* has been translated as a "buddha resembling [his] cause" in the *Laṅkāvatāra[sūtra].* This is the *sambhogakāya.* As to the body of maturation, the maturation of the six *pāramitās* appears as the body of a buddha—at the time of "[single]-moment comprehension" *(ekakṣaṇikābhisamaya).*[1105] As to [the buddha of] samādhi, since it is [also] taught in the introduction of the *Prajñāpāramitā,* it is like the appearance of an assembly of tathāgatas teaching the Dharma, seated on many lotuses of jewels at the head of light [rays] emerging from the displayed sense faculty of the tongue, after [the buddha] has become absorbed in the king of samādhis. As to the buddha of aspiration, through their aspiration, bodhisattvas appear as buddhas to others. As to the buddha of the mind, bodhisattvas who gained control over the mind see that they can discipline others if they turn into the form of a buddha, and do so accordingly.

[19.17–24] Among these [five], the first three are [buddha] kāyas of those described as a buddha on the tenth [bodhisattva] level and above. The latter two are bodhisattvas who have gained control [over all phenomena].[1106] The *svābhāvika-*, *sambhoga-*, and *nirmāṇakāya,* all three, will be explained in this [treatise, i.e., the *Ratnagotravibhāga*]. On account of their resembling a buddha, the last two are metaphorically labeled as buddhas in order to generate respect for [your] teacher and statues of the Buddha. Moreover, as for the name buddha, it [applies, strictly speaking, to] the buddha of no more learning, but those on the tenth level are [also] called buddhas. In the commentary on this [present work, the *Ratnagotravibhāga*], those from the eighth level onward are called buddhas. Even those from the [bodhisattva] levels onward are [sometimes] called [buddhas]. In the *Tarkajvālā* it is explained that you are called a buddha when you possess a steady bodhicitta. Also all sentient beings are declared to be buddhas in view of [their mind]streams. Such explanations serve a particular aim. Further, [even] some men and medicines have arbitrarily been labeled as buddhas metaphorically. But here [in the *Ratnagotravibhāga,*] it should be understood that [only] those on the eighth level onward are called buddhas.

[19.24–25] As to [the vajra point of] the Dharma, in the *Vyākhyāyukti* it has been said, [in the paragraph on] comprehending the ten meanings [of the word dharma]:

> [The word] *dharma* has the following meanings: knowable objects, the path, nirvāṇa, the objects of the mental faculty,[1107] merit, life,[1108] the discourses [of the Buddha], what will happen in the future,[1109] certainty, and law.[1110]

[19.25–26] From among these [ten] you must choose, here in the context of the Jewel of the Dharma, the path, nirvāṇa, and the discourses.

[19.26–20.2] As to [the vajra point of] the Community, it is a synonym of assembly. Here it is the Saṅgha in terms of the ultimate, [that is,] liberation [and] cessation. The noble ones, [that is,] śrāvakas, pratyekabuddhas, and bodhisattvas, who have this [ultimate] as their basis, are also called [this].

[20.2–4] As to [the vajra point of] the [buddha] element *(dhātu),* it has the meaning of *substantial [cause] (nye bar len pa)* [or] *source ('byung khungs)* of the fruit. In the present context, [that is,] with regard to the pure and impure, which manifest themselves [respectively] as the Three Jewels and saṁsāra, [the element] is, according to circumstances, explained as *potential (gotra).*

[20.4–5] As to [the vajra point of] enlightenment, [Skt.] *bodhi,* since [the term] is used for the purified faults and the thorough knowledge of [all] phenomena, it should be understood as being like a buddha, [that is, it applies to bodhisattvas] from the eighth level onward.

[20.5–6] As to [the vajra point of] qualities, in general they are properties *(dharma).* They are what particular [properties] clearly differentiated from other properties are called. Here, accordingly, they are properties such as the [ten] strengths, clearly distinguished from [those of] other teachers. [Such properties] should be called [qualities] only from the eighth level onward.

[20.6–9] As to [the vajra point of] buddha activity (Tib. *phrin las*), *phrin* is a honorific word. [Skt.] *karma[n]* means *action (las).* Action is involved here because [the progression] from wholesome worldly deeds up to the state of a buddha is necessarily accomplished through [the assistance of] other buddhas. The cause of this, wisdom and compassion, is called activity *(phrin las),* in the [same] way that the cause is metaphorically termed the fruit.[1111]

[20.9–14] As to [the word] *finally* [in RGV I.1b], activity is the seventh [and] last [vajra point], starting from the first [vajra point], the Jewel that is the Buddha. Also, with regard to the body of meaning [in the treatise], since activity is the final fruit of generating a mind set on attaining enlightenment (bodhicitta), it is [qualified by] *finally.* If the body of the treatise is [taken], as explained in the commentary on master Dignāga's *Nyāyabindu,* to [mean] both the "body of meaning" and the "body of words," then the seven *vajras* are "the body of meaning," and the collectivity of discourse that expresses them is the body of words or terms, and this is precisely [what] this stanza [(RGV I.1) is about]. In the present treatise, [the text] from [stanza RGV I.4 starting with] "Which has [neither] beginning..." up to [stanza RGV V.28 ending with] "...in short, the two results are taught by the last [stanza]"

> **[20.15] ...is the entire treatise. The body of this entire [treatise] is, in short, all seven vajra points.**[1112] [RGV I.1cd]

[20.16–18] The stanza starting with "[The seven vajra points must be known,] together with their own defining characteristics...." (RGV I.2)[1113] explains that the source of this body [is] like the mother of a child. The stanza starting with "From the Buddha [comes] the teaching..." [RGV I.3] explains the connection by which the body is, like veins and sinews, stitched together.

[The *Ratnagotravibhāgavyākhyā* says:[1114]]

> **[They are "vajra bases"[1115] in that they are the basis or support of the vajra-like meaning, [namely the object] of realization. In this regard, it should be known that [what] by nature [is] the ineffable meaning (i.e., object) of self-realization is like a vajra, since it is difficult to understand with a knowledge that results from listening and reflection. The letters that express this meaning by teaching the [most] favorable path for attaining it are called the *base* because they are the support of this [meaning]. Thus, as [the meaning] is difficult to understand and [the syllables are its] support, the meaning and syllables should be known as a *vajra base (vajrapada)*. What is here the meaning and what are the syllables? [First] the meaning is mentioned: it is the sevenfold meaning (i.e., object) of realization, that is to say, the meaning of Buddha, Dharma, Saṅgha, the [buddha] element, enlightenment, qualities, and activity. This is called the meaning. The letters by which the sevenfold meaning (i.e., object) of realization is made known [or] elucidated are called syllables. This teaching of the vajra points should be known in detail according to the sūtras.**[1116]]

[20.18–22] Now the *[Ratnagotravibhāga]vyākhyā* on this stanza [I.1] will be explained. In this regard there is an explanation of the term *vajra point* (lit. "vajra base") and a presentation of canonical sources making the vajra[-like] meanings known. First, the seven meanings (i.e., objects), which must be realized on the basis of the [corresponding] words, are ultimate ones, and thus vajra-like. The words expressing these [meanings] are a basis because they are [their] foundation. Thus all seven words are called *vajra bases.* To explain them again: since [Tib.] *de la* ("in this regard"), [in Sanskrit] *tatra,*[1117] is the seventh case, it [can] be taken to imply [Tib.] *de na* ("at that place," "there") and [means]: when explaining this vajra *base.*

[20.22–21.1] "Listening" means arisen from listening, that is to say, knowing the meaning from scriptures. "Reflection" means arisen from reflection, that is, knowing the meaning from having reflected on reasons and arguments. "Difficult to understand on the basis of these two [types of] knowledge" means that when directly distinguishing the meaning, it is very difficult to actualize it, because these two [forms of knowledge] are conceptual. Therefore you should take [the meaning] to be an indistinguishable quality and [likewise] understand that the seven ultimate [points] are like a vajra. However [the meaning] is understood, since an expression is [always] referring to a thought, the meaning should not be taken as the actual object of the thought. Within the direct [perceptions] of any knowable object whatsoever, it is the meaning and object of comprehension that have the nature of self-realization, [that is,] a direct [perception] arisen from meditation.

[21.1–7] If you object then that, "The seven meanings are what is experienced in self-realization, and if these seven meanings are, on the other hand, ineffable, they [cannot] be the subject matter of the treatise. Thus, the treatise [meant for discourse] is devoid of subject matter." It is not so. As for the self-realization that realizes the seven meanings: even though it cannot arise primarily on the basis of words, the knowledge arisen from listening and reflection is a cause favoring the attainment of the fruit, [or] self-realization. Through teaching it, since [this favorable cause] is the path that leads you to the attainment of self-realization, self-realization is taught as well. This in the same way as [the city of] Pāṭaliputra is expressed when you say: "This is the way leading to Pāṭaliputra." This has been also said [in the *Ratnagotravibhāga* V.16]:

> Thus, on the basis of authoritative scripture and reason,
> [This doctrine] has been explained [by me] only for my own purification
> And for helping those endowed with marvelous virtues
> In terms of their intelligence and devotion.[1118]

[21.7–9] Thus, the insight arising from listening is brought forth by explanations based on scripture, and the insight arising from reflection by ones based on reasoning. In this respect it is stated in the *Laṅkāvatāra[sūtra]:*

> [21.9–13] Now further, the bodhisattva and great being Mahāmati requested the illustrious one to speak on this subject: "Illustrious one, may it please the illustrious one to explain to me again where, from where, and how thoughts of the cognitive forms *(vijñapti)* of phrases[1119] among the people occur, [and] the experiential object that manifests as the thoughts of words." The illustrious one said: "The occurrences of syllables,[1120] Mahāmati, come about from a combination of the head, chest, nose, throat, palate, lips, tongue, and teeth."[1121]

[21.13–15] This is in accordance with what is explained in the *Vacanamukh[āyudhopama]:*

> [Sounds are produced from] the chest, throat, palate, tongue, nose, head, teeth, and the lips—from all and each of these places.[1122]

[Tib.] *mgo bo* ("head") means *spyi bo* [a synonym of head], and *brang* ("chest") means *khog pa* [a synonym of chest].

[21.15–23] It is again stated in the *[Laṅkāvatārasūtra]:*

> Further, Mahāmati, we will explain the defining characteristics of the accumulations that go to make up words, phrases, and syllables. When these accumulations are well understood, bodhisattvas and great beings who delve into meaning, phrases, and syllables swiftly awaken to unsurpassable complete enlightenment and cause all sentient beings to awaken in the same way. Mahāmati, *word-body* (that is, the "accumulation that goes to make up words")[1123] is the thing on the basis of which a word is coined. The accumulation is a thing. [Here,] *accumulation* (Skt. *kāya*) does not have a different meaning than body. Mahāmati, this is the *word-body.* The *phrase-body,* Mahāmati, does not have a different meaning than "the existence of many[1124] meanings of phrases," "[their] ascertainment," and "definite objects [of reference]." Mahāmati, this is what I taught to be the *phrase-body.* The *syllable-body,* Mahāmati, is that by which words and sentences are

made manifest and does not have a different meaning than syllables, symbols, characteristic signs, objects [of reference], and designation.[1125]

[21.23–22.3] Again, Mahāmati, the *phrase-body* is a definite product[1126] that constitutes phrases.[1127] Mahāmati, *words* are different specific words consisting of letters, [namely, the ones] from *a* to *ha*. Mahāmati, the *syllable-body*[1128] here refers to short, long, and extended syllables.[1129] Mahāmati, the *phrase-body* here is: regarding the phrase*(pada)*-body, the idea of it is obtained from the walkers on the trails *(padavīthī)*—elephants, horses, humans, deer, cows,[1130] buffalos, sheep,[1131] cattle, and so forth. Moreover, Mahāmati, words and syllables are the four formless skandhas. [The latter,] being expressed by [the term] *word,* are in fact word.[1132] Insofar as they are manifest *(vyajyate)* by virtue of their specific defining characteristic, they are syllables *(vyañjana).* Mahāmati, these are the defining characteristics of the expressions *word* and *phrase* with regard to the accumulations/bodies of words, phrases, and syllables. You should familiarize yourself with this [topic].[1133]

[22.3–11] Any term for any thing—the labeling [of the latter] as if it were a reality—is a word. A collection of many of these is called the "accumulation," "body," or "thing." A phrase is called true when it elucidates [something], not, [that is,] by scattering words in a general way, [but] by using different [grammatical] cases. Syllables are letters that form words and phrases. *Syllable* is *vyañjana* in Sanskrit, and means "letter," "mark," or "consonant." [In the case of] these, the meaning of the three accumulations is straightforward. As to "definite [product[1134] that constitutes] phrases," when explaining it in terms of the other synonyms, it is as explained before. The accumulation that goes to make up words (i.e., the word-body) is the cause of words. "From *a* to *ha*" means the sixteen vowels and the thirty-three consonants. The accumulation that goes to make up syllables (i.e., the syllable-body) is also the cause of syllables; [these are pronounced] in three ways, [namely with] a long, short, and average span of breath. As to the other synonyms, the walkers on the footpaths (elephants and so forth),[1135] they [refer] to the phrase-body, because phrase is in Sanskrit *pada* and means "foot." The word-body consists of the four formless skandhas beginning with sensation, given that they make you comprehend the meaning. The specific defining characteristics necessarily involved in comprehending meaning, since they are unchangeable, are called syllables.

[22.11–14] Jñānaśrībhadra has stated [in his *Laṅkāvatāravṛtti*][1136] that words are terms that express, and phrases are the subject matter [to be expressed]. Having explained these three bodies/accumulations together with their separate defining characteristics according to this same *[Laṅkāvatāra]sūtra*, the Abhidharma, and the treatises on grammar, I shall again explain the three together on the basis of one foundation.

[22.14] Furthermore, in the *[Mahāyāna]sūtrālaṁkāra* [I.4cd] it is stated:

> It should be known that the Dharma has two aspects as well: meaning and syllables.[1137]

[22.14–17] Therefore the entire treatise is explained as being [mere] syllables. Here [in the *Ratnagotravibhāga*] it is the same. The syllables that express the seven meanings,[1138] [namely,] the underlying nature of the terms of the entire treatise, are called the *base* of the seven meanings, for they are the foundation of these seven meanings. Moreover, the knowledge involving thoroughly understanding the seven meanings is called *meaning,* because this knowledge arises on the basis of the terms and terms are its basis. This is the stage when understanding *(rtog pa)* arises in the listener.

[22.17–19] With regard to the one who is explaining [the Dharma], it is stated [in *Mūlamadhyamakakārikā* XXIV.8ab]:

> The teaching of the Dharma by the buddhas is based on the two truths.[1139]

[22.19–25] Accordingly, the meaning is posited as the support and the terms as the supported, since the terms used by the one who explains arise from a knowledge that thoroughly understands the meaning. To sum up, it is in view of them being difficult to grasp that the [seven] meanings should be understood to be vajra[-like]. It is in view of their being the support of the meaning that the syllables should be understood to be the "base" of the meaning. "In view of" means "by reason of." [This is] "the conventional meaning of explaining [the seven vajra points] as vajra and base." As to the [question], "What is here the meaning and what are the syllables?" it is clarified by: "the sevenfold [meaning of realization is called meaning]." The Sanskrit is here: *tatra katamo 'rthaḥ katamad vyañjanam.* Since *katama* is [an interrogative particle calling for a relation expressed by] *as* [Tib. *du*], we must translate here: "[What is] meaning [and what are] syllables [taken] as here?" Therefore it is clear that a suitable translation of the answer [must be]: "As to the meaning of realization, it must be expressed[1140] as the sevenfold meaning."

[22.25–23.4] As to the meaning of *buddha*, it is the meaning of the term *buddha*. The rest follows accordingly. "The letters *(akṣara)* by which the sevenfold meaning (i.e., object) of realization is made known [or] elucidated are called syllables *(vyañjana)*." Since there is a sevenfold meaning, the [expressive] words [lit. "syllables"] are [also] sevenfold. [Sanskrit] *vyañjana* is "syllable" or "consonant," because the essence of the seven[fold] meaning is made known and, more particularly, elucidated.[1141] Thus it is said. As to the presentation of canonical sources justifying the vajra meaning[s], this teaching of the vajra bases has been expressed in a condensed form, but now it should be known in detail according to the sūtras.

[The next passage in the *Ratnagotravibhāgavyākhyā* is:]

> **[Ānanda, the Tathāgata is invisible. He cannot be seen with eyes. Ānanda, the Dharma is ineffable. It cannot be heard with ears. Ānanda, the Saṅgha[1142] is not conditioned. It cannot be worshipped either by body or by mind.[1143] Thus the [first] three vajra points should be understood according to the *Dṛḍhādhyāśayaparivarta*.[1144]]**

[23.4–8] When in the sūtra the illustrious one told Ānanda to teach the Dharma with regard to the invisible Tathāgata, the ineffable Dharma, and the Saṅgha that cannot be worshipped, Ānanda replied the following to the illustrious one: "How is it, illustrious one, that the Tathāgata is invisible, that the Dharma in ineffable, and that the Saṅgha cannot be worshipped?" [The Buddha answered] "Ānanda, the Tathāgata is invisible," because he must be taken in terms of [his] dharmatā, as has been said in the *Vajracchedika:*

> The buddhas are the dharmakāya; the leaders see the dharmatā.

[23.8–12] [In the *Dṛḍhādhyāśayaparivarta* the Buddha said, speaking of himself in the third person:][1145] "He cannot be seen with the eyes as the marvelous marks [of a buddha]. The Dharma, too, Ānanda, is ineffable, inasmuch as it must be taken in terms of [its] dharmatā. It cannot be heard with ears, that is, as the sixty[fold] melodious speech. The Saṅgha, too, Ānanda, is not conditioned, inasmuch as it must be taken in terms of [its] dharmatā. It can neither be venerated by the body nor worshipped by a mind that longs [to do so] upon seeing [the Saṅgha]."

[23.12–16] Immediately after this teaching Ānanda said: "Illustrious one, it is amazing [how] difficult it is to realize in such a way the dharmatā of the buddhas, the illustrious ones." Since [the Buddha] gave his consent, it is obvious that the Three Jewels must be taken with reference to [their] dharmatā [here]. Thus the first three vajra points under discussion here should be understood according to the *Dṛḍhādhyāśayasūtra*, since [their explanation] was requested by the bodhisattva Dṛḍhādhyāśaya.

[The next passage in the *Ratnagotravibhāgavyākhyā* is:]

> **[Śāriputra, this [ultimate] meaning is the [cognitive] object of the Tathāgata; it comes under the range of the Tathāgata['s awareness].[1146] Śāriputra, it cannot, to start with, be known, seen, or examined correctly even by śrāvakas or pratyekabuddhas on the basis of their own insight, much less by fools and ordinary people,[1147] unless they [i.e., śrāvakas, pratyekabuddhas, fools, and ordinary persons] realize it by faith in the Tathāgata. Śāriputra, that which must be realized by faith is the ultimate. Śāriputra, *ultimate* is an expression for the [buddha] element in sentient beings. The *[buddha] element in sentient beings,* Śāriputra, is an expression for buddha nature. Buddha nature, Śāriputra, is an expression for the dharmakāya.[1148] Thus the fourth vajra point should be understood according to the *Anūnatvāpūrṇatvanirdeśa.*[1149]]**

[23.16–20] [It has been said:][1150] "Śāriputra, this ultimate meaning is the [cognitive] object of omniscience whose nature is [that of] the Tathāgata; it comes under the range of the Tathāgata's wisdom, which apprehends all knowable objects. For these reasons it is called ultimate. Śāriputra, it cannot, to start with, be correctly known (as the [buddha] element of sentient beings), seen (as buddha nature), or examined (as being the dharmakāya), even by śrāvakas or pratyekabuddhas on the basis of their own insight rather then on what others say; how much less can fools and ordinary people, who are prone to view the transitory collection [as a real *I* and *mine*], realize it by their own knowledge."

[23.20–22] "They realize it by faith in the Tathāgata" means by following his discourses and merely trusting [his words]. Since śrāvakas, pratyekabuddhas, and ordinary persons [can have such a realization], they are not included among those who do not realize it [at all]. [The Buddha thus said:][1151] "Śāriputra, even though the ultimate is difficult to realize, it must be realized by faith in the words of the Buddha."

[23.22–24.2] [It has been further said:][1152] "Śāriputra, the name *vase* and the material of [its] huge bulb are not identical by nature, and [their] relation is not such that they are inseparable in terms of the four elements. Were that so, it would follow that even a cow would think of the word *vase* upon seeing the huge bulb [of one]. Therefore, since all words are subsequent labels *(btags pa)* for this and that meaning, they are called *expressions (bla dvags)*.[1153] In this sense, the word *ultimate* is an expression for the emptiness [of] sentient beings that is, in a certain respect, synonymous with the phrase '[buddha] element in sentient beings.'[1154] Likewise, the phrase '[buddha] element in sentient beings' is, in a certain respect, an expression for buddha nature. The term *buddha nature*, Śāriputra, is synonymous with the term *dharmakāya*. It is an expression of a subsequent label."

[24.2–5] Thus the fourth vajra point should be understood on the basis of its five defining characteristics of the ultimate in accordance with the *Anūnatvāpūrṇatvanirdeśasūtra*, implying that the element of sentient beings is like a vajra. The explanation of the three [reasons for the existence of buddha nature in sentient beings]—being embraced and pervaded *(spharaṇa)* by the embodiment of the perfect Buddha and so forth—in the chapter on suchness mingled with stains, is also based on this treatise (i.e., sūtra).

[The next passage in the *Ratnagotravibhāgavyākhyā* is:]

> **[Illustrious one, *unsurpassable enlightenment* is an expression for the sphere (Tib. *dbyings*) of nirvāṇa. *Sphere of nirvāṇa*, illustrious one, is an expression for the Tathāgata's dharmakāya. Thus the fifth vajra point should be known according to the *Āryaśrīmālā[devī]sūtra*.[1155]]**

[24.5–14] Further down in [RGV I.89 (J I.87)] it is stated:

> Perfect enlightenment/awakening to all aspects is the removal of
> [all] stains together with the [corresponding] mental imprints.
> Moreover, it is buddhahood, nirvāṇa, and nonduality on the ultimate [level].[1156]

Similarly,[1157] unsurpassable enlightenment (Tib. *byang chub*) has the same meaning as buddha (Tib. *sangs rgyas*), inasmuch as cleansing *(byang)* and awakening *(sangs)* have the same meaning, as do blossoming *(rgyas)* and achieving *(chub)*.[1158] [Buddha in turn] has the same meaning as the sphere of nirvāṇa (Tib. *mya ngan 'das*), since stains together with the [corresponding] mental imprints are misery (Tib. *mya ngan*), while their removal [is expressed by] "beyond" (Tib. *'das*). Therefore, the name *enlight-*

enment is an expression for the sphere of nirvāṇa. Therefore, both enlightenment [or] buddha and removal [or] nirvāṇa are the same as nonduality and the ultimate [truth] of the transformation of the basis. As for the sphere of nirvāṇa, it is an expression for a tathāgata's dharmakāya, the way [nirvāṇa] exists when it is the element of sentient beings, thus it came[1159] (Tib. *de bzhin gshegs*, Skt. *tathāgata*) and was attained, and a [tathāgata's] body *(kāya)* is inseparable from the qualities of the properties *(dharma)* of the [ten] strengths and so forth. Thus the fifth vajra point should be known according to the *Āryaśrīmālādevīsiṁhanādasūtra*, *ārya* being a general title for a sūtra, while the particular sūtra itself is called *Śrīmālādevīsiṁhanāda*.

[The next passage in the *Ratnagotravibhāgavyākhyā* is:]

> **[Śāriputra, the dharmakāya taught by the Tathāgata possesses inseparable properties and qualities, [impossible] to recognize as something disconnected,[1160] actually in the form of properties of the Tathāgata, which surpass in number the grains of sand of the river Gaṅgā. Thus the sixth vajra point should be understood according to the *Anūnatvāpūrṇatvanirdeśa[sūtra]*.[1161]]**

[24.14–18] The dharmakāya[1162] taught by [our] teacher the Tathāgata has the following meaning. The [qualities], such as the [ten] strengths, which surpass in number the grains of sand of the river Gaṅgā, are the properties *(dharma)* of a tathāgata. Since the wisdom of the Buddha is identical with them, it [i.e., the wisdom or the dharmakāya] possesses inseparable properties. Even at a time when defilements prevail, it possesses qualities that are [impossible] to recognize as something disconnected.[1163] In short, since the qualities and the element are connected in a relation of identity, the term *kāya* must [refer] to [their] true nature.[1164] [Thus] the sixth vajra point should be understood according to the *Anūnatvāpūrṇatvanirdeśasūtra*.

[The next passage in the *Ratnagotravibhāgavyākhyā* is:]

> **[Mañjuśrī, the Tathāgata does not engage in conceptualizing or imagining. Still, such effectiveness unfolds without effort in him who neither conceptualizes nor imagines. Thus the seventh vajra point should be understood according to the *Tathāgataguṇajñānācintyaviṣayāvatāranirdeśa*. Such are, to sum up, the seven vajra points. It should be understood that they are the body of the entire treatise, in the form of collected topics that are the [seven] doors to the [present] teaching.[1165]]**

[24.18–21] [The Buddha said in the *Tathāgataguṇajñānācintyaviṣayāvatāranirdeśa:*][1166]

> Mañjuśrī, the Tathāgata does not engage in conceptualizing in general, when chastening disciples, or in imagining anything in particular, such as objects and time. Still, even without [these] concepts, such an effectiveness—[namely] the display of the kāyas of a tathāgata, the sounding of the melody of [his] speech and so forth—does not depend on effort. Thus it unfolds [in him who] is neither conceptualizing nor imagining, without effort and uninterruptedly, as long as space exists.

[24.21–24] This [defines] the seventh vajra point or word, which refers to the ultimate [level] of a buddha as an agent of unfolding activity. It should be understood according to the *Tathāgataguṇajñānācintyaviṣayāvatāranirdeśasūtra.* [According to its title] the sūtra teaches how you enter the inconceivable experiential sphere of the Tathāgata's qualities and wisdom by virtue of the insight gained by hearing[, reflecting on, and meditating upon this sphere].

[24.24–26] Such are, to sum up, the seven vajra points. It should be understood that they are the body that summarizes and accumulates all branches of the treatise in the form of collected topics, these collected topics being the seven doors through which you comprehend the [present] teaching in detail.

The Explanation of RGV I.2

[24.26–25.3] Now, in order to teach what connection this treatise (i.e., the *Ratnagotravibhāga*) has with a canonical source that states these seven topics uninterruptedly in one sūtra, it is said [in RGV I.2]:

> **These [seven vajra points] should be understood,[1167] each together with its own defining characteristics, [as explained] in sequential order in the *Dhāraṇīśvararājasūtra*—**
> **The [first] three in the introductory chapter,**
> **And the [remaining] four in the [chapters on] a "Distinction of the Qualities of a Bodhisattva" and on a "[Distinction of the Qualities of a] Buddha."**[1168]

[25.3–7] [Ngog Loden Sherab's] "together with" *(rjes su 'brel ba)* is *anugata* in Sanskrit. Since it can mean "to follow," "to be similar" *(rjes su 'gro ba),*[1169] "to abide together" *(rjes su gnas pa),* and "in accordance" *(rjes su 'brangs pa),* it is [also] possible to translate it as "in accordance." There are three [points] to explaining this stanza: a brief explanation, a detailed presentation, and a summarized meaning. With regard to the first it has been said [in the *Ratnagotravibhāgavyākhyā:*]

> **The [first] three from among these seven vajra points together with the specification of [their] own defining characteristics should be understood, in respective order, from the introductory chapter of the *Āryadhāraṇīśvararājasūtra.*** [1170]

[25.7–10] "Together with" *(rjes su 'brel ba)* [must] be deleted here [in Ngog Loden Sherab's translation] and [the sentence corrected to:] "must be understood in accordance *(rjes su 'brangs)* with the [introductory] chapter." If we delete "together with" and translate instead: "must be understood in accordance with the introductory chapter," [the result] is in accordance with the Indian text. As to "the specification of [their] own defining characteristics," this sūtra does not specify mere terms of the Three Jewels and so forth; *specify,* rather, is used because [the text] elucidates the defining characteristics of the actual meaning [of the vajra points]. In this sūtra, the seven meanings [of the vajra points] are taught under the aspect of both truths.

[The next passage in the *Ratnagotravibhāgavyākhyā* is:]

> **[After that, the remaining four [vajra points] are from the [chapters on] a "Distinction of the Qualities of a Bodhisattva" and on a "[Distinction of the Qualities of a] Buddha."]** [1171]

[25.10–11] After that, [as to] the remaining four, i.e., the [buddha] element, enlightenment, qualities, and activity, it should be understood that one is from the [chapter on] a "Distinction of the Qualities of a Bodhisattva" and that three are from a "Distinction of the Qualities of a Buddha."

The Three Jewels: Buddha, Dharma, and Saṅgha

[25.11–17] As to the detailed presentation, there are two [stages]: the presentation of the words of the sūtra and an explanation of their meaning. As to the first:[1172]

> **In this *[Dhāraṇīśvararājasūtra]* it has been said: "The illustrious one completely awakened to the sameness of all phenomena**

and duly set the wheel of teaching *(dharmacakra)* in motion. [Thus] he had a limitless, well-disciplined crowd of disciples."[1173] As for an explanation of this: **from these three phrases of the root** [**text**] or treatise **you should understand the presentation of** [**how**] **you arrive at full knowledge about the gradual arising of the Three Jewels in successive order**. This refers to when the teacher [himself] is on the path. From among **the remaining four** [**vajra**] **points**, one (i.e., the buddha element) is the **substantial cause** and three are the attending causes **of that which corresponds to the arising of the Three Jewels.**[1174] It is in terms of [these four] that **you should understand the specification of** [**how**] **you arrive at a full knowledge** [**of the cause corresponding to the arising of the Three Jewels**].[1175]

[25.17–19] **In this respect, when abiding on the eighth bodhisattva level, he attained the** tenfold **power over all phenomena. Therefore he,** the illustrious one, who **went to the supreme seat of enlightenment, has been called "he who completely awakened to the sameness of all phenomena."**[1176]

[25.19–26.3] It is said that the illustrious one, having gone to the vajra seat [in Bodhgayā], completely awakened to the sameness of all phenomena. This is said because earlier, [namely,] from the time he abided on the eighth level onward, he was [already] awake to the sameness of all phenomena. This is like saying that he conquered Māra again at the time he abided on Vulture Peak (Gṛdhrakūṭa), having [already] conquered Māra before when abiding on the vajra seat. On the eighth [level] he attained the complete realization that phenomenal existence and quiescence are the same. [Moreover, he attained on this level] the excellence of pure [buddha]fields and activity. Thus greatly resembling a buddha, he was called a buddha. "All phenomena" refers to saṁsāra and nirvāṇa, and he completely awakened toward [their] sameness in the form of the one wisdom, which is able to endure that both (saṁsāra and nirvāṇa) lack an own-being. In fact, phenomenal existence is the [state in which] forms appear to the intellect of sentient beings and bodhisattvas up to the seventh level. A mind that does not [experience] an arising in terms of an own-being and [thus] lacks [mentally created] characteristic signs is called *natural luminosity.* On the eighth level these two (i.e., the intellect of phenomenal existence and luminosity) are realized as being of one taste. As for the mastery of all phenomena, it has been taught as the attainment of the ten powers in passages such as the following from the [chapter] on the eighth level in the *Daśabhūmikasūtra:*

> He who has perfected in such a way body and wisdom [has control over all sentient beings. Moreover,][1177] he attains mastery over his life for having been blessed with a lifespan[1178] that [lasts] for a truly inexpressible [number of] eons.[1179]

[26.3–6] There are two supreme "seats" (according to the Tib: *essences*) of enlightenment: Akaniṣṭha and the vajra seat [in Bodhgayā]. Since the solid Akaniṣṭha is never destroyed, and since the vajra seat is not destroyed even by the three [elements of] fire, water, and earth at the end of an eon, [these two] are very firm and thus called an *essence.* "Went" is *gata* in Sanskrit. Since *[gata]* can also mean "abided," [the phrase "he went to the supreme seat of enlightenment"] is also understood in the sense of "he abided in the supreme essence of enlightenment."

[26.6–9] An illustrious one who has completely awakened is called "one who has set the wheel of teaching in proper motion." [In the *Ratnagotravibhāgavyākhyā* it is stated:]

> **When abiding on the ninth bodhisattva level, he knew well the mental dispositions of all sentient beings, attained the highest perfection [in making use of] the faculties [of sentient beings], and was skilled in destroying in all sentient beings the series of mental imprints of defilements. [Therefore he who has completely awakened is called "one who has set the wheel of teaching *(dharmacakra)* well in motion"].**[1180, 1181]

[26.9–16] Having attained discriminative awareness on the ninth level, he sets the vast dharmacakra in motion. Knowing well the many forms of all sentient beings' dispositions and devotion, he turns the [dharma]cakra in accordance with [these] dispositions. Given his highest perfection in making use of sentient beings' faculties—it being possible that some have strong devotion but inferior faculties, while others have little devotion but sharp faculties—he knows the [range of] objects [experienced by his] disciples. [Thus] he knows now to turn the dharma[cakra] with discriminative awareness. This is for the following reason. He destroys the series of three realms [caused] by *karman* and defilements, the series of thoughts [occurring] on account of the mental imprints of designations, and the series of mental bodies [brought forth] by the mental imprints of ignorance. Being expert [in employing to this end] these temporary remedies and even the final [one]—the vajra-like samādhi—he is an expert in the fruit of the dharmacakra.

[The next passage in the *Ratnagotravibhāgavyākhyā* is:]

[While abiding on the tenth bodhisattva level, he underwent the consecration of a crown prince of the unsurpassable teaching of the Tathāgata, and immediately after that he ceased to be hindered with regard to effortless buddha activity. Therefore, he who set the wheel of teaching in proper motion is called "the one who had a limitless well-disciplined crowd of disciples."][1182]

[26.16–21] The Buddha, the illustrious one, who set the wheel of teaching in proper motion, is called "the one who had a limitless well-disciplined crowd of disciples." For when he was abiding on the tenth level, immediately after he had reached this level [in fact], he underwent the consecration of a crown prince of the unsurpassable teaching of the Tathāgata. [Moreover,] immediately after he obtained [this status], his [activity, which was then already] in accordance with buddha activity, became effortless and uninterrupted. How he was consecrated is not mentioned here, but this can be learned from the *Daśabhūmikasūtra*. For [there] it is said that during the consecration there were innumerable followers who sat on innumerable lotuses, wherefore he led a limitless crowd of disciples on the tenth level.

[The next passage in the *Ratnagotravibhāgavyākhyā* is:]

[Again, [the author] teaches this leading a limitless well-disciplined crowd of disciples in the portion of the treatise that immediately follows, namely from "he was together with a great assembly of monks"[1183] up to "he was together with an immeasurable assembly of bodhisattvas";[1184] and as to [the meaning of] "those [disciples] who possess such qualities,"[1185] he perfectly led [them][1186] in successive order to the enlightenment of śrāvakas and buddhas, wherefore "[the illustrious one] was together with those who possess such qualities."][1187]

[26.21–27.2] Now, the leading of a limitless crowd of disciples is taught in this treatise immediately after the teaching of [how] you arrive at a full knowledge[1188] of the arising of the Three Jewels, namely, from "he was together with a great assembly of monks," sixty thousand in number, up to "he was together with an immeasurable assembly of bodhisattvas." For those who have been led to the enlightenment of śrāvakas possess the qualities [described in the passage] from "those who know all" up to "those who penetrate the words of the Tathāgata,"[1189] and those who have been led to the enlightenment of buddhas possess the qualities [described in the passage] from "renunciation for the sake[1190] of the experiential object of unobstructed omniscience" up to "the unlimited, uninterrupted activity[1191] of a bodhisattva."[1192] He dwelt together with [disciples] who possessed such qualities. "Together with" means [their] activity was in accordance [with his].

[The next passage in the *Ratnagotravibhāgavyākhyā* is:]

> **[Then, immediately after the teaching of the praiseworthy qualities of śrāvakas and bodhisattvas, the proper analysis of the qualities of the Buddha Jewel should be understood: based on the excellence of the Buddha's meditative stabilization,[1193] which is inconceivable, he manifested a spacious circular hall [adorned with] an array of jewels and caused the circle of the Tathāgata to assemble[1194] in it. They offered various divine substances and poured down clouds of praise.]**[1195]

[27.2–10] Then, immediately after the teaching of the praiseworthy qualities of śrāvakas and bodhisattvas, the illustrious one taught the Dharma teaching called "the door to renunciation [and] being without hindrances [that opens up] by adopting a bodhisattva's conduct."[1196] [The following passage from the *Dhāraṇīśvararājasūtra* starting with:]

> At this time the illustrious one entered into a meditative absorption called *the samādhi of the Tathāgata that illuminates the experiential objects of a buddha just the way they are emanated.* Thereupon, at this time, [he made manifest] through the power of the Buddha—in the upper intermediate space, [that is,] in the desire realm up to the form realm—a spacious circular hall that is the abode of the Buddha, made of the Tathāgata's roots of virtue.[1197]

Up to

> And in all world realms with their [respective] four continents, [namely,] all world realms of [the universe called] Huge Thousand,[1198] which consists of one thousand to the faculty of three [worlds], huge staircases of this kind occur.[1199]

[is summarized in the *Ratnagotravibhāgavyākhyā* in the sentence:] By the excellence of his inconceivable meditative stabilization, the Buddha manifested a spacious circular hall [adorned with] an array of jewels.

[27.10–18] Then the six classes of gods of the desire realm made offerings to, praised, and served the illustrious one together with his retinue. [The illustrious one] then proceeded [together with his retinue] up the staircases to the spacious circular hall. He took his seat on the lion throne, and his retinue sat down on seats appropriate to them.[1200] Then the illustrious one entered into the meditative absorption of a samādhi called *play of the Buddha in [a state of] liberation and unhinderedness.* From him, that is, from all the pores of [his] body, emanated light rays surpassing in number the grains of sand of the river Gaṅgā, illuminating the world realms in the ten directions. This light pacified [the suffering of] the lower realms, and from this light the stanzas "[The light of Śākyamuni] by which the force of diligence has been firmly established—without limit and openly"[1201] up to "Look at those today who exert themselves in open faith and devotion"[1202] resounded in order to encourage the bodhisattvas. [This light and these stanzas] made [them] understand all buddhafields, and having [thus] encouraged all bodhisattvas, [the light] descended to the crown of the head of the illustrious one.

[27.18–24] Then, from the world realms of the ten directions, bodhisattvas such as *Kusumaśrīgarbha came to this spacious hall together with their retinues, which surpass in number the grains of sand of ten river Gaṅgās. They poured down clouds of offerings and praises, and sat down on seats that had emanated in their directions. Likewise, an immeasurable assembly of bodhisattvas, which was encouraged by the light, and the four groups,[1203] and [other] humans and nonhumans from the [universe called] Huge Thousand, [attracted] by the sounds of clear speech, came up the staircases to the spacious hall and sat down on seats appropriate to them. Even the gods up to Akaniṣṭha [Heaven] assembled, wherefore all this [has been summarized in the *Ratnagotravibhāgavyākhyā* by the following passage:] "and had the circle of the Tathāgata to assemble in it. They offered various divine substances and poured down clouds of praise. This is how the proper analysis of the qualities of the Buddha Jewel should be understood."

[The next passage in the *Ratnagotravibhāgavyākhyā* is:]

> **After that, the proper analysis of the qualities of the Dharma Jewel should be understood as follows: He [manifested] the appearance of an array of high Dharma seats, emanated light,**

and announced the names and qualities of [various] Dharma teachings.[1204]

[27.24–28.5] After that, the illustrious one became aware of this huge assembly of retinues, and from a circle of hair between [his] eyebrows, light rays called *demonstration of the bodhisattva's strength* shone forth, circled seven times around the assembly of bodhisattvas, and descended onto the crowns of their [heads]. Then, as soon as this light touched the bodhisattva *Kusumaśrīgarbha, he got absorbed into a samādhi [called] *display of all ornaments.* By the power of this [samādhi] the lion throne of [Śākya]muni appeared in the middle of this hall, many millions[1205] of palmyra [trees][1206] in height and adorned with jewels...and endowed with all manner of ornaments.[1207] In this [passage] "an array of high Dharma seats" (Skt. *udāradharmāsanavyūha*) is taught. Then the bodhisattva *Kusumaśrīgarbha spoke the [following] stanza to the illustrious one:

> Kindly fulfill the needs of sentient beings with [your] sunlight![1208]

[28.5–9] In this and the passage up to "the light was praised, and [the illustrious one was requested to explain the Dharma while still] seated on the lion throne"[1209] "the praise of light"[1210] is taught. It is taught [in the *Dhāraṇīśvararājasūtra*] that the [illustrious one] remained on the lion throne in order to teach what is endowed with immeasurable qualities—starting with:

> Having found [by himself] the liberation of being without hindrances, the illustrious one then focused on planning the bodhisattva's path, namely the Dharma teachings called *the door to renunciation and being without hindrance [entered] by adopting a bodhisattva's conduct.*[1211]

[This has been summarized in the *Ratnagotravibhāgavyākhyā*:] "[The illustrious one] announced the names and qualities of [various] Dharma teachings, and thus the proper analysis of the qualities of the Dharma Jewel should be understood."

[28.9–13] By the power of the Buddha, the ten bodhisattvas *Ratnayaṣṭi, etc., [entered their respective] samādhis,[1212] and it is the power resulting from the experiential object [of these samādhis] that is taught next. In view of this and the passage from "Then the bodhisattva *Dharmeśvara"[1213] up to [the conclusion of] the chapter on the assembled "array of ornaments,"[1214] [it is stated in the *Ratnagotravibhāgavyākhyā*:]

> **After that the proper analysis of the qualities of the Saṅgha Jewel should be understood as follows: [The Buddha] displayed the mutual power that results from the experiential objects of the samādhis of bodhisattvas and taught a praise of their manifold qualities.**[1215]

[The next passage in the *Ratnagotravibhāgavyākhyā* is:]

> **[After that, again, the proper analysis of the qualities of these Three Jewels should be seen in successive order, and this is included in the concluding portion of the introductory chapter. The most excellent prince of the Dharma, [Dhāraṇīśvararāja,] having been fitted out in a buddha-ray initiation with supreme fearlessness and quick-wittedness, taught a praise of the ultimate, which is possessed of the real qualities of a tathāgata, and announced the topics of the supreme teaching of the Mahāyāna. [The illustrious one then] showed how to attain perfect mastery of the Dharma, namely the fruit resulting in [being able] to cause [the Saṅgha] to realize the [Mahāyāna].]**[1216]

[28.13–20] After that, the illustrious one saw the assemblies of the retinues of the [ten] bodhisattvas as large receptacles of the Dharma, and since the most excellent prince [of the Dharma], Dhāraṇīśvararāja, was not afraid, a light ray called *quick-wittedness* emanated from the top of the teacher's head, circled seven times around the maṇḍala of retinues, then a hundred times around the body of Dhāraṇīśvararāja, and descended onto the crown of his [head]. This is [referred to in the *Ratna-gotravibhāgavyākhyā* with the words] "he was initiated by a buddha ray." Immediately after this light had touched the bodhisattva Dhāraṇīśvararāja, through [this] power of the Buddha, he outshone by a hundred times the bodies, light, and lion thrones of the retinues. [Having received this blessing] he rose,[1217] put on his upper wear, made offerings in the form of an umbrella the size of the three-thousand-world [universe] in width, flowers, cymbals, and so forth, praised the light ray, and pronounced [the following stanzas]:

> [28.20–23] Being touched by the light of the leader of men,
> I remember any [virtue] attained before,
> [And my] intellectual brilliance, quick-wittedness, and retentive power

Exceeds [those of others] by many thousands.
My body is healthy and my mind pure,
My intellect happy and balanced.
On top of that, a buddha's full omniscience
And quick-wittedness have entered my body.[1218]

[28.23–24] Up to these stanzas [corresponds to] "the most excellent prince of the Dharma was fitted out with supreme fearlessness and quick-wittedness in a buddha-ray initiation" [in the *Ratnagotravibhāgavyākhyā*].

[28.24–29.1] From:

Since it is difficult to gain the great power of a buddha,
Weak ones cannot take delight [in it].
The Buddha having granted it for the sake of all sentient beings,
I request it from the Buddha.[1219]

up to

Kindly explain the experiential objects of the leaders.[1220]

[corresponds to] "Based on the attainment of quick-wittedness, he taught a praise of the ultimate, which is possessed of the real qualities of a tathāgata" [in the *Ratnagotravibhāgavyākhyā*].

[29.1–3] From "After the bodhisattva Dhāraṇīśvararāja had praised the illustrious one with these stanzas, he said the following to the illustrious one:"[1221] up to "[It is the ornament of bodhisattvas that the] accomplishment of work does not torment [them]"[1222] [corresponds to] "and he announced the topics of the supreme teaching of the Mahāyāna" [in the *Ratnagotravibhāgavyākhyā*].

[29.3–7] In view of [the passage] "illustrious one, why does a bodhisattva [first] conquer Māra and foes and rid himself of doubt, and [only] then [enter into the sphere of a tathāgata]?"[1223] up to "I will explain to you how one swiftly attains perfect mastery of the Dharma"[1224] [the following is stated in the *Ratnagotravibhāgavyākhyā*:] "[The illustrious one then] showed [him] how to attain perfect mastery of the Dharma, namely the fruit resulting in [being able] to cause [the Saṅgha] to realize the [Mahāyāna]. Thus the proper analysis of the unsurpassable qualities of these Three Jewels should be viewed in sequential order, and this is included in the concluding portion of the introductory chapter."

[29.7–12] By the power of the Buddha, Dhāraṇīśvararāja surpassed his own kind and also others a hundred times over, and having attained the height of quick-wittedness, he taught a praise of the Buddha, teaching [therein] his unsurpassable qualities. He announced the topics, wherefore the unsurpassable qualities of the Dharma were taught. He taught the fruit resulting in [being able] to cause [the Saṅgha] to realize the [Mahāyāna], wherefore the unsurpassable qualities of the Saṅgha were taught. As to these three teachings of qualities, since they are given immediately after the introductory chapter, titled "Array of Ornaments," it should be known that they are included in the concluding portion [of this chapter]. It goes up to "Then the bodhisattva Dhāraṇīśvararāja said to the illustrious one: 'Well so.'"[1225]

Buddha Nature and Its Purification through the Three Dharmacakras
[29.12–14] [The *Ratnagotravibhāgavyākhyā* further says:]

> **Then, after the introductory chapter of the *[Dhāraṇīśvara-rāja]sūtra*, the buddha element is elucidated by way of a description of the application of sixty purifying factors to this [element], the process of purification making sense [only] if the object to be purified possesses [buddha] qualities.**[1226]

[29.15–18] Generally, the simple expression *cleansing properties* does not pervade (i.e., coincide with the domain covered by) the expression *properties to be cleansed,* just as no [such pervasion] is ascertained when expressing gold by the term *fibroferrite.*[1227] On the other hand, if a knowledgeable [person] looks closely, he is able to ascertain, "There is a fruit."[1228] This is explained in [*Pramāṇavārttika* I.7[1229]]:

> The arising of the fruit (i.e., effect), [a process] that is inferred
> From[1230] the complete cause [as being a logical reason],
> Is described as the nature *(svabhāva)* [of this cause],[1231]
> Since [this fruition] does not depend on other things.[1232]

[29.18–25] Given such [a relationship], as expressed in the example, [we must concede that] in general the object to be purified, or the fruit, is endowed with qualities[, which means] "is connected with qualities." In the same way, Vinayadeva explains *connection ('brel pa)* in [his] *Hevajra* commentary[1233] as a synonym of "being endowed" *(ldan pa),* "contact" *(phrad pa),* and "being linked" *(sbyor ba).* This needs to be understood, even though it is explained here, in the ten presentations [of the element], as "being endowed" *(ldan pa)*. This is because it is proper to say that the cause that gives rise to a fruit that is pure for having been cleansed is a cleansing [factor], if such an object or fruit is endowed and [thus] connected with qualities. It is like an expert prospector sifting the earth [for] gold, or an alchemist cleansing a precious *vaiḍūrya* stone. The meaning is such. It has been said: "The buddhas, who think in terms of many eons, see that when bodhisattvas, great beings, apply these sixty factors [of cleansing] for the sake of all sentient beings, [the result] is beneficial." And: "Whatever has been investigated with great insight, I, too, have investigated [it]."

[29.25–30.7] In this way, the learned masters, the buddhas, caused the learned students, the bodhisattvas, to exert themselves in [applying] the sixty factors and strung the precious threefold training on the thread of remembrance. [Thus] they put on the [four] ornaments of the body of intellect, seized the eight great lamps of recollection, and so forth, and produced the power of sixteenfold great compassion, and as they sift the great earth of sentient beings and perform the thirty-two acts[1234] of cleansing some of the stones [which stand for] sentient beings, it is certain that these sentient beings [will be found to] possess [such] a nature that special marvelous qualities are bound to come forth. Since that nature is the cause that brings forth the qualities, it is given the name *element*. Since this is for the sake of all sentient beings, and not only for one type of earth, ground, or [precious] stone—of sentient beings—there are no sentient beings with a definite cut-off potential. This elucidates the meaning of [the sentence]: "It is not the case that [arhats] fall [into the extreme of] peace and cannot rise [from it any more]."

[30.7–9] [Now, as to the reason why] gold and the [buddha] element of sentient beings [are taken to be] similar in the *Daśabhūmikasūtra*, [the *Ratnagotravibhāgavyākhyā* continues:]

> **This motive having been taken up [as the subject matter],[1235] again a particular example, namely the [purification] process[1236] of gold, is used for the ten bodhisattva levels.[1237]**

[30.9–14] [In the *Daśabhūmikasūtra*] it is stated:[1238]

> For example, O sons of the victorious ones, gold that is heated in fire by a skilled [gold]smith[1239] to a certain extent becomes to that same extent thoroughly refined,[1240] completely pure, and pliable [for the purpose of decorations and ornaments].[1241] Likewise, O sons of the victorious ones, the extent to which a bodhisattva[1242]

makes offerings to the buddhas and illustrious ones, makes efforts with regard to the development of sentient beings, and "is in a state of having absorbed"[1243] the purifying factors of the [ten] levels,[1244] to that same extent the roots of his virtues, which are dedicated to omniscience, will make [him][1245] [even more][1246] thoroughly refined, completely pure, and pliable at will.[1247]

[30.14–15] Likewise in [the chapter on] the second level [in the *Daśabhūmikasūtra*] it is stated:

O sons of the victorious ones, when this gold is put into fibroferrite, it will be even more freed from all impurities.[1249]

[30.15–16] Also on the third level and higher levels, it is said [to be cleaned] by other specific acts of purification each in turn. [In the *Ratnagotravibhāgavyākhyā* it is further stated:]

[In this sūtra, too, immediately after the presentation of the activity of a tathāgata, the example of an impure *vaiḍūrya* stone is given.][1249]

[30.16–22] It has been taught in this same *Dhāraṇīśvararājasūtra* using the example of the *vaiḍūrya* gem.[1250] The example of an impure *vaiḍūrya* gem is given immediately after the presentation of the thirty-two-[fold] activity of a tathāgata, which is [related to] the thirty-two qualities of dissociation, such as the [ten] strengths. It has been taught starting with "Son of a noble family, it is like this." With regard to the stages of unfolding activity, everything—the [entire] activity of speech, all turnings of dharmacakras—have been summarized and taught as the threefold [dharma]cakra. Since it (i.e., the dharmacakra) is a great teaching, the foundation of these [turnings] must be spread out. [The sentence:] "[A tathāgata] has completely awakened [to all phenomena]"[1251] in the commentary on the Jewel of the Buddha, [means:] "after he has come to know reality as it is with the nonconceptual wisdom of a buddha."

[30.22–23] The heap of *vaiḍūrya* gems [refers to] all the [buddha] elements of sentient beings, inasmuch as it is stated [in the *Ratnagotravibhāgavyākhyā* on I.8]:

"Of the sentient beings" means "[sentient beings] who are among those who have committed themselves [to one of the three *yānas*], those have not committed themselves [to one of the three *yānas*], or those who have committed themselves to something wrong."[1252]

[30.23–31.1] The stains of all the [buddha] elements of sentient beings from among those not committed or those committed to the right [path] are cleansed by the [teachings of] the dharmacakra. The stains—the hindrances of defilements among ordinary persons, the hindrances of the knowable among the śrāvakas and pratyekabuddhas, both these hindrances that bodhisattvas as ordinary persons may [still] have, and the hindrances of any remaining [mental] imprints that noble ones still have after subduing the rough form of both hindrances—[all these] hindrances are cleansed.

[31.1–5] The path, in as far as it is a remedy against the stains, has been taught in the *[Abhidharma]samuccaya:*

> What is the truth of the path? The path by which you thoroughly come to understand [the truth of] suffering, abandon origination, actualize cessation, and meditate on the path—these are, in short, the defining characteristics of the path. The path is fivefold: the path of accumulation, the path of preparation, the path of seeing, the path of meditation, and the path of completion.[1253]

[31.5–7] In the *Abhisamayālaṁkāra* these have been taught as the paths conducing to liberation, to penetration, to seeing, to meditation, and to no more learning. The purifying paths [are reflected in] five divisions in each of the three *yānas*.

[31.7–19] As for the stages of bodhisattvas established on the path, they have been taught in the presentation of the ten bodhisattva levels[1254] [in the twentieth chapter] of the *Avataṁsaka[sūtra]:*[1255]

> O sons of the victorious one, since this bodhisattva potential, as it is called, extends as far as the dharmadhātu and reaches the limits of space, it is vast. Bodhisattvas abiding in it are born into the [great] family *(rigs)*[1256] of the past, future, and present buddhas. O sons of the victorious ones, if you ask what things [the buddhas] thought bodhisattvas should strive for and [what they] proclaimed, these are, O sons of the victorious ones, the ten bodhisattva levels. It is what past, present, and future buddhas taught, teach, and will teach. If you ask which ten,

> they are: the bodhisattva level of generating [bodhi]citta for the first time, the bodhisattva level of the beginner, the bodhisattva level of yoga conduct, the bodhisattva level of growing up, the bodhisattva level of sublime preparation, the bodhisattva level of sublime resolution, the irreversible bodhisattva level,[1257] the bodhisattva level of youthfulness,[1258] the bodhisattva level of the regent,[1259] and the bodhisattva level of consecration.[1260]

[31.19–20] [Thus] it is taught that the ten [types of] bodhisattvas abide in the potential (or belong to the [buddha] family). As for the potential in this [passage], it has been taught in the *Laṅkāvatārasūtra:*[1261]

> [31.20–23] Furthermore, Mahāmati, there are five potentials leading[1262] to [different] realizations. Which five? They are: the potential leading to the realization of the Śrāvakayāna, the potential leading to the realization of the Pratyekabuddhayāna, the potential leading to the realization of the Tathāgatayāna, the [uncertain] potential of not being committed to any one [of the three], and the fifth, the [potential of] being without a potential.[1263]
>
> [31.23–32.5] Mahāmati, how should you thoroughly come to understand the potential that leads to the realization of the Śrāvakayāna? Somebody whose body hairs stand on end when realization on the basis of a thorough knowledge of the skandhas, *dhātus*, *āyatanas*, and specific and general characteristics is being taught, whose mind takes immediate interest in the knowledge [automatically obtained] by becoming familiar with defining characteristics, but is not [interested in] becoming familiar with the defining characteristic of being inseparable from dependent arising—such a person, Mahāmati, has the potential that leads to the realization of the Śrāvakayāna. Someone who has, based on [his] view of the realization of the Śrāvakayāna, totally abandoned the rising (i.e., active) defilements on the sixth and fifth levels, [but] not the defilements of the mental imprints, [namely,] someone who is [still] subject to inconceivable transmigration[1264] truly utters the lion roar: "My [future] rebirth is uprooted, [my] morality *(brahmacarya)* established. I have done what has to be done."[1265] Having said this and the like, he becomes familiar with the fact that persons lack a [true] self, to the point where, as a consequence, he becomes someone whose mind [embraces] nirvāṇa.[1266]

[32.5–9] Others, Mahāmati, thoroughly understand existence in terms of a self, a sentient being, a vital life force, a nourisher, a noble being, and an individual, and thus seek nirvāṇa [in them]. Others again, Mahāmati, seeing that all phenomena depend on causes, are ones whose mind [may] take [that] to be nirvāṇa. [But] since they do not see the selflessness of phenomena, they do not attain[1267] liberation, Mahāmati. Mahāmati, such a mind, which takes[1268] nonemancipation as emancipation, belongs to those who have the potential that leads to the realization of the Śrāvakayāna and [the potential of] tīrthikas.[1269] Here, Mahāmati, you[1270] must make an effort in order to [help them] overcome [their] unsound views.[1271]

[32.9–14] Then, Mahāmati, a person possessing the potential that leads to the realization of the Pratyekabuddhayāna is somebody whose body hairs stand on end, rejoicing[1272] with tears [in his eyes], when realization only for oneself is being taught. When the obstinate clinging to entities owing to the causal condition of not socializing, the being confounded by the manifold variety of his own body's magical power and the display of a magical partition [of his body] into two [parts] are pointed out, [such a person] is pleased. Knowing that he has a potential that leads to the realization of the Pratyekabuddhayāna, he should engage in discourse that is in keeping with the realization of the Pratyekabuddhayāna. This, Mahāmati, is the defining characteristic of somebody with the potential that leads to the realization of the Pratyekabuddhayāna.[1273]

[32.14–21] Then, Mahāmati, there is the threefold potential that leads to the realization of the Tathāgatayāna. This is [1] the potential that leads to the realization of phenomena, which by their nature lack an own-being, [2] the potential that leads to the noble ones' realization, which [is attained] by themselves individually in the form of thorough understanding, and [3] the potential that leads to the realization of the vastness[1274] of outer buddhafields. Mahāmati, if somebody is not afraid, frightened, or terrified when any of these three is being taught, when the inconceivable notion that [everything in the world merely consists] of the appearances of his own mind—body, *ālaya[vijñāna]*, property, and abode—is being taught, he should be known as one who possesses the potential that leads to the realization of the Tathāgatayāna. This, Mahāmati, is the defining characteristic of someone with the potential leading to the realization of the Tathāgatayāna.[1275]

[32.21–25] Mahāmati, when these three are being taught, somebody with the [uncertain] potential of not being committed should be engaged there, wherever his mind tends. Mahāmati, such[1276] a tapping of the potential is the level of purification. This tapping needs to be done in order to proceed to the level of no more appearance. Having been cleansed of the [mental] imprints of his own defilements in his individual *ālayavijñāna*, a śrāvaka will see the selflessness of phenomena and obtain as a consequence the abode of the bliss of samādhi, and finally the embodiment of a victorious one (i.e., the dharmakāya).[1277]

[32.25–33.2] Thus the sources of the [description of the] potential as taught in the *Avataṁsaka[sūtra]* and the explanation of the subdivisions of the potential in the *Laṅkāvatārasūtra* have been presented. Now they will be explained a little [more]. As to [the expression] "this bodhisattva potential,"[1278] it is a *buddha potential,* given that it is a cause similar [to the fruit]. For roughly speaking, a bodhisattva is the cause—the substantial [cause]—of a buddha, as has been said in the *Madhyamakāvatāra* [I.1b]:

Buddhas were born from bodhisattvas.[1279]

[33.2–6] Well then, even though the grain of a *lungtang* (tree?) is [taken to be] the seed of a *lungtang* trunk, when carefully analyzed, you come to know that it is [only] the kernel inside of it that is the seed of the trunk. Likewise, if carefully analyzed, it is the essence of a bodhisattva's mindstream that is the potential. If you ask how so, [the answer is that] this very essence functions as the seed of the buddha properties, wherefore it is called *dharmadhātu* (lit., source of the [buddha] properties). As has been said in the *Dharmadhātustotra* [stanza 17]:

I maintain that, as a seed, this [buddha] element is itself the support of all [buddha] properties *(dharmas).*[1280]

[33.6–8] As to "extends as far as the [dharmadhātu],"[1281] [it means that] the part that [consists of] seeds delimits the [buddha] potential from other knowable objects. If you wonder whether only bodhisattvas have [such seeds], this is explained [in RGV I.16b–d]:

> [The wisdom that knows] the extent [of the dharmadhātu] *(yāvadbhāvikatā)* results from the fact that they see [with their intelligence, which realizes the limits of the knowable,][1282] that the true nature of omniscience exists in all sentient beings.[1283]

[33.8–13] Since [this wisdom] accordingly exists in all sentient beings, it is vast and broad, reaching the limits of space. It is the seed of the dharmakāya, in the same way as the sprout that emerges from the kernel becomes the potential [bringing forth] the trunk. In the *Dharmadhātustotra* [66–68] it is said:[1284]

> The generosity [that involves] undergoing various hardships,
> The discipline [of] gathering [wholesome *karman*] for the sake of sentient beings,
> And the patience that benefits others—
> I maintain that by these [three] the [buddha] element is fortified.[1285]
>
> Diligence with regard to all [positive] properties,
> Applying the mind to meditation,
> And permanently relying on insight—
> These, too, cause enlightenment to blossom.
>
> Insight together with skillful means,
> Very pure aspiration,
> And wisdom well established in strength
> Are four qualities (*dharmas*) that strengthen the [buddha] element.

[33.13–15] Similarly, since the root of wholesome deeds that are in accordance with the ten perfections is fortified, that which has been fortified is called the fortified or appropriated potential.

[33.15–16] With regard to this, too, it has been stated in the *Laṅkāvatārasūtra*:[1286]

> Mahāmati, the potential of the noble ones is divided into three types, according to the distinction made among śrāvakas, pratyekabuddhas, and buddhas.[1287]

[33.16–21] Likewise, the three potentials, each of which are certain, and the uncertain potential, which changes depending on which conditions are met, are the four potentials of the noble ones. To teach being without a potential [means to be] without a fortified potential. This was not made clear in the previous words [quoted from the *Laṅkāvatārasūtra*]. You may wonder why being without a fortified potential is [still] taken as a potential. [The reason] is not that the absence of a fortified potential is itself called a potential. It is rather that not everyone possesses a fortified potential [just] because everybody has a natural potential. Since [anyone] possessing a mind has a natural potential, he is [also] spoken of in these terms, in the same way as a noble being is meant by "tonsured" (i.e., a monk).[1288] Some Yogācāras take the expression "without a potential" literally.

[33.21–24] Here, in the teachings in the *Dharmadhātustotra* on the strengthening of the potential, the similarity of a person's[1289] skandhas, sense faculties, and so forth—their being made similar[1290] to the Buddha himself—is the potential, and therefore they (i.e., the skandhas, etc.) are the cause of [such a] potential at that time. When, by this similarity, wholesome deeds are performed naturally or automatically, this is a sign of the potential. The cause is illustrated by the fruit, as has been stated in, among other places, the *Bodhisattvabhūmi:*

> In this regard, the sign of the potential of the bodhisattva's perfection of generosity is that the bodhisattva naturally rejoices in generosity.[1291]

[33.25–34.7] Passages such as "[Somebody whose] body hair stands on end when the realization of skandhas, *dhātus*, *āyatanas*, and specific and general characteristics is being taught" teach the sign of a potential, as in the case of the potential of generosity and so forth. As to "internalization [based on] thorough knowledge," it is a name for realization. Based on the potential, "its mind takes immediate interest in the knowledge [automatically obtained] by becoming familiar with defining characteristics,"[1292] and this is the cause of realization. Since both types of those with a Hīnayāna potential exhibit such a [cause], [but] since those whose minds take immediate interest in becoming familiar with the defining characteristic of being inseparable from dependent arising are exclusively endowed with the pratyekabuddha [potential],[1293] it has been said that [śrāvakas] are not [similarly interested] and are cut off from it. By [internalizing] the view of realization on the Śrāvakayāna, they abandon the causes of manifest defilements at the time of fruition [but] not [their] mental imprints. By abandoning the causes for manifest [defilements], they have abandoned transmigration and rebirth following [normal] death. Knowing this directly, they utter the lion roar, utilizing the strength that has come from the right knowledge that [their] existence and so forth are destroyed. The main point along the path on which you achieve this is the knowledge that a person lacks an own [independent] self.

[34.7–14] Not having abandoned mental imprints, they obtain a mental body at the time of "no remainder" but are [still] subject to inconceivable transmigration. As to the explanation of "on the sixth and fifth level," bodhisattvas also have [recourse to] the path, [or] potential, of the śrāvakas and pratyekabuddhas. On the fifth [level] they reverse [something that] is similar to the defilements to be abandoned by śrāvakas through their knowledge of truth. On the sixth [level] they reverse [something that] is similar to what must be abandoned by pratyekabuddhas through their knowledge of dependent arising. This is the reversal, in the [mind]stream of bodhisattvas, of thoughts that are metaphorically called defilements, but in reality there are no [more] real defilements from the first bodhisattva level onward. Ārya Vimuktisena has said in this regard that [this level] is the śrāvakas' and pratyekabuddhas' perfection of abandonment and realization. From the seventh level onward, they outshine by the strength of [their] mind the śrāvakas and pratyekabuddhas.

[34.14–18] Although the teaching of the Buddha has many [different] presentations of nirvāṇa, [and] even if it is the lowest among these, the nirvāṇa of the śrāvakas, [attained when] defilements and a rebirth following [normal] death are reversed by meditating on the lack of an [independent] self in a person, it is [still] known by its main difference vis-à-vis outsiders, [such as the] Sāṁkhya, who claim the existence of a self, and therefore [can still] be taken to be liberation. As for the Vaiśeṣikas,[1294] they argue along the lines that liberation [is achieved] by eliminating the qualities of the personal self—earth and the like—so they are not liberated. In our own judgment, however, this is but the extinction of what is merely imputed.

[34.18–24] Again, others assert ([and this is reinforced] by their having attained the actual base of meditation) that once attachment is abandoned, the actual base of successively higher [states] is attained. In view of that, outsiders (i.e., non-Buddhists) who [become] free from attachment to the corresponding lower [states] see that all entities [that cause] suffering on the lower levels depend on the causes of attachment on these levels. Reversing this attachment through meditation, they enter a state of mind in which they claim [to have attained] nirvāṇa. Some in particular become proud, thinking that they are arhats for having reversed attachment with the help of the actual base of meditation. Seeing that they connect with another existence at the moment of death, they come to know that they are not arhats and give rise to the mistaken view that others are not arhats either. [Thus] it is explained in the *Bsam gtan pa'i dpe mkhyud kyi mdo.* Therefore it is said that śrāvakas, pratyekabuddhas, and outsiders have not [attained] supreme liberation since they do not see the selflessness of phenomena.

[34.24–35.1] The signs of the pratyekabuddha potential are that when the discourses of this vehicle are explained, [their body] hair stands on end and so forth. As for the path, it is taught [in the *Abhisamayālaṁkāravṛttiḥ Sphuṭārthā* II.8] by Ācārya Haribhadra:

> On the path of the pratyekabuddhas, there is simple meditation on the truth as it has been explained, and having meditated on entities as they really are, [that is,] arising in dependence....[1295]

[35.1–3] Not having completely realized the selflessness of phenomena, they obstinately cling to entities. Therefore it is not the nirvāṇa of the supreme. It has been said in many sūtras, however, that their magical clairvoyance and so forth is far superior to the clairvoyance of the śrāvakas.

[35.3–4] There is [a distinction] among three potentials of the Tathāgatayāna in the larger [version] of the *[Laṅkāvatāra]sūtra,* but there is a distinction among four potentials in the [version with] eight chapters:[1296]

> The potential leading to the realization of naturally [established?] phenomena, [the potential leading to the realization of phenomena that lack an own-being....][1297]

[35.4–7] This is no doubt correct. We can postulate that the *Cittamātrikas, who say that [mind] is established in terms of its nature or own-being—and, according to Maitrīpa, the Sautrāntikas, too—have a realization superior to the śrāvakas. As to the realization that phenomena lack an own-being, it starts from the Mahāyāna path of seeing. Mādhyamikas are the ones with a potential for this [realization].

[35.7–8] Here in [RGV II.7] it is stated:

> [The cause of the separation from the two hindrances is again the two types of wisdom,] which are taken to be nonconceptual wisdom and the one obtained after that.[1298]

[35.8–10] With regard to this wisdom obtained after [meditation], it is stated [in RGV II.19a–20a]:

> [Buddhahood is always[1299] the cause][1300] of seeing visible objects not made from elements,[1301] purely hearing the good discourses, smelling the pure scent of the Tathāgata's discipline, tasting the flavor of the right Dharma of the great noble ones, and experiencing the bliss of touching meditative stabilization.[1302]

[35.10–16] Likewise, the five sense faculties, collected together within the mental faculty of a bodhisattva, exhibit appearances with particular forms. With the manifestation of a few, many, [or] limitless buddhafields, which are characterized by [such particular appearances], the two accumulations are brought to completion, and this is the realization of exalted outer buddhafields. Since [this] depends on that which precedes it, [namely,] the direct realization of buddha nature—which is the nonconceptual wisdom free from mental fabrication—the thorough understanding [or] generation of [the bodhisattva's] own realization, it is expressed by the term *attained after [meditation]*. In the same way as the two stages of training (the perfection of wisdom and skillful means) emerge during the middle [dharma]-cakra, the two stages of nonconceptual [wisdom] and [wisdom] obtained after that have been explained in the last [dharmacakra] as well. These were the explanations of the certain potentials.

[35.16–17] As for the uncertain one, even though it is certain with regard to the potential of the noble ones in general, it is not certain with respect to any of the three *yānas*. As is said in the *[Mahāyāna]sūtrālaṁkāra* [XI.55ab]:

> There are two kinds of uncertain śrāvakas: those who have seen the meaning of [their own] *yāna* and those who have not.[1303]

[35.17–19] In the same way, somebody with an uncertain potential does not generate the bodhicitta of aspiration, and thus is said to be a śrāvaka who is uncertain, in that he acts like a śrāvaka, meditating on the noble truths and so forth, even though he is a bodhisattva.

[35.19–25] Next, the ten states, or conditions, of bodhisattvas[1304] from the *Avataṁsaka[sūtra]* will be explained.

1. As to generating [bodhi]citta for the first time, it [involves] seeing the Tathāgata's marvelous characteristics, seeing his miracles, seeing sentient beings' suffering, and seeing (i.e., reading) the scriptures. The generation of bodhicitta for the first time is based on whatever is suitable. It is the generation of [bodhi]citta that is full of aspiration. As a result of this generation of [bodhi]citta for the first time, the seed of the ten strengths is

generated. You rejoice [in it] by expressing the benefit of, among other things, the superior generation of [bodhi]citta by honoring the Buddha, and exert yourself with regard to the practice of [bodhi]citta. As has been said in [*Bodhicaryāvatāra* V.97]:

> The deeds of a bodhisattva may be vast,
> But first you must purify your mind.[1305]

[35.25–36.3] 2. With regard to the bodhisattva [level] of the beginner, Ācārya Haribhadra has stated [in his *Abhisamayālaṁkāravṛttiḥ Sphuṭārthā* I.22]:

> Similarly, in order for a bodhisattva to generate bodhicitta for the first time and so forth, and in order for him to generate the bodhicitta of exertion at the proper time and practice the Dharma implied by it....[1306]

Accordingly, you learn the instructions when you are in a state of generating the bodhicitta of aspiration. The way to learn [them] is to listen when they are first read out. After that you learn to meditate in an isolated place, and having attained [a stable] meditation, [you learn how to become] expert in teaching the Dharma to others.

[36.3–6] 3. The bodhisattvas whose practice is yoga[1307] abide on [the level of] the third generation of [bodhi]citta. It has been said that they meditate [according to] many [practices], such as the *presence of mindfulness* (Skt. *smṛtyupasthāna*). Accordingly, they exert themselves with regard to the yoga of the two types of selflessness, from "impermanence" up to "without action." By virtue of this, eyes that do not depend on other [factors] arise, together with clairvoyance.

[36.6–9] 4. "[The bodhisattva level of] growing up" is also called *having been born in an existence with changed conditions. Jāta*[1308] in Sanskrit [means] having been born into a family [of good ancestry]. Thus, having attained a [new] birth in a form [that reflects your] fully matured knowledgeable faith in such things as the Three Jewels, deeds, and fruit, as [taught] in the discourses of the Buddha, you acquire [the ability] to listen to the Dharma from the buddhas of the three times. Abiding on the great path of accumulation, you can listen to the Dharma directly from a tathāgata.

[36.9–12] 5. [A bodhisattva on the level of] sublime preparation abides, during the fourth generation of [bodhi]citta, on the part [of the path characterized by] penetration. In [the *Abhisamayālaṁkāra* IV.35ab] it has been stated:

The observed object of [different] types of heat[1309]
Are here praised as being all sentient beings.[1310]

Accordingly, whatever [practice] you begin upon attaining penetration, it is connected with the benefit of sentient beings. You ascertain that sentient beings, buddhafields, and so forth are immeasurable.

[36.12–16] 6. The bodhisattva [on the level of] sublime resolution has [become] certain by virtue of his very stable resolution with regard to the Three Jewels and so forth, and attains the state of patience on the level of being in partial concordance with penetration.[1311] For it has been said [in the *Abhisamayālaṁkāra* V.3]:

Unsurpassably perfecting the properties of threefold omniscience
Without ever abandoning the benefit of sentient beings is called *stability*.[1312]

This is the state of the fourth generation of [bodhi]citta. Since it has [also] been expressed as "comprehending the ten aspects, [namely,] signlessness and so forth," it should be referred to as *generating perseverance in not being afraid of emptiness*.

[36.16–18] 7. The bodhisattva on the irreversible [level] has attained the first [bodhisattva] level, [on which] he does not retreat from knowledgeable [faith] in the Three Jewels and his own level, as has been stated in the *[Prajñāpāramitāratnaguṇa]saṁcaya[gāthā]* [XVII.7b]:

...always free from doubts about their own level, like Mount Meru....[1313]

This [accounts for] the first level up to the seventh.

[36.18–20] 8. The bodhisattva [on the level of] the youthfulness abides on the eighth level. Being faultless, he is called *youthful*. As to fault, it [has the meaning of] defect, and [the bodhisattva on this level is called youthful] because he does not have any [faults] or [their] roots. The buddhas and illustrious ones instruct them by means of sublime [buddha]fields.

[36.20–22] 9. The bodhisattva [on the level of] a regent abides on the ninth level, since in the same way as a regent knows the activities of a king, [the bodhisattva on this level] is an expert with regard to the activities of a buddha, [such as] the preaching of the Dharma.

[36.22–24] 10. The bodhisattva [on the level of] consecration abides on the tenth level and has attained [the ability to perform] the innumerable deeds of a buddha. On the basis of these [points], the ten bodhisattva levels [of the *Avataṁsakasūtra*] have been explained.

[36.24–37.1] Now the way the buddha potential is purified by the three [dharma]cakras will be explained. Among the three *yānas*, even those who have obtained the four fruits on the Śrāvakayāna differ considerably in terms of qualities. Although they have [all] attained arhat[ship], there are many differences [among them]: [one] is with ornaments[1314] and [another] without,[1315] the body [of one] is frail and [that of another] is not. The situation is similar with regard to the pratyekabuddhas.

[37.1–6] Since bodhisattvas below the seventh level have many different faculties, there are many potentials functioning as their causes, and this is what is called the fortified potential. Although the natural potential has, among others, fortified and nonfortified [and] pure and impure [forms], these are, in terms of their nature, not very different, inasmuch as [the natural potential] has been taught as being of the nature of suchness, which is not different in buddhas and any sentient being. Therefore it has been said in the *Śrīmālā[devī]sūtra* [221b][1316] that whoever has no doubts [that what is covered by the extremity of the sheath of all defilements is] buddha nature also has no doubts about the dharmakāya of the buddhas. Thus they are not different, and since the fundamental substantial cause of a buddha is [buddha] nature alone, this latter must be purified. Toward that end the limitless activity of the light and emanations of the buddhas purifies the [buddha] element of sentient beings.

[37.6–8] All of these three stages, which have been taught by way of the example of refining a *vaiḍūrya* gem in the *Dhāraṇīśvararājasūtra*, are the purification by means of the teaching [wheels] *(dharmacakra)* of the noble one, which have not been set in motion before by humans or gods. With regard to the example, [the *Dhāraṇīśvararājasūtra* (as quoted in the *Ratnagotravibhāgavyākhyā*)] states:

> [37.8–13] **Son of noble family, take an expert jeweler who knows how to refine jewels well. He extracts impure jewels from a mine, washes them in salty acidic water, and polishes them with a black haircloth. But he does not cease his efforts there. After that he washes them in a sharp gravy and polishes them with a woolen blanket. But he does not cease his efforts there. After that he washes them in a medicinal liquid and polishes them with a finely woven cotton cloth. [Thus] polished and rid of impure substances, [such a gem] is called a precious *vaiḍūrya* stone.**[1317]

[37.13–16] The three stages of purifying the coarse, middle, and subtle stains is an example of the purification by way of the three turnings [of the dharmacakra]. When a specialist in the worldly sense analyzes an impure precious gem, he [finds that] it is worth purifying. The meaning [illustrated] is the fortified potential. [But] a specialist in the worldly sense does not know their [i.e., sentient beings'] potential, and it is [rather] the ability to purify by the power of meditative concentration that [serves as] an example for the naturally present potential.[1318] In [Bhavya's] *Prajñāpradīpa* it is stated:

> [37.16–20] Moreover, some think the following: "Since it has been said in the scriptures: 'In a tree or a trunk of a tree there are various elements,' [you are also entitled to say that] hotness exists in water. Therefore this is not a [proper] example." [Answer:] With regard to this, [a magician] who possesses magical powers or has gained control over sentient beings [may say:] "May there be riches, gold, silver, and so forth wherever there is grass, chaff, cow dung, and so forth." Magically empowered by this [declaration], [the grass and the rest] are [all transformed] in a like manner. [This also] permitted with regard to a tree, it has been said: "There are various elements in a tree and in the trunk of a tree."[1319]

[37.20–24] Such an ability to transform chaff into gold by the power of meditation is not a generally accepted way that causal relation works. Rather, when the power of meditation is involved, it is only the spatial element of the chaff that can be transformed into gold by this power, so that it is not a mutual transformation of an own-being of the two elements. The spatial element was used by the illustrious one as a simile of the naturally present [buddha] potential. Since it is obvious that in a generally accepted valid cognition, absolute darkness does not arise from a flame, it is not possible to claim [such and incur the undesired consequence in *Madhyamakāvatāra* VI.14b]:

> Then absolute darkness arises even from a flame.[1320]

[37.24–38.1] Likewise, you can certainly distinguish between objects that can be [produced by] the magical power of meditation and not, for if it were not so, the power of the buddhas' meditation would transform all sentient beings into buddhas in one moment, as is said in the *Tarkajvālā* (that is, *Madhyamakahṛdaya* X.3ab):

> If it could by achieved by the power of [Śākya]muni, all sentient beings would have passed into nirvāṇa.[1321]

[38.1–5] When an individual person has accepted the moral precepts and [first] established himself as a lay practitioner, [then] as a novice monk, and [then as] a [fully ordained] monk, it is not certain that this monk has obtained the fruit of a stream-enterer and so forth, even though it is said that entering into the teaching is completed when the *upasaṁpādana* vows of a monk[1322] have been taken. Likewise, even though the three dharma-cakras are set in motion, the three stages, namely, the nirvāṇa of the Hīnayāna, the attainment of the Mahāyāna levels of the nobles ones, and the attainment of the eighth [bodhisattva] level, have set temporary limits. In this regard, [the following is the presentation of] the first stage of purification [in the *Ratnagotravibhāgavyākhyā*]:

> [38.5–8] **Son of a noble family, a tathāgata, too, knows the unpurified element of sentient beings and creates disgust in those who rejoice in saṁsāra with the alarming teaching of impermanence, suffering, no-self, and impurity. [In such a way] he causes them to enter the noble discipline of the Dharma.**[1323]

[38.8–11] Thus it is stated [in the *Dhāraṇīśvararājasūtra* (as quoted in the *Ratnagotravibhāgavyākhyā*)]. A tathāgata is like a jeweler because he knows the [buddha] element of sentient beings precisely and completely. This is in accordance with:

> Then, as to the śrāvakas, he wishes to know all [of them]—because of his continuous engagement—as though he wanted, for example, to burn everything with fire, but it is not that he knows them instantaneously.[1324]

So, it is claimed that he comes to know the [buddha] elements of sentient beings gradually, not instantaneously.

[38.11–12] You may ask what is [meant] by the following statement:

> In the Mahāyāna it is said that he is someone whose pervasion of the entire maṇḍala of knowable objects [occurs] in a single moment of knowledge *(mkhyen pa)*.[1325]

[38.12–16] The jeweler, who [in this example] is the Tathāgata, is uninterruptedly engaged in his activity [of looking for the jewels of sentient beings] in the innumerable world systems. This is shown [in the text], for it is said further down[1326] in this teaching [of the *Dhāraṇīśvararājasūtra*?]:

> The doubt as to whether the dharmacakras were turned all at once or sequentially is removed. In the limitless world systems, they were turned all at once, and with regard to the individual persons, they were turned sequentially.[1327]

[38.16–19] Well then, for those who possess more roots of virtue at the stage of being in partial concordance with liberation *(mokṣabhāgīya)*, the second [dharma]cakra is first set in motion. For those who possess many more [roots of virtue], the first to be set in motion is the third [dharma]cakra. This should be understood in accordance with the *Ajātaśatrukaukṛtyavinodana[sūtra]*, the *Śūraṁgamasamādhi[sūtra]*, the *Aṅgulimālīya [sūtra]*, and others.

[38.19–26] Likewise, if you take the *Saddharmapuṇḍarīka[sūtra]* as a measure, at the time when many arhats, such as Śāriputra, were on the śrāvaka path, they were made to mature with the roots of virtue that pertain to the Mahāyāna and were granted a prophecy through the third [dharma]cakra. Thus whoever abides on the śrāvaka path is also prompted to embrace the third [dharma]cakra, so that somebody with such a potential becomes a disciple of the first and third [dharma]cakras. You may ask, is it not taught in the *Saddharmapuṇḍarīka[sūtra]* that it [itself] is the second [dharma]cakra? How can it then be the third [dharma]cakra? This [results] from a different way of counting. When presenting [the turnings] as two, the [dharma]cakra of the Hīnayāna and the Mahāyāna, the *Saddharmapuṇḍarīka[sūtra]* is the second [dharmacakra]. In the *Saṁdhinirmocana[sūtra]* it is described as the third, in accordance with the classification of the teachings for those who have entered the Śrāvakayāna, the Mahāyāna, and all *yānas*.

[38.26–39.4] This [particular] description as three stages[1328] is found in the present treatise (RGV II.41a–c), too:

> The nirmāṇakāya, which is the [primary] cause of [people] in the worlds entering
> The path of peace, bringing [them] to maturity, and granting [them] prophecies,[1329]
> Always abides in it,[1330]
> [Like the form elements in the spatial element.][1331]

and in the detailed explanation [of this stanza] as the last stage of the presentation as three stages, it is stated [in RGV II.58c–59d] that [the *Saddharmapuṇḍarīka*] is the third stage:

> Through the teachings of the reality of the Dharma
> In the *Saddharmapuṇḍarīka* and other [sūtras],
> He diverts [the śrāvakas] from their former conviction,
> And by using insight and skillful means,
> Makes them mature on the ultimate *yāna*
> And utters a prophecy with regard to [their] supreme enlightenment.[1332]

[39.4–11] When you first enter the Śrāvakayāna, aspects of the truth of suffering arise, and because of frightening impermanence [you realize] the suffering of being overpowered like chaff blown around by the wind. Because you have clung to the existence of a creator such as Īśvara and a substantial self that is different from the mere accumulation of skandhas even though they do not exist, [your life] has become pure suffering. Having seen that the stainlessness of what is in reality bliss has become immersed in impure mud, he creates—through his teaching that makes you weary of saṁsāra—disgust in sentient beings who are attached to saṁsāra, rejoicing in it, seeing it as something possessing good qualities. At the stage of being in partial concordance with liberation and the stage of being in partial concordance with penetration, he creates disgust in a general way. [For] when you directly come to know the aspects of the truth of suffering mentioned above and the twelve aspects of the remaining three truths on the path of seeing, you attain a state of great weariness[—in this way] he creates disgust [on this level]. Having [thus] made it a direct remedy for defilements, [the Buddha] causes you to embrace the disciplinary doctrine of the noble ones, the truth of the path.

[39.12–15] From that weariness he causes you [to go on to] attain [the level of] no more learning that is free from attachment, and from the latter to become established in the nirvāṇa without remainder, which is also the cessation of the polluted skandhas. The first [dharma]cakra has thereby partially reached fruition. That this is not entirely so is because the Buddha's activities are for the sake of establishing [everybody] in omniscience; the first [dharma]cakra was set in motion for this purpose.

[39.15–17] With regard to the second [dharma]cakra it is stated [in the *Dhāraṇīśvararājasūtra* (as quoted in the *Ratnagotravibhāgavyākhyā*)]:

But a tathāgata does not cease his efforts there. After that he makes them realize his guiding principle *(netrī)* through his teaching of emptiness, signlessness, and wishlessness.[1333, 1334]

[39.17–21] The sentence "But a tathāgata does not cease his efforts there" excludes the possibility that the Śrāvakayāna has reached the end with a defining characteristic of not [being able to] proceed to other [*yānas*]. You may ask, "Well then, for what reason does he make again effort?" A tathāgata is endowed with the realization of omniscience for [the sake, too, of] those who, after that [practice of the first dharmacakra], have entered the Mahāyāna, having generated bodhicitta together with the [corresponding] conduct. As for his guiding principle, it is the path.

[39.21] [As] is stated [in *Abhisamayālaṁkāra* I.2a:]

> The path [leading to] omniscience,
> [Is what has been taught here (i.e., in the *prajñāpāramitā* sūtras) by the teacher.][1335]

[39.21–22] The essence of this path is the three doors to liberation, and so he makes them realize the guiding principle through his teaching of emptiness, signlessness, and wishlessness.

[39.22–40.4] In the *prajñāpāramitā*, too, also these three [doors] have been taught:[1336]

> Moreover, Subhūti, the Mahāyāna of the bodhisattvas, the great beings, is the three samādhis. If you ask what these three are, they are the samādhi of emptiness, the samādhi of signlessness, and the samādhi of wishlessness. If you ask what the samādhi of emptiness is, it is that which abides in a mind fully realizing that all phenomena are empty of their own defining characteristics, [and that which is] emptiness as a door to liberation. This is the samādhi of emptiness. If you ask what the samādhi of signlessness is, it is that which abides in a mind fully realizing that all phenomena are without [characteristic] signs, [and that which is] signlessness as a door to liberation. This is the samādhi of signlessness. If you ask what the samādhi of wishlessness is, it is that which abides in the mind fully realizing that all phenomena are not to be "mentally elaborated,"[1337] [and that which is] wishlessness as a door to liberation. This is the samādhi of wishlessness.

[40.4–5] This defines it—the entire path taught in the *prajñāpāramitā*. But the "highest fruit"[1338] of the levels proper to this [second] dharmacakra is obtained [only] by [a bodhisattva] on the seventh level.

[40.5–8] With regard to the third [dharma]cakra it is stated [in the *Dhāraṇīśvararājasūtra* (as quoted in the *Ratnagotravibhāgavyākhyā*)]:

> **But a tathāgata does not cease his efforts there. Thereafter he causes sentient beings, who have by origin various natures, to enter the sphere of a tathāgata through the teaching of the irreversible [turning of] the dharmacakra, the teaching of the threefold purity. Those who have entered[1339] [the sphere] realize the true nature of a tathāgata and are called the unsurpassable venerable ones.**[1340]

[40.8–10] "But a tathāgata does not cease his efforts there" is explained in the *Ratnāvalī* [V.40]:

> In the same way as eight śrāvaka levels are explained according to the Śrāvakayāna,[1341] there are ten bodhisattva levels according to the Mahāyāna.[1342]

[40.10–15] The sixth śrāvaka level in the *Laṅkāvatāra[sūtra]* passage ("Mahāmati, from the sixth level onward, the bodhisattvas, great beings, śrāvakas, and pratyekabuddhas enter cessation."[1343]) is the level of the fruit of a "never returner." Even though it is not at all the same as the sixth bodhisattva level in terms of qualities, etc., it has been subsumed under the same name, *sixth level*. The śrāvakas' and bodhisattvas' respective enterings into cessation are explained in this way as being the same in name [only].

[40.15–18] If, however, based on the commentary of the *Aṣṭasāhasrikā Prajñāpāramitā* (which says that since on the bodhisattva path of seeing the abandonment and realization of śrāvakas and pratyekabuddhas are perfect), they are *enemy destroyers (arhats),* because they have destroyed the enemies on the path of seeing, and *[practitioners] in whom the outflows are exhausted,* because they have exhausted the outflows on the path of seeing—[if] you think [on this basis] that you do not have to learn any more after having attained arhatship, [you should consider that it was said:] "But a tathāgata does not cease his efforts with that." Thereafter, those bodhisattvas are introduced into the sphere of a tathāgata.

[40.18–19] If you ask what the sphere of a tathāgata is like, it is engaged within itself in working for the sake of sentient beings, with neither effort nor concepts, because it has been said in this [RGV I.77]:

> [40.19–21] As to the way of the bodhisattva, in the state obtained after meditation[1344]
> He becomes equal to the Tathāgata on account of having liberated sentient beings in [various] worlds.[1345]

[40.21–23] Since this [ability] is obtained from the eighth level onward, that bodhisattva is also called a tathāgata. In the *[Prajñāpāramitāratnaguṇa]-saṁcaya[gāthā]* [XII.4cd], too, it has been said:

> Bodhisattva[s] thoroughly realize this [dharmatā][1346] as suchness
> And are therefore called *buddha* by the tathāgatas.[1347]

[40.23–24] Not having attained the sphere of such a tathāgata, [a bodhisattva] on the seventh level should not to be said to be without defilements. With regard to the notion that there is [still] attachment to the wisdom of a tathāgata and that [his] intentions have not been completely perfected, it is stated in *Daśabhūmikasūtra:*

> [40.24–41.3] O son of the victorious one, a bodhisattva on the seventh level has left for the most part all the accumulations of defilements—attachment and the rest[1348]—behind him. A bodhisattva practicing on the [seventh] level, "having gone far," should to be said to be someone neither with defilements nor without defilements. If you ask why that is, [it is for the following reason:] as no defilements occur, he should not be said to be with defilements. But since [he still] longs for the wisdom of a tathāgata, and since [his] intentions are not completely perfected, he should not be said to be without defilements either.[1349]

[41.3–7] It is said that because of this, the conduct arisen from practice, and attachment to the wisdom of a tathāgata, are from the first to the seventh level given the name *defilement,* and it is the purification of this a tathāgata puts his effort into. As for the skillful means by which he does this, it is by the teaching of the irreversible [dharma]cakra. Because this teaching is one of threefold purity,[1350] it is, firstly, a perfect teaching.

[41.7–10] As for this threefold purity, it has been said in the *Mahāyānasūtrālaṁkāra* [and the corresponding *bhāṣya* XII.11]:

> This teaching of the buddhas is pure in terms of the three circles.
> It should also be known to be free from the eight faults.

> "Pure in terms of the three circles" means [the purity of that] by which he teaches, [that is, in] speech and words; [the purity of] how [it is taught]—the kind of statements and so forth—and [the purity of the disciples] to whom [it is taught], who know the condensed statements and detailed explanations.[1351]

[41.10–11] Therefore, it is threefold—the purity of the speech of teachers, famous among [the monks of] Nālanda; of the teachings to be explained; and of the [mind]streams of the disciples.

[41.11–19] Since wisdom on the eighth level is irreversible, it is called the irreversible level. The meaning of this teaching is that some people get tired of the [meditation] cushion and are not able to sit for a long time [on it], and in the same way as they [can]not endure the cushion, they rise again from meditative equipoise, and this means not being able to endure meditative equipoise. Since, on the eighth level, you do not rise [any longer] from meditative equipoise, [which is focused] on nonorigination, it is called the *endurance of nonorigination*. Nor do you turn away from the wisdom of nonorigination. From this [eighth] level onward, the teaching in its main part is therefore said to be irreversible. Since it is transmitted into the [mind]stream of the disciple, it is called a [dharma]cakra, namely the *Dhāraṇīśvararājasūtra* itself and the other sūtras of the irreversible [dharma]cakra. Moreover, the actual students of this [dharma]cakra are sentient beings who by origin have various natures. Since the term *nature* is a synonym of the term *potential*, you need [to understand] potential. "Various" [means] "different." As [sentient beings] are the fruit arisen from different potentials, they have [these] as [their] origin. The explanation in the *Saṁdhinirmocanasūtra* (VII.30) "those who have entered all vehicles"[1352] [refers] precisely to this.

[41.19–21] The fruit of this [dharma]cakra is [the state of] having entered the sphere of a tathāgata. As for the true nature of a tathāgata, it is said [in *Abhisamayālaṁkāra* IV.16cd]:

> And that which is different from that ([knowledge of minds] called active and so forth[1353])
> Is the knowledge of these [forms of mind] in [their] aspect of suchness.[1354]

And it is [further] said [in *Abhisamayālaṁkāra* IV.17a]:

> The sage[s] realize suchness [and teach it to others].[1355]

[41.21–24] In this manner you realize the true nature of a tathāgata, which [means that] you know the mind of sentient beings in terms of its true nature and so forth, become enlightened, attain the arhat[ship] of the unsurpassable *yāna*, and you are thus said to be an unsurpassable object of veneration. In this regard, it has been said in [the chapter on] the eighth level in the *Daśabhūmika[sūtra]* that [a bodhisattva on the eighth level] is honored by all worldly protectors.[1356]

[41.24–42.10] As for how stains are thereby cleared away, it is stated in the *Laṅkāvatārasūtra:*

> "Illustrious one, how is the stream of appearances, which are your own mind, purified—instantaneously or gradually?" The illustrious one replied: "The stream of appearances, which are your own mind, is purified gradually and not instantaneously. "Mahāmati, it is like the mango fruit, which ripens gradually and not instantaneously. It is in this way, Mahāmati, that sentient beings' streams of appearances, which are their own mind, are purified. Mahāmati, it is like a potter, who makes pots gradually and not instantaneously; in the same way, Mahāmati, a tathāgata causes sentient beings' streams of appearances...to be purified gradually and not instantaneously. Mahāmati, it is like grass, a thicket, medicinal herbs, and forest trees, which grow up gradually from the earth[1357] and not instantaneously; in the same way, Mahāmati, a tathāgata causes sentient beings' streams of appearances...to be purified gradually and not instantaneously. Mahāmati, it is like someone who becomes a master of comedy, dancing, music, singing, lute,[1358] cymbals,[1359] and painting gradually and not instantaneously; in the same way, Mahāmati, a tathāgata causes all sentient beings' streams of appearances...to be purified gradually and not instantaneously."[1360]

> [42.10–15] Mahāmati, it is like all manifestations of forms in a mirror, which appear instantaneously without concepts;[1361] in the same way, Mahāmati, a tathāgata causes all sentient beings' streams of appearances...to be purified instantaneously, [namely in a stream] free from concepts and [in] a [tathāgata's] experiential object that lacks appearances. Mahāmati, it is like the disks of the moon and the sun, which illuminate with [their] rays all manifestations of forms instantaneously; in the same way, Mahāmati, a tathāgata instantaneously shows the experiential object of the victorious one, [that is, of] his inconceivable wisdom, to those sentient beings[1362] who are free from the mental imprints of bad states, [namely,] their own minds' appearances.[1363]

[42.15–19] Here, the stream of appearances that are your own mind is the basic consciousness, which is comparable with the stone of the *vaiḍūrya* family. It is similar to the water of the ocean. From it arise the forms of active consciousness, which are similar to waves. When the active consciousness becomes pure, it does so gradually. The gradual ripening of fruit of the mango tree is an example of gradually increasing [the dosage] of a remedy to purify the mind. The potter stands for the tathāgata. By his fashioning, that is, by his teaching of the Dharma, the path gradually arises. [This is what the *Laṅkāvatārasūtra*] is saying [here].[1364]

[42.19–21] As to the example of the great earth, in the same way as everything arises in dependence on the earth, which is by nature void of concepts, so too the qualities arise gradually from the nonconceptual dharmakāya of the tathāgata and the nonconceptual meditative concentration of the bodhisattvas. [This is what the *Laṅkāvatārasūtra*] is saying [here].

[42.21–22] In the same way as vocal music, comedy, and instrumental music are mastered gradually, so too the qualities arise gradually even from the conceptual state together with performance that is attained after [meditative concentration]. [This is what the *Laṅkāvatārasūtra*] is saying [here].

[42.22–23] The example of the mirror stands for the instantaneous appearance of all objects of knowledge in your mindstream after it is liberated from base states on the pure [bodhisattva] levels. [This is what the *Laṅkāvatārasūtra*] is saying [here].

[42.23–24] The example of the sun and moon stands for the instantaneous diffusion of brilliance of teaching the Dharma to other disciples. [This is what the *Laṅkāvatārasūtra*] is saying [here].

[42.24–25] Therefore the gradual purification of stains by way of the three [dharma]cakras goes up to the seventh level. [This is what the *Laṅkāvatārasūtra*] is saying [here].

[42.25–43.2] The first turning washes away defilements that have arisen through the [wrong] view of a self. The middle turning purifies [both] coarse and subtle concepts that come from clinging to things. The last turning purifies the so-called object appearances that appear to the mind, for they are a hindrance to seeing [your own] buddha nature properly.

[43.2–4] Furthermore, [it is stated] in the *Laṅkāvatārasūtra* [II.99–100]:

> Like the waves of the ocean, set in motion under windy conditions,
> Arising like a dance—and there is no interruption—
> The stream of the basic [consciousness] is in a similar manner set
> constantly in motion by the wind of [cognitive] objects,
> And the varied waves[1365] of consciousness arise as in a dance.[1366]

[43.4–7] The continuum is the basic consciousness, which is without interruption. In the same way as dance-like waves arise when a flow of water has been stirred by winds, so too the waves of the eye consciousness and so forth arise under the conditions of [cognitive] objects, which [in this] resemble the wind. Assuming the forms of a dancer, deities, and the like, [the waves] dance. Likewise, the basic consciousness assumes the forms of [cognitive] objects and arises as the consciousness of the eyes and so forth. This is like a dancer. [This is what these stanzas] are saying [here].

[43.7–10 In the *Laṅkāvatārasūtra* (II.101–2) it is further said:]

> Blue,[1367] red, salt, conch shells, milk, sugar,
> Astringent fruits, and flowers,
> These are known to be neither identical nor different,[1368]
> Like rays of the sun and the moon,
> And waves of the ocean.[1369]
> Likewise the seven types of consciousness, too,
> Are connected with the mind.[1370]

[43.10–16] If you consider what the forms of an object are like when they appear to consciousness, they appear as blue and so forth. As to blue and red, they appear to the eye consciousness. [Here] it is being said that they appear as the aspects of conch shells, milk, flowers, sun rays, and so forth. As to salt, sugar, and the astringent myrobalan fruit, these characterize what appears in the form of taste. Furthermore, when a pot appears in the sunlight,[1371] the manifested pot is not substantially different from the [actual] pot. [But] if it were substantially identical with the [material] continuum [of the pot], a pot would appear also in the darkness. Therefore, it is free from identity and difference. Likewise, when blue appears to the eye consciousness, it is the eye consciousness itself that takes on the appearance of blue. Therefore, this appearance of blue is not substantially different from consciousness *(shes pa)*. The fact that the stream of this consciousness appears also as yellow [shows that] this appearance as blue does not [totally] conform with the continuum of consciousness. [This is what these stanzas] are saying [here].

[43.16–17] Likewise, since the seven types of consciousness occur as these very seven types of consciousness themselves in a stream of the type that basic [consciousness] is, they are not different from the basic [consciousness] in terms of substance [or] type. [But] it is not the case that they permanently abide as a [continuous] stream.

[43.17–18] Thus, the master Vasubandhu said [in his *Triṁśikākārikā*, stanza 16]:

> The manifestation of mental consciousness takes place at all times,
> Except in an unconscious state, in a state without mind *(citta)*,
> sleep, or fainting.[1372]

[43.18–22] ...and thus explained three states without [active consciousness]. As for the defiled mind, it does not exist during absorption on the supramundane path and cessation. Thus the defiled mind and the consciousness of the five doors[1373] are completely tainted, but since the mental consciousness has both a tainted and untainted [part], it can abandon the tainted [part]. [This is what the stanza] is saying [here].[1374]

[43.22–24] [It is further said in the *Laṅkāvatārasūtra* (II.103–4):]

> The change of the ocean [produces] the variety of waves.
> Likewise, the basic [consciousness] moves on as the variety of what are called [active forms of] consciousness.
> Mind, [defiled] mind, and [active] consciousness are [conventionally] determined for the sake of defining characteristics,
> [But in reality] the eight [types of consciousness], whose [only] defining characteristic is not to be separate, can neither be the basis for definition nor possess defining characteristics [as distinct types].[1375]

[43.24–44.2] In the same way as the flat expanse of the ocean [may] turn about, change, and appear as waves, so too the basic consciousness becomes a sevenfold variety of consciousnesses. Thus the mind (as a consequence of having accumulated mental imprints in the basic [consciousness]), the defiled mind (as a consequence of egocentricity), and the active mind (as a consequence of the mental faculty and its corresponding cognition of objects) are [all] labeled "consciousnesses," having acquired their names and meaning by virtue of their distinct defining characteristics. In reality, all of these are types of the same basic [consciousness], and as types, they should therefore not be associated with defining characteristics or a basis for definition. The eight have the defining characteristic or nature of not being different types.

[44.2–3] [It is further said in the *Laṅkāvatārasūtra* (II.105):]

> In the same way as there is no difference between waves and the ocean,
> A development (i.e., in the sense of a real distinction)[1376] from the mind of the types of consciousness is not found.[1377]

[44.3–5] When waves have "returned to" and "developed" into the ocean, they are [indeed still] waves. [But] in the same way as you do not apprehend [them as distinct entities, thinking rather that] they are the ocean, so too the eight types of consciousness are not apprehended [as something separate] when mind has "developed" into the eighth [bodhisattva] level. [This is what this stanza] is saying [here].

[44.5–7] Likewise, with regard to these [eight forms of consciousness], Saraha said [in his *Dohākośagīti*, stanza 74]:[1378]

> Whatever emanates from the mind, [and however long such thoughts do so,]
> So long will their nature be that of the protector [of all beings].[1379]
> Are water and waves different or not?
> [His] equality with worldly existence is by nature [that of] space.[1380]

[44.7–9] Zhang [Tsalpa Tsöndrü] (Zhang [Tshal pa Brtson 'grus]) said:

> Do not think that these thoughts—suddenly arisen
> From within the state of thus positing [your] mind—
> Are themselves different
> From luminosity and the dharmakāya.

In the same way, waves stirred up with a crashing sound
From the unmoved clear ocean
Are nothing different [from the ocean].[1381]

[44.9–13] Chegom (Lce sgom) (ca. 1140/50– 1220)[1437] said:

Even though a variety of dual appearances appear to the mind,
With regard to their abiding nature they have never been different and are of one taste.
It is like water and ice: even though they appear to be two,
They have the same taste, for the nature of ice is water.
Therefore, the nature of water and ice is not different.
You should know that all phenomena that appear as [subject-object] duality are like that.[1382]
It is like the ocean and the waves: even though they appear as two,
They have the same taste, in that by their nature waves are the ocean.
Therefore, the nature of the ocean and the waves is not different,
And you should know that [all] phenomena that appear as [subject-object] duality are like that.[1383]

[Thus] the discourse of the victorious one (i.e., the *Laṅkāvatārasūtra*) is a basis for such [mahāmudrā teachings].

[44.13–16] [Next, the *Ratnagotravibhāgavyākhyā* says:]

> With regard to the example of gold, it too refers to [the potential]: "**Thinking of this potential, which is purity** by nature, even though it has been hindered by the adventitious stains...." If you ask, the potential of what? [the answer] is the **element,** the potential, and the cause **of a tathāgata.**[1384] The proof in the scripture for this [is:] **Just as gold is not seen in crumbled stone but [first] becomes visible through a process of purification, similarly tathāgatas [become visible by purification] in the world of living beings. Thus it has been stated** in the *Ghanavyūha[sūtra].*[1385]

[44.17–20] A variant reading [?][1386] of this sūtra [passage] is: "The presence of gold does not become apparent by pulverizing stones to dust; the gold appears by a particular process of purification." The example of gold teaches that the naturally present potential, [namely] suchness, is purified.

Here [in the *Ratnagotravibhāga* I.151 (J I.148)] it is said:

> Since it is unchanging by nature, [full of] virtue, and perfectly pure,
> Suchness is [well] illustrated by the analogy of a piece of gold.[1387]

[44.20–45.5] Somebody may remark that if you explain the gradual purification of stains by means of the three [dharma]cakras together with the examples, [and] if it is easy to understand the differences between the first and the second [dharma]cakras, in that they [respectively] teach the [four] noble truths and emptiness, what is then the difference between the second and the third [dharma]cakras? In the *Saṁdhinirmocanasūtra*, the last two [dharma]cakras are both taught in terms of the lack of own-being, absence of production, absence of cessation, quiescence from the start, and being naturally in a state of nirvāṇa. Therefore, they appear not to be different in reality. If, on the other hand, a difference is evident, inasmuch as the second [dharmacakra] has been taught as being provisional and the third as being definitive, is it the case that, in terms of compassion, the extent of a bodhisattva's conduct is greater or smaller in [either of the] two? Or is there a difference of a higher and lower view in terms of insight? Or a difference in being expert or not in cultivating [the view] in meditation? Or a difference in having completed the [bodhisattva] levels or not? If there is no difference, how are you to understand that the purity in terms of the three circles[1388] of the discourses in the third [dharmacakra] are mentioned in particular, and that the Tathāgata's effort [in the third dharmacakra] surpasses the previous ones? If there are differences, say them!

[45.5–7] If this is a worthwhile question, those disciplined according to the works of the Śrāvakayāna and those exclusively disciplined according to the Madhyamaka treatises of Nāgārjuna and his disciples will become terrified. Nevertheless, since obviously many, even persons with marvelous devotion, have had [this question], an answer must be given.

[45.7–21] In the *Saṁdhinirmocanasūtra* (VII.31–32) it is stated:

> [Paramārthasamudgata] asked: "Illustrious one, how much merit do those sons or daughters of good origin generate who hear this illustrious one's teaching of the definitive meaning—beginning with phenomena lacking an own-being up to being naturally in a state of nirvāṇa—and then develop devotion, write it down, memorize it, read it, venerate it, propagate it, receive an oral transmission of it, recite it to others, reflect on it, and unite with it in the form of meditation?" The illustrious one

> replied to the bodhisattva Paramārthasamudgata: "Paramārthasamudgata, those sons or daughters of good origin will generate immeasurable, incalculable merit. It is not easy to give an example of this, but I will explain it to you briefly. Paramārthasamudgata, it is like this: If you compare, for example, the particles of earth on the tip of a fingernail to all the particles of earth in the earth, they do not approach even a hundredth part, they do not approach even a thousandth part [or] even a hundred-thousandth part—any part, any approximation, any comparison. If you compare the water in a cow's hoof print to the water in the four great oceans, it does not approach even a hundredth part, and so on. Paramārthasamudgata, I have explained the merit of those who are devoted to the sūtras of provisional meaning up to being united [with them] in the form of meditation. If you compare it to the merit of having completely realized the [bodhisattva] levels by devotion,[1389] to the teaching of definitive meaning up to complete realization from being united [with it] in the form of meditation, it does not even approach a hundredth part (and so on) up to 'it does not bear any comparison.'"[1390]

[45.21–22] Given that the difference in benefit from [only] hearing these provisional and definitive meanings is already so great, you may conceive that the difference [between them and] the profound and vast meaning of the last [dharma]cakra is also on the same order.

[45.22–46.5] There is a distinction [among the three dharmacakras] resulting from a difference in compassion. With regard to the second [dharma]cakra, you are focused—according to the three aspects of compassion, which is [either directed] toward sentient beings [or] phenomena, [or] is without any objective support—on [either] sentient beings with their suffering of suffering, [or] on their being encumbered with the suffering of impermanence, [or] on the nature of emptiness. Here in the third [dharmacakra] the nature of mind is [taken to be] the nature of bliss, permanence, the true self, and essential purity. Outside of this [nature, however], it has been temporarily[1391] hindered by ignorance, and as a result appears to be encumbered with suffering. Thinking that this is amazing, you develop compassion in order to remove this confusion. Likewise, knowing that you are yourself of the same kind as [this buddha] potential, you develop friendliness and love, and seeing the nature of sentient beings, you rejoice and respect them as if they were teachers. [Finally,] you generate the equanimity[1392] in which you see the sameness of all sentient beings. You work, as a result of this, much more expeditiously for the benefit of others, and this is considered to be the attainment of the four special immeasurable [qualities]. This is taught from "So it was presented before" (RGV I.163a (J I.160a)) up to "you obtain buddhahood quickly" (RGV I.170d (J I.167d)).[1393]

[46.5–11] With regard to generating bodhicitta, which arises from the [four] immeasurable [qualities], it has been said in the *Bodhicittavivaraṇa*:[1394] It has been stated [in the *Guhyasamājatantra*]:[1395]

> [Your own mind][1396] is free from all entities.
> It is exempt from the skandhas, *dhātus*, and *āyatanas*,[1397]
> The perceived object and the perceiving subject.
> Being equanimous [in keeping with] the selflessness of
> phenomena,
> Your own mind has never arisen since the beginning
> And has emptiness as its nature.[1398]

> In the same way as the illustrious buddhas and the great bodhisattvas generated a mind [committed] to great enlightenment, I too shall generate such a mind from now on until I am [in the heart of] enlightenment, so that sentient beings who are unsaved may be saved, those who are not liberated may be liberated, those who are not consoled may be consoled, and those who have not completely passed into nirvāṇa may completely pass into nirvāṇa.

[46.11–12] It has been [further] said in the *[Bodhicittavivaraṇa]*:[1399]

> Having thus generated the bodhicitta that in terms of apparent [truth] has the nature of aspiration, [bodhisattvas] must generate ultimate bodhicitta by the power of meditation.[1400]

[46.12–14] [This power of meditation is] the supreme generation of bodhicitta, since it arises through the power of seeing the similarity between the enlightenment to be attained, and the [cognitive] object, [namely,] sentient beings' luminosity of mind.

[46.14–16] This ultimate [bodhi]citta is also called emptiness, for it is stated in the *Bodhicittavivaraṇa* [71]:

[A blissful mind] has been also explained as suchness, the limit of reality,
Signlessness, and the ultimate, the very supreme bodhicitta, and emptiness.[1401]

[46.16–17] It is even more exalted when you train yourself, based on this generation of [bodhi]citta, to observe the conduct of a bodhisattva. When you familiarize yourself with the [bodhi]citta of focusing on the nature of mind, you realize that the nature of the six active forms of consciousness is luminosity.

[46.17–24] In the *Dharmadhātustotra* [38–43] it is stated:[1402]

Based on eyes and forms,
Stainless appearances occur.
Since these neither arise nor cease,
They are rightly known as the *dharmadhātu.*[1403]

Based on sound and ears,
[The corresponding] consciousness [occurs]; the mind of these three[1404]
Is the *dharmadhātu* without defining characteristics,
Obtained without any concepts at all.[1405]

Based on the nose and odor,
An olfactory consciousness [occurs]; [all three are] suchness.
This makes you realize that [they are] the *dharmadhātu*
That is without forms and unteachable.[1406]

The nature of the tongue is emptiness.
The tasted object, too, is an "isolated [phenomenon]."[1407]
And given their *dharmadhātu* nature,
Their [corresponding] consciousness is without abiding.[1408]

Pure tangible objects with the defining characteristic of being a condition,
[That which] by [its] nature [is] the pure body,
[And the corresponding consciousness that is] free from conditions—
[These are what] I call the *dharmadhātu.*[1409]

Having completely abandoned thoughts and imagined [objects][1410]

With regard to phenomena that appear to the mental
[consciousness],[1411]
You should meditate on phenomena being the *dharmadhātu,*
Given[1412] that they lack an own-being.

[46.24–47.2] Accordingly, the six collections of consciousness, their support (the six faculties), and the six objects [constitute] the eighteen *dhātus*. When the eighteen [types of] mental movement[1413] occur in them, you [may] meditate on these [mental] movements as luminosity, and once you are used [to doing so], the eighteen *dhātus* themselves appear as luminosity. When they do appear [as luminosity], you are said to be accomplished.

[47.2–10] Based on this, you obtain the qualities of the pure sense fields *(āyatana)* as taught in the *Saddharmapuṇḍarīka[sūtra]*. It has been said that 112 or 108 qualities arise with regard to each *āyatana*. There are twenty "world realms"[1414] of the desire [realm], sixteen of the form [realm], and four of the formless [realm]—altogether forty. [Forty] each in the ten directions makes four hundred, and this in each of the three times makes 1,200. When you see the forms[1415] that abide in the four hundred worlds in the ten directions of the present, they are seen as if assembled at the gate of the eyes. In a like manner are seen the forms of the past and the future of these world realms. For a bodhisattva, they are first seen with the eyes of flesh, not with clairvoyance. Thus it has been explained in the sūtra, which repeats [this description] with regard to the other [sense] faculties as well. When he sees such a variety of objects, the conduct of a bodhisattva becomes very exalted. Extensive clairvoyance is also quickly achieved by accomplishing eyes[1416] of flesh [that see that]. Thus a vast amount of merit can be created.

[47.10–12] [In the same way] as the venerable Dīpaṁkāraśrījñāna (i.e., Atiśa) said [in his *Bodhipathapradīpa* 37]:

The merit of [only] one day and night accruing to those possessing
clairvoyance
Somebody devoid of clairvoyance does not have even in
a hundred lives.[1417]

[47.12–13] [The third dharmacakra] is more distinguished also by reason of [its] view. There it is asserted, among other things, that all phenomena, subject as they are to worldly existence and nirvāṇa, lack an own-being from the very beginning and are free from the eight extremes of mental fabrication.

[47.13–17] In the *Dharmadhātustotra* [30–33] it is said:[1418]

Just as a horn on the head of a rabbit
Is only imagined[1419] and does not exist,
So all phenomena, too,
Are only imagined and do not exist.

If you analyze down to minute atoms,[1420]
Even the horn of an ox does not exist.
As it was before, so it will be later;
So why imagine here [that anything exists]?[1421]

If [things] arise in dependence
And cease in dependence—
If a single [independent thing] does not arise[1422]—
How do fools conceive of one?

The defining characteristics of imagined origination[1423]
Must be understood as [conforming to] the middle [way],
In accordance with the examples of the horn of a rabbit and
an ox—
Just like the properties of the Sugata himself.[1424]

[47.17–19] In this way it is taught that phenomena lack a single own-being, [and] with recourse to [the arguments of] neither one nor many, interdependence, and the interdependence of impermanence. Just as in the corpus of analytical works, so it is here [in the third dharmacakra], too.

[47.19–25] Nevertheless, in whatever way they are [determined through] investigation as being emptiness, [it is stated in *Dharmadhātustotra* 18–22:][1425]

Even the stainless sun and moon
Become obstructed by the five hindrances:
Clouds, mist, smoke,
Eclipses,[1426] and dust.[1427]

Similarly, the luminous mind
Becomes obstructed by the five hindrances:
Attachment, malignancy, laziness,
Dissipation, and doubt.[1428]

Like cloth purified by fire,
[That is,] when one puts [a cloth]
Sullied with various stains over a fire,
The stains are burnt but not the cloth,[1429]

Similarly, with the luminous mind,
Sullied with stains arisen from desire,
The stains are burnt by wisdom
But not the luminous [mind].[1430]

Those sūtras taught by the victorious ones
In order to reveal emptiness—
All eliminate defilements
But do not diminish the [buddha] element.[1431]

[47.25–26] This means that luminosity that is not annihilated, even though it is accompanied by defilements throughout beginningless time, cannot be rejected even by the sūtras that reveal emptiness or [by] the numerous analytical [works].

[47.26–48.4] Therefore, the view here [in the third dharmacakra] is that if you take the way things appear as the measure, without considering the essential mode of phenomena, they exist in the modes of saṁsāra and nirvāṇa, material things and consciousness, the material world and beings. If, on the other hand, the essential mode serves as the measure, nothing whatsoever exists as something different from the mind, and it (i.e., the view) is the insight *(prajñā)*—the knowledge—that even the true nature of mind *(sems nyid)* is the natural mind,[1432] which in no way exists as a phenomenon that possesses [characteristic] signs. The emptiness that is examined by reasoning and that which is grounded in luminosity—[neither] can be destroyed by anything; [both] are buddha nature.

[48.4–10] Reasoning that establishes that no own-being exists at all and a [treatment of] the mind abiding as luminosity occur in many scriptures, but they are explained particularly extensively in the *Ghanavyūha* and the *Laṅkāvatāra*. In these it is [explained] in the same way as the emptiness of an own-being is taught in the Madhyamaka treatises. On the other hand, if you persistently investigate in a direct manner, without depending on logical reason, the mind and the mental factors that are included in defilements and thoughts, [you again find that] nothing exists at all, in the same way as when you approach a cloud that looks like a mountain and [find out that] it is not like one, or a moving fata morgana, which is not perceived when you go up close, or a heap of stones that is not a man. Therefore it is difficult to distinguish [on such a level] even the difference between an apparent [truth] that is correct and one that is false. If this-worldly [criteria] serve as the measure, [however,] they can be distinguished.

[48.10] These points were taught by former lamas as well. Zhang [Tsalpa Tsöndrü] stated:[1433]

> [48.11–13] O Mother who gives birth to all the victorious ones and their sons!
> [You] who need to be realized by fortunate practitioners!
> Heart treasure of those descending from [you,] venerable [Mother]!
> Elixir of the vehicles, [namely] all scriptures, logical works, and pith instructions!
> Dharmakāya, essence of the final definitive meaning!
> Sphere of naturally pure luminosity!
>
> [48.13–15] In the three times, whether buddhas come or not,
> Whether the noble community realizes [the ultimate] or not,
> Whether the wise ones preach or not,
> Whether those learned in commenting on intention are to explain [these discourses] or not—
> This true nature, [this] luminosity, free from mental fabrications and pure,
> Has ever been spontaneously present and abides without increase or diminution.
>
> [48.15–17] Even though harm has been wrought over immeasurably many eons on pure space,
> By the burning of the fire [element] and the blowing of the wind [element],
> [And] by the generation and destruction of worlds, for example,
> This has not harmed space—it was neither increased nor diminished.
>
> [48.17–18] [Sometimes] clear sunlight is completely obstructed by clouds;
> It may thus appear to increase, becoming more clear, or to diminish
> When the clouds dissolve or when it is overcast,
> But the essence of the sun can neither increase nor diminish.

[48.18–21] The unchangeable dharmakāya, which abides like that,
Is nothing other than your own mind.
The whole of saṁsāra and nirvāṇa appears in all its variety in the mind.
When this is not realized, your own mind is disturbed
By the power of mistaken delusion, and [the mind] therefore appears as the suffering [of the] material world and the beings of saṁsāra.
When it is realized with certainty, your own mind appears as
The limitless wisdom of nirvāṇa and great bliss.

[48.21–22] Therefore, since everything emanates from your own mind,
You know the true nature of all sentient beings
If[1434] you recognize the true nature of your own mind;
Knowing that, you know all[1435] phenomena, such as nirvāṇa.

[48.22–24] By knowing all phenomena completely, you transcend all three realms;
By knowing one (i.e., the nature of your own mind), you become versed in all.
The leaves and petals of [a plant whose] roots are cut fall by themselves;
Therefore, your own mind will ascertain [all] alone.[1436]

[48.24–25] The true nature of your own mind, which is the seed of everything,
Has never been different from the mind of all victorious ones and [their] sons.
It appears as the unborn dharmakāya;
It is not something material, but self-awareness, [that is,] natural clarity.

[48.25–49.1] It is not established as an entity and is devoid of color, shape, and measure;
It is not a nonentity [either] but [can] manifest as anything according to conditions;
It is not something eternal [but rather is] empty of an own-being;
It is not something completely nonexistent [either], being self[-revelatory] clarity that is empty by nature.

[49.1–2] It is not established as a self; when investigated, it is without essence;
It is not a "no-self" [either], being the great self free from mental fabrications;
It is not established as [any] extreme and is without any perceiving subject.
It is not established as a middle and is beyond all points of reference.

[49.2–3] It cannot be illustrated by an example, nor can it even go by the name [of its possible] parts;s
But neither does it lack exemplification, being like space.
It is not established as [something that can be called by] words, and it cannot be denoted by an expression;
But neither is it free of words, being the cause of all expressions.

[49.3–7] Existent and nonexistent, true and false,
Empty and nonempty, quiescent and not quiescent,
Mentally fabricated and not,
Imaginable and not,
Bliss and suffering, existing as a cognitive object and not,
Duality and nonduality, beyond the intellect and not,
Isolated and not, established and not,
Pure and impure, spontaneously present and not—
Uttering clusters of words like these does not get at it.
Even though it is expressed in the form of many synonyms,
No matter how profound and acute the clusters of words,
These cannot bring you any closer to the true nature of mind.

[49.7–9] Though you may investigate and examine for eons,
No matter how skilled and profound your investigations and examinations,
That which is original by nature cannot be an object of investigation,
And therefore you cannot realize the true nature of mind [by such means].

[49.9–10] For example, the planets and stars that appear [as a reflection] in the ocean:
Even if you thoroughly sift with a sieve made of silk,
In the end you will not be able to get hold of a single star,

Because the planets and stars [in the ocean] are not cognitive objects
[corresponding directly to] entities.

[49.10–12] As long as [something] can be expressed in words, for that long
It may be [supplied] with names, but no matter how well supplied it is, these are not the nature [of the mind];
As long as there is a grasping of the duality "to be seen" and "seer,"
The nondual nature [of the mind] cannot be realized.

[49.12] Chegom Sherab Dorjé (Lce sgom Shes rab rdo rje) said:

[49.12–14] The root of all phenomena is the mind of enlightenment *(bodhicitta),*
And since clarity, which is the mind's nature *(rang bzhin),* is not obstructed,
The magical display of the mind is unimaginable;
Nevertheless, the true nature *(ngo bo)* of the mind is not established as anything.

[49.14–15] It has ever been empty, without a self, and free from mental fabrications;
Being coemergent great bliss free from mental fabrication,
It is free from the thorns and dust of [characteristic] signs, is stainless,
Has never arisen, and is naturally pure.

[49.15–16] It is the perfection of wisdom, inexpressible in word or thought;
Not being an object [that can be] recollected by the consciousness, mind, mental faculty, or intellect,
It lacks, like the true nature of phenomena, an example illustrative of it.
A metaphor that fits [only] partially is that it resembles space.

[49.16–19] Lacking the shapes and colors that are the [characteristic] signs of things,
It has neither limits nor a middle and transcends all [possible] sides and parts.

It has neither beginning nor end, and it does not become used up or increase.
It knows no going or coming, [and yet it is] all-pervading—the expanse over which it is spread out;
Devoid of change in the three times: it neither increases nor decreases.
Outside the three times of past, future, and present,
It goes beyond the extremes of existence and nonexistence, eternalism and nihilism, true and false.
It has ever been separated from good and bad, being and not being, [wrong] assertion and denial.

[49.19–21] It is beyond causes and conditions of origination, destruction, and change.
It may be disturbed and affected by conditions,
But it does not deviate from [its] nature of emptiness;
However great the variety [of its appearances], in its aspect of empti[ness] it is one.

[49.21–22] It is empty of self [and] empty of other—and within the equality of being empty,
The surface is empty and the deep [inside] as well; in the sphere of profound empti[ness],
The outside is empty, the inside is empty, and empty is the huge expanse.
Therefore the true nature of mind is like space.

[49.22–24] It pervades everything but cannot be defined as such.
If the mind has not been seen, will not be seen, and is not being seen
Even by all the buddhas of the three times,
This is all the more true of bodhisattvas, pratyekabuddhas, and śrāvakas.
How much more, therefore, of ordinary beings?

[49.24–25] The mind is without duality, and neither is it established as unitary;
Thus it is empty. How, then, can this empti[ness] be seen?
If the mind were seen or realized,
It would be a thought and therefore not the real mind.

[49.25–50.1] However much you investigate, the real mind cannot be known.
If it ever were known *(rig)*, this would be ignorance *(ma rig)*.
Therefore, the true nature of mind *(sems nyid)* has always been empty,
And so, certainly, the mental factors as well.
Thus the intellect, clinging to things and adhering to illusions,
Should be known as primordial emptiness.

[50.1–3] In emptiness nothing exists as duality,
And even emptiness has always been empty.
"Empty" and "not empty"—this knowledge is a thought,
And the nature of this very thought is primordial empti[ness].
The nature of primordial empti[ness] is beyond the intellect, free of thought and expression.

[50.3–4] The innermost part of knowledge is empti[ness], and if you realize deeply—
[And] not only verbally—that in which the limits of the mind *(yid)* are exhausted,
You see the true nature *(dharmatā)* of mind *(sems)*, the ultimate truth.
You realize the essence of all buddha words and pith instructions,
And you fathom the [underlying] intention of the victorious ones of the three times.

[50.5–7] This must be seen as the dharmakāya and [its] being pointed out.
The experience and realization [that comes from] seeing the nature of mind
Are not within the grasp of those [only] learned in the words of the scriptures and the Dharma.
It is not understood as a result of sharp logical reasoning
Or realized within the higher [state of] concentration [called] *calm abiding.*
It does not appear because of a greater activation of body and speech.

[50.7–8] The fortunate consequence of strength from your own former practice,
The blessing of a right wise lama,

And great devotion and respect—[realization] is within the grasp of these three
[Special forms of] interdependence coming together at one time.

[50.9] Pagmo Drupa said in the *Rin chen rgyan 'dra zhes bya ba'i bstan bcos*:[1438]

[50.9–10] With regard to the mind there are two [points]: [it is] not established and not obstructed;
"Not established" [refers to] the pure luminosity
And "not obstructed" [to] the spontaneously present united into a pair [with luminosity].

[50.10–11] [This] union into a pair is taught as a view
[That acts] as a remedy for clinging to an individual self.
As for the way to enter[1439] pure luminosity,
[Which is a remedy] for the clinging to the self of phenomena:

[50.11–12] The root of both saṁsāra and nirvāṇa is the mind;
And the mind is primordially pure, suchness.
Since[1440] it is primordially quiescent and has not arisen,
The mind has been ever free from the extremes of mental fabrication.

[50.12–13] Primordially pure and pure by nature,
Gradually [becoming] pure and spontaneously present,
It is free from the extremes of thought, expression, and difference,
Uninterrupted and not conditioned.

[50.13–15] Free from the three [stages] of origination, destruction, and abiding,
It is all-pervading but not established as a thing.
Not going and coming, and uninterrupted,
It is self-arisen great bliss without outflows;
It is coemergent wisdom.

[50.15–23] The [expression] "not established" [in the line] "With regard to the mind there are two [points], not established and not obstructed" is not a nonaffirming negation, but [refers] rather to the true nature of mind *(sems nyid),*[1441] which is not established as [something with] characteristic signs. The [expression] "not obstructed" [refers to] forms that appear among the objects of the sense faculties. "The clinging to an individual self" is explained in the great treatises as clinging to the mind as a self. Furthermore, you cling to the mind, which appears in [multiform] variety, as to a self, and since it (i.e., the self) is then nothing other than that variety without characteristic signs, the basis for a self is undermined. If clinging to the self of phenomena is the clinging to the existence of an own-being of the mind, its basis is withdrawn in view of the mind being luminosity. "Uninterrupted" means the "continuation in a continuum [of moments]" from beginningless time till buddhahood. A continuation in a continuum it is, but this does not mean that it arises as forms with characteristic signs. The characteristic signs having disappeared, [its] flowing (lit. "going") is not obstructed, and neither does it abide as phenomena with characteristic signs. "Self-arisen" means that it arises from within itself, without the necessity of various conditions. Not being a mental faculty *(yid)* or a body either, it is bliss. Since both the mind without characteristic signs and the unobstructed appearances arise simultaneously, it is also called "coemergent."

[50.23] [Pagmo Drupa] further [said in the *Rin chen rgyan 'dra*]:[1442]

> [50.23–25] As for how the cause [of the ordinary mind]—the two aspects of ignorance—
> Arose from the original mind, [that is,] self-arisen wisdom:
> The true nature of mind *(sems nyid),* mixed with the true nature of phenomena,
> Is coemergently arisen wisdom;
> It appears as this latter, [but cannot itself] be ascertained.[1443]
>
> [50.25–26] [Mind] that does not recognize itself by itself
> Is coemergent ignorance.
> Through the knowledge that perceives clarity to be your own [self],
> Knowledge [in the form of] self-awareness will be perceived as I.
> That which appears to you as objects will be perceived as other.[1444]
>
> [50.26–51.1] Without the insight that realizes [this],
> The true nature of phenomena is not realized—
> Which results in the ignorance of the imagined.

Under whatever conditions it (i.e., the imagined) was produced, it is [still] the mental faculty *(yid)* of the original [mind].

[51.1–3] The outward-looking [mind] is the mental consciousness *(manovijñānam),*
And the inward-looking mind is the defiled mind *(kliṣṭaṁ manaḥ).*[1445]
The wisdom of the natural [or uncontrived] ground[1446]
And the wisdom [of] the consciousness of the five doors (i.e., the eyes, etc.) are caused by these two "minds" *(manovijñānam* and *kliṣṭaṁ manaḥ)* being in discord
And [the resulting inner and outer] are kept from meeting or [coming] very close.

[51.3–4] The defiled mind looks inside
And perceives the original [mind], which is without an I as an I.
[The consciousness of] the five doors is nonconceptual;
[Still,] the mental consciousness perceives it as [endowed with] characteristic signs.

[51.4–5] Perceiving object and consciousness as two,
You accumulate defilements and *karman* of attachment and hate.
Just as in the examples of the threads of the silkworm
Or the objects in a dream,
You become entangled in yourself.

[51.5–10] Original mind, [that is,] self-arisen wisdom, is only the way mind is in [terms of] its own nature. It is not the case that first wisdom free of ignorance arose, and later ignorance arose from it, since if you reacquire stains from a stainless mind, it would follow that even a buddha [would return] to saṁsāra. The former mind, too, was mingled with ignorance; but [since its] true nature is not enveloped in ignorance, [it makes sense to say that] a twofold ignorance has arisen from this [original mind].[1447] The first [appearance of] ignorance is when the [primordial] ground (or basic [consciousness]?) simply does not recognize itself. This is what the *Śrīmālādevīsūtra* calls the "level of mental imprints of ignorance."

[51.10–13] "It appears [as this, but] cannot be ascertained" means that even though it appears as something without established nature at all, it cannot be ascertained [as being such]. "The imagined" means a thought within the mental [consciousness]. It is attachment to a perceived object and a perceiving subject and so forth. "Defiled mind" is a very subtle form of knowledge, being the mere appearance of the [primordial] ground (or basic [consciousness]?) as the [personal] self. Therefore, the worldly shrewd are not aware of it. The direct substantial cause of the entire mental consciousness and the consciousness of the five doors is the basic [consciousness] that has become the defiled mind.[1448] The defiled mind causes dualistic appearances in the form of the six accumulations [of consciousness].

[51.13–16] To sum up, the abiding nature of the phenomena of saṁsāra and nirvāṇa is the true nature of mind *(sems nyid),* which has no characteristic signs. It is the svābhāvikakāya, because even when you become a buddha, it is precisely that mind, [and that mind] alone, whose nature it is to have no characteristic signs. It is also called the dharmakāya, because in essence it is the [ten] strengths and so forth [of a buddha]. The two form kāyas shine forth as a reflection of the svābhāvikakāya for disciples.

[51.16–18] This same meaning is taught by Saraha [in his *Dohākośagīti*]:[1449]

> [They are like] two trunks from one seed;
> For this reason there is only one fruit.
> And whoever thinks of them as being undivided
> Is liberated from saṁsāra and nirvāṇa.[1450]

[51.18–19] [Saraha further said in his *Dohākośagīti,* stanza 74]:[1451]

> The true nature of mind *(sems nyid)* alone is the seed of
> everything;
> I prostrate to [this] mind,
> In which worldly existence and nirvāṇa spreads,
> And that is like a wish-fulfilling jewel in bestowing desired fruit.[1452]

[51.19–22] Also [with regard to] meditation, there are both—a root and branches. The root in turn has two aspects: meditation on the lama and meditation on the mind. As to meditation on the lama, it is mainly found in the traditions of Dampa Sangyé and Jé Gampopa. It is not that it does not exist in other [traditions as well]. In the "instructions encompassing the path and the fruit,"[1453] for example, the extensive yogas such as "inner heat" *(gtum mo)* have been explained as inferior, the *samaya*s and vows as middle, and the profound path as superior *(bla ma).*[1454]

[51.23–25] Dependence on a right person as the root of the path is generally even found in the Śrāvakayāna, but much more so in the Mahāyāna. But not only mere respectful reliance on a lama—meditation on the lama

[may] be [also] made the [essential] nature of the path. Both traditions expressing [this][1455] are very clear [on the matter].

[51.25–52.3] In the *Tathāgataguṇajñānācintyaviṣayāvatāra[nirdeśa]sūtra* it has been said:

> Mañjuśrī, a bodhisattva who is supported by a spiritual friend outshines in one morning the roots of virtue that have arisen from ten million, one hundred thousand million, immeasurable hundreds of thousands of buddhas. [He outshines] what has arisen from giving, from making offerings, and from upholding the training relating to them. Thus [a bodhisattva] who venerates [his] spiritual friend possesses inconceivable qualities.[1456]

[52.3–6] Even though the Tathāgata is not surpassed [by] the lama in terms of [actual] qualities, [the roots of virtue from] one morning of being supported by the lama outshines the roots of virtue that have arisen from [being supported by] innumerable [buddhas]—ten million, one hundred thousand million, immeasurable hundreds of thousands—from giving material offerings to them, and from upholding the training [relating to them]. It is clear that this [results] from having taken as [your] path meditation on [your] lama.

[52.6] Jigten [Sum]gön said in [his] *Cintāmaṇi:*

> [52.6–13] In general terms, Pagmo Drupa [has said]: "As for the instruction on how to practice in accordance with the sūtras and tantras, with devotion to, and respect for, the lamas of the profound path, the previous lineage [holders, such as] the master of yogins Virūpa,[1457] the protector of beings Nāgārjuna, the venerable [pair] Tīlo[pa] and Nāro[pa], the supreme accomplishment [can be realized] in this life, and also great bliss appears in an instant by their kindness. [Thus] it has been taught by Vajradhara in the secret mantra [tradition] of the Mahāyāna. Jinas [in the form of] space vajras[1458] fill, as if an agglomeration of sesame seeds, [the space in front of] all buddhas of the past, present, and future. [All] the time they practice austere asceticism and they teach the Dharma of attaining enlightenment: '[Your] meditation is not pure; you have not attained the ultimate with it. Focus on luminosity, which is pure like the face of space. If you focus on luminosity,

it will reveal itself in the form of its own [inherent] bliss.' Thus they tame demons and [become] perfect buddhas under the tree of supreme enlightenment."

[52.13–15] [My] lama [who is like a] jewel (i.e., Pagmo Drupa)[1459] repeatedly said: "All the buddhas of the three times even have their individual principal deity[1460] as an ornament at the top of the head. [Thus] I have been paying respect to the right lama who shows [me] that my own mind is a buddha."

[52.15–24] The qualities of both saṁsāra and nirvāṇa—this [fruit] arising from that [cause]—are immeasurable, [and their causal relation is only known by the lama].[1461] Everything, the accumulations of merit and wisdom, the [bodhisattva] levels, the [five] paths, and buddha[hood], can only be obtained from the lama and from no one else. Having ascertained that the only life[-blood] of benefit and happiness is [your] lama, you do not succumb to the first root infraction [of despising your lama, but rather] venerate him as the crown of [your] head, as [you] do the "king of wish-fulfilling jewels" *(rin chen dbang gi rgyal po).*[1462] Having made offerings [to him] with a mind bent on enlightenment, I will pray for all desired [qualities]. [From him,] too, now that he resides in the middle of [my] heart, I will seek advice with regard to both saṁsāra and nirvāṇa. On the throne of a fearless lion, a red lotus, and a sun and moon [seat] in the joyous [throat] cakra sits the precious protective lama, [who is in essence] Amitāyus, in great meditative equipoise. He teaches the Dharma under the aspect of [the letters] *a* and *nga.*[1463] I will listen to him, and also others ought to be satisfied with this profound Dharma. A right lama shows the cakras of body, speech, and mind, and the cakra of jewel[-like] wisdom, and also, like Śrī Kṛṣṇācarya, the twenty-four sacred places.[1464] The lord of the Dharma, the protector, (i.e., Pagmo Drupa)[1465] teaches the *tripiṭaka* and the four tantra classes, [that is,] the entire scriptures of the victorious one.[1466]

[52.24–53.1] Zhang [Tsalpa Tsöndrü], too, frequently said:

The state of nonduality arising from within [your mind] [depends] only [on] the blessing of [your] lama. The wisdom of realization arises among those with faith and respect for the lama. Those expert in investigation and examination[, however,] "grope in the dark" *(chi cha yod).*

[53.1–4] Also the great master of *siddhas* Dampa Sangyé said:

> The path that is in essence *prajñāpāramitā* has the name *mahāmudrā* and is completely in accordance with the Mantra[yāna]. This teaching, called the "calming of suffering," was taught to many fortunate ones here in the country of Tibet.

[53.4–8] In the *Avataṁsaka[sūtra]* [it is explained that] the bodhisattva as a beginner first applies himself to studying, then remains in a solitary place, and [finally] becomes a spiritual friend. Similar to these stages, three stages corresponding to when he is a studying śrāvaka, a practicing pratyekabuddha, and a helping bodhisattva are explained [in the sūtra]. The first stage is to listen to instructions from the lama, [the second] to meditate on the lama, while by reciting the lama's *mantra* on top of that, he completes [the third stage] of the lama. This is called *mind training.* Therefore, meditation on the lama is the root or essence of the path in the tradition of instructions.

[53.8–9] You may ask, in what sense is it the root? Dampa [Sangyé] said:

> If you commend yourself to the lama, you reach wherever you like.
> People of Dingri, show devotion and respect to the lama[, who is like your] feet.

[53.9–11] Accordingly he is the guiding [condition] or root cause that makes you traverse the path. In the *Ratnāvalī* [II.98] it is stated:[1467]

> The major and minor marks
> Of a universal monarch, however good [they may be],
> Are said to arise [only] from a single act[1468]—
> Faith[1469] in the king of subduers (i.e., Śākyamuni).[1470]

[53.11–13] This means that with faith in the major and minor marks of the king of subduers as cause, you will obtain the major and minor marks of a universal monarch. When you have faith in the king of subduers, reflections of the major and minor marks of [Śākya]muni shine forth. These are stored as imprints in the mind, and from their maturation they develop into the major and minor marks of a universal monarch.

[53.13–16] Likewise, if the lama on whom you are here meditating in order to realize emptiness directly has had no such direct realization of emptiness himself, it will not appear in his disciples either. Therefore Dampa [Sangyé] said:

> If a mold has no carvings, [the molded figure] will be blank[1471] [and] not a [proper] *tsha tsha.*[1472]

[53.16–17] The venerable Gampopa said many times:

> It is necessary that the lama himself have a direct realization of emptiness.

[53.17–19] Likewise, if [a disciple's] attention is frequently focused on the body, speech, and mind of a lama who sees the truth, his mind will be really the lama, in the sense that the mental faculty *(yid)* of the disciple will become very similar to [that of] the lama. This is what the above[-mentioned teacher] (i.e., Gampopa) thinks in the main. This meaning is [expressed in the following line] taught in the *Saṁpuṭi[tantra]:*

> The [vajra] master is the king of the mind.[1473]

[53.19–20] In this regard Jigten Gönpo said:

> As long as they have not become Vajradharas themselves, nobody should meditate on my disciples but only on the root lama. [Otherwise] great confusion is added to confusion.

[53.20–22] Also Götsangpa said:

> Often it is seen that the mind[1474] of the disciple is wasted by praying to a lama who has not the [proper] defining characteristics. If a lama has attachments, it will increase those of a disciple.

[53.22–24] In the same way as the sense faculty of the eye is the guiding condition of eye consciousness, so too a lama, who is the king of the mind, functions as the guiding condition for directly realizing emptiness. The meaning of the excellent [beings] who take [their] lama to be like the [wisdom] eye of the forehead is precisely this.

[53.24–54.2] The scriptures depict some who killed [their] parents and then took up a life of homelessness, studied the *tripiṭaka,* but because they were still engulfed in saṁsāra, did not even attain the mere path of the noble ones. Their disciples, however, attained the fruit of arhatship. The faculty that gave rise to their flawless wisdom resulted from faith in the scriptures. Among the followers of pith instructions it is known as the lama of scriptures.

[54.2–4] Also in this [*Ratnagotravibhāga* (IV.54 (J IV.51))] we find:

> Realizing that there is the suffering[1475] of death and transmigration in the gods' [realm] and the suffering of constant striving in the human [realm],
> Those with insight do not desire the greatest glory among gods or humans.
> This is because of their insight and their persistent faith in the words of the Tathāgata,
> And [consequently], because of their seeing on the basis of their knowledge that "this is suffering, this is its cause, and this is [its] cessation."[1476]

[54.4–7] "They see on the basis of their knowledge" means directly seeing on the basis of their insight, while on the other hand, the guiding condition of this insight of directly seeing, [namely,] what is brought about by the power of faith is called *persistent faith.* That which is brought about by the guiding condition of insight is called *persisting in the Dharma.*

[54.7–13] The second stage is the stage of meditating on the mind. In the *[Āryaḍākinīvajra]pañjarā[tantra]* it is stated:

> In this birth you will become a buddha
> By meditating on the mind as the supreme buddha.
> Apart from [this] jewel mind
> There are neither buddhas nor sentient beings.
> Apart from that which is the basis[1477] and the different forms of consciousness,
> There is nothing whatsoever.
> The mightiest beings in the three realms,
> All the buddhas, are brought about by the mental faculty.
> The greatest king in the three realms
> Is the true nature of mind *(sems nyid);* by it alone [kingship] is obtained.
> Entities arisen as form, sound,

And smell alike, taste, and tangible object, are here called the jewel mind.
They are quiescent in the supreme dharmadhātu.
[Śākya]muni said that
Form, feeling, discrimination,
Formative forces, and consciousness—
None of them is different from the entity of mind.[1478]

[54.13–16] The meditation on the precious mind is as stated. Moreover, there is [the meditation of] special insight, which is called *analytical meditation* by many scholars, including Kamalaśīla, wherein, based on reasoning such as being beyond one and many, you cultivate a continuum of inferential knowledge. This is preceded by the attainment of calm abiding, [a meditation wherein] you focus on a statue of the Buddha[, for instance]. This is not rejected here, but more profound than that is meditation on the path without conceptual examination.

[54.16–23] That has been also stated in Sahajavajra's commentary on [stanza no. 6 of] Maitrīpa's *Tattvadaśaka:*

> Being accordingly firmly anchored in the accumulations of calm abiding, [namely,] discipline and the like, you straighten your body upright in an agreeable place,[1479] and having taken a seat on the cushion of wished-for bliss, you actualize great compassion. Then you need to generate a one-pointed mind. In order to do this, the yogin first of all focuses, as well as he can, on all phenomena [that appear in his mind] just exactly as they are, that is, in any of their possible differentiations, such as skandhas, *dhātus*, *āyatanas*, or as having form or not. Then he ascertains that they are empty of the own-being of one and many, whereupon he needs to imbue [his] mind[1480] by continuously [ascertaining that they are] that way again and again. He must [so] direct [his] mind until body and mind have become very pure. Once they have become very pure, calm abiding is achieved, [as] has been stated [in the following stanza]:
>
> By distinguishing skandhas, etc., you correctly perceive all phenomena,
> And analyze [and conclude them] to be empty.

[54.23–55.5] As long as you are in meditative stabilization *(samādhi),* the mental faculty apprehends them as they really are. Then, coming out of meditative stabilization, you analyze again all phenomena with the eye of insight. Having analyzed [them], you need to meditate again.[1481] Thanks to this [practice], you rid yourself of the seeds of doubt. When the mind has become steady by focusing in calm abiding, then, if you analyze with insight *(shes rab),* the right appearance of wisdom arises, for it is said: "[In] meditative equipoise you know [reality] as it is."[1482] Insight and calm abiding are continually concordant. In this regard, the path of calm abiding and deep insight united into a pair properly endowed with such skillful means as generosity and discipline is widely known as *engaged [bodhi]citta* in the tradition of *pāramitā.* This is the state of preparation, inasmuch as you attain through the [progressive] stages of meditative stabilization—such as the appearance of the marvelous—[the levels] of heat and the like [on the path of] "connecting with definite differentiation" *(nirvedhabhāgīya).*

[55.5–8] Once you have next attained the path of seeing, you are in the causal state, and afterward, through the [progressive] stages of meditation, in the state of fruition. Here, in this regard, the distinctions made with respect to engaged [bodhi]citta within the tradition of *pāramitā* are presented both concisely and at length in the *Bhāvanākrama* and other works of Kamalaśīla. You should look them up there; they are not written here for reasons of space.

[55.8–12] No such engaged [bodhi]citta is intended here [in the *Tattvadaśaka,* however,] since in the *[Bhāvanākrama]* it is [only] pure by having been produced on the basis of analysis, whereas here [in the *Tattvadaśaka*] meditation is [performed] with a non-analytical mind right from the beginning.[1483] When somebody who possesses *pāramitā* pith instructions, which are adorned with the words of the guru, internalizes the *Yuganaddha-Madhyamaka, then [his] very insight into the ultimate, [namely,] the emptiness endowed with all excellent forms, [spontaneously] continues in a continuum [of moments].[1484] This is calm abiding and nothing else, for it has been said [in *Hevajratantra* I.8.44cd]:

> When you thoroughly know all phenomena,
> [Your] meditation is actually nonmeditation.[1485]

[55.12–15] For this reason, such a calm abiding and special insight united into a pair are the path; and to be sure, an engaged [bodhi]citta together with devotion toward a goal different [from this path] is not being asserted here. This is [also] taught in [Maitrīpa's *Mahāyānaviṁśikā*, stanza 12]:

> [The quintessence] to be realized in the thousands of collections of teachings is emptiness.
> [Emptiness] is not realized through analysis. The meaning of destruction (i.e., emptiness) [is rather attained] from the guru.[1486]

[55.15–16] It is further stated [in *Mahāyānaviṁśikā*, stanza 18]:

> Whose practice of continuous meditation [remains undisturbed, even] when apprehending [forms] such as a vase,[1487]
> Will become a great buddha whose single body [of compassion and emptiness pervades] all forms.[1488]

[55.16–17] In order to elucidate these two [stanzas], [it should be remembered that Maitrīpa] said [in *Tattvadaśaka*, stanza 6cd]:

> [The samādhi of realizing reality as it is *(yathābhūtasamādhi)* occurs through engaged [bodhi]citta,][1489]
> Because reality arises without interruption for those acquainted with its abode.[1490]

[55.17–20] For those who, thanks to the pith instructions of the right guru, are aware of the basis of this engaged [bodhi]citta, whose nature is the suchness of [the two truths] united into a pair, there arise uninterruptedly, that is, in every moment, emptiness and compassion inseparable, [these being] the defining characteristics of ultimate bodhicitta. They are called yogins, because they are of this very nature.

[55.20–22] Thus it is said, and this is therefore what the venerable Maitrīpa thought. The way the *Ratnagotravibhāga* [explains it] here is similar. Among the four principles, namely those of dependence *(apekṣāyukti)*, cause and effect *(kāryakāraṇayukti)*, proving on the basis of feasibility *(upapattisādhanayukti)*, and true nature *(dharmatāyukti)*,[1491] it is the last, the principle of true nature, by which [the *Ratnagotravibhāga*] thoroughly examines reality. As for the principle of true nature in this regard, in the *Saṁdhinirmocanasūtra* (X.7) we find:

> [55.22–24] Whether tathāgatas appear [in this world] or not, there is, to support the Dharma, the dharmadhātu [as] a support, and this is the principle of true nature.[1492]

[55.24–56.5] In line with this, it has been said in the present commentary (i.e., the *Ratnagotravibhāgavyākhyā*):

> Now, this buddha nature, whose reach is as great as the dharmakāya's, whose defining characteristics are not different from [those of] suchness, and that has the nature of a definite potential, exists always and everywhere without any difference. This needs to be seen against the backdrop of [our] taking true nature as the measure. As has been stated [in the *Tathāgatagarbhasūtra*]:[1493] "Son of a noble family, the true nature of phenomena is this: whether tathāgatas appear [in this world] or not, these sentient beings always possess buddha nature." This true nature of phenomena is here principle, argument, and method.[1494] By virtue of which (i.e., true nature of phenomena) this (i.e., contents of perception) is this way (i.e., an accurate realization of mind)[1495] and not otherwise. Everywhere it is precisely the true nature of phenomena that is relied upon[1496]—the principle underlying an accurate realization [and] a correct knowledge of mind. The true nature of phenomena is inconceivable and unthinkable; it must rather be simply believed in.[1497]

[56.5–12] As for the reality of the mind, when generated under the guiding condition of respectful faith in, and devotion to, the lama, the nonconceptual mind grows in its clarity. As a result of this you accurately realize the mind's quality of nonorigination and come to know [its] unobstructedness or [its] luminosity completely. When the eyes [cannot see clearly] or a lamp is not bright [enough], you do not see even the gross outlines of a form. If both are clear [and bright], even the minute details of a form can become clear. Similarly, when the concepts of internalized words and meanings are not clear, you will never be able to actualize the reality of mind. As for the realization, owing to the true nature of pure mind's clarity, that mind is without origination: given that they are the true nature of dependent arising, the phenomena (i.e., dharmas, namely the contents of perception, etc.) of [mind's] clarity simply are like the accurate realization of mind based on it (i.e., true nature). Not being [further] modified, however, by wrong assertions and denials, they are what is accurately determined by [what is designated by the affixed suffix] *tā*. Therefore they become "true nature" *(dharmatā)*.

[56.12–16] This is not like expectations based on a proof that establishes the apprehension of fire from [a direct perception of] smoke by means of inferential cognition. Therefore, the true nature *(dharmatā)* is taken as the measure when meditating on the mind. Since measure (i.e., valid cognition) has the connotation of "not perverting," the phenomena of mind's clarity are not perverted by it (i.e., dharmatā as measure). The learned need to ascertain this. Even in the matter of inferential cognition, the force of the inference is exactly as great as the [power of] recalling the three modes of proof. Moreover, the power of recalling is altered by [your] very clear statement of proof for the other party. Therefore Dignāga said: "I make it clear!"

[56.16–18] As for cultivating a direct [cognition] that sees reality, a lama who directly sees the true nature [of the mind] is needed, and as for cultivating inferential [cognitions], you need to see what a disputant must [still] establish on his own. The two are obviously similar. Also, Candragomin said:

> [56.18–19] Reasoning itself is to extract the essence, to extract what is supreme. If there is no [proper] reliance, it is not [properly done].[1498]

[56.19–21] Accordingly, the reliance on a disputant is needed. Especially in order to realize the emptiness of all phenomena on the basis of proofs, such as being beyond one and many or [that of] dependent [arising], a strength of conviction must certainly be generated. [Thus] it is stated in the commentary on the *[Madhyamaka-]avatāra* (XI.55):

> [56.21–23] Likewise it is obvious that even nowadays some who in former lives formed the mental imprint of a strong conviction regarding emptiness realize the depth of emptiness on the strength of [this] cause alone. [Moreover,] it is seen that even those who have failed—in that they regard as true that [which is taught] according to the textual traditions of the "non-Buddhists" *(tīrthikas)*—fathom the depth of emptiness on the strength of [that] cause alone.[1499]

[56.23–25] Thus, wishing [your practice] to be preceded by the force of conviction and merit, you by all means need to accumulate merit through dependence on a lama in order to realize the properties of natural luminosity. As it has been said [in *Hevajratantra* I.8.36cd]:

> [The coemergent is neither taught by anyone else nor found anywhere (i.e., in scriptures)]. It must be known by yourself, from [having accumulated] merit by taking recourse to the skillful means of [pith instructions obtained] while passing time with the master.[1500]

[56.25–57.1] Well then, somebody may ask in what way emptiness is realized by way of direct [cognition] only, unpreceded by inferential [reasoning]. This has to be [further] explained. In the *Madhyamakālaṁkāra* (stanza 73) [it is stated]:

> [57.1–2] Now, since the nature of it (i.e., a vase, etc.) is directly manifest
> By having realized it,
> Why is it that unwise people
> Do not realize in this way the nature *(dngos po)*[1501] of entities?[1502]

[57.2–5] You may object: when these [things] are realized, it does not make sense that their own-being is not realized. It is as if you look at a piece of land devoid of vases and realize that its essence is to be devoid of vases. If ordinary beings, even the worst [of them], whose view is not good (lit., "white"), perceive things that are merely free from all possible [wrong] superimpositions [baselessly arrived at] from the formlessness of entities and the like, why do they not realize them as they are?

[57.5–6] [The *Madhyamakālaṁkāra* (stanza 74) answers]:

> [In fact] they do not. Having a burdensome [mind]stream without beginning,
> They are overpowered by [their habit of] of imagining entities as real;
> Therefore no living beings
> Directly realize it (i.e., the nature of entities).[1503]

[57.6–14] Those entering into worldly existence without beginning, whose intellect is disturbed by the poison of an obstinate adherence to entities, are not able to thoroughly understand [their] form, in the sense of perceiving [reality] in a simple direct way. This is like people with an impaired intellect who do not realize momentariness because they focus on a continuum of similar events. Moreover, [ordinary direct perception] is not very amazing. Even though the shapes of a vase, an ox, and so forth, which are devoid [of the universal properties] of an ox and so forth, are clearly seen, those who have a mistaken understanding, [viewing as they do things] according to the traditions of Kapila, Kaṇāda, and the like, do not perceive [them] in this way (i.e., as being empty of universal properties). Thus all sentient beings possess a knowledge of [direct] appearances [even] on the basis of not having ascertained natural emptiness. Nevertheless, owing to the confusion that has arisen throughout beginningless time, ascertainment is lacking. It is like the Sāṁkhyas and others, who possess a knowledge [of things] that clearly appear to be devoid of real universal properties, and still a [corresponding] ascertainment does not arise [in them]. Thus it has been said. Master Haribhadra, too, [said,] when explaining the defining characteristics of an own-being in [his] commentary on the *Aṣṭasāhasrikā Prajñāpāramitā*, that all sentient beings possess a knowledge that [is capable of] directly seeing emptiness.

[57.14–15] Götsangpa said:

> The [latent] knowledge at the time [you are an ordinary] being
> Exists in the form of the dharmakāya;
> Even though it is taught by the lama, this is not [really] necessary—
> It is suitable for being realized by yourself.

[57.15–17] With that in mind, venerable Koṭali, too, said:

> Eye consciousness, without the duality [imagined] by thought,
> Is wisdom—fantastic!

[57.17–20] The Ven. Dharmakīrti said [in his *Pramāṇavārttikakārikā* I.68–70[1504]]:

> The other form *(pararūpa)* is concealed
> By [thought's] own form *(svarūpa),* [imputed] by the intellect,
> Which, [while] basing itself on different entities,
> Reflects a single object.
>
> Through [such] a concealing[1505] [thought]
> The concealed manifold objects appear—even though discrete
> in themselves—

As if they were not different entities,
In some form [suggestive of a universal property].[1506]

Under the constraint of [such] thinking on the part of it [i.e., the intellect],
[This] universal is [then] declared to be [something] existent.
Ultimately, [however,] it does not exist
The way it is imagined by that [intellect].[1507]

[57.20–26] The meaning of this quote [is]: To a conceptual knowledge controlled by direct cognitions that take in different entities, such as sandalwood and *nyagrodha* [trees], there appears the form of a single universal called *tree,* into which all distinctive features of a tree are gathered. When it appears, you think that that form is external, and cling to the existence of a single object universal. Even though such objects do not relate to a single universal, these objects' nonexistence becomes obscured by the thought's own form, and the [concrete] entities of trees are seen as something not different from the single entity of the universal *tree.* Since a great number of sentient beings possess such thoughts, the existence of universals is proclaimed in accordance with the ideas of the many. The intellect that contains the form of the universal *tree* thus corresponds to the apparent (lit., "concealing") [truth], concealing as it does the ultimate. Such a universal of a tree is a mere convention, but apart from that it does not exist in any ultimate sense. To sum up, it may be said that the universal [called] *tree* is imputed to the set of trees taken as the basis of imputation.

[58.1–5] Sentient beings face two [types of] confusion: perceptual confusion, such as the yellow appearance of a [white] conch shell, and the confusion of adherence, such as adhering to the universal *tree* as an entity. Inferential knowledge removes the confusion of adherence but not perceptual confusion. Inferences are thoughts, and it is obvious that thoughts are like the conception of entities,[1508] which naturally is confusion. This is what Dharmakīrti said, and Kamalaśīla asserted [this] as well:

Naturally these thoughts
Are in the end the nature of ignorance.[1509]

Therefore, with respect to the ultimate, appearances are only confusion.

[58.5–6] Likewise, all apprehensions involving obstinately adhering to entities, which must be refuted by the Mādhyamikas, are simply like these universals grasped at by thought. In the *Hastavālavṛtti* it is stated:[1510]

> [58.6–12] You regard and perceive a rope as a snake. To see it as a rope would be meaningless. Here, in a not so fortunate land, you apprehend at dusk the form of a rope simply as the property of a universal and thus become confused. Because you do not thoroughly grasp the nature of [its] distinctive features, a [false] knowledge arises that certifies: "This [can be] only a snake!" [Even] if you perceive its distinctive features, this knowledge too is confused knowledge, and in the end meaningless, given the tedious mental fabrication caused by imagining it not the way it really is. The knowledge with regard to that [rope] is also confused, as [in the case of seeing] a snake, when you see its parts [and still cling to the rope as a single entity]. Also with regard to that rope, if you divide it into its parts and examine it, an own-being of a rope is not apprehended. This being the case, the apprehension of a rope is nothing but mere confusion, like the intellect thinking that it is a snake.

[58.12–13] Thus it is said that the seeing of different parts while clinging to the existence of a single phenomenon is the systematized confusion of all confusions. Likewise it is stated in the *[Bodhisattvayogācāra]catuḥśataka[ṭīkā]:*

> [58.13–20] Just as you say that something permanent exists[1511] when looking at a continuum wrongly, you [also] say that an entity exists when looking at an accumulation wrongly. The flame of a butter lamp passes out of existence every single moment; [still,] the earlier and later moments are based on an uninterrupted connection of cause and effect. When there is an accumulation of causes and conditions, an existing continuum comes forth. Similarly, if everything conditioned that passes out of existence as soon as it has arisen has an accumulation of causes and conditions of such a nature, then existent continua, which are based on the uninterrupted connection of cause and effect, have been coming forth throughout beginningless time. Therefore you can infer[1512] with certainty how the own-being of these continua abides. As for the non-Buddhist *ṛṣis*, who ascertain [their existence] in a mistaken way, they remember a former basis; since they do not directly [perceive] the momentary destruction within it, they see the continua, which pass from one skandha to the next, in a wrong

> way, and accept both a self and an other. [Thus] they think that entities exist as something permanent.[1513]

[58.20–23] It is further stated:

> Specifically and generally characterized phenomena are [here] merely being imputed. But when these [phenomena] arise, it is only an accumulation that arises and only an accumulation that passes out of existence. Since opponents do not know the accumulation the way it really is and see [it] wrongly, they consider that discrete [entities], such as earth, are established in terms of an own-being and realize only an entity that, besides being simply mistaken, is also unjustified logically.[1514]

[58.23–26] Likewise, all imputations that a nature of entities exists are made on the basis of different parts. All perceptions of permanence, such as the thought that "the man of last year is this one [here]" are merely imputations to different earlier and later parts. Therefore, [whereas] Dharmakīrti [applies this critique] only to how universals are [wrongly] imputed to be real, it is applied in the Madhyamaka treatises to assertions concerning particulars[1515] as well, and [then] it is determined that all entities are without an own-being.[1516]

[58.26–59.5] Such being the case, when you come close to something that appears from [afar, as from] the other side [of a valley], to be a single small [entity], you see different [things], such as grass, trees, and stones, and not a single [entity]. Looking at a stream of water from a long distance, you see it as [something] immovable as if it were a stick. Coming close to it, you see only a series of former and later waves, and not that it is immovable. Likewise, when the direct [perception] arisen from the yoga of one-pointedness thoroughly investigates the mind and outer [objects] in any of their temporal differences, it realizes that no own-being whatsoever can be apprehended in any entity. This is the way to directly realize nonorigination.

[59.5–6] The continuum of direct [perceptions] repudiates concepts, which involve words and meanings. When these are overcome, [the result is] the entire overcoming of appearances. With regard to this, the Ven. [Maitrīpa?] said:

> You realize that they (i.e., appearances) came forth through the cause of expressing forms of objects.

[59.6–10] Therefore the fruit, [namely,] all mistaken appearances, have ceased. With regard to this, former [masters] explained: "Appearances have dissolved in the mind." When you perform an analytical meditation based on inferential [cognitions], it is not the case that a direct [cognition] that realizes reality arises immediately after these same [inferential] thoughts have ceased, but rather [only] when [all] thoughts disappear. Only then does a mere nonconceptual direct [cognition] arise, and from this arises a direct [cognition] that realizes reality. These two differ only in being far and close.

[59.10–11] These stages were taught by the Ven. [Maitrīpa?], who said:

> Constantly search and thoroughly investigate
> With the help of mental expressions *(manojalpa)*![1517]
> There is nothing to be internalized or expressed.
> Analyze with the yoga of one taste as well!

[59.11–12] Kamalaśīla, too, explained in the [three] *Bhāvanākrama*s and the commentary on the *Nirvikalpapraveśadhāraṇī* that at the end of analysis you rest in nonconceptuality only.

[59.12–22] Atiśa said in the *Madhyamakopadeśa:*[1518]

> Likewise, the mind of the past has ceased and passed out of existence. The future mind has not yet arisen and come forth. It is very difficult to investigate the present mind under such [circumstances]. It has no color and lacks shape. Being like space it is not established [as anything]. In other words, if you analyze and break it down with the weapons of reasoning, such as that it is beyond one and many, or has not arisen, or natural luminosity, you realize that it is not established [as anything]. Likewise, if neither [color nor shape] are established as entities in terms of any own-being whatsoever, and [both are] nonexistent only, the thoroughly cognitive insight itself is not established either. For example, being subject to the condition of a fire kindled by rubbing two pieces of wood, these two pieces, too, are burned, and afterward there is nothing left; even the very fire that burnt [them] goes out. Similarly, when all phenomena, inasmuch as they are specifically and generally characterized, are simply established as nonexistent, even that insight does not appear, and since this is luminosity that is not established in terms of any own-being whatsoever, all mistakes,

such as laxity and excitement, are removed. During this time no knowledge whatsoever is conceptualized, nothing whatsoever is perceived, and all mindfulness *(dran pa)* and attention *(yid la byed pa)* have been given up. The knowledge (namely, consciousness) should remain in such a mode until the enemies and thieves, namely, [characteristic] signs and thoughts, come up [again].

[59.22–24] In this respect, Götsangpa said:

As for the analytical meditation of the scholars and the *kusulu* meditation of resting—if the two are taken by themselves, the path in the *kusulu* tradition is faster.

[59.24–60.5] If you [intend to use] such a yoga in meditation, then in the *Laṅkāvatārasūtra* it has been explained as meditation in five stages. It has been said:

Moreover, Mahāmati, I will explain the turning back of the conditions of ignorance, thirst, and *karman;* the turning back of thoughts, [namely,] the suffering of the three worlds;[1519] and the view[1520] that objects as appearances of your own mind are an illusion. Mahāmati, there are some Śramaṇas or Brāhmaṇas who assert that something exists without having existed before, [namely,] the manifest fruit of a cause and an entity abiding in time;[1521] [further] that, depending on conditions, skandhas, elements, and sense spheres arise, remain, and, also after coming into existence, cease.[1522] Mahāmati, they uphold a destructive and nihilist [view] with regard to [things like a mental] continuum, action, origination [and destruction],[1523] worldly existence, nirvāṇa, the path, *karman,* effects, and truth. Why is that? It is because they do not apprehend directly and thus lack fundamental insight.[1524]

[60.5–7] From that [passage] up to

Mahāmati, the bodhisattvas, the great beings, will attain before long the sameness of saṁsāra and nirvāṇa,[1525] it states that having turned away from a nihilist view, you meditate on the sameness of saṁsāra and nirvāṇa, on the strength of minutely analyzing the causal and resultant phenomena of saṁsāra.

[60.7–9] Immediately after that, the "physical isolation"[1526] is taught in [the passage]:

> Mahāmati, through [their] right practice, which is connected with the effortless [accomplishment] of great compassion and skillful means, through [their practice of seeing] that all sentient beings[1527] are the same as an illusion and a reflection....[1528]

[60.9–10] The "mental isolation" is taught in [the passage]:

> Through [their practice of seeing[1529] that the original state] has not started from [causes and] conditions[1530] and is beyond [the duality of] an internal and external object.[1531]

[60.10–13] Immediately after that, the blessing by themselves, [namely,] the meditative stabilization [of experiencing phenomena to be] illusion-like, is taught in [the passage]:

> [Bodhisattvas] who, through [their practice of] not seeing [objects] outside of the mind, become endowed with the blessing of being without characteristic signs, who deeply meditate as part of [their practice of] gradually pursuing [their chosen] object[s] of meditative stabilization along the stages represented by the [bodhisattva] levels, and who are convinced that the threefold world is an illusion [produced by] their own mind, they attain the meditative stabilization [of experiencing phenomena to be] illusion-like.[1532]

[60.13–14] After that, "luminosity without appearance" is taught in [the passage]:

> By entering [a state that consists of] only their own mind without appearance, they attain the abode of *prajñāpāramitā*.[1533]

[60.14–18] "Union into a pair" is taught in [the passage]:

> Mahāmati, the bodhisattvas who are free from origination and action[1534] fully attain what conforms to the body of a tathāgata, which is like the form of a vajra in meditative stabilization. [This body] is endowed with the emanation [body] of suchness [and thus][1535] adorned with power, clairvoyance, control, love, compassion, and skillful means, a body of a tathāgata, which has arrived at the place that offers passage to all the buddhafields, is beyond the mind, mental faculty, and mental consciousness, and whose basis has been gradually transformed.[1536, 1537]

[60.18–20] Also, the three meditative stabilizations *(samādhi)* that are taught in [the stanza:] "May the perfection of meditation be completed by the samādhi [of experiencing phenomena to be] illusion-like, the samādhi of becoming a hero, and the vajra-like samādhi,"[1538] are united into a pair with the *prajñāpāramitā* [of experiencing phenomena to be] illusion-like and [the experience] without appearance.

[60.20–25] With respect to this, the utmost among purposeful objects of bodhisattvas is the activity of a tathāgata. This activity must be performed with compassion in accordance with the way it is taught [in the *Ratnagotravibhāga*] as "[pouring down] from the clouds of compassion."[1539] Therefore, it is said here [in the *Laṅkāvatārasūtra*, quoted above]:[1540] "great compassion." [The *pāda* RGV IV.4b]: "By which, [that is,] by [which of] the numerous means for those to be guided"[1541] is taught [in the *Laṅkāvatārasūtra*] by way of "skillful means." [The *pāda* RGV IV.3d]: "The wise one[s] are always without effort" is taught by way of the "effortless [accomplishment]." [The *Laṅkāvatāra* passage] "The right practice, which is connected [with...]"[1542] [means] the right practice of meditation on the activity that possesses [these] three particular [qualities]. It is said to possess five stages.

[60.25–61.7] Even though the body of all the [buddha] elements of sentient beings has no [independent] self, it has nevertheless arisen, by the spell and medicine of mere ignorance, and is thus illusory. Since it is only an appearance in the mind, the isolation of the body from a [wrong] view is taught. If analyzed, it has arisen from the pure mind, and did not start from causes and conditions that consist of elements or anything formed from elements.[1543] This is the isolation [of the mind] from the ordinary. The essential mind is isolated from an outer perceived object and an inner perceiving, and this is the isolation of the mind. No characteristic signs or forms of an outward looking mind exist, and being blessed by [such] nonconceptuality, the bodhisattvas who are endowed with it go with [their] body of meditative stabilization to the pure abode,[1544] etc., until they gradually go to the tenth level. They pursue, [that is, they become] concordant with, the objects of meditative stabilization [on various levels] and are convinced that the entire mind of the three worlds[1545] is their own mind, [the three worlds being] an illusion. In view of that, they deeply meditate and attain a meditative stabilization where one of the defining characteristics is the perception that all the buddha realms are like an illusion.

[61.7–13] Having entered suchness, which means that forms or appearances of characteristic signs simply do not exist in their mind, they attain the abode of *prajñāpāramitā*, which embodies the eighteen types of emptiness. This amounts to full enlightenment. Having attained enlightenment, the bodhisattvas, who are free from the activity of striving to be born with a pure body, do not conceptually differentiate between the two "doors" of enlightenment and appearance when, from the state of full enlightenment, the door to the appearance of the limitless objects of knowledge opens. This [state] is therefore said to be like the form of a vajra [in] meditative stabilization. It is [also] called the vajra-like meditative stabilization or the "union into a pair." Its qualities conform with [those of] a tathāgata's dharmakāya. The suchness is endowed with such emanations[1546] that appear in [different] forms to sentient beings. This demonstrates [the matter] in short.

[61.13–18] When explained in detail, [the word] *dharma* in *dharmakāya* [stands for] strength, clairvoyance, ten types of control, love toward concrete [beings], and compassion in general. The own-being of these is [expressed by] *kāya*. They are adorned with [skillful] means for the sake of others, and have arrived at the place that offers a passage to all the buddhafields. A characteristic of them is that they teach to some as to disciples and to others as to teachers.[1547] An emanation is the assuming of forms for the sake of limitless sentient beings. Not depending on another path, they have reversed the mind, [that is,] the basic consciousness, the defiled [consciousness], and the mental consciousness. Free from these three, they gradually—[that is, by] progressing *('pho ba)* from one [bodhisattva] level to the next—[but] fully attain the three kāyas of a tathāgata of a transformed *('phos pa)* basis.

[61.18–22] It was the master Āryadeva who said that this text teaches the five stages. Therefore I have followed the words of this master and explained matters accordingly. Lamas who practice the pith instructions of this text [i.e., the *Ratnagotravibhāga*] explain [these instructions in terms of] stages of meditation on [buddha] nature called the *four yogas.* I cannot say with certainty that their literal expressions are nowhere [found] in the scriptures, only that I did not see them. [Their] meaning[, however,] is explained in the *Laṅkāvatārasūtra.*

[61.22–26] Even though there are many [explanations on] the stages of the four yogas composed by lamas, [I quote here] Zhang [Tsalpa Tsöndrü Drag (grags)], [who] said:[1548]

> The meditative equipoise of realizing your mind is known in the stages of the four yogas. When the yoga of one-pointedness has arisen, you realize the nature *(rang bzhin)* of your own mind. Clarity and emptiness are not obstructed, and are without middle and extreme, like the vault of pure space. To remain in a vibrant *(sing ge)*[1549] and crisp *(ye re)*[1550] state is the meditative equipoise of the first yoga. The spreading of thoughts from it is [already] the [state] attained after [meditation], even though you may have meditated seated. When you remain in [this] vibrant and crisp state of clarity and emptiness, there may be internal chatter [and] movement, but you remain within the meditative equipoise.
>
> [61.26–62.3] When the yoga of freedom from mental fabrication has arisen, you realize the true nature *(ngo bo)* of your own mind. It is uninterrupted awareness, free from mental fabrication. Your own mind, which is without origination and cessation, adopting and discarding, is grounded in the dharmakāya, and this is the meditative equipoise of the second yoga. When you remain in this, there may be mental movement, chatter, and talk, but you are still in meditative equipoise. When distracted by the characteristic signs of mental fabrication, you may meditate seated, but this is [already the state] attained after [meditation].
>
> [62.3–9] When the yoga of one taste has arisen, you realize the defining characteristics of your own mind. You realize that manifold saṁsāra and nirvāṇa arise from your own mind, which is the dharmakāya [and] free from mental fabrication. The entire multiplicity, [including] thoughts and the nonconceptual, appearances and nonappearance, abiding and not, being empty and not, being clear and not, has, as luminosity and dharmakāya, one taste. Therefore, you see the appearance of the great dharmakāya but not the conceptual, which is not luminosity. The realization of a sameness of taste in this way, [that is,] the moment of capturing it with the mental faculty *(yid),* is the meditative

equipoise of the third yoga. When it is captured by the uncontrived mental faculty, there may be mental jumping, running, chatter, and talk, but you still remain within the meditative equipoise. When separated from the uncontrived mental faculty, you may meditate seated, but this is [already the state] attained after [meditation].

[62.9–17] When the yoga of nonmeditation has arisen, the yogin does not need to meditate, the true nature of awareness [now] being free of [the need for any] support. There is no meditator; he has disappeared. It is said that the Buddha with his three kāyas and five types of wisdom has become fully complete in yourself. Now [you realize your] primordial knowledge that this [Buddha] is yourself. This is the accomplishment of mahāmudrā. You are certain that this [Buddha] is yourself. The thought that you have attained [this] primordially present accomplishment is not [the product of] a conceited mind. There is neither retaining nor not retaining by mindfulness, neither mental engagement nor lack thereof, neither one taste nor not [one taste]. There is no duality. When [you let] consciousness [rest] in its own place, there are neither stages of meditative equipoise nor [the state] obtained afterward. In uninterrupted awareness and emptiness there is no dying and no being born. The strength of a *garuḍa* comes to completion within the eggshell. When it leaves the eggshell it [immediately] flies off into space. [Likewise,] the qualities of the three kāyas are [already] complete within [your] mind. [The powers of working] for the benefit of others arise after the [constraining] "seal" of the body[1551] has been destroyed [at death].[1552] [When they] arise in such a way without meditation, there are no [separate] stages of meditative equipoise and a [state] attained afterward. As long as there is something to become familiar with, [such as] how elevated a realization may be, there is a duality of meditative equipoise and a [state] attained afterward, there is a retaining and not retaining by mindfulness, and there is the duality of being distracted and not. When there is nothing to become familiar with, [and this is] the only [thing that] arises, this should be called *nothing to meditate on.*

[62.17–23] Also in the *Laṅkāvatārasūtra*, in the answer to Mañjughoṣa's (i.e., Mahāmati's) question on the great yoga *(mahāyoga),* it has been said:

> The Buddha replied: "Mahāmati, the great bodhisattvas, great beings who are in possession of the four dharmas,[1553] are yogins of the great yoga. What are their four [dharmas]? They are: the ascertainment[1554] that appearances are your own mind; abandoning the view of origination, abiding, and destruction; the realization[1555] that external entities do not exist; and the strong wish[1556] to internalize the wisdom of the noble ones by yourself.[1557] Mahāmati, bodhisattvas, great beings who possess these four dharmas, are yogins of the great yoga.
>
> [62.23–63.2] If somebody asks, Mahāmati, how a bodhisattva, a great being, then becomes expert in ascertaining that appearances are his own mind, [the answer] is: he looks[1558] at it in the following way: this threefold world is only your own mind. The mind is devoid of an *I* and a *mine,* [subsists] without motion, and without adopting or discarding. Throughout beginningless time it is permeated by [the inclination to] adhere to imprints of baseness left by mental fabrications.[1559] It is [closely][1560] connected with indulging in the variegated forms of the triple world. It appears[1561] to be in concordance with the concepts (i.e., the mental fabrications) of body, property, dwelling place, and existence.[1562] In this way, Mahāmati, a bodhisattva, a great being, is expert in ascertaining that appearances are his own mind."[1563]

[63.2–7] Thereby is the yoga of one-pointedness taught. It has five distinctive features: the meditation [that everything is] mind only; neither adopting nor discarding; being permeated by the imprints of mental fabrication; connection; and concordance. The first is the meditative stabilization of realizing that clarity and emptiness are like space. As for the appearances of the threefold world, everything appears as the nature of this clarity and emptiness itself. You realize that only this much is wandering about in saṁsāra. The *I* or its *mine* of a *goer* from here to the other side is not different from this [clarity and emptiness]. Therefore, even when you pass into the next world, it is only the mind that is passing [away]; there is nothing else apart from it that wanders to the other world.

[63.7–9] Second, you think that the abiding in clarity and emptiness and the wandering of thoughts—these two—are not different categories in terms of their substance. Since precisely clarity and emptiness move about as thoughts, nothing whatsoever must be adopted or discarded with regard to thought and clarity.

[63.9–10] Third, you know that the imprints of mental fabrication have not been given up when many thoughts occur again, even though you have seen [mind] as clarity and emptiness.

[63.10–11] Fourth, you know that even the indulging subject, [that is,] the various forms of intellect, which indulge in the [world] of objects when it is not resting in meditative equipoise, is the mind of clarity and emptiness itself.

[63.11–13] Fifth, you know that all the appearances of a body, property, a dwelling place, and the realms of the six types [of beings] are bound up with this same mind, in that they share the same identity.

Thus, it has been said in many ways that all thoughts [arising by way] of the doors of appearance are known to have the nature of nonthought. One [stanza] in accordance with this has been taught in *Pramāṇavārttika* [III.287[1564]]:

> [63.13–14] That which clings to word and meaning with regard to any [object]—
> This very knowledge is a mental construct with regard to [this object].
> [Its] nature is not word or meaning;
> Therefore, in this respect all types [of knowledge] are direct.[1565]

[63.14–17] In the sūtras and śāstras it is explained that you understand mind only because it has been ascertained that the connection between a noun and its referent is imagined. This [fifth point] is nothing more than this. Götsangpa takes this yoga of one-pointedness to be the essence of [the path of] accumulation and the four branches [of the path] of penetration, namely heat and the rest.

[63.17–24] [The *Laṅkāvatārasūtra* further says:]

> If somebody asks, Mahāmati, how a bodhisattva, a great being, abandons[1566] the view of origination, abiding, and destruction, [the answer] is: as [in the case of] the [apparent] arising of forms in an illusion or a dream, no entities arise, since [their true nature] does not exist in terms of either self, other, or [a combination of] both. Bodhisattvas follow [the fact that entities] are only appearances of their own mind, and see the nonexistence of external entities.[1567] Having seen this, they see that the forms of consciousness are not active, and that the conditions [for these forms] are not heaped up, wherefore they see that the triple world has arisen from conditions of thought; and because of not

> apprehending any inner or outer phenomena, they truly see that [the triple world] lacks an own-being, and the view of origination is discarded. They realize that the own-being of phenomena is an illusion or the like, and thereby fully attain [the ability] to endure that phenomena do not arise. Mahāmati,[1568] in this way a bodhisattva, a great being, abandons the view of origination, abiding, and destruction.[1569]

[63.24–26] This is the yoga of freedom from mental fabrication:

> When the yoga of freedom from mental fabrication has arisen, you realize the true nature *(ngo bo)* of your own mind. It is uninterrupted awareness, free from mental fabrication. Your own mind, which is without origination and cessation, adopting and discarding, is grounded in the dharmakāya, and this is the meditative equipoise of the second yoga.[1570]

[63.26–64.2] It is as explained in these [stanzas]. All entities are like the forms in an illusion or a dream. Even though they appear to arise, they do not do so [in reality]. If no true nature can be established [for them] as a self, other, or [a combination of] both, they simply do not arise. You realize that they are altogether baseless and without root.

[64.2–9] [The yoga] increases to [encompass] five distinctive features of that realization. First, seeing that the appearances are in accordance with the mind, you realize that the totality of all appearances are mind, in that when the mind is happy or suffering, [its] appearances are similar. Second, seeing that the mind lacks an own-being, you see that appearances are the mind's "doors of appearance" and you realize[, in addition,] that appearances lack an own-being. Third, because this realization has arisen, the sense faculties turn inward, and the five [forms of] consciousness no longer engage with objects. Fourth, the conditions for consciousness to arise are the five sense faculties, [their] objects, and nonperception *(avijñapti).* These eleven piled-up heaps are mere imagining[1571] and, moreover, lack an own-being. You see, further, that these eleven, [that is,] any heaps to be piled up, are without an own-being or basis. Fifth, the yogin increasingly sees that the outer and inner heaps (skandhas) lack an own-being and realizes that the entire threefold world has also arisen from what is made under the conditions of inner thought. It is said:

> [64.9–10] The three forms of existence are simply imagined and do not exist as entities with an own-being.[1572]

[64.10–15] This path of realization has two fruits. As to the first, the unconditioned fruit [or] cessation, because [the bodhisattvas] do not apprehend any outer and inner phenomena and truly see that [phenomena] lack an own-being, the view or notion that entities arise in terms of [an] own-being is contradicted. Therefore, [this view] is discarded, and so everything to be abandoned on [the path of] seeing, such as the sixty-two base views, is abandoned. As to the conditioned [fruit], they realize that it [has] the nature of things like illusions, and thereby fully attain the essence of the path of liberation, [that is, the ability] to endure that phenomena do not arise[, which in turn is the ability to endure] that which follows the proclamation [of emptiness].[1573] The way it has been explained [here] is: "Mahāmati, in this way a bodhisattva, a great being, abandons the view of origination, abiding, and destruction."[1574] Götsangpa thinks that this realization [amounts to the same] as attaining the first [bodhisattva] level.[1575]

[64.15–21 In the *Laṅkāvatārasūtra* it is further said:]

> If somebody asks, Mahāmati, how then a bodhisattva, a great being, becomes expert in realizing that external entities do not exist, [the answer] is: Mahāmati, all entities[1576] are like a fata morgana, a dream, and the apparitions of falling hairs.[1577] All entities lack an own-being[1578] and are caused by adhering to [what arises from] the imprints[1579] of thoughts—[from] the ripening,[1580] in various forms,[1581] of the baseness of mental fabrication, [and such ripening occurs] throughout beginningless time. Bodhisattvas[1582] and great beings who correctly see this realize that external entities do not exist in such a way. This is [the meaning of the sentence]: "A bodhisattva, a great being, is expert in realizing that external entities do not exist."[1583]

[64.21–65.4] In this [passage from the *Laṅkāvatārasūtra*] the yoga of one taste is taught. In the same way as [Zhang] explained [the yoga of one taste],[1584] all entities that are subsumed under [the categories] object and mind are only false appearances, since they resemble a fata morgana, a dream, and the apparitions of falling hairs. A dam is not needed for the water of a fata morgana, and it is not necessary to take care of a son from a dream, nor is it necessary to tie apparitions of falling hairs into a knot.

Likewise, when you see the essential nature of mind, not the slightest endeavor of view is needed to repel appearances. Therefore, you realize that all appearances in the form of entities are this very true nature of mind *(sems nyid)* that lacks an own-being. Because you realize, as a consequence of this, that *-appearances and dharmatā are of one taste, you do not abandon or adopt anything.

[65.4–7] You may wonder, if that is the way it is, what is it, then, that appears in different forms, without having an own-being? It [is what] appears owing to the power of the baseness of mental fabrications [that occur] throughout beginningless time. "Baseness of mental fabrications" in turn [means:] Thoughts are mental fabrications, and their imprints are baseness. Also the appearances in various forms, such as mountains and houses, that [arise] from these [imprints] are called—using the name of the cause for the fruit—imprints. It is like saying "This is poison" when seeing the [already manifest] disease [caused by it].

[65.7–9] Thoughts of adhering to manifold [appearances and the like] arise, and from the imprints left by them, similar [appearances] arise in turn. Such a mechanism of alternating imprints and thoughts has no beginning in time. [As] has been said [in the *Mahāyānābhidharmasūtra*]:[1585]

> The beginningless sphere (i.e., the buddha element) is the basis of all phenomena.[1586]

[65.9–13] Thus the support of imprints is the true nature of mind *(sems nyid)* in its natural luminosity. It is because you thus realize that mind and appearances are of one taste that this is called the yoga of one taste. Götsangpa thinks that this [ranges] from the second to the seventh [bodhisattva] level. Accordingly, bodhisattvas and great beings realize that external entities do not exist. [And this is the meaning of the sentence]: "A bodhisattva, a great being, is expert in realizing that external entities do not exist."

[65.13–16] [The *Laṅkāvatārasūtra* further says]:

> Somebody might ask: How does a bodhisattva, a great being, [get] the strong wish to internalize the wisdom of the noble ones himself? [The answer] is: having fully attained [the ability to] endure that phenomena do not arise, [bodhisattvas] dwelling on the eighth level obtain the mental body owing to their thorough understanding of final perfection,[1587] which is the realization[1588] of the mind, the mental faculty, the mental consciousness, the five categories, the [three] natures, and the two types of selflessness.[1589]

[65.16–25] In this [passage,] the yoga of nonmeditation is taught....[1590] The "wisdom [of the noble ones understood] by yourself" is precisely this [same yoga of nonmeditation] as explained [by Zhang].

[65.25–66.2] With regard to [this wisdom], it is stated in this [*Laṅkāvatārasūtra* II.202]:

> [Mahāmati, a bodhisattva or great being] who has withdrawn alone to a solitary place analyzes[1591] himself with his own intellect, because he does not consider valid and reliable words of the Buddha [any more]. Not relying on anybody else, he has abandoned [wrong] views and concepts, and exerts himself to gradually advance [through the bodhisattva levels] and [finally] reach the level of a tathāgata. Mahāmati, this is the defining characteristic of having realized the wisdom of the noble ones by himself.[1592]

[66.2–5] Therefore, because the yogin becomes aware on his own, [and] not by way of direct and inferential valid cognitions or the reliable words of the Buddha—since there is no relying on the valid cognitions of any person whatsoever—this is called "having internalized by yourself." This [fact] is called *nonmeditation,* because what is called *meditation* is the force of the desire to meditate and the cognition of the characteristic signs of meditation, and these do not exist here [from this level on].

[66.5–12] [The expression] "being resolved" in [the sentence] "being resolved to [attain your experiential] object of realizing the wisdom of the noble ones by yourself"[1593] denotes [a kind of] provisional self-realization in which you internalize conviction, even though this conviction is not manifest from the eighth level onward. Also [the expression] "endurance of the fact that phenomena do not arise" occurs many times in the scriptures. Having thoroughly investigated with the insight of reflection, you [learn to] endure that there is no origination in terms of an own-being. This is called the first endurance. On the first level it is called the endurance that follows the proclamation [of emptiness]. On the sixth level, it is called the concordant endurance. As to the eighth level attainment of the [ability] to endure that phenomena do not arise, on former levels [bodhisattvas] realize in meditative equipoise that phenomena do not arise, and [the endurance of this fact] started from that [realization]. [Though] you realize on the eighth level that phenomena do not arise, [the endurance of this fact] did not start [only] from that [level][1594] and is thus [already] a great endurance [by the eighth level]. Therefore, supreme endurance is given the name of endurance, in the same way as a person capable of good deeds is [only] called a person.

[66.12–19] Some [yogins] may be able to sit on one cushion for up to one month, but when the second month starts, they have to get up, and in this case do not have the slightest endurance any more. It is like that also on the former [bodhisattva] levels. Because of that endurance, the mind, [that is,] the five types of consciousness together with the basic consciousness, the defiled mind, and the mental faculty with thoughts, is transformed on the eighth level. Among the five dharmas, it is names, characteristic signs, and thoughts that are transformed, and even the three natures and the two types of selflessness are fully realized here. On the seventh level and below, the appearances of the mental consciousness—and therefore the imagined [nature]—are not reversed. Since the thoughts of the mental faculty are not reversed, the dependent [nature] is not reversed. Although the imprints of imagining the two types of self have not been abandoned up to the seventh level, they are reversed here on the eighth level. Because of the perfect realization following from that, the [three] natures and the two types of selflessness are realized, [which is] the thorough understanding [characteristic of] final perfection.[1595]

[66.19–21] [As for] the attaining of the mental body: you attain on this level the mental body, which [amounts to] the realization of the svābhāvikakāya, and [this] distinctive [goal] is named [accordingly] and explained in these terms. As to the mental body in detail, when this text explains the mental body, it does so by taking its lead from this sūtra.[1596]

[66.21–26] With regard to the *Laṅkāvatārasūtra*, there are two [translations], a shorter one, the so-called essence of the discourse, and one longer than it—longer in that it contains in the first part the teachings to the lord of Laṅka and more than nine hundred stanzas in the final part.[1597] It is obvious that in [their presentation of] the great yoga, both are in some disorder. In the shorter [translation, from the Chinese,] the realization that external entities do not exist is taken as the second yoga,[1598] whereas in the longer [version] it is taken to be the third. It is better to take it as the third, in accordance with the commentary of Jñānaśrībhadra.[1599] It is [further] obvious that the detailed explanation of the individual [yogas] is mixed up in the longer text, but not in the shorter one. A simple attainment of the mental body is [achieved] from the lower [levels] onward.

[66.26–67.3] If you ask why, among the three mental bodies of arhats, pratyekabuddhas, and powerful bodhisattvas, as taught in the *Śrīmālā-[devīsūtra]*, the mental bodies of an arhat and pratyekabuddha are obtained when no skandhas are left over, Ācārya Buddhaguhya explained that when these two, who are endowed with mental bodies, enter the Mahāyāna, it is at the stage of engagement based on conviction. Thus it has been said that a mental body is obtained even at the stage of engagement based on conviction.

[67.3–10] Now, the [following] explanations will be taken from the teachings in the *Vairocanābhisambodhitantra* and [its] commentary [called the] *[Vairocanābhisambodhitantra]piṇḍārtha:* The extent to which śrāvakas and pratyekabuddhas obtain the fruit; the difference between their mistaken and unmistaken path; how they gradually realize selflessness; the point in time when they and the bodhisattvas who have entered the Mahāyāna right from the beginning transcend the one hundred sixty worldly [forms of] mind; how there is a vision of the truth at the stage of engagement based on conviction; [how] this stage is in accordance with the ten levels of the fruit; and how [these] ten levels, which are their branches,[1600] exist—[these points are explained] so that those who possess the faith that arises from having obtained the eyes of seeing the vastness of the Dharma will not deprecate the Dharma.

[67.10–18] In [Buddhaguhya's] commentary *Vairocanābhisambodhitantrapiṇḍārtha* it is stated:[1601]

> As to this, the understanding[1602] has accordingly been taught as being twofold—realizing the selflessness of a person and realizing the selflessness of a person and phenomena—in line with the difference between sentient beings with dull and sharp faculties. In this regard, those with dull faculties first enter the path of realizing the selflessness of a person after abandoning a path that is solely a worldly path.[1603] After that they grow weary of things such as the manifestation of the hundred sixty [kinds] of worldly mind, which have the defining characteristics of a mind of attachment and so forth, and realize the selflessness of a person. [This sentence] must be extended to "mind of attachment, mind of hatred, mind of love, mind of delusion, and so forth." After the one hundred sixty [kinds of] worldly mind have been left behind for three eons, a supramundane mind is generated. It is like this: it (i.e., the person) [consists] of skandhas only, and a self never exists; [it is like] the thought that the world is meaningless given [the existence of] the city of Indra [together with its] realms and so on. Up to here [the first type of understanding] has been taught.

[67.18–25] The yogins with sharp faculties first remove concepts of a self and so forth: skandhas, *dhātus*, *āyatanas*, and [any duality of] a perceived and perceiver. Having left the one hundred sixty [kinds of] worldly mind behind, they enter [the realization of] the selflessness of persons and phenomena. It is stated [in the root tantra]: "Moreover, Guhyakādhipati, in those who have no regard for other modes of progress than the Mahāyāna, a mind [that realizes] the selflessness of phenomena arises. If you ask, why it is, [the answer is:] a form of discrimination[1604] arises that [sees that everything is] like an illusion, a fata morgana, a reflection, an echo, a fire-wheel,[1605] or the city of Gandharvas since their nature is thoroughly known once your former mode of conduct and the abode of the skandhas are completely abolished. Therefore, Guhyakādhipati, even the selflessness of phenomena in terms of a mind[1606] must be abandoned."

[67.25–68.10] Therefore, when those with dull faculties and those with other-than-sharp faculties cultivate in such a way the path of the selflessness of a person, and while those with sharp faculties cultivate the path of realizing the selflessness of a person and phenomena, yogins with dull faculties gradually attain eight fruits, such as entering the fruit of the "stream-enterer," which is preceded by the abandonment of the one hundred sixty [kinds of] worldly mind—attachment and the like; and later they understand that skandhas and so forth are like the nature of an illusion, a fata morgana, and similar [examples]. Being completely free from the distinctions made among skandhas, *dhātus*, and *āyatanas*, they realize that these three have quiescence and emptiness as their only defining characteristics. As has been said in detail, among other things, in the [root tantra]: "Guhyakādhipati, even with regard to those who abide in a supramundane [state of] mind, an intellect is produced that thinks: 'The skandhas possess it (i.e., the supramundane mind).' The moment freedom from attachment to skandhas arises, you are liberated, owing to [their] destruction similar to [the destruction of] foam, water bubbles, and a fata morgana. It is like this: having abandoned[1607] skandhas, *dhātus*, *āyatanas*, and [the duality of a] perceived and perceiver, you realize the sphere of quiescence, whose own-being is the true nature of phenomena. Guhyakādhipati, those who are connected to the supramundane mind [and] the eight features distinguishing a mistaken and unmistaken mind [and] are free from the net of deeds and defilements are yogins."

[68.10–18] Those with dull faculties are śrāvakas and pratyekabuddhas; those with sharp faculties bodhisattvas. "First" means to have freshly entered the Śrāvakayāna, not indirectly from one *yāna* to the other. As for the merely worldly path, it is, among others, the view that there is merely a self that is free from the qualities, [as] postulated by the Vaiśeṣikas. It is the views of a self [entertained] by the tīrthikas. As to the one hundred sixty [forms of] worldly mind, they are sixty defilements, starting from a mind of attachment and going up to a mind of [re]birth.[1608] The sixty are taken singly, in pairs, [and then] in groups of three, four, five, six, eight, and ten, so that there are altogether one hundred sixty,[1609] but in reality there are only sixty. "Such as" means other defilements different from these. "To renounce" [means] to abandon them. "After [the one hundred sixty worldly kinds of mind] have been left behind for three eons, a supramundane mind is generated" [means:] "Having newly entered the *yāna*, you become an arhat [in the state of] no more learning at best within three lifetimes and at most within three eons."

[68.18–26] "[Consists] of skandhas only," and so forth, is the way to realize the selflessness of persons. You know that a self of persons does not exist; it is only skandhas that wander in saṁsāra. "[Yogins with sharp faculties] first remove concepts of a self and so forth: skandhas, *dhātus*, *āyatanas*, and [any duality of] a perceived and perceiver. Having left the one hundred sixty worldly [kinds of] mind behind, they enter [the realization of] the selflessness of persons and phenomena" [means that] even that which is [wrongly] imagined by the tīrthikas, such as that beings are pervaded by the self of a person and so forth, are removed. Having removed, with the view of mind only, the clinging to phenomena—skandhas, *āyatanas*, and elements up to perceived [objects] and perceiving [subjects]—you leave the one hundred sixty worldly [kinds of] mind behind and comprehend the selflessness of persons and phenomena. Just as śrāvakas are able to leave behind the worldly mind with the view of the selflessness of persons, you know that [the equivalent] can also be done on the bodhisattva path with the view of mind only. Those with sharp faculties demonstrate this at the time of passing beyond the worldly mind.

[68.26–69.5] "Those who have no regard for other [modes of progress]" in [the sentence] "Moreover, Guhyakādhipati...." are Mādhyamikas, ones with very sharp faculties. [The passage] "The abode of skandhas" [provides] the basis upon which skandhas are so designated. They are destroyed [the moment their] nonexistence is realized. As for the selflessness of phenomena here, there are two types: the one realized by the followers of Cittamātra[, who] postulate the ultimate [existence of] a mind free from a perceived [object] and a perceiving [subject], [while] the Mādhyamikas realize that even this [mind] does not exist. Therefore, such a selflessness of phenomena in terms of a mind that is free from a perceived [object] and a perceiving [subject] is necessarily abandoned by the Mādhyamikas. "Even" [means:] It is not that the clinging to a self of phenomena is abandoned only to the extent of [no longer] adhering to perceived [objects] and perceiving [subjects].

[69.5–10] [The paragraph] from "Therefore" up to "sphere of quiescence"[1610] [states that] after attaining arhat[ship] on the Śrāvakayāna, you enter the Mahāyāna upon realizing the selflessness of phenomena. In the preceding states of the "stream-enterer" and the rest you still cling to skandhas and so forth [as things that] exist, and therefore it is said that there is a clinging to phenomena. There are eight [noble persons who have tasted] the fruit of the supramundane mind: the four enterers and the four abiders, [namely the stream-enterer and so forth.[1611]] As to their path, when the sixteen [attributes of the four noble truths]—impermanence and the rest—are realized,[1612] it is stated that they are seen with regard to the world. Because you thus realize the yoga [on the level of] apparent [truth], [this realization] is unmistaken with regard to the correct apparent [truth], but since you do not realize the ultimate truth, [namely,] the selflessness of phenomena, it is [also] linked with what is mistaken.

[69.10–12] For it is stated in *Laṅkāvatārasūtra* [II.128]:

> The fruit of the stream-enterer, that of the once-to-come,
> That of the not-to-come, and even that of arhatship [still represent]
> impaired [states of] mind.[1613]

[69.12–14] "Who are free from the net of deeds and defilements" [means that] in the state of remainder you are free from the net of the defilements, which have completely ripened. In the state without remainder you are free from the net of deeds *(karman),* but not free from the mental imprints of defilements.

[69.14–23] The commentary *[Vairocanābhisambodhitantra]piṇḍārtha*[1614] [notes]:

> As explained before, the yogins enter the path [of realizing] the selflessness of persons and phenomena according to their [individual] stage of dull or sharp faculties, and both are [still] in a state in which all phenomena, as illusion-like appearances, obscure [their] mind, [so that] they are encouraged to start to

make efforts to realize the level of engagement based on conviction. This is the stage they are at. In the same way that they thoroughly internalize the path of realizing the selflessness of persons and phenomena, so too they are made familiar with this very [selflessness] through the meditation of actualizing the mind of entering, abiding, and awakening [others],[1615] and being looked after [in this way][1616]—[an activity] that precedes [their] future attainment of the conduct of the perfections of generosity and the rest by the four means of attracting sentient beings—they are made to enter the ten [levels]. For these, and for those instructed with the Dharma words of [how to] enter these [levels] on the strength of insight acquired by listening and reflecting, even though their (i.e., the *pāramitās*'?) outflow, [namely,] the qualities of body, speech, and mind, have not been attained [yet],[1617] [the levels] are as if they were a reality.[1618] Being convinced of this is the "conviction" [in the expression "engagement based on conviction"]. The essence of a bodhisattva's benefiting himself and others is engagement based on conviction, no matter what form the preceding conviction takes in his engagement. This essence is a [bodhisattva] level, in the sense of a foundation. It is taught that you spend one eon on the level of engagement based on conviction.

[69.23–70.1] The level of engagement based on conviction is the development of three [kinds of] mind, as has been said: "Given its engagement with the 'perfections' *(pāramitā)* and the four [means of] attracting [sentient beings], the [bodhisattva] level of conviction is unequalled, immeasurable, and inconceivable, the source of immeasurable wisdom, and obtained by ten [kinds of] mind. What I will mention briefly is that all [levels] are attained by way of it. Therefore [even] the level of omniscience[1619] is explained as *conviction.* The wise leave [this] level behind them in [only] one eon."

[70.1–4] Moreover, the development of three [kinds of] mind, explained as the level of engagement based on conviction, and the elucidation of the ten [kinds of] mind on the level of conviction, in the "practices" that complete the ten levels of wisdom, have been correctly taught in this treatise, in the chapters [XIII–XVI] on the secret [maṇḍala][1620] in connection with the tantra attached[1621] to this *Vairocanābhisambodhitantra:*

[70.4–8] Then, Guhyakādhipati, if you ask what the thorough knowledge of the three [forms of] mind[1622] [operative on the level of] engagement based on conviction is, [the answer is:] Guhyakādhipati, the defining characteristic of internalizing that the mind is neither arising nor passing out of existence is the first realization, since you realize the first instant of the mind [of engagement based on conviction]. The second is nonconceptuality, wholly leaving behind the entire net of thoughts. Great compassion arises upon thinking that having realized a state without hindrances, sentient beings must be established on the right path. This is the third [type of] mind operative on [the level of engagement based on conviction]. Guhyakādhipati, through the attainment of [these] three [forms of] mind, the levels *(bhūmi),* perfections *(pāramitā),* and means of attracting [sentient beings] will be attained.

[70.9–12] Guhyakādhipati, as to the preparations for attaining the levels and perfections, the bodhisattva follows the conduct of a bodhisattva according to the secret Mantra[yāna], and once he possesses skillful means and insight, he is induced to engage in proper [activity] in the form of the four means of attracting [sentient beings]. To give the gift of Dharma with a joyful mind is the [path of] preparation, which is a branch of the levels and perfections of this [engagement based on conviction].

[70.12–14] Guhyakādhipati, having given them [the gift of] Dharma, a bodhisattva who abides in the discipline of a pure and unconditioned mind establishes sentient beings in the discipline at their wish. He himself abides in it. This is regarded as the [path of] preparation, which is a branch of the levels and perfections of this [engagement based on conviction].

[70.14–16] Guhyakādhipati, when a bodhisattva pervades luminosity[1623] and, with his mind, the phenomena of the ten directions, he himself obtains the [ability to] endure that phenomena do not arise. To establish others in this [state] is regarded as the [path of] preparation, which is a branch of the levels and perfections of this [engagement based on conviction].

[70.16–19] Moreover, Guhyakādhipati, [a bodhisattva who] possesses rays of wisdom initiates effort by the force of an intellect skilled in the eventual and gradually increasing realization by this same mind and establishes others in this [state]. Guhyakādhipati, this is regarded as the [path of] preparation, which is the attainment of a branch[1624] of the levels and perfections of this [engagement based on conviction].

[70.19–21] Guhyakādhipati, when a bodhisattva observes the conduct of a bodhisattva according to the secret Mantra[yāna], he "stabilizes his mind"[1625] with an intellect that possesses wisdom [but] without paying attention to any of the meditations; and when he causes others, too, to properly adopt this [state], this is regarded as the [path of] preparation, which is the attainment of a branch of the levels and perfections of this [engagement based on conviction].

[70.21–24] Guhyakādhipati, [the bodhisattva] himself abides in it (i.e., the perfection of meditation) with this same mind, [namely,] an intellect endowed with wisdom, [but] without paying attention to the worldly or the supramundane meditations, or the immeasurable [attitudes] of the śrāvakas; when he causes others to correctly adopt this [state], this is regarded as the [path of] preparation, which is the attainment of a branch of the levels and perfections of this [engagement based on conviction].

[70.24–71.2] Guhyakādhipati, a bodhisattva who observes the conduct of a bodhisattva according to the secret Mantra[yāna], [and] who is endowed with such an earnest intention of meditation, is himself—owing to this same mind, [namely,] an intellect endowed with wisdom—grounded in [a state in which] he is induced to apply[1626] worldly and supramundane insight, and establishes others in it too. Such [a state] is regarded as the attainment of a branch of the perfection of insight and the actualized level [corresponding to it].

[71.2–5] Guhyakādhipati, a bodhisattva, being expert in perfectly attracting [sentient beings] by skillful means [and] well blessed with spiritual friends, is induced to make prayer wishes for [attaining] all properties of a buddha and—starting with the first mind [of enlightenment]—to

> attract sentient beings by the four means of attraction. This is regarded as the attainment of the [path of] preparation,[1627] which is the perfection of skillful means and the "far-reaching" [level] of this [engagement based on conviction].
>
> [71.5–7] Guhyakādhipati, [a bodhisattva who,] thanks to an intellect endowed with wisdom, is motionless and not the least agitated is not subdued by any adversary or by gods or by [any] from among the hosts of demons. This is regarded as the [path of] preparation, which is the "motionless" level of this [engagement based on conviction] and [its corresponding] perfection.
>
> [71.7–13] Guhyakādhipati, a bodhisattva who is well looked after by spiritual friends, who [has realized] with regard to all phenomena their equality with illusory phenomena, and who is endowed with the perfection of great compassion is induced to pervade the buddhafields in the ten directions with the perfection of great compassion, to fully rejoice equally with body, speech, and mind, and to see—with body hairs standing on end and much joy—the tathāgatas residing in the ten directions. He is endowed with great compassion extending to the extreme of the far-thest] sentient being, and is induced to pervade all sentient beings with the extremity of space, the extremity of [the scope of all] sentient beings, [and] the ultimate of wisdom and consciousness.
>
> [71.13–15] When he has thus obtained the generation of the power of faith, diligence, and insight, he sees, both in dreams and directly, buddhas and bodhisattvas, and even obtains the meditative stabilization of not forgetting bodhicitta. He should be known as a bodhisattva who has entered the "circle" (maṇḍala) of conviction.[1628]

[71.15–21] By quoting this [passage], I have taught the buddhahood of [the level called] *engagement based on conviction.* "[All phenomena, as] illusion-like appearances, [still] obscure [their] mind"[1629] [means that] when śrāvakas and arhats enter [the path of realizing] the selflessness of phenomena after attaining [their] goal, [they still perceive] illusion-like appearances. Even those with sharp faculties are like them, and thus [such] appearances obscure [their] mind, in that they are conceptual hindrances. With "both also"[1630] it is clearly taught that you are encouraged to enter [the stage of] engagement based on conviction[1631] even though you have [already] entered the Mahāyāna [after] reaching the śrāvakas' and pratyekabuddhas' [path of] no more learning. "Are the first realization"[1632] means: [are] the first moment or the first state of the mind [of enlightenment]. At that time, you realize by means of analytical knowledge—in the form of special insight [still] accompanied by thoughts—that the mind does not arise and cease. This is the first mind, [that] of entering, because it makes you enter the main part [of the practice].

[71.21–24] As to the second mind[, that] of abiding, it is a nonconceptual direct [awareness], since the entire net of thoughts together with their words and meanings has been left behind completely. To some extent it is as taught in [the explanation of] the Jewel of the Saṅgha [in RGV I.13c]:

> [The community, which] sees with an unobstructed intellect
> that buddhahood is all-pervading.... [1633]

[71.24–26] In the same way as you realize that your own mind is emptiness, you see that the mind of every sentient being is also emptiness. This is a realization without hindrances. Thanks to its power, great compassion toward sentient beings arises, and you [help] to establish [them] on the path. This is the mind of awakening [others], the state attained after [meditation].

[71.26–72.5] Moreover, [this is shown in] the four meditations taught in the *Laṅkāvatārasūtra.*[1634] The meditation of the śrāvakas and what is less advanced than the yoga practice of bodhisattvas are proper for fools. It is clear that the three [states, as in the mind of] entering and so on, are, respectively: [the meditation devoted to the] examination of meaning, [the meditation with] suchness as its object, and the meditation of a tathāgata. As to the formulation "...to be the [path of] preparation, which is a branch of the [bodhisattva] levels and perfections," the supramundane, real levels, and real perfections are [states you arrive at] after you have attained the ultimate mind. When you meditate on the branch [called] *the cause that is in partial concordance with these [states],* [namely,] the ultimate, this is said to be yoga. It should be understood that this [applies] to all of them.[1635]

[72.5–6] *Dharmadhātustotra* [stanza 78 says]:[1636]

> Because you have taken full possession of the foundation of the white,
> After completely abandoning the foundation of the black,
> This [first level] is at that time definite realization
> And called *joyful.*

Accordingly, [the first bodhisattva level] is joyful because you are generous to others.

[72.6–8] [The *Dharmadhātustotra* further says (stanza 79)]:

> That which is permanently stained
> By various stains such as attachment
> Has become stainlessly[1637] pure,
> [And this level] is called *stainless.*[1638]

Likewise, [the second level] is stainless in virtue of your having purified the stains of the mind.

[72.8–10] [The *Dharmadhātustotra* further says (stanza 80)]:

> Because stainless insight becomes very clear,
> After you have stopped the net of defilements completely,
> Limitless darkness is dispelled;[1639]
> Therefore [this level] is the *luminous [one].*

Likewise, [the third level] is called *luminous* because phenomena in the ten directions are illuminated by the light of stainless insight. [Moreover,] you endure phenomena, which are explained in all the discourses as nonarising.

[72.10–12] [The *Dharmadhātustotra* further says (stanza 81)]:

> The ever pure and luminous
> Is entirely surrounded by the light of wisdom
> Of having completely avoided distraction;
> Therefore this level is called[1640] the *radiant one.*

Likewise, [the fourth level] is called *radiant* because the light rays of the wisdom that realizes the mind radiate to the [mind]streams of others.

[72.12–14] [The *Dharmadhātustotra* further says (stanza 82)]:

> All sciences, arts, and crafts [are mastered here],
> [Along with] all[1641] the various forms of meditation,
> And defilements difficult to overcome
> Have been vanquished; therefore [this level] is called *difficult to overcome.*

Likewise, [the fifth level] is called *difficult to overcome* because you vanquish the defilements of clinging to meditation [in terms of] self and other.

[72.14–16] [The *Dharmadhātustotra* further says (stanza 83)]:

> All the marvels of the three aspects[1642]
> Of enlightenment are gathered,
> And the profound arising and passing out of existence is exhausted;
> Therefore[1643] this level is called *actualization.*

Likewise, [the sixth level] is called *actualization* because you actualize the perfection of insight that realizes [that phenomena] neither arise nor pass out of existence.[1644]

[72.16–18] [The *Dharmadhātustotra* further says (stanza 84)]:

> A web of [wisdom] light [like] the design of a wheel[1645]
> Plays about everywhere;[1646]
> The swamp of the ocean of saṁsāra has been crossed over.
> Therefore this [level] is called *gone far.*

Likewise, [the seventh level] is called *far going* because it includes [everything] between the first [enlightened] mind—attracting [sentient beings] and aspiration—up to a buddha.

[72.18–20] [The *Dharmadhātustotra* further says (stanza 85)]:

> Firmly held by the Buddha,
> [The bodhisattvas] entered into an ocean of wisdom.
> And attained the power of effortless [activity];
> Therefore [this level] is *immovable* for the messenger of Māra.[1647]

Likewise, [the eighth level] is called *immovable* because it is not moved by Mārā or [other] enemies.

[72.20–22] [The *Dharmadhātustotra* further says (stanza 86)]:

> Because the yogin has reached perfection[1648]
> In [his] discourses of teaching the Dharma
> In all [fields of] correct knowledge,
> This [level] is called *excellent intelligence.*

Likewise, [the ninth level] is called *excellent intelligence* because you have been well looked after by a spiritual friend, and have thus obtained an intellect that [realizes that everything] is like an illusion, and [you are thus endowed with] great compassion.

[72.22–24] [The *Dharmadhātustotra* further says (stanza 87)]:

From the kāya of this nature of wisdom,
Which is equivalent to stainless space
And held by the buddhas,[1649]
The *cloud of the Dharma* fully arises.

Likewise, [the tenth level] is called the *cloud of Dharma teachings* because from the kāya of buddha wisdom arises the cloud of Dharma teachings, which pervades all sentient beings.

[72.24–73.1] That there is also a seeing of truth on the level of engagement based on conviction has been explained in the [following stanza]:

Those whose mind abides, like a mountain,
In what is quiescent
And without an own-being from the beginning
See the truth.[1650]

[73.1–3] For it is stated in the word-for-word commentary: "As for 'see the truth,' it is explained as the bodhicitta of abiding." This [bodhi]citta of abiding and the realization of freedom from mental fabrications are only different terms having the same meaning, since both of them express realization that nothing arises in terms of an own-being.

[73.3] Zhang [Tsalpa Tsöndrü] said in [his *Phyag rgya chen po lam zab mthar thug*]:[1651]

[73.3–5] Mahāmudrā is attained in one go.
The confused err when they reckon it in terms of levels and paths.
Still, in order to please the confused,
The levels and paths of the vehicle of defining characteristics
Must be reckoned as a substitute even here.

[73.5–6] The special dawning of [that] realization
Is the level of the path of seeing [called] *extremely joyful*.[1652]
Cultivating this realization of equal taste is the path of meditation.
When there is nothing to meditate upon [any more], this is the path of completion.

[73.6–7] Although suffering is not done away with,
And qualities and abilities do not immediately arise

> Upon the realization of nonduality,
> No one would object and say that this is not the path of seeing.
>
> [73.7–8] Although the ice cannot be melted
> And the ground and stones do not turn warm
> Immediately after the sun has risen at dawn,
> No one would object and say that this is not the sun.

[73.8–10] Since mahāmudrā is attained in one go, you must not reckon in terms of the levels and paths. This means that since the [bodhisattva] levels are the direct realization of the true nature of phenomena and there is no division in the true nature of phenomena, it is not possible to count the individual levels as [distinct] parts of it.

[73.10–12] This is in accordance with what has been said in the *Madhyamakāvatārabhāṣya* [on I.5] together with the quotation [of a stanza from the *Daśabhūmikasūtra*]:

> Being the true nature of consciousness, they (i.e., the bodhisattva levels) cannot be distinguished in terms of an own-being.[1653] Just as a trail of a bird in the sky cannot be expressed or seen by the wise, in the same way no bodhisattva levels can be expressed, [and if this is the case,] how can they be heard of?[1654]

[73.12–14] In meaning this accords, too, with what Haribhadra said:

> Since you apprehend nothing other than what has been actualized on the path of seeing, as has been explained, [the paths of] seeing and meditation are not different. Thus a real path of meditation is not presented.

[73.14–18] As to the [passage]: "Still, in order to please the confused, the levels and paths of the vehicle of defining characteristics must be reckoned as a substitute even here," it has to be evaluated against the background of the presentation of the ten *pāramitās* and ten levels on the level of engagement based on conviction—[a presentation] based on the "attached tantra"[1655] in the commentary *Vairocanābhisambodhitantrapiṇḍārtha*. This being the case, some advocate then that it is not appropriate to present the first mind of "abiding or realization without mental fabrication of the [level of] engagement based on conviction" as the first [bodhisattva] level[1656] because it does not have the 112 qualities.[1657]

[73.18–19] In this regard, however, Chöjé Drigungpa said:

> If you find definitive sūtras and śāstras in support of your entailment, I will give you a good horse.

[73.19–74.2] In [the chapter in the] *Daśabhūmikasūtra* on the first level it is stated:

> A bodhisattva abiding on this [first level] has to a great extent mastered the world and obtained great power....[1658] Wishing [all this], he starts with that kind of effort by which[1659] you abandon everything—house, wife, and property—and set out for the teaching of the Tathāgata. Having done so, he attains and enters into a hundred samādhis within the period of one moment;[1660] sees a hundred buddhas; understands well [that he has] their blessing; causes a hundred worlds to tremble; passes through a hundred [buddha]fields; illuminates a hundred worlds; causes a hundred sentient beings to mature; remains for a hundred eons; reaches one hundred eons into the past and the future; investigates a hundred doors of Dharma; displays a hundred bodies; and displays each body with an entourage of a hundred bodhisattvas.[1661] Such are the efforts he starts to make.[1662]

[74.2–5] In this passage the 112 qualities of a bodhisattva on the first level are taught.[1663] When you have obtained the first level in this life, you become a king [with the standing of a] cakravartin in the next [life]; and having renounced your family life,[1664] you meditate in the forest. Because it has been taught that these qualities arise from that, it is said that the attainment of the first level and the attainment of the 112 qualities do not coincide.

[74.5–14] [Moreover], it would follow that the sun has not risen [only] because the qualities of the [just-]risen sun are not [yet] complete. It is clear that this accords with both Zhang and Drigungpa.[1665] It is not only appropriate to present the abiding mind as the ten levels; it is [also] seen to be appropriate to relate it with the four stages of penetration and the four yogas, for the following reasons: (1) It is taught as being ineffable in the *Abhisamayālaṁkāra* in the paragraph on heat, and it is seen during [the yoga of] one-pointedness that thoughts are not as they really are. (2) It is taught that during the yoga of freedom from mental fabrications, after [your] insight has increased, you see that everything, both outer and inner, is empty, and in the paragraph on the peak it is taught: "If thoroughly investigated by insight, nothing is apprehended [any more]." (3) The realization during the yoga of one taste that the mind is without origination and that the appearances of the mind are of identical taste is in line with the explanation in the paragraph on forbearance: "The lack of an own-being in such things as forms—this very lack [is] its own-being." (4) Nonmeditation is called such because there is no [further] thought of wishing to meditate. Such a meditation is supreme. This is in line with what is called "nonconceptual meditative stabilization" in the paragraph on the supreme [mundane] quality.

[74.14–18] Moreover, in the life story of Drigungpa's disciple Nyö Gyalwa Lhanangpa (Gnyos Rgyal ba Lha nang pa) (1164–1224),[1666] a disciple of Nyö Gyalwa, Yeshé Dorjé (Ye shes rdo rje), says:

> In terms of the four stages of penetration on the path of preparation, they only accord with the Pāramitāyāna. Nevertheless, here again all properties of the path and the fruit are completely perfect. One-pointedness is the actualization during the meditative stabilization of heat. Freedom from mental fabrications is the seeing during the meditative stabilization of the peak of dharmatā. Forbearance is the direct realization of one taste, [that is,] the actualization of the equality of all phenomena. The supreme mundane quality is the actualization of qualities; [that is,] all worldly beings have matured and been liberated through the deeds of the buddhas and because of [their] activity.

[74.18–22] In this way it is claimed that it is appropriate to relate the four penetrations with the four yogas, but also on other occasions it is not inappropriate to do so. It is also appropriate [to say] that from the eighth level onward all four yogas are completed in one instant. The *Ratnamegha[sūtra]* explains that engagement based on conviction is in accordance with the [four] states of penetration. The scholar Asvabhāva also explained it as such. It is very good [that he did so].

[74.22–25] Notwithstanding, it is obvious that they must be taken to be [a feature of] the path of accumulation [as well], because it is said in the *Vairocanābhisambodhi[tantra]* that you ascend in a quarter of an eon to the path of preparation, which is called *entering the levels after getting beyond engagement based on conviction.* I do not think that these different presentations contradict each other. In the same way, the explanations that both the prior generation of an enlightened attitude by a beginner and the first level are the generation of the first enlightened attitude do not contradict each other.

[74.25–26] The last two dharmacakras differ in that the [bodhisattva] levels become completely perfected [only in the third dharmacakra, and] not [in the second one]. The levels of the fruit of the last dharmacakra are the [three] pure levels. The levels of the fruit of the second dharmacakra are only said to be the seventh level and below.

[The next sentence of the *Ratnagotravibhāgavyākhyā* to be explained is:]

> **[What are, in this regard, the qualities of the sixtyfold process of purifying the buddha element?]**[1667]

[74.26–75.4] Thus, the way to realize what must be cleansed has been explained with an explanation of the [process of] cleansing.[1668] In this regard, the processes that purify the three stains of the [buddha] element are the [sixty] qualities,[1669] so that you should become accordingly familiar [with them], and obtain that which possesses the light of pure qualities, by applying the sixty purifying processes to the [buddha] element of sentient beings, in the same way as the quality of redness [is obtained] by bringing together turmeric powder and lime ($CaCO_3$). You may ask, what are these sixty distinctions among its aspects?

[75.4–5] [The next sentence in the *Ratnagotravibhāgavyākhyā* is:]

> **They are: the fourfold ornament of bodhisattvas, the eightfold brilliance of bodhisattvas, the sixteenfold compassion of bodhisattvas, and the thirty-two-fold activity of bodhisattvas.**[1670]

[75.5–8] Among these, the main activity of all the buddhas and bodhisattvas is to teach the Dharma, for it is said:

> The *munis* do not wash off sins with water,
> Nor do they clear away the stains of beings with [their] hands,
> Nor do they transfer their own realization to others.
> They rather liberate [beings] by teaching the true nature of
> phenomena [and] peace.

[75.8–9] Moreover:

> "I will explain to you the path
> That cuts off [all] fear of [cyclic] existence;

You must accomplish it on your own."
This is what the Tathāgata has taught.

[75.9–13] Even though the Dharma is being taught, the teacher is like a carpenter; the instrument of the teaching is like a tool—an axe or a saw; and the product or the fruit of the work is like the [wooden] figure of a man or a woman. As for the qualities of the teacher of the Dharma, among these three phenomena, it is said in the *Mahāyānasūtrālaṁkāra* [XVII.10]:

> You should rely on a [spiritual] friend who is controlled, peaceful, pacified,
> Superior in virtue, diligent, rich in discourses,
> Who has realized them,[1671] [and] who is eloquent,
> Loving, and free from distress.[1672]

[75.13–16] In accordance with that, the [first three] of the four ornaments—[namely,] discipline *(śīla),*[1673] meditative stabilization *(samādhi),* and insight *(prajñā)*—[refer to the qualities of being] controlled, peaceful, and pacified. As to [the fourth ornament,] retentive power *(dhāraṇī),* in view of [properties of] a marvelous memory, it is explained that you are adept in retaining words and are quick-witted, and for these reasons you are eloquent. As to the eight [types of] brilliance—memory and the rest—they are [responsible for] the penetration of reality. The sixteen[fold] compassion is that whose nature is kindness; these [sixteen aspects of compassion] are the great[ness] of those explaining the Dharma.

[75.16–20] The [first] three, discipline and so forth, are the threefold training. As to insight, [the third] among them, it has been explained in the sūtras as the ascertainment of meaning; that is, the insight that ascertains the meaning of the subject matter *(abhidheya).* Retentive power is the memory retaining the words of the text *(abhidhāna)* without forgetting [anything]. Just as people rejoice if someone puts on body ornaments, the circle of [your] retinue rejoices if you are endowed with these four ornaments. That is why they are called *ornaments.* Both insight and compassion are the tools for teaching the Dharma, the eight[fold] brilliance being insight, and the sixteen[fold] compassion [being] compassion.

[75.20–25] The eight[fold] brilliance is: the brilliance of memory *(smṛti),*[1674] the intellect *(mati),* understanding,[1675] phenomena *(dharma),* knowledge,[1676] truth *(satya),* clairvoyance *(abhijñā),* and accomplishment *(pratipatti). [Brilliance of] memory* is the memory of the proper way [to ensure that you] do not forget the virtuous deeds performed by a bodhisattva and [that you] perform new ones not performed [before]. It is also the memory that does not forget which nonvirtuous [deeds] have been given up and of the [need to] abandon what has not been given up [before]. This is the marvelous [memory], the essence of perfect abandoning. The marvelous insight, which has arisen from [this] essence of abandoning, has the power to seize the city of the Buddha's Dharma. Based on [this] memory, the vast brilliance [illuminating all] knowable objects arises.

[75.25–76.1] [The *brilliance of the] intellect* refers to the certain understanding of activities relating to the teaching of the Dharma. This is [a kind of] brilliance, and—since such activities are informed by an intellect [that applies] the four hermeneutical principles[1677]—the Hīnayāna and the action of Māra are overcome.

[76.1] [The *brilliance of] realization* is the direct realization by yourself of the different types of Dharma to be taught. In view of this you are skilled in teaching the Dharma to others.

[76.2–4] The *brilliance of phenomena:* here, phenomena are [either] mundane or supramundane, depending on the various ways of knowable objects—in view of the [various] ways phenomena [appear as] knowable objects. Having come to understand the four noble truths (in which these two types of phenomena are addressed), you fully realize that the phenomena of defilements are adventitious, and, by the mind's natural luminosity, know the phenomena of purification to be nirvāṇa.

[76.4–5] As to what is called the *brilliance of knowledge,* it is how the noble ones of the three *yānas* know knowable objects; it is what is called[1678] knowledge of a stream-enterer up to a buddha.

[76.5–8] As to what is called the *brilliance of truth,* it is—given that you know the four noble truths and the qualities resulting from having meditated on them—the individual knowledge of the way to meditate on the four truths, this being the cause of your entering [a state of] certainty, obtaining the four fruits, and obtaining the patience of a pratyekabuddha and a bodhisattva and the enlightenment of a buddha.

[76.8–9] The *brilliance of clairvoyance* is the six[fold] clairvoyance, and based on this, it is knowing the skillful means of gathering the two accumulations.

[76.9–10] The *brilliance of accomplishment* is the accomplishment of calm abiding, deep insight, and a marvelous intellect in your own [mental] continuum, and the accomplishment of the skillful means of ripening and liberating others. Since the entire Mahāyāna path is seen by means of these eight, they are called *brilliances.*

[76.10–15] The sixteen[fold] compassion of a bodhisattva is: Having seen [the various situations people are in, compassion] takes the form of wishing [that sentient beings] may be free from the [following defects]: (1) various views, (2) the four errors, (3) the notion of mine,[1679] (4) the five hindrances, (5) the attachment to the objects of the six sense spheres, (6) seven[fold] pride, (7) straying from the noble path, (8) lack of independence,[1680] (9) anger, (10) being influenced by sinful friends, (11) lacking the potential of the noble ones,[1681] (12) mistaken views,[1682] (13) a view of a self caused by ignorance, (14) being seized by the executioner [in the hire] of the skandhas,[1683] (15) being tied in the noose of Māra, and (16) straying from the higher realms and liberation.

[76.15–18] In this regard, the mixing of various views with the view of the transitory collection [as a real *I* and *mine*] makes you a heretic who has mistakenly entered [a wrong path]. The four errors and the view of the transitory collection entailing the notion of a mine are coemergent. Those who have not embraced tenets share them. These [first] three (i.e., various views, the four errors, and the notion of a mine) are discordant with insight. Being hindered by both the five hindrances and an attachment to the objects of the six sense spheres are discordant with meditation. They are the defilements of desire.

[76.18–21] As to the seven[fold] pride: since it hinders you from becoming distinguished, it is discordant with diligence. You strive along a low path that is at odds with the noble path, you lack independence, being attached to your house, and you do not rejoice in virtue. For these reasons, [sevenfold pride] is discordant with diligence. Anger, hatred, and harmful intent are the discordances of patience.

[76.21–23] Being separated from a spiritual friend and performing sinful acts are what is called *being influenced by sinful friends*. It is discordant with discipline. Being overpowered by lust, you lack the potential of the noble ones, which is without attachment. This is discordant with generosity.

[76.23–77.1] The wrong view of action *(karman)* as being without fruit and the ignorant view of a self are respectively the obstacles on the paths leading to the higher realms and liberation. *Being seized by the executioner [in the hire] of the skandhas* is discordant with the [state of] nirvāṇa without remainder. Since a wavering and conceited mind is Māra's noose, it is discordant with [the state of nirvāṇa] with remainder. In this way, these fifteen forms of suffering are, according to circumstances, an obstacle [to attaining] the higher realms and liberation, where the sixteenth form of suffering should be taken as a general summary.

[77.1–3] As to the [thirty-two-fold] activity of a bodhisattva—activity whose essence lies in deeds consisting in generating the good path of virtue in support of sentient beings: These [deeds] are performed by teaching the Dharma, it having been said in the *[Dhāraṇīśvararājasūtra]:*

> ...thinking that the Dharma should be taught to them so that they abandon all views.[1684]

[77.3–17] [The thirty-two-fold activity is:] (1) [The bodhisattva][1685] awakes [sentient beings from] the sleep of delusion [by applying insight].[1686] (2) He places[1687] those [beings inclined toward] the Hīnayāna[1688] [in the Mahāyāna]. (3) He gives those wishing things other than Dharma the wish for Dharma. (4) He furnishes[1689] those who have an improper livelihood with a proper livelihood. (5) He establishes those sunk in [bad] views in the right view of the noble ones.[1690] (6) He establishes those with an inappropriate mental disposition, [one] caused by ignorance, in an appropriate mental disposition. (7) He establishes those who abide in a wrong dharma in the right Dharma. (8) He establishes the stingy in [the practice of] generosity. (9) He establishes those with poor behavior in discipline. (10) He establishes those with overriding harmful intent in [the practice of] patience [and love].[1691] (11) He establishes the lazy in the [exertion of] effort.[1692] (12) He establishes the distracted in meditation.[1693] (13) He establishes those with faulty knowledge in knowledge. (14) He establishes those who perform inadequate activities in right activities. (15) He establishes those overcome by defilements in the [practice of] abandoning defilements. (16) He sets[1694] those who are bound by the view of the transitory collection [as a real *I* and *mine*] to the [practice of] nonapprehension. (17) He establishes the undisciplined in discipline. (18) He establishes the ungrateful in [the habit of] being grateful. (19) He pulls out those who have fallen in the [four] currents.[1695] (20) He forces those who do not speak well [about each other] to abide in harmony. (21) He connects those deprived of virtue to the roots of virtue. (22) He sets[1696] those without the wealth of the noble ones to [the practice of] obtaining the wealth of the noble ones. (23) He furnishes[1697] those who are overcome by diseases of the four elements with [a life] without disease. (24) He illuminates with wisdom those who are surrounded by the darkness of ignorance. (25) He brings those who are attached to the three realms in contact with a thorough knowledge of the three realms. (26) He establishes[1698] those who are on the left-hand path onto the right-hand path. (27) He establishes those attached to [their present] life in [the practice of] seeing its disadvantages. (28) He leads those who are bereft of the Three Jewels to the uninterrupted lineage of the Three Jewels. (29) He connects those who have fallen off from the right Dharma with [the practice of] upholding the right Dharma. (30) He establishes those who are bereft of the six recollections[1699] in [these] six recollections.[1700] (31) He establishes those with the hindrances of *karman* and defilements in [the practice of] remedying these [hindrances]. (32) He establishes those who possess nothing but lack of virtue in the completely perfected Dharma of virtue.[1701]

[77.17–20] These [thirty-two] are the activity resulting from what is done on the basis of sixteen[fold] compassion, and hence they must be referred to [their] respective categories. As to leading those who have devotion to the Hīnayāna to the Mahāyāna—since the Hīnayāna is, in the view of the Mahāyāna, a low path, and since bodhisattvas are caused to fall [back] to the Hīnayāna through sinful friends and Māra—this is the activity of the seventh, tenth, and fifteenth [points of] compassion. The others are easy to understand.

Enlightenment, Buddha Qualities, and Activity

[The next sentence in the *Ratnagotravibhāgavyākhyā* is:

> **Immediately after teaching the [thirty-two-fold activity], the enlightenment of the Buddha is illustrated through a presentation of the sixteenfold compassion of great enlightenment.**][1702]

[77.20–22] After teaching the thirty-two-fold activity, King Dhāraṇīśvara said to the illustrious one [in the *Dhāraṇīśvararājasūtra*]:

> Illustrious one, how does the great compassion of the buddhas and the illustrious ones enter sentient beings?[1703]

[77.22–23] In reply to this question [the latter] said:

> Son of a noble family, the great compassion of the buddhas and the illustrious ones neither arises in nor enters sentient beings.[1704]

[77.23–24] It is through such statements, [namely,] through the presentation of the sixteenfold compassion of great enlightenment, that the enlightenment of the Buddha is illustrated.

[77.24–78.6] The sixteen[fold] enlightenment is: (1)[1705] Being enlightened in the view of having neither root nor foundation. (2) Being enlightened in terms of quiescence and utmost quiescence. (3) Being enlightened in terms of enlightenment's natural luminosity, given that the mind is naturally luminous. (4) Being enlightened in view of not adopting or discarding [anything]. (5) Being enlightened in terms of no characteristic signs and nonapprehension. (6) Being enlightened in that the three circles [of agent, object, and action] are cut off. (7) Being enlightened in view of neither having a body nor being conditioned. (8) Being enlightened in view of neither having a foundation nor undergoing differentiation. (9) Being enlightened with respect to the fact that [enlightenment] can be expressed as neither body nor mind. (10) Being enlightened with respect to the fact that it cannot be grasped and is without a basis. (11) Being enlightened in terms of emptiness. (12) Being enlightened in being equal to space. (13) Being enlightened in view of the true [primordial] ground. (14) Being enlightened in that there is "no [longer any] mode of apprehension" *(anākāra)*[1706] from the perception of forms *(ākāra)*. (15) Being enlightened in being uncontaminated and not having appropriated [the skandhas]. (16) Being enlightened in being pure, stainless, and without defilements.[1707]

[78.6–8] These [points] are not realized, and it is in order that sentient beings [be able to] realize [them] that the great compassion of the buddhas arises. The explanation of the sixteen[fold] enlightenment explains suchness mingled with stains, too. Therefore, the [sixteen points] are [automatically] explained on the occasions of explaining "suchness mingled with stains" and "stainless enlightenment."

[78.8–12] [The next sentence in the *Ratnagotravibhāgavyākhyā* is:]

> **Immediately after [the sixteenfold compassion of great enlightenment] is taught, the qualities of the Buddha are illustrated through a presentation of the ten strengths, the four fearlessnesses, and the eighteen exclusive features.**[1708]

This is because it has been said [in the *Dhāraṇīśvararājasūtra*]:

> Son of a noble family, if you ask what the activity of a buddha is, it is, son of a noble family, the thirty-two[fold] activity of a tathāgata. If you ask what these thirty-two [activities] are, then, son of a noble family, with regard to that, [first of all] on the basis of his unsurpassable wisdom, a tathāgata perfectly knows the "right as [precisely something] right."[1709]

And so forth. [The next sentence in the *Ratnagotravibhāgavyākhyā* is:

> **Immediately after the [qualities of a buddha] are taught, the thirty-two-fold activity of a buddha is illustrated through a presentation of the unsurpassable activity of a tathāgata.**[1710]

[78.12–15] "After...are taught" does not mean that the activity of a buddha is taught immediately after the thirty-two qualities of a buddha have been completely taught. Rather, the performance of the activity of teaching the Dharma is explained each time immediately after one of [the thirty-two] qualities has been explained. Thus the thirty-two-fold activity of a buddha is illustrated through a presentation of the unsurpassable activity of a tathāgata.

[78.15–16] As for a summary, thirdly, [it is given in the next sentence of the *Ratnagotravibhāgavyākhyā*:]

> **In this way the seven vajra points should come to be known in detail, [namely] through the illustration of their own defining characteristics in accordance with the *[Dhāraṇīśvararāja]-sūtra*.**[1711]

[78.16–19] [Objection:] The defining characteristics proper to things different from the seven [vajra] points have been taught. Still, is the [buddha] element—in having been illustrated [by way of] the sixty [purifying] factors—not established as existing as a single element; or, how are its own defining characteristics taught? [Answer:] The potential of the noble one is explained in terms of the ornament of meditative stabilization; and the apprehension of the element is taught in terms of the ornament of insight, since [in insight] you apprehend an element as vast as space. [The buddha element] is mainly taught on the basis of these and the remaining [ornaments] [and] even [on the basis] of its own defining characteristics.

[78.19–20] Third, as to the connection between the [respective] former and later subjects, it has been asked [in the *Ratnagotravibhāgavyākhyā*:]

> **And then what is the connection between these [subjects]?**[1712]

[78.20–24] There are two types of connections: the connection between the subject matter and the text, and the connection regarding how the meaning of the [seven] subjects are related to each other. As to the first, it was stated just above [that] the seven meanings (i.e., the seven vajra points) have been explained through a presentation of their own defining characteristics in the *Dhāraṇīśvararājasūtra.* As to how the meanings of the subjects are related to each other, this is expressed through the connection of the seven meanings (i.e., the seven vajra points)—the Buddha and so forth—in terms of how the [respective] former and latter [function as] cause and effect.

A Short Explanation of RGV I.3

[78.25–79.7] To put this in wholly general [terms, it has been said in *Ratnagotravibhāga* I.3]:[1713]

> **[From the Buddha [comes] the teaching, and from the teaching the noble community.**
> **Within [the setting of] the community, [buddha] nature leads to the attainment of the [buddha] element of wisdom.**
> **And the attainment of this wisdom is the highest enlightenment,**
> **Which is endowed with properties, such as the [ten] strengths, that benefit all sentient beings.]**[1714]

When the Buddha came into the world, it happened as a consequence that the wheel of the Dharma was set in motion in places like Vārāṇasī. From that the noble community formed, and it is stated that within[1715] [the setting of the] matured community, [buddha] nature leads to the realization or attainment of the [buddha] element of wisdom. [Your] enlightenment is prophesied on the basis of this, [namely,] of finally[1716] having attained wisdom. Thus you attain, as prophesied, buddhahood, the supreme among the three [types of] enlightenment. It is stated that omniscience is attained on the strength of this enlightenment, wherefore the qualities such as the [ten] strengths are attained [as well]. Thanks to these qualities the properties, [or] activities, that benefit all sentient beings without exception occur. Therefore [this stanza] perfectly encapsulates the seven meanings and [establishes] the connection [among the topics] of the treatise.

[79.7–9] Likewise, this text teaches not only the connection among these seven meanings but also the connection in terms of their [natural] order. As to calling the buddha activity a "property" *(dharma),* from among the ten meanings of the word *dharma,* it is the [last one], "law."[1717] It is stated that to act for the benefit of others after [attaining] enlightenment is the law in the realm of all buddhas.

[79.9–16] The teacher [found] perfect enlightenment, and after forty-nine days had passed, he turned the wheel of the Dharma of the four truths in Vārāṇasī, Ājñātakauṇḍinya being the first in whom the path of seeing arose. When others, too, gradually attained the noble paths, the gods took refuge in the Buddha, the Dharma, and the future Saṅgha. This is taken, in its meaning, from the scriptures. [The Buddha] taught to the directly manifest noble ones as if they were śrāvakas, causing them to gradually mature in the Mahāyāna, and when they realized the [buddha] element the way it really is, he prophesied in the *Saddharmapuṇḍarika[sūtra]* that Śāripūtra and others [would become] buddhas. After becoming buddhas, they, too, would work for the benefit of sentient beings in virtue of the fact that they [themselves] would possess qualities such as the [ten] strengths. Thus it is said.

[79.16–24] The sequence of enlightenment and [subsequent] omniscience has been also stated in the commentary on Buddhagupta's *Piṇḍārtha*:[1718]

> The immediate cause is enlightenment and omniscience. In this regard, the defining characteristics of enlightenment and omniscience have been stated in the *[Ārya]buddhabhūmisūtra*. They are explained in the following way: "enlightenment is the wisdom of equality, and omniscience is the wisdom of individual investigation, and so on." Having taken up the conduct of a bodhisattva, the illustrious one made himself over a long period of time familiar with both the fact that the various sentient beings are like an illusion and the fact that in reality all phenomena are emptiness. The effect of this twofold cause is therefore the wisdom of individual investigation and so forth and the wisdom of equality, and these two only. At the moment of clear realization, [that is,] in the first moment [of it], arise the five wisdoms of equality, individual investigation, and so forth, which are without any mode of apprehension and have the suchness of all phenomena as their objective support. They are called *enlightenment* and *omniscience*. After that they assume the name of *dharmakāya*.

[79.24–80.8] Since enlightenment and omniscience have therefore been explained as being the immediate cause of the dharmakāya, the connection between enlightenment and the qualities—the ten strengths and the like—has [also] been explained, inasmuch as [the qualities] arise from it. In this regard, the translator (Ngog Loden Sherab) made a twofold circle *('khor lo)* with respect to the seven meanings of the subject matter of the *Mahāyānottaratantra [Ratnagotravibhāga]:* the [circle] of nonabiding nirvāṇa and [the circle of] the [Three] Jewels.[1719] With regard to [the first], with the [buddha] element of some sentient beings functioning as a cause, with the Three Jewels functioning as an attendant condition, and with the aid of meditation, the three properties—enlightenment and so forth—are attained. Since other disciples are in turn guided by these three, and by these still others, [the whole] is called a *circle.* This is taught in the present stanza on the series [of the seven vajra points]. Again, [with] the [buddha] element of sentient beings functioning as a cause, with the three [properties of] somebody else's enlightenment and so forth functioning as a condition, and with the aid of meditation, [a new set of] Three Jewels is attained. Having attained [the state of] Three Jewels, they in turn again act similarly. Therefore, this is called the *circle of the [Three] Jewels.* I do not see any fault in claiming that such has been taught, since it has been stated in [*Ratnagotravibhāga* I.24ab] and other [places]:

> The potential of [these] Three Jewels
> Is the object of those who see everything.[1720]

[80.8–11] In the introduction of the *[Dhāraṇīśvararāja]sūtra,* the meaning of "completely awakened toward the sameness of all phenomena" is explained as the attainment of buddha[hood] on the eighth level, [the attainment of the] Dharma on the ninth [is also explained], and [that of] the Saṅgha on the tenth, at which time the Saṅgha, as a circle that has attained the tenth level, sees its own [buddha] element. Having cleansed [the buddha element] by means of the sixty [purifying] qualities, [this Saṅgha] attains the three [properties]—enlightenment and so forth. Thus this [point] is also explained. These [remarks] conclude the explanation of the connection among [the topics of] the treatise.

Part III
Zhönu Pal's Views on Buddha Qualities, Emptiness, and Mahāmudrā

5. Buddha Qualities

THE TRANSLATION of the commentary on the first two introductory stanzas (RGVV I.1–2) in the previous chapter has laid a broad foundation for the following analysis of Zhönu Pal's *Ratnagotravibhāga* commentary. It has become clear that the mahāmudrā teachings of direct cognition are preferred to the approach of an intellectually understood emptiness. But before we turn to the question of how Zhönu Pal presents emptiness and mahāmudrā, we will investigate his distinctive theory of subtle buddha qualities, which lies at the heart of his mahāmudrā approach.

General Remarks

One of the main issues useful in pinning down an exegete's position on the *tathāgatagarbha* teachings is the question of how the qualities of a buddha are to be explained. In the third chapter of the *Ratnagotravibhāga*, the claim is made that the stainless buddha qualities are based on, and indivisible from, stainless suchness, and are compared with the brightness, color, and shape of a jewel.[1721] Thirty-two qualities of dissociation—the ten strengths, four fearlessnesses, and eighteen exclusive features—are distinguished from thirty-two qualities of maturation, which are the thirty-two marks of a perfect being. While the qualities of dissociation are connected with the ultimate kāya,[1722] the qualities of maturation are related to the body of conventional truth, or the form kāyas that are based on the ultimate kāya.[1723]

In his commentary, Zhönu Pal replaces without comment "stainless suchness" with dharmakāya,[1724] and thus explains the dharmakāya as the support of all qualities, in the same way as forms are supported[1725] by space.[1726] This is of course not wrong, given that the form kāyas are themselves supported by the dharmakāya, as are, consequentially, the qualities of maturation of the form kāyas. The qualities of dissociation do not depend on a newly created substantial cause, but nevertheless blossom, for Zhönu Pal, during the process of being freed from hindrances. The qualities of the form kāyas, on the other hand, are explained as depending on a substantial cause:

> The qualities of the dharmakāya are called the *fruit of dissociation.* They are like the spreading appearance of the light of a lamp [located in a vase] when the vase is broken, since that which abides primordially and without depending on a newly created substantial cause for them (i.e., the qualities) appears directly and blossoms merely by becoming free from hindrances. (DRSM, 509.7–9)
>
> The qualities of the form kāyas are the *fruit of maturation.* As for their substantial cause, they are established on the basis of a substantial cause, [namely,] on the basis of continued individual merit, which is based [in turn] on an artificially appropriated potential, so that they are like the picture painted by the artists.[1727] (DRSM, 509.9–11)

What Zhönu Pal usually means by buddha qualities in the following discussion are the qualities of dissociation—the ten strengths and so forth. Only they, in his eyes, have ever been naturally present in a subtle form as something that resembles the svābhāvikakāya, and thus not produced by artificial causes and under artificial conditions.

In his commentary on the second vajra point (the Jewel of the Dharma that possesses an eightfold quality), Zhönu Pal shows that the semantic field of the word *quality* (Tib. *yon tan*) naturally implies increment or growth. Thus, we are told that the Sanskrit equivalent *guṇa* is also used as a multiplier. *Triguṇa*, for example, means "three times." As the outcome of a causal relationship, the fruit or benefit is sometimes called a quality, such as the color red resulting from mixing turmeric powder and lime[1728]—an example used several times to illustrate the natural growth of the qualities of the dharmakāya within their own sphere through the interaction of the buddha element in sentient beings with the sixty cleansing factors.[1729]

Different Views on Buddha Qualities

Faced with presentations that teach that buddha qualities already exist in ordinary persons, Zhönu Pal follows mainstream Mahāyāna and takes such passages to refer to the seeds of the qualities only. Thus he concludes a discussion of the path under the second vajra point:

> Here the teaching in the tathāgatagarbha sūtras and treatises that the [buddha] nature of sentient beings is naturally endowed with qualities such as the [ten] strengths, I take [to refer to their] seeds. (DRSM, 121.6–7)

In different parts of the commentary we are told that *being endowed* (Tib. *ldan pa*) needs to be understood in the sense of *connected* (Tib. *'brel pa*).[1730] To support his view, Zhönu Pal quotes Vinayadeva's *Hevajravajrapadoddharaṇanāmapañjikā,* explaining that defining the relation between buddha nature and the qualities in terms of connected *('brel pa)* underscores both that the qualities have arisen from buddha nature and that the two have an identical nature.[1731]

In his explanation of the second vajra point, Zhönu Pal lists five different ways that the teaching that sentient beings are "endowed" or "connected" with buddha qualities may be interpreted.

> [1.] That which is naturally "endowed" (Tib. *ldan pa*) is taken by some to be the qualities of focusing, since these qualities arise by focusing and meditating on it (i.e., emptiness or that which is naturally endowed with qualities).[1732] (DRSM, 121.7–8)
>
> [2.] Some assert that the body of the [ten] strengths, etc., exists completely [within ordinary people], and even assert that it exists ultimately. (DRSM, 121.8–9)
>
> [3.] Some say that the body [of the qualities] exists in a[n already] perfected [state] but not that it exists ultimately. (DRSM, 121.9)
>
> [4.] Some say that "only to be suitable" is called *to possess all qualities,* since [conditions] are suitable for the [ten] strengths, etc., to arise in the mindstream. (DRSM, 121.9–10)
>
> [5.] Some say that not all sentient beings are suitable for becoming buddhas, since the accumulation of causes necessary for becoming a buddha is not complete. Therefore *suitable* means simply that the accumulation [of necessary causes] is complete and not merely the [corresponding] possibility. (DRSM, 121.10–12)

In his lengthy commentary on the four inconceivable aspects of the last four vajra points, Zhönu Pal admits that there are many passages in the treatises and profound sūtras to the effect that innumerable buddha qualities exist in sentient beings, and lists another six possible explanations that overlap to some extent with the list of the first five points:

[6.] Some think that it is like saying that Subhūti "takes after" the Tathāgata because the suchness of the Tathāgata is not different from the suchness of Subhūti. The meaning [of the phrase that] a buddha exists in sentient beings because the Tathāgata's suchness is present in sentient beings is like that. (DRSM, 237.26–238.2)

[7.] Some say that the buddha qualities exist only to the extent that sentient beings are suitable for attaining buddha[hood]. (DRSM, 238.2–3)

[8.] Some think that it has been explained that the view of the transitory collection of *I* and *mine* is the lineage of the Buddha because [this wrong view] is [also] known to be stainless. For this reason even the contaminated skandhas, elements, and *āyatanas* of sentient beings are the buddha potential, and therefore it is appropriate to refer to them as the buddha qualities existing in sentient beings. (DRSM, 238.3–5)

[9.] Some say that when yogins experience themselves, they see the reality of the nonartificial mind and think that the mind (Tib. *thugs*) of a buddha and the minds of all sentient beings, too, are of this nature, and even say that this is precisely what buddha[hood] is. Moreover, they say that the teaching that sentient beings possess the buddha qualities follows exactly along the same lines. (DRSM, 238.5–8)

[10.] Some think that sentient beings permanently possess the [ten] strengths and so forth of the Tathāgata exactly as they are found [in him]. It is just that they are not seen, being obstructed by hindrances. (DRSM, 238.8–9)

[11.] Some think that even though sentient beings do not possess buddha qualities in their own [mind]stream, it is not the case that a buddha, who is distinct from other [mind]streams, does not exist everywhere, for it is said in the *Gsang ba bsam mi khyab pa*:[1733] The body, speech, and mind of the Tathāgata pervade the expanse of space. (DRSM, 238.9–12)

The Blossoming of Subtle Qualities

The unusually large variety of differing positions on the teaching of buddha nature reflects the problematic stance that most of the sūtras this teaching is based upon have, which is that all sentient beings possess the nature of a buddha (doubtlessly in the sense that they are already complete buddhas but do not know it because of their adventitious defilements). Following the *Laṅkāvatārasūtra*, Zhönu Pal points out that statements to the effect that even the major and minor marks of a buddha exist in sentient beings come dangerously close to the non-Buddhist view of an *ātman*. Still, Zhönu Pal does not want to write off the theory of buddha nature completely, postulating as he does the primordial existence of subtle buddha qualities.[1734]

In his commentary on RGV I.12 Zhönu Pal further takes buddha nature to be a primordial subtle seed of purification and compares it to the continuum of a grain of rice that, given that it is beginningless, must exist in a subtle way in the empty space that is destined to form another world again after the former world has vanished. The coarse seed of a grain of rice is compared to the fortified [bodhisattva] potential that is produced by the same subtle seed or root of conditioned virtue.[1735] The space-like aspect of a subtle seed or quality is again referred to in Zhönu Pal's commentary on RGV I.161–70 (J I.158–67), where the ultimate buddha element within sentient beings is related with the nonartifical svābhāvikakāya and explained as something in the ordinary mindstream that resembles the potential of the svābhāvikakāya.[1736]

In his explanation of the strengthening of the potential in DhS 66–68, Zhönu Pal takes the potential as including the skandhas, sense faculties, and so on, which are made up in a way similar to the Buddha himself.[1737] He seemingly explained buddha nature along the same lines in his Kālacakra commentary *Rgyud gsum gsang ba*, for the Eighth Karmapa Mikyö Dorjé criticizes him for asserting, with reference to the Third Karmapa Rangjung Dorjé, that buddha nature in sentient beings resembles a buddha, in that the Buddha is similar to the six *āyatanas* of sentient beings.[1738] But here in his *Ratnagotravibhāga* commentary on I.25, Zhönu Pal rules out that the skandhas (i.e., the view of the transitory collection of *I* and *mine*) are the lineage of the buddhas (see the above-mentioned explanation no. 8) on the grounds that this is too far removed from the underlying intention of the teaching that the buddha qualities are never recognized (unlike defilements such as attachment) as something separable from the mind.[1739]

At the end of both of his lists of different views about the buddha qualities, Zhönu Pal tells us that he personally prefers to compare the buddha qualities to the sense faculties of a future monarch still in the womb of a destitute woman, which is the eighth of nine examples taught in the *Tathāgatagarbhasūtra*. He takes this to mean that the qualities are already present, but only in a subtle form. In other words, they still have to mature naturally.

In the commentary on the second vajra point it becomes clear that Zhönu Pal calls the sum of all causes and conditions relating to a quality *subtle quality* (in the same way as a mixture of turmeric powder and lime would be called the *subtle quality of redness,* since such a mixture is bound to manifest the actual quality of redness once the two ingredients are in contact):

> ...it is not the case that that which has become like a mixture of semen, blood, and milk in the mother's womb does not possess the six sense faculties [at all]; [rather,] they exist in a subtle way.... (DRSM, 121.12–13)

Zhönu Pal attempts to read his understanding into RGVV I.2, where the relation between the sixty cleansing factors and the buddha element, which naturally possesses qualities, is explained. The passage in the *Ratnagotravibhāgavyākhyā* is:

> Then, after the introductory chapter of the *[Dhāraṇīśvararāja]-sūtra,* the buddha element is elucidated by way of a description of the application of sixty purifying factors to this [element], the process of purification making sense [only] if the object to be purified possesses [buddha] qualities.[1740]

Zhönu Pal comments:

> Generally, the simple expression "cleansing properties" does not pervade (i.e., coincide with the domain covered by) the expression "properties to be cleansed," just as no [such pervasion] is ascertained when expressing gold by the term *fibroferrite.* On the other hand, if a knowledgeable [person] looks closely, he is able to ascertain, "There is a fruit."[1741] This is explained in [*Pramāṇavārttika* I.7[1742]]: "The arising of the fruit (i.e., effect), [a process] that is inferred from[1743] the complete cause [as a logical reason], is described as the nature *(svabhāva)* [of this cause],[1744] since [the arising of the effect] does not depend on other things."[1745] Being [related] in such a way, as it is also expressed in the example, [you must concede that] in general the object to be purified, or the fruit, is endowed with qualities[, which means] "is connected with qualities." (DRSM, 29.15–19)

In other words, gold ore (the buddha element of sentient beings) is only connected with the actual qualities of purified gold (a buddha). A mixture of gold ore with fibroferrite (the cleansing factors of buddha activity), however, constitutes a complete cause for the arising of purified gold. Thus it can be claimed on the basis of PV I.7 that this mixture has the nature conducive to the arising of the fruit. To be sure, only the assisting buddhas literally possess qualities in Zhönu Pal's eyes, and it is due to the power of these buddhas that similar qualities can naturally mature in the mindstream of ordinary sentient beings. The clause "the process of purification making sense [only] if the object to be purified possesses [buddha] qualities" does not mean, then, for Zhönu Pal, that the buddha element literally possesses buddha qualities. It is, rather, merely "connected" *(ldan pa = 'brel pa)* with them in such a way that in the presence of the cleansing factors the buddha element is a complete cause for the arising of buddha qualities.

Zhönu Pal must have been aware that this is not the picture the example involving gold draws (after all, fibroferrite must have been cheaper than gold ore) and thus illustrates the above-mentioned cleansing process further down in his commentary by means of turmeric powder and lime, a mixture that manifests the quality "redness." Similarly, he is uncomfortable with the comparison to a *vaiḍūrya* gem, and suggests in his commentary on the relevant passage in RGVV I.2 that the process of spiritual purification is better exemplified by the magical transformation of grass into riches, because such a magic is said to depend on the spatial nature of grass, it being the example of space that is repeatedly used to illustrate the buddha element.[1746]

In his commentary on the second vajra point, Zhönu Pal further argues:

> I assert that [the buddha qualities in sentient beings] are like the six sense faculties of the [future] universal monarch who is [still] an embryo in the belly of a destitute woman. Such subtle strengths (i.e., buddha qualities) increase as you ascend the [bodhisattva] levels, and thus become the ten strengths of the completely perfected body. (DRSM, 121.18–20)

And at the end of the six explanations listed in the commentary on the four inconceivable points, Zhönu Pal says:

> I think that the actual (i.e., fully blossomed) wisdom of the buddhas with its [ten] strengths and so forth is not contained in the [mind]stream of sentient beings, in the same way as the sense

> faculties and the major and minor marks of the [universal monarch in the womb] exist [only] in a subtle way (i.e., not fully blossomed). The "different forms of wisdom"[1747] exist rather as something subtle, like the painting spoken of in the example.[1748] (DRSM, 239.12–14)

Also interesting is the way the example of the universal monarch in the womb is explained in the context of correlating the nine examples from the *Tathāgatagarbhasūtra* with nine defilements.[1749] The Tibetan translation of the relevant stanza in the root text is problematic and has given rise to different interpretations. If we follow the Sanskrit and take, as de Jong does, *vipākavat* as a possessive adjective modifying *jñāna*,[1750] the translation would be:

> The stains on the seven [impure] levels
> Resemble the stains of the womb's confinement.
> And the ripened nonconceptual wisdom
> Is like being delivered from the womb's confinement.[1751]
> (RGV I.144 (J I.141))

Even though Zhönu Pal does not criticize the Tibetan translation here, he too subordinates *ripened* to *wisdom:*

> The stains of those on the seven impure levels resemble the womb's confinement, whose nature is that of impure stains. The nonconceptual wisdom experienced on these levels is like the sentient being in the womb. Even though the potential of all the sense faculties of a noble being has [already] arisen, it is not [yet] activated. Once the child is delivered from its confinement in the mother's womb, its sense faculties become activated. Likewise nonconceptual wisdom ripens beyond the seventh level, and the buddha kāyas fully ripen and become perfect.... (DRSM, 418.18–22)

Together with the sixth of the nine examples, which compares buddha nature to a seed that develops into a tree under the proper conditions, the example of the universal monarch is the strongest one supporting a development of the buddha qualities, or upholding a difference between the subtle qualities of buddha nature and the fully ripened ones of the dharmakāya. Thus, Zhönu Pal concludes his explanation of the eighth example with the following remark:

> Those who ignore the way in which the fully manifest marks of a king are not complete in the state of being an embryo and how the seed, which stands for the [buddha] element, gradually grows in the example before,[1752] and also hold that a completely perfect body of a buddha exists in all sentient beings, and that there is no increment, do not thoroughly understand these meanings. (DRSM, 406.7–10)

Taken in this way, the example of the future universal monarch excludes, on the one hand, the view that the qualities of buddha nature have to be newly created from scratch,[1753] and on the other hand, the view that the qualities exist primordially in a fully developed way.[1754]

The remaining seven examples from the *Tathāgatagarbhasūtra*, such as the Buddha in the lotus or the gold in the filth, paint a different picture, however. A complete Buddha is already present in sentient beings but simply not recognized because of the defilements. Similar examples quoted in the *Ratnagotravibhāgavyākhyā* from the *Dhāraṇīśvararājasūtra* or the *Anūnatvāpurṇatvanirdeśasūtra* are so abundant that we are tempted to reinterpret the examples of the universal monarch and the tree rather than reading a subtle development of the buddha element into the entire *Ratnagotravibhāga*.[1755] Zhönu Pal does go for a subtle reading nonetheless. He claims that the nature of your mind and the dharmakāya[1756] are so similar as to prompt an unchanging substance such as a *vaiḍūrya* stone to be taken as an example.[1757] In support he quotes the most essential stanza of the *Ratnagotravibhāga*, I.27, which states that the cause, buddha nature, was given the name of its fruit. Zhönu Pal follows from this clause that these two are not exactly identical.[1758]

The status of stanza I.27, which is at the center of Zhönu Pal's hermeneutics, is the subject of dispute. In the Tengyur it is not contained in the root text of the *Ratnagotravibhāga*, but it appears in the *Ratnagotravibhāgavyākhyā* on a similar stanza.[1759] Zhönu Pal is supported, however, by the Sanskrit manuscripts edited by Johnston, who includes RGV I.27 as part of the root text.[1760] It is:

> By virtue of the presence of buddha wisdom in [all] kinds of sentient beings,
> The fact that stainlessness is by nature without duality,
> And the fact that its (i.e., the buddha potential's) fruit has been "metaphorically" applied[1761] to the buddha potential [itself],
> All sentient beings are said to possess the essence of a buddha.[1762]

Zhönu Pal comments:

> First of all, by virtue of the presence of buddha wisdom in all kinds of sentient beings, this buddha wisdom, which is present in sentient beings, is called *buddha nature*. Even though this wisdom is the real tathāgata, it is only metaphorically called the *nature* of sentient beings, since it is not contained in the [mind] stream of sentient beings.[1763] (DRSM, 262.12–14)
>
> Second, since suchness, i.e., the mind's true nature without adventitious stains, is not different in either buddhas or sentient beings, it is said to be buddha nature. The suchness that exists in a buddha is a real buddha. The suchness of sentient beings is a buddha metaphorically. Therefore, [suchness] abides as [if having] two parts. (DRSM, 262.14–17)
>
> Third, the parts in sentient beings that resemble a buddha—such things as their skandhas—are the buddha potential. Its fruit has been metaphorically applied to it, as [if it were] a tathāgata, and that potential is said to be of the nature of a tathāgata. Therefore, even if it is of this nature in the real [sense of the word], it is a tathāgata [only] metaphorically. (DRSM, 262.17–19)

The assertion in the third reason that the tathāgata nature needs to be understood as being a tathāgata only metaphorically, but is nevertheless nature in the real sense of the word, is already found in Ngog Loden Sherab's commentary,[1764] even though Loden Sherab quotes the less explicit RGV I.28, in which the third reason is only "because of the potential." That Zhönu Pal's interpretation of this crucial stanza was greatly influenced by Ngog Loden Sherab is shown a little further down, where he explicitly states that Loden Sherab's distinction of three buddha natures corresponding to the aspects of cause, nature, and fruit is a very good one.[1765]

How is this hermeneutic strategy of avoiding the extremes of denying the buddha element altogether on the one hand and ascribing fully developed qualities to it on the other applied to the famous passage that with regard to the buddha element nothing needs to be removed or added? The two most quoted stanzas of the *Ratnagotravibhāga* are:

> There is nothing to be removed from it and absolutely nothing to be added.
> The real should be seen as real, and seeing the real, you become liberated.[1766] (I.157 (J I.154))

> The buddha element is empty of adventitious [stains], which have the defining characteristic of being separable;
> But it is not empty of unsurpassable qualities, which have the defining characteristic of not being separable.[1767] (I.158 (J I.155))

As we have seen above, Zhönu Pal is very much concerned about reading a too ontological understanding into the *tathāgatagarbha* theory and therefore attempts to remove the thorns of problematic passages by embedding these passages in mainstream Mahāyāna. Indeed, the first stanza is one of the most famous ones in Mahāyāna literature.[1768] Zhönu Pal wants us first to grasp how it is explained in the second dharmacakra:

> The first stanza is [shared] in common with the *Abhisamayālaṁkāra* (V.21). Therefore you should first thoroughly understand how the commentary of Master Haribhadra explains it in accordance with the second dharmacakra. In the commentary (i.e., the *Abhisamayālaṁkāravṛtti*) it is said: "Since, [then,][1769] liberation is not possible with an obstinate clinging to entities, you should ascertain that forms and so forth, as things dependently arisen, exist [only] conventionally and that they lack an own-being and so forth. In doing so, you have not, with regard to any phenomenon, either removed or added anything by way of [wrong] denial or reification. When you see reality[1770] by virtue of having repudiated your mistake, in the same way as one illusionary elephant conquers another one, you become liberated."[1771] (DRSM, 440.3–8)

In other words, "nothing should be removed" refers to dependent arising, and "nothing should be added," to the phenomena's emptiness—its quality of lacking an independent existence. That both the obstinate clinging to entities and the remedy for it, namely wisdom, exist on the level of apparent truth is expressed by the example of an illusory elephant conquered by another illusory elephant.[1772]

It is such an understanding that led exegetes like some followers of Ngog Loden Sherab to construe buddha nature as emptiness with the defining characteristics of a nonaffirming negation. In his introduction, Zhönu Pal summarizes such a view by pointing out that all qualities are gathered as if called by focusing on that with which the qualities are naturally endowed (i.e., connected), namely the emptiness of a nonaffirming negation. This emptiness is the cause of purification, or the object of wisdom conducive to purification. Since this emptiness has always been present nothing needs to be added to it. Moreover, the objects of all defilements, namely the self of a person and phenomena, do not need to be removed, since they have been wrongly superimposed by virtue of all the defilements and hence are nonexistent throughout beginningless time.[1773] With such an understanding of RGV I.157 (J I.154), the phrase "there is nothing to be added" can be related with emptiness, or the cause of the qualities, rather than the qualities themselves.

The way of the third dharmacakra starts for Zhönu Pal from the naturally pure buddha element, which is called *emptiness* (decomposed by him into "empti-" and "-ness"):

> Since no characteristic sign at all (in the way of any defilements to be removed) exists as the nature [of the buddha element], the buddha element is called *empti-*. Nor are there any qualities, not even the slightest, that did not exist [before] and have to be newly created and added. It has ever been the nature of qualities, and is thus called *-ness*. Therefore the nature of the buddha element is empty of adventitious stains whose defining characteristics are: to be separable from the buddha element itself, and to be suitable to abandon. As for the unsurpassable properties, such as the [ten] strengths, whose defining characteristics are: to be inseparable from the buddha element and to be natural (i.e., not fabricated), the buddha element is not empty of them in their subtle form. This refers to "-ness." (DRSM, 441.5–9)

It is interesting to note that Zhönu Pal alters the whole purport of the two stanzas by adding here, without any commentary, the tiny word *phra mos* ("in [their] subtle form"). We have the impression that he wants to slip his interpretation across unnoticed, the root text being so clearly against him in this stanza. Such an exegetic strategy would explain why the problematic part of the compound "wisdom, which is not separate from the dharmadhātu" in the *Ratnagotravibhāgavyākhyā* has been transformed into "wisdom's cause, which is not separate from the dharmadhātu."[1774] The *vyākhyā* reads:

> Having reached (that is, realized (Tib. *rtogs*)) the door of wisdom, which is not separate from the dharmadhātu, [whose nature it is to have] a single mode....[1775]

Zhönu Pal comments:

> ...the door of what has become the cause of wisdom that is not separate from the dharmadhātu that [in turn] is identical with the dharmakāya in terms of *empti-* and *-ness*.... (DRSM, 445.13–14)

In other words, it is the cause of wisdom (i.e., the subtle qualities) that is not separate from the dharmadhātu. The dharmadhātu is identical with the dharmakāya only in terms of *empti-* and *-ness,* in the way described above: adventitious stains are not part of the nature of either the dharmadhātu or dharmakāya *(empti-).* But neither in turn is empty of inseparable buddha qualities *(-ness)*—with the restriction of "in their subtle form," of course, with regard to the dharmadhātu.

Of particular interest in this respect are some parts of Zhönu Pal's commentary on the corresponding *Ratnagotravibhāgavyākhyā,* which starts with an explanation of the sentence in RGV I.157ab (J I.154ab) that nothing needs to be removed or added:

> What is taught by that? That there is no characteristic sign (or cause)[1776] of any of the defilements *(saṁkleśa)* whatsoever to be removed from this naturally pure buddha element, because it is naturally devoid of adventitious stains.[1777]

Zhönu Pal comments:

> Given the buddha element, there is no cause *(rgyu mtshan)* whatsoever of any defilements that need to be removed, for the following reasons: (1) Any assertion in this respect that stains that have become [part of its] nature must be removed is opposed [to the nine examples,] for it is explained during the teaching of the nine examples that [buddha] nature is pulled out of the sheath of stains. (2) The statement: "The stains being removed, [buddha] nature necessarily arises" belongs to the level of apparent [truth]. (3) Ultimately, [false] imagining, being the cause that brings forth all defilements, does not have to be removed. And (4) [The element] is pure in terms of its own nature. The applicability (lit., "pervasion") [of this syllogism is established] inasmuch as the element is by nature free from adventitious stains. Whatever is the [buddha element's] nature is not artificial; there-

> fore [the element] is not adventitious—in the [same] way, for example, as parts of the sky that [are covered] by clouds do not change in the slightest into something else when the clouds have formed in [those parts of] the sky. What is established by such an explanation is that [real] stains of [false] imagining cannot be removed, given that they lack an own-being [in the first place]. (DRSM, 442.22–443.3)

When the buddha element is described as "nonartificial," which is also an attribute of the svābhāvikakāya,[1778] an allusion is being made to the ultimate or space-like aspect of the qualities. It is these aspects that are not affected by defilements, in the same way as clouds do not change the sky. The *vyākhyā* continues:[1779]

> Also, nothing needs to be added to it in the way of a characteristic sign of purification, since it is by nature in a state of possessing the inseparable pure properties [of a buddha].[1780]

Zhönu Pal restricts the inseparability of the qualities as applying only to their ultimate aspect or true nature, thereby following the Tibetan translation *rnam par dbye ba med pa'i chos dag pa'i chos nyid*[1781] (true nature of the inseparable pure buddha properties) for Skt. *avinirbhāgaśuddhadharmatā:*

> Given the element of the tathāgata, there is not the slightest cause *(rgyu mtshan)* of purification that needs to be added to it. The reason is "...because the dharmatā of the inseparable pure properties (i.e., qualities) is [its] nature." Purification is [both] the path and cessation. Its cause is proper mental engagement. When you meditate on this [element], unsurpassable qualities do not have to be added by focusing on something previously nonexistent being newly [acquired]. "Inseparable" means that the unsurpassable qualities and the buddha element have never been divided. Therefore the proper engagement is merely to focus on the buddha element as it is. (DRSM, 443.4–8)

In other words, it is only the true nature of the buddha qualities that needs to exist primordially, not the qualities themselves—that is, their emptiness—to which nothing needs to be added. For Ngog Loden Sherab, the qualities collect as if called when you focus on emptiness;[1782] in other words, they are more or less automatically obtained when meditating on the cause of purification. Zhönu Pal maintains something similar when he explains that qualities do not have to be added when you meditate on the cause of purification; it is not necessary, according to him, to meditate on something becoming newly created.

The *Ratnagotravibhāgavyākhyā* continues with a quotation from the *Śrīmālādevīsūtra:*

> Buddha nature is empty of the sheath of all defilements, which are separable and recognized as being separate. It is not empty of the inconceivable buddha qualities,[1783] which are inseparable, recognized as not being separate and far beyond the sands of the Gaṅgā in number.[1784]

Zhönu Pal comments:

> With regard to the nature of mind, no faults have to be removed, nor any qualities newly added. For this reason buddha nature is "empti- "of the sheath of stains (that possess the two special features of being separable and recognizable as being separate), [that is, empty] of what does not touch upon [its] nature. An element that possesses the two special features of being inseparable—because it is identical [with its qualities]—and of being continuously recognizable as not being separate [from these] is inconceivable in terms of an own-being. The fact that it is not empty of what is beyond the object of imagination, [namely,] the buddha qualities, which are far beyond the sands on the banks of the Gaṅgā in number, [stands] for [the syllable] *-ness* [in the word *emptiness*]. (DRSM, 443.11–15)
>
> If they are far beyond the sands of Gaṅgā in number, do they have the same identity among themselves, or are they different? They have strictly the same identity. To be sure, the ten strengths[1785] are posited as ten forms in accordance with the difference of objects. There are, however, not ten different [strengths] with regard to their own-being. (DRSM, 443.15–17)

The *Śrīmālādevīsūtra* clearly states that the buddha qualities are inseparably connected with the buddha element. But Zhönu Pal explains this with reference to their identical nature, which means that there are no different qualities in terms of own-being. Thus, elucidating the content of this passage on the level of dharmatā allows Zhönu Pal to maintain his theory of naturally growing subtle qualities in the same way as it allows the more extreme position of Gyaltsab Jé, for example, who denies the primordial existence of qualities altogether.[1786]

That this is indeed Zhönu Pal's strategy (i.e., to explain the inseparable buddha qualities on the level of dharmatā) becomes clearer a little further down in the same part of the commentary, where he does not tire of emphasizing the growth or blossoming of the qualities:

> It is not necessary to search in something other than [buddha] nature for the wisdom that realizes emptiness. After becoming acquainted with, and accustomed to, [the fact] on the path that it is empty of adventitious [stains] from the beginning, the unsurpassable qualities that exist in this very buddha nature "blossom" *(rgyas)* to become the wisdom of emptiness, and that is all. (DRSM, 444.24–26)

Also interesting in this context is a discussion of Haribhadra's statement in his commentary on the *Aṣṭasāhasrikā Prajñāpāramitā* that the entire dharmadhātu is seen on the first bodhisattva level.[1787] In reply to the challenge that this contradicts the *Dharmadhātustotra*, according to which only a tiny part of the dharmakāya is seen even on the tenth level, Zhönu Pal says that Haribhadra explains the dharmadhātu as being the selflessness of phenomena, as something whose defining characteristics are a negation. Therefore, it makes sense to say that it is seen completely on the first level. But the *Dharmadhātustotra* is concerned with attaining the dharmakāya of the Buddha, and that is a different matter. The name dharmadhātu stands only for something similar to the dharmakāya. In fact, there is an important divergence. On the first level, on which the entire dharmadhātu is seen, you see only your own buddha nature directly, but not that of others:

> As to the meaning here of "[only seeing] a little," at the time when knowledge that sees its nature (i.e., the buddha nature) has arisen, its (i.e., the buddha nature's) qualities have not [yet] blossomed. Therefore, you see [only] a little. Even though you see an increasing number of qualities of your buddha nature on the higher levels, in comparison with a buddha, even the qualities of the tenth level are [but] a little. (DRSM, 446.19–21)

The theory of blossoming qualities could be challenged on the grounds that a buddha is thought of as "unconditioned, it being his nature to be without beginning, middle, or end."[1788]

Zhönu Pal comments:

> With "unconditioned" it is taught that buddha nature is not artificially (Tib. *'phral du*) conditioned by adventitious causes and conditions but rather is permanent in the sense that it has ever been contained in its own sphere. This is taught by way of the nine examples, such as the body of the tathāgata inside a lotus. With "the quality of being without effort" is taught permanence, in that the wisdom of the buddhas remains present as long as space [exists], until the end of time. This is taught in the ten presentations of essence, cause, fruit, etc. (DRSM, 83.11–15)

It is further explained that that which possesses the six qualities (unconditioned, effortless, not to realize [the true nature] through other conditions, wisdom, love, and power) is not the sambhogakāya, which belongs to the apparent truth; it is rather the ultimate buddha, since the form kāyas are conditioned.[1789]

The discussion of in what sense exactly the dharmakāya is unconditioned is introduced by a reference to the *Mahāyānasūtrālaṁkāra* and texts by other Indian masters:

> The ultimate buddha in the stanza [IX.65]: "The summary of [all] buddha bodies should be understood in terms of the three kāyas"[1790] of the *Mahāyānasūtrālaṁkāra* refers to the dharmakāya, and (i.e., that is) the svābhāvikakāya among the three bodies taught in this [*Mahāyānasūtrālaṁkāra*].[1791] (DRSM, 83.23–25)

Zhönu Pal continues that according to the *Satyadvayavibhāga*, emptiness is taught as being the Madhyamaka path as well as the dharmakāya.[1792] Vimuktisena and Haribhadra call emptiness the potential when on the path and svābhāvikakāya at the time of fruition. The meaning of *svabhāva*, Zhönu Pal writes, is to be "nonartificial," and to attain the fruit means to realize it, in that it is not something new that has arisen. Still, Āryadeva says that it would follow that the dharmakāya is conditioned since it is an object experienced by the noble ones.[1793]

The learned master, Zhönu Pal holds, did very well to present emptiness as dharmakāya. But the *unconditioned* explained here in the *Ratnagotravibhāga* is not like "the emptiness of the nonaffirming negation." In the *Jñānālokālaṁkārasūtra* and the *Laṅkāvatārasūtra* it is clear that *unconditioned* refers to the fact that a tathāgata neither arises nor ceases to exist. Moreover, according to the former sūtra, a tathāgata is momentary but a never-ending continuum all the same. For Buddhagupta, too, the dharmakāya is the nonabiding nirvāṇa, which is an accumulation of a momentary continuous flow.[1794]

Zhönu Pal sums up:

> Thus the dharmakāya is taught as being momentary and a continuation in a continuum [of moments]. In short, since it would have no power if it did not possess moments, and since here it is said to possess power, you must retreat from the view that it is completely unconditioned. This is explained by the *[Ratnagotravibhāga]vyākhyā:* "Unconditioned must be taken as the opposite of conditioned. Here, conditioned is called that in which origination, abiding, and destruction can be observed. Since these do not exist, buddhahood has to be seen as something without beginning, middle, or end, and as being constituted by the unconditioned dharmakāya."[1795] That means that the Buddha himself is the basis of predication. He must be seen as being distinguished from other phenomena by the singular nature of the dharmakāya. The dharmakāya [is able to] evolve within its own sphere, even though it is without artificial conditions. Therefore it is called *unconditioned* because it is like space and not like clouds, which arise, abide, and cease. (DRSM, 86.13–20)

This is the key to how Zhönu Pal understands the unchangeability of the buddha element. Later on, when commenting, for example, on how the unchangeable dharmakāya is permanent (RGV I.84),[1796] he admits that the definitive treatises explain buddha nature as unchangeable in all stages and that this has to be understood as above.[1797]

For Zhönu Pal it is important to analyze the relation between buddha nature and the dharmakāya in line with mainstream Mahāyāna, a procedure that is, at least in some parts, supported by the *Ratnagotravibhāgavyākhyā*. This becomes clear in the commentary on the last stanza of the second vajra point, which is on the truth of cessation:

> Since in such a way you do not see the nonexisting characteristic sign or cognitive object [any more] and since you see the existing ultimate truth as it is, nothing is removed or added with regard to either of them. The realization of the equality of all phenomena on the basis of such a wisdom of equality should be known as a remedy for what is opposed, in all its forms, to seeing reality. Since [the remedy] has arisen, the opposite is known as not at all connected or present together. This is the path of seeing and meditation—of the nonconceptual wisdom—which causes you to attain the dharmakāya. It should be known in detail, as in the sūtra[s], and in accordance with the *prajñāpāramitā* [sūtras].[1798]

The last remark in particular, that you should understand the attainment of the dharmakāya according the *prajñāpāramitā* [sūtras], rules out a too ontological view of buddha nature. What is identical is thus only the true nature of both buddha nature and the enlightenment of a tathāgata.[1799] In his commentary on the second vajra point, Zhönu Pal makes the interesting remark that buddha nature is, roughly speaking, the seed or basis of all phenomena belonging to nirvāṇa.[1800] In the following Zhönu Pal addresses the problem of how buddha nature in its space-like aspect (namely in being suchness mingled with stains) can function as a seed of qualities:[1801]

> You may ask: "Well then, if you called buddha nature a seed with regard to the stage of purification, then space,[1802] too, would become the seed of rice or the like in the outer world. But how can it (i.e., space) become the grain planted under the earth? If it is that grain of rice[, rather,] that is the seed, must you [not] then think that the seed of the stage of purification is not [buddha] nature either, [that is, that it is] something else?" This is a well-formulated question. Grains of the outer [world] are of two kinds: subtle and coarse seeds. As to the subtle one, in the *Catuḥśataka* [VIII.25] it is said: "Just as the end of a seed (i.e., the seed as an end product) is seen but its beginning is not found, so too arising does not occur, since [any possible] cause [of it would be] incomplete."[1803] [Candrakīrti's] commentary on this is: "Just as [the end stage of] the beginningless continuum of a seed that endures since a long time as cause and fruit, one following the other, [is seen]...."[1804] Likewise, the continuum of a grain of rice must exist in a subtle way in empty space, which

> is bound to form again [another] world, after the [former] world has vanished. For were it not so, [its] continuity would be impossible. Likewise, [too,] it is the subtle seed of the stage of purification that I posit as [buddha] nature. As to the coarse seed, I take it to be the fortified [bodhisattva] potential, which is made by that same subtle [seed] inasmuch as it has become the root of conditioned virtue. (DRSM, 119.26–120.10)

And in his commentary on stanza RGV I.20, which states that the teaching and the community are not the ultimate refuge, Zhönu Pal later explains:

> Even though such qualities of the dharmakāya as the [ten] strengths are present in sentient beings as the properties of seeds, they must be nourished and supported[1805] by the fortified [bodhisattva] potential at the beginning, and the accumulation of merit on the tenth level at the end. Thus it is not the case that the dharmakāya is not labeled "conditioned." It is like the image of a king produced [on canvas] by an assembly of numerous painters. (DRSM, 200.16–19)

In other words, the subtle seed is not only the root of the fortified bodhisattva potential and conditioned virtue, but in turn is also nourished and supported by them.

With buddha nature being posited as a seed, the question arises how it is that the fruit, the dharmakāya, is not subject to change, since it would be the result of mutable entities functioning as substantial causes. Zhönu Pal counters by postulating both a coarse and subtle relation between cause and effect in the phenomenal world. The relation between clay and a clay pot is a coarse one, but there are also continua in the outer world that evolve within their own sphere—and this, for Zhönu Pal, does not really constitute change. In fact, not even space, or, as we have seen above, the dharmakāya, is absolutely unconditioned in his eyes:

> You may ask: "If space is absolutely unconditioned, how can there be a continuum?" Nothing expressed by the word *space* is absolutely unconditioned. The intermediate sky seen by the eyes is also called space, and "what belongs to the realm of mental objects" *(dharmāyatanika)*[1806]—whose nature is merely that of being enclosed space—as well. (DRSM, 120.13–15)

In order to prove that space was taught as a "continuous substance" *(rgyun gyi rdzas)*, Zhönu Pal quotes the examples of the transformation of the basis in Vasubandhu's *Dharmadharmatāvibhāgavṛtti.*[1807] All three examples—space, gold, and water—demonstrate the primordial luminosity that must be discovered (that is, not newly created) by removing adventitious stains, but space is nowhere described there as a "continuous substance." Only in the last example does Vasubandhu explain that the clarity of formerly muddy water does not newly occur in the substance water, which is a "continuation in a continuum [of moments]" (Tib. *rgyun gyis 'jug pa*). It is difficult, though, to apply this predication, as Zhönu Pal obviously expects us to do, to all three examples, since Vasubandhu distinguishes space from gold and water:

> Here, with the examples of gold and water, only a quality [of the example] was taught to be equivalent [to the transformation], [but] not [its] substance. With the example of space it (i.e., the transformation) was taught completely.[1808]

The preceding sentence, to which this remark refers, states:

> Since that [change] does not take place, the true nature of phenomena, and the transformation of the basis, which is constituted by it, are permanent.[1809]

Nevertheless, Zhönu Pal concludes:

> You may ask: "Well then, are any particular features of the properties pertaining to [buddha] nature called a seed?" Here in the *[tathāgata]garbha sūtras* and [related] treatises, the nature of sentient beings has been taught as being naturally endowed (i.e., connected) with such qualities as the [ten] strengths. That is what I take to be the seed. (DRSM, 121.5–7)

One possible way of understanding the passage quoted from the *Dharmadharmatāvibhāgavṛtti* would be to interpret, along the lines of Zhönu Pal, the permanence of the dharmatā and the transformation of the basis as an endless continuation of a continuum of moments, of which only the continuum of space is a fully valid example, as opposed to the continua of gold and water particles. That his understanding is such becomes clear when he again quotes the same passage of the *Dharmadharmatāvibhāgavṛtti* to bring his exegesis into line with the *Ratnagotravibhāgā*'s teaching that buddha nature is all-pervading in all three states (impure, partly pure, and perfectly pure) and thus, as shown in the following paragraph of the *Ratnagotravibhāga*, without change. Of particular interest here is a portion of Zhönu Pal's commentary in which he deals with a quotation from the *Anūnatvāpūrṇatvanirdeśasūtra* in the *vyākhyā* on RGV I.50:

> Therefore, Śāriputra, the [buddha] element of sentient beings and the dharmakāya are not different. The very *(eva)* [buddha] element of sentient beings is the dharmakāya. It is precisely *(eva)* the dharmakāya that is the [buddha] element of sentient beings. They are not two in their meaning, differing merely by letter.[1810]

This statement is very explicit. The use of the particle *eva* allows only one interpretation—absolute identity. Still, Zhönu Pal explains:

> Since it is space-like nonconceptuality that is the general defining characteristic, the [buddha] element of sentient beings is not different from the dharmakāya, or the dharmakāya from the element of sentient beings, in the same way as the space inside a golden receptacle and the space inside an earthen receptacle are not different in terms of the feature of being without hindrances. It is precisely the general defining characteristic of the [buddha] element of sentient beings that is the nature of the dharmakāya, and it is precisely the general defining characteristic of the dharmakāya that is the element of sentient beings. These are not different in terms of the expressed meaning; it is only the letters that are different. This is how [the equation of the buddha element with the dharmakāya] must be understood. (DRSM, 338.23–339.2)
>
> When presented as suchness in a nonaffirming negation, the lack of an own-being in a buddha is the lack of an own-being in sentient beings, and vice versa. There is no difference with regard to [their] nature. When the Sautrāntikas posit space as being the absence of obstructing tangible objects, the absence of obstructing tangible objects inside an earthen receptacle is [the same as] the absence of obstructing tangible objects inside a golden receptacle. (DRSM, 339.2–5)
>
> When the transformation of the basis is taught in the *Dharmadharmatāvibhāgavṛtti* with the examples of water, gold, and space, in all three it is explained that there is a continuum. There-

> fore, it is not the case that space that exists only as enclosed space does not partake of the nature of momentariness along a continuum. If you take time into account here, space at the beginning of an eon *(kalpa)* is not the [same] space at the time of [its] destruction. In terms of location, the substance that exists as the enclosed space of a golden receptacle is not that which exists as the enclosed space of an earthen receptacle. Likewise, a moment in the continuation of a continuum having the quality of the [buddha] element's awareness of sentient beings is not a moment in the wisdom of a buddha. Notwithstanding, in the same way as the existence of the enclosed space of a golden and earthen receptacle is not different in terms of type *(rigs),* the nonconceptuality of a buddha and the nonconceptuality of sentient beings are of a very similar type. They even admit of the conventional designation "identity"—in the same way as saying that I and the buddhas share the same speech. (DRSM, 339.6–13)

Having shown that even space possesses the nature of momentariness, Zhönu Pal seems to be well prepared to comment in the following chapter on the unchangeable character of buddha nature in all its different states. The introductory stanza basically heralds the main stance of the entire treatise:

> Because it is endowed with faults in an adventitious way and naturally endowed with qualities,
> It is of an unchangeable nature—as it was before, so it is after.[1811] (RGV I.51)

Zhönu Pal explains:

> The [buddha] element remains in the sheath of faults throughout beginningless time, but later it is endowed with qualities purified of those faults. It thus appears to be subject to change. Nevertheless, it is unchangeable by nature, even though it goes through stages. This is because the former faults, being adventitious, are contained in the [buddha] element but not [in its] nature. The qualities blossom *(rgyas)* later, but they blossom as the nature of the [buddha] element, not as something entirely separate; therefore their connection [with the buddha element] is one of identity.[1812] (DRSM, 339.20–23)

Having restricted the unchangeability of the buddha element to its nature, or dharmatā, Zhönu Pal explains the natural growth of the qualities within the sphere of the buddha element. In doing so, he quotes Rangjung Dorjé's *Snying po bstan pa:*

> This unfabricated natural mind[1813] is called the *dharmadhātu* [or] the *nature of the victorious ones* (i.e., *buddha nature*). It is not improved on by the noble ones, or vulgarized by sentient beings. (DRSM, 339.26–340.2)

Even though this contradicts the theory propounding a natural growth,[1814] Zhönu Pal goes on to explain:

> Therefore, even though it is disturbed by the higher and lower realms of beings and the manifold mental defilements, [its] nature does not change. Thus the mind remains within itself, and so is at peace and is pure with regard to all [those defilements]. When purified, it is the nature of the qualities. Therefore [the qualities] increase naturally within it *(ngang gis),* like space when a house is being destroyed. (DRSM, 340.2–5)

Interesting, too, is Zhönu Pal's commentary on the third inconceivable point (that inseparable qualities are present even in ordinary beings):

> The earlier qualities in sentient beings and the later qualities of the stainless state exist in the same way as the dharmatā, because neither the earlier nor the later ones are different in terms of being or not being the dharmatā. Therefore here, too, it is difficult to realize that [buddha nature] is unchangeable, even though the qualities in the state of sentient beings and the qualities at the level of a buddha are different in terms of having blossomed or not. To express this in an example that is only partially true, the space in the state of being of an existing world and the space in the state of being devoid of a world (after its dissolution) differ in that [the latter is] spacious and [the former] congested. Still, the two never diverge from the nature of space. (DRSM, 236.3–8)

In other words, the different states of buddha nature have in common that they are inseparable from the dharmatā, which makes buddha nature unchangeable in its most important aspect.

To shed further light on how Zhönu Pal understands the natural growth of buddha nature into enlightenment and buddha activity, we have to return once more to his interesting explanation of the second vajra point of the Dharma. Here not only buddha nature, but also the *ālayavijñāna*, is taken to be the root:

> To sum up, it has been taught that without a support [and] something supported, an uninterrupted saṁsāra from beginningless time up to now is not admissible. If saṁsāra is not admissible, neither is the remedy for it, nirvāṇa. Since this [combination of] support and supported is the stained *ālayavijñāna*, this *ālayavijñāna* will be reversed when you become a buddha. Even though it has been reversed, there is, after you become a buddha, activity for the sake of sentient beings for as long as space exists. Because this is not possible without a support [and] a supported, the root [must] be the actual buddha nature. It has been established [in the *Laṅkāvatārasūtra*] that the *ālayavijñāna* is the second root. (DRSM, 131.5–9)
>
> You may think, "Well then, this [reasoning] may be allowed inasmuch as buddha nature has been taught as that first support. But why is it necessary to teach the so-called *ālayavijñāna* expressly as a second support?" It is because buddha nature possesses two features: being naturally empty from mental fabrication and abiding as a quality of the mind. The part about being empty from mental fabrications is taught in the analytical corpus for those given to reasoning....(DRSM, 131.9–12)
>
> When the feature of the mind that is [buddha] nature appears during a direct [realization of it] in your own [perceiving] subject, you see it, and so not only realize that the mind itself is free from mental fabrication; by its power, you also realize that the whole of saṁsāra and nirvāṇa is without an own-being. What is in perfect harmony with the workings of such a mind is the subtle inside of the mind of sentient beings, [namely,] the *ālayavijñāna*. Therefore it is further explained as being focused on the dharmadhātu. In view of the teaching that "the *ālayavijñāna* is an unconscious perception (or, representation) [of the outer world, etc.],"[1815] it cannot be perceived in the form of an experience even by those wise in the ways of the world. Therefore, it is difficult to say "that what is similar to that *[ālayavijñāna]*, [namely,] the kāya[s?] and the nonconceptual mental consciousness that is free

> from the three parts of time, is like this [or that]." This difficulty will be experienced by those who are not crazy. It is in view of only this much [ascertainment] that the experts in pith instructions say, "This is the *ālaya[vijñāna].*" (DRSM, 131.14–21)

It is important to note that Zhönu Pal follows the *Laṅkāvatārasūtra* and sees in the *ālayavijñāna* not only the basis of saṁsāra but in the end also the cause of it being reversed into nirvāṇa. If both the *ālayavijñāna* and buddha nature are taken to be the root of saṁsāra and enlightenment, you may wonder how the relation between the two is explained. In his commentary on the third vajra point, the Saṅgha, Zhönu Pal says:

> To sum up, I have explained the mind, [that is,] the *ālaya[vijñāna].* I explained it, among other things, as [buddha] nature. I explained it not in the sense that it is actual buddha nature. I explained it as a reflection of [buddha] nature. (DRSM, 178.2–3)

The fact that the *ālayavijñāna* is presented as a reflection of buddha nature and, like buddha nature, taken as a root of enlightenment, precludes a strict distinction between the buddha element and the adventitious stains, and thus an interpretation along the lines of Jonang zhentong.

The Examples Used to Illustrate the Growth of the Qualities

Most of the examples used in the *Ratnagotravibhāga* and its *vyākhyā* clearly paint a picture of a primordially present buddha who only needs to be discovered and cleansed from adventitious stains. Zhönu Pal's understanding is different, namely that the qualities exist only in a subtle form, as seeds of the fully blossomed buddha qualities. To support his stance, he follows a double strategy. First, he picks out the few examples that allow an interpretation in line with his view. The two examples he chooses from the *Ratnagotravibhāga*, namely that of the tree and the future monarch, do indeed have features that suggest a growth of subtle qualities. But the main focus of the example of the tree lies not on the growing tree, but on the imperishability of its seed and that the result, namely the tree, is already contained in the seed. Similarly, in the second example adduced, that the future monarch is still an embryo does not seem to be crucial for an understanding of it. His nature of being a cakravartin will not change, in that his future role is already programmed and his poor mother already protected.

But Zhönu Pal emphasizes that the embryo still has to develop in the same way as the tree still has to grow from its seed.

Zhönu Pal also compares the subtle forms of wisdom inside sentient beings with the painting used in another example, probably the one of the silk cloth and the universe from the *Avataṁsakasūtra.*[1816] In addition, Zhönu Pal cites a number of examples that, while not found in the *Ratnagotravibhāga* and its *vyākhyā,* fully support his point. One of the most quoted ones is that of the waxing moon in the *Dharmadhātustotra:*

> [Practitioners] on the [bodhisattva] levels are seen to grow gradually, in the same way as you see the fine [crescent] moon growing day after day. In the same way as the moon is full on the fifteenth day, so too is the dharmakāya complete and clear on the final [bodhisattva] level. (DRSM, 121.20–22)

Obviously Zhönu Pal compares the qualities with the waxing illumination of the moon, and not with the moon itself. Most of the remaining examples illustrate a change in quantity but not in quality—for example, the space inside a house that widens when the house is torn down;[1817] and space in the two states of containing a universe and not containing one (after its dissolution);[1818] or the light of a lamp inside a vase that spreads after the vase is broken.[1819] In other words, buddha qualities increase as ever more hindrances that cover the qualities with defilements are removed:

> Even though there is a difference between [the buddha qualities] in terms of being subtle and having increased, depending on the extent to which adventitious stains are purified or not, they do not have the attribute of being changeable by nature. (DRSM, 122.1–2)

One example falls out of line, that of the red color produced by mixing turmeric powder and lime. Zhönu Pal uses it to illustrate the cultivation of qualities by bringing together the sixty purifying factors with the buddha element in sentient beings.[1820] The quality red, however, is the result of a chemical process between two substances, something entirely conditioned. In this respect it is also interesting how Zhönu Pal understands the example of the gold. The customary scenario of naturally present qualities that become manifest during the process of purification is replaced by a complete causal nexus involving mixing gold ore and fibroferrite. This mixture can be ascertained as having the nature of the arising of the fruit or pure gold.[1821]

The Ontological Status of the Buddha Qualities

Ontology in the *Ratnagotravibhāga* is based primarily not on the two truths of the Madhyamaka but rather on a distinction between a buddha element (or buddha nature) with its inseparable qualities on the one hand and adventitious stains that can be separated from the buddha element on the other. If you wish to relate this to the two truths in Madhyamaka, the most obvious thing to do would be to take the buddha element with its inseparable qualities as the ultimate truth and the adventitious stains as the apparent truth. Indeed, in a quotation from the *Anūnatvāpūrṇatvanirdeśasūtra*,[1822] which is one of the main sources of *tathāgatagarbha* theory, the ultimate is equated with the buddha element in its different states:

> Śāriputra, that which must be realized by faith is the ultimate. Śāriputra, *ultimate* is an expression for the [buddha] element in sentient beings. The *[buddha] element in sentient beings*, Śāriputra, is an expression for buddha nature. *Buddha nature*, Śāriputra, is an expression for the dharmakāya.[1823]

On the other hand, RGV I.21 says that:

> Ultimately, buddhahood is the only refuge for the world, given that the Sage has the Dharma as his body, and the Community sets it as its ultimate goal.[1824]

And the paragraph on the endowment or connection with qualities in the second chapter of the *vyākhyā* (RGV II.29–37) is introduced the following way:

> The explanation that a buddha has the defining characteristics of space was taught with the underlying intention of the ultimate and exclusive buddha characteristic of the tathāgatas.[1825]

Based on this, you could claim that it is only the space-like characteristic, or the emptiness, of a buddha that qualifies for ultimate truth.

That Zhönu Pal has problems with sūtras like the *Anūnatvāpūrṇatvanirdeśasūtra* must be clear by now. In his commentary on the passage from this sūtra (quoted above), he diplomatically refers to the three reasons for the presence of buddha nature in sentient beings (RGV I.27–28).[1826] The equation of buddha nature with dharmakāya can be relativized by the explanation that the fruit of buddha nature has been only "metaphorically" applied to the buddha potential.

In his commentary on RGV I.1, Zhönu Pal explains all seven vajra points in terms of the ultimate and the apparent truths. In this context he calls the thirty-two qualities of dissociation ultimate (otherwise called qualities of the dharmakāya), but assigns the thirty-two qualities of maturation to the level of apparent truth.[1827] The question arises, of course, in what way the thirty-two qualities of dissociation are ultimate. RGV III.3 states that the first kāya, which is there said to be ultimate, is endowed with them, so that it makes sense to call the qualities of dissociation ultimate, especially in the broader context of explaining each of the seven vajra points on an ultimate or apparent level of truth.

In his commentary on RGV I.26, Zhönu Pal argues that suchness mingled with stains must be realized, since it includes all knowable objects that fully exhaust the two truths:

> The adventitious stains, [that is,] the mind and the mental factors, both of which are dominated by the ignorance that conceals reality, belong to the apparent, because they are contained within the entire apparent truth. (DRSM, 242.10–11)
>
> In contrast suchness is contained within ultimate truth. (DRSM, 242.11–12)

A further explanation of ultimate truth is found in the commentary on the introductory stanza to the ten aspects of the buddha element:

> And this [buddha] element is the sphere *(dbyings)* of the ultimate. As to the ultimate, it is the right wisdom, which knows reality. Its object is the sphere; it [itself] is a synonym of the [buddha] element. This is the meaning of *ultimate truth.* (DRSM, 270.1–3)

In other words, the right wisdom, which knows reality is included within the ultimate or suchness. Thus the qualities of the dharmakāya are only ultimate inasmuch as they partake of this suchness. That ultimately buddha nature, and hence its qualities, are understood in this way becomes clear in Zhönu Pal's discussion of the statement in the *Laṅkāvatārasūtra* that buddha nature has provisional meaning:

> Some say that because of [the phrase] "in order to guide (i.e., discipline) the heretics" buddha nature was taught in this

> *[Laṅkāvatārasūtra]* as having provisional meaning. Others have replied that the goal of teaching buddha nature is explained, but it is not explained as having provisional meaning. In my opinion neither is correct, since the underlying intention here is that terms such as *[buddha] nature, sentient beings, self,* and *lord* have a provisional meaning. Once you have come to be guided by them, the meaning of buddha nature must be thought of in terms of selflessness. [On the other hand,] the *Laṅkāvatārasūtra* does not teach [the ultimate aspect of] buddha nature, which is explained here in the *[Ratnagotravibhāga Mahāyāna-]Uttara [tantra]*, [from] beginning [to] end, and is thus unable to attain final certainty, but as for the goal to which you are guided [through the teaching of buddha nature in the *Laṅkāvatārasūtra*], it is taught as being the suchness [also] explained here [in the *Ratnagotravibhāga*]. (DRSM, 267.15–21)

In terms of enlightenment, Zhönu Pal accepts only the svābhāvikakāya as a fit candidate for the ultimate truth, the form kāyas being enlightenment on the level of apparent truth.[1828] In this context, an explanation of how the qualities are endowed with the ultimate kāya in the paragraph on endowment or connection[1829] in the chapter on enlightenment is of particular interest:

> Since here *ldan pa* (lit., *endowment*) has the meaning of "being connected," the qualities are connected with activity, and activity with the dharmakāya, which is [also] endowed with the defining characteristics of the two [form] kāyas. (DRSM, 482.26–483.1)

And in his following paragraph on manifestation *(vṛtti),* Zhönu Pal explains:

> It (i.e., buddhahood or enlightenment in terms of dharmatā) manifests itself while [at the same time] being inseparably endowed (i.e., connected) with inconceivable qualities that are, like space, unconditioned. Although its nature is thus unconditioned, it manifests itself in different kāyas that are [both] conditioned and unconditioned. (DRSM, 483.3–4)

For Zhönu Pal, the conditioned kāyas are the form kāyas, with their qualities of maturation, but also the dharmakāya inasmuch as it consists of discourses taught in profound and diverse ways.[1830] Thus only the unconditioned svābhāvikakāya aspect of the dharmakāya correlates with the ultimate. *Unconditioned* is not understood as a static state but as a mode of being not produced by artificial causes and under artificial conditions (this does not exclude qualities that blossom naturally). Zhönu Pal points out that *ngo bo nyid (svabhāva)* in svābhāvikakāya means "nonartificial."[1831] Does this mean, then, that the naturally growing qualities are ultimate in every respect? When confronted with such an objection that the buddha element undergoes change if his theory of natural growth is followed, Zhönu Pal points out the true nature of the qualities, namely their general defining characteristic of being nonconceptual. Thus he comments on a passage from the *Anūnatvāpurṇatvanirdeśasūtra* to the effect that the nature of the dharmakāya is the general defining characteristic of the buddha element. He compares the buddha element in different states to the space enclosed by golden and earthen receptacles.[1832] Similarly you could say that the emptiness of buddha nature is not different from the emptiness of a buddha. In addition, in his commentary on RGV I.158 (J I.155) Zhönu Pal explains that the innumerable qualities are identical, not different. Thus the ten strengths (which are different *jñānas*) differ only with regard to their perceived object but not in essence. About the dharmakāya he says in this context:

> Even though the endless number of forms of all knowable objects are not mixed with each other, it (i.e., the dharmakāya) is free of the fault of being many, since [all forms] have an identical own-being. It is also free of the fault of being one, since that own-being is the complete pacification of mental fabrications and [since] it is not characterized by [any] characteristic sign. (DRSM, 443.18–20)

This amounts to saying that the dharmakāya is empty because it is beyond one and many. In other words, the ten strengths of buddha nature are not different because they are the same wisdom apprehending different objects. On the other hand, this wisdom does not constitute an independently existing entity with specific characteristics, and this avoids the fault of being one. Taken in such a way, the existence of buddha qualities does not contradict the Madhyamaka notion of emptiness.

Emptiness, however, is not only a nonaffirming negation, but is also positively described as awareness-emptiness.[1833] Zhönu Pal adduces Maitrīpa to support his view that this awareness and emptiness of the third dharmacakra is supreme,[1834] which is also more in accordance with the *Ratnagotravibhāga.* This "awareness-emptiness" is not simply the emptiness of an awareness; buddha nature has the double feature of being both free from mental fabrications (emptiness) and aware.[1835]

In Zhönu Pal's explanation of the second example from the *Tathāgatagarbhasūtra,* honey represents buddha nature and also, according to him, the buddha element of primordial awareness, which is explicitly called by him "ultimate truth."[1836] What Zhönu Pal means by *awareness* becomes clear in a discussion of the truth of the path and the truth of cessation in the second vajra point. In this context, he observes that the movement of mind has ceased on the level of a buddha, and goes on to explain:

> The Mādhyamikas assert that a mind to which only entities appear displays mental movement, but a buddha definitely does not display this movement. This is also the underlying purport of the *Jñānālokālaṁkārasūtra.* Given that both nirvāṇa and buddha are explained as a single ground in the *Śrīmālādevī[sūtra]* and this treatise here (i.e., the *Ratnagotravibhāga*), [these texts] explain [this ground] as awareness only. But in asserting that it is the awareness aspect of [buddha] nature, they therefore do not assert that it is the wisdom of the path. (DRSM, 100.12–15)

Thus awareness is not only clearly distinguished from mind, but also from the wisdom of the path. Moreover, in the explanation of emptiness in the last dharmacakra, awareness is taken to be a residual part of emptiness, whereas it is only the lack of an own-being in the second dharmacakra. You do not find any kind of own-being in entities by searching with inferential reasoning. What remains, the lack of an own-being, abides as the object of an inferential valid cognition. On the path of the third dharmacakra you do not find any adventitious phenomena by relying on direct valid cognitions. Thus [the nature of mind] is said to be empty of these phenomena. What remains rests as mere awareness without any characteristic signs.[1837]

Further support for the thesis that both aspects of buddha nature, the emptiness of adventitious stains (i.e., freedom from mental fabrication) and awareness-emptiness, correlate with the ultimate is found in the commentary on RGV I.51, where Zhönu Pal describes the reality of definitive meaning in terms of self-awareness,[1838] which is free from mental fabrication:

> You may ask: "Well then, what is reality in its definitive meaning?" It is very self-awareness itself, which is free from all forms of mental fabrication. You may object: "Well, if you [implicitly] call it momentary, how is it then not apparent [truth]?" It is not [apparent truth] because it does not "conceal reality," which is the meaning of the term *apparent [truth]*. Moreover, it cannot produce defilements when focused on. Also, not [everything] that does not withstand logical analysis comes under apparent [truth], because if logical analysis is needed when, in assessing a sprout, etc., your valid cognition [can]not stop the superimposition of taking that [sprout, etc.] for a [real] thing, then it is a [direct] valid cognition by which you apprehend very awareness itself, which is without any [characteristic] signs and mental fabrications whatsoever; and you can counteract all fabrications by precisely this valid cognition. So what can be generated by again using analytic reasoning? This is the reason why the master Āryadeva said that you must apply many synonyms for the ultimate truth. (DRSM, 340.18–25)

In other words, soteriological awareness (which includes the object of self-awareness) is but a synonym of the ultimate. Even though it does not stand up to logical analysis, it helps to counteract mental fabrication. For Zhönu Pal then, the ultimate is not the object of reasoning or inferential knowledge; it is rather the object of the wisdom of the noble ones.[1839] As we have seen above, momentariness is not really a problem for Zhönu Pal either, since he goes so far as to assign this predicate even to space.

In conclusion, the Madhyamaka concept of the two truths does not undergird the *Ratnagotravibhāga;* in fact, it is alien to it. Thus, in order to answer the question whether the buddha qualities exist on the level of ultimate truth, you have first to be aware of which two truths you are talking about. In the second dharmacakra, the ultimate is taken to be the absence of an own-being. Since Zhönu Pal carefully avoids claiming such an existence, the buddha qualities are of course also empty of such an own-being. Still, the qualities of the dharmakāya are taken to be ultimate, but, as has been shown above, only in the sense that they partake of suchness. When Zhönu Pal explains that the buddha element does not change, even though its primordial subtle qualities blossom in a natural way on the path, he does so on this level. In the third dharmacakra, which for Zhönu Pal is superior, positive descriptions of the ultimate are used and, as we have seen above, both aspects of buddha nature, which are freedom from mental fabrication (emptiness) and awareness, are explained as corresponding to the ultimate truth. Because qualities are described as naturally growing within their own sphere and as being even momentary, however, this guards against a too ontological understanding of the third dharmacakra.

6. Two Types of Emptiness

A first glance at Zhönu Pal's introductory explanation of the buddha element (DRSM, 14.22–17.24) immediately reveals one of his main aims, which is to embed the theory of *tathāgatagarbha* into mainstream Mahāyāna in general, and into the Madhyamaka tradition of Maitrīpa in particular. Zhönu Pal claims that Maitrīpa called the emptiness taught in the *Madhyamakāvatāra* middling Madhyamaka, and "awareness-emptiness" *(rig stong)* supreme Madhyamaka. Even though the term itself is not found in Maitrīpa's *Tattvadaśaka*, it is said in TD 5 that all phenomena, which are of one taste, are unobstructed, without an abode, and experienced in the *yathābhūtasamādhi* as being luminous.[1840] Maitrīpa's disciple Sahajavajra, in his *Tattvadaśakaṭīkā*, defines *one taste* as "the one taste in terms of suchness," *unobstructed* as "without a superimposed own-being," and *without an abode* as "not arisen."[1841] It goes without saying that these terms define emptiness in accordance with Nāgārjuna and Candrakīrti. What makes Maitrīpa's Madhyamaka supreme is the experience of this emptiness as natural luminosity, which is equated with self-awareness by Sahajavajra.[1842] In his *Sākārasiddhi* Jñānaśrīmitra (one of Maitrīpa's teachers) summarizes stanza I.9 of the RGV and equates the crucial term *pratyātmavedyaḥ* (which is the same as *pratyātmavedanīya* in RGVV I.1, i.e., "to be realized by yourself") with *svasaṁvedana* (Tib. *rang rig*, self-awareness).[1843] It is obvious that Sahajavajra's self-awareness *(rang rig)* should be understood in terms of *pratyātmavedanīya* as well, and it is this kind of *(rang) rig* that is—in its luminous experience[1844] of the nature of phenomena—also the emptiness of the nature of phenomena, and thus "awareness-emptiness."

In his *Ratnagotravibhāga* commentary[1845] Zhönu Pal explains that the emptiness of middling Madhyamaka is approached by the method of nonaffirming negation and assigned to the middle (or second) dharmacakra, whereas supreme Madhyamaka with its "awareness-emptiness" is said to follow the path of affirming negation and belong to the third dharmacakra. In his exposition for those with average faculties,[1846] Zhönu Pal defines the emptiness of the second dharmacakra as a nonaffirming negation along the lines of the common assertion that phenomena are empty of any own-being.[1847] In this context he quotes *Mūlamadhyamakakārikā* XV.2ab, which posits that something created cannot be the own-being *(svabhāva)* of anything. Even in this world, according to the *Prasannapadā*, something created, such as the "hotness" of water, is not considered to be an own-being, whereas the "hotness" of fire is. Only something that does not arise from contact with other things can be an own-being.

Candrakīrti is quick to point out that the "hotness of fire" is an example of an own-being only in the common sense, or, to use the technical term, on the level of conventional truth. In reality, the hotness of fire is created, and in the final analysis it is in no way different from the hotness of water.[1848] For Candrakīrti the six elements (i.e., earth, water, fire, wind, space, and consciousness)[1849] cannot be imagined in terms of the categories of existence and nonexistence, of objects to be defined, or of defining characteristics.[1850] In other words, a material world and consciousness cannot be grasped in any known way. As soon as you identify a defining characteristic, such as the hotness of fire, you have already altered your experienced reality by false imagining.[1851] The own-being of entities can, however, become the object of the noble ones. In his commentary on MMK XV.2cd, Candrakīrti explains:

> Entities that have come[1852] under the influence of the eye disease [known as] ignorance—in which form they attain, through the practice of not seeing [them], the state of being the object of the noble ones, whose eye disease, ignorance, has been removed—this very [form] is their own-being, their essential nature. This is what has been established, and this is the defining characteristic [of own-being].[1853]

In other words, the own-being of entities is not only defined in a negative way (it is neither artificially created nor dependent on anything) but also in terms of being the object of the noble ones, who perceive reality without subjectively distorting it by false imagining. In his commentary on the same stanza, Candrakīrti equates the own-being of entities with their true nature *(dharmatā)*, natural state *(prakṛti)*, emptiness, lack of essence *(naiḥsvabhāvya)*, suchness, existence as it is *(tathābhāva)*, and the continuous nonarising of things such as fire.[1854] Candrakīrti is careful enough to explain that such an own-being of nonarising is but the nonexistence of anything whatsoever.[1855]

From what has been said above, however, you could argue in line with Dölpopa or Zhönu Pal[1856] that this negation only excludes predicates pertaining to the realm of conventional truth.[1857] How else could the own-being of entities be experienced in a nonconceptual way by the noble ones, and reality also be positively defined by using the term *peaceful*?[1858] In other words, in the second dharmacakra, on the path of Madhyamaka reasoning, it is possible to negate theories (or reifications of any theory) of reality, but doing so has no implications for the validity of what is opposed to the negation. Once all misleading concepts are removed, a direct cognition or experience of reality is possible, as described positively in the third dharmacakra. This carries constant warnings concerning both the limitations of language and the danger of mental fabrication and the subjective alteration of reality that is usually created by the process of imputation and labeling. Thus the language of the third dharmacakra usually consists of pairs of paradoxes, in which a positive statement of your direct experience of reality is combined with a negation of any possible reification that could be produced by this statement if it is taken on an ordinary intellectual level of understanding. To support his point, Zhönu Pal quotes the conclusion of Bhavya's *Prajñāpradīpa*, which states that people who are used to imagining truly existent things apprehend reality mainly by inferential cognitions, but this is not the way a buddha apprehends reality.[1859]

Moreover, Zhönu Pal points out that the example of the hotness of fire is also used in the teachings of the third dharmacakra to illustrate that emptiness is the nature of all phenomena.[1860] In other words, Zhönu Pal does not want us to believe that hotness is really accepted as the own-being of fire in the *Prasannapadā*. That Candrakīrti uses the example at all, rather, indicates for Zhönu Pal that an own-being is not entirely to be excluded. In fact, you could argue that in the *Prasannapadā* unconditioned nirvāṇa, which is free from mental fabrication, fulfills these criteria.[1861] It would, however, not be right to label nirvāṇa *own-being*, since this would be again a mental fabrication, from which ultimate reality is supposed to be free. As stated above, the goal of the analytical Madhyamaka works of the second dharmacakra is to exclude any conceptual reification of reality by showing the internal contradictions of any theory of reality. But for Zhönu Pal this does not mean that a positive description of a nonconceptual experience of reality, as found in the third dharmacakra, is entirely excluded by the analytical Madhyamaka works of the second dharmacakra. For him, these analytical works are rather a possible preparation for the direct approach described in texts like the *Ratnagotravibhāga*.

On the basis of such argumentation, Zhönu Pal introduces two different types of emptiness. In the third dharmacakra, the emptiness of an own-being (that is, the emptiness of the second dharmacakra) is first established in an outer husk, namely the adventitious stains. Then the emptiness that is buddha nature is ascertained in a direct valid cognition, not, that is, as a nonaffirming negation of an own-being. Even though buddha nature has not arisen from causes and conditions, it is not the case that it does not arise at all, in Zhönu Pal's opinion. It simply does not depend on other phenomena in its natural flow, and in this it is like the element of space evolving within its own sphere. In other words, Candrakīrti's emptiness of an own-being does not apply to the buddha element, in Zhönu Pal's eyes, "because it (i.e., the buddha element) does not arise from contact with other things"—the criterion for an own-being in the *Prasannapadā*.[1862] It should be noted, however, that for Zhönu Pal the word *ngo bo nyid* in *ngo bo nyid kyi sku (svābhāvikakāya)* means "nonartificial."[1863] The "natural character" of buddha nature is such a "nonartificial" *(ngo bo nyid,* Skt. *svabhāva)* that it turns, in the state of a buddha, into a "kāya consisting of this *svabhāva*," that is, a svābhāvikakāya. But since the svābhāvikakāya denotes the ultimate aspect of a buddha, this *svabhāva* consists wholly of space-like qualities and is nothing other than Candrakīrti's *svabhāva* (or *prakṛti*) of entities.

This is as far as Zhönu Pal is willing to go. He strictly opposes statements to the effect that fully developed qualities of the dharmakāya or even the major and minor marks of a buddha exist in sentient beings. That would come too close to the non-Buddhist view of an *ātman* for him.[1864] In other words, he holds that in sentient beings, something that at most resembles the svābhāvikakāya really exists,[1865] and speaks in this context of "subtle buddha qualities" or "seeds."[1866] Consequently, he takes the buddha element to be momentary, and only unconditioned in the sense of not being artificially conditioned by adventitious causes and conditions.[1867] Confronted with the objection that its momentariness entails that it belongs to the apparent truth, he explains that focusing on it does not produce defilements or obscure reality. Moreover, not everything that does not stand up to logical analysis is therefore apparent truth.[1868] A logical analysis of the buddha element only yields its being free from mental fabrications and characteristic signs. How it relates to awareness must be experienced in a direct cognition. Zhönu Pal suggests this when he distinguishes two different types of emptiness in the context of explaining three reasons why the truth of cessation is inconceivable:

> In this treatise (i.e., the *Ratnagotravibhāga*) in particular, there are two [types of] emptiness to be distinguished. [First is] the nonaffirming negation, in which entities are empty of any kind of own-being. [Secondly,] it is not enough that an obstinate clinging to entities does not arise when you see [reality] yourself on the basis of a valid cognition of the perceiving subject. But when you see [reality yourself on the basis of such a valid cognition], the awareness that is a remedy for all kinds of mind *(blo)* possessing characteristic signs [also] abides as a mere property. This is the case whether buddhas appear or not. Therefore it is called *abiding nature.* Thoughts and the resulting defilements, skandhas, etc., are not the fundamental nature *(gshis);* still, the fundamental nature is the basis of defilements and thoughts, and even [this] is not seen. Therefore, when you teach emptiness, [the canonical formula is]: "You truly see that something is empty of that which does not exist in it, and that that which remains in place exists." The defining characteristics of emptiness as taught in this [passage] inhere in both [types of] emptiness. By searching with inferential reasoning, you will not see any kind of own-being in entities. What remains is the lack of an own-being, which abides as the object of [inferential reasoning]. When searching on the basis of direct, correct [cognition], you do not see any adventitious phenomena. Thus [the fundamental nature] is said to be empty of these phenomena. What remains abides as mere awareness without [any] characteristic signs. Since both [types of] emptiness are thus grounded in the two types of valid cognition, they are never deceptive and are therefore "true." (DRSM, 101.14–24)

The difference between the two dharmacakras is thus more one of method than of philosophical tenet. While an analytical investigation of reality in the second dharmacakra reveals nothing but the lack of an own-being, a direct cognition of your buddha nature reveals not only the emptiness of adventitious stains but also an awareness that cannot be grasped by intellectual reasoning. To postulate that this awareness is a substantial own-being with an independent existence, though, would make it an object of the intellect and bring it within range of the Madhyamaka criticism.

The realization of this awareness or "awareness-emptiness" is further explained by Zhönu Pal a little further down:

> In terms of "awareness-emptiness" *(rig stong),* the skandhas and the like are adventitious, because in a correct direct [cognition] of entities such as the skandhas arising into existence, sinking into nonexistence, [a combination] of both, or neither one nor the other are not perceived. Since [arising entities and the like] are artificial and coerced, they are said not to be the fundamental nature of the uncontrived mind. Thus, not only is the uncontrived mind not the object of coemergent or imaginative thought, since all thoughts are adventitious, but it cannot be conceptualized or defined by them [either]. It must be realized in an unfabricated, direct way. (DRSM, 102.4–9)

What is then the relation between the lack of an own-being and awareness, the two things left over, in the second and third dharmacakras? In the same paragraph of the commentary Zhönu Pal gives a precise answer to this question:

> Even though the emptiness of nonaffirming negation taught in the middle dharmacakra and the truth of [buddha] nature taught in the last [dharmacakra] are very different with regard to the object of understanding, I do not assert that the difference is that, whereas [the reality ascertained through] nonaffirming negation is directly realized, [buddha] nature is not directly realized. Even though there is a difference with regard to the referents of these words, there is no difference when the happiness of direct [cognition] is realized. This follows from a number of supreme pith instructions, and [in these] I put faith. (DRSM, 110.13–17)

In other words, positive descriptions of the ultimate in the third dharmacakra are in reality, or ontologically, not different from emptiness. This is clear, too, from Zhönu Pal's discussion of the expression "self-awareness (i.e., self-realization) that is free from mental fabrications." As we have seen above, he defends such descriptions of the ultimate by pointing out that not everything that does not stand up to logical analysis is automatically invalidated on the ultimate level. In the conclusion of this particular discussion (in his commentary on RGV I.51) he seeks support from Āryadeva, who said that many synonyms of the ultimate truth must be used.[1869] For Zhönu Pal, they are not only as valid as the expression "emptiness of nonaffirming negation," but also needed as descriptions of direct experiences resulting from special meditation techniques. This point is discussed in the chapter on mahāmudrā.[1870]

Here it is important to note that Zhönu Pal understands the corpus of the *prajñāpāramitā* teaching as implying that something is left over after the negation of an own-being. In his comment on the reason why it is inconceivable that the true nature *(ngo bo)* of attachment is buddha nature, whereas attachment itself is adventitious,[1871] the famous passage from the *Aṣṭasāhasrikā Prajñāpāramitā* is quoted:

> This mind is not mind, the nature of mind being luminosity. (DRSM, 216.2–3)

This passage is explained in line with the *Bṛhaṭṭīkā* from the perspective of the three natures *(trisvabhāva)*. "This mind" denotes the imagined nature. The perfect nature, which is the mind of unsurpassable enlightenment, or the dharmakāya, is beyond all defining characteristics of imagining and thought, so it is said not to be that mind. Therefore the nature of mind is luminosity.[1872]

This is very consequential, for such an interpretation of the *prajñāpāramitā* literature in accordance with the *Bṛhaṭṭīkā*—that is, the perfect nature being empty of the imagined and dependent natures—is one of the most important hermeneutic moves of the Jonangpas. It endorses, or at least does not exclude, an understanding to the effect that the ultimate possesses qualities that are not empty.

That Zhönu Pal seeks the purport of the *prajñāpāramitā* corpus in this direction is also supported by the following passage:

> The teaching of being like clouds and the like in the *prajñāpāramitā*[1873] does not mean that all knowable objects were taught as being like clouds and the like. As for the limit of reality, the ultimate truth in the teaching of the two truths in the *prajñāpāramitā*, it was taught that it is, as the basis that is empty *(stong pa'i gzhi)*, devoid of all conditioned forms. [It has been said:]
>
>> Whatever is conditioned is not the ultimate.
>
> Having thus rejected that [conditioned forms] are the ultimate, the ultimate is called "empty of the conditioned." On the other hand, the opposite of the conditioned, that is, the ultimate, does

> not exist as something essentially different either, for it has been said:
>
> > Subhūti, it is not "that the apparent of the world and the ultimate are entirely different things"; rather, the very suchness of the apparent is the ultimate truth.
>
> It is not the case that the basis of negation is not the ultimate just because the notion that phenomena of the apparent [truth] are ultimate is negated. The ultimate is also said to be [experienced] directly and clearly. (DRSM, 448.17–24)

And there is no doubt that this ultimate, which is empty of conditioned phenomena, is buddha nature, or as Zhönu Pal puts it:

> The fact that the present mind lacks an own-being in reality does not negate mind, which is [buddha] nature. (DRSM, 217.17–18)

In his commentary on the final stanzas of the first chapter of the *Ratnagotravibhāga*, which explain the necessity to teach buddha nature in a third dharmacakra, Zhönu Pal explains that the substantial cause (Tib. *nye bar len pa'i rgyu*) of buddhahood was not clearly taught in the second dharmacakra, and that

> it (i.e., buddha nature) does not incur the slightest harm from [either] reasoning or the canonical scriptures of the *prajñāpāramitā* if you postulate that it is empty of any kind of "substantial own-being" *(dngos po'i ngo bo nyid).* (DRSM, 449.4–5)

Consequently, what is left over in such an emptiness—buddha nature, awareness, and so forth—cannot possess a substantial own-being.[1874] This is also made clear in the commentary on RGV I.159–60 (J I.156–57), where Zhönu Pal explains that the teachings of the second and third dharmacakras do not contradict each other:

> If somebody wonders how this explanation regarding particular features of buddha nature—as being permanent, stable, and so forth—does not contradict [the *prajñāpāramitā*], the answer is as follows: The explanation here that sentient beings possess buddha nature does not contradict the explanation in the

> *prajñāpāramitā* that [everything] lacks an own-being in the same way as an illusion. It is only that something that has not been clearly taught before is now being taught. As to the purpose of this [teaching, it was given because] some sentient beings are unable, given their despair, to enter the enlightened [mind].[1875] (DRSM, 447.14–17)

How Zhönu Pal imagines the condition "lack of an own-being" being fulfilled becomes clearer from how he takes the Mādhyamikas' stance that there is no view called emptiness and Nāgārjuna's famous statement that there is not the slightest thing that is not empty:

> That emptiness is the ultimate truth is not negated even by the statement that there never can be a view called emptiness. [This view] negates rather a [form of] emptiness deliberately imagined by thoughts. This is also what has been taught in the [following passage of] the *Mūlamadhyamakakārikā:* "When there is not the slightest thing[1876] that is not empty, where will the empty then be?"[1877] The meaning of this was taught by Candrakīrti when he said, with regard to emptiness, that no support for them (i.e., phenomena) can be established in terms of specific characteristics.[1878] (DRSM, 449.5–9)

Even though the ultimate lacks an own-being and specific characteristics in Zhönu Pal's eyes, it still must be properly ascertained in a third dharmacakra as being "awareness-emptiness," or buddha nature. These terms may be used as long as they do not violate the dictum of emptiness in the second dharmacakra.

As already shown in the previous chapter, for Zhönu Pal, buddha nature and its qualities are not something fully developed right from the beginning but grow naturally within their own sphere. They are thus not statically permanent but in a sense momentary. In order to uphold a distinction between them and ordinary phenomena, Zhönu Pal is forced to differentiate between artificial and nonartificial causes, with buddha nature being thus explained as nonconditioned, given that it is not produced by artificial causes. The notion that something brought forth, such as the nonconceptual wisdom of the path, is still considered to be unconditioned, can be also found in the *Madhyāntavibhāgaṭīkā.*[1879]

Zhönu Pal's distinction between natural and artificial properties reflects his mahāmudrā background. Thus he follows the Third Karmapa Rangjung

Dorjé in describing the dharmadhātu, or buddha nature, with the mahāmudrā term *unfabricated* or *natural mind.*[1880] In line with this, he explains the negandum in the third dharmacakra as meaning that the natural mind, or the original state of mind *(sems kyi gnyug ma),* is empty of everything fabricated:

> The negandum, too, that of which something is empty, is [here] a little different from [how it is defined in] the middle [dharma-]cakra. From sentient beings up to the Buddha [something] exists [that is] established as the nature of mind in virtue of being neither impaired by, nor fabricated under, other conditions. It is called *empty of fabricated adventitious phenomena*.... All these are, according to the circumstances, fabricated from [cognitive] objects, [mental] imprints, and impaired sense faculties, and thus not the way the original mind is. Therefore the original mind is said to be empty of them. (DRSM, 15.20–16.5)

To be sure, having directly realized emptiness within the framework of the last dharmacakra, you do not rest in a vacuum-like nothingness, the true nature of things being characterized by the awareness of natural luminosity:

> Here, too, in the last dharmacakra, when you investigate[1881] the nature of adventitious attachment and so forth, you see neither any object to become attached to nor any subject that becomes attached. You simply abide in the fundamental nature of attachment—the mere awareness of natural luminosity. If you abide so, even qualities such as clairvoyance appear without any special effort. (DRSM, 441.14–17)

The distinction between the adventitious stains and buddha nature in the second type of emptiness gives rise to the question about their exact relation. In his commentary on the compatibility of the buddha element with the *prajñāpāramitā* (RGV I.160–70 (J I.157–67), Zhönu Pal explains:

> Here, too, in the last dharmacakra, the ultimate is called *empty of adventitious stains,* since phenomena such as attachment are adventitious and thus not ultimate. On the other hand, even though it is pure of adventitious [stains], it is not at all acceptable [to think that the adventitious] abides somewhere other

> than in the ultimate buddha element, since the ultimate buddha element has been taught as being the basis of all defilements. Likewise, the svābhāvikakāya of a buddha, it is stated, is not artificial. It is taught that only something that resembles it exists in sentient beings. Moreover, the fact that a direct vision of the noble ones alone enters it, allows it to be called ultimate, as well. (DRSM, 448.24–449.2)

Throughout the commentary, Zhönu Pal uses several examples to bring home that the apparent and ultimate truths and related pairs, such as thought and luminosity, or saṁsāra and nirvāṇa, are not different in the sense of being separate things. That thought and luminosity share the same nature is compared, for instance, to the same nature of ice and water, or waves and the ocean.[1882] Similarly, adventitious stains and buddha nature are not considered two different things that happen to be mixed up or occur together; rather, buddha nature actually possesses, temporarily, the properties of the stains, in the same way as iron can be temporarily hot. If it did not have these properties, it could not be called the basis of defilements. In his commentary on the first inconceivable point,[1883] Zhönu Pal explains:

> When cold iron is brought in contact with fire, the cold substance changes into something else—hot [iron]. Without the condition presented by fire, it will change again into a cold [substance], but it is not the case that the mind apprehends as one, without differentiating, a mixture of two different substances provided that neither hot nor cold is within the nature of iron. Likewise the mind is also turned into defilements by the fire of [mental] imprints. When the imprints are reversed, there are no [longer] any defilements. Thus, even though the mind is thereby known to be associated with defilements, it is not the case that at the time of the defilements, both the pure mind and the defiled one are mixed as two separate substances and simply not differentiated by the mind. (DRSM, 218.8–12)

In other words, adventitious stains and the buddha element are not two substances that have become mixed up; rather buddha nature itself manifests as defilements in the same way as the property of heat is not different from hot iron. In a saṁsāric state of mind, buddha nature possesses two types of properties: defilements and buddha qualities. These differ, however, in that the defilements can be separated out whereas the buddha qualities are inseparable. Here the comparison drawn in *Prasannapadā* XV.2 is brought in. Whereas the property of heat as manifested in water or iron can be separated by letting the substance cool down, the hotness of fire is inseparable. In the same way as you cannot have a fire without heat, buddha nature never occurs without the buddha qualities, but it can be separated from the "heat" of defilements.

It is therefore no surprise that Zhönu Pal favors the *Laṅkāvatārasūtra*'s equation of buddha nature with the basic consciousness (which is taken by him as the reflection of buddha nature).[1884] He quotes and discusses at length the pertinent passage of the *Laṅkāvatārasūtra*[1885] after his commentary on the crucial stanzas RGV I.27–28, which presents three reasons for the presence of buddha nature in sentient beings.[1886] While the *Laṅkāvatārasūtra* is not quoted in the *Ratnagotravibhāgavyākhyā* at all, Zhönu Pal's commentary contains nearly the entire sūtra in the form of frequent quotes. He considers it a Madhyamaka work[1887] and endorses its assertion that emptiness was taught as buddha nature for those who are not capable of grasping emptiness.[1888]

This is how buddha nature can be explained as a manifestation of defilements. Even though the buddha qualities exist in a subtle form or as something that resembles the svābhāvikakāya, for Zhönu Pal they are at the same time emptiness, and as such identical in essence with the defilements, which are also empty. As we have already seen above, the difference between the adventitious and the buddha element is further characterized by their occurring artificially and naturally, respectively. Whereas the heat of water depends on outer conditions, such as a fire, a natural quality does not.

Another example that illustrates the relation between artificial phenomena (adventitious stains) and the buddha element is that of clouds and space. In his general introduction, based on the first stanza of the first chapter of the *Ratnagotravibhāga*, Zhönu Pal explains:

> On the other hand, they do not arise as something entirely different from the nature of mind. It is like space, for example. Even though it does not turn into phenomena like clouds and mountains, and is thus termed empty, it would not be appropriate to say that these clouds and so forth abide somewhere else than in space. Moreover, in view of their being produced out of ignorance, even the outer material world and the bodies of sentient beings are artificial [or fabricated] and thus [themselves] neganda, things of which [the buddha element] is empty. (DRSM, 16.4–7)

Even though the dharmakāya is explained as the fruit of buddha nature, it is said:

> The dharmakāya evolves in its own sphere, even though it is not subject to artificial conditions. Thus, it is called unconditioned because it is like space and not like clouds, which arise, abide, and cease. (DRSM, 86.18–20)

The sense in which the buddha element is still not contrived and adventitious is illustrated by the unchangeable nature of space, which is not affected by clouds:

> The saying: "The stains being removed, the essence necessarily arises" belongs to the apparent [truth]. Ultimately, [false] imagining, which is the characteristic sign bringing forth all defilements, does not have to be removed, because it is pure in terms of its own-being. The validity of this [syllogism is established] by virtue of the fact that the [buddha] element is by nature free from adventitious stains. Whatever belongs to [this] nature is uncontrived and therefore not adventitious—even as, for example, some parts of the sky that [are covered] by clouds do not change in the slightest way into something else when the clouds have formed in it. (DRSM, 442.24–443.2)

And, we might add, the disappearance of clouds does not change space either, even though the volume of visible "openness" increases within its own sphere. A change in quantity does not affect the quality of space:

> Even though there is a difference between subtle [buddha qualities] and increased ones by virtue of [buddha nature possessing] parts in which adventitious stains have been purified or not, they do not have the attribute of being changeable by nature. This should be understood, [for example,] in the same way as space enclosed by a house: [the space] becomes wider by tearing down the house, but the nature of space itself does not thereby become subject to change. (DRSM, 122.1–3)

In his introduction to the second chapter of the *Ratnagotravibhāga*, Zhönu Pal discusses at length the *Dharmadharmatāvibhāga* and its *vṛtti*, in both of which the distinction between dharmas and the dharmatā closely parallels that between adventitious stains and buddha qualities in the *Ratnagotravibhāga:*

> The root text (the *Dharmadharmatāvibhāga*) itself accords well with the explanation in the *Ratnagotravibhāga* that [the buddha element] is empty of adventitious stains but not empty of [buddha] qualities, for it (i.e., the *Dharmadharmatāvibhāga*) clearly teaches a distinction between the existing dharmatā and the nonexisting dharmas. (DRSM, 470.15–16)

The *Dharmadharmatāvibhāga* describes the relation between dharmas and the dharmatā in the following way:

> The two are neither identical nor different, since there is [both] a difference and not a difference between the existent and nonexistent. (DhDhVK 38–41)

Vasubandhu's commentary explains that the difference follows from the fact that the dharmatā exists whereas dharmas do not. On the other hand, they are also not different, because the dharmatā is only characterized by the nonexistence of dharmas,[1889] which means that both are empty.

The relation between dharmas and the dharmatā is a key to the understanding of emptiness in the third dharmacakra. Thus Dölpopa bases his zhentong definition of the two truths as "different in the sense that identity is negated" *(gcig pa bkag pa'i tha dad pa)* on this passage of the *Dharmadharmatāvibhāga.*[1890] Zhönu Pal understands the dharmatā, which is beyond duality, as being a continuity of stainless mind, but not in such a way that the absence of duality implies the existence of something. It does not even go beyond saṁsāra, given that it is the nature of all phenomena:

> The dharmatā is free from the knowledge of eyes, etc., of ordinary people and even [its] support, [namely,] the experiential object. Since it is [also] free from the imaginations that are accompanied by words and meanings—together with [their] modes of apprehension—the mindstream that is, like the sphere of space, of one taste, is called *dharmatā.* This is because even all phenomena of saṁsāra are not beyond this nature. With regard to this, some say that it is a nonaffirming negation [concerning] the nonexistence as perceived object and perceiving subject, and that even an affirming negation would be allowable, in that it

> would exist as nonduality. Such [negations] may be taken to be the dharmatā, but here it is not like that, since the commentary explains [the dharmatā] as the continuity of a stainless mind only. (DRSM, 456.14–18)

Basing himself on *Mahāyānasūtrālaṁkāra* XIII.19[1891] and the *Dharmadharmatāvibhāga*, Zhönu Pal describes the stainless mind as natural luminosity, and this nature of mind as empty of duality and thought.[1892] For him, the explanation that natural luminosity coexists with all the defilements shows that Vasubandhu's *Dharmadharmatāvibhāgavṛtti* belongs to the Madhyamaka tradition:

> This teaching [in the *Dharmadharmatāvibhāgavṛtti*] of a qualitative similarity between the transformation of the basis and two qualities, those of space as a substance that continues in a continuum and of [natural luminosity that] is apprehended after previously not being apprehended, shows clearly that the *[Dharmadharmatāvibhāga]vṛtti* of the master [Vasubandhu] belongs to the Madhyamaka tradition. In the major Yogācāra treatises it is not explained that there is a naturally pure continuation within the continuum of all defilements—ignorance and the like[1893]—but here it is so explained.[1894] (DRSM, 470.12–15)

In the same way as in the *Ratnagotravibhāga*, Zhönu Pal thus avoids describing the ultimate as a static and permanent entity. This is one reason why he does not see the dharmatā as a negation that affirms the existence of something that is nondualistic, such as a static space-like entity of natural luminosity. Understood as a continuum, natural luminosity is the true nature in every moment of ordinary mind. In other words, natural luminosity is also the true nature of defiled mental events—a stance that Dölpopa vehemently rejects. That which is empty, then, is in reality not different from the basis of emptiness in which something is left over (the adventitious stains and the buddha element, or dharmas and the dharmatā)—any more than hot iron is from cold iron. This is made clear in Zhönu Pal's explanation of the transformation of the basis in the *Dharmadharmatāvibhāga:*

> The meaning of "you comprehend the nature *(svabhāva)*[1895] [of the transformation when you understand that it is] the stainlessness of suchness, in that adventitious stains no [longer] appear at all, while suchness appears in every form" is: Having reverted

> from [a state in which it] provides the basis of adventitious stains, it provides the basis of the nature that appears as suchness. (DRSM, 458.4–6)

In other words, the nature of the transformation of the basis is not newly created, but only revealed after its adventitious stains have been removed. That this is in accordance with the *Ratnagotravibhāga* is explained by the *vyākhyā* in the first point *(svabhāva)* of the second chapter on enlightenment (RGVV II.1):

> The element that was taught by the Buddha as being buddha nature when not freed from the sheath of defilements should be known as the nature of the transformation of the basis when purified from them.[1896]

Zhönu Pal comments:

> ...the element, or cause, that is given the name *buddha nature* when it is not freed from the sheath of defilements, that is, when it has become the basis *(āśraya)* bringing forth defilements, is the basis *(āśraya)* [in the expression "transformation of the basis"], providing as it does the support of all defilements. When it is irreversibly purified from its stains, including the mental imprints, it does not function as a basis of defilements [any more] and has therefore reverted from [its] former state. Since it provides the support of purification only, you should know it to be the nature of the transformation of the basis. The two, the element and the transformation of the basis, are only differentiated on the basis of possessing stains or not, [for their] nature is very suchness. (DRSM, 471.24–472.2)

To conclude, contrary to the zhentong of the Jonangpas and the position of Rangjung Dorjé, Zhönu Pal explains the two truths, which in the *Ratnagotravibhāga* are represented by adventitious stains and the buddha element, as one in essence. This is probably also the reason why he did not use the Jonang terms rangtong and zhentong for his two types of emptiness.

7. Zhönu Pal's Mahāmudrā Interpretation of the *Ratnagotravibhāga*

The Ratnagotravibhāga *as a Basis for Mahāmudrā Instructions*

At the very beginning of his commentary on the *Ratnagotravibhāga*, Zhönu Pal makes it clear that he has aligned himself with, or at least explains the *Ratnagotravibhāga* from within, the mahāmudrā traditions of Maitrīpa, Dampa Sangyé, and Gampopa. Thus, after praising lamas who exemplify compassion and the perfection of wisdom in general and Maitreya in particular, he

> bow[s] to Maitrīpa in whom the treatise of the *[Ratnagotravibhāga Mahāyāna]-Uttaratantra* [began to] blaze, as a consequence of having found [the realization of] mahāmudrā through the kindness of the venerable Śabaripa. (DRSM, 2.6–7)

That the commentary's main purpose is to teach and justify a sūtra-based form of mahāmudrā is also shown by the fact that the following stanzas of Zhönu Pal's initial praise are dedicated to Dampa Sangyé[1897] and Gampopa.[1898] It was Gampopa who made the famous statement that the *Ratnagotravibhāga* was the basic text of their mahāmudrā tradition.[1899] As a doctrinal support for his sūtra- or *pāramitā*-based mahāmudrā, Zhönu Pal repeatedly adduces Sahajavajra's *Tattvadaśakaṭīkā* and Jñānakīrti's *Tattvāvatāra.*[1900] In the introduction to his *Ratnagotravibhāga* commentary, Zhönu Pal informs us that these *pāramitā*-based pith instructions, called mahāmudrā, were further explained by Maitrīpa's heart disciples Vajrapāṇi and Dampa Sangyé. Tsen Kawoché, who—based on teachings from Sajjana—founded the "meditation tradition" of the Maitreya works, is also considered to have followed exclusively the tradition of Maitrīpa.[1901] This is the tradition, too, in which Zhönu Pal's *Ratnagotravibhāga* commentary stands. Thus, Kongtrül Lodrö Tayé says in the introduction of his *Ratnagotravibhāga* commentary:

Zu Gawai Dorjé composed, in accordance with Sajjana's teaching, a commentary on the *Ratnagotravibhāga*, and also translated the root text of the *Dharmadharmatāvibhāga* and its *vṛtti*. They (i.e., Zu Gawai Dorjé and Tsen Kawoché) also became well known as followers of the meditation tradition of the Maitreya works, which was very special in terms of [both] uncommon explanations and practice. Among those grounded in this[1902] tradition was the Omniscient Rangjung Dorjé, who, through his vision of wisdom, precisely realized the underlying intention of the invincible [Maitreya and] composed a summary of the contents of the *Ratnagotravibhāga*. Karma Könzhön (b. 1333) and others commented at length [on it], while the great Karma Trinlepa composed a commentary containing corrections [to the *Ratnagotravibhāga*]. The great translator from Gö, Zhönu Pal, composed a very expanded commentary on Asaṅga's *vyākhyā*.

The great omniscient Dölpopa introduced an extraordinary tradition, which accords with this tradition,[1903] and adhering to [his] commentary, his lineage of disciples in general, and the omniscient Tāranātha and others in particular, established a textual tradition based on explanation and practice. The oral transmission of these commentaries continues up to the present day.[1904]

The Three Dharmacakras: Mahāmudrā Hermeneutics

That Zhönu Pal comments on the *Ratnagotravibhāga* from within the tradition of meditation is also clear from his colophon:

> The Dharma master Drigungpa [Jigten Sumgön] rejoiced in Jé Gampopa's statement that the basic text of these mahāmudrā instructions of ours is the *[Ratnagotravibhāga] Mahāyānottaratantraśāstra* composed by the illustrious Maitreya; and since it is evident that the notes to [his] *Uttaratantra* explanations, the points he makes when presenting the three dharmacakras, and also the explanations deriving from Sajjana's heart disciple Tsen Kawoché, are [all] in accordance with mahāmudrā proper, I have relied on them and have made [this] clear to others as best as I could. (DRSM, 574.9–12)

Unfortunately, I have not been able to locate any *Ratnagotravibhāga* notes by Jigten Sumgön, but as we have already seen in part I of this study, the *Chos kyi 'khor lo legs par gtan la phab pa* states that the mahāmudrā practiced by Jigten Sumgön is in accordance with the *Ratnagotravibhāga*,[1905] its seven vajra points being a commentary on the meaning of the third dharmacakra,[1906] which is described as the dharmacakra of definitive meaning.[1907] In his *Dgongs gcig*, Jigten Sumgön further explains that the three dharmacakras differ with regard to the concepts of different groups of disciples, that all three dharmacakras are contained in each dharmacakra, and that the seed of any subsequent dharmacakras is already latent in the previous ones.[1908] The seed of the three dharmacakras is of definitive meaning, and in this sense all dharmacakras have definitive meaning. Still, the third dharmacakra is considered superior in its effectiveness.[1909]

Zhönu Pal embeds most of his mahāmudrā exposition in his commentary on RGVV I.2, where the three dharmacakras are compared to three successive, ever-finer processes of purifying a *vaiḍūrya* stone in the *Dhāraṇīśvararājasūtra*.[1910] He follows the *Saṁdhinirmocanasūtra* in putting the third dharmacakra at the top of his hermeneutical ladder. According to *Saṁdhinirmocanasūtra* VII.30,[1911] the Buddha taught the four noble truths in the first dharmacakra. He taught both the second and the third dharmacakras beginning with the lack of an own-being in phenomena—that they neither arise nor pass out of existence, that they are quiescent from the beginning, and that they are naturally in a state of nirvāṇa—in other words, emptiness as taught in the *prajñāpāramitā* sūtras and the analytical Madhyamaka works of Nāgārjuna. Thus the last two dharmacakras are not different in terms of ontology. Still, the third dharmacakra differs in the fine distinctions it offers, and for this reason alone it has—contrary to the first two—definitive meaning *(nītārtha)*, and so outshines the second dharmacakra by an uncountable factor.[1912] In VII.3 the *Saṁdhinirmocanasūtra* explains that the Buddha was thinking of the three types of "lack of own-being" *(niḥsvabhāvatā)* when he turned the dharmacakra beginning with the lack of an own-being in phenomena. In the following paragraphs (SNS VII.3–13) it becomes clear that the three *niḥsvabhāvatā*s are the three natures of the Yogācāra (that is, the imagined, dependent, and perfect natures), while SNS VII.24 states that the formula "beginning with the lack of own-being, etc.," is intentional—in other words, must be understood in terms of the three *niḥsvabhāvatā*s. It is therefore reasonable to conclude that the correct distinction between them is what makes the third dharmacakra definitive.

Confronted with the conclusion that the *Saṁdhinirmocanasūtra* then teaches, that the *prajñāpāramitā* and Nāgārjuna's Madhyamaka are provisional and the *cittamātra* view is definitive, Candrakīrti tries to show in his *Madhyamakāvatāra* that the central Yogācāra tenets, on which the hermeneutics of the *Saṁdhinirmocanasūtra* rest, are provisional notwithstanding that this sūtra explicitly claims the contrary. Kamalaśīla affirms in his *Madhyamakāloka,* however, that the hermeneutics of the *Akṣayamatinirdeśa* and the *Saṁdhinirmocanasūtra* are compatible. The teaching of nonarising in the *prajñāpāramitā* (i.e., the emptiness of the *Akṣayamatinirdeśa*) refers exclusively to the ultimate, while the *Saṁdhinirmocanasūtra*'s clarification of this emptiness with the help of the three *niḥsvabhāvatā*s helps to avoid the two extremes of wrong denial and superimposition on the Madhyamaka path.[1913]

It is clear that Zhönu Pal adopts the hermeneutics of the *Saṁdhinirmocanasūtra.* Not only does he not mention the competing *Akṣayamatinirdeśasūtra* at all; he even dedicates some thirty pages of his introductory study to showing that the third dharmacakra is superior in every respect, whether compassion, view, or meditation.[1914] Technically, his long explanations are part of a commentary on the comparison of the threefold spiritual purification to the gradually more refined polishing of a *vaiḍūrya* made in the *Dharaṇīśvararājasūtra,* which is quoted by the *Ratnagotravibhāgavyākhyā* on I.2. This example shows, in line with the *Saṁdhinirmocanasūtra,* that there is ultimately only one vehicle for all sentient beings,[1915] and that everybody eventually becomes purified with the help of the three dharmacakras.

This is made clearer in the commentary following the third quotation from the *Dhāraṇīśvararājasūtra,* where it is said that you enter the sphere of a tathāgata with the help of the irreversible (i.e., third) dharmacakra, or the teaching of threefold purity.[1916] According to the *Daśabhūmikasūtra,* Zhönu Pal notes, the seventh level is still defiled in a sense, because you still long for the wisdom of a tathāgata at this stage. It is, of course, the *Ratnagotravibhāga* with its teaching of a buddha element empty of adventitious stains that is the main commentary on the third dharmacakra.[1917] That Zhönu Pal follows the distinction made in the *Saṁdhinirmocanasūtra* between *neyārtha* and *nītārtha* is evident from his comment on RGV V.5, which says that only hearing one word of these teachings on the buddha element yields much more merit than anything else.[1918] Zhönu Pal explains:

> The meaning [of this] should be understood according to the teaching in the *Saṁdhinirmocanasūtra* on the difference in merit [resulting] from devotion to sūtras of provisional meaning and [to those of] definitive meaning. (DRSM, 561.22–23)

There is not the slightest attempt to elevate the second dharmacakra to the same level as the third; Zhönu Pal goes so far as to quote in full length the *Saṁdhinirmocanasūtra*'s description of how the third dharmacakra is superior, and concludes that, since the benefit derived from merely hearing its definitive meaning is that great, the profound and vast meaning of the last dharmacakra stands out accordingly.[1919] Thus, having determined the nature of mind in the third dharmacakra, Zhönu Pal now finds the generation of compassion much more effective; for you can rejoice in the fact that everybody including yourself already possesses amazing qualities.[1920] Referring to the *Bodhicittavivaraṇa* (a work ascribed by tradition to Nāgārjuna), he further contends that the ultimate bodhicitta is the supreme generation of bodhicitta, since it arises through the power of seeing the similarity between your own enlightenment and sentient beings' luminosity of mind. In other words, the superior conduct of a bodhisattva in the third dharmacakra is directly linked with his realization of luminosity.[1921]

The related view is corroborated by a famous passage from the *Dharmadhātustotra* (stanzas 18–22) in which the fire of wisdom is said to burn away the adventitious stains of the ordinary mind but not mind's luminous nature. Moreover, the luminous nature (equated with the [buddha] element) is not diminished by those sūtras that were taught in order to reveal emptiness.[1922] Based on such considerations, Zhönu Pal defines the view of the third dharmacakra:

> If you take the way things appear as the measure, without considering the essential mode of phenomena, they exist in the modes of saṁsāra and nirvāṇa, material things and consciousness, the material world and beings. If, on the other hand, the essential mode serves as the measure, nothing whatsoever exists as something different from the mind, and it (i.e., the view) is the insight *(prajñā)*—the knowledge—that even the true nature of mind *(sems nyid)* is the natural mind, which in no way exists as a phenomenon that possesses [characteristic] signs. The emptiness that is examined by reasoning and that which is grounded in luminosity—[neither] can be destroyed by anything; [both] are buddha nature. (DRSM, 47.26–48.4)

Zhönu Pal stresses that mind's luminosity is taught in many scriptures, such as the *Ghanavyūhasūtra* and the *Laṅkāvatārasūtra*. In the latter it is explained in the same way as the emptiness of an own-being is taught in the Madhyamaka treatises.[1923] The superior meditation of the third dharmacakra is then mainly justified as a direct approach to natural luminosity, as explained in mahāmudrā pith instructions.

Still, in his commentary on RGV I.159–60 (J I.156–57), Zhönu Pal points out that the teachings of the second and third dharmacakras, namely of emptiness and buddha nature respectively, do not contradict each other. It is only that the teachings of the second dharmacakra do not clearly formulate what ultimate truth really is.[1924]

The superiority of the third dharmacakra is mainly based on special mahāmudrā techniques, particularly ones that lead to a sudden realization of your nature of mind, and not on an ontological zhentong distinction in the manner of Dölpopa. At the end of his long demonstration of the superiority of the third dharmacakra, Zhönu Pal clearly states that you can reach only the seventh bodhisattva level with the teachings of the second dharmacakra, whereas the fruit of the third dharmacakra is the three final, pure levels.[1925] This is perfectly in line with what Jigten Sumgön taught in his autocommentary on the *Chos 'khor gtan phab:*

> Even our teacher, the illustrious Buddha, first generated a mind directed toward unsurpassable enlightenment, and during an incalculable eon traversed the path up to the first [bodhisattva] level by means of the first dharmacakra. During [another] incalculable [eon] he traversed the path up to the seventh level by means of the second dharmacakra, and during a [third] incalculable [eon] he traversed the three pure levels by means of the third dharmacakra.[1926]

Zhönu Pal also adopted a distinction between the gradualist and simultaneist. Quoting the *Laṅkāvatārasūtra* passage on the gradual and instantaneous purification of the mindstream, he explains in his commentary on the description of the third dharmacakra in the *Dhāraṇīśvararājasūtra* that on the pure bodhisattva levels all objects of knowledge appear instantaneously, the gradual purification of stains through the three dharmacakras going up only to the seventh level.[1927] Referring to the *Vairocanābhisambodhitantra*, Zhönu Pal further argues that this seventh level may be also a provisional one already found on the path of accumulation,[1928] one that brings sudden realization within the reach of more ordinary practitioners.

This latter explanation seems to contradict the *Chos 'khor gtan phab*, which contends that all sentient beings attain enlightenment gradually, while only someone who has accumulated merit previously and who attains enlightenment at the time of the fruit is called a simultaneist. Still, Jigten

Sumgön claims in his *Dgongs gcig* (IV.18) that "all levels and paths are traversed with the same realization,"[1929] while in the sixth chapter of the *Dgongs gcig* he explains that this realization, which is at the same time the supreme view, is created by devotion (VI.6–7), with meditation taken to be the cultivation of this view (VI.10).[1930] In other words, a devoted practitioner can rely at a relatively early stage on the one realization of the true nature of his mind, which leads him through all the levels to buddhahood.[1931] This brings sudden realization within the reach of more ordinary practitioners who are well short of the actual path of seeing. In support of such an interpretation, Zhönu Pal refers to a statement in the biography of Jigten Sumgön's disciple Nyö Gyalwa Lhanangpa written by a certain Yeshé Dorjé.[1932] Even more important for Zhönu Pal's simultaneist mahāmudrā, however, is a passage from Zhang Tsalpa Tsöndrü's *Phyag rgya chen po lam zab mthar thug* to the effect that mahāmudrā is attained in one go, so that the confused err when they reckon it in terms of levels and paths.[1933]

To conclude, the *Phyag chen lam zab mthar thug* and similar mahāmudrā works are quoted in Zhönu Pal's discussion of the three dharmacakras in RGVV I.2 in order to establish a connection between the *Ratnagotravibhāga* and his mahāmudrā tradition. The determination of the ultimate as buddha nature or natural luminosity in the third dharmacakra is taken to be the direct mahāmudrā approach to the nature of mind. This approach is not really different from the emptiness of the second dharmacakra. While the analytical methods of the second dharmacakra deflate all concepts, coarse and subtle, about things, the third one purifies phenomenal appearances that hinder the proper perception of buddha nature.[1934]

The Mahāmudrā Approach of Yogic Direct Valid Cognitions

The key to understanding how the *Ratnagotravibhāga* can be used to support a *pāramitā*-based mahāmudrā tradition is Rangjung Dorjé's equation of buddha nature with the mahāmudrā term *unfabricated natural mind,* which is—like buddha nature—neither improved by the noble ones nor demolished by sentient beings.[1935] The fact that this unfabricated natural mind is empty of fabricated adventitious stains is also described as "awareness-emptiness," which Maitrīpa, according to Zhönu Pal, equates with the supreme Madhyamaka of the third dharmacakra. This awareness[1936] cannot be grasped by relying on the inferential valid cognitions of Madhyamaka reasoning in the second dharmacakra but must be realized directly.[1937]

The intellectual approach to the ultimate can only negate without implying anything, and the result is a nonaffirming negation that is realized by means of an inferential valid cognition. Zhönu Pal follows Bhavya's *Tarkajvālā* in pointing out that this cannot be the ultimate that is beyond the intellect, but only the ultimate taken as the qualification of a thesis. It is the ultimate that is attainable when you are engaged in performance, the ultimate that is in accordance with the accumulation of merit and wisdom, and is called worldly wisdom endowed with mental fabrications.[1938]

In the third dharmacakra, the scope of such a nonaffirming negation is restricted to the adventitious stains, whose lack of an own-being has been established by inferential valid cognitions. The ultimate that is beyond the intellect is taken to be the emptiness that is buddha nature, or the element of awareness. To support his stance, Zhönu Pal quotes Bhavya, who concludes his *Prajñāpradīpa* with the statement that the ultimate, or the reality, of nonconceptual wisdom must be realized in such a way that for the perceiving subject all mental fabrications are pacified. Someone, however, who imagines truly existent things does not perceive reality like a buddha, but has for the time being to rely on inferential cognitions.[1939]

In his commentary on how the example of the piece of gold in the mud (the fourth example from the *Tathāgatagarbhasūtra*) illustrates the suchness of buddha nature,[1940] Zhönu Pal explains that realizing the selflessness of persons and phenomena with the help of a nonaffirming negation removes coarse ignorance only:

> You may ponder the question: "It is through knowledge of both [types of] selflessness endowed with the defining characteristics of a nonaffirming negation that the root of [saṁsāric] existence is removed, and if this [knowledge] yields liberation as well, why call it *buddha nature,* a second [kind of] suchness?" [Answer:] Knowledge that possesses the defining characteristics of a nonaffirming negation removes coarse ignorance but not [its] subtle form, for when meditating on this [negation], you search for another object, without thoroughly knowing yourself by yourself, and that is why dualistic appearances are not uprooted. Therefore mere [nonaffirming negation] does not get one beyond the stage characterized by the mental imprints of ignorance. (DRSM, 426.9–13)

On the other hand, it is important to note that for Zhönu Pal the emptiness of nonaffirming negation taught in the middle dharmacakra and the truth of buddha nature taught in the last dharmacakra are different with regard to the objects of discourse, but he does not assert that there is a difference when there is direct realization:

> Even though there is a difference with regard to the objects these words (i.e., *nonaffirming negation* and *buddha nature*) refer to, there is no difference when the joy of direct [perception] is realized. This follows from a number of pith instructions, and [in these] I have placed faith. (DRSM, 110.15–17)

In other words, it is only on the level of intellectual understanding that a difference is made between buddha nature and adventitious stains (with only the stains being subject to nonaffirming negations). Against the background of the previous explanation, this must mean that as long as the process of investigating emptiness through inferential valid cognitions continues, there are still subtle forms of ignorance, so that reality (or buddha nature) cannot be directly realized. From this it does not follow, however, that there is an ontological difference between an ultimate true nature and an apparent truth. According to Thrangu Rinpoche, this also explains the difference between zhentong and mahāmudrā. In analysis the adventitious stains and buddha nature are necessarily differentiated, since buddha nature is empty of what does not belong to it (i.e., it is "empty of other," or *zhentong*). But when buddha nature is directly realized (mahāmudrā), there is no longer any difference between it and the adventitious stains or apparent truth.[1941]

In the paragraph on the superiority of the third dharmacakra in terms of meditation, Zhönu Pal states that a direct cognition that realizes reality does not arise during an analytical meditation immediately after the thought processes of inferences have ceased but rather only when all thoughts disappear.[1942] Thus it is important not to view Madhyamaka reasoning as an end in itself, but as a means to get one as expeditiously as possible to a state allowing direct access to the nature of mind. This sets the stage for the mahāmudrā pith instructions, which enable such a practical direct approach to the true nature of mind, or buddha nature.

The direct cognition within awareness-emptiness of the third dharmacakra is taken to be investigative and nonconceptual at the same time. Zhönu Pal compares it to fixedly watching water in order to determine whether there are sentient beings in it. Such a direct realization can be induced by first telling the disciple to investigate his mind day and night. Then he may be told to give up all unnecessary thinking and to settle in his mind without wavering, and this gives rise to the mahāmudrā yoga of one-pointedness. Once this has been achieved, he goes on to watch the meditating mind by turning his direct cognition inward,[1943] and this gives rise in turn to a direct perception that all phenomena lack a truly existent self.[1944]

Such pith instructions enable an immediate approach to the true nature of mind, or awareness-emptiness. By investigating in a direct way without depending on logical reasoning, you can see that everything lacks an own-being, in a way similar to approaching a cloud that looks like a mountain and finding out that it is not like one at all. It is not that the validity of analytical meditation is denied, but rather that in order to reach your goal, it is not necessary to resort to inferential cognitions again and again once you have established that all phenomena lack a true existence. You need to study a map only once or twice in order to know how to get from A to B. Once the way is familiar, you ride along without being constantly conscious of the entire itinerary.[1945] Similarly, nonconceptual meditation does not necessarily go astray even if not constantly informed by an intellectual ascertainment of emptiness.

In the paragraph on the superior meditation of the third dharmacakra, Zhönu Pal compares those who use this mahāmudrā approach to someone on a mountain ridge to whom a stream of water below appears to be immovable, like a stick. Descending into the valley, he sees from close up that the river is only a series of former and later waves, and that it is constantly moving. Likewise, when a direct perception arisen from the yoga of one-pointedness captures the mind and outer objects in any of their temporal differences, you realize that no own-being whatsoever can be apprehended in any entity. This is the way of directly realizing nonorigination.[1946] This direct realization of nonorigination is achieved in the second mahāmudrā yoga, the yoga of freedom from mental fabrication.[1947]

The continuum of direct perception that has been cultivated in the way described above repudiates concepts tied to words and meanings, and it is by virtue of this that all appearances are overcome. Zhönu Pal quotes earlier masters who explained that all appearances dissolve in the mind, and that you should constantly verify that nothing can be internalized or expressed with the help of mental constructs. This process should continue into the third mahāmudrā yoga, the yoga of one taste. In order to hammer home his point, Zhönu Pal notes that even Kamalaśīla, whose works are normally not the best support of special mahāmudrā instructions, explains in his three *Bhāvanākramas* and the commentary on the *Nirvikalpapraveśadhāraṇī* that at the end of analysis you rest in nonconceptuality.

Even Atiśa states in the *Madhyamakopadeśa* that once you have established that all phenomena are nonexistent, then no consciousness whatsoever is conceptualized, nothing whatsoever is perceived, and all mindfulness *(dran pa)* and concentration *(yid la byed pa)*[1948] is given up.[1949] Thus Atiśa, too, accepts a nonconceptual meditation after analysis.

In quoting Götsangpa, Zhönu Pal leaves no doubt that his immediate mahāmudrā approach outshines any analytical meditation:

> As for the analytical meditation of the scholars and the *kusulu* meditation of resting—if the two are taken by themselves, the path in the *kusulu* tradition is faster. (DRSM, 59.22–23)

Just how low Zhönu Pal's opinion of the analytical approach of the second dharmacakra is can be seen from a remark in his commentary on RGV I.156 (J I.153):

> Among the bodhisattvas, [some] find the emptiness of non-affirming negation through inferential valid cognition, but even this valid cognition is taken to be ignorance inasmuch as it is conceptual by nature. Therefore, here, the manner of the last dharmacakra is supreme, because you are mainly engaged in the nonconceptual. (DRSM, 438.23–26)

The mahāmudrā approach is the only way for ordinary sentient beings to directly experience reality as it is. On the ordinary Mahāyāna path, this is only possible on the first bodhisattva level, the path of seeing, which is attained after eons of accumulating merit and wisdom. For a direct mahāmudrā experience of the true nature of your mind, Madhyamaka reasoning can be helpful in the beginning as a preparation for meditation, but it is not an indispensable condition for its success. On the contrary, clinging to an intellectual understanding of emptiness can become an obstacle.[1950]

Sūtra-Based Mahāmudrā Meditation

The way mahāmudrā meditation is doctrinally supported can be best understood in Zhönu Pal's extensive commentary on the superiority of the meditation practice of the third dharmacakra. This meditation practice, according to the *Dhāraṇīśvararājasūtra* (and thus the *Ratnagotravibhāga*) assumes that everybody, even those who were first supported by the teachings of the first two dharmacakras, eventually enters into the experiential sphere of a tathāgata and realizes the nature of the third dharmacakra.[1951] It is to this that the phrase "those who have entered all vehicles" in the definition of the third dharmacakra of the *Saṁdhinirmocanasūtra* refers.[1952] The experience a tathāgata shares with the practitioners of the third, irreversible dharmacakra is classically described by a passage of the *Laṅkā-vatārasūtra* (LAS II.99–105), in which the *ālayavijñāna* and the remaining seven forms of consciousness (including their phenomenal content) are compared to the ocean and its waves.[1953] As we have already seen in the chapter on buddha qualities,[1954] Zhönu Pal follows the *Laṅkāvatārasūtra* in seeing the *ālayavijñāna* as not only the basis of saṁsāra but in the end also the cause of saṁsāra being reversed into nirvāṇa—in seeing the *ālaya-vijñāna*, then, as a reflection of buddha nature. As already pointed out, Zhönu Pal considers the *Laṅkāvatārasūtra* a Madhyamaka work,[1955] stressing its assertion that emptiness was taught as buddha nature for those who were not capable of grasping emptiness.[1956] In other words, the *ālayavijñāna* is implicitly equated with emptiness as well, and this enables LAS II.99–105 to be tied in with the mahāmudrā teachings of Saraha, who adopts the simile of water and waves in his *Dohākośagīti,* stanza 74:

> Whatever emanates from the mind, [and however long such thoughts do so,]
> So long will their nature be that of the protector [of all beings].[1957]
> Are water and waves different or not?
> [His] equality with worldly existence is by nature [that of] space.[1958]

Thus the *Laṅkāvatārasūtra* plays an important role in linking mahāmudrā with the teaching of buddha nature and the *Ratnagotravibhāga.* Mahāmudrā practice requires, however, working with direct perceptions of the true nature of your mind right from the beginning, whereas in RGVV on I.157–58 (J I.154–55) buddha nature (or the buddha element) is said to be difficult to apprehend and not a fully experiential object for even the highest saints.[1959] Moreover, the direct perception of reality required by the mahāmudrā approach is traditionally only possible from the first bodhisattva level onward or else through tantric practice.

Besides referring to the *Tattvadaśakaṭīkā* and the *Tattvāvatāra* as doctrinal support for a path of direct perceptions outside the tantras, Zhönu Pal elaborates in detail on a sūtra-based interpretation of the five stages in the *Pañcakrama,* which normally involve a formal tantric practice of the completion stage in highest yogatantra. The passage into which the five stages are read is from the second chapter of the *Laṅkāvatārasūtra* (namely from the prose portion following LAS II.98).[1960] The first stage is called *physical isolation,* because it protects the yogin from the ordinary appearances of skandhas and the like by replacing the skandhas with manifestations of bliss and emptiness (that is, deities).[1961] The sentence from the *Laṅkāvatārasūtra* that Zhönu Pal claims this stage describes, runs:

> Mahāmati, through [their] right practice, which is connected with the effortless [accomplishment] of great compassion and skillful means, through [their practice of seeing] that all sentient beings are the same as an illusion and a reflection....[1962]

Of particular interest is also the interpretation of the third stage, "blessing from within" *(svādhiṣṭhāna),* during which an initiated yogin who has already practiced the generation stage solicits his tantric master's pith instructions on the *svādhiṣṭhāna* level[1963] in order attain the luminous state.[1964] This third stage can be reasonably read into the phrase "being endowed with the blessing of being without characteristic signs." The passage adduced from the *Laṅkāvatārasūtra* for the *svādhiṣṭhāna* level is:

> [Bodhisattvas] who, through [their practice of] not seeing [objects] outside of the mind, become endowed with the blessing of being without characteristic signs, who deeply meditate as part of [their practice of] gradually pursuing [their chosen] object[s] of meditative stabilization along the stages represented by the [bodhisattva] levels, and who are convinced that the threefold world is an illusion [produced by] their own mind, they attain the meditative stabilization [of experiencing phenomena to be] illusion-like.[1965]

It should be noted that Sahajavajra explains *svādhiṣṭhāna* in a similar way:

> He is "adorned by being blessed from within" means that he is blessed within himself by the nature of his mindstream, which is bound up with the nature of uncontrived reality. That which emanates from [his] nature of suchness naturally adorns him.[1966]

For Sahajavajra the yogin of mahāmudrā experiences uncontrived reality after abandoning characteristic signs by not becoming mentally engaged,[1967] and this is not really different from saying that the bodhisattva is "endowed with the blessing of being without characteristic signs."

Now we are in a position to understand Zhönu Pal's strategy: by showing that the *Laṅkāvatārasūtra* teaches *(sva-)adhiṣṭhāna* as the third of five stages forestalls the possible objection that the *Tattvadaśaka* and its *ṭīkā*, which offer the best support for his *pāramitā*-based mahāmudrā, are in reality tantric, describing as they do the yogin is "adorned with the blessing from within *(svādhiṣṭhāna)*" in TD 9cd. But much more importantly than this, Zhönu Pal reads the five stages of the *Pañcakrama* into the fourth chapter of the *Ratnagotravibhāga* (RGV IV.3–4)—the one on activity. The stanzas RGV IV.3–4 read:

> The wise one[s] are always without effort,
> Since thoughts about what guidance [should be undertaken],
> For whom, by which [means], where,
> And when do not arise [in them]. (IV.3)
>
> For whom, [that is,] for [which] element (i.e., type of) [of sentient being] guidance is required,
> By which, [that is,] by [which of the] numerous skillful means,
> What, [that is, what] guidance,
> Where and when, [that is, in this or] that place and at [this or that] time. (IV.4)[1968]

In Zhönu Pal's "*Pañcakrama* passage" of the *Laṅkāvatārasūtra*, the "fivefold" practice of bodhisattvas is "connected with the effortless [accomplishment] of great compassion and skillful means" (see above). As described in RGV IV.45a (J IV.43a) buddha activity pours down from the clouds of compassion. The *pāda* RGV IV.4b: "By which, [that is,] by [which of] the numerous means for those to be guided" is taught by use of the *Laṅkāvatāra* term *skillful means;* and the *pāda* RGV IV.3d: "The wise one[s] are always without effort" is taught by way of *effortless [accomplishment]*. The *Laṅkāvatāra* passage "The right practice, which is connected [with…]" means the right practice of meditation on the activity that possesses these three particular qualities, and this practice is said to possess five stages.[1969]

Zhönu Pal justifies his interpretation of this *Laṅkāvatāra* passage by pointing out that it goes back to Āryadeva. We are further informed that lamas who practice the pith instructions of the *Ratnagotravibhāga* explain the *Ratnagotravibhāga* in terms of stages of meditation on buddha nature called the *four [mahāmudrā] yogas*. Zhönu Pal admits that he has not found literal echoes of them in the scriptures, but suggests that their meaning is explained in a prose passage following stanza II.137 in the *Laṅkāvatarasūtra* (LAS 79.16ff.).[1970] In support of Zhönu Pal, it should be noted that Jñānakīrti had earlier related mahāmudrā practice with the traditional fourfold Mahāyāna meditation by equating *Mahāyāna* in *Laṅkāvatārasūtra* X.257d with mahāmudrā. The *pādas* X.257cd ("A yogin who is established in a state without appearances, sees Mahāyāna"[1971]) thus mean that you finally see or realize mahāmudrā.[1972] The prose passage following LAS II.137[1973] introduces four meditation techniques, called *dharmas,* that a great bodhisattva must possess. Zhönu Pal compares them to the presentation of the four mahāmudrā yogas from Zhang Tsalpa Tsöndrü's *Phyag rgya chen po lam zab mthar thug zhang gi man ngag.*[1974]

In the introduction to his commentary on the second chapter of the *Ratnagotravibhāga,* Zhönu Pal discusses at length the dharmatā chapter in the *Dharmadharmatāvibhāgakārikās*, because its ten points relating to the transformation of the basis *(āśrayaparivṛtti)* are similar to the *Ratnagotravibhāga's* presentation of enlightenment. During his exposition of the four "meditation practices" *(prayoga)* in the *Dharmadharmatāvibhāga,* Zhönu Pal maintains that these four *prayogas*, which are also found in the *Laṅkāvatārasūtra,* the *Mahāyānasūtrālaṁkāra,* and the *Madhyāntavibhāga,* correspond to the four yogas of mahāmudrā. This is why he sees in the Maitreya works a basis for mahāmudrā practice.[1975]

The First Mahāmudrā Yoga of One-Pointedness

The yoga of one-pointedness is compared to the first dharma in the prose passage following LAS II.137, that is, the meditation that appearances are your own mind. Your own mind is said to lack an *I* or *mine,* and does not adopt or discard. It is permeated by mental imprints of baseness and indulges in the manifold forms of the triple world that appear bound up with such concepts as body and property. In accordance with these five points of the first dharma in the *Laṅkāvatārasūtra,* the first mahāmudrā yoga of one-pointedness is described as having five distinctive features as well. The first is the meditation that everything is mind only, which means that all appearances of the threefold world have the nature of mind's clarity and emptiness. Second is to ponder that the abiding in clarity and emptiness and the wandering of thoughts are not substantially different categories in terms of their substance. Since clarity and emptiness are in motion as thoughts, nothing whatsoever must be adopted or discarded with regard to thoughts and clarity. Third, when many thoughts occur again, know that the imprints of mental fabrication have not been given up, even though you have seen [mind] as clarity and emptiness. The fourth is to know that the perceiving subject, which indulges in various objects, is this mind of clarity and emptiness. Fifth is to know that all the appearances of a body, property, a dwelling place, and the realms of the six types [of beings] are bound up with this same mind, in that they share the same identity. In the sūtras and śāstras it is explained that you can understand mind only because the connection between names and their referents is ascertained to be imagined. The mind possesses the ability to clearly display the phenomenal world, including all other mental events, with all these appearances being empty. This is how Zhang Tsalpa Tsöndrü explains the first mahāmudrā yoga:

> When the yoga of one-pointedness has arisen, you realize the nature *(rang bzhin)* of your own mind. Clarity and emptiness are not obstructed and are without middle and extreme, like the vault of pure space. To remain in this brightness is the meditative equipoise of the first yoga. (DRSM, 61.23–25)

In his commentary on the dharmatā chapter of the *Dharmadharmatāvibhāgakārikās*,[1976] Zhönu Pal reads this first mahāmudrā yoga into the first *prayoga* of the *Dharmadharmatāvibhāga*, which consists of the practice of apprehending that everything is a mere image. From the latter commentary it is clear that Zhönu Pal interprets the *cittamātra* denial of an outer material world and a perceiving subject on the basis of the Madhyamaka negation of an own-being or independent existence of an own-being. In other words, wherever the *Dharmadharmatāvibhāga* negates outright the existence of outer objects, Zhönu Pal restricts this negation to the own-being of such objects.[1977] Consequently, it is also not the objective of the first mahāmudrā yoga to establish that everything is mind or perception only. The yogin rather directs his investigative attention inward, as called for in the pith instructions, and only deals with what appears in the mind. In his *Dharmadharmatāvibhāga* commentary, Zhönu Pal defines the first yoga:

> The first [mahāmudrā yoga] is to look inward and to apprehend that [everything] is your own mind only *(cittamātra)*. (DRSM, 465.13)

The Second Mahāmudrā Yoga of Freedom from Mental Fabrications

The second dharma of the *Laṅkāvatārasūtra*[1978] answers well to the mahāmudrā yoga of freedom from mental fabrications, since you have to abandon the wrong view that phenomena arise, abide, and pass out of existence. This results in the realization that external entities do not exist. Not apprehending any inner or outer phenomena, the bodhisattva really sees that the triple world lacks an own-being. Here in the second dharma or mahāmudrā yoga, Zhönu Pal distinguishes again five levels. The yoga of freedom from mental fabrication starts by realizing that the totality of all appearances is mind, for when the mind is happy or suffering, its appearances are similar. Second, having thus seen that the mind lacks an own-being, you realize that appearances are the mind's "doors of appearance" and also that appearances lack an own-being. Third, once this realization has arisen, the sense faculties turn inward, and the five forms of consciousness no longer engage with objects. Fourth, the five sense faculties, their respective objects, and nonperception *(avijñapti)* are understood as lacking an own-being.[1979] Finally, the yogin increasingly sees on the fifth level of this second yoga that the outer and inner skandhas lack an own-being, and realizes that the entire threefold world has arisen under the conditions of inner thought.

A little disturbing for Zhönu Pal's enterprise is that you attain the endurance of nonorigination in the second dharma of the *Laṅkāvatārasūtra,* since this usually happens on the eighth bodhisattva level, whereas according to Götsangpa, the yoga of freedom from mental fabrications corresponds to the first level. This is probably one reason why this passage of the *Laṅkāvatārasūtra* was slightly distorted in both Tibetan translations, the one directly from the Sanskrit and the other from the Chinese.[1980] Apart from this, the second dharma fits well with Zhang Tsalpa Tsöndrü's presentation of the second mahāmudrā yoga:

> When the yoga of freedom from mental fabrication has arisen, you realize the true nature *(ngo bo)* of your own mind. It is uninterrupted awareness, free from mental fabrication. Your own mind, which is without origination and cessation, adopting and discarding, is based in the dharmakāya, and this is the meditative equipoise of the second yoga. (DRSM, 61.26–62.2)

The second step in the *Dharmadharmatāvibhāga* is to realize the nonexistence of mere external entities. The nonapprehension of the perceiving subject comes with the third *prayoga.* In his *Dharmadharmatāvibhāga* commentary, Zhönu Pal presents the second yoga:

> As for the explanation in the second *[prayoga]* that there is nothing outside, it is the [mahāmudrā yoga of] freedom from mental

> fabrications, in which you realize that all phenomena that have become the object of mind lack any basis. (DRSM 465.14–15)

It is only by understanding this second *prayoga* as meaning that the nonexistence of external objects refers to the lack of their own-being that it can be brought into line with the second mahāmudrā yoga, freedom from mental fabrications.

The Third Mahāmudrā Yoga of One Taste

The objective of the third dharma in the *Laṅkāvatārasūtra* is to establish that external entities do not exist in reality but only as in a dream. The difference from the first dharma is the emphasis placed on the nonexistence of external entities rather than simply saying that appearances are your own mind. Unlike the first and second dharmas, the third one is clearly based on the notion that all phenomena are caused by mental imprints[1981] and lack an own-being. Zhönu Pal explains that a dam is not needed for the water of a fata morgana, and likewise, once you see into the essential nature of mind, not the slightest endeavor to establish a view is needed to repel appearances. Therefore, you realize that all appearances in the form of entities are this very true nature of mind *(sems nyid),* which lacks an own-being. Realizing, as a consequence of this, that appearances and dharmatā are of one taste, you do not abandon or adopt anything. Still, manifold appearances arise due to mental imprints. It is interesting that Zhönu Pal refers here to the *Mahāyānābhidharmasūtra* ("The beginningless sphere (i.e., buddha element) is the basis of all phenomena"),[1982] which reflects his particular understanding of buddha nature as possessing mental imprints in the same way as the basic consciousness. Since you thus realize that mind and appearances are of one taste, such a meditation is called the *yoga of one taste.* In order to induce the experience of one taste, Zhang Tsalpa Tsöndrü's description of the third mahāmudrā yoga stresses the point that everything arises from your own mind:

> When the yoga of one taste has arisen, you realize the defining characteristics of your own mind. You realize that from your own mind, which is the dharmakāya and free from mental fabrication, manifold saṁsāra and nirvāṇa arise. The entire multiplicity [including] thoughts and the nonconceptual, appearances and nonappearance, abiding and not, being empty and not, has, in terms of luminosity and dharmakāya, one taste. Therefore,

> you see the appearance of the great dharmakāya but not the conceptual, which is not luminosity. The realization of the sameness of taste in this way, [that is,] the moment of capturing it with the mental faculty *(yid)*, is the meditative equipoise of the third yoga. (DRSM, 62.3–7)

Since phenomena caused by mental imprints include inner ones as well, this third mahāmudrā yoga is indeed similar to the third *prayoga* in the *Dharmadharmatāvibhāga*, which proceeds from the nonexistence of a perceived object to the nonapprehension of a perceiving subject.

In the third stage of the *Dharmadharmatāvibhāga* even mind-only is no longer apprehended. It is therein explained as no longer apprehending even a perceiving subject, since without a perceived object such a subject simply does not make sense. That everything, inside and outside, is no longer apprehended amounts for Zhönu Pal to the same thing as realizing that both lack an own-being. In other words, both are free from mental fabrication, and it is in this sense that everything is of one taste. In his *Dharmadharmatāvibhāga* commentary, Zhönu Pal says about the third yoga:

> The realization that outside appearances and the inner mind are free from mental fabrications and of one taste (i.e., of the same nature) is the *prayoga* of the nonapprehension of apprehension (that is, the apprehension of mind-only is not apprehended). (DRSM, 465.15)

It should be noted that in this explanation of the third *prayoga*, outer appearances are not completely negated either.

The Fourth Mahāmudrā Yoga of Nonmeditation

The fourth dharma in the passage following LAS II.137 is the determination to realize the noble wisdom within yourself. It corresponds to the eighth bodhisattva level, on which you realize the mind, the mental faculty, the mental consciousness, the five dharmas, the three natures, and the two types of selflessness. In addition, a mental body is attained. Zhönu Pal explains that on this advanced level the yogin thoroughly understands by himself, and this is called *nonmeditation*, for what is called *meditation* is the vigor of the wish to meditate, and this vigor does not exist from this level on. Given this advanced stage, it is reasonable to compare the fourth dharma of the *Laṅkāvatārasūtra* to the corresponding mahāmudrā yoga of nonmeditation:

> When the yoga of nonmeditation has arisen, the yogin does not need to meditate, the nature of awareness [now] being free of [the need for any] support. There is no meditator; he has disappeared. It is said that the Buddha with his three kāyas and five types of wisdom has become fully complete in you. Now you [realize your] primordial knowledge, that this [Buddha] is you. This is the accomplishment of mahāmudrā. (DRSM, 62.9–11)

The fourth stage of the *Dharmadharmatāvibhāga* reflects the common Yogācāra practice of referring to the absence of duality as something positive as well. Thus, the nonapprehension of a perceived object and perceiving subject leads to the apprehension of nonduality. In the *Laṅkāvatārasūtra* (X.257) it is taken to be wisdom seeing the most excellent, in the *Mahāyānasūtrālaṁkāra* as the abiding in dharmadhātu. Since Zhönu Pal does not want to see in the absence of duality an affirming negation, he explains that on the level of this *prayoga* you simply perceive again in a special way that object and subject do not exist as two, and this is called the yoga of nonmeditation. In his *Dharmadharmatāvibhāga* commentary, he says about the fourth yoga:

> Perceiving again in a special way that the perceived object and the perceiving subject do not exist as two, you do not meditate, and this is called *nonmeditation,* the fourth [mahāmudrā] yoga. (DRSM, 465.16)

The Four Mahāmudrā Yogas and the Ratnagotravibhāga

The four yogas cannot be read directly into the *Ratnagotravibhāga.* But since the dharmatā portion of the *Dharmadharmatāvibhāga* is considered to be a commentary on the second chapter of the *Ratnagotravibhāga,* this does not really make a difference to Zhönu Pal. Moreover, Tibetan tradition has it that the *Dharmadharmatāvibhāga* was rediscovered together with the *Ratnagotravibhāga* by Maitrīpa. Thus there is not only a close connection between these two works but also a common link to the Indian mahāsiddha who taught the mahāmudrā pith instructions being discussed here. Indeed, Zhönu Pal finds passages in the *Ratnagotravibhāga* itself that back up the teaching of the four yogas.

Having explained the nonconceptual nature of awareness-emptiness with the aid of pith instructions in the introduction of his *Ratnagotravibhāga* commentary, Zhönu Pal goes on to maintain that the first two *padas* of RGV I.13 teach the first two mahāmudrā yogas, i.e., the yoga of one-pointedness and the yoga of freedom from mental fabrications. He repeats this assertion in his commentary on the corresponding passage in the *Ratnagotravibhāgavyākhyā*.[1983] The stanza introduces the third vajra point, the Jewel of the Saṅgha:

> I bow before those who see that—in view of the natural luminosity of their mind—defilements lack an own-being, (I.13a)
> And, as a consequence of that, have completely realized the extreme limit of selflessness of all sentient beings and the world as quiescent, (I.13b)
> Who see that buddhahood is all-pervading, whose intellect is unobstructed, (I.13c)
> And whose vision of wisdom embraces the purity and infinitude of sentient beings. (I.13d)[1984]

For Zhönu Pal, the first line teaches the yoga of one-pointedness and the second line the yoga of freedom from mental fabrication. The following stanza is an explanation of the preceding one:

> Because of the purity of their vision [attained] through an inner wisdom embracing both the quality and the extent [of the nature of mind],
> The assembly of the wise ones on the irreversible [level] possesses unsurpassable qualities.[1985] (RGV I.14)

Thus the first half of RGV I.13 teaches the wisdom that embraces the quality, while the second half elucidates the wisdom that embraces the extent of the true nature of mind. In other words, Zhönu Pal identifies the inner wisdom that reveals the quality of the nature of mind with the first two mahāmudrā yogas. It is explained by the following stanza and its *vyākhyā*:

> [The wisdom that embraces] the quality results from [the] realization [of the wise ones] that the world is quiescent in its true nature, and this [realization] results from the fact that [their mind] is naturally pure, and that they see that all defilements have been removed [from the true nature of mind] throughout beginningless time.[1986] (RGV I.15)

The corresponding portion of the *vyākhyā* is:

> In this regard, you should know that [the wisdom that embraces] the quality results from realizing the extreme limit of selflessness of the entire world, which is called *persons and phenomena.*[1987]

For Zhönu Pal, the second part of this sentence, starting with "results from...," teaches the yoga of freedom from mental fabrication; and the sentence that follows in the *vyākhyā*, the yoga of one-pointedness:

> In short, the realization that persons and phenomena are not destroyed because it has always been their nature to be quiescent arises from two causes: that they see the natural luminosity of mind and that the mind's defilements have been removed and stopped [in the true nature of mind] throughout beginningless time.[1988]

The remaining portion of the *vyākhyā* goes into greater detail:

> Here, the natural luminosity of mind and its [simultaneous] defilement—it is very difficult to realize that these two [properties coexist] in the immaculate element, for [it is a common Buddhist opinion that] a virtuous and nonvirtuous mind [always] occur [only] one at a time, given that [the one cannot] unite with the other (lit., "second"). Therefore it is said [in the *Śrīmālādevīsūtra*]: "Illustrious one, momentary is the virtuous mind; it is not impaired by defilements. Momentary, too, is the nonvirtuous mind; this mind is not impaired by defilements [either]. Illustrious one, the defilements do not touch this mind, nor does the mind [touch] the defilements. How is it possible, then, illustrious one, that the mind, which has the property of not being touched, is defiled by darkness? Illustrious one, defilements exist. The defiled mind exists. It is in such a way, illustrious one, that defilements of a naturally pure mind are difficult to understand."[1989]

Here the momentariness of the mind is its true nature, which is natural luminosity. In other words, the true nature of both the virtuous and nonvirtuous mind is natural luminosity.[1990] Thus the yoga of one-pointedness consists in seeing the natural luminosity of the immaculate element that contains defilements, even though it is not defiled by nature, just as—to use one of Zhönu Pal's examples—iron can be hot even though heat is not the natural property of iron.

Both mahāmudrā yogas result in the vision of the wisdom of equality, which sees that the entire world is empty of a self of persons and phenomena. The question, though, is how you attain this vision of selflessness. It is possible to refute the self of a phenomenon through reasoning followed by a meditation on its selflessness. But in Zhönu Pal's opinion it is much better to follow the *Kāśyapaparivartasūtra* and destroy the view of a self through nonconceptual mind, and this is what practitioners of mahāmudrā do.[1991] Zhönu Pal explains:

> The followers of mahāmudrā uphold the tradition [of destroying the view of a self through nonconceptual mind]. When the thought of viewing a self has arisen, the very same mind that has attained the yoga of one-pointedness before merely gazes at that thought of viewing a self. This occurs without the arising of a thought afterward—one that gives up that thought [of a self] and analyzes it by reasoning.[1992] Nevertheless, for those who are not devoted to this tradition and also lack the mental strength, the cultivation of selflessness on the basis of analytical inferences is a good path. (DRSM, 144.18–22)

The dominant role of direct valid cognitions in the mahāmudrā approach is further elucidated in the following passage, a little further down in the same section, on the lack of a self in persons:

> As for the remedy that prevents such a view of the transitory collection [as a real *I* and *mine*] from arising [again] later, valid cognitions are what is definitely needed, for it is said in the *Pramāṇa]vārttika* [IV.99cd]: "Whoever has valid cognitions invalidates the other [who is without such cognitions]." In this regard, the followers of mahāmudrā operate strictly with direct valid cognitions while others operate with inferential valid cognitions. (DRSM, 149.17–20)

Again, with regard to the meditation on the selflessness of phenomena, two different approaches are distinguished in accord with the different capacities of practitioners:

> The first is to generate insight *(prajñā)*, [that] of realizing the lack of an own-being—which arises from a valid cognition as a remedy for the [wrong] notion that outer and inner phenomena

> possess an own-being. The second is to see that the root of the threefold world, [that is,] the clinging to characteristic signs and the notion that entities have an own-being, has arisen merely from appearances of the mind, and then to meditate on pure appearances with the mahāmudrā yoga of self-realization. As a result of this, obstinate clinging to all knowable objects as entities does not occur. [This is achieved] by eliminating the effect, [which is achieved] by reversing the cause. In this connection, it is said many times in the *Laṅkāvatārasūtra* that the mental appearances [that are] your own mindstream are pure. As for the stages of meditation, they are the five stages explained before.[1993] (DRSM, 166.14–19)

The key to this nonconceptual mahāmudrā approach is a particular understanding of nonconceptual wisdom in the *Dharmadharmatāvibhāga*, namely Maitrīpa's and Sahajavajra's explanation of it. In his commentary on the second vajra point, Zhönu Pal explains the path in terms of nonconceptual wisdom by first quoting its five negative defining characteristics from the *Dharmadharmatāvibhāgavṛtti*. According to this, nonconceptual wisdom means (1) not only ceasing to direct your attention to concepts, since otherwise fools and small children would also possess nonconceptual wisdom. (2) It means not simply going beyond concepts, unless you include the second *dhyāna* here as well. (3) Nor is it only the nature of quiescence, since this state is also attained during sleep or drunkenness. (4) Nor is it the actual nonconceptual itself; otherwise visible objects such as stones would possess nonconceptual wisdom. (5) Finally, it is not the act of imagining the nonconceptual either, for imagination is again a concept.[1994] Zhönu Pal then comments:

> With regard to the meaning [of these five negative defining characteristics] here, they have been determined as [being] concepts that possess words and meanings, for nonconceptual wisdom must refer to a direct [cognition] free from such concepts. Its negative [component], "nonconceptual," is a remedy, the remedy for the four types of clinging to characteristic signs. These are the four characteristic signs of [what is] opposite [to liberation (for example, attachment)]; of the remedy; of suchness; and [of] the property of realization. The underlying thrust [of this teaching] is that the obstinate clinging to these four characteristic signs [yields] "concepts"; and being a remedy for this, [wisdom] is "nonconceptual." (DRSM, 114.4–8)

> As to what has been taught in the *Dharmadharmatāvibhāga* along these lines, the meaning of entering the nonconceptual is established. There are obviously two traditions[, however,] of fathoming the meaning of this sūtra:[1995] Kamalaśīla maintains that the [interpretive] imaginations that must be given up can only be given up on the strength of the insight of thorough investigation. [On the other hand,] it is maintained in the commentary on Maitrīpa's *Tattvadaśaka* that they are given up on the strength not of thorough investigation, but of the meditative stabilization [during] which [you experience] reality exactly as it is.[1996] [To be in] this meditation [is] to know the intrinsic nature of [even] what must be given up as luminosity. Here, it is reasonable to follow Maitrīpa, who [re]discovered this treatise. (DRSM, 114.8–12)

In this context, Zhönu Pal explains that according to the *Vairocanābhisambodhitantra* nonconceptual wisdom is present already well below the first bodhisattva level:

> There are two different types of nonconceptual: the paths of seeing and meditation. The path of seeing is well known under that name, given that you directly see the true nature that was not seen before, but nevertheless, based on the *Vairocanābhisambodhitantra*, there is [already] a direct seeing of the true nature when on the level [called] *engagement based on conviction.* Therefore, the consciousness *(shes pa)* that sees the true nature on the first level refers to what has arisen as the direct [cognition] of self-realization. With regard to the continuous cultivation of this seeing, there is also a consciousness that is not direct, but here, concerning what is to be taken as the defining basis of the truth of the path, you should refer to direct [cognition] only. (DRSM, 114.12–17)

The abandoning of the four characteristic signs is also discussed in Zhönu Pal's explanation of the *Dharmadharmatāvibhāga* at the beginning of the second chapter of his *Ratnagotravibhāga* commentary. After a long quote from Sahajavajra's *Tattvadaśakaṭīkā* on the seventh stanza, which teaches that the world is empty of duality and that the vain intellectual approach to emptiness is itself nothing other than luminosity, Zhönu Pal addresses the possible objection brought forth by Sahajavajra that Maitrīpa postulates characteristic signs in the guise of such concepts as nondual bodhicitta (the characteristic sign of reality or suchness), *yathābhūtasamādhi* (the characteristic sign of the remedy[1997]), and realization (the characteristic sign of the fruit), whereas according to the *Nirvikalpapraveśadhāraṇī* all characteristic signs must be abandoned on the strength of not becoming mentally engaged. After presenting Kamalaśīla's reply, which he considers inadequate for adepts with sharp faculties, he presents his own tradition, in line with Maitrīpa's *Tattvadaśaka:*

> If an [inferential] valid cognition did not arise, the teaching that [characteristic signs] must be abandoned would be fruitless, because there would be no other means of abandoning the four characteristic signs. Later on, having familiarized yourself [with this cognition] in meditation, you abandon even the characteristic signs related to what must be accomplished and so forth. Thus it has been said. Since inferences are a remedy for characteristic signs, they are said to be "without characteristic signs." This also [follows], among other things, from the yoga of abandonment. If you take [such inferential] knowledge without characteristic signs as the beginning [of meditation], how does this contradict the sūtra? ...Even though this first reply reflects the position of Kamalaśīla, it is not meant for those with sharp faculties. As for my own tradition, even though you vainly adhere to the nonexistence of dualities such as knowledge and knowable objects, [the mental event that is this vain adhering] is not [really] different from luminosity. Thus, after becoming acquainted with [vain adhering] in the form of luminosity, you meditate [on it]. Since you meditate on the fact that even thoughts of what must be accomplished and what accomplishes [it] are luminosity, you know that the intrinsic nature of [their] corresponding appearances is luminosity, and [so automatically] abandon characteristic signs. This is the tradition for those with sharp faculties. (DRSM, 464.7–15)

Contrary to Kamalaśīla, Maitrīpa's tradition employs direct perceptions of the luminous nature of all characteristic signs, as a result of which the characteristic signs simply disappear, or rather appear as what they really are—luminosity. Sahajavajra's *Tattvadaśakaṭīkā* is again quoted at length when Zhönu Pal explains the superiority of meditation in the third dharmacakra. While analysis is said to play an important role for Kamalaśīla, you should start in on meditation without an analytical mind right from the beginning after receiving *pāramitā*-based mahāmudrā instruction. Based on the lama's special instruction, you investigate the nature of your mind by directly observing it. Zhönu Pal compares the momentum of recalling the three modes of proof and the disputant who sees what has to be established on the analytical path to your conviction and the lama's realization of emptiness on the path of direct perception. To be sure, for Zhönu Pal it is better not to precede a direct cognition of emptiness with inferential reasoning.[1998]

Zhönu Pal points out that such a nonanalytical approach to reality is supported by the *Ratnagotravibhāgavyākhyā*. Indeed in the introduction to the crucial paragraph on the defining characteristics of buddha nature (RGV I.156–58 [J I.153–55]), the statement that buddha nature exists always and everywhere without a difference is based on the principle of true nature *(dharmatāyukti)*. This true nature is said to be reliance and principle at the same time:

> Everywhere it is precisely the true nature of phenomena that is what is relied upon:[1999] the principle underlying an accurate realization of the mind [and] a correct knowledge of it. The true nature of phenomena is inconceivable and unthinkable; it must be rather believed in.[2000]

For Zhönu Pal, this means that the nonconceptualizing mind is generated by respectful faith in, and devotion to, the lama. This is the only way for a beginner to directly realize with certainty the mind's quality of nonorigination and luminosity.[2001]

A good explanation of how you begin the nonanalytical approach to emptiness or natural luminosity is found in the commentary on the second vajra point, where Zhönu Pal explains the first mahāmudrā yoga of one-pointedness:

> The practitioners of the mahāmudrā pith instructions deriving from Maitrīpa say that when you abide in that which is not anything, being free from [unnecessary] thinking about the past, present, and future, a thought that distracts you from this may arise. In this case, you gaze at it without getting agitated about what exactly has arisen. This very gazing is a thorough searching of how [the mind operates] with regard to that thought. Thus it is said. Even though all other thoughts become completely pacified in this way, you must [continue to] meditate. The mind

> meditates and a subtle thought of abiding arises. When you gaze [with] naked [awareness] also at this, this subtle thought too ceases, and a mind arises that is like space in being free from a middle and extremes. This is called the yoga of one-pointedness. [DRSM, 137.23–138.2]
>
> Also Nāgārjuna has said [in his *Bodhicittavivaraṇa*, stanza 51]: "The defining characteristics of abiding in [a state of] mind without apprehension are those of space. I assert that whoever meditates on space meditates on emptiness." Having realized that the forms of the objects of all thoughts wandering about as the objects of the external [world] are false, the subject too melts into the sphere of this very same mind, which is like space. When you see this, [neither] the [false] imagining, which is the cause of the defilements, [nor] the focus of this [false] imagining is seen as something at all permanent, joyful, or the like. Such a yoga must be practiced once it is seen in this way. [DRSM, 138.2–6]

A little further down, after quoting *Laṅkāvatārasūtra* X.256ab and *Mahāyānasūtrālaṁkāra* XIV.23–27 in support, Zhönu Pal shows that his mahāmudrā approach can be brought into line with Haribhadra but not Kamalaśīla:

> The master Haribhadra maintains that through meditation on the Madhyamaka view that all phenomena completely lack an own-being, the three clear appearances—small, middle, and large—of being without a perceived object and the one clear appearance of being without a perceiving subject arise when on [the path] of penetration, while the clear appearance of realizing the lack of own-being arises on the first level. The followers of mahāmudrā claim that the clear appearances of the four [levels of the path of] preparation arise gradually from a single direct cultivation of abiding in a state of not directing your mind on anything. In this regard the great scholar Kamalaśīla has said: "When the form of the perceiving subject and even nondual knowledge are destroyed, this [level] is called the supreme quality on [the path of] partial concordance with penetration (i.e., its fourth level)." I think that the explicit teaching to meditate on the stage of the supreme quality, [namely,] that nondual knowledge is not true, does not exactly accord with Haribhadra. (DRSM, 138.21–139.2)

At the end of his explanation of the stanza RGV I.31, in which the own-being of buddha nature is said to resemble the qualities of a wish-fulfilling jewel, the sky, and water, Zhönu Pal quotes Dampa Sangyé, who teaches the four mahāmudrā yogas based on this stanza:

> In view of its (i.e., the buddha element's) nature of power, unchangingness, and adhesiveness,
> It bears resemblance, in these, to the qualities of a wish-fulfilling jewel, the sky, and water.[2002] (RGV I.31)

Dampa Sangyé maintains the following:

> Through the yoga of one-pointedness you settle [your] mind [in such a way that it is] not moved by thoughts, like [unstirred] water [becoming] clear. By doing so, you realize space-like suchness that is free from mental fabrication. With this as the base, you [practice] the yoga of one taste, and in doing so, you may be [again] focused on the outside with the eyes and the other [senses], but you realize the suchness of pure aspects. When the jewel-like, effortless yoga of nonmeditation has arisen, compassion arises without effort for the master of meditation. This is therefore the state of a great bodhisattva hero, who works liberally for the sake of others. (DRSM, 272.6–10)

Zhönu Pal elucidates the first three of the four yogas once more in connection with his presentation of the three natures of the buddha element, namely those associated with its being the dharmakāya, suchness, and the buddha potential (RGV I.147–52 [J I.144–52]). These three aspects are illustrated by the nine examples from the *Tathāgatagarbhasūtra*. The first three examples illustrate the dharmakāya, the fourth suchness, and the remaining five the buddha potential. In meditation practice, however, this threefold classification does not matter for Zhönu Pal:

> Even though the [buddha] element was explained in terms of separate [aspects] in line with the distinction among its three natures, in [meditation] practice these may be taken to be identical. (DRSM, 430.25–26)

Nevertheless, Zhönu Pal links the three mahāmudrā yogas with these three aspects, and with the three particular features of the buddha qualities that are gradually realized in the three yogas. The three particular features are explained in a passage from the *Śrīmālādevīsūtra* quoted in the *vyākhyā* on I.152–55 (J I.149–52):

> Therefore, illustrious one, buddha nature is the basis, foundation, and support of the unconditioned [buddha] qualities, which are connected [with it], inseparable [from it], and which [can]not be recognized as being disconnected [from it].[2003]

Zhönu Pal explains the particular feature of being connected with the gloss "in the sense of having the same identity *(bdag nyid gcig);*" inseparable means that "they are not different in essence"; and the last feature implies that "even though a long period of time has passed nobody knows of a method to separate them."[2004] The following explanation of the three yogas is a commentary on a subsequent passage of the *vyākhyā* that introduces a section dealing with the defining characteristics of buddha nature:[2005]

> The yogins of mahāmudrā gradually come to see the three particular features [of the buddha qualities]. Here, through the yoga of great one-pointedness, you see the vastness [of buddha nature],[2006] seeing as you do your own mind to be without extremes and a middle, just like space. When you realize as it indeed is, the [extreme] limit of the selflessness of all phenomena through the yoga of freedom from mental fabrication, [you see that] nothing becomes empty later that was not [already] empty before. Since you realize that the nature of the fundamental state has ever been like this, and that nothing deviates from this fundamental state even when you become a buddha later, you see [buddha nature] as not being separate [from] suchness. Because you realize through the yoga of one taste that appearances and [their] empty [nature] are of one taste, you know that the mind of all sentient beings is like your own mind. Since you know that the mind of sentient beings is very similar to the pure dharmakāya of the buddhas, you see [buddha nature] as the nature of a definite potential. (DRSM, 431.6–13)

In the following, Zhönu Pal stresses that in the *Ratnagotravibhāga* the approach to reality or the buddha element is based on the principle of true nature *(dharmatāyukti),* which means that reality is simply of a certain nature. It is inconceivable and cannot be realized through an ordinary direct cognition obtained on the basis of familiarity with the content of inferences:

> Well then, you may ask whether such a seeing is one that has become a direct [cognition] from first realizing [buddha nature] in an inferential valid cognition based on the principle of proving on the basis of feasibility, and [then] becoming continuously used to it (i.e., the content of the inferential cognition); or whether it is a seeing that [occurs] for no major reason, [that is,] adventitiously? It is neither a seeing based on [the principle of] proving on the basis of feasibility nor a seeing without reason. It is a seeing based on the principle of true nature *(dharmatāyukti)*. (DRSM, 431.13–16)

The yoga of nonmeditation is explained a little further down:

> You realize that the mind has never arisen, as time itself is free from mental fabrication. In consideration, however, that [mind] appears as if the mind to be meditated upon and the meditating mind were different, the conventional expression "nothing to meditate upon" (or *nonmeditation*) is used when you have actualized [the truth] that the two forms of an object and a subject do not exist, in the same way as a lamp does not illuminate itself. This [level] of nonmeditation, moreover, has states that are small, middle, and large according to differences in gross, average, or subtle [degrees of] abandoning what must be given up. As for Maitrīpa, who said that there are no stages, he did not think that there are no differentiations according to small and average; he thought that everything has one single taste—the taste of emptiness. (DRSM, 433.7–12)

Zhönu Pal's Justification of a Sudden Mahāmudrā Path

In the description of the four mahāmudrā yogas above, Zhönu Pal quotes Götsangpa because he relates them with the more common system of the five paths and ten bodhisattva levels. The yoga of one-pointedness corresponds to the path of accumulation and preparation, the yoga of freedom from mental fabrications to the path of seeing and the first bodhisattva level, the yoga of one taste to the subsequent impure bodhisattva levels up to the seventh, and the yoga of nonmeditation to the last three pure levels.

On the other hand, the stance that mahāmudrā is attained in one go is also endorsed: Zhönu Pal quotes a pertinent passage from Zhang's *Phyag rgya chen po lam zab mthar thug*[2007] to the effect that the true nature of phenomena *(dharmatā)* is directly realized on the path of seeing and that the ensuing bodhisattva levels cannot be distinguished so as to correspond to various parts of the dharmatā, for the dharmatā is indivisible. As Zhang says, once the sun has risen, nobody will stand up and say it is not the sun because it cannot melt ice immediately. To support this point, Zhönu Pal refers to Haribhadra, who says that nothing new is actualized on the path of meditation that has not already been seen on the path of seeing.[2008] As further support, Zhönu Pal quotes Candrakīrti's *Madhyamakāvatārabhāṣya*, which compares advancement on the bodhisattva levels to the trail of a bird in the sky, which cannot be expressed or seen even by the wise.[2009]

Zhönu Pal goes one step further and contends that the levels of the vehicle of defining characteristics are not real levels but only "preliminary levels," that is, levels on the path of preparation. Under this assumption, it is not only the real bodhisattva levels of the paths of seeing and meditation that are like the trail of a bird in the sky but also the preliminary ones. To support his argumentation, Zhönu Pal draws our attention to a presentation of the ten *pāramitās* on the level of engagement based on conviction in the *Vairocanābhisambodhitantra*.[2010] According to the *Vairocanābhisambodhitantrapiṇḍārtha*, these correspond to the preliminary bodhisattva levels and so are below the actual path of seeing or the first true bodhisattva level.[2011] Zhönu Pal further tries to show that the four yogas of mahāmudrā are in accordance with the four states of penetration as explained in the *Abhisamayālaṁkāra*,[2012] and claims that from the eighth [preliminary] level onward, all four yogas are completed in one instant.[2013] Finally, Zhönu Pal holds that it is even possible to include the path of accumulation under "engagement based on conviction."

In order to establish that the levels and paths of the vehicle of defining characteristics belong in reality to the path of preparation, it is necessary to show that the arhats enter the bodhisattva path below the actual path of seeing. Zhönu Pal explains that there are different opinions about the level on which arhats join the Mahāyāna:

> ...before, in my own tradition, this used to be explained by adducing the discourses *(lung)* of Buddhaguhya.[2014] But as to this "entering on the eighth level"—if an arhat of the Śrāvaka[yāna]

> entered the Mahāyāna, [and] if you maintained that his conversion to the Mahāyāna and the arising of the wisdom of the eighth level were simultaneous, and if you achieved in three lifetimes of an arhat what has to be accomplished on the basis of your conduct [over] many incalculable eons from the first to the seventh level, then you would fall prey to error, [namely,] the unacceptable consequence that arhats have sharper faculties then bodhisattvas, and this would be completely against reason. (DRSM, 500.7–11)

The entering into the Mahāyāna on the eighth level has to be understood rather in the following way:

> In the same way as beginner bodhisattvas are said to enter [the state of] buddhahood on account of having generated a mind that wishes to enter buddhahood, some arhats who generate the wish to attain the eighth level of the Mahāyāna by focusing [on it], and who are said to learn as much as they can [to attain it], are called "the ones who enter the eighth level." In this case I do not see any contradiction. (DRSM, 500.12–14)

Thus, based on the *Vairocanābhisambodhitantra*, Zhönu Pal relegates the five paths and ten levels commonly explained in Mahāyāna and the four yogas of mahāmudrā to a level called *engagement based on conviction*, which in reality corresponds to the paths of accumulation and preparation. If this is accepted, you can maintain that even a beginner can have a direct experience of the true nature of his mind, and this is what is referred to as attaining mahāmudrā in one go.

A combination of gradual and spontaneous aspects of the path of purification can be found in a prose passage following stanza II.127 in the *Laṅkāvatārasūtra* (LAS 55.3–56.6),[2015] which illustrates the gradual aspects with examples such as the growing of grass or the mastery of skills, and the spontaneous with reflections in a mirror and the brilliance of the sun and the moon. Basing himself on this, Zhönu Pal explains that the stains are gradually purified up to the seventh bodhisattva level, while after that the objects of knowledge appear instantaneously, as in a mirror.

From what has been said above, it follows that Zhönu Pal interprets the seventh bodhisattva level of the *Laṅkāvatārasūtra* as the *Vairocanābhisambodhitantra* does, namely as a preliminary one. It follows further that the gradual process of purification of stains within the three dharmacakras goes only up to the preliminary seventh level. Does this also mean, however, that the nonconceptual wisdom fully ripens after the preliminary seventh level,[2016] that is, that complete buddhahood is attained, instantaneously, already at that level? The example of the rising sun, used by Zhang to illustrate the attainment of mahāmudrā in one go, does not suggest an instantaneous attainment of complete buddhahood entirely; for even though nobody maintains that the newly risen sun is not the sun, the ice does not immediately melt.[2017]

In a discussion of a supposed tension between Haribhadra's statement that the entire dharmadhātu is seen on the first bodhisattva level on the one hand, and the *Dharmadhātustotra* on the other, according to which only a tiny part of the dharmakāya is seen even on the tenth level, Zhönu Pal says that Haribhadra takes the dharmadhātu as the selflessness of phenomena, as something that has the defining characteristics of a negation. Therefore, it makes sense to say that it is seen completely on the first level. But attaining the dharmakāya of a buddha is something else again, because for Zhönu Pal dharmadhātu is not just a different name for the dharmakāya. The difference is that on the first level you see only your own buddha nature directly, but not that of others.[2018] Attaining mahāmudrā thus means for Zhönu Pal that the direct vision of emptiness on the first level is not different from seeing it on the tenth level. But the extent of perceived reality or buddha nature necessarily increases, so that the buddha nature of other beings are seen as well, in the same way as Zhang's newly risen sun still gets stronger and melts the ice.

We can now better appreciate Zhönu Pal's great effort to interpret the *Ratnagotravibhāga* as implying that there is a difference between the three aspects of the buddha element, namely the dharmakāya, suchness, and the buddha potential, and that accordingly, buddha qualities exist in ordinary beings only in a subtle form and must naturally mature. During meditation practice, however, these three aspects can be taken to be identical, according to Zhönu Pal.[2019] In other words, with regard to gazing at your true nature of mind in meditation,[2020] there is no difference on the various bodhisattva levels; still, the buddha qualities mature gradually on these levels,[2021] in the same way as Zhang's sun gradually gains strength. For Zhönu Pal, such a view is in perfect harmony with scholars such as Haribhadra or Candrakīrti, and thus with mainstream Indian Mahāyāna.[2022]

To be sure, an instantaneous experience of mahāmudrā, which occurs once the mind first becomes free from mental fabrication on the level of engagement based on conviction, does not entail that the buddha qualities have already matured on this early level. Referring to Zhang Tsalpa

Tsöndrü and Drigung Jigten Sumgön, Zhönu Pal argues that it would follow therefore that the sun has not risen because its qualities (such as melting ice) are not yet in evidence during the first hours of the day.[2023] As a further support, Zhönu Pal adduces the *Daśabhūmikasūtra* according to which you attain 112 qualities only in the life after the one in which you have reached the first level.[2024] It is only against this background that we can fully understand the importance of maintaining that the buddha qualities have to grow naturally. By taking such an approach, Zhönu Pal protects his understanding of mahāmudrā from being classified as "Chinese Buddhism."

Zhönu Pal does not seek open controversy over his mahāmudrā interpretation of buddha nature and avoids the controversial mahāmudrā term *white panacea (dkar po chig thub)*, which stands for the self-sufficient means of directly realizing your natural mind. He is also not much concerned with directly justifying his mahāmudrā explanations, the mere possibility of interpreting the *Ratnagotravibhāga* in line with mahāmudrā being justification enough for him. Only once does he indirectly address the criticism that his mahāmudrā is "Chinese Buddhism."[2025]

This charge of being "Chinese Buddhism" is addressed in the commentary on RGV I.15, in which the wisdom of "quality" *(yathāvadbhāvikatā)*, that is, the realization of natural luminosity and the two types of selflessness, is understood in terms of the first two mahāmudrā yogas. Zhönu Pal leads into the topic "selflessness of phenomena" with a quote from Śāntideva's *Bodhicaryāvatāra*, stanza IX.55:

> The remedy for the darkness of the hindrances of defilements and the knowable is emptiness. Why does not [the yogin] who wishes [to obtain] omniscience quickly meditate on it?[2026] (DRSM, 165.21–22)

...and skillfully directs the matter of "Chinese Buddhism" away from his mahāmudrā tradition toward Śāntideva by asking:

> Well then, is the explanation of the Chinese monk called Mahāyāna not appropriate? The Chinese monk said, "Everything that must be given up is only eliminated by meditating on emptiness, and since doing so confers the ability to realize everything knowable, the teachings relating to skillful means—such as compassion, the generation of an enlightened attitude, the [first] five *pāramitās*, and the four [means of] conversion—are only for the

> sake of guiding foolish low-class [practitioners], but they are not for those with sharp faculties." (DRSM, 165.22–25)

Zhönu Pal comes to the aid of Śāntideva with three arguments:

> This is not the case. The first reply is [as follows]: Master Nāgārjuna says [in his *Bodhicittavivaraṇa*, stanza 73]: "When yogins have thus meditated on emptiness, [their] mind will, beyond all doubt, rejoice in benefiting others."[2027] Thus meditation on emptiness gives rise to compassion, and through it you become engaged in applying skillful means. (DRSM, 165.25–166.1)
>
> The second reply: It is not only that by meditating on emptiness you finally achieve omniscience; along the way, you come to know many things not known before by becoming free from gross hindrances. Therefore Śāntideva says [in his *Bodhicaryāvatāra* VIII.94ab]: "I must remove the suffering of others, because it is suffering like my own suffering."[2028] From this reasoning, therefore, an inferential valid cognition arises involving the realization that the suffering of others must be removed, and it is [further] taught that you become active for the sake of others. When many knowable objects appear as a result of meditation, you realize by means of valid cognition that it is inappropriate not to work for the sake of others. (DRSM, 166.1–6)
>
> The third reply: Also, the great compassion of a tathāgata is included in the teaching of the last dharmacakra that sentient beings are naturally endowed with the qualities of a buddha. As both insight and compassion have always been connected in terms of their nature, you [automatically] apply abundant skillful means by merely realizing emptiness and exhausting all hindrances—[even in the case of] those who [first] abandon neither the hindrances of not attending to the benefit of sentient beings nor the ignorance [of the need] to benefit the countless sentient beings, the abundant skillful means of benefiting others not having been taught [to them]. (DRSM, 166.6–10)

In other words, there is nothing wrong with the strong emphasis on "gazing at your own nature" in mahāmudrā practice, since it is nothing other than the direct perception of emptiness[2029] in mainstream Madhyamaka. According to the *Bodhicaryāvatāra* itself, the need for the first five *pāramitās* is in no way questioned by seeing meditation on emptiness as the remedy that removes all defilements.

The Fourth Zhamarpa Chödrag Yeshé expresses the following complaint in his commentary on the *Bodhicittavivaraṇa,* which he had composed on the basis of explanations by his teacher Zhönu Pal:

> Such a meditation (i.e., nonconceptual meditation on emptiness), which was praised by Ārya Nāgārjuna, was proclaimed by some [masters] during the earlier and later [diffusion of the Dharma] in Tibet as being the meditation of the Chinese Hva shang; still, here in this treatise (i.e., the *Bodhicittavivaraṇa*) it is taken as the tradition of the great bodhisattvas.[2030]

In order to support the stance that mahāmudrā is attained in one go, it is necessary to show that the qualities of the dharmakāya (at least in their subtle form) are already present in ordinary beings as the very nature of their adventitious defilements.[2031] For Zhönu Pal, the four qualities of the dharmakāya, namely the perfections of purity, self, bliss, and permanence, are a key to understanding this. They are explained in RGV I.35–36 as the fruit of four causes within buddha nature: conviction, insight, meditative stabilization, and compassion.

> The perfection of the qualities purity, self, bliss, and permanence are its fruit.
> [To attain this fruit] it acts with aversion to suffering and longing and praying for the attainment of peace. (RGV I.35)

What is taught here in the first half of the stanza?

> The fruit (i.e., the four qualities) of these [four causes] is, in short, constituted by the antidote to what has [again] become a fourfold mistaken [view], the opposite [of the four mistaken views concerning saṁsāra having been wrongly applied] to the dharmakāya.[2032] (RGV I.36)

Ordinary people usually think that the conditioned phenomena of worldly existence are pure, possessing a self, blissful, and permanent. These mistaken views are cured by the correct notions that such phenomena are impure, without a self, suffering, and impermanent. It would be wrong, however, to extend these predications to the dharmakāya. Generating the perfections of purity, self, bliss, and permanence is the way to correct such a mistake.

Zhönu Pal points out that this is not achieved by a contrary mode of apprehension but by cultivating the path that appears as bliss:

> You internalize that here, in the last dharmacakra, notions of impurity and the like are abandoned with the aid of the notions of purity and so forth. Therefore, when the entire world appears to the noble śrāvakas as suffering, [such a notion] is abandoned by cultivating its antidote, [that is,] the path that appears as bliss but not a path involving a contrary mode of apprehension. (DRSM, 290.10–13)

Liberation through the appearance of the path as bliss is compared to the liberation that comes from seeing emptiness. In order to remove wrong notions, which can be compared to the eye sickness of seeing falling hairs, it is the medicine of emptiness that must be relied on to cure ailing eyes, and not inferential valid cognitions. Such an application of emptiness is the practice of mahāmudrā:

> To abide in the sphere in which appearances [simply] occur as they are, without disturbing the mental faculty with thoughts, with something involving the cognitive modes of removing and negating or positing and establishing, is mahāmudrā yoga. [Another] name for it is emptiness, and here it is [like] eye medicine. Moreover, the teaching of the four notions of purity and the rest with regard to the dharmakāya relates to the path of mahāmudrā. Apart from this, they are not notions that fix on [any] characteristic sign. (DRSM, 290.19–23)
>
> If you ask how [this can be], in [RGV I. 140 (J I.137) it is said]: "Just like filth is repulsive [even for ordinary people], the active states [of defilements are repulsive] for those possessed by desire; [they are] like filth, for they are the cause of their indulging in [unpleasant objects of] desire."[2033] This has been said with regard to the path of apparent [truth]. Here, [in such a state,] when terrible imaginings of attachment have arisen, you are disturbed by them, and a mind turned away from them does not arise. When you rest within the very thought of attachment, then that disturbed mental faculty itself, the condition that gives rise to attachment, calms down.[2034] (DRSM, 290.23–26)

> Something like that is called meditation on purity; and it is not impurity. Nor is it to internalize the thought of blindly labeling it ultimate purity. (DRSM, 290.26–291.2)
>
> Likewise, when you abide in that same sphere, abiding as in the former continuous flow of mind, there is no high and low of dualistic appearances, and therefore you attach notionally [to the mind] the name *permanent.* (DRSM, 291.2–3)
>
> Likewise, when you abide in a single continuity, like space, after such an abiding mind (i.e., abiding within attachment) has become free from the clouds of mistaken appearances, the mind is said to have attained independence, and is notionally labeled as *self.* (DRSM, 291.3–5)
>
> When you abide within this same sphere [of attachment] after gaining the certainty that all mistaken appearances [result] from an object and subject, [that is, from] dualistic appearances, nondual wisdom, [that is,] thorough self-realization, arises. By virtue of it, all thoughts, such as the wish to abandon saṁsāra or attain nirvāṇa, are pacified, and the mind has no more thorns. You are free from all appearances of suffering, and this is called meditation on bliss. (DRSM, 291.5–8)

Thus, every samsaric state of mind can be the starting point of mahāmudrā, even the wildest forms of defilement can be experienced as the perfection of purity, bliss, and the like by simply abiding and relaxing within them and calming down. The qualities of buddha nature are not something other than or somewhere else than in defilements. This requires that both of them, namely the two truths, are not taken to be different with regard to their nature.[2035] Thus Zhönu Pal explains a little further down:

> As for the definitive meaning, attachment and so forth are ultimately of the nature *(rang bzhin)* of the dharmakāya. The noble śrāvakas make a mistake in clinging to attachment as something real.... (DRSM, 292.17–19)

This is also clear from the commentary on the two stanzas RGV I.157–58 (J I.154–55), which teach the defining characteristics of the two types of emptiness:

> A bodhisattva who is versed in the two modes of the particular features of emptiness, namely being empty of adventitious stains

> but not empty of qualities, is somebody in possession of the full meaning of emptiness. As for the mode of identity [and] difference—not [a form of] emptiness, [namely,] the interruption [of attachment to a desired object] as something different from, or outside of, the mind—you are distracted and very perplexed by a mind that is engaged in many forms. In terms of the view, [when holding] such views, [and] this view [in particular], you do not dwell in meditative equipoise [focused] on full meaning, nor do you even obtain deep insight. Since the calm abiding of one-pointedness is not obtained either, the mind is said to be distracted from emptiness in the states of both view and meditation. (DRSM, 444.9–14)
>
> If you know the emptiness explained here, you do not think that the interruption of attachment is emptiness. Nor do you think that attachment itself is emptiness. Because you do not see emptiness existing as something different from attachment either, you let [your mind] rest in that very attachment, just as it appears, without refuting or establishing [anything]. By doing so, you also come to see the natural luminosity [of attachment] through deep insight. Whatever thought arises becomes a friend of meditative stabilization and therefore becomes [the mahāmudrā yoga of] one-pointedness as well. Moreover, emptiness is here declared to be ultimate emptiness. It is the very buddha nature itself, declared to be the ultimate truth, that is, the truth of the noble ones. (DRSM, 444.14–19)

The assertion that ultimate emptiness (equated with buddha nature) and defilements, or nirvāṇa and saṁsāra, are in reality inseparable, and both your own mind, is one of the central tenets in mahāmudrā. It goes back to Saraha, who compares the two with two trunks growing from one seed.[2036]

Pairs of Paradoxes

By maintaining that the buddha element and the adventitious stains are identical in terms of their empty nature, Zhönu Pal protects himself against a too-ontological interpretation of the third dharmacakra's positive predications of the ultimate. According to his mahāmudrā tradition, such cataphatic statements, as Seyfort Ruegg and Schaeffer[2037] proposed calling them, are usually contrasted with or, more accurately, complemented by a negation. Such an *apophasis*, to use the Greek term for this kind of negation, ensures that cataphatic statements do not mislead you into thinking that the true nature of mind consists of independently existing entities. Since the true nature of mind is beyond the reach of language or logical forms of expression, it can be only tentatively expressed, by pairs of paradoxes. Thus, mahāmudrā descriptions of the ultimate consist of sheer endlessly creative play between cataphatic and apophatic terms. They are not a senseless repetition of paradoxes but pith instructions that directly point to your own true nature.

Cataphatic terms can be subsumed under *freedom from mental fabrications* and apophatic terms under *awareness*. The awareness has nothing to do with ordinary consciousness but rather is a synonym of the ultimate. For Zhönu Pal buddha nature is best described by a combination of both: "awareness that is free of mental fabrication." The first problem is that any statement about the ultimate harbors a paradox, in that it is necessarily an object of the intellect (being labeled as *buddha nature*, for example), as reflected in its being able to function as a grammatical substantive. Something that is termed *free from mental fabrications* is being mentally fabricated in the very process of calling it such. This paradox is only heightened by combining the predication *free from mental fabrication* with the predication *awareness*. Understood as a stream of moments, awareness is momentary and thus, strictly speaking, an apparent truth (and so, according to Buddhist terminology, a mental fabrication).[2038] The combination of two terms that are *prima facie* paradoxical not only points to the limitations of logical forms of expression but also works toward transcending the limited capacity of the intellect and realizing the paradoxical nature of the ultimate in a direct valid cognition. Such pairs of paradoxes go back to the *prajñāpāramitā* literature, where the cataphatic term *form* is combined with the apophatic term *empty*. The endless repetition of this paradox in different variants may be tiring for the reader bent on a purely intellectual approach, but the constant confrontation with the paradoxical nature of the ultimate during a traditional recitation is a skillful practice designed to make emptiness realizable.

The inconceivable nature of the relation between the two members of such paradoxical pairs is dealt with in the stanzas RGV I.23–25, which provides for each of the four objects of the omniscient—namely, suchness mingled with stains (buddha nature), stainless suchness (enlightenment), qualities, and activity—a reason why they are inconceivable.

> Suchness mingled with stains and then suchness apart from stains,
> The stainless buddha qualities and buddha activity,

Are the objects for those who see the ultimate [truth];
From them the sublime Three Jewels arise.[2039] (RGV I.23)

The potential of [these] Three Jewels
Is the object of those who see everything;
This fourfold [object] is inconceivable
For four reasons in sequence:[2040] (RGV I.24)

Because [suchness] is endowed with both purity and defilements;
Because [suchness] has [ever been] free from all defilements and [still] has been purified;
Because the properties [of a buddha] are inseparable;
And because [buddha activity] is without effort and thought.[2041] (RGV I.25)

The *vyākhyā* explains the four reasons in the following way:

1. The [first] point here is inconceivable, because suchness mingled with stains is simultaneously—at one and the same time—pure and defiled, being an object of experience not even for pratyekabuddhas, who are convinced of what the profound Dharma is like.[2042]
2. The [second] point here is inconceivable, because suchness, which is free from stains, is first defiled with stains and [only] later is pure.[2043]
3. The [third] point here is inconceivable, because stainless buddha qualities are found to be not different in terms of their inseparable true nature, before and later, even on the level of ordinary people, which is invariably defiled.[2044]
4. The [fourth] point here is inconceivable, because buddha activity unfolds in sentient beings simultaneously, everywhere, at all times, and without effort and thought in accordance with their mental disposition and [the capacity of the] disciples, and this without fault and in an appropriate way each time.[2045]

The first two points are inconceivable because suchness that has ever been naturally pure can be mingled with stains. Related to this paradox, of course, are the stainless buddha qualities, which are inseparable from suchness even on the level of ordinary beings. The unlimited activity that unfolds on the basis of these qualities just adds to the inconceivable nature of the buddha element, which in its purity possesses these qualities and is nevertheless the basis of saṁsāra.

Based on the explanation in stanzas RGV I.157–58 (J I.154–55) that it is the adventitious stains, not the qualities, that are separable, we might imagine that the buddha element is something essentially different from the stains. Even though the two can mix with one another and coexist, they do not interfere with each other, except that the stains prevent the manifestation of the primordial buddha nature with its inseparable qualities. This would be the Jonangpa zhentong view.

For Zhönu Pal, the buddha qualities and the stains are properties of exactly the same buddha element,[2046] and what is really inconceivable is that the true nature of mind can have such contradictory or paradoxical properties at the same time. Of particular interest is Zhönu Pal's concluding commentary on RGVV I.25, in which the first two reasons of why the stages of purification (buddha nature and enlightenment) are inconceivable are related with awakening *(sangs),* cleansing *(byang),* and freedom from mental fabrications, while the second two reasons—why the naturally present qualities and activity are inconceivable—illustrate blossoming *(rgyas),* accomplishment *(chub),* and awareness:

> The main subject discussed in this treatise is the enlightenment of the Buddha. In this regard, the first two reasons show the [Buddha's] awakening *(sangs)* and cleansing *(byang),* in that they show the stages of purification. The second two show the [Buddha's] blossoming and accomplishment *(chub),* in that they show the qualities and the activities associated with them. With regard to the basis, the first two reasons mainly show the mode of being free from mental fabrication; they show that [the element] has been ever empty of suffering and the origin [of suffering], [which are] the characteristic signs of what is adventitious. The second two reasons mainly show the element in its mode of abiding in the form of awareness; they show the qualities and their activities. [As to what results] from the element's freedom from mental fabrication [it is the three nirvāṇas], for based on whether [only] one side of it is realized or it is completely realized, it [can] become [any of] the nirvāṇas of the three vehicles. From its mode as awareness, the element develops into the phenomena of saṁsāra, given that the whole of saṁsāra arises from the basic consciousness, which is a reflection of this appearing mode [of awareness]. (ZhP 241.6–14)

That the same buddha element is able to turn into saṁsāra and nirvāṇa in its respective modes of awareness and freedom from mental fabrication pointedly illustrates the paradoxical nature of *awareness that is free from mental fabrication,* or to be more exact, "the element that is both awareness and freedom from mental fabrication." This can be sensed in the very terms for Buddha *(sangs rgyas)* and enlightenment *(byang chub)* in Tibetan. While the first syllables *sangs* and *byang* are apophatic, expressing the nonexistence or negation of defilements, the second syllables denote the blossoming of qualities and the accomplishment of the activity associated with them and are cataphatic in nature, that is to say, they assert something.

Mahāmudrā descriptions of the true nature of mind normally suggest that the true nature of mind is not really different from the mind of buddhas.[2047] Even Zhönu Pal, who otherwise carefully distinguishes the subtle qualities of ordinary beings from the blossomed qualities of buddhas, says that there is no difference in meditation practice.[2048] Enlightenment is thus, as awareness, the true nature of suffering.

Pairs of paradoxes can also be identified in the explanation of the four qualities of the dharmakāya. Awareness, whose reflection is the basic consciousness with all the mental imprints, can manifest saṁsāric states of mind, such as suffering.[2049] Since ordinary people cling to such states as something supposedly blissful, the first step is to negate such a wrong perception. Indeed the śrāvakas realize that suffering is not blissful. The true nature of suffering is, however, the dharmakāya's perfections of bliss, etc., but this is recognized neither by simply clinging to suffering as bliss nor by simply negating the notion that it is bliss. By resting your mind in suffering just as it is, you actualize the emptiness of the suffering, or you gain freedom from mental fabrication, transcend the level on which bliss and nonbliss form a paradoxical pair, and attain the perfection of bliss beyond bliss and nonbliss. The same holds true for the dharmakāya's perfections of self, purity, and permanence.[2050]

The crux that paradoxes boil down to is to serve the purpose of transcending the ordinary. Thus a simple predication is not enough to point out the true nature of mind. Even the most accurate terms, including *spontaneous presence, coemergent, magical display,* and *luminosity,* do not do this entirely, unless they are complemented by a corresponding apophatic formulation, such as *free from the extremes of thought and expression; without origination, abiding, and cessation; having no form, shape, or color;* or *not being established as anything.* Still, paradoxical pairs can only point to something beyond words.

8. Conclusion

ZHÖNU PAL, as his biography shows, commanded a wide range of knowledge. Not only did he enjoy a full-fledged Kadampa education at Chenyé, he also studied at nearly every monastic or religious center in Ü and Tsang. Zhönu Pal wrote his *Ratnagotravibhāga* commentary when he was eighty-one years old, and he must have considered the various views of his teachers in doing so. Our study confirms what Zhönu Pal claims in the colophon, namely that he combined the commentarial tradition of Loden Sherab with Gampopa's and Drigung Jigten Sumgön's mahāmudrā interpretation of the *Ratnagotravibhāga*. Zhönu Pal's close relation to the Pagmo Drupa rulers could be an explanation for this preference.

When the six positions described in part 1 of this work are compared, it can be said that Zhönu Pal's way of interpreting the *Ratnagotravibhāga* most resembles the position of the Drugpa Kagyü master Barawa Gyaltsen Palzang. Both hold that only the svābhāvikakāya partakes of the ultimate truth, which means that for them there is not only a blank nothingness in the end but also an aspect of clarity or awareness. Consequently, they only accept that the ultimate space-like qualities that resemble the svābhāvikakāya, namely the natural luminosity of the dharmatā of the mind, exist throughout beginningless time. For both, the inseparability of buddha qualities is related to this dharmatā, which cannot be differentiated in terms of shape, color, or quantifiable numbers. As I have shown in the introduction, a few passages in the *Ratnagotravibhāgavyākhyā* do indeed suggest that this was the intention of its author.

Barawa restricts the inseparability of the qualities to their true nature, however, and concludes that the qualities of both the dharmakāya and the form kāyas are themselves separable, the former (namely the ten strengths, etc.) being multiple and the latter (namely the major and minor marks of a buddha) having shape and color.[2051] Zhönu Pal disagrees at least with regard to the qualities of the dharmakāya, contending that the ten strengths only differ in terms of how wisdom experiences different objects, which does not have the undesired consequence that the dharmakāya consists of multiple features.[2052] On the other hand, Zhönu Pal is far from endorsing the view of the zhentongpas or Longchenpa that the qualities of both the dharmakāya and the form kāyas exist throughout beginningless time.

If anything, it is the qualities of the dharmakāya, in the eyes of Zhönu Pal, that abide primordially, because they do not depend on a newly attained substantial cause for their abiding nature. They appear directly and blossom merely by becoming free from hindrances. Still, they exist in an ordinary mindstream only in a subtle form. The qualities of the form kāyas do not primordially exist even in a subtle form, because they depend on a substantial cause in the form of an artificially appropriated potential.[2053] Zhönu Pal's theory of subtle qualities is a compromise between the clear statements of the *Tathāgatagarbhasūtra*, *Śrīmālādevīsūtra,* and other texts to the effect that buddha nature is inseparably endowed with innumerable qualities and the various attempts to bring the teaching of buddha nature into line with mainstream Madhyamaka. When we consider how these subtle qualities are explained, though, they are seen to be compared to the subtle seeds of empty space that is due to form another world after the current world has vanished. These space-like subtle seeds are said to resemble the svābhāvikakāya and its ultimate qualities, and in the final analysis this theory of subtle qualities does not differ from Barawa's position. In other words, both Barawa and Zhönu Pal are careful enough not to violate the Mādhyamika's dictum of emptiness.

A similar approach can be observed in the case of Ngog Loden Sherab, for whom nothing is newly acquired in terms of the essence of enlightenment. Nevertheless, the realization of the ultimate is taken as the cause of all qualities, which gather as if called, and are thus naturally connected. It seems very likely that Zhönu Pal's theory of subtle qualities is a further development of Loden Sherab's "gathering of naturally connected qualities." Loden Sherab's interpretation was at least helpful in getting the notion of a natural growth of qualities accepted.

In view of this theory of subtle qualities, it is difficult to see how Zhönu Pal could have adopted Tsongkhapa's explanations of the *Ratnagotravibhāga*, as the Fourth Zhamarpa Chödrag Yeshé suggested he did when he reported that Zhönu Pal was fond of Tsongkhapa's *Ratnagotravibhāga*-based hermeneutics.[2054] Mikyö Dorjé, too, informs us that Zhönu Pal was influenced by Tsongkhapa in his presentation of the natural and fortified potentials in the Kālacakra commentary *Rgyud gsum gsang ba*.[2055] In that commentary, Zhönu Pal seems to claim further that buddha nature in sentient beings is merely their six *āyatanas*, which resemble a buddha.[2056] Zhönu Pal clearly rules out such an interpretation in his commentary on RGV I.25.[2057] His commentary on RGV I.26, for its part, shows that he followed Loden Sherab's explanation of the buddha element as a cause, and thus differed from Gyaltsab Jé.[2058] Zhönu Pal may indeed have written his *Rgyud gsum gsang ba* (in 1442) while still under the strong influence of his teacher Rimibabpa Sönam Rinchen, who advised him to abandon neither the mahāmudrā view nor the tradition of the Gelugpas.[2059] But in the *Ratnagotravibhāga* commentary, which Zhönu Pal wrote in 1473, Tsongkhapa is not referred to even once.[2060]

To be sure, Zhönu Pal's subtle qualities refer to the natural luminosity of an ordinary mindstream and not to distinct entities on the order of the ten strengths and the like. In this respect it is interesting that Barawa claims that even Dölpopa was thinking of natural luminosity or the ultimate qualities of the svābhāvikakāya (i.e., the qualities described in RGV II.46c–47d) when he said that buddha nature is not empty of the ten strengths and so on (i.e., the qualities of both the dharmakāya and the form kāyas). Moreover, it is noteworthy that Longchenpa speaks of "luminous major and minor marks of the Buddha" *('od mtshan dpe)* when referring to primordial qualities.[2061]

Various passages show that in the eyes of Zhönu Pal, every mindstream has its own subtle qualities that naturally blossom into their own enlightened dharmakāya. In other words, he adheres to explanation number 9 in my list of Zhönu Pal's own summary of possible positions on buddha nature: you realize your own natural mind and so understand that the mind of a buddha and the mind of all sentient beings are of a similar nature.[2062] This means that the fully blossomed wisdom of the buddhas with its ten strengths and so forth is not contained in the mindstream of sentient beings, and the real buddha kāyas do not pervade sentient beings (in the sense of sharing a common part of space).[2063] This is clear from Zhönu Pal's explanation of the example of the *vaiḍūrya* stone (which illustrates the dharmakāya) and the mud in the *Sāgaramatiparipṛcchā:* the example of a *vaiḍūrya* stone is chosen in order to reinforce the notion that sentient beings' nature of mind and the dharmakāya are very much similar in type (but not the same thing).[2064]

Zhönu Pal informs us himself that he is here following Ngog Loden Sherab who distinguished a twofold "circle" *('khor lo)* with regard to the sevenfold subject matter in the *Ratnagotravibhāga:* the circle of the nonabiding nirvāṇa and the circle of the Three Jewels. In the first circle, sentient beings attain enlightenment through their practice, with their buddha nature functioning as a cause *(rgyu)* and the Three Jewels as an attendant condition *(lhan cig byed pa'i rkyen).* Since by these three still other disciples are guided, and by the next set of three again still others, the whole is called a circle. Once disciples have become buddhas themselves, they assist other sentient beings in a second "circle" by acting as attendant conditions for these other's enlightenment.[2065]

Zhönu Pal's and Ngog Loden Sherab's understanding of distinct mindstreams that become buddhas on their own is supported by a passage from the *Avataṁsakasūtra* quoted in RGVV I.25.[2066] This early stage of the *tathāgatagarbha* doctrine does not vindicate monism, since enlightenment is described as being equal to but not identical with an already existing tathāgata.[2067] This is in sharp contrast to the zhentong of Dölpopa, and, if you follow Mikyö Dorjé, also of Rangjung Dorjé, who maintains that the ultimate buddha kāyas literally pervade the entire universe, including all sentient beings.[2068] According to Dölpopa, it is in this sense that all buddha qualities are already complete in you. Still, the buddha kāyas, or buddha nature (which is the same thing in this form of zhentong), are not considered to inhere in the mindstreams of sentient beings. On this point, zhentong is similar to the view of Loden Sherab. Both have in common the belief that wisdom or luminosity is in reality the enlightened mind of a tathāgata. The difference, of course, is that for Loden Sherab individual mindstreams generate their own buddha qualities.

Zhönu Pal does not follow Loden Sherab in every respect, though. For Loden Sherab, awareness of wisdom or luminosity results from the enlightened mind penetrating the emptiness of all phenomena, including the mental factors of an ordinary mindstream,[2069] whereas for Zhönu Pal, and also Barawa, the emptiness of such a mind has also an aspect of clarity. In this respect, Zhönu Pal's subtle qualities amount to something more than the emptiness of a blank nothingness.[2070] The process of natural growth undergone by these subtle qualities is compared to turmeric powder turning red when it comes into contact with lime,[2071] which stands for the purifying factors of the buddhas. In other words, the individual mindstream and the activity of the buddhas both contribute substantially to your enlightenment.

A slightly different picture is drawn when Zhönu Pal explains, based on Rangjung Dorjé's equation of the unfabricated "natural mind" *(tha mal gyi shes pa)* with the dharmadhātu and the nature of the victorious ones (i.e., buddha nature), that the mind does not alter its nature even when disturbed by defilements. Zhönu Pal comments that the mind remains natural and pure with regard to all those defilements; and since purity is the nature of the qualities, these qualities increase naturally within it, like space when a house is being destroyed.[2072] This picture is more in line with zhentong, in that the qualities are compared to space, which increases by removing the enclosure of defilements. In other words, something that is omnipresent and fully developed throughout beginningless time is only being revealed, and thus only appears to grow in your individual mindstream.

You could argue that it is unlikely that a scholar like Zhönu Pal did not see the obvious contradictions between these two examples and the exegetical traditions they represent, and that he therefore followed a strategy similar to that of Dölpopa, who would call Loden Sherab's commentarial tradition ordinary, the extraordinary explanation being tantric and one only hinted at occasionally in general Mahāyāna presentations. In order to settle this question it would be necessary to consult Zhönu Pal's works on the tantras, especially the *Kālacakratantra,* which are unfortunately not available at present. But Zhamar Chödrag Yeshé does describe Zhönu Pal's view on the "reflections of emptiness" *(śūnyatābimba),* which are experienced during the Kālacakra practice of the six-branch yoga. Thus the reflections of emptiness cannot be established by analysis as not truly existing; to see them rather means to see the true nature of your mind.[2073] This seems to be in line with the Jonang position. In fact, one of Zhönu Pal's Kālacakra teachers, Lhakhang Tengpa Sangyé Rinchen, was a disciple of the great Jonang abbot Choglé Namgyal, and Zhönu Pal must have known through Sangyé Rinchen (whom he greatly respected) the extraordinary zhentong interpretation of the Kālacakra as propounded by the Jonangpas. Moreover, Zhönu Pal is described by Zhamar Chödrag Yeshé as having blended the teachings of various traditions including the one by Yumowa Mikyö Dorjé, whom Tuken Lozang Chökyi Nyima considers as the originator of zhentong teachings.[2074] If Zhönu Pal was in reality a zhentongpa, he would definitely have been one in the same mold as Rangjung Dorjé, for both claim, contrary to the Jonangpas, that buddha nature undergoes momentariness. In fact, Zhönu Pal tries to show at length that even space is momentary in some sense.

Mikyö Dorjé for his part observes no such similarity between Rangjung Dorjé and Zhönu Pal, but rather criticizes Zhönu Pal for citing Rangjung Dorjé in support of his claim that buddha nature in sentient beings is merely their six sense fields *(āyatanas),* which resemble a buddha.[2075] Mikyö Dorjé makes it clear that the "[buddha] element" (Skt. *dhātu*), or the potential, is nothing less than the dharmadhātu, or rather, the dharmadhātu wisdom,[2076] and not a cause in any real sense of the word. Thus, he rejects any attempt to see in the buddha element a real cause.[2077] But most importantly, Mikyö Dorjé does not approve of Zhönu Pal quoting Rangjung Dorjé in support of his explanation of buddha nature. Right at the beginning of his review of the *Rgyud gsum gsang ba*, Mikyö Dorjé makes it clear in what way he takes the positions of Rangjung Dorjé and Zhönu Pal to be different. After summarizing his and Rangjung Dorjé's view that buddha nature is identical with the all-pervading buddha kāyas, he deals at length with a possible objection from Zhönu Pal's side:

> In your proposed way of how buddha nature exists in sentient beings, the husk of sentient beings does not exist...Well, it would then be proper to take a vase as the essence of a rabbit's horn.[2078]

This raises the question of how Zhönu Pal defines the relationship between the ordinary impure mind and buddha nature, or apparent and ultimate truths. In chapter 2 we saw that Dölpopa regards the two as being different in that their identity is negated *(gcig pa bkag ba'i tha dad pa)*, whereas Barawa's mahāmudrā stance of equating buddha nature with the *ālayavijñāna* requires the two truths to be one in essence. Basing himself on the *Laṅkāvatārasūtra*, Barawa maintains that the *ālayavijñāna* and buddha nature are the same in essence but bear different names,[2079] and even accepts the consequence that buddha nature experiences suffering in virtue of its awareness.[2080] According to Mikyö Dorjé, Zhönu Pal claims in his *Rgyud gsum gsang ba* that buddha nature is identical with the *ālayavijñāna* and that it also experiences suffering.[2081] But in his *Ratnagotravibhāga* commentary there is nothing to this effect, and even though the *Laṅkāvatārasūtra* is repeatedly quoted, Zhönu Pal refrains from fully endorsing the sūtra's equation of buddha nature with the *ālayavijñāna* but rather takes the *ālayavijñāna* to be a reflection of buddha nature.[2082] Here again, Zhönu Pal follows Loden Sherab, who brings the buddha element into relation with the *ālayavijñāna*, maintaining that all sentient beings arise from the buddha element under certain specific conditions.[2083]

As we saw in chapter 2, Rangjung Dorjé combines a strict Yogācāra distinction between the *ālayavijñāna* and the supramundane pure mind (similar to zhentong) with Saraha's mahāmudrā explanation (the mind is the basis of saṁsāra and nirvāṇa), including as he does—based on the works of Maitreya—mere appearances empty of duality, or the stainlessness of the eight types of consciousness, within buddha nature. Once apparent truth has been restricted to these mere appearances, the distinction between a pure and impure mind no longer affects the question of the relationship between the two truths, since the two truths are only distinguished from that of which both are empty: duality. Rangjung Dorjé is thus in a position to assert in his mahāmudrā works that both truths are one in essence, notwithstanding his predilection for Yogācāra.

In a similar way, Zhönu Pal explains that the two truths, or adventitious stains and buddha nature, are not separate entities, and repeatedly illustrates this with examples such as ice and water or waves and the ocean.[2084] In other words, adventitious stains and buddha nature are not two substances that have become mixed up (this is how Zhönu Pal describes the Jonang position);[2085] it is buddha nature itself that manifests as defilements, just as the property of heat is not different from that of hot iron. In his commentary on the transformation of the basis in RGVV II.1, Zhönu Pal explains that in an ordinary state buddha nature functions as a basis that brings forth all defilements. When it is irreversibly purified from its stains, it no longer functions as a basis of defilements, which is called the transformation of the basis *(āśrayaparivṛtti)*. The two, the buddha element and the transformed basis, are only differentiated on the basis of whether they possess stains or not, for their own-being is very suchness.[2086]

Still, for Zhönu Pal the teaching of a buddha nature that is both not empty of qualities and empty of adventitious stains is nothing other than the explanation in the *Dharmadharmatāvibhāga* according to which the existing dharmatā differs from nonexisting dharmas.[2087] In other words, even though buddha nature can be the basis for adventitious stains, there is still a difference between buddha nature and the adventitious stains, in that buddha nature exists and adventitious stains do not. Dharmatā is defined by Zhönu Pal as the continuity of the stainless mind, which is free from thought but still not beyond all phenomena of saṁsāra.[2088] In the eyes of Zhönu Pal, Vasubandhu's *Dharmadharmatāvibhāgavṛtti* belongs to the Madhyamaka tradition, because it teaches, contrary to the Yogācāra treatises, that there is a naturally pure continuation of natural luminosity within the continuum of all defilements.[2089] What Zhönu Pal had in mind here were probably Yogācāra works, such as Asaṅga's *Mahāyānasaṁgraha,* where a clear line is drawn between an impure *ālayavijñāna* and a pure supramundane mind, or pure dharmadhātu[2090]—in other words, passages such as the one Rangjung Dorjé incorporated into his interpretation of buddha nature in his autocommentary on the *Zab mo nang gi don.*

The differences Mikyö Dorjé detected between Zhönu Pal and Rangjung Dorjé can thus be traced back to differences between the Maitreya works and the *Mahāyānasaṁgraha*. Rangjung Dorjé, however, also defines the relationship between the two truths, along the lines of the *Dharmadharmatāvibhāga*, as being neither identical nor different, and includes his notion of "mere appearances" or "stainlessness of the eight types of consciousness" in buddha nature.[2091] In other words, here we have again a continuum of the stainless mind within the continuum of defilements, and in the same way as (according to Zhönu Pal) buddha nature can be the basis of defilements, Rangjung Dorjé's mere appearances can be the basis of defilements if misunderstood and perceived dualistically.

It is difficult, though, to compare two masters who have both drawn on different strands of Buddhist thought. Given the central place the *Mahāyānasaṁgraha* has in Rangjung Dorjé's autocommentary on the *Zab mo nang gi don*, it is safe to say that Zhönu Pal ends up closer to Barawa than to the Third Karmapa.

The position of Zhönu Pal, who after all received so great a number of Nyingma teachings that Khetsun Sangpo considers him a Nyingma lineage holder,[2092] also differs considerably from the way Longchen Rabjampa explains the *Ratnagotravibhāga* in the *Grub mtha' mdzod*. In this work, Longchenpa shows that, with regard to the ground *(gzhi)*, dzogchen does not differ from the teaching of the *Ratnagotravibhāga*, which means that buddha nature is such that you already possess all spontaneously present buddha qualities of the three kāyas (with the restriction that your own major and minor marks of a buddha are only of a luminous nature).[2093] The particular role the *Ratnagotravibhāga* plays in the *Grub mtha' mdzod* can best be inferred from the fact that Longchenpa justifies the superiority of dzogchen over the sūtras by quoting RGV I.5a, which states that buddhahood is unconditioned and spontaneously present.[2094]

In a similar way, Zhönu Pal explains that "unconditioned" buddhahood refers to primordially present (but subtle) qualities that do not depend on a newly attained substantial cause for them.[2095] *Unconditioned* further means for Zhönu Pal that buddha nature is not artificially *('phral du)* conditioned or influenced by adventitious causes and conditions.[2096] But this only applies to the qualities of the dharmakāya, the qualities of the form kāyas (the major and minor marks of a buddha) being established by a substantial cause that comes into play through a continuation of individual merit, which is in turn based on an artificially appropriated potential.[2097] Another difference is that Longchenpa reads the dzogchen meaning of *spontaneously present (lhun grub)* into the *Ratnagotravibhāga*, namely, as referring to the buddha qualities, while Zhönu Pal holds the traditional view that it qualifies the activity of a buddha, which is without effort *(lhun grub).* In a sense, the way Zhönu Pal explains the buddha qualities is similar to Lodrö Tsungmé's. In the eyes of Lodrö Tsungmé, the qualities of the form kāyas are artificially created through the accumulation of merit. Even though this does not apply to the qualities of the dharmakāya, Lodrö Tsungmé distinguishes between the ten strengths and the like of ordinary beings and the ones of a buddha. But again, we do not yet know Zhönu Pal's tantric explanation of buddha nature.

It is true that Zhönu Pal does not make use of the term *zhentong*, but he does, based on the teachings of the second and third dharmacakras, distinguish two types of emptiness. Emptiness is thus not only the nonaffirming negation of the analytical Madhyamaka works, but also positively described as awareness-emptiness in the teachings of the third dharmacakra, to which the *Ratnagotravibhāga* belongs. Following the tradition of Maitrīpa, Zhönu Pal defines emptiness as awareness or buddha nature when directly experienced (in the same way as phenomena are also experienced as luminosity in *yathābhūtasamādhi* in TD 5). In the third dharmacakra, the emptiness of an own-being (that is, the emptiness of the second dharmacakra) is applied to the outer husk of the adventitious stains. Then the emptiness that is buddha nature is ascertained in a direct valid cognition, not, that is, as a nonaffirming negation of an own-being. In his commentary on the fourth point (buddha nature) of the topical outline in RGV I.1ab, Zhönu Pal brings this to the point:

> From sentient beings up to a buddha [something] exists [that is] established as the nature of mind because it is neither impaired nor fabricated by other conditions. It is called *empty of fabricated adventitious phenomena.* (DRSM, 15.20–22)

He could have equally said that an existing true nature of mind is zhentong, "empty of other," that is, empty of fabricated adventitious phenomena. The adventitious phenomena do not arise as something entirely different from the nature of mind, though. It is like space, for example. Even though space does not turn into phenomena like clouds and mountains, and is thus termed "empty," it would be wrong to say that these clouds and the rest abide anywhere else than in space. Similarly, buddha nature is empty of, but not different from, everything artificial, including what is produced out of ignorance—even the outer material world. It should be noted that such a positively defined true nature of mind is not established as something possessing characteristic signs,[2098] and as we have seen above, the qualities of the true nature of mind are only space-like seeds. If you want to call this *zhentong*, you should be aware that it differs from both the Jonang and Kagyü[2099] versions of it. In his biography, Zhönu Pal is thus said to have criticized Dölpopa for taking the appearances [produced by] *karman* and the appearance related to wisdom as two separate individual entities that have been mixed together. Zhönu Pal prefers to define the relation between the two in accordance with the example of ice and water, which are only two different states of the same substance (H_2O).[2100] In a similar way, Zhönu Pal prefers the equation of buddha nature with the *ālayavijñāna* in the *Laṅkāvatārasūtra* (even though he takes the *ālayavijñāna* as only a reflection of buddha nature), and not the distinction in the *Mahāyānasaṃgraha* between an impure *ālayavijñāna* and a pure dharmadhātu, this distinction being the preference of the Third Karmapa Rangjung Dorjé. This definitely reflects Zhönu Pal's Kadam and Sakya education, which prevented him from being overly influenced by the views of the Jonangpas or Rangjung Dorjé in this matter. Thus he was indeed being careful when he shored up his presentation of buddha nature with the commentarial tradition of Loden Sherab.

When it came to mahāmudrā hermeneutics, however, Zhönu Pal did not pay heed to the commentarial tradition of either Loden Sherab or the Kadampas and Sakyapas to any great extent. Guided by Gampopa and Drigung Jigten Sumgön, Zhönu Pal claims that the gradual purification of the three dharmacakras only leads up to a provisional seventh bodhisattva level, well below the actual bodhisattva levels. As can be seen from my translation (DRSM, 36.24–74.26), Zhönu Pal justifies the superiority of the third dharmacakra on the basis of mahāmudrā explanations given by various Indian and Tibetan masters. In doing so, he tries to show that two controversial currents within Kagyü mahāmudrā, namely the ones later classified as sūtra-based mahāmudrā and essence mahāmudrā, stem from Indian traditions and are not Chinese Ch'an Buddhism in disguise, a charge mainly leveled by the Sakyapas. Writing a commentary on the *Ratnagotravibhāga*, Zhönu Pal could not enter directly into this debate. Nevertheless, under the pretext of showing the superiority of the third dharmacakra, he goes so far as to endorse Zhang Tsalpa Tsöndrü's controversial statement that mahāmudrā is attained in one go, and that the confused err when they reckon in terms of levels and paths. Such a teaching, which belongs to the later category of essence mahāmudrā, can be justified, according to Zhönu Pal, by combining the *Laṅkāvatārasūtra* passage[2101] on the gradual and instantaneous purification of the mindstream with the presentation of provisional bodhisattva levels in the *Vairocanābhisambodhitantra*. For Zhönu Pal, all objects of knowledge appear instantaneously on the pure bodhisattva levels (namely from the eighth level onward), and since there are already "provisional pure levels" even on the path of accumulation, an instantaneous realization of mahāmudrā comes within the reach of practitioners well below the actual bodhisattva levels. In terms of "sūtra-based mahāmudrā," Zhönu Pal shows how the four mahāmudrā yogas are already latently contained in the *Laṅkāvatārasūtra* and various passages of the *Ratnagotravibhāga*, and it is with this in mind that his *Ratnagotravibhāga* commentary can be called a "direct path to the buddha within."

Notes

1 Skt. *tathāgatagarbha*. For a discussion of this term see Zimmermann 2002:43–46.

2 Tatz 1994:65. For a detailed description of Maitrīpa's life see Tatz 1987:695–711.

3 See Kong sprul Blo gros mtha' yas: *Shes bya kun khyab mdzod*, vol. 3, 375.18–20.

4 See DRSM, 7.24–8.1.

5 According to the Chinese tradition, the *Ratnagotravibhāga* was written by Sāramati (Frauwallner 1969:255–56). For a discussion of the authorship of the Maitreya works see Mathes 1996:11–17.

6 The date of translation is some time between 511–15 (see Ui 1959:21). On the dating 515 A.D., see Ui 1959:17.

7 See the final section of the introduction.

8 See Keira 2004:6.

9 Jñānakīrti's *Tattvāvatāra* was translated by Rin chen bzang po (958–1055).

10 See Tatz 1987:698.

11 The Sanskrit original of DhDhV 18–19 is quoted in JNĀ, 432.10–13, while RGV I.9 is summarized in JNĀ 478.11.

12 The verses II.95c–97b (JNĀ, 537.4–7) are nearly identical with RGV I.154–55 (J I.151–52).

13 This will be discussed in detail in Kano's forthcoming dissertation.

14 See Mathes 1996:163–68.

15 Dol po pa only informs us in his *Ri chos nges don rgya mtsho* that his final view of *gzhan stong* is an extraordinary Vajrayāna explanation of buddha nature (see "The Position of Dölpopa Sherab Gyaltsen" in chapter 2 of this work).

16 It should by noted, however, that at the beginning of his commentary for those with average faculties, Gzhon nu dpal remarks that the full-fledged commentary (for those with "inferior faculties") is meant to be for those who are clever and faithful (DRSM, 13.9–10).

17 The hermeneutic device in question divides the entire Buddhist teaching into three groups or dharmacakras, the first group consisting of the Hīnayāna, the second of the *prajñāpāramitā* and Madhyamaka, and the third of the Yogācāra, buddha nature, mahāmudrā, and tantra (see also Mathes 1996:155–56).

18 See Perler (2002:23–30) for similar methodological principles defined in order to structure and evaluate text material in the context of describing theories of intentionality in medieval Europe.

19 Gzhon nu dpal not only enjoyed a full-fledged Bka' gdams education, but studied at nearly every important monastic or religious center in Dbus and Gtsang. See chapter 3 in this work.

20 See DRSM, 574.10–12.

21 According to Kong sprul Blo gros mtha' yas's introduction to his *Ratnagotravibhāga* commentary (*Rgyud bla ma'i bshad srol*, 9b1–10a1).

22 To be precise, my presentation of Klong chen pa's position on buddha nature is limited to the one expounded in the *Grub mtha' mdzod* (see the section on Klong chen pa's position in chapter 2).

23 See Ehrhard 2002:41, fn. 9.

24 Zhva dmar Chos grags ye shes: *Gzhon nu dpal gyi rnam thar*, 18a3–6.
25 Roerich 1949–53:524.
26 In fact, Rang byung rdo rje studied under Shāk gzhon, among other texts, the Maitreya works (see Situ Paṇ chen Chos kyi 'byung gnas and 'Be lo Tshe dbang kun khyab: *Sgrub brgyud karma kaṁ tshang brgyud pa rin po che'i rnam par thar pa*, 199a1–4).
27 The stanza numbering of the RGV refers to the one used in my edition of Gzhon nu dpal's commentary on the RGVV, and the one in parentheses to Johnston's edition of the Sanskrit text.
28 Seyfort Ruegg 1969 and 1973.
29 Zhva dmar Chos grags ye shes: *Gzhon nu dpal gyi rnam thar*, 10b1–2. The Eighth Karmapa Mi bskyod rdo rje ("Rje Yid[a] bzang rtse ba'i Rgyud gsum gsang ba...", 998.6: *...khyod rang gi bla ma tsong kha (text: ga) pas...*) even refers to Gzhon nu dpal as a disciple of Tsong kha pa.
a The text has the wrong spelling *ye*. 'Gos Lo tsā ba Gzhon nu dpal is occasionally called "the man from Yid bzang rtse," which was his retreat place (see Zhva dmar Chos grags ye shes: *Gzhon nu dpal gyi rnam thar*, 32b6–7).
30 Zhva dmar Chos grags ye shes: *Gzhon nu dpal gyi rnam thar*, 10b7–11a2 (see pp. 136–37 in this work).
31 Anyone who has worked with prints from the Patna films of both *Ratnagotravibhāgavyākhyā* manuscripts must admit that Johnston's edition is surprisingly good.
32 For a detailed review of Seyfort Ruegg's study on buddha nature, see Schmithausen 1973.
33 RGVV, 3.4–6: *yo 'yam śāriputra tathāgatanirdiṣṭo dharmakāyaḥ so 'yam avinirbhāgadharmā / avinirmuktajñānaguṇo yad uta gaṅgānadīvālikāvyatikrāntais tathāgatadharmaiḥ / itīdaṁ ṣaṣṭhaṁ vajrapadam anūnatvā[a]pūrṇatvanirdeśānusāreṇā[b]nugantavyam /*.
a B (2b1) reads *-nā-* instead of *-natvā-*.
b B (2b1) reads *-ṇevā-* (i.e., *-ṇaivā-*) instead of *-ṇā-*.
For a description of the RGV manuscripts A and B, see pp. 154–55 in this work and Bandurski et al. 1994:31–33.
34 As also correctly understood by Seyfort Ruegg 1969:314.
35 For a detailed discussion of both compounds, see Schmithausen 1971:131–32.
36 See "Observations de Rgyal tshab rje" in Seyfort Ruegg 1969:294–96.
37 Zimmermann 2002:64.
38 See the section "Buddha Qualities" in chapter 5 of this study.
39 Zimmermann 2002:63–64.
40 Gzhon nu dpal views this equation in the context of RGV I.27, where the fruit, or the dharmakāya, has been only metaphorically applied to buddha nature (DRSM, 24.2–5). In RGV I.27 the third reason for the presence of a buddha nature in sentient beings is that "its (i.e., buddha nature's) fruit has been metaphorically applied to the buddha potential." (RGVV, 26.3–4: *bauddhe gotre tatphalasyopacārād.*)
41 RGVV, 2.11–14: *paramārtha iti śāri[putra]*[a] *sattvadhātor etad adhivacanam / sattvadhātur iti śāriputra tathāgatagarbhasyaitad adhivacanam / tathāgatagarbha iti śāriputra dharmakāyasyaitad adhivacanam / itīdaṁ caturthaṁ vajrapadam /*[b] *anūnatvāpūrṇatvanirdeśaparivartānusāreṇānugantavyam /*.
a Missing in B (2a3); A is not available.
b According to B (2a4); Johnston omits the *daṇḍa*.
42 RGVV, 76.1–2: *nāpaneyam ataḥ kiṁcid upaneyaṁ na kiṁcana / draṣṭavyaṁ bhūtato bhūtaṁ bhūtadarśī vimucyate //*.

43 RGVV, 76.3–4: *śūnya āgantukair dhātuḥ savinirbhāgalakṣaṇaiḥ / aśūnyo 'nuttarair dharmair avinirbhāgalakṣaṇaiḥ //.*

44 The Derge Tengyur and DRSM, 441.24 translate *chos dag pa'i chos nyid* (Nakamura 1967:149.7): ...inseparable from the "true nature of Buddha properties." But in view of the following quotation of the *Śrīmālādevīsūtra*, the reading of the Narthang and Peking editions *(chos dag nyid)* are preferred, with the compound *avinirbhāgaśuddhadharmatā* taken as the abstract of a *bahuvrīhi.*

45 RGVV, 76.5–7: *kim anena paridīpitam / yato na kiṁcid apaneyam asty ataḥ prakṛtipariśuddhāt tathāgatadhātoḥ saṁkleśanimittam āgantukamalaśūnyatāprakṛtitvād asya / nāpy atra kiṁcid upaneyam asti vyavadānanimittam avinirbhāgaśuddhadharmatā*[a]*prakṛtitvāt / tata ucyate / śūnyas tathāgatagarbho vinirbhāgair muktajñaiḥ sarvakleśakośaiḥ / aśūnyo gaṅgānadīvālikāvyativṛttair avinirbhāgair amuktajñair acintyair buddhadharmair iti / evaṁ yad yatra nāsti tat tena śūnyam iti samanupaśyati / yat punar atrāvaśiṣṭaṁ bhavati tat sad ihāstīti yathābhūtaṁ prajānāti / samāropāpavādāntaparivarjanād aviparītaṁ*[b] *śūnyatālakṣaṇam anena ślokadvayena paridīpitam /.*

a See A (19a4) and B (39b3). Johnston omits, probably inadvertently, *-tā-*.

b Corrected according to A (19a4) and B (39b5).

46 See Chalmers 1899; Seyfort Ruegg 1969:319–20.

47 It is difficult to see how space-like qualities could be left over in emptiness. Would such a remainder make any difference in terms of the nature of emptiness?

48 RGVV, 76.15: *tathāgatagarbhajñānam eva tathāgatānāṁ śūnyatājñānam.*

49 Seyfort Ruegg 1969:346.

50 Schmithausen 1973:133.

51 RGVV, 26.11–15: *svabhāvahetvoḥ phalakarmayogavṛttiṣv avasthāsv atha sarvagatve*[a] *sadāvikārikatvaguṇeṣv abhede jñeyo 'rthasaṁdhiḥ paramārthadhātoḥ /.*

a B (15a1) has *avasthāneṣv atha sarvatve*, which is against the meter; A is not available. According to the Tibetan (Nakamura 1967:49.17): "[the ten points] have the intended meaning of the ultimate [buddha] element."

52 Strictly speaking, the ten strengths, etc., belong to the ultimate kāya, which is, according to RGV I.148 (J I.145), only the first aspect of the dharmakāya, i.e., the pure dharmadhātu. Its second aspect corresponds to the sambhogakāya. The latter forms together with the nirmāṇakāya the so-called form kāyas, which possess the thirty-two marks of a great being. This lack of a consistent presentation of the kāyas in the RGV reflects its different layers. For convenience sake I follow the common usage in Tibetan scholarly discourse and call the ten strengths, etc., the *qualities of the dharmakāya.*

53 According to RGV III.1–3. See below in this paragraph.

54 These stanzas present the fifteen defining characteristics of the ultimate. These are explained as buddhahood that is (1) inconceivable, (2) eternal, (3) everlasting, (4) quiescent, (5) constant, (6) perfectly pacified, (7) all pervading, (8) nondiscriminative, (9) without attachment, (10) without hindrance, (11) devoid of gross sensation, (12) imperceptible, (13) incognizable, (14) pure, and (15) immaculate (see Takasaki 1966:323–24).

55 RGVV, 84.3–4: *yad uktam ākāśalakṣaṇo buddha iti tat pāramārthikam āveṇikaṁ tathāgatānāṁ buddhalakṣaṇam abhisaṁdhāyoktam /.*

56 RGVV, 87.2–4: *prabhāsvaraṁ viśuddhaṁ ca dharmadhātu*[a]*svabhāvataḥ / aprameyair asaṁkhyeyair acintyair asamair guṇaiḥ / viśuddhipārami*[b]*prāptair yuktaṁ svābhāvikaṁ vapuḥ /.*

a Schmithausen (1971:164) proposes reading *dharmadhātu* in compound against B (44a5).

b B (44a5) and Johnston read *-mī-*.

57 For the *Tathāgatagarbhasūtra* see Zimmermann 2002:121.

58 See RGVV, 63.18.

59 See Takasaki 1966:14 and Schmithausen 1971:126–29.

60 RGVV, 26.1–4: *buddhajñānā[ntargam]*[a]*āt sattvarāśes tannairmalyasyādvayatvāt prakṛtyā / bauddhe gotre tatphalasyopacārād uktāḥ sarve dehino buddhagarbhāḥ //*.

a Not readable in B (15a4); A is not available.

61 DRSM, 150.10–12.

62 See also Schmithausen 1973:131.

63 RGVV, 91.5–13: *svārthaḥ parārthaḥ paramārthakāyatā*[a] *tadāśritā saṁvṛtikāyatā ca / phalaṁ visaṁyogavipākabhāvād etac catuḥṣaṣṭiguṇaprabhedam // ātmasaṁpattyadhiṣṭhānaṁ śarīraṁ pāramārthikam / parasaṁpattyadhiṣṭhānaṁ ṛṣeḥ sāṁketikaṁ vapuḥ // visaṁyogaguṇair yuktaṁ vapur ādyaṁ balādibhiḥ / vaipākikair dvitīyaṁ tu mahāpuruṣalakṣaṇaiḥ //*.

a According to B (45b2); A is not available. Johnston reads, probably for metrical reasons, *-kāyas* instead of *-kāyatā*. But the *upajāti* meter allows twelve for the normal eleven syllables in a *pāda*. B is supported by the *Jñānaśrīmitranibandhāvali*, which quotes RGV II.1 on p. 502, ll.9–13 and p. 536, ll.13–16.

64 The *paripuṣṭagotra* is equated with the *samudānītagotra* in MSABh III.4.

65 Skt. *āśraya;* the Tibetan has "source" *(gter)*. This is in accordance with a variant reading of this stanza (RGV I.154 (J I.151)) in the *Sākārasaṁgraha* (see JNĀ, 537.5 and 537, fn. 1): *-ratnākare tva-* (read: *-ratnākaratva-*).

66 RGVV, 71.18–72.6: *gotraṁ tad dvividhaṁ jñeyaṁ nidhānaphalavṛkṣavat / anādiprakṛtisthaṁ ca samudānītam uttaram // buddhakāyatrayāvāptir asmād gotradvayān matā / prathamāt prathamaḥ kāyo dvitīyād dvau tu paścimau // ratnavigrahavaj jñeyaḥ kāyaḥ svābhāvikaḥ śubhaḥ / akṛtrimatvāt prakṛter guṇaratnāśrayatvataḥ // mahādharmādhirājya*[a]*tvāt sāmbhogaś cakravartivat / pratibimbasvabhāvatvān nirmāṇaṁ hemabimbavat //*.

a Johnston reads *-ja-;* corrected according to Takasaki 1966:289.

67 I.e., in many sūtras, such as the *prajñāpāramitā* sūtras.

68 RGVV, 77.9–19: *āha*[a] *yady evam asaṅganiṣṭhābhūmipratiṣṭhitānām api paramāryāṇām asarvaviṣaya eṣa durdṛśo dhātuḥ / tat kim anena bāla*[b]*janam ārabhya deśiteneti / deśanāprayojanasaṁgrahe ślokau / ekena praśno dvitīyena vyākaraṇam / śūnyaṁ sarvaṁ sarvathā tatra tatra jñeyaṁ meghasvapnamāyākṛtābham / ity uktvaivaṁ buddhadhātuḥ punaḥ kiṁ sattve sattve 'stīti*[c] *buddhair ihoktam // līnaṁ cittaṁ hīnasattveṣv avajñā 'bhūtagrāho bhūtadharmāpavādaḥ / ātmasnehaś cādhikaḥ pañca doṣā yeṣāṁ teṣāṁ tatprahāṇārtham uktam //.*

a According to both manuscripts (A 19b2; B 40b5). Johnston's omission of *āha* is probably only a reading mistake (see also Schmithausen 1971:160).

b Johnston inserts between *bāla-* and *-janam*, against both manuscripts (A 19b2; B 40a5), *-pṛthag-*.

c Both manuscripts (A 19b3; B 40a6) have *astīti,* which violates both sandhi and meter.

69 It should be noted that *abhiprāya* in *ābhiprāyika* refers either to the hidden intention of a *neyārtha* statement (and this is the common usage in Madhyamaka hermeneutics) or to the thought content of what is really true. While the first meaning is found in Candrakīrti's *Madhyamakāvatāra* (see MA VI.94), the second is more common in Yogācāra (see, for example, Vasubandhu's *Viṁśatikā* 9–10).

70 See Seyfort Ruegg 1985:309–11 and 1988b:1–4; and Cabezón 1992:226–27.

71 According to the *Prasphuṭapadā*, the canonical allusions to an *ātman* and *ālayavijñāna* are provisional statements *(neyārtha)* motivated by specific salvific goals

(prayojana) of the Buddha, and have as their "intentional ground" (Tib. *dgongs gzhi*) emptiness (see Seyfort Ruegg 1988b:2).

72 This is the view of Sa skya Paṇḍita and Bu ston Rin chen grub (Seyfort Ruegg 1973:29–33).

73 These principles are laid out in a famous stanza (see below) quoted in the *Vyākhyāyukti* (see VY, 6.13–16). Gzhon nu dpal (DRSM, 13.2–6) quotes the same stanza from an unknown work by Vasubandhu, namely the *Rje btsun gyi man ngag thob pa, rje btsun* standing for Maitreya. This is an indication that the Yogācāra principles of exegesis were taken as having been set forth by Maitreya.

74 Thanks to a quotation in Haribhadra's *Abhisamayālaṁkārāloka* (AAA, 15.24–25) the Sanskrit of the stanza at the beginning of Vasubandhu's *Vyākhyāyukti* (VY, 6.13–16) is available: *prayojanaṁ sapiṇḍārthaṁ padārthaḥ sānusaṁdhikaḥ / sacodyaparihāraś ca vācyaḥ sūtrārthavādibhiḥ //.*

75 See the beginning of RGVV I.1 (RGVV, 1.6–10): "They are *vajra words* (otherwise translated as *vajra base* or *vajra point*) in view of being the words or support of the vajra-like meaning, [in the sense of the object] of realization. With regard to this, it should be known that [this] naturally ineffable meaning (or object) of self-realization is like a vajra, because it is difficult to understand with a knowledge that results from listening and reflection. The letters that express this meaning by teaching the favorable path for attaining it are called the *base* inasmuch as they are the support of this [meaning]. Thus, in view of its being difficult to understand and being the support as well, it should be known in terms of meaning and syllables, as the *vajra base (vajrapada).*" *(vajropamasyādhigamārthasya padaṁ sthānam iti vajrapadam / tatra śruta*[a]*cintāmayajñānaduṣprative[dhatvād ana]*[b]*bhilāpyasvabhāvaḥ pratyātmavedanīyo 'rtho vajravad veditavyaḥ / yāny akṣarāṇi tam artham anu*[c]*vadanti tatprāptyanukūlamārgābhidyotanatas tāni tatpratiṣṭhā[bhūtatvāt padam ity ucyante /]*[d] *iti duṣprativedhārthena pratiṣṭhārthena ca vajrapadatvam arthavyañjanayor anugantavyam /).*

a Johnston wrongly reads *śruti* (cf. B (1b2)).

b In B (1b2) four *akṣara*s are missing; A is not available. The gap is therefore filled in with the grammatically more correct *-dhatvād ana-* (Johnston proposes: *-dhād ana-*). Cf. also Schmithausen 1971:131.

c Johnston wrongly reads *abhi-* in preference to *anu-* (cf. B (1b2)). In fact, *anu-vad*, ("to tell," "to say," or "to narrate"), fits much better the context here.

d Not readable and partly missing in B (1b3); A is not available.

76 This, at least, is what Gzhon nu dpal claims in his commentary on RGV I.1. Having quoted the stanza with the five principles, he prefers, however, to define the goal in line with Haribhadra's four *anubandha*s (Tib *dgos 'brel*, "goal and connection"), which are applied in Haribhadra's *Abhisamayālaṁkārāloka* (see DRSM, 13.3–18). These four are (1) the connection [between the subject matter and the goal] (Skt. *sambandha*); (2) the subject matter (Skt. *abhideya*), (3) the goal/motive (Skt. *prayojana*), and (4) the "goal of the goal" or the "goal that is also attainable" (Skt. *prayojanaprayojana*) (see AAA, 2.3–5). For a Tibetan explanation of these four *dgos 'brel* see *Bod rgya tshig mdzod chen mo*, s.v.

77 This depends on whether one follows Haribhadra's way of explaining the *prayojana* of the *Vyākhyāyukti* in terms of his four *anubandha*s (see AAA, 15.26–27).

78 VY, 8.13–16: "[Possible goals are:] to correctly teach those who are completely confused, to cause the unattentive to adopt [virtues], to praise [virtues] to those who are disheartened, and to cheer up those who have correctly entered the path." *(kun tu rmongs pa la yang dag par bstan pa dang / bag med pa rnams la yang dag par len du gzhug pa dang / kun tu zhum pa rnams la yang dag par gzeng bstod pa dang / yang dag par zhugs pa rnams la yang dag par dga' bar bya ste /.)*

79 The first rule of the *Vyākhyāyukti* (the goal of the sūtra must be stated) applies in general to all sūtras one wishes to comment upon (see VY, 8.11–12.26).

80 In the context of Yogācāra, the thought content *(abhiprāya)* of what is really true.

81 See VY, 212.19–224.13 and Cabezón 1992:227–28.

82 See VY, 229.8–20: "It is just like having taught [stanzas] such as 'having killed father and mother, [...the Brahmin remains without sin] (= *Udānavarga* XXIX.24).' Without doubt this needs [further] explanation.... Passages such as 'All phenomena lack an own-being, do not arise nor cease' need [further] explanation, too. Why is that? It is in order to remove the clinging of the foolish to the existence of the imagined nature,...and to remove the clinging of the ignorant[a] to the nonexistence of phenonmena, which are inexpressible by nature (=dependent nature)." *(pha dang ma ni bsad byas shing / / zhes bya ba de lta bu la sogs pa bstan pa ji lta bu yin / de ni gdon mi za bar bshad par bya ste / ... chos thams cad ni ngo bo med pa / ma skyes pa ma 'gags pa zhes bya ba de lta bu la sogs pa 'di yang bshad par bya'o // ci'i phyir zhe na / byis pas kun tu brtags pa'i ngo bo nyid yod pa nyid du 'dzin pa bsal pa'i phyir / ... mgo smos pa mi shes pa rnams brjod du med pa'i ngo bo'i chos med par 'dzin pa bsal ba'i phyir).* In other words, the teaching of emptiness needs further clarification in terms of the *trisvabhāva*-theory.

a Guṇamati glosses Tib. *mgo smos pa mi shes pa rnams* in his *Vyākhyāyuktiṭīkā* (Peking Tengyur no. 5570, *sems tsam*, vol. *i*, fol. 154a3) as *gang dag don rnam ma phye ba mi rtogs pa de dag* (Skt. **ye avibhaktārtham apratipadyante te*) "those who do not realize the undetermined meaning"; in other words, those who do not understand *neyārthasūtras* (see Lee 2001a:80).

83 See VY, 225.8–16.

84 See my translation of DRSM, 37.8–40.8.

85 A similar line of thought is followed by the Dge lugs scholar Gung thang 'Jam pa'i dbyangs (1762–1823) (see Seyfort Ruegg 1969:402). It is interesting in this context to note that Tsong kha pa, according to Zhva dmar Chos grags ye shes (*Gzhon nu dpal gyi rnam thar*, 10b1), said in Gnyal in 1415: "One way to distinguish the provisional and definitive [meanings] that does not contradict what has been explained here is to do the explaining according to the *Mahāyānottaratantra* (=*Ratnagotravibhāga*)." *(... 'dir bshad pa dang 'gal ba min pa'i drang nges kyi 'byed lugs shig theg pa chen po rgyud bla ma nas bshad 'dug.)*

86 See Takasaki 1966:381.

87 See DRSM, 45.7–21.

88 The context clearly requires a past participle with the meaning of "taught" or "expounded." Skt. *nīta* (translated as *bzhag* in Tibetan) does not exactly have this meaning (Skt. *praṇītam* would be better in fact), but it does have the advantage of alluding to the adjective *nītārtham*, which modifies *sūtram*. This stylistic device (known as *tantra* in Sanskrit grammar) is used to hint at the hermeneutic term "definitive meaning" *(nītārtha)*. See also de Jong (1979:579), who translates the word as "taught as definitive."

89 RGVV, 118.3–6: *yasmān neha jināt supaṇḍitatamo loke 'sti kaścit kvacit sarvajñaḥ sakalaṁ sa veda vidhivat tattvaṁ paraṁ nāparaḥ / tasmād yat svayam eva nītam ṛṣiṇā sūtraṁ vicālyaṁ na tat saddharmapratibādhanaṁ hi tad api syān nītibhedān muneḥ //.*

90 See DRSM, 7.9–13.

91 Schmithausen 1973:131.

92 RGVV, 24.4–6: *yan nv aham eṣāṁ sattvānām ārya*[a] *mārgopadeśena sarvasaṁjñākṛtabandha*[b] *nāpanayanaṁ kuryāṁ yathā svayam evāryamārgabalādhānena mahatīṁ saṁjñāgranthiṁ vinivartya tathāgatajñānaṁ pratyabhijānīran / tathāgatasamatāṁ cānuprāpnuyuḥ /.*

a Johnston reads *āryeṇa* (corrected according to Takasaki 1966:192).

b B (14a4) inserts against A (17a2) the letter *na*.

93 LAS, 77.15–17: "You illustrated it as being pure in terms of the purity of natural luminosity and so forth and as being the bearer of the thirty-two marks and as being inside the body of all sentient beings." *(sa ca kila tvayā prakṛtiprabhāsvaraviśuddhyādiviśuddha eva varṇyate dvātriṁśallakṣaṇadharaḥ sarvasattvadehāntargato....)*

94 Skt. *mahāmate* is only rendered once.

95 LAS, 78.5–11: *na hi mahāmate tīrthakarātmavādatulyo mama tathāgatagarbhopadeśaḥ / kiṁ tu mahāmate tathāgatāḥ śūnyatābhūtakoṭinirvāṇānutpādānimittāpraṇihitādyānāṁ mahāmate padārthānāṁ tathāgatagarbhopadeśaṁ kṛtvā tathāgatā arhantaḥ samyaksaṁbuddhā bālānāṁ nairātmyasaṁtrāsapadavivarjanā*[a]*rthaṁ nirvikalpanirābhāsagocaraṁ tathāgatagarbhamukhopadeśena deśayanti /.*

a According the ms. T (17a4) of Nanjio's edition.

96 LAS, 220.9–16 (see also Takasaki 1981:2–4): *bhagavāṁs tasyaitad avocat / tathāgatagarbho mahāmate kuśalākuśalasahetukaḥ*[a] *sarvajanmagatikartā / pravartate naṭavad gatisaṁkaṭa ātmātmīyavarjitaḥ /*[b] *tadanavabodhāt triṁsaṅgatipratyayakriyāyogaḥ pravartate / na ca tīrthyā avabudhyante kāraṇābhiniveśābhiniviṣṭāḥ / anādikālavividhaprapañcadauṣṭhulyavāsanāvāsita ālayavijñānasaṁśabdito 'vidyāvāsanabhūmijaiḥ saptabhir vijñānaiḥ saha mahodadhitaraṁgavan nityam avyucchinnaśarīraḥ pravartate.*

a The private copy of Hemraj Shakya (NGMPP reel no. A 917/6, fol. 105b2) has *-sahetukaḥ* instead of *-hetukaḥ* in the other manuscripts.

b Nanjio has *-varjitas* without *daṇḍa;* but the revised edition of Takasaki (1981:3) is followed here.

97 I.e., the passage that claims that buddha nature teaches emptiness.

98 MA, 198.13–15: *rnam pa de lta bu'i mdo sde rnam par shes par smra ba rnams kyi nges pa'i don nyid du khas blangs pa thams cad drang ba'i don nyid yin par lung 'dis mngon par gsal bar byas nas....*

99 MA, 131.17–19.

100 LAS, 49.2–3: *āture āture yadvad bhiṣag dravyaṁ prayacchati / buddhā hi tadvat sattvānāṁ cittamātraṁ vadanti vai //.*

101 LAS, 49.4–5: *tārkikāṇām aviṣayaṁ śrāvakāṇāṁ na caiva hi / yaṁ deśayanti vai nāthāḥ pratyātmagatigocaram //.*

102 MSA, 40.13–14: *sarveṣām aviśiṣṭāpi tathatā śuddhim āgatā / tathāgatatvaṁ tasmāc ca tadgarbhāḥ sarvadehinaḥ //.*

103 MAVBh, 27.5–9: *na kliṣṭā nāpi vākliṣṭā śuddhā 'śuddhā na caiva sā / kathaṁ na kliṣṭā nāpi cāśuddhā / prakṛtyaiva / prabhāsvaratvāc cittasya / kathaṁ nākliṣṭā na śuddhā / kleśasyāgantukatvataḥ /.*

104 MAVBh, 24.4–13: *kathaṁ śūnyatāyāḥ prabhedo jñeyaḥ / saṁkliṣṭā ca viśuddhā ca / ity asyāḥ prabhedaḥ / kasyām avasthāyāṁ saṁkliṣṭā kasyāṁ viśuddhā / samalā nirmalā ca sā / yadā saha malena varttate tadā saṁkliṣṭā / yadā prahīṇamalā tadā viśuddhā / yadi samalā bhūtvā nirmalā bhavati kathaṁ vikāradharmiṇītvād anityā na bhavati / yasmād asyāḥ abdhātukanakākāśaśuddhivac chuddir iṣyate // āgantukamalāpagamān na tu tasyāḥ svabhāvānyatvaṁ bhavati /.*

105 See Mathes 1996:20–21. Gzhon nu dpal (DRSM, 455.24–470.24) explains convincingly that the part of the *Dharmadharmatāvibhāga* dealing with *āśrayaparivṛtti* is a commentary on the second chapter of the *Ratnagotravibhāga.*

106 Mathes 1996:152–53.

107 Pāsādika 1989:129–30.

108 It is quoted in full length in RGVV I.2. For a translation see DRSM, 37.8–40.8.

109 See Cabezón 2003:294.

110 This gap will be filled, however, by the forthcoming thesis of Kazuo Kano.

111 In July 1994 I managed to find a complete block print of this commentary in the library of the Shel ri sprul skus in Dolpo and could thus restore the first folio, which was missing in the copy of Dvags po Rin po che (the NGMPP reel number of the text from Dolpo is L 519/4).

112 Seyfort Ruegg 1969:302–4.

113 Lit., "actually."

114 But they are, in fact. In other words, the ultimate does even not appear in a nonconceptual direct cognition. Thus, it does not become the basis for a verbal ascertainment in the same way as a vase.

115 Rngog Blo ldan shes rab: *Theg chen rgyud bla'i don bsdus pa*, 6b1–2: *don dam pa ni Ngagi yul ma yin pa'i phyir te / rnam par rtog pa ni kun rdzob yin pas don dam pa rtog pa'i yul ma yin pa'i phyir ro / / ngagis brjod du med pa'i don yang 'dir sgra dang rtog pa'i zhen gzhi ma yin pa la dgongs te / dngos su sgra'i shes pa la mi snang ba tsam ni ma yin no / / 'di ltar yin na ni kun rdzob pa bum pa la sogs pa yang de ltar thal ba'i phyir ro //.* See also Jackson 1994:18–19.

116 Jackson 1994:19.

117 This translation as a relative clause requires taking the preceding clauses ending in *ston pa* as (genitive?) attributes depending on the following *Mahāyānottaratantra.*

118 Tib. *tshul gcig* (Skt. *ekanaya*) "single mode" refers to the theory of *ekayāna* (see Blo ldan shes rab's (*op. cit.*, 44b1–2) explanation of *ekanayadharmadhātu* [RGVV, 77.7]).

119 Rngog Blo ldan shes rab: *Theg chen rgyud bla'i don bsdus pa*, 1b2–4: *bcom ldan 'das byams pas bde bar gshegs pa'i bka'i dgongs pa phyin ci ma log par gsal bar mdzad pa na / nges pa'i don gyi mdo sde rin po che phyir mi ldog pa'i chos kyi 'khor lo / chos kyi dbyings tshul gcig tu ston pa / shin tu rnam par dag pa gdon mi za ba'i chos kyi rnam grangs thams cad kyi don rab tu ston pa / theg pa chen po rgyud bla ma'i bstan bcos 'di mdzad pas / theg pa chen po'i don gyi de kho na rnam par gzhag pa yin no /.*

That the *Ratnagotravibhāga* has definitive meaning for Blo ldan shes rab is also clear from his commentary on RGV I.159–60 (J I.156–57); see Rngog Blo ldan shes rab: *op. cit.*, 44b6–46a5.

120 Rngog Blo ldan shes rab: *op. cit.*, 1b4–2a1.

121 Gzhon nu dpal: *Deb ther sngon po*, 309.5–7: *...lo tsā ba chen po dang slob dpon gtsang nag pa ni de bzhin gshegs pa'i snying po zhes bya ba don dam pa'i bden pa la zer mod kyi / don dam pa'i bden pa ni sgra dang rtog (text: rtogs) pa'i dngos kyi yul ma yin pa lta zhog / zhen pa'i yul tsam yang ma yin zhes gsung / slob dpon Phya pa ni dngos po rnams bden pas stong pa'i med pa dgag pa ni don dam pa'i bden pa yin zhing / de sgra rtog gi zhen pa'i yul du yang bzhed /.*

122 Rngog Blo ldan shes rab: *op. cit.*, 22b4–23a1: *ji snyed yod pa nyid rig pa ni thams cad la rdzogs pa'i sangs rgyas rjes zhugs gzigs pa zhes bya ba ste / thun mong gyi mtshan nyid chos dang gang zag gi bdag med pa de nyid ni / de bzhin gshegs pa'i rang bzhin sangs rgyas kyi snying po yin la / de'ang rten sems can gyi khams thams cad la khyab par rjes su zhugs par rig pa ni ji snyed yod pa shes pa'o / / de la 'gro ba thams cad la yod pa'i bdag med pa nyid de kho na phyin ci ma log par rig pa ni ji lta ba rig pa yin la / des rten thams cad la khyab par dmigs pa ni ji snyed pa rig pa yin no / / gnyis ka yang 'jig rten las 'das pa'i shes rab don dam pa'i yul yin gyi / kun rdzob kyi yul can ni ma yin no /.*

123 Otherwise translated as "buddha nature."

124 I take Tib. *btags pa* in the sense of Skt. *prājñaptika* (Tib. *btags pa ba*), which is usually opposed to Skt. *lākṣaṇika* (Tib. *mtshan nyid pa*) "the real one" (see Ārya Vimuktisena's *Abhisamayālaṁkāravṛtti* on I.39 and Kano 2003:109–11).

125 Rngog Blo ldan shes rab: *op. cit.*, 29a4–29b2: */ de la rnam par dag pa'i de bzhin*

nyid rdzogs pa'i sangs rgyas kyi sku yin la / de la 'phro ba ni des khyab pa ste / sems can thams cad kyis thob tu rung ba'i phyir khyab pa yin no / / phyogs 'di la ni de bzhin gshegs pa ni dngos po yin la / sems can 'di'i snying po can du ni btags pa yin te / de thob pa'i skal ba yod pa la des khyab par btags pa'i phyir ro / / . . . rigs yod pa'i phyir na zhes bya ba ni / de bzhin nyid rnam par dag pa'i gnas skabs thob pa'i rgyu dge ba'i bag chags shes rab dang snying rje'i sa bon ni de bzhin gshegs pa'i rgyu yin pas de bzhin gshegs pa zhes btags pa yin la / sems can gyi snying po ni dngos po kho na yin no /.

126 This is quoted in RGVV I.25. The immeasurable qualities are compared to a one-to-one scale painting of the universe on a silk cloth that has been put inside an atom.

127 Rngog Blo ldan shes rab: *op. cit.*, 28b4–6: */ 'dir dar yug gi ri mo rdul phra rab la yod pa de bzhin du / sangs rgyas kyi ye shes sems can gyi rgyud la yod pa de gang zhe na / chos kyi dbyings so / / de ji ltar ye shes yin zhe na / bcom ldan 'das kyis chos thams cad mtshan nyid med par skad cig gcig dang ldan pa'i shes rab kyis mkhyen pas (text: bais) na / shes rab de shes bya dang dbyer med do / / des na don dam pa chos kyi dbyings nyid de rig pa'i ye shes yin la / de yang sems can thams cad la ma tshang ba med par gnas pas dpe don 'di ni shin tu 'thad pa'o /.*

128 Ibid., 41a6–b1: *lus pa med pa'i sems can gyi khams khyab pa zhes bya ba ni / de bzhin gshegs pa snga ma rnams kyi rtogs pa'i chos dpag tu med pa'i tshogs las yang dag par grub pa / shin tu rnam par dag pa'i de bzhin nyid dang / de dmigs pa'i ye shes tha dad pa'i rang bzhin des sems can thams cad la khyab pa ste / chos sku de ni stong pa nyid yin la / stong pa nyid kyang sems can la yod pa'i phyir ro /.*

129 Ibid., 49b3–50a3.

130 Ibid., 19b5–6 and 20a5.

131 Ibid., 5b3: "The continuum of mind, which has the nature of emptiness, is the [buddha] element" *(. . . stong pa nyid kyi rang bzhin du gyur pa'i sems kyi rgyud ni khams yin no).*

132 Ibid., 4a2–3: *. . . med par dgag pa'i tha snyad kyi yul du gyur pa'i khams ni med par dgag pa'i tha snyad kyi yul du gyur pa'i nyer len du brjod kyi skyes bu byed pa'i don nyid ni dngos su yod pa ma yin no / / tha snyad kyi yul zhes bya ba ni / med par dgag pa rang bzhin du grub pa de kho nar med pa'i don te /.*

133 RGVV, 148.2–4: *buddhatvam. . . sarvair buddhaguṇair upetam amalair nityaṁ dhruvaṁ śāśvataṁ /.*

134 Rngog Blo ldan shes rab: *op. cit.*, 47a6–b2: *. . . dri med sangs rgyas yon tan kun ldan / rtag brtag g.yung drung ni sangs rgyas nyid do // zhes bya bas ye shes dang spangs pa dang / de la brten pa'i yon tan dang / de yang sngon med pa skyes pa ni ma yin te / sngon gyi sgrib pa dang bcas pa'i gnas skabs na yod pa nyid du brjod pas ni ngo bo bstan pa to // de'i rgyu ni de la chos la mi rtog pa'i ye shes dang / de'i rjes las thob pa rnam 'byed ye shes te /.*

135 "Because it is endowed with the state of having adventitious faults, and naturally endowed with qualities, it is of an unchangeable nature—as it was before, so it is after." (RGVV, 41.20–21: *doṣāgantukatāyogād guṇaprakṛtiyogataḥ / yathā pūrvaṁ tathā paścād avikāritvadharmatā //.*)

136 Gzhon nu dpal explains in this context that "endowed" (Tib. *ldan pa*) has to be understood in the sense of "being connected" *('brel pa)*. To support his interpretation, Gzhon nu dpal quotes Vinayadeva's *Hevajravajrapadoddharaṇanāma-pañjikā*, and explains that defining the relation between buddha nature and the qualities in terms of *'brel pa* underscores both that the qualities have arisen from buddha nature and that the two have an identical nature (see DRSM, 29.18–21 and DRSM, 323.19–23).

137 Tib. *yon tan rang bzhin* is difficult to construe. Either *yon tan* is taken as a genitive attribute *(yon tan gyi rang bzhin)*, or *rang bzhin* as an adverb *(rang bzhin gyis).*

138 Rngog Blo ldan shes rab: *op. cit.*, 33a6–33b3: */ yon tan rang bzhin nyid ldan phyir*

// zhes bya ba ni shin tu rnam par dag pa'i gnas skabs na yon tan gyi chos kyi mi 'gyur ba'i 'thad pa bstan te / yon tan glo bur du gsal ba'i gnas skabs kyi rang bzhin la ma gos pa'i don te / rang bzhin gyi yon tan mtha' dag dang bral ba ma myong ba'o // dper na ma dag pa'i gnas skabs na sngon med pa'i yon tan gyi khyad par can du ma bsgrubs pa bzhin no // yon tan rang bzhin gyis grub pa'i don yang / yon tan rang bzhin dmigs pa sgro ma btags par grub pa'am / yon tan gyi rgyu'i dmigs pa rab tu grub pa'i phyir te / yang dag pa'i kun rdzob sgro ma btags par gnas pa'am / don dam pa de ltar gnas pa'i phyir / rim (text: rigs)[a] *pa bzhin no / don dam pa rtogs pa ni yon tan kun gyi rgyu yin te / chos kyi dbyings rtogs na sangs rgyas kyi yon tan thams cad bos pa bzhin du 'du pa'i phyir ro //.*

a The conjecture is according to Kano.

139 Tib. *kun rdzob*, otherwise translated as "apparent."

140 According to the Skt. and DRSM, 439.25: *'di las bsal bya ci yang med /.*

141 Rngog Blo ldan shes rab: *op. cit.*, 42b3–6: *kun nas nyon mongs pa'i dmigs pa don dam par yod par sgro mi 'dogs pa dang / rnam par byang ba'i sems dang sems las byung ba'i dmigs pa kun rdzob tu yod pa la skur ba mi 'debs pas / bden pa gnyis ji lta ba bzhin gnas pa ni / stong pa'i don phyin ci ma log pa yin no zhes brjod pa ni / 'di la bsal bya ci yang med ces bya ba'o // de kho na nyid 'di la bsal bar bya ba kun nas nyon mongs pa'i dmigs pa ni ci yang med de / gdod ma nas ma grub pa'i phyir ro // de kho na nyid 'dir gzhag par bya ba rnam par byang ba'i mtshan ma stobs dang mngon par shes pa la sogs pa'ang cung zad med do // stobs la sogs pa rnam par byang ba'i dmigs pa kun rdzob tu yod pa ni / thog ma med pa nas gnas pa'i phyir ro /.*

142 Ibid., 43a3–5: *rnam dbyer med pa'i mtshan nyid can / zhes bya ba ni bla na med pa'i yon tan mi dmigs pa kun rdzob tu yod pa ste / de kho na nyid dang kun rdzob tu yod pa mi 'gal ba'i phyir / rang bzhin nyid la yod par brjod do // des na kun rdzob sgyu ma lta bu de mngon sum du rtogs na yon tan de dag 'grub pa yin te / yon tan gyi rang bzhin ni de dag la dmigs pa kho na yin pa'i phyir ro /.*

143 Śākya mchog ldan: "Blo mchog pa'i dri lan," 568.6–7: *dang po la gnyis te / snying po'i ngos 'dzin stobs la sogs yon tan gyis khyad par du ma byas pa'i med dgag gi cha la bzhed pa dang...dang po ni rngog lo tsa chen po rjes 'brang dang bcas pa'o.* For a discussion of this *dri lan* see also Kano 2001:55–56.

144 "The beginningless [buddha] element is the basis of all phenomena." (RGVV, 72.13: *anādikāliko dhātuḥ sarvadharmasamāśrayaḥ /.*)

145 Rngog Blo ldan shes rab: *op. cit.*, 42a4–6.

146 DRSM, 4.14–20.

147 Gzhon nu dpal: *Deb ther sngon po*, 309.7: *btsan lugs pa rnams ni sems kyi rang bzhin 'od gsal ba bde bar gshegs pa'i snying po yin pas / de sangs rgyas kyi rgyu yang grung por bzhed.* Śākya mchog ldan, too, informs us in his *Dbu ma'i 'byung tshul* (p. 240) that Btsan Kha bo che takes buddha nature to be natural luminosity (for a short description of Śākya mchog ldan's position see Tillemans and Tomabechi 1995: 891–96).

148 Shes rab rgya mtsho mentions in his list of rare texts (cf. Lokesh Chandra 1963, vol. 3, no. 11338) "an explanation of the *Uttaratantra* recorded (in the form of notes) by the translator Gzu Dga '[ba] rdo [rje] on the basis of teachings given by the Paṇḍita Sajjana" *(paṇḍita sajjana'i gsung la lo tsā ba gzu dga' rdor gyi zin bris byas pa'i rgyud bla ma'i rnam bshad).*

149 Kong sprul Blo gros mtha' yas: *Rgyud bla ma'i bshad srol*, 9b1–4.

150 These include "not specifically tantric" mahāmudrā meditation techniques that do not require any initiation or formal tantric practice.

151 DRSM, 574.5–12.

152 Śākya mchog ldan: "Blo mchog pa'i dri lan," 569.1–3: *snying po'i ngos 'dzin rang bzhin rnam dag rkyang pa'i cha la bzhed pa dang / de dang yon tan dbyer med kyi*

tshogs don la bzhed pa'o / / gnyis pa la'ang / yon tan de dag rtogs pa chos sku'i yon tan go chod por 'dod pa dang / rang bzhin chos sku'i yon tan du 'dod pa'o / ... / gnyis pa ni rje phag mo gru pa sogs rje dvags po'i bka' brgyud 'dzin pa mang po dag go.

I have to thank Kazuo Kano for drawing my attention to this reference.

153 Rang byung rdo rje: *Dbu ma chos dbyings bstod pa'i rnam par bshad pa*, 22a3–4.

154 The text in the Peking Tengyur (TA, 43b5) reads *phyag rgya chen po las byung ba* ("what has arisen from mahāmudrā") instead of *phyag rgya chen po*.

155 Gzhon nu dpal: *Deb ther sngon po*, 632.6–633.4: *de yang dvags po rin po ches dpal phag mo gru pa la / 'o skol gyi phyag rgya chen po 'di'i gzhung ni bcom ldan 'das byams pas mdzad pa'i theg pa chen po rgyud bla ma'i bstan bcos 'di yin zhes gsungs shing / dpal phag mo gru pas kyang rje 'bri gung (text: khung) pa la de skad du gsungs pas / rje 'bri gung (text: khung) pa dpon slob kyi gsung rab rnams su theg pa chen po rgyud bla ma'i bshad pa mang du 'byung ba de yin no / 'di la chos rje sa skya pas pha rol tu phyin pa'i lugs la phyag rgya chen po'i tha snyad med cing / phyag rgya chen po'i ye shes gang yin pa de ni dbang las skyes pa'i ye shes kho na yin no zhes bzhed mod kyi / slob dpon ye shes grags pas mdzad pa'i de kho na nyid la 'jug par / pha rol tu phyin pa la mngon par brtson pa'i dbang po rab ni / zhi gnas dang lhag mthong bsgoms pas so so'i skye bo'i gnas skabs nyid na phyag rgya chen po dang nges par ldan pa yang dag par rtogs pas phyir mi ldog pa'i rtags nyid dang / zhes gsungs la / de kho na nyid bcu pa'i 'grel pa (text: 'brel ba) lhan cig skyes pa'i rdo rjes mdzad par yang / ngo bo pha rol tu phyin pa / sngags dang rjes su mthun pa / ming phyag rgya chen po zhes bya ba'i khyad par gsum dang ldan pa'i de bzhin nyid rtogs pa'i ye shes gsal bar bshad do / de bas na rje sgam po pa'i pha rol tu (text: du) phyin pa'i phyag rgya chen po ni mnga' bdag mai trī (text: tri) pa'i bzhed pa yin par rje rgod tshang pas kyang bshad do /.* See also Roerich 1949–53:724–25.

156 See also Jackson 1994:17–19.

157 Sa skya Paṇḍita claims in his *Sdom gsum rab dbye* that there is no substantial difference between such a mahāmudrā and the rdzogs chen of the Chinese tradition (see Rhoton 2002:118).

158 See Roerich 1949–53:402.

159 See my translation of DRSM, 5.12–15.

160 Mi bskyod rdo rje: *Dbu ma la 'jug pa'i rnam bshad*, 5.4–5.

161 Lhalungpa 1993:101.

162 DRSM, 343.2.

163 According to the colophon, the *Tattvāvatāra* was translated by Rin chen bzang po (958–1055).

164 TA, 46a2–3: *yum chen mo shes rab kyi pha rol tu phyin pa nyid kyi mtshan gzhan ni phyag rgya chen po ste / de ni gnyis su med pa'i ye shes kyi ngo bo nyid yin pa'i phyir ro /.*

165 These *pāda*s mark the end of a traditional description of the fourfold Mahāyāna meditation in the *Laṅkāvatārasūtra* (LAS 298.15–299.1): "Based on the apprehension of suchness, one should pass beyond [even] mind only (X.256cd). Having passed beyond mind only, one should pass beyond a state that is without appearances. A yogin who is established in a state without appearances, sees the Mahāyāna (X.257)." (*cittamātraṁ samāruhya bāhyam arthaṁ na kalpayet / tathatālambane sthitvā cittamātram atikramet //* (X.256) *cittamātram atikramya nirābhāsam atikramet / nirābhāsasthito yogī mahāyānaṁ sa*[a] *paśyati //* (X.257).)

a According to ms. T in Nanjio's edition.

This passage is cited in Seyfort Ruegg 1981:90; Mimaki 1982:236–40; Eckel 1987:60; Lindtner 1997:160; and Bentor 2002:44–45.

166 TA, 71b8–72a1: ... *theg pa chen po zhes bya ba la / mtshan gyi rnam pa gzhan du na phyag rgya chen po zhes bya ba ste / de mthong bar 'gyur ro zhes gsungs pa ni / snang med gnas pa'i rnal 'byor pa / de yis theg pa chen po mthong.*

167 See LAS, 79.16–82.4.

168 See Mathes 2005:16–19.

169 *Tattvadaśaka* stanza no. 9 is as follows (TD, 94.7–8): "[The yogin] who has left the [eight] worldly dharmas behind and adopted a yogic conduct does everything without a reference point, being adorned with the blessing from within." *(lokadharmavyatīto 'sau unmattavratam āśritaḥ / sarvaṁ karoty anālambaḥ svādhiṣṭhānavibhūṣitaḥ //.)*

170 KDN, 14.10–15.

171 TDṬ, 193b6: "Yogic conduct *(unmattavrata)* means acting without the thoughts of the mental faculty" *(smyon pa'i brtul zhugs ni yid kyis bsam pa med par byed nyid do /);* and TDṬ, 194a3–4: "He is adorned by his being blessed from within means that he is blessed by himself in the nature of his mindstream, which is connected with the nature of uncontrived reality. That which emanates from [his] nature of suchness naturally adorns him." *(rang byin brlabs pas rnam brgyan pa'o zhes bya ba ni rang nyid gnyug ma'i de kho na nyid kyi bdag nyid du 'byor pa'i sems kyi rgyun de'i bdag nyid du byin gyis brlabs pa'o / / de bzhin nyid kyi rang bzhin las 'phro ba rang bzhin gyis rgyan pa....)*

172 PK III, introduction (31.3–7): *utpattikramānusāreṇa prāptābhiṣekhaḥ...vajraguruṁ samyag ārādhya / ...tadanantaraṁ guruvaktrād āptasvādhiṣṭhānakramopadeśaḥ /.*

173 PK III.14: *svādhiṣṭhānānupūrveṇa prāpyate hi prabhāsvaram / tasmād vajraguruḥ pūrvaṁ svādhiṣṭhānaṁ pradarśayet //.*

174 See Tatz 1994:98.

175 See the translation of DRSM, 61.18 below.

176 TD, 92.9–94.2: *evam ekarasā dharmā nirāsaṅgā nirāspadāḥ / prabhāsvarā amī sarve yathābhūtasamādhinā // yathābhūtasamādhiś ca bhavet prasthānacittataḥ / ajasraṁ jāyate tattvaṁ yasmāt tatpadavedinām //.*

177 See Mathes 2006:222–23.

178 I.e., the works of Kamalaśīla.

179 According to the reading in Gzhon nu dpal's quote: "right from the beginning" *(dang po nas);* see DRSM, 55.9.

180 TDṬ, 189a1–2: *...'jug pa'i sems pha rol tu phyin pa'i tshul gyi rab tu dbye ba rnams ni ka ma la shī la'i sgom pa'i rim pa la sogs par bsdus pa dang rgyas par bzhag ste* (corrected according to Gzhon nu dpal's quote (see DRSM, 55.6–7); the Peking Tengyur reads *kā ma la shī la la sogs pa'i sgo nas bstan te*) */ de nyid du rtogs par bya'o / / 'dir rgyas pa'i 'jigs pas ma bris so / / de lta bur gyur pa'i 'jug pa'i sems ni 'dir dgongs pa ma yin no / 'dir de dpyad pa las byas pas yongs su ma dag pa'i phyir ro / / 'dir dpyad pa med pa'i sems kyis mngon (text: kyi sngon) du bsgom bya ba nyid do /.*

181 MV, 76.11–12: *dharmaskandhasahasreṣu bu*[a]*dhyatāṁ nāma śūnyatā / bu*[b]*ddhā nāsau parāmarśād vināśārthaṁ bhaved guroḥ //.*

a According to the manuscript (NGMPP reel no. B 22/24, fol. 34b5); the Japanese edition has *ba-*.

b The manuscript (NGMPP reel no. B 22/24, fol. 34b5) and the Japanese edition have *bu-*.

182 TDṬ, 189b6: *thabs dang shes rab bdag nyid kyi shes pa gnyis med pa'i de kho na nyid byang chub kyi sems so /.*

183 TD, 94.4: *dvayahīnābhimāna*[a]*ś ca tathaiva hi prabhāsvaraḥ //.*

a According to the Japanese edition. The manuscript reads *-noya-*, Bhattacharya *-ropa-*.

My translation follows the Sanskrit here.

184 SN, 58.13–14: *pratipakṣe sthito naiva tattvāsakto 'pi naiva yaḥ / gārddhyaṁ naiva phale yasya mahāmudrāṁ sa vindati //.*

185 TDṬ, 190a4–6: */ gnyis dang bral bar rlom pa yang / / gang phyir de ni 'od gsal 'dod*

[/] ces bya ba smras te / [a] *'di (text: 'dir) ni 'dir dgongs pa yin te / de yongs su shes pas de kho na nyid do*[a] *[/] de kho na nyid rtogs par bya ba'i phyir dpyod pa gsum rnam par spang bar bya bar (text: ba) bstan pa yin te / mtha' bzhi yongs su spong ba bzhin no / / gnyen po'i phyogs la mi gnas shing / / de nyid la yang chags min gang (text: mi chags pas) / / gang gi'ang 'bras bu mi 'dod pa (text: pas) / / de yis (text: yi) phyag rgya chen po shes / / zhes bya ba'i tshig gis so / / 'dir yang phyag rgya chen po zhes bya ba ni phyag rgya chen po'i de kho na nyid kyi man ngag ste /.* My emendations are according to DRSM, 462.16–19.

a Gzhon nu dpal, who quotes this passage (DRSM, 462.15–16), has a different reading: *'dir dgongs pa ni 'di yin te / de kho na nyid yongs su mi shes pa dag gis ni....* The translation follows this reading.

186 TDṬ, 190b8–191a2.

187 Sahajavajra (TDṬ, 191b8) glosses *gang des (yena tena)* as "by [living on] any food. Whether it is [good] food or not, it must be eaten as found. One should not cling thereby to any thoughts about what one likes and what not" *(zas kyis so / / bza' dang bza' min de bzhin du / / ji ltar rnyed pa bza' bar bya / / 'dod dang mi 'dod rnam rtog rnams / / 'dzin pa 'dir mi bya'o /).*

188 Sahajavajra (TDṬ, 191b8–192a1) glosses *ji ltar de ltar (yathā tathā)* as "whoever it is, by the aspects of his body, speech, and mind" *(gang dang gang de'i lus dang / ngag dang / yid kyi rnam pas so /).* In other words, the yogin fully experiences the nondual reality of every moment in any situation without any thought as to what he likes.

189 TD, 94.5–6: *etattattvāvabodhena*[a] *yena tena yathā tathā / vivṛtākṣo bhramed yogī keśarīva samantataḥ.*

a Shastri 1927:59 reads *-rodhena.*

190 The instrumental *(rnal 'byor pas)* indicates that the subject of the root text is glossed where *yogin* together with its attribute is in this case *(rnal 'byor mig ni rgyas 'gyur pas).*

191 TDṬ, 191b5–6: *...sngar bstan pa'i gnyis su med pa'i de kho na nyid du (omit du?) bla ma dam pa'i man ngagis nges par rtogs pa'i rnal 'byor pas so /.*

192 TDṬ, 192a5–b1: *'o na gsang sngags kyi tshul gyi rnal 'byor pa dang bye brag ci yod ce na / / phyag rgya bzhi'i rjes su 'gro ba med pa'i phyir dang / lha'i nga rgyal gyi bde ba chen po'i ro med pas / / btang snyoms kyi rnam pas mngon par byang chub pa dus ring pos rdzogs pa'i phyir / bsgrub par bya ba dang sgrub par byed pa nyid kyi rnam pas (text: pa) bye brag nyid shin tu che'o / / gzhan gyis (text: gyi) pha rol tu phyin pa'i tshul gyi rnal 'byor pa las 'di khyad par yod de / bla ma dam pa'i man ngagis dpyad pa'i stong pa nyid zung du 'jug pa'i de bzhin nyid nges par rtogs pas shin tu khyad par 'phags pa'i phyir ro / / de'i phyir 'di nyid dka' ba'i spyod pa med pa 'di nyid ni stong pa nyid du ro gcig pa'i de kho na nyid shin tu nges pa dag ni yul gyi grong gis sbrul 'dzin pa ltar sbrul la rtse yang de'i 'bigs par mi 'gyur ro / / 'di nyid la de kho na nyid kyi ye shes phyag rgya chen po zhes kha cig brjod /.*

193 This means that phenomena cannot be ascertained to be either single individuals (wholes) or plural composites (parts).

194 Sgam po pa: "Tshogs chos yon tan phun tshogs," 556.4–557.3: *de la rjes dpag lam du byed pa ni / chos thams cad gcig dang du bral gyi gtan tshigs kyis gzhig (text: gzhigs) nas / 'gro sa 'di las med zer nas thams cad stong par byas nas 'jog pa ni rjes dpag go / lha'i sku bskyed pa'i rim pa la brten nas rtsa rlung dang thig le dang / sngags kyi bzlas brjod la sogs pa byin rlabs kyi lam mo / / mngon sum lam du byed pa ni bla ma dam pa cig gis sems nyid lhan cig skyes pa chos kyi sku 'od gsal bya ba yin gsung ba de lta bu nges pa'i don gyi gdams ngag phyin ci ma log bstan pas / rang la nges pa'i shes pa lhan cig skyes pa de la lta spyod sgom gsum ya ma bral bar gnyug ma'i shes pa lam du khyer ba....*

195 Jackson 1994:34.

196 Lit., "somebody whose [realization] is instantaneous." The term *simultaneeist* takes into account that realization may already occur together with otherwise ordinary modes of consciousness.

197 The date is according to Karmay 1988:102.

198 See Karmay 1988:95. For a detailed discussion of the *cig car ba* tradition in Tibet, see Seyfort Ruegg 1989.

199 See Sgam po pa "Tshogs chos bkra shis phun tshogs," 290.2–3.

200 Kapstein (2000:77) suggests that Sgam po pa did not quote directly from sūtras in support of his mahāmudrā, but was culling them from pre-existing meditation manuals, such as the *Bsam gtan mig sgron.* Indeed, he was careful to employ only passages attributed to sūtras in order to avoid being accused of propagating Chinese Ch'an Buddhism. But several of the sūtras were Ch'an apocryphal writings.

201 'Jig rten gsum mgon: "Chos 'khor 'ong ges zhus pa'i gzhung gi rtsa ba," 15.12–14: *phyag rgya chen po theg chen bla ma'i rgyud / 'di yi khrid la 'bad pas nan tan byas / / 'jig rten mgon las yang dang yang du thos.*

202 "Chos 'khor 'ong ges zhus pa'i gzhung gi 'grel pa," 317.9–12: *dpal 'bri gung pa chen po kho (text: khong) rang nyid kyis thugs dam mdzad pa'i phyag rgya chen po de ni theg pa chen po rgyud bla ma 'di nyid dang mthun te / phyag rgya chen po yon tan de ni theg pa chen po rgyud bla mar yang don de nyid bstan pa'o.*

203 'Jig rten gsum mgon: "Chos 'khor 'ong ges zhus pa'i gzhung gi rtsa ba," 14.17–15.2: "This supreme summary of the seven vajra points was made by the illustrious [Maitreya]nātha as a commentary on the third dharmacakra." *(/ rdo rje gnas bdun mchog tu bsdus pa 'di / / chos kyi 'khor lo gsum pa'i don 'grel du / bcom ldan mgon pos mdzad par gyur....)*

204 Ibid., 10.17: "This [third] dharmacakra of definitive meaning...." *(/ nges pa'i don gyi chos kyi 'khor lo 'di /)*

205 In fact, the "Dam chos dgongs pa gcig pa'i gzhung" was written down by 'Bri gung 'Jig rten gsum mgon's disciple Spyan snga Shes rab 'byung gnas (1187–1241).

206 'Jig rten gsum mgon: "Dam chos dgongs pa gcig pa'i gzhung," 11.11–13: "The three aspects of the dharmacakra ('dharma circle') differ in accordance with the thought [characteristic of] the circle of disciples. In each dharmacakra all three are complete. The seed of the following [dharmacakra] already abides in the previous one" *(chos 'khor rnam gsum 'khor gyi rtog pa'i khyad / / 'khor lo re re la yang gsum ga tshang / / phyi ma'i sa bon snga ma snga mar gnas /).* See also Rig 'dzin Chos kyi grags pa: "Dam pa'i chos dgongs pa gcig pa'i rnam bshad lung don gsal byed nyi ma'i snang ba," 43.8–52.14.

207 'Jig rten gsum mgon: "Chos 'khor 'ong ges zhus pa'i gzhung gi 'grel pa," 330.17–331.3: "In general, it is the seed of the three dharmacakras, and in particular the subject matter of the dharmacakra of definitive meaning.... All *yānas*—such can be definitely ascertained—[lead] ultimately [to] a uniform path, the single *yāna*" *(spyir 'khor lo gsum gyi sa bon / bye brag tu nges don chos kyi 'khor lo'i brjod bya / ... theg pa thams cad mthar thug tshul gcig pa theg pa gcig tu nges par gtan la phabs te /).*

208 It is said, for example, the first dharmacakra makes one mature *(smin);* the second one makes one mature very much *(shin tu smin);* and the third one makes one mature to the utmost *(shin tu rab tu smin)* (Ibid., 346.19–347.6).

209 'Jig rten gsum mgon: "Chos 'khor 'ong ges zhus pa'i gzhung gi rtsa ba," 18.10–14: */ cig car ba dang rim gyis pa zhes pa / / sems can khams kyis (text: kyi) byang chub thob byed pa / / rim gyis thob kyi cig car ma yin zhes / ... / dang por byang chub mchog tu sems bskyed nas / / 'khor lo gsum po rim gyis bgrod pa dang /.*

210 'Jig rten gsum mgon: "Chos 'khor 'ong ges zhus pa'i gzhung gi 'grel pa," 338.1–7: *cig car ni rnam pa thams cad du mi srid pa yin / 'o na cig car ba gang la zer snyam na / sngon bsod nams bsags pa'i 'bras bu tshe 'dir thob pa la cig car ba zhes btags / de ltar na bdag cag gi ston pa sangs rgyas bcom ldan 'das kyang cig car ba yin te / sngon bskal pa grangs med pa rnams su tshogs bsags pa'i 'bras bus tshe 'dir sangs rgyas pa yin / 'on kyang sngon bsod nams bsags pa la ma ltos pa'i tshe 'dir 'bras bu thob pa mi 'ong bas de ltar na lam thams cad rim gyis pa yin te /.*

211 Ibid., 338.12–17: *bdag cag gi ston pa sangs rgyas bcom ldan 'das 'di nyid kyang / ...dang po bla na med pa'i byang chub tu sems bskyed nas / sa dang po man chad bskal pa grangs med gcig 'khor lo dang po'i tshul gyis lam bgrod / sa bdun man chad du grangs med gcig 'khor lo gnyis pa'i tshul gyis lam bgrod / dag pa'i sa gsum gyi grangs med gcig 'khor lo gsum pa'i tshul gyis lam bgrod pa yin....*

212 'Jig rten gsum mgon: "Dam chos dgongs pa gcig pa'i gzhung," 12.4–5: *ji snyed lam rnams sa bcus bgrod pa ste / de yang rim gyis 'jug pa.*

213 Rig 'dzin Chos kyi grags pa: "Dam pa'i chos dgongs pa gcig pa'i rnam bshad lung don gsal byed nyi ma'i snang ba," 75.9–15: */ gzhan yang dpal phag mo gru pas / / cig car 'jug pa'i gang zag de / / tshogs bsags bsags pa yi gang zag yin / / rgyud sbyangs sbyangs pa yi gang zag yin / / blo btul btul ba yi gang zag yin / / nyams skyes skyes pa yi gang zag yin / zhes gsungs pa ni skye ba 'di'i rim gyis pa yang ma zad par skye ba mang po'i snga rol nas bsags sbyang byas pa la dgongs pas tshe 'di'i rtogs pa skye myur gcig car ba zhes bod pa de yang skye ba snga ma nas rim gyis sbyangs pa la dgongs so /.*

214 'Jig rten gsum mgon: "Dam chos dgongs pa gcig pa'i gzhung," 12.4–5: */ shes bya'i sgrib pa thog mar spong ba'ang yod /.*

215 Ibid., 15.4: */ rtogs pa gcig gis sa lam ma lus bgrod /.*

216 Ibid., 17.1–2: */ rtogs pa skyed thabs mos gus kho nar nges /.*

217 Ibid., 17.2: */ lta ba'i mchog gyur rtogs pa dang ldan pa /.*

218 Ibid., 17.4: */ rtogs pa goms par byed pa sgom pa ste /.*

219 According to oral explanations of Lama Jorphel (Kathmandu).

220 DRSM, 73.3–5. See also Martin 1992:287 and Jackson 1990:52–53.

221 DRSM, 74.18–25.

222 DRSM, 272.6–10; see chapter 7 of this work.

223 Kong sprul Blo gros mtha' yas: *Shes bya kun khyab mdzod*, vol. 3, 375–94; and Ponlob Rinpoche in Callahan 2002:xxiiif.

224 Oral information by Ponlob Rinpoche.

225 DRSM, 73.8–10.

226 See also Broido 1987:67.

227 See DRSM, 74–75.

228 See Mathes 2000:195–223.

229 Hookham (1991) and Stearns (1999) have already described Dol po pa's system of interpretation at length. Moreover, Stearns has given a detailed account of Dol po pa's life, based on two early biographies written by his disciples Lha'i rgyal mtshan (1319–1401) and Kun spangs Chos grags dpal bzang (1283–1363?) (Stearns 1999:11–39).

230 Dol po pa: *Ri chos nges don rgya mtsho*, 150.4–6: *kun btags dang gzhan dbang gis stong pa'i chos nyid yongs grub don dam du yod par gsungs pa'i phyir don dam gzhan stong nyid du legs par grub po /.*

231 This point used to be misrepresented by the Dge lugs pas. See for example the description of the Jo nang position in the *Grub mtha' shel gyi me long* (Seyfort Ruegg 1963:73–91).

232 Dol po pa: *Ri chos nges don rgya mtsho*, 446.26–447.1: *chos sku de ni gdod nas spros dang bral / spros dang bral ngo shes pas bden par grub /.*

233 Cf. also Dol po pa's definition of ultimate truth in the *Ri chos nges don rgya mtsho*

(258.11–12): "Ultimate truth means that [something] is true ultimately, and not on the level of apparent [truth]." *(don dam bden pa gang yin pa de don dam du bden gyi kun rdzob tu bden pa ma yin.)*

234 Stearns 1995:829–31.

235 See Tāranātha: "Gzhan stong snying po," 502.5–503.1.

236 It is important to note that Sajjana himself does not use the term *gzhan stong* within his system of interpretation, it being Kun dga' grol mchog who uses this term to describe it.

237 This and the following are of course allusions to the *Madhyāntavibhāga* and *Dharmadharmatāvibhāga.*

238 Kun dga' grol mchog: "Khrid brgya'i brgyud pa'i lo rgyus bzhugs so," 83.6–84.1 (See also *Jo nang kun dga' grol mchog gi khrid brgya'i skor*, 104.3–5): */ kha che paṇḍita sajjana'i gsung gis rgyal bas 'khor lo dang po bden bzhi / bar pa mtshan nyid med pa / mthar legs par rnam par phye ba'i chos kyi 'khor lo bzlas pa lan gsum bskor ba las snga ma gnyis dngos btags ma phye ba / phyi ma don dam par nges pa'i tshe / dbus dang mtha' phye / chos dang chos nyid phye nas gsungs zhing /.* My translation follows closely the one by Stearns (1999:42–43). In the following, Kun dga' grol mchog tells us that this statement appears in an old notebook written by Btsan Kha bo che himself and called *Padma lcags kyu* (Ibid.).

239 See van der Kuijp 1983:41.

240 See Dol po pa: *Ri chos nges don rgya mtsho*, 341.4–344.16.

241 Such a hermeneutic strategy is also referred to in the introduction of Kong sprul Blo gros mtha' yas's *Ratnagotravibhāga* commentary, where it is stated with regard to the Btsan tradition of interpreting the same text: "In accordance with this tradition, the great Omniscient Dol po pa introduced an extraordinary tradition, and following [his] commentary, [his] lineage of disciples in general, and such masters as the Omniscient Tāranātha in particular, established a textual tradition based on explanation and practice. The oral transmission of these commentaries continues up to the present day" (Kong sprul Blo gros mtha' yas: *Rgyud bla ma'i bshad srol*, 9b5–10a1: *...lugs 'di dang mthun pa / kun mkhyen dol po pa chen pos thun mong ma yin pa'i srol phye ste (text: phyes te) 'grel pa'i rjes su 'brangs nas slob brgyud spyi dang bye brag thams cad mkhyen pa tāranātha sogs kyis bshad pa dang nyams len gyis gzhung btsugs pa'i 'grel pa'i lung rgyun da ltar bar bzhugs pa dang /*).

242 See Mathes 1996:160–61.

243 Kong sprul Blo gros mtha' yas: *Shes bya kun khyab mdzod*, vol. 1, 460–61.

244 See Tsultrim Gyamtsho and Fuchs 2000:103–4.

245 This restriction is also explained in Tāranātha's *Gzhan stong snying po* (see Mathes 2000:219–20).

246 See Mathes 2004:285–328.

247 Lamotte 1938:19–20; see "The Position of the Third Karmapa Rangjung Dorjé" in chapter 2 of this work, where MS I.48 is quoted and discussed.

248 See Frauwallner 1951:148–59. Seyfort Ruegg (1973:7) took this distinction to be a forerunner of *gzhan stong.*

249 Closely related to this topic are, of course, the questions of *gzhan stong*, two types of emptiness, and the relationship between the two truths.

250 See Zhva dmar Chos grags ye shes: *Gzhon nu dpal gyi rnam thar*, 10b1f. and 19a4–6 (see chapter 3).

251 Thus, for Rong ston, the buddha element is not empty of the selflessness of phenomena and persons, whereas Gzhon nu dpal propounds his "subtle qualities," of which the buddha element is not empty. (Rong ston: *Theg pa chen po rgyud bla ma'i bstan bcos legs par bshad pa*, 143.20–146.19.)

252 Zhva dmar Chos grags ye shes reports (*Gzhon nu dpal gyi rnam thar*, 19a4–5) that

Gzhon nu dpal received *Ratnagotravibhāga* explanations from Rong ston in Thang po che in 1421.

253 Ibid., 10b1–2.

254 Ri mi 'babs pa, who was a disciple of the second Zhva dmar pa, eventually became a follower of the Dge lugs pa (see Roerich 1949–53:546).

255 Zhva dmar Chos grags ye shes: *Gzhon nu dpal gyi rnam thar*, 30b5–31a5.

256 Mi bskyod rdo rje: "Rje yid bzang rtse ba'i Rgyud gsum gsang ba...," 989.2–3: *yang bla ma rin po che blo bzang grags pa'i lta grub tshad mar yang khas blangs nas / mnyam med dvags po bka' brgyud kyi srol 'dzin du bzhed pa dpon slob yid (text: yig) bzang rtse pa dag /.*

257 Zhva dmar Chos grags ye shes: *Gzhon nu dpal gyi rnam thar*, 29a2–3.

258 Ibid., 10b7–11a2.

259 RGVV, 25.11–13: *tatraiṣāṁ caturṇāṁ padānāṁ prathamaṁ lokottaradharmabījatvāt pratyātmayoniśomanasikārasaṁniśrayeṇa tadviśuddhim upādāya triratnotpattihetur anugantavyaḥ /.*

260 DRSM, 261.13–4 and rNgog Blo ldan shes rab: *Theg chen rgyud bla'i bsdus don*, 3a1.

261 According to the 'Bras spungs dkar chag (vol. 1, p. 3, *phyi ka*, no. 000012) the full title is: *Dpal dus kyi 'khor lo'i rgyud bshad pa la 'jug pa rgyud gsum gyi gsang ba rnam par phye ba.* Unfortunately, this text has not been available to me.

262 This is at least what follows from the way Mi bskyod rdo rje criticizes the *Rgyud gsum gsang ba.* His own view (which he claims is in accordance with Rang byung rdo rje) is as follows ("Rje yid bzang rtse ba'i Rgyud gsum gsang ba... ," 984.5–6): "[It is true that buddha nature] has been also taught as a term for the cause of a buddha. But to give buddha nature the names of cause and fruit is [to engage in] mere metaphor. As to buddha nature, it cannot be the fruit of anything, because no distinctions can be made on the basis of it in terms of a substantial cause and attendant conditions." *(sangs rgyas kyi rgyu'i ming gis kyang gsungs la / sangs rgyas kyi snying po de la rgyu dang 'bras bu'i ming gis btags pa ni btags pa tsam du zad kyi / sangs rgyas kyi snying po ni gang gi'ang 'bras bur mi rung ste sangs rgyas kyi snying po de nyid la skyed byed kyi nyer len gyi rgyu dang lhan cig byed pa'i rkyen gyi khyad par du byar med pa'i phyir.)*

263 The fortified potential is usually explained as the accumulation of merit.

264 Seyfort Ruegg 1969:294–96. Rgyal tshab rje prefers to call the buddha element a "substantial basis" *(nye bar len pa'i gnas)*, given that it does not produce anything in a strict sense.

265 Mi bskyod rdo rje: *op. cit.*, 1007.6–1008.2: *rang bzhin gnas rigs dang rgyas 'gyur gyi rigs ngos ma zin pas 'khrul dngos ma yin pa ji ltar 'dra yang de mi 'gyur bar bstan / des ni 'di dpon slob kyi lugs la rje Tsong kha pa dpon slob kyi lta grub kyi 'dres yod pas 'dod pa ni kha cig la tshad mar mi 'gro bar bstan pa'o /.*

266 Ibid., 1003.3–5: *khyod kyi sems can thams cad la sangs rgyas kyi snying po gnas pa'i tshe / sangs rgyas de gnas pa min / sangs rgyas de'i rigs dang 'dra ba zhig gnas pa yin / 'dra ba de la skye mched drug gi khyad par ba yin pas 'di lta bu zhig sems can la yod pa yin zer nas / dpal karmapa rang byung rdo rje gi lung drangs mod / 'di mi 'thad pa la /....*

267 DRSM, 239.15–18: "Utterances that the view of the transitory collection [as *I* and *mine*] is the lineage of the Buddha do not have any effect.... I think that [such a position] is too far removed from the underlying intention of the teaching that the properties of the qualities are never known as something separate from the mind, [contrary to] attachment, etc., which are. Well then, the qualities of realization, such as the [ten] strengths, are present in the sentient beings in a subtle form."

268 DRSM, 5.10–11.

269 Ibid., 574.7–8.

270 Kong sprul Blo gros mtha' yas: *Rgyud bla ma'i bshad srol*, 9b1–4.

271 Rang byung rdo rje: *Dbu ma chos dbyings bstod pa'i rnam par bshad pa*, 8a5–7: "The form kāyas of the buddhas have arisen from the accumulation of merit, and the dharmakāya, in short, is born from the king, the accumulation of wisdom. Likewise these two accumulations are the cause for [one's] attainment of buddhahood. This has been [taught] extensively in the *Uttaratantra* and Candrakīrti, too, taught it in [his] *Madhyamakāvatāra*" *(sangs rgyas rnams kyi gzugs sku 'di / bsod nams tshogs las byung ba ste / chos kyi sku ni mdor bsdus na / rgyal po ye shes tshogs las 'khrungs / de lta bas na tshogs 'di gnyis / sangs rgyas nyid ni thob pa'i rgyu / zhes bya ba dang rgya cher rgyud bla ma dang slob dpon zla ba grags pas kyang dbu ma 'jug par bstan te).*

272 Ibid., 3a5–6: "That which abides in a naturally pure and stainless way in all those who have these hindrances is the dharmadhātu, and since it is quite simply the Buddha, I pay homage [to it]" *(sgrib pa de dang ldan pa kun la rang bzhin gyis dag cing dri ma med par bzhugs pa ni chos kyi dbyings te [text: ste] sangs rgyas ni de yin pas phyag 'tshal lo).*

273 Ibid., 9 *(gong ma)*b7–8: "Hindrances are cleared through the [causal] condition of practicing the path. Therefore one speaks of the [resulting] appearance as a buddha, but it is not that he has arisen on his own, through another, a combination of both, or from no cause" *(lam rnam par bsgrub pa'i rkyen las bsgrib pa gsal bas sangs rgyas su snang bar brjod kyi bdag dang gzhan dang gnyis ka dang / rgyu med pa las byung ba ma yin no).*

274 RGVV, 55.8–9 and 55.12–13: *dharmakāyādiparyāyā veditavyāḥ samasataḥ / catvāro 'nāsrave dhātau caturarthaprabhedataḥ // buddhadharmāvinirbhāgas tadgotrasya tathāgamaḥ / amṛṣāmoṣadharmitvam ādiprakṛtiśāntatā //.*

275 Rang byung rdo rje: *op. cit.*, 9a2–6: *'di'i nges pa ni / mdor na zag med dbyings la ni / don gyi rab tu dbye ba bzhi / chos kyi sku la sogs pa'i / rnam grangs bzhir ni rig par bya / sangs rgyas chos dbyer med pa dang / de rigs de bzhin nyid thob dang / brdzun med bslu med chos nyid dang / gdod nas rang bzhin zhi nyid do / zhes rgyud bla ma las gsungs te / 'bras bu'i cha nas sangs rgyas chos dang dbye ba med pa dang / rgyu'i cha nas rang bzhin dang / rgyas 'gyur gyi rigs dang / bden pa gnyis kyi cha nas mi brdzun mi bslu ba'i tshad ma dang / spangs pa'i cha nas rang bzhin gyis zhi ba dang / glo bur gyis zhi ba zhes bstan gyi ngo bo tha dad pa ma yin no / rgyas par ni 'grib pa med pa dang / 'phel ba med pa'i mdo las gsungs so /.*

276 Ibid., 11b5–8: *ji ltar chu shing snying po phye na med kyang / de'i 'bras bu dang po smin nas za ba ltar / brtag na snying po cung zad kyang med pa ni 'khor ba yin la / 'khor ba de yang rnam par rtog pa ste / ... rnam par rtog pa ni snying po med pa sgyu ma dang / smig rgyu lta bu yin mod kyi / de nyid gnas yongs su gyur pa las / sems can thams cad la phan par byed pa'i gzugs kyi sku 'byung ste / de'i phyir rnam par shes pa nyon mongs pa'i dra bas 'dres pa 'khor ba zhes bya la / nyon mongs pa dang bral bas bya ba grub pa'i ye shes su gyur te / sems can rnams kyi bdud rtsir 'gyur ro /.*

277 This is clear from Rang byung rdo rje's summary of the seven examples; the banana tree and its fruits being said to illustrate the transformation of the basis of thoughts and the fruit of the nirmāṇakāya (see further below).

278 Śākya mchog ldan: "Chos kyi dbyings su bstod pa zhes bya ba'i bstan bcos kyi rnam par bshad pa," 310.2 and 310.5–6: *dpe'i skabs su 'bras bu mngar po nyid chu shing gi snying por bstan no snyam du bsam par mi bya ste / ... de'i tshe na sems can la sangs rgyas kyi khams yod par bshad kyi / sangs rgyas nyid sems can gyi snying por ma bshad do /.*

279 Rang byung rdo rje: *op. cit.*, 12a1–6: *de ltar khams rang bzhin gyis rnam par dag pa dpe rnams kyis (text: kyi) bstan pa'i rim pa 'di yang mar gyi dpes ni sems can gyi dus na 'o ma la chu dang mar gcig tu 'dres par snang ba ltar sems can nyid snang gi / sangs rgyas ni mi snang la / sangs rgyas par gyur pa na dri ma dang 'dres pa med de / mar chu la gtan mi 'dre bar snang ba bzhin du ngo bo bstan pa'o / mar me'i dpes ni yon tan gyi 'od la ma dag pa dang dag pa'i dus thams cad du khyad med kyang / sgrib g.yog gi rkyen gyis che ba dang chung ba ltar snang ba la 'gal ba med pa'i ldan pa'i yon tan bstan to / nor bu'i dpes ni chos sku rang gi yon tan sgrib pa thams cad bral ba dang / rnam par rtog pa med pa'i 'phrin las 'jug pa'i yon tan can du bstan no / gser gyi dpes ni / byas pa ma yin pa dang / dge ba dang rnam par dag pa'i yid kyi rang bzhin longs spyod rdzogs pa'i rgyu 'bras ston to / 'bras shun gyi dpes ma rig pa bag chags kyis ma grol gyi bar la blos mi mthong bar bstan no / chu shing gi dpes 'dzin pa dang rnam par rtog pa gnas gyur pa'i sprul pa'i sku'i 'bras bu'i dpe ste /.*

280 According to Stearns 1999:47–48.

281 Kong sprul Blo gros mtha' yas: *Rgyud bla ma'i bshad srol*, 180a3–4 and 181b5.

282 Kong sprul Blo gros mtha' yas: *Shes bya kun khyab mdzod*, vol. 1, 460.2–461.6. See also the last section of chapter 1.

283 It should be noted that the term *gzhan stong* does not occur in Rang byung rdo rje's works even once. Kong sprul himself uses Jo nang terminology in order to impart his particular interpretation of Nāgārjuna's hymns and the Maitreya works.

284 See Kong sprul Blo gros mtha' yas: *Shes bya kun khyab mdzod*, vol. 1, 460.2–13. Tauscher (1999:vii) notes that Gtsang nag pa was one of the "eight mighty lions" who were disciples of Phya pa Chos kyi seng ge (1109–69). He held the office of abbot at Gsang phu Sne'u thog and was, according to Tauscher, a strict follower of Rngog Blo ldan shes rab's Svātantrika tradition (Tauscher 1999:vii–viii). Gzhon nu dpal informs us in his *Blue Annals* that there is a difference, however, in the two masters' presentation of the ultimate truth (see *Deb ther sngon po*, 309.5–7). According to van der Kuijp (1978:357), Phya pa Chos kyi seng ge was nonsectarian, although in fact he is frequently mentioned in Bka' gdams pa biographies.

285 See Karma Thinley 1980:83–7.

286 That is, if the buddha nature of ordinary beings is taken to be identical with a "perfect Buddha whose wisdom is fully blossomed."

287 The trilogy of texts known as the *Sems 'grel skor gsum* comprises the *Vimalaprabhā* (Peking Tengyur no. 2064), the *Hevajrapiṇḍārthaṭīkā* (Peking Tengyur no. 2310) and a *Cakrasaṁvara* commentary with the title **Lakṣābhidhanād uddhṛta*[a] *laghutantrapiṇḍārthavivaraṇa* (Peking Tengyur no. 2117) (see Stearns 1999:178).

a According to the catalogue of the Peking Tengyur: *-hrita-*. The Sanskrit title is probably a reconstruction from the Tibetan.

288 Karma 'Phrin las pa : "Dris lan yid kyi mun sel zhes bya ba lcags mo'i dris lan bzhugs," 91.1–4: */ bdag gi bla ma thams cad mkhyen pa gsung / / ding sang gzhan stong smra bar rlom pa 'ga' / / don dam rtag brtan ther zug mi 'gyur ba / / bden par grub 'di gzung 'dzin glo (text: blo) bur bas / / stong phyir gzhan stong zab mo 'di yin lo / / 'di 'dra rtag pa'i lta ba la dga' bas / / mthar 'dzin stong nyid zab mor smra byed pa'i / / brdzun gyi zol tshig yin gyi mdo sde las / / gsungs pa'i gzhan stong rnam dag de ma yin / / bla med chos kyis sems nyid mi stong zhes / rgyal ba byams pas gsungs pa la 'khrul nas / / gzhi la bzhugs pa'i yon tan drug bcu bzhi / / glo (text: blo) bur dri mas stong la gzhan stong zhes / / sgrib pa kun zad ye shes rab rgyas pa'i / / rdzogs pa'i sangs rgyas dmyal ba la sogs pa / / 'gro ba drug gi sdug bsngal myong ba'i phyir / / 'khor bar 'khor zhes rgyal la skur btab bo / / rgyud dang sems 'grel mdo sde du ma dang / / byams chos rjes 'brang bcas las gsungs pa'i don / / rang byung rdo rje bzhed pa'i gzhan stong ni / / rgyal ba'i dbang po'i gsung las 'di skad thos /.*

289 According to Thrangu Rinpoche they refer to the tantric forms of the sambhogakāya such as Rdo rje 'chang.

290 Mi bskyod rdo rje: "Yid bzang rtse ba'i Rgyud gsum gsang ba...," 976.3–6: "The Sugata is the Buddha endowed with both purities. As for its essence (i.e., buddha nature), it is the mind of the Buddha, nonconceptual wisdom, and suchness. In view of his possessing both purities, the Sugata is the tantric form kāya and the display of the indestructible illusory [body]. In view of [his possessing] the indestructible illusory body, he is the dharmakāya of luminosity and indestructible wisdom. With the former in mind it has been said [in RGV I.28a]: 'because of being pervaded by the body of the perfect Buddha'; and thinking of this: 'because its suchness cannot be differentiated' (RGV I.28b)." *(bde bar gshegs pa ni dag pa gnyis dang ldan gyi sangs rgyas yin la / de'i snying po ni / sangs rgyas kyi thugs rnam par mi rtog pa'i ye shes de bzhin nyid yin la / dag pa gnyis ldan 'di nyid kyi dbang du byas pa'i bde bar gshegs pa ni rdo rje'i gzugs sku dang / sgyu 'phrul mi shigs pa'i bkod pa / gnyis pa'i dbang du byas nas 'od gsal ba'i chos sku dang / gzhig du med pa'i ye shes yin la / 'di yi snga ma la dgongs nas / / rdzogs sangs sku ni 'phro phyir dang / / zhes dang / phyi ma la dgongs nas / de bzhin nyid dbyer med phyir dang / zhes 'byung la /.)*

291 See Tsultrim Gyamtsho and Fuchs 2000:103–4.

292 See my sections on the positions of Dol po pa and Sa bzang Mati paṇ chen in chapter 2.

293 Stearns, who elaborates the two positions in a section in his *The Buddha from Dolpo* (1999:98–105), points out that Dol po pa did not depart from the position of the founders of Sa skya, the first of whom, Sa chen Kun dga' snying po (1092–1158), maintained (in a tantric doctrinal context) that birth in saṁsāra occurs because the vital winds have not been drawn into the central channel. For Dol po pa, it is thus not enough to simply recognize deluded appearances for what they are.

294 Smith 1970:34.

295 So, for example, Kurtis Schaeffer (1995) in his unpublished M.A. thesis.

296 Stearns 1999:49–52.

297 The term *ālaya* without *vijñāna* is already being used in the *Ghanavyūha* to denote the different bodhisattva levels (see Seyfort Ruegg 1973:35). According to Frauwallner (1951:148), this distinction reflects an old quarrel between two Indian missionaries, Bodhiruci and Ratnamati (the latter came to China in 508). While Bodhiruci claimed that it is the *ālayavijñāna* that is the basis of all perceptions, Ratnamati thought that it was "suchness" *(tathatā).*

298 Otherwise translated as "basic consciousness."

299 Rang byung rdo rje: *Zab mo nang gi don gsal bar byed pa'i 'grel pa bzhugs so*, 8a6–7: *'di la kun gzhi zhes bya ba rnam par shes pa'i sgra ma smos na de bzhin nyid la yang kun gzhi brjod du rung ba'i phyir rnam par shes pa smos so /.*

300 Rang byung rdo rje: *Zab mo nang gi don zhes bya ba'i gzhung bzhugs*, 2b4: *rgyu ni sems nyid thog med la / / rgya chad phyogs lhung ma mchis kyang / / de nyid ma 'gags rol pa las /.*

301 The Tibetan has no equivalent for Skt. *sadā.*

302 RGVV, 42.12–17: *pṛthivy ambau jalaṁ vāyau vāyur vyomni pratiṣṭhitaḥ / apratiṣṭhitam ākāśaṁ vāyvambukṣitidhātuṣu // skandhadhātvindriyaṁ tadvat karmakleśapratiṣṭhitaṁ / karmakleśāḥ sadāyoniśomanaskārapratiṣṭhitāḥ // ayoniśomanaskāraś cittaśuddhipratiṣṭhitaḥ / sarvadharmeṣu cittasya prakṛtis tv apratiṣṭhitā //.*

303 Usually the translation of *de bzhin gshegs pa'i snying po*. Rang byung rdo rje prefers the terms *sangs rgyas kyi snying po, rgyal ba'i snying po,* or simply *snying po* (in order to hint at his extraordinary tantric interpretation of buddha nature?).

304 Rang byung rdo rje: *Zab mo nang gi don gsal bar byed pa'i 'grel pa*, 7b6–8a1: */ rgyud bla ma las /* [RGV I.55–57] */ ces gsungs te 'di ni sangs rgyas kyi snying po la sems su brjod cing 'khor 'das thams cad kyi gzhi'i don yin no /.*

305 The quoted stanza is from the "Dohās for the People" ("Do ha mdzod kyi glu bzhugs so," 289.5). The Apabhraṁsa version of this stanza is as follows: cittekka saala bīaṁ bhavanivvāṇā vi jaṁsi viphuranti / taṁ cintāmaṇi-rūaṁ paṇamaha icchāphalaṁ dei //. (Shahidullah 1928:140, stanza 43).

306 And not like 'Ba' ra ba, for example, who follows the *Laṅkāvatārasūtra*, which fully equates the *ālayavijñāna* with buddha nature (see above in the last section of chapter 1).

307 Rang byung rdo rje: *op. cit.*, 8a3–4.

308 Ibid., 9b3: *rnam par byang ba'i chos de dag ci ltar bskyed ce na / 'di ni sngar brjod pa'i sems kyi dag pa'i chos kyi sku de bzhin gshegs pa'i snying po la brten pa ste.*

309 Lamotte (1938: vol. 1, 19) adds a genitive between *bag chags* and *sa bon*: "the seed of the mental imprint...."

310 Lit., "hearing."

311 Rang byung rdo rje: *Rang 'grel*, 9b4–6 (cf. Lamotte 1938: vol. 1, 19.1–8): *sa bon thams cad pa rnam par smin pa'i rnam par shes pa ni kun nas nyon mongs pa'i rgyu yin na / de'i gnyen po 'jig rten las 'das pa'i sems kyi sa bon ji ltar rung [/] 'jig rten las 'das pa'i sems ni ma 'dris (text: 'dres) pas de'i bag chags med pa nyid do / / bag chags de med na sa bon gang las 'byung*[a] *(text: byung) ba brjod dgos so zhe na / chos kyi dbyings shin tu rnam par dag pa'i rgyu mthun pa thos pa'i bag chags sa bon*[a] *(text: son pa) las de 'byung*[a] *(text: byung) ngo /.*

a According to Lamotte.

312 See Lamotte 1938: vol. 1, 66 : "est-elle identique à la connaissance-réceptable...."

313 Rang byung rdo rje drops the *nyid* after *ngo bo* here (cf. Lamotte 1938: vol. 1, 19.10).

314 My translation follows Rang byung rdo rje (see below). Lamotte (1938: vol. 2, 67) translates: "Jusqu'à ce qu'on obtienne l'illumination des buddhas...." The reason for the difference here is that Lamotte's translation follows the Chinese.

315 Here again, Rang byung rdo rje reads *ngo bo* instead of *ngo bo nyid* (cf. Lamotte 1938: vol. 1, 19.26). But in Mi bskyod rdo rje's *Abhisamayālaṁkāra* commentary (*Shes rab kyi pha rol tu phyin pa'i lung...*, 239.5), in which this passage is quoted, we have the correct reading *ngo bo nyid.*

316 Rang byung rdo rje: *Rang 'grel*, 9b6–10a4 (cf. Lamotte 1938: vol. 1, 19.9–20.4): *thos pa'i bag chags gang yin pa de yang / ci kun gzhi'i rnam par shes pa'i ngo bo nyid yin nam / 'on te ma yin / gal te kun gzhi rnam par shes pa'i ngo bo yin na ni ji ltar de'i gnyen po'i sa bon du rung / ci ste de'i ngo bo nyid ma yin na ni* [a]*thos pa'i bag chags de yi sa bon gyi gnas gang zhig yin par lta*[a] *zhe na / sangs rgyas kyi byang chub la brten nas thos pa'i bag chags* [b]*su gyur ste /*[b] *gnas gang la 'jug pa de lhan cig 'byung ba'i tshul gyis rnam par smin pa'i rnam par shes pa la* [c]*chu dang 'o ma bzhin du 'jug kyang /*[c] *de ni kun gzhi'i rnam par shes pa ma yin te / de'i gnyen po'i sa bon nyid yin pa'i phyir ro /* [d]*de yang bag chags chung ngu las 'brings dang de las chen por 'gyur te / thos bsam bsgom pa la lan mang du byas pa dang ldan pa'i phyir / de ni*[d] *chos kyi sku'i sa bon du blta ste / kun gzhi'i rnam shes kyi gnyen po yin pas kun gzhi'i rnam shes kyi* [e]*ngo bo*[e] *ma yin pa dang / 'jig rten pa yin yang 'jig rten las 'das pa yi chos kyi dbyings shin tu rnam par dag pa'i rgyu mthun pa yin pas 'jig rten las 'das pa'i sems kyi sa bon du gyur pa'o / de ni 'jig rten las 'das pa'i sems ma byung du zin kyang nyon mongs pa'i kun nas dkris* [f]*pa dang ngan 'gro dang / nyes pa*[f] *thams cad dengs par byed pa'i gnyen po yin no / sangs rgyas dang byang chub sems dpa' dang phrad pa'i rjes su mthun pa'o /.*

a Lamotte (19.12–13): *des thos pa'i bag chags kyi sa bon de'i gnas ci zhig yin par blta* (as translated here).

b Lamotte (19.15): *'jug par 'gyur gang yin pa.*

c Lamotte (19.16–17): *'jug te / 'o ma dang chu bzhin no /.*

d Lamotte (19.19–24): *bag chags chung ngu la brten nas bag chags 'bring por 'gyur ro / / bags chags 'bring po la brten nas bag chags chen po 'gyur ste / thos pa dang bsam pa dang / bsgom pa lan mang du bya ba dang ldan pa'i phyir ro / / de la thos pa'i bag chags kyi sa bon chung ngu dang 'bring dang chen po yang.*

e Lamotte (19.26): *ngo bo nyid.*

f Lamotte (19.31–20.1): *pa'i gnyen po dang / ngan song du 'gro ba'i gnyen po dang / nyes par byas pa.*

317 The *vimuktikāya* of the śrāvakas and pratyekabuddhas.

318 It is interesting that Mi bskyod rdo rje, who incorporated this passage into his *Abhisamayālaṁkāra* commentary (*Shes rab kyi pha rol tu phyin pa'i lung...*, 240.2) replaced *'phel* ("develop") with *'bar* ("blaze"), thereby giving the sentence a stronger *gzhan stong* connotation.

319 Rang byung rdo rje: *Rang 'grel*, 10a4–6 (cf. Lamotte 1938: vol. 1, 20.5–14): */ byang chub sems dpa' las dang po pa rnams kyi (text: kyis)*[a] *'jig rten pa yin yang / chos kyi skur bsdus pa dang / nyan thos dang rang sangs rgyas rnams kyi rnam par grol ba'i lus su bsdus par yang blta'o / / de ni kun gzhi'i rnam par shes pa ma yin gyi / chos kyi sku dang rnam par grol ba'i lus kyis*[b] *bsdus pas /* [c]*chung 'bring chen por rim gyis 'phel ba ltar / rnam par smin pa'i shes la 'bri (text: 'bring) zhing / gnas rnam pa thams cad du gyur pa dang / sa bon thams cad pa yang med par gyur te / rnam pa thams cad du spangs pa yin no.*[c]

a Lamotte (20.5): *kyi.*

b Lamotte (20.9): *su.*

c Lamotte (20.10–14): *chung ngu dang 'bring dang chen po ji lta ji lta bur rim gyis 'phel ba de lta de lta bur rnam par smin pa'i rnam par shes pa yang 'bri zhing gnas kyang 'gyur ro // gnas rnam pa thams cad du gyur na rnam par smin pa'i rnam par shes pa sa bon thams cad pa yang sa bon med par gyur pa dang rnam pa thams cad du spangs pa yang yin no /.*

320 The four wisdoms are the mirror-like wisdom, the wisdom of equality, and the discriminating and all-accomplishing wisdoms, which manifest as a result of transforming the eight consciousnesses.

321 Rang byung rdo rje: *Rang 'grel*, 10a6–10b1: ...*rgyas 'gyur kyi rigs de gsar du byung ba snyam du kha cig sems na / de ltar ma yin te [/] rang bzhin du gnas pa'i rigs chos kyi dbyings de la / kun gzhi'i rnam shes la sogs pa brgyad rnam par bzhag pa de ni yang dag pa ma yin pa'i kun tu rtog pas (text: pa) bzhag cing phye ba de ltar / tshogs brgyad po de rnams kyi dri ma med pa'i rang gi ngo bo ye shes bzhi'i rang bzhin du yod do / de yang yang dag pa'i kun tu rtog pas bzhag cing sangs rgyas kyi byang chub la brten pa'i dkar po'i chos kyis sngar gyi dri ma de bcom pa las tshogs brgyad kyi 'khrul pa med pas gnas gyur pa'i ye shes kyi ming thob ste / ...dri ma med pa ni ye shes yin la dri ma dang bcas pa ni rnam par shes pa yin par blta'o /.*

322 Mi bskyod rdo rje: *Shes rab kyi pha rol tu phyin pa'i lung...*, 234–59. I am indebted to Karl Brunnhölzl for drawing my attention to this passage.

323 Mi bskyod rdo rje (*Shes rab kyi pha rol tu phyin pa'i lung...*, 238.3) uses this term.

324 Ibid., 235.6.

325 In MAV I.14 the following synonyms for emptiness are given: suchness, the extreme limit of reality, signlessness, ultimate truth, and the dharmadhātu. (See Nagao 1964:23). The reference in Mi bskyod rdo rje's *Abhisamayālaṁkāra* commentary is on p. 238, ll. 3–4, where the term *kun gzhi'i ye shes* is expressly mentioned.

326 Kong sprul Blo gros mtha' yas: *Zab mo nang gi don gyi 'grel pa*, 17b4–6: *'dir rang 'grel las / 'khor 'das thams cad kyi gzhir gyur pa'i chos nyid de bzhin nyid la kun gzhi'i sgrar gsungs nas de'i nang gses dag pa dang bcas pa la kun gzhi'i ye shes dang sa bon*

thams cad pa'i cha nas kun gzhi'i rnam shes su gsungs te [/] sems la dag ma dag gnyis su dbye / .

327 A comparison of the *Ratnagotravibhāga* commentaries of Dol po pa and Kong sprul shows that Kong sprul was well aware of the difference between his *gzhan stong* view and that of the Jo nang pas (see above and my section on Sa bzang Mati paṇ chen in chapter 2).

328 Mathes 2001:313.

329 Stearns 1999:52.

330 Ibid., 47–48.

331 The first *pāda* of the first chapter is: "As for the [first] cause [of everything], it is the beginningless true nature of mind *(sems nyid)*" (my additions are according to the context of the first chapter of the *Zab mo nang gi don*).

332 Rang byung rdo rje: *Rang 'grel*, 10b3–4: *thog med la zhes bya ba ni / dus kyi thog ma dang tha ma ni rtog pas sgro btags pa yin pas 'dir ni dri ma med pa dang dri ma dang bcas pa'i rang gi ngo bo ni rten cing 'brel bar 'byung ba de nyid dang gzhan las rnam par grol ba ste / de las thog ma gzhan med pa'i phyir thog ma med pa'i dus zhes bya ste /.*

333 The term *gzhan stong* was not invented by Dol po pa but already in use at the time Rang byung rdo rje wrote his autocommentary. Thus Dol po pa refers to a certain Pho ri ba who also defines the ultimate as *gzhan gyis stong pa* (see Stearns 1999:50).

334 Mi bskyod rdo rje: *Shes rab kyi pha rol tu phyin pa'i lung*, 250.1–5: *blun po la la zhig sems can gyi sems kyi chos dbyings la bde gshegs snying po de dbyer mi phyed pa'i tshul gyis yod pa ni theg pa chen po rgyud bla ma'i dgongs par thams cad mkhyen pa karma pa dpal rang byung gis bzhed pa yin zhes zer ro / / dam pa de nyid ni de ltar bzhed pa ma yin te / zab mo nang don gyi rang 'grel du dag pa la sems su brjod pa dang / ma dag pa la sems su brjod pa zhes rnam pa gnyis su dbye bar mdzad de / ma dag pa'i sems pa can de la sems can du bshad nas de lta bu'i sems can la chos kyi dbyings med par bshad pa dang / sems can de nyid chos dbyings las phyin ci log tu gyur pa'i yang dag pa ma yin pa'i kun rtog gis bskyed pa glo bur ba'i dri mar bzhag go / / dag pa'i sems de ni tha mal gyi shes pa dang / dang po'i mgon po dang / dang po'i sangs rgyas sogs su mtshan gsol nas de nyid la sangs rgyas kyi yon tan rnams dang dbyer mi phyed pa'i tshul can yin par gsungs pa dang /.* My translation of this quote follows Karl Brunnhölzl's unpublished translation of Mi bskyod rdo rje's commentary, except that some terms have been altered in order to maintain consistency with the rest of the work.

335 Stearns (1999:203), who ponders the same question (except that he is comparing Dol po pa's *gzhan stong* with these mahāmudrā stanzas), must have had these stanzas in mind when he referred to pages 97–98 of the *Mgur rnams.*

336 *Rang byung rdo rje'i mgur rnams*, 97.6–98.3: *kun gzhi 'khor 'das kun gyi gzhi / ma rtogs (text: rtog) dus na 'khor ba ste / rtogs na de bzhin gshegs pa'i thugs / kun gzhi'i ngo bo brjod pa lags / dper na me long g.ya' dag la / gzugs brnyan 'char ba ji lta bar / rang sems dri med dbyings nyid la / sna tshogs shes pa ldang zhing 'gag / yul dang yul can gnyis 'dzin 'di / rang gis dbyings la snang ldang phyir / 'khor 'das gnyis med ngo bo gcig / ma rtogs (text: rtog) 'khrul zhing rtogs nas grol / rtog bya rtog byed gnyis med kyang / gnyis su bzung bas 'khor ba'i gzhi / gnyis med ngo bo mthong ba na / rgyal ba'i snying po mngon du gyur.*

337 Since the meaning of Tib. *ngo bo* varies considerably according to context, it is impossible to use a single English word consistently. As a *rdzogs chen* category, *ngo bo* refers to the essential nature of primordial awareness.

338 That "compassionate responsiveness" *(thugs rje)* is intended here is clear from the commentary on the beginning of the fifth chapter, where the seminal drops

(bindu), seen as being free from mental fabrications, are explained as one's own coemergent nature of mind. This mind is explained in the commentary (Rang byung rdo rje: *Rang 'grel,* 41a2) in the following way: " …[its] essence is empty, [its] nature is clear, and [its compassionate responsiveness] is unimpeded. These three are [respectively]: (a) the dharmakāya, which is free from mental fabrications, (b) clarity, namely the sambhogakāya, and (c) compassionate responsiveness, [which can] accomplish anything, namely the nirmāṇakāya" *(ngo bo stong / rang bzhin gsal / rnam pa 'gag pa med pa gsum po spros pa dang bral ba'i chos kyi sku dang / gsal ba longs spyod rdzogs pa'i sku dang / thugs rje cir yang grub pa sprul pa'i sku ste /).*

339 Rang byung rdo rje: *Zab mo nang di don,* 2b4–5: *rgyu ni sems nyid thog med la / / rgya chad phyogs lhung ma mchis kyang / de nyid ma 'gags rol pa las / / ngo bo stong la rang bzhin gsal / / rnam pa 'gag med cir yang 'char / /.* The first three *pāda*s are repeated here.

340 This expresses the *rdzogs chen* idea that the qualities of the mind are spontaneously present *(lhun grub).*

341 Rang byung rdo rje: *Rang 'grel,* 11a3–5: *sems de nyid rnam par shes pa skad cig gis rang ngo ma 'gags pa'i rnam par rol pa'i cha las / rang bzhin stong pa nyid du gnas pa dang / rang bzhin gyis gsal bar gnas pa ni thams cad kyi gzhir gyur pa dang / de las sems byung gi tshogs dang rnam par shes pa'i tshogs bdun kyi rang rang gi rnam pa 'gag pa med par skad cig tu 'char ba'i phyir / ma dag pa'i gnas skabs na sems dang yid dang rnam par shes pa zhes bya bar gsungs pa dang / dag pa na sku gsum dang ye shes gyi ming gis brjod pa yin no /.*

342 Translated as " …identical with the *ālayavijñāna*" above.

343 Mi bskyod rdo rje: *Shes rab kyi pha rol tu phyin pa'i lung…,* 236.5–6.

344 By using the nonhonorific form *mngon sum du byas* (instead of *mngon du mdzad,* as in the previous term), Mi bskyod rdo rje makes it clear that this is not the realization of the dharmakāya per se (in which case the honorific form would have been obligatory).

345 Mi bskyod rdo rje: *Dbu ma la 'jug pa'i rnam bshad,* 6b1–2: *'di'i dbu ma'i lta ba rgyud la skyes pa na tha mal gyi shes pa mngon du mdzad ces pa dang / chos sku mngon sum du byas zer ba dang / chos can myu gu dang rnam rtog sogs de dag de'i chos nyid las gzhan du ma grub par rtogs pa na rnam rtog chos skur shar ba zhes tha snyad mdzad nas /.*

346 As Stearns (1999:52) and Schaeffer (1995) have done.

347 Rang byung rdo rje: *Zab mo nang gi don,* 22b6–23a1: */ sems can khams ni sangs rgyas kyi / / snying po dri med bden gnyis ldan / / 'di ni ye shes rdo rje ru / / kun rdzob gzung 'dzin snang ba ste / / bden pa chu zla lta bu 'o / / don dam stong nyid bco brgyad de / / bden pa gnyis med ye shes brjod /.*

348 In the remaining portion of this quote buddha nature is expressed by the term *sangs rgyas kyi snying po.*

349 The particle *dag* after *sangs rgyas kyi snying po* suggests that the buddha nature and the pure element are considered to be two different things, or rather two aspects of what exists ultimately.

350 See further up, where the stainlessness of the eight consciousnesses is related to the four wisdoms.

351 I.e., regard the two truths as being separate?

352 Rang byung rdo rje: *Rang 'grel,* 62a7–62b3: *don dam par gang zhig yod na / rtog pa'i drva ba thams cad las 'das pa'i sems rang bzhin gyis dag pa'i sems can gyi khams sangs rgyas kyi snying po dag ni yod pas de'i tshul brjod pas / sems can khams ni sangs rgyas kyi / snying po dri med bden gnyis ldan zhes smos so / / de la sangs rgyas kyi snying po ni sngar smos pa'i tshogs brgyad kyi 'khrul pa dri ma med pa kho na yin*

mod kyi 'on kyang bden pa gnyis kyi don mngon sum du ma byas pa dag rten cing 'brel bar 'byung ba'i tshul la rmongs nas / / lta ba tha dad pa dag 'dzin pas 'khor bar gyur to.

353 This is what Schaeffer (1995) claims on the basis of the root text. And indeed it is understandable why one might reach such a conclusion in the absence of Rang byung rdo rje's commentary.

354 Rang byung rdo rje: *Rang 'grel,* 62b6–7.

355 For a translation of this quote see my translation below of Gzhon nu dpal's commentary for those with average faculties (DRSM, 46.5–11).

356 MAVBh, 18.21–22: *arthasattvātmavijñaptipratibhāsam prajāyate / vijñānaṁ nāsti cāsyārthas tadabhāvāt tad apy asat.* My additions in brackets are according to Vasubandhu's *bhāṣya.*

357 Rang byung rdo rje: *Rang 'grel,* 63a3–5: */ gzung ba dang 'dzin pa gnyis su kun brtags pa ni rnam pa thams cad du med pa dag yin te / 'phags pa byams pa'i zhal snga nas kyang /* [MAV I.3] */ ces kun brtags pa'i gzung ba dang 'dzin pa thams cad rnam pa thams cad du med pa nyid du gsungs so / / 'o na bden pa ji ltar bzhag ce na / med bzhin du yang snang ba tsam de ni kun rdzob kyi bden pa zhes bya ste / bslu ba med pa'i rang gi ngo bo nyid yin pa'i phyir ro /.*

358 Ibid., 63a5–6: *'di yang rnam grangs kyi don dam par bzhag pa yod mod kyi / chos nyid kyi rigs pa'i rjes su 'brel pa dag ni stong pa nyid chen po bco brgyad kyi rnam par bshad pa'i rang bzhin stong pa nyid sngar smos pa de nyid don dam pa'i bden pa yin no /.* For the meaning of *chos nyid kyi rigs (dharmatāyukti)* see the introductory remarks on RGV I.156–58 (J I.153–55), which is quoted in the part of Gzhon nu dpal's commentary I have translated (DRSM, 55.24–56.5).

359 Rang byung rdo rje: *Dbu ma chos dbyings bstod pa'i rnam par bshad pa,* 7b1–2: *bden pa gnyis kyi rang gi mtshan nyid kyis 'gyur ba med pa dang phyin ci ma log pa gnyis so / 'jig rten pa dang rigs pa'i grags pa ni / kun rdzob bden pa'i bye brag ste /.*

360 Ibid., 63b1–2: *de ltar bshad pa'i bden pa gnyis po 'di yang chos rnams dang chos nyid ji lta ba bzhin du de bzhin nyid dang gzhan las rnam par grol ba yin pa gcig pa dang tha dad gang du'ang brjod du med do / tshul 'di ni sangs rgyas bcom ldan rnams kyis rtogs shing bstan pa'i chos thams cad kyi don kyang yin te /.*

361 As found in the *Majjhimanikāya.* See Chalmers 1899; and Seyfort Ruegg 1969:319–20.

362 So expressed in Vasubandhu's *Madhyāntavibhāgabhāṣya* on I.1–2 (see Mathes 2000:200–201).

363 MAVBh, 18.2–3: *śūnyatā tasyābhūtaparikalpasya grāhyagrāhakabhāvena virahitatā (stong pa nyid ni yang dag pa ma yin pa'i kun tu rtog pa de gzung ba dang 'dzin pa'i dngos po dang bral ba nyid do,* Peking Tengyur, *sems tsam,* vol. *bi,* fol. 2b2).

364 For example, in SNS VII.7 (see Mathes 2000:216).

365 See the section on Dol po pa's position below.

366 See Dol po pa: "Bden pa gnyis gsal ba'i nyi ma," 13ff. According to Dol po pa, a buddha still knows the world in the same way as one remembers the appearances of a dream but no longer sees them after waking up (see Mathes 1998:464–65).

367 This is made particularly clear in Tāranātha's *gzhan stong snying po* (see Mathes 2000:195–223).

368 Mathes 2000:220.

369 See MAV III.10cd, where "ultimate," or literally the "highest object" *(paramārtha),* is taken to have three different meanings according to the three possible ways of analyzing a compound in Sanskrit. (1) Tatpuruṣa: "The ultimate in terms of object is suchness in the sense of being the object of the highest wisdom" *(arthaparamārthas tathatā paramasya jñānasyārtha iti kṛtvā).* (2) Karmadhāraya: "The ultimate in terms of attainment is nirvāṇa in the sense of being the highest

object" *(prāptiparamārtho nirvāṇaṁ paramo 'rtha iti kṛtvā).* (3) Bahuvrīhi: "The ultimate in terms of practice is the path in the sense that the highest is its object" *(pratipattiparamārtho mārgaḥ paramo 'syārtha iti kṛtvā).* The path on the higher levels is taken as the nonconceptual cognition of suchness in the *Madhyāntavibhāga.* For the Sanskrit see MAVBh, 41.18–21.

370 Rang byung rdo rje: *Rang 'grel,* 10b3–4: *thog med la zhes bya ba ni / ... 'dir ni dri ma med pa dang dri ma dang bcas pa'i rang gi ngo bo ni rten cing 'brel bar 'byung ba de nyid dang gzhan las rnam par grol ba ste /.*

371 Seyfort Ruegg (1971:466): *śūnyatāhārakāḥ sūtrā ye kecid bhāṣitā jinaiḥ / sarvais taiḥ kleśavyāvṛttir naiva dhātuvināśanam //* (DhS 22).

372 The first quoted *pāda* is not in the root text of the *Ratnagotravibhāga.* The remaining two are RGV I.147ab (J I.144ab): *svabhāvo dharmakāyo 'sya tathatā gotram ity api /* (RGVV, 69.19). Rang byung rdo rje's insertion does not alter the meaning, but simply clarifies what the demonstrative pronoun *asya* refers to.

373 Rang byung rdo rje: *Rang 'grel,* 64a6–64b1: *stong pa nyid ni ston pa'i mdo / / rgyal bas ji snyed gsungs pa de / / de dag kun gyis nyon mongs ldog / khams de nyams par byed ma yin / / shes bya ba la sogs pa rgyas par gsungs shing / 'di'i ming gi rnam grangs ni / rgyud bla ma las / sems kyi rnam par dag pa'i khams / / 'di yi rang bzhin chos sku dang / / de bzhin nyid dang rigs kyang ste / / zhes bya ba la sogs pa shin tu rgyas par gsungs shing / dpe dgus nyon mongs pa ji snyed pa mdor bsdus pas drug cu rtsa bzhi rnam par sbyangs pa las dri ma med pa'i sangs rgyas kyi yon tan drug cu rtsa bzhi snang bar byed pa /.*

374 Such an understanding could be based on the *Laṅkāvatārasūtra* (see LAS, 77.15–78.11 and section 4 of my introduction), where buddha nature, which bears the thirty-two marks, is compared to a gem enveloped in the garment of *skandhas.*

375 Rang byung rdo rje: *Zab mo nang gi don,* 1b3–2a1: */ lhan skyes gcig dngos gnyis kyi bdag / / sku gsum rtsa rlung thig le can / / gnas skabs bzhi po sku bzhi nyid / / sku lnga'i bdag nyid la phyag 'tshal /.*

376 Rang byung rdo rje: *Rang 'grel,* 3b6–4a3: *lhan cig skyes pa gcig dngos ni / sems can thams cad la dbye ba med par dri ma dang bcas te gnas pa sangs rgyas thams cad kyi chos sku yon tan phrin las dang bcas pa yin la / gnyis kyi bdag ni thabs dang shes rab dang / kun rdzob dang don dam pa'i rang bzhin 'bras bu chos kyi dbyings shin tu dri ma med pa dang de'i rgyu mthun pa rab tu zab pa'i sku gnyis so / / sku gsum rtsa rlung thig le can zhes pa ni don dam pa bde ba chen po chos kyi dbyings ni chos kyi sku yin la kun rdzob kyi bden pa la brten pa'i rgyu mthun par rab tu zab pa'i sku de la rmi lam dag pa dang kun gzhi la brten pa'i yid srog gi rlung dang bcas pa gnas gyur pa longs spyod rdzogs pa'i sku dang / tha mal gyi snang ba dngos po la 'jug pa'i rnam par shes pa dag pas sprul pa'i sku 'byung ste / 'di yang rtsa ni sku / rlung gsung / thig le thugs rdo rje ste / 'di gsum rnam par sbyangs pas thob par gsungs pa'i phyir sangs rgyas thams cad kyi sku gsung thugs kyi ngo bor gsungs so /.*

377 RGV I.152–55 (J I.149–52) and III.1–3.

378 Rang byung rdo rje: *op. cit.,* 4a4: *...ye shes kyi sku ste sems can rnams kyi sgrib pa dang bcas pa'o.*

379 Rang byung rdo rje: *Snying po bstan pa,* 35a6–35b3.

380 RGVV, 37.6–9: *anādibhūto 'pi hi sā*[a]*vasānikaḥ svabhāvaśuddho dhruvadharmasaṁhitaḥ / anādikośair ni*[b]*vṛto na dṛśyate suvarṇabimbaṁ paricchāditaṁ yathā //.* This stanza of unknown origin is quoted in RGVV I.41 and resembles the ninth simile in the *Tathāgatagarbhasūtra.*

a Johnston and A (21b4) read *cā-,* which is difficult to construe.

b Johnston and A (21b4) read *bahir-* in place of *ni-,* which goes against the meter and the Tibetan.

381 Kong sprul Blo gros mtha' yas makes this important distinction in his commentary on RGV I.6 (see Tsultrim Gyamtsho and Fuchs 2000:103–4).

382 Rang byung rdo rje: *Snying po bstan pa*, 35b1–2: */ thog ma med pa'i dus kyi khams / chos rnams kun gyi gnas yin te / / 'di yod pas na 'gro kun dang / / mya ngan 'das pa'ang thob pa yin /.* Cf. RGVV, 72.13–14: *anādikāliko dhātuḥ sarvadharma-samāśrayaḥ / tasmin sati gatiḥ sarvā nirvāṇādhigamo 'pi ca //.*

383 HT, 188.5–6.

384 See HT, 183.3–4 (*Hevajratantra*, part 2, IV.51): "The three kāyas are said to be located within the body in the form of *cakras*. The fivefold wisdom of the three kāyas is known as the *cakra* of great bliss *(mahāsukhacakra)" (trikāyaṁ dehamadhye tu cakrarūpeṇa kathyate / trikāyasya pañcajñānaṁ cakra[ṁ] mahāsukhaṁ matam //).*

385 Rang byung rdo rje: *Snying po bstan pa*, 36a4–6.

386 Ibid., 36a6–37a1.

387 See Kong sprul Blo gros mtha' yas: *Rnam par shes pa dang ye shes 'byed pa'i bstan bcos kyi tshig don go gsal du 'grel pa*, 8a2: "In Tibet [some] claim that the outer world and its content (i.e., sentient beings), all good and bad, were created by a certain Sgam pa phyva." *(bod du snod bcud legs nyes thams cad sgam pa phya (=phyva?) zhes ba bas byas par 'dod pa....)*

388 Ibid., 37a2–5: *de la gzugs sku gnyis rang bzhin / / sum cu rtsa gnyis mtshan dpe byad / / thob pa'i yon tan rang lus te / / lus de bdag dang phyva dbang phyug / tshangs dang phyi rol bden pa'i rdul / / phag na mo yis byas pa min / / sgo lnga gzung dang 'dzin pa yi / / rnam 'gyur ma dag de sbyangs pas / / de tshe thob par tha snyad byas / / de bas rtsa rlung thig le rnams / / dag pa dag pa'i gzugs sku ste / / ma sbyang ma dag gzugs sku'o /.*

389 According to the above-quoted passage from the *Zab mo nang gi don* and its autocommentary it would be only the *nāḍīs* and *prāṇa* which correspond to the form kāyas, though.

390 Which is quoted in RGVV I.2 (see my translation of Gzhon nu dpal's *Ratnagotravibhāga* commentary DRSM, 37.8–13).

391 It is interesting that Rang byung rdo rje chooses *'du byed (saṁskāra, saṁskṛta)* instead of *'dus byas (saṁskṛta)*—probably because buddhahood is said to be *'dus ma byas* in RGV I.5. Gzhon nu dpal, who adheres to the same view as Rang byung rdo rje, solves this apparent contradiction in his *Ratnagotravibhāga* commentary (DRSM, 83.11–13) by restricting the predicate "unconditioned" with the help of the adverb "not artificially" *(ma 'phral du),* which does not exclude momentariness altogether.

392 Rang byung rdo rje: *Snying po bstan pa*, 37b4–6: */ gang dag lta ngan zhugs pa rnams / / sangs rgyas yon tan rgyu med dang / / yang na rang min phyi rol gyi (text: gyis) / / rgyu rkyen gyis bskyed rtogs pa ni / / phyi rol rtag chad khyad ci yod / / 'du byed skad gcig skye 'gag snang / / ma dag 'du byed dag dang mtshungs / / gal te de ltar ma yin na / / gzugs sku'i phrin las rgyun chad 'gyur / / 'on kyang 'du byed ming mi brjod /.*

393 Hookham (1991): *The Buddha Within;* and Stearns (1999): *The Buddha from Dolpo.*

394 Stearns 1999:11–39.

395 Stearns 1995:829–31.

396 Stearns 1999:22.

397 The entire Buddhist tradition accepts only three great councils in India held for the purpose of consolidating the teaching after the Buddha's nirvāṇa.

398 Stearns 1999:123.

399 Cf. VPṬ, 74.5–8 (stanza I.22).

400 Kapstein 2000:115–16.

401 Kapstein 1992:24–25.
402 Mathes 2000:195–223.
403 Stearns 1999:26.
404 Kapstein: *The 'Dzam-thang Edition of the Collected Works of Kun-mkhyen Dol-po-pa Shes-rab rgyal-mtshan*, vol. 4 *(ma)*, 883–1161.
405 Dol po pa: "Nyi ma'i 'od zer," 990.6–7.
406 See the commentary on I.155 (J I.152) (Ibid., 988.3–4).
407 Namely on the grounds that it was copied by Kong sprul Blo gros mtha' yas nearly *verbatim* (Hookham 1991:173–74). But such an assumption is not only baseless but also unlikely, since the text is signed by the "One Endowed with the Four Reliances" *(rton pa bzhi ldan)*, which was the most common pseudonym used by Dol po pa in his works (Stearns 1999:201).
408 Hookham (1991:183) early on observed that Dol po pa did not read his *gzhan stong* view explicitly into the *Ratnagotravibhāga*. In fact, she even criticizes the *Ratnagotravibhāga* and the *vyākhyā* itself for not being more consistent with *gzhan stong*. Thus she writes: "One feels that, in Shentong terms, all this (i.e., RGV I.30–34) deviates from the essential message of the RGV" (Ibid., 200). And about the following paragraph on the *guṇapāramitās* (RGV I.35–39), too, she is less than happy: "Again the explanations [of the *vyākhyā*] in this section are rather disappointing from a Shentong point of view. They give the impression that the four transcendental qualities are separate results of different contributory causes of buddhahood; even transcendental permanence is explained as continuous activity rather than nonarising, nondwelling, nonceasing, noncompounded, and so on."—and then goes on to quote the *Ri chos nges don rgya mtsho* for a correct presentation of this point (Ibid., 202). In my opinion, Hookham does not sufficiently appreciate the fact that the *Ratnagotravibhāga* consists of different layers with at times heterogeneous structures (even though she observed that according to Takasaki RGV I.32–33 does not belong to the original text), or the elegant way Dol po pa (who was of course aware of these inconsistencies) handles these problems.
409 For a translation of RGV III.1–3 see p. 12.
410 This statement indicates that Dol po pa is reporting the conventional Mahāyāna explanation of this topic.
411 Dol po pa: *Ri chos nges don rgya mtsho*, 340.15–341.3: *zhes bral 'bras chos sku gang yin pa 'gyur med yongs grub dang de bzhin nyid kyi sku la bral ba'i yon tan stobs la sogs pa tshang ba dang / bskyed 'bras gzugs sku gang yin pa phyin ci ma log pa'i yongs grub dang yang dag ye shes ldan pa la bskyed pa'i yon tan mtshan la sogs pa yod par gsungs so / / 'di dag gis ni kha cig chos sku 'ang bskyed 'bras kun rdzob tu 'dod pa dang / kha cig gzugs sku'ang bral 'bras don dam du 'dod pa bsal ba yin no / ... de bzhin du kha cig chos sku'ang sems can rnams la dang po nas med par 'dod pa dang / kha cig gzugs sku'ang sems can rnams la dang po nas yod par 'dod pa (text: par) yang shin tu 'khrul te gter dang 'bras bu'i shing bzhin du / zhes sogs rgya cher gsungs pa'i phyir ro /.*
412 Ibid., 341–42.
413 Kapstein 1992:24–25.
414 Dol po pa: *Ri chos nges don rgya mtsho*, 343.19–21 and 344.8–9: *de la gzugs sku rnam pa gnyis ni kun rdzob kyi longs spyod rdzogs pa dang sprul pa'i sku ste thun mong du rab tu grags pa'o / / don dam pa'i longs spyod rdzogs pa dang sprul pa'i sku ni chos nyid yongs grub de bzhin nyid la tshang ste / ... des na don dam gyi longs spyod rdzogs pa dang sprul pa'i sku ni thun mong ma yin pa sngags kyi tshul la grags pa'o /.*
415 Cf. Ibid., 284.9–12.

416 The second chapter on the path is introduced in the following way (Ibid., 128.17–21): "In this way, even though the ultimate Buddha, [or] dharmakāya, whose nature is the endless inseparable qualities, exists intrinsically in all sentient beings, it is not the case that the two accumulations of the path are not needed, given that the adventitious stains must be removed, and the purpose of all sentient beings fulfilled, once the apparent form kāyas have been generated." *(de ltar don dam pa'i sangs rgyas chos kyi sku mi 'bral ba'i yon tan mtha' yas pa'i bdag nyid sems can thams cad la rang chas su bzhugs kyang lam tshogs gnyis mi dgos pa ma yin te / glo bur dri ma bsal dgos pa'i phyir dang / kun rdzob gzugs sku bskyed nas sems can thams cad kyi don bya dgos pa'i phyir ro /.)*

417 Ibid., 118.22–24 and 119.19–22: *...spangs pa la yang gnyis te / dri ma thams cad gdod nas rang bzhin gyis ma grub pa'i spangs pa dang dri ma glo bur ba gnyen pos bcom nas zad pa'o / ...de bzhin du sangs rgyas kyi rtogs pa la yang gnyis te / gdod nas chos nyid rang gis rang rig pa'i rtogs pa rang byung ye shes dang / lam zab mo bsgom pa las skyes pa'i rtogs pa gzhan byung ye shes so / /.*

418 This negation of identity has been often misunderstood and represented in a wrong way. (Cf. Newland, who writes that for Dol po pa the two truths are different entities *(ngo bo tha dad pa)*. Instead of referring to the Jo nang material, however, he quotes Seyfort Ruegg, Hopkins, and Thurman (Newland 1992:30 and 260). Thus, Dol po pa negates not only identity but also difference. In his "Bden gnyis gsal ba'i nyi ma," 23.2–3) Dol po pa explains that "the two truths should be called neither identical *(de nyid)* in terms of their nature nor different *(gzhan)* [in terms of their nature]."[a]

a For Tib. *de nyid dang gzhan*, Skt. *tattvānyatva*, see MAVBh, 23.10.

419 See Mathes 1996:122–23.

420 Lamotte (ed.) 1935:47.

421 Dol po pa: *Ri chos nges don rgya mtsho*, 323.16–324.6: *des na thams cad kyis stong pa dang chos thams cad kyis stong pa ni khyad par shin tu che ste / gnas lugs la chos kyis stong yang chos nyid kyis mi stong pa'i phyir ro / / 'dis ni chos dang chos nyid ngo bo gcig la ldog pa tha dad du 'dod pa dang tha dad gtan med du 'dod pa yang bsal ba yin te / de gnyis la ngo bo gcig pa bkag pa'i tha dad yin pa'i phyir ro / / 'o na dgongs 'grel du / 'du byed khams dang don dam mtshan nyid dag / / gcig dang tha dad bral ba'i mtshan nyid de / / gcig dang tha dad nyid du gang rtog pa / / de dag tshul bzhin ma yin zhugs pa yin / / zhes bden gnyis gcig dang tha dad gang yang ma yin par gsungs pa dang 'gal lo zhe na / lung des ni bden gnyis ngo bo gcig pa dang ngo bo tha dad pa bkag pa yin te / gnas lugs la don dam gyi ngo bo grub kyang kun rdzob kyi ngo bo ma grub pa'i phyir ro / / 'di las gzhan du 'chad pa thams cad ni bden pa gnyis la bden lugs gnyis dang snang lugs gnyis dang stong lugs gnyis dang (omit dang?) de dag med par 'dod na chad par lta lugs gnyis kyi khyad par gtan nas ma phyed par gcig tu 'dres pa'i dug gis myos pa'i bab col kho na yin no /.*

422 See also Broido (1989:88) who has made the same observation with regard to two sets of *skandha*s in the *Ri chos nges don rgya mtsho*.

423 RGVV, 12.14: *ayam eva ca bhagavaṁs tathāgatadharmakāyo 'vinirmuktakleśakośas tathāgatagarbha ity ucyate*.[a]

a Schmithausen (1971:137) proposes reading *ity ucyate* instead of *sūcyate* (B is not clear, A not available).

424 *Ri chos nges don rgya mtsho*, 324.9–21.

425 Ibid., 142.17–19: *sangs rgyas rtag pa dang sangs rgyas kyi thar pa gzugs yin pa dang nam mkha' yang sangs rgyas kyi gzugs yin / zhes pa la sogs pa'i don ni...de bzhin nyid kyi gzugs sogs dang / khams gsum dang dus gsum las 'das pa'i gzugs sogs zhes pa la sogs pa 'chad par 'gyur pa'i skabs su rig par bya....*

426 RGVV, 7.14–15: *asaṁskṛtam anābhogam [aparapratyayoditam / buddhatvaṁ jñānakāruṇyaśaktyupetaṁ dvayārthavat //].*

427 Dol po pa: *Ri chos nges don rgya mtsho*, 97.15–17: *'dus ma byas shing lhun gyis grub / ces pa la sogs pas mthar thug gi sangs rgyas 'dus ma byas su gsungs pa yang skad cig dang bral ba la dgongs pa yin no /.*

428 Dol po pa: "Nyi ma'i 'od zer," 908.6–909.1: *dri ma med pa'i sangs rgyas gyi yon tan ni / chos sku de nyid dang 'brel pa'i stobs bcu dang / mi 'jigs pa bzhi dang / ma 'dres pa bco brgyad la sogs pa bral ba'i 'bras bu dang / mtshan dpe so (omit so?) sum cu rtsa gnyis la sogs pa smin pa'i 'bras bus bsdus pa'i sangs rgyas kyi chos gang yin pa'o /.*

429 Ibid., 909.1: *rgyal ba'i mdzad pa ni stobs bcu la sogs pa'i yon tan de rnams yang dag par 'grub pa'i nus pas.*

430 In RGV I.25 four reasons are presented why exactly the four points of RGV I.23 are inconceivable.

431 Dol po pa: "Nyi ma'i 'od zer," 911.3–4: *dri ma med pa'i sangs rgyas kyi yon tan gyi don ni / stobs bcu la sogs pa don dam pa'i yon tan rnams mtha' gcig tu kun nas nyon mongs pa dang bcas pa so so'i skye bo'i gnas skabs na yang rnam par dbye ba med pa'i chos nyid du yod pa yang yin la / mngon du gyur yang ma yin pa'i phyir 'gal ba ltar snang bas bsam gyis mi khyab pa ste /.*

432 Ibid., 914.2–5: *rdzogs pa'i sangs rgyas kyi chos kyi sku ni / chos thams cad la 'phro zhing khyab pa'i phyir dang / 'khor 'das thams cad kyi chos nyid la rnam par dbye ba med pa'i phyir dang / de bzhin gshegs pa'i rigs / chos kyi dbyings rang bzhin gyis dag pa sgrib pa sbyang rung du sems can thams cad la yod pa'i phyir na lus can kun kyang thog ma med pa nyid nas dus rtag tu rgyun ma chad par don dam pa'i sangs rgyas kyi snying po can yin te /.*

433 Ibid., 989.6.

434 Compare, for example, Klong chen pa's commentary on these stanzas.

435 Dol po pa: "Nyi ma'i 'od zer," 986.6–987.3: *dper na 'bad rtsol gyis gsar du ma bsgrubs shing longs spyod zad mi shes pa dang ldan pa'i gter chen sa'i 'og na rang bzhin gyis gnas pa dang 'bad rtsol gyis bsgrubs pas 'bras bu dang bcas pa'i shing ljon sa skyed mos tshal du rim gyis skye ba ji lta ba bzhin du sku gsum 'byung du rung ba'i sangs rgyas kyi rigs de yang rnam gnyis su shes par bya ste / thog ma med pa'i dus nas sems kyi rang bzhin du nye bar gnas pa'i chos kyi dbyings rnam par dag pa rang bzhin gyi rigs dang / de la dmigs te thos pa la sogs pa byas pas 'bad rtsol gyis gsar du yang dag par blangs pa las byung ba'i dge ba thar pa'i cha dang mthun pas mchog tu gyur pa rgyas gyur gyi rigs nyid do.*

436 Ibid., 987.3–6: *sku gsum thob tshul ni / rgyu rang bzhin dang rgyas pa'i rigs 'di gnyis las 'bras bu rdzogs pa'i sangs rgyas kyi sku gsum thob par 'dod pa yin la / de yang dang por rang bzhin du gnas pa'i rigs de nyid ye shes kyi tshogs mang pos mthar phyin par byas nas glo bur gyi dri ma mtha' dag dang bral ba las sku ni dang po dag gnyis ldan chos nyid ngo bo nyid kyi sku ni 'thob pa ste / gnyis pa rgyas 'gyur gyi rigs 'phel ba las bsod nams kyi tshogs mthar phyin pa yis ni sku phyi ma gdul bya nye ba dang ring ba la snang ba longs spyod rdzogs pa'i sku dang sprul pa'i sku gnyis po thob bo /.*

437 Cf. Stearns 1995:829 and 1999:13–16.

438 Tsultrim Gyamtsho and Fuchs 2000:171–72.

439 *Sa skya pa'i mkhas pa rnams kyi gsung skor*, vol. 4, 1–520.

440 Mati Paṇ chen: "Nges don rab gsal," 518.6–519.1.

441 He appears under this name in the colophon of the new Jo nang translation of the *Kālacakratantra* made by him together with Blo gros dpal (see Stearns 1999:24 and 185).

442 Oral information from Khenpo Abbey.

443 Ngag dbang blo gros grags pa: *Jo nang chos 'byung zla ba'i sgron me*, 33.21–22.

444 Mati Paṇ chen: "Nges don rab gsal," 16.1–17.2.

445 HT, 188.4–5 (*Hevajratantra* part 2, IV.69): *sattvā buddhā eva kiṁ tu āgantukamalāvṛtāḥ / tasyāpakarṣaṇāt sattvā buddhā eva na saṁśayaḥ.*

446 Mati paṇ chen: "Nges don rab gsal," 8.3–9.1: *thob par bya ba don dam pa'i sangs rgyas chos kyi sku rang byung lhan cig skyes pa'i ye shes de nyid sems can thams cad kyi sems kyi rang bzhin du khyab par gnas pas sgrib pa spangs pa tsam gyis mngon du 'gyur ba'i phyir sgrub par dka' ba yang ma yin te / dpal dus kyi 'khor lo bsdus pa'i rgyud kyi rgyal po las / sems can rnams ni sangs rgyas nyid de chen po'i sangs rgyas gzhan 'dir 'jig rten khams na yod ma yin / . . . ces gsungs shing / kye'i rdo rje las kyang / sems can rnams ni sangs rgyas nyid / 'on kyang glo bur dri mas sgrib / de bsal nas ni sangs rgyas nyid / ces gsungs la / chos kyi dbyings su bstod pa las kyang / nyon mongs dra bas g.yogs pa la / / sems can zhes ni brjod pa yin / / de nyid nyon mongs bral gyur na / / sangs rgyas zhes ni brjod par bya / / zhes la sogs pa rgya cher gsungs pa ltar ro /.*

447 See HT, 183.3–4 (part 2, stanza IV.51): *trikāyaṁ dehamadhye tu cakrarūpeṇa kathyate / trikāyasya pañcajñānaṁ cakramahāsukhaṁ matam //.*

448 Lit., "explanations and so forth."

449 Mati paṇ chen: "Nges don rab gsal," 48.5–49.1, 49.4–5, and 50.3: *gal te rgyud las bshad pa la sogs ni rnam par snang mdzad la sogs par gsungs pa'i phyir lus 'di nyid lha'i ngo bor shes na ni sangs rgyas kyi sku'o snyam du mngon par zhen na / de yang de dag gi chos nyid la dgongs pa yin gyi / chos can ma dag pa'i lus 'di ni sangs rgyas nyid ma yin te / de ni 'dus byas snying po med pa nyid yin pa'i phyir dang / sangs rgyas ni 'dus ma byas pa rang byung gi sku yin pa'i phyir ro / . . . don dam gzugs kyi skur 'dod pa spong ba ni / gzhan yang 'di snyam du mdzad pa bcu gnyis spro ba la sogs bstan pa'i phyir don dam pa'i sangs rgyas ni gzugs kyi sku'o snyam du sems na de ltar yang mi bsam ste / gzugs kyi sku ni skal pa la ltos nas gzhan snang la grub pa 'dus byas kyi dngos por ston pa yin gyi 'dus ma byas pa la sogs pa don dam pa'i yon tan rnams dang mi ldan pa'i phyir ro / . . . don dam pa'i sangs rgyas ni chos kyi sku kho na yin te /.*

450 Ibid., 243.2–4.

451 Ibid., 111.3–4: *don dam pa'i yon tan thams cad kyang ma tshang ba med pa'i sems can mtha' dag la (text: las) rjes su zhugs par de bzhin gshegs pas mkhyen nas.*

452 Ibid., 55.2–3: *sangs rgyas nyid thog ma dang dbus dang mtha' mar 'dus byas kyi chos skye ba dang gnas pa dang 'jig pa rnams med pa'i rang bzhin can yin pa'i phyir 'dus ma byas pa ste / mya ngan las 'das pa'i mdo las / rtag tu gnas pa'i chos ni dus gsum la (text: las) ma gtogs te / de bzhin gshegs pa yang de dang 'dra bar dus gsum la ma gtogs pa de bas na rtag pa'o zhes gsungs pa ltar ro.*

453 See Tsultrim Gyamtsho and Fuchs 2000:103–4.

454 RGVV, 25.11–13: *tatraiṣāṁ caturṇāṁ padānāṁ prathamaṁ lokottaradharmabījatvāt pratyātmayoniśomanasikārasaṁniśrayeṇa tadviśuddhim upādāya triratnotpattihetur anugantavyaḥ /.*

455 Mati paṇ chen: "Nges don rab gsal," 112.6: . . .*gnas gcig dri ma dang bcas pa'i de bzhin nyid de ni dag par bya ba'i rgyu yin te / de dri mas rnam par dag pa las dkon mchog gsum 'byung ba'i phyir.*

456 Ibid., 121.1–3: . . .*sems can gyi gnas skabs na ni / don dam pa'i yon tan thams cad dang ldan pa'i sangs rgyas nyid med la yod par gsungs pa ni sa bon tsam la dgongs pa'o zhes bya ba de yang 'thad pa ma yin te / sa bon 'phel zhing yongs su smin pa las skyed pa'i 'bras bu de ni 'dus byas su 'gyur zhing /.*

457 Ibid., 115.3–116.6.

458 Ibid., 116.6–117.1: *de lta bas na don dam pa'i sangs rgyas ni yod pa mngon sum du gyur par blta yi / med pa gsar du bskyed par ni rnam yang 'dod par mi bya'o / / rnam grangs ni chos kyi dbyings de nyid las / rigs dang zag pa med pa'i sa bon dang sems can gyi khams dang thams cad kyi rang bzhin zhes kyang bya ste /.*

459 Ibid., 251.2–4: *gzhan yang rang bzhin gsum la don dgur phye ba'i nang nas bstan pa*

chos sku gnyis dang / yang dag par blangs pa las byung ba'i rigs dang / gzugs sku ni zhar las byung ba dbye ba la mkhas pa'i ched du yin gyi thams cad la khyab pa'i phyir ni ma yin no / / 'on kyang de dag gi rten zag pa med pa'i dbyings ni thams cad la khyab pa nyid do /.

460 Skt. *upacāra.* Gzhon nu dpal explains this term by citing the example of a Brahmin boy who is called a lion because he is a hero and fearless (DRSM, 150.10–12). Whereas a real lion is an animal, here the word *lion* is only metaphorically applied to the brave boy.

461 RGVV, 26.3: *bauddhe gotre tatphalasyopacārād.*

462 See Mati paṇ chen: "Nges don rab gsal," 515.5–516.1: "Motivated by [my] strong devotion to the very profound principle [of the RGV] I also made, based on the Indian text, a few changes and carefully proofread [the translation]." *(bdag gis kyang mchog tu zab pa'i tshul la lhag par mos pa'i dbang gis rgya gar 'phags pa'i yul gyi dpe la gtugs te / cung zad bcos shing shin tu dag par bgyis pa'o /.)*

463 Mati paṇ chen: "Nges don rab gsal," 128.5–6: *sangs rgyas nyid 'grub pa'i rigs khams sgrib pa dang bcas pa'i gnas skabs la yang de dri ma dang bral ba'i 'bras bu chos sku tha dad med par nye bar spyod cing yod pa'i phyir na / 'gro ba ma lus pa kun don dam pa'i sangs rgyas kyi snying po can....*

464 See Stearns 1999:67.

465 Mati paṇ chen: "Nges don rab gsal," 122.6–123.5: *rtag dngos su thal ba spong ba ni / 'on te snga ma phyi ma khyad par med pa yang yin la rgyu dang rkyen la ltos nas 'bras bu grub pa yang yin pa'i phyir dbyings gang yin pa de ni rtag pa'i dngos por 'gyur ro zhe na / 'dus ma byas pa nyid kyi phyir rtag pa ni 'gyur mod / skye ba dang 'jig pa dang gnas pa'i mtshan nyid gsum dang bral ba'i phyir 'dus byas kyi dngos por ni lta ga la 'gyur / ... de lta na yang don byed nus pa'i phyir dngos por 'gyur ro zhe na / rnam pa thams cad du don gnyis mthar phyin par byed pa'i nus pa dang ni ldan mod / de nyid kyi phyir nyi tshe ba 'dus byas kyi dngos por ni mi 'gyur te / 'dus byas thams cad ni brdzun pa slu ba snying po med pa nyid yin pa'i phyir ro / 'on kyang rtag pa yang yin la 'dus ma byas pa'i dngos po yang yin pa zhes brjod pa la ni 'gal ba med de /.*

466 In defense of the Jo nang pas it should be noted that an "entity" (Skt. *bhāva,* Tib. *dngos po*)—or better, "state of being" in this context—described as the nonexistence of duality is taken as a defining characteristic of emptiness in MAV I.12 (see MAVBh 22.23).

467 Stearns 1999:48.

468 An exception is Kazuo Kano's unpublished Master's thesis (Kyoto 2001), which includes an edition and a Japanese translation. Seyfort Ruegg (2000:78–79) stresses the importance of this commentary in his recent publication on the history of Indian and Tibetan Madhyamaka philosophy.

469 The actual commentary is exactly identical with what Tsetan Dorji reproduced in 1974, namely the ancient manuscript from the library of Ri bo che Rje drung Rin po che of Padma bkod. In the colophon that Paldan Sherab added to this text (p. 686, ll. 2–5), he claims that he revealed this profound *gter ma* in America ("This profound treasure, which remained hidden...for more than six hundred human years...was later revealed from the rich country of America by...Paldan Sherab." *mi lo drug brgya lhag tsam nyer brgal ba'i / mi snang rgyas btab gzims pa'i zab gter gang / phyi ma'i dus 'dir mkhan slob chos gsum dang / kun mkhyen chos kyi rgyal pos thugs bskyed las / 'byor rgyas a mi ri ka'i rgyal khab nas / sangs rgyas padma'i thugs rjes nyer 'tsho mkhan / dpal ldan shes rab gang gis slar yang bton /.*)

470 Gter bdag gling pa 'Gyur med rdo rje: *Dus gsum rgyal ba...,* 5b5. In this *stotra,* Klong chen rab 'byams pa is praised under a number of different names.

471 A copy of this "fabricated text" found its way into the Newark Museum. Gene Smith informed me that the late Bdud 'joms Rin po che became aware of the ex-

istence of this text while visiting the museum (the first page with the handwritten *dbu med* title looks very authentic indeed) and took a copy of it back to Nepal. In December 1997 I located this legendary *Rgyud bla ma* commentary by Klong chen pa in the Bla brang of Bdud 'joms Rin po che in Kathmandu.

472 I.e., the *Byams chos sde lngar spyi don sher mdo* and the *Rgyud blar 'grel pa rin chen sgron me* (see p. 687 of Paldan Sherab's altered text).

473 Glag bla Chos 'grub and Chos grags bzang po: *Kun mkhyen klong chen rab 'byams kyi rnam thar*, 208–26.

474 Gzhon nu dpal: *Deb ther sngon po*, 456.7–458.3. According to the *Deb ther dmar po* (p. 70.15–20), Blo gros mtshungs med studied under Shāk gzhon, when the latter held the seat of Sne'u thog.

475 Gzhon nu dpal: *Deb ther sngon po*, 458.3–4.

476 Situ Paṇ chen Chos kyi 'byung gnas and 'Be lo Tshe dbang kun khyab: *Sgrub brgyud karma kaṁ tshang brgyud pa rin po che'i rnam par thar pa...*, 204.6–205.4.

477 Gzhon nu dpal: *op. cit.*, 463.7–464.7.

478 Both the author Blo gros mtshungs med and the place Gsang phu Sne'u thog are mentioned in the colophon of the "Nges don gsal byed sgron me," 565.3–4.

479 Klong chen pa went to Gsang phu when he was nineteen and studied under the fifteenth abbot Slob dpon Btsan dgon and the sixteenth abbot Bla brang pa Chos dpal rgyal mtshan (*Kun mkhyen klong chen rab 'byams kyi rnam thar*, 26.13–21 and 172.20–173.6).

480 Dorji Wangchuk (Hamburg) has informed me that a previous teacher of his, Pema Sherab from the Ngagyur Rnying ma Institute in Mysore, is of the same opinion. In fact, Dorji Wangchuk has seen a copy of Paldan Sherab's fabricated Klong chen pa commentary, to which Pema Sherab had added his own refutation of Paldan Sherab's hypothesis on the basis of internal evidence. See also Wangchuk 2004:187–88 (When Dorji Wangchuk's article appeared, I had already completed my work and could thus not appreciate his observations, which fully corroborate my point).

481 Khenpo Abbey included Blo gros mtshungs med's *Ratnagotravibhāga* commentary in his recently published collection of works of ancient Sa skya scholars (see *Sa skya pa'i mkhas pa rnams kyi gsung skor*, vol. 3, 239–565). In the table of contents of the third volume (Ibid., vol. 3, 1), the author of Blo gros mtshungs med's *Ratnagotravibhāga* commentary is referred to as "a disciple of Bla ma Dam pa [Bsod nams rgyal mtshan], Blo gros mtshungs med of Gnas phrug" (in the margins of the commentary spelled *gnas drug*).

482 In the collected works of Dam pa Bsod nams rgyal mtshan, Gnas drug pa Blo gros mtshungs med is repeatedly mentioned as a scribe, and once even as the spiritual friend who requested Bla ma Dam pa to compose an exegesis of the *Hevajratantra*. See van der Kuijp 1993:127–28 and 141–42 and Kano 2001:32–36. There is still another lama, a certain Ri khrod pa Blo gros brtan pa (1316–58), who is called Blo gros mtshungs med, but it can be excluded that this one is the Blo gros mtshungs med from Gnas drug (Kuijp 1993:128, fn. 32).

483 Kong sprul Blo gros mtha' yas: *Rgyud bla ma'i bshad srol*, 9a2–3.

484 Ibid., 9a4: *...thams cad rngog lo chen po'i rjes su 'brangs pa la chos skad zar zur mi mthun pa mang ngo /.*

485 See Bu ston Rin chen 'grub: *Bu ston chos 'byung*, 363.17–21; Seyfort Ruegg 1966:152; and Kano 2001:35. It was because of this argument that Bu ston composed his *Bde gshegs snying po'i mdzes rgyan* (translated and analyzed by Seyfort Ruegg (1973)).

486 Blo gros mtshungs med: "Nges don gsal byed sgron me," 251.2–3.

487 See Schmithausen 1971:142.

488 RGVV, 26.5–6: *saṁbuddhakāyaspharaṇāt tathatāvyatibhedataḥ / gotrataś ca sadā sarve buddhagarbhāḥ śarīriṇaḥ //.*

489 And my edition of the DRSM.

490 RGVV, 26.3: *bauddhe gotre tatphalasyopacārād.*

491 Technically speaking, Blo gros mtshungs med does not agree that in the first reason *tathāgata* is real and *garbha* metaphorical; or that in the third reason *tathāgata* is metaphorical and *garbha* real (Blo gros mtshungs med: "Nges don gsal byed sgron me," 345.4–346.2).

492 I.e., the fortified potential.

493 See Blo gros mtshungs med ("Nges don gsal byed sgron me," 419.3) on RGV I.154: "the fortified potential does not exist as something pervading all sentient beings, since it is a potential that has been newly accomplished through conditions." *(rgyas 'gyur gyi rigs ni rkyen gyis rigs gsar du bsgrubs pa yin pas sems can thams cad la khyab byed du med do /.)*

494 Ibid., 346.3–347.1: *chos kyi sku ni yon tan dang dbyer med pa'i chos kyi dbyings yin la de sems can thams cad la bdag gcig tu khyab byed du yod pa'i dngos yin pa la gnod byed med pa'i phyir btags pa bar 'jog pa de mi 'thad pa dang / chos sku 'phro ba'i don de thob tu rung ba yin na rigs yod pa las logs su byar med pa'i phyir ro / gal te rigs yod pa bsgrubs pa las byung ba yin no zhe na / 'o na de sems can thams cad la khyab byed du yod par 'gyur te / de khyab byed du yod pa'i rgyu mtshan gyis sems can thams cad de bzhin gshegs pa'i snying po can du bsgrub nus pa'i phyir ro / ... de gnyis las sems can la khyab pa ni rang bzhin du gnas pa'i rigs yin no / des na dngos su gsungs pa'i de bzhin gshegs pa'i snying po dor nas sems can gyi snying po 'chad pa ni nges pa'i don gyi gsung rab kyi dgongs pa ma yin no /.*

495 See Blo gros mtshungs med's (Ibid., 342.5–343.1) refutation of Phya pa's stance that the potential acquired by practice is the actual cause of the Three Jewels (the naturally present potential being a cause only in a metaphorical sense) in his commentary on RGV I.23: "This is not appropriate. The fruit, the Three Jewels, would not arise from the naturally present potential, for it would not be their cause.... Moreover, the cause from which the Three Jewels arise would have a beginning, since the fortified potential has a beginning." *(de ni mi 'thad de / rang bzhin du gnas pa'i rigs las 'bras bu dkon mchog gsum mi 'byung ste de dag gi rgyu ma yin pa'i phyir / ... gzhan yang dkon mchog gsum 'byung ba'i rgyu la thog ma yod par 'gyur te / rgyas 'gyur gyi rigs la thog ma yod pa'i phyir ro /.)*

On Blo gros mtshungs med's presentation of Phya pa's stance see also Kano 2003:109–11.

496 RGVV, 41.21: *yathā pūrvaṁ tathā paścād avikāritvadharmatā //.*

497 RGVV, 76.1: *nāpaneyam ataḥ kiṁcid upaneyaṁ na kiṁcana /.*

498 See the commentary (Blo gros mtshungs med: "Nges don gsal byed sgron me," 367.3) on RGV I.51cd: "...since [buddha nature] is naturally endowed with qualities such as the [ten] strengths throughout beginningless time." *(...stobs sogs kyi yon tan rnams rang bzhin kyis gdod ma nyid nas ldan pa'i phyir....);* and on RGV I.154ab (Ibid., 421.6): "...since previously nonexistent qualities such as the [ten] strengths need not be newly accomplished at all...." *(stobs sogs kyi yon tan sngar med gsar du bsgrub bya cung zad kyang med.)*

499 In his introduction, Blo gros mtshungs med (*op. cit.*, 257.5–258.1) describes apparent truth with regard to the seven vajra points: "The ultimate buddha element is the naturally present pure dharmatā of the mind; its [corresponding] apparent [truth] is that aspect of it that has the ability to generate undefiled [buddha] properties, which possess the primordial mental imprints of virtue. [These imprints] are [the potential] that has arisen from practice. With regard to enlightenment, the ultimate is the dharmakāya and the apparent [truth] the form kāyas. With re-

gard to the qualities, the ultimate is the [ten] strengths, etc., and the apparent [truth] the thirty-two marks [of a buddha]." *(khams don dam pa ni sems kyi chos nyid rnam par dag pa rang bzhin du gnas pa'o / kun rdzob pa ni dge ba'i bag chags thog ma med pa can zag pa med pa'i chos skyed pa'i nus pa'i cha ste bsgrubs pa las byung ba'o / byang chub la yang don dam pa ni chos sku yin la kun rdzob pa ni gzugs sku yin no / yon tan yang don dam pa ni stobs la sogs pa yin la kun rdzob pa ni mtshan sum cu rtsa gnyis yin no /).*

500 Ibid., 343.4–6: *gal te rang bzhin du gnas pa'i rigs rgyu mtshan nyid pa yin na dngos por 'gyur ro zhe na / de la rang bzhin du gnas pa'i rigs ni thog ma med pa'i dus can gyi dri ma dang bcas pa'i chos nyid stong pa nyid yon tan tshad med pa dbyer med du gnas pa yin cing / de la chos nyid stong pa nyid kyi cha ni dri ma med pa'i chos kyi sku'i gnas gyur pa'i rgyu yin yang skyed byed kyi rgyu ma yin pas dngos por mi 'gyur ro / ye shes kyi cha ni / rigs 'dra phyi ma sangs rgyas kyi stobs sogs skyed par byed pa'i rgyu yin pas dngos po yin pa la gnod pa med do /.*

501 Blo gros mtshungs med comments (Ibid., 319.6) on RGV I.16: *sems rang bzhin gyis 'od gsal ba ni rang bzhin gyis gnas pa'i ye shes yin la.*

502 Ibid., 334.6–335.1: *snying po ni dbyings kyi cha nas ngos bzung na dri ma dang bcas pa'i sems kyi chos nyid bsam gyis mi khyab pa'i sangs rgyas kyi yon tan rnams dang dbyer med pa / gdod ma nas grub pa'i chos sku yin te /.*

503 On the question whether primordial wisdom can be subsumed under the naturally present potential, see Blo gros mtshungs med's (*op. cit.*, 336.1) commentary on RGV I.16: "The sphere and wisdom, which exist throughout beginningless time, are the naturally present potential." *(dbyings dang ye shes gdod ma nas grub pa ni rang bzhin du gnas pa'i rigs yin la.)*

504 Ibid., 337.3: *rgyu la 'bras bu gnas par 'gyur ro zhe na / mi 'gyur te dri ma thams cad kyi rnam par dag pa'i ye shes 'bras bu yin yang sems can la med cing dri ma dang bcas pa'i ye shes sems can gyi rgyud la yod kyang de 'bras bu ma yin no /.*

505 For a translation of these stanzas see above, introduction, section 3 ("The *Ratnagotravibhāga* and its *Vyākhyā*").

506 Tib. *dngos po ngo bo nyid kyi sku;* translated in accordance with an explanation given (orally) by Thrangu Rinpoche.

507 The Tibetan renders Skt. *iti* by means of a causal construction.

508 Blo gros mtshungs med: "Nges don gsal byed sgron me," 416.4–417.2: *rang bzhin du gnas pa dang bsgrubs pa las byung ba'i rigs 'di gnyis las 'bras bu rdzogs pa'i sangs rgyas kyi rnam par dag pa'i sku gsum thob par 'gyur bas de dag gi rgyu yin par 'dod pa yin / des na khams sam rigs ni rgyu yin no / rigs gang las 'bras bu sku gang thob ce na dang po rang bzhin du gnas pas sku ni dngos po ngo bo nyid kyi sku thob ste sngar dri ma dang bcas pa'i de bzhin nyid yod na de'i dri ma sbyangs pas rnam par dag par gyur pa'i chos kyi skur gnas gyur pa 'thob pa'i phyir ro / blo gros chen po kha cig na re / stong pa nyid la dmigs pa'i tshul bzhin yid la byed pa la goms pas rnam par mi rtog pa'i shes rab skye bas ye shes kyi rgyur btags pa yin zhes gsungs pa ni mi 'thad de / 'grel pa las / de bzhin gshegs pa nyid*[a] *sangs rgyas kyi sku rnam pa gsum gyis (text: gyi) rab tu phye ba yin te / des na de bzhin gshegs pa'i khams ni de thob pa'i rgyu yin pas 'dir khams kyi don ni rgyu'i*[b] *don to.* The corresponding Sanskrit of the quotation from the *vyākhyā* is as follows (RGVV, 72.9–10: *trividhabuddhakāyaprabhāvitatvaṁ hi tathāgatatvam / atas tatprāptaye hetus tathāgatadhātur iti / hetvartho 'tra dhātvarthaḥ /*).

a Corrected according to Nakamura (1967:141.10). Blo gros mtshungs med reads *de bzhin gshegs pas ni.*

b Corrected according to Nakamura (1967:141.12). Blo gros mtshungs med reads *rgyu'am.*

509 Blo gros mtshungs med: "Nges don gsal byed sgron me," 417.4–5 and 418.2–3:

gnyis pa rgyas 'gyur gyi rigs kyis ni phyi ma gzugs kyi sku gnyis thob pa ste thar pa'i rgyur gyur pa'i dge ba bsgrubs shing smon lam btab pas sangs rgyas pa'i tshe / gdul bya nye ba dang ring ba la gzugs sku gnyis su snang ba'i phyir ro / … sprul pa'i sku ni longs spyod rdzogs pa'i sku'i dbang gis gdul bya'i blo ngor de'i gzugs rnyan shar ba'i tshul gyis ni rang bzhin yin pa'i phyir / gser las byas pa'i bcos ma'i gzugs lta bu'o /.

510 I.e., the three natures of the buddha element.

511 Ibid., 418.6–419.3: … *chos kyi sku dang de bzhin nyid dang rang bzhin du gnas pa'i rigs gsum ni sgra ji bzhin du sems can thams cad la khyab par yod la chos kyi sku'i rgyu mthun par zab pa dang rgya che bar ston pa gnyis dang rigs kyi 'bras bu sku gsum ni 'bras bu'i sa na yod pa bstan pa yin la / de dag sems can la yod pa dang yod kyang sgrib pas bsgribs pa ni gsung rab gnyis kyi bdag rkyen ji lta ba dang ji snyed pa mkhyen pa'i ye shes gnyis dang / sku gnyis 'byung ba'i bdag po ye shes bzhi yod pas de ltar gsungs te ye shes de dag dri ma glo bus dag pa na de'i dbang gis gdul bya la gsung rab gnyis dang sku gnyis su snang bar 'byung ba'i phyir ro / / ngo bo nyid kyi sku ni chos kyi sku dang don gcig yin cing / rgyas 'gyur gyi rigs ni rkyen gyis rigs gsar du bsgrubs pa yin pas sems can thams cad la khyab byed du med do /.*

512 Ibid., 277.5–6: "Since the dharmakāya of a tathāgata is free from all conditioned phenomena, it is not conditioned." *(de bzhin gshegs pa'i chos kyi sku de 'dus byas kyi chos thams cad kyis dben pas na 'dus ma byas pa….)*

513 Klong chen pa: *Grub mtha' mdzod*, 161–90.

514 Thus, the buddha element or sphere *(dhātu)* in the *Ratnagotravibhāga* is systematically brought into relation with the *rdzogs chen* notions of primordial ground of manifestation *('char gzhi)*, self-arisen wisdom *(rang byung ye shes)*, and awareness *(rig pa)* in the *Grub mtha' mdzod*. Germano (1992:79) has observed that "the entirety of [Klong chen pa's] *Tshig don mdzod* can be understood as an innovative commentary on the significance of the… 'buddha nature,' which the beginning of the *Tshig don mdzod* refers to as 'the adamantine nucleus of radiant light.'"

515 Klong chen pa: *Grub mtha' mdzod*, 190.1–2: "Instead of viewing this presentation of a [buddha] potential as having provisional meaning, one should know that it has definitive meaning only." *(rigs kyi rnam par gzhag pa 'di ni drang don du mi lta bar / nges pa'i don 'ba' zhig tu bzung ste shes par bya'o /.)*

516 See below.

517 Kong sprul Blo gros mtha' yas: *Shes bya kun khyab mdzod*, vol. 1, 460.2–461.6.

518 See Mathes 2004:285–328.

519 They are: (1–2) The two *yāna*s of gods and men, (3–4) the two non-Buddhist *yāna*s, (5–6) the two *yāna*s of the śrāvakas, namely Vaibhāṣika and Sautrāntika, (7–8) the two *yāna*s of the followers of Cittamātra and the Svātāntrika-Mādhyamikas, (9) the *yāna* of the Prāsaṅgika-Mādhyamikas, (10–15) the *yāna*s of Krīya, Cārya, Yoga, Mahā, Anu and Ati, and (16) the *yāna* of the spontaneously present clear light, the vajra essence (Klong chen pa: *Grub mtha' mdzod*, 59.1–3).

520 The eight chapters of the treatise are:

1. How the teacher, the Buddha, came [into the world] (8.3)
2. A presentation of the nature of [his] teaching, the correct Dharma (25.3)
3. A detailed explanation of the divisions of the ocean of one's own and other tenets (55.6).
4. A precise explanation of how to proceed on the paths of these [tenets] (137.5)
5. A presentation of the secret *mantra* [path], or Vajrayāna (257.6)
6. A presentation of the secret *mantra* [path] (282.1)
7. A presentation of the old [tradition of] the secret *mantra* [path] (310.4)
8. A precise explanation of the path of clear light, [or] vajra essence (361.3)

521 That is, the eighth chapter starting on p. 361.

522 Klong chen pa: *Grub mtha' mdzod*, 364.4–6.
523 Ibid., 364.6–365.1; cf. RGVV, 72.13–14 and Takasaki 1966:290.
524 The quoted stanza is from the "Dohās for the People" ("Do ha mdzod kyi glu bzhugs so," 289.4).
525 Shahidullah (1928:173) translates on the basis of the Apabhraṁsa: "Faites obéissance à celui qui est comme la pierre magique...."
526 Klong chen pa: *Grub mtha' mdzod*, 365.1–2: *sems nyid gcig pu kun gyi sa bon te / gang la srid dang mya ngan 'das 'phro ba / / 'dod pa'i 'bras bu ster bar byed pa yi / / yid bzhin nor 'dra'i sems la phyag 'tshal lo /*. The translation follows Karma Phrin las pa's commentary (see my note on the translation of DRSM, 51.18–19). See Shahidullah 1928:140.
527 Klong chen pa: *op. cit.*, 365.5.
528 Equated with buddha nature on the same page (Ibid., 369.6).
529 As denoting a hindrance, the term *kun gzhi* must here stand for *kun gzhi rnam shes*, one of the eight accumulations.
530 Klong chen pa: *Grub mtha' mdzod*, 369.2–5: *rig pa de yang ngo bo stong / rang bzhin 'od lngar gnas la / thugs rje zer du khyab pa sku dang ye shes kyi 'byung gnas chen por bzhugs kyang / ngo bo chos sku stong pa ye shes gzigs pa dag pa'i cha la kun gzhi dang tshogs brgyad kyis bsgribs / rang bzhin 'od lngar gsal ba la / gdos (text: rdos) bcas sha khrag gi phung pos bsgribs / thugs rje zer dang rig pa 'char byed du gnas pa la las dang bag chags kyis bsgribs te / shin tu blta bar dka' ba'i bdag nyid du bzhugs na yang / med pa ma yin te sems can kun la khyab par rang rang gi lus la rten bcas nas yod de /*.
531 Ibid., at the beginning of chapter 6, on p. 282.1.
532 Lit., "without union and separation."
533 As in the quotation above, *kun gzhi* must be taken as *kun gzhi rnam shes*, which is one of the eight accumulations.
534 Klong chen pa: *Grub mtha' mdzod*, 282.3–6: *...mtshan gzhi ni / 'od gsal ba'i rang bzhin sku dang ye shes 'du 'bral med pa'i dbyings rang bzhin gyis dag pa dang de la brten pa'i chos sbyang bya sbyong byed dang bcas pa thams cad yin no / ...dbyings 'od gsal ba'i chos nyid rang bzhin rnam dag ni sbyang ba'i gzhi'o / / glo (text: blo) bur gyi sgrib pa las dang nyon mongs pa 'khor ba'i chos kun gzhi tshogs brgyad dang bcas pa ni sbyang bar bya ba'i dri ma'o / de'ang bag chags sna tshogs pa'i kun gzhi ni 'khor ba'i rtsa ba yin pas ldog la / gnas lugs don gyi kun gzhi'i don mi ldog kyang / tha snyad gzhir btags pa'i ming gi cha de log nas chos kyi dbyings kyi ye shes zhes bya bar 'gyur ba'o /*.
535 Both Tib. *dbyings* and *khams* are used to translate Skt. *dhātu*, the term employed in the *Ratnagotravibhāga* for the buddha element that is not empty of qualities. Cf. the different Tibetan translations of the stanza from the *Mahāyānābhidharmasūtra* (RGVV, 72.13: *anādikāliko dhātuḥ sarvadharmasamāśrayaḥ /*). In the quotation in the *Ratnagotravibhāgavyākhyā*, the Tibetan for *dhātu* is *khams*, whereas it is *dbyings* in the translation of this stanza in the *Triṁśikābhāṣya* (see Takasaki 1966:290).
536 In his autocommentary on the *Zab mo nang gi don*, Rang byung rdo rje distinguishes, based on *Mahāyānasaṁgraha* I.45–48, an impure *kun gzhi rnam par shes pa* from a pure dharmadhātu in a similar way, and remarks that in this context the term *kun gzhi* alone can also refer to suchness, and thus to the pure dharmadhātu (see above, "The Position of the Third Karmapa Rangjung Dorjé").
537 I am indebted to Stearns (1999:51) for this reference. Without translating or further analyzing the passage, Stearns observes that this passage "has none of the connotations inherent in Dol po pa's usage."
538 Further down, Klong chen pa explains that the actual sun is empty of what is

referred to by synonyms such as "light-maker" or "[the one drawn by] seven horses," neither of which captures its real meaning (*Rdzogs pa chen po sems nyid ngal gso'i 'grel pa*, 221.6–222.1).

539 Such as *skandhas*, *dhātus*, and *āyatanas* (Ibid., 222.1–2).

540 Klong chen pa: *Rdzogs pa chen po sems nyid ngal gso'i 'grel pa*, 220.1–221.5: *rang gis stong pa ni med bzhin snang ba chu'i zla ba lta bu rang gi mtshan nyid spangs pa dang / rang gzhan du dbye ba'i cha shas med kyang lhun gyis grub pa'i chos mi 'dor bas btags pa rang gi ngo bos stong pa gnyis so / / gzhan gyis stong pa'ang / mi ldan pa gzhan gyis stong pa dang rnam grangs gzhan gyis stong pa'o / / gnyis kas stong pa la'ang / gnyis bcas rnam grangs pas stong pa dang sgra don rang mtshan pas stong pa'o / de la sems kyi chos nyid 'od gsal ba snying po'i khams kyi rang bzhin 'di ni skyon gyi dngos po mtha' dag gis stong la / yon tan gyi mtshan nyid ldan pa / ngo bo nyid kyis (text: kyi) dag pa'i cha nas skyon yon grub bsal las 'das pa'o / . . . kun tu rtog pa'am rnam shes tshogs brgyad po 'di dag ni gshis la med pas rang gi ngo bos kyang stong la / . . . mdor bsdu na / rang gis stong pa ni chos gang dang gang yin pa de'i rang bzhin bden pa med pa'o / . . . gzhan gyis stong pa ni chos de la chos gzhan med pa'i cha nas btags pa'o.*

541 Klong chen pa: *Grub mtha' mdzod*, 219.5.

542 Ibid., 185.6–186.2: *de'ang don dam pa'i bden pa dbyings yin la / 'di'i rang bzhin mthong bas don dam bden pa mthong zhes bya'i / cir yang med pa'i stong nyid kyang don dam bden pa ma yin no / de'ang byis pa so so skye bo daṇg / las dang po dag bdag tu zhen pa'i gnyen por bdag med pa la sogs pa bstan pa yin gyi (text: gyis) / don la dbyings 'od gsal ba 'dus ma byas shing lhun grub tu yod pa shes par bya ste /.*

543 In this rhetorical question (Klong chen pa: *Grub mtha' mdzod*, 329.4) the Tibetan term *khams* is used for the buddha element (Skt. *dhātu*), just as in the *Ratnagotravibhāga* (Klong chen pa otherwise uses *dbyings*). Apart from the doctrinally close *Mahāratnakūṭasūtra*, the *Ratnagotravibhāga* is the only nontantric work quoted in the chapters on Vajrayāna and *rdzogs chen* in the *Grub mtha' mdzod*.

544 Klong chen pa: *Grub mtha' mdzod*, 329.5: *rang byung gi ye shes rdzogs pa chen po nyid ye nas sangs rgyas kyi che ba'i yon tan lhun grub tu yod pas / sku gsum rang chas su tshang ba'i phyir logs nas btsal mi dgos. . . .*

545 Ibid., 325.5–6.

546 Ibid., 326.6–327.1: *rang bzhin rdzogs pa chen po 'od gsal dbyings kyi ngo bo rang byung gi ye shes te / 'di la bskyed bya skyed byed kyi rgyu 'bras rkyen dang bcas pa med pas nam mkha' lta bu'i rang bzhin du ye nas yod pa. . . .*

547 A cycle of tantras of the *sems sde* (see Achard 1999:60).

548 Klong chen pa: *Grub mtha' mdzod*, 327.2: *ji ltar sngon (RGV: sngar) bzhin phyis de bzhin / 'gyur ba med pa'i chos nyid do* (RGVV, 41.21: *yathā pūrvaṁ tathā paścād avikāritvadharmatā //*).

549 Klong chen pa: *op. cit.*, 327.2.

550 RGVV, 7.14–15: *asaṁskṛtam anābhogam [aparapratyayoditam / buddhatvaṁ jñānakāruṇyaśaktyupetaṁ dvayārthavat //].*

551 Klong chen pa: *op. cit.*, 55–137.

552 For the combination of the *trisvabhāva* with the *tathāgatagarbha* theory see Mathes 2000:218–20.

553 See Klong chen pa: *op. cit.*, 282.5–6, where the actual basis of everything is clearly distinguished from the *kun gzhi* as *ālayavijñāna*. Whereas the *kun gzhi* is not affected by the transformation of the basis, the *ālayavijñāna* is turned back.

554 On *dbu ma chen po*, see van der Kuijp 1983:35–45.

555 See Mathes 2000:196.

556 Klong chen pa: *Yid bzhin rin po che'i mdzod kyi 'grel pa padma dkar po*, 840.1–3. (I am indebted to F.-K. Ehrhard for this reference.)

557 Klong chen pa: *Grub mtha' mdzod*, 126.3: *don dam pa'i bden pa'i mtshan nyid ni gzung 'dzin spros pa dang bral ba'i ngo bo ste /.*

558 See Mathes 1996:19.

559 Strictly speaking, nothing is really transformed for Klong chen pa, who explains (*Grub mtha' mdzod*, 240.4–5): "In terms of that which appears by virtue of [becoming] free from the hindering [stains] on the basis of the wisdom that exists in oneself, a transformation of the basis [occurs only] in a metaphorical sense" *(rang la yod pa'i ye shes de'i steng gi sgrib byed bral stobs kyis snang ba'i cha nas gnas gyur du btags pa ste /).*

560 Cf. MA 361.14, which reads *sems 'gags pas* instead of *sems 'gags pa* (Klong chen pa: *Grub mtha' mdzod*, 244.6).

561 Lit., "presentation."

562 Klong chen pa: *op. cit.*, 244.4–245.3: *dbu ma par 'dod pa kha cig sangs rgyas la ye shes med pas / ye shes kyi mkhyen pa'ang med de shes bya spros pa yin la / de dang bral ba'i phyir dang / ... 'jug pa las / sems 'gags pa de sku yis mngon sum mdzad / ces gsungs pa'i phyir ro zhe na / de ni mi rigs te / stong ngos chos sku la ltos na ye shes yod med gnyis kar ma grub pas yod ces bzhag kyang 'gog la / med ces 'dod kyang 'gog pa mtshungs pa'i phyir med pa'ang mi 'thad la / snang ngos gzugs sku la ltos nas / gdul bya snang nas don mdzad pa snang dgos pas ye shes kyang snang dgos pa'i phyir dang / shes bya shes byed la sogs pa'i grub mtha' btags pa thams cad spros pa yin yang / gang gis kyang ma btags par snang ba'i rnam gzhag gi yul rnams spros pa zhes gzhag tu med pa....*

563 Sa skya Paṇḍita: *Thub pa dgongs gsal*, 72b2–3: *ye shes rang rgyud la bden par grub pa yod na mu stegs rtag smra dang mtshungs pa dang / ... / ye shes rang rgyud la med par gzhan snang yin na sangs rgyas la yon tan med par 'gyur ro /.*

564 Kong sprul: *Shes bya kun khyab mdzod*, vol. 2, 540.23–541.1: *don dam par sangs rgyas kyi sa na ye shes yod med 'das shing / tha snyad du ni ye shes yod....*

565 Klong chen pa: *Grub mtha' mdzod*, 137–257.

566 RGVV, 43.9–10: *cittasya yāsau prakṛtiḥ prabhāsvarā na jātu*[a] *sā dyaur iva yāti vikriyām.* The Tibetan does not render *jātu.*

a B (24b5) reads *yātu;* ms. A is not complete here.

567 Klong chen pa: *Grub mtha' mdzod*, 161.6–162.1: *dbyings dang rang bzhin gyis rnam par dag pa don dam pa'i bden pa rang byung gi ye shes de ni / dri ma dang bcas pa'i dus na rigs sam khams sam de bzhin gshegs pa'i snying po zhes bya la / dri ma dang bral ba'i tshe byang chub bam de bzhin gshegs pa zhes bya ba....*

568 RGVV, 76.1–2: *nāpaneyam ataḥ kiṁcid upaneyaṁ na kiṁcana / draṣṭavyaṁ bhūtato bhūtaṁ bhūtadarśī vimucyate //.*

569 Klong chen pa: *op. cit.*, 162.3–4: *dbyings snying po 'di'i ngo bo la dor bya'i dri ma ye nas med de rang bzhin gyis 'od gsal zhing dri ma med pa'i phyir ro / / sngar med kyi yon tan phyi nas gsar du bsgrub pa med de yon tan lhun grub yin pa'i phyir ro /.*

570 RGV I.25 reads as follows: "Because [suchness] is endowed with purity and defilements; because [suchness] has [always been] apart from all defilements and [nevertheless] has been purified; because the properties [of the Buddha] are inseparable; and because [the buddha activity] is without effort and thought." (RGVV, 21.15–16: *śuddhyupakliṣṭatāyogāt niḥsaṁkleśaviśuddhitaḥ / avinirbhāgadharmatvād anābhogāvikalpataḥ //.*) The *vyākhyā* on the third and fourth points is as follows: "The [third] point here is inconceivable, in that stainless buddha qualities are found to be not different in terms of their inseparable true nature, before and later, even on the level of ordinary people, which [level] is wholly defiled. The [fourth] point here is inconceivable, in that buddha activity unfolds in sentient beings simultaneously, everywhere, at all times, and without effort and thought in accordance with their mental disposition and [the capacity of

the] disciples—and this without fail and in an appropriate way each time. (RGVV, 22.8–10 and 24.9–10: *tatra vimalā buddhaguṇāḥ paurvāparyeṇaikāntasaṁkliṣṭāyām api pṛthagjanabhūmāvavinirbhāgadharmatayā nirviśiṣṭā vidyanta ity acintyam etat sthānam / …tatra jinakriyā yugapat sarvatra sarvakālam anābhogenāvikalpato yathāśayeṣu yathāvaineyikeṣu*[a] *sattveṣv akṣūṇam*[b] *anuguṇaṁ pravartata ity acintyam etat sthānam /.*)

a A (7a3) reads *yathāvainaiyikeṣu*, B (14a6) *yathāvainai(*or *-ne-)keṣu.* The conjecture is according to Takasaki 1966:192 and Schmithausen 1971:141.

b B (14a6) reads *akṣūṇṇam* or *akṣūṇatvam.*

571 The Sanskrit root *tar* usually means "to come out," "to arise." The Tibetan rendition of *tar* as *sgrol* suggests to take a causative form of *tar.*

572 Klong chen pa: *Grub mtha' mdzod,* 170.2–3: *gautra zhes pa'i go guṇa zhes bsgyur na yon tan yin la / tra tara zhes bsgyur na sgrol ba ste / yon tan gyis (text: gyi sa?) rten byas nas 'khor na'i pha rol du sgrol bas te / de nyid las / yon tan ni / sgrol ba'i don shes par bya zhes so /.*

573 My translation follows the Tibetan and the way Klong chen pa obviously interprets this stanza. If one does not take the Sanskrit or Vasubandhu's *bhāṣya* into account, this is the most reasonable way to do so. For a paraphrase of the Sanskrit (MSABh, 11.8–9: *prakṛtyā paripuṣṭaṁ ca āśrayaś cāśritaṁ ca tat / sad asac caiva vijñeyaṁ guṇottāraṇatārthataḥ*) see Seyfort Ruegg 1969:79: "La Lignée [Tib. *rigs,* Skt. *gotra,* is translated by me as 'potential'] existant par nature et la developée, ou le support et le supporté; de plus, le *gotra* est existant en tant que cause mais inexistant en tant que fruit; enfin ce facteur reçoit le nom de *gotra* puisqu'il réalise les qualités." Seyfort Ruegg notes that *uttāraṇa* has the meaning of "to realize" or "to carry out [a promise]." The *bhāṣya* explains the compound *guṇottāraṇatā-* in the following way: "the qualities come out in the sense that they arise from it (sc. the potential)" (*guṇā uttaranty asmād udbhavantīti kṛtvā* (MSABh, 11.12)).

574 I.e., the cause liberating the dharmakāya and the svābhāvikakāya from the adventitious stains.

575 I.e., the cause liberating the form kāyas from the adventitious stains.

576 Klong chen pa: *Grub mtha' mdzod,* 170.5–6: *dbyings stong pa ni chos sku ngo bo nyid sku'i bral rgyu rten yin la / ye shes snang ba rang 'od mtshan dpe dang bcas pa ni brten pa gzugs sku gnyis kyi bral rgyur gnas pa ste /.*

577 Lit., "accomplishment."

578 I.e., taking a causative form of *tar.*

579 Tib. *sgrol.*

580 Blo gros mtshungs med: "Nges don gsal byed sgron me," 332.2–4: *bsgrubs pa las byung ba ni 'phags pa'i rigs tha dad pa la sogs pa'i rkyen gyis gsar du bsgrubs pa'o / de la rang bzhin du gnas pa ni rten yin cing bsgrubs pa las byung ba ni brten pa yin no / rigs kyi mtshan nyid ni / dri ma dang bcas pa'i gnas skabs kyi chos gang zhig 'phags pa'i spang rtogs 'byung du rung ba'o / sgra don ni gotra zhes pa la go'i bar nas gu byung ste / gu ṇa (text: na) zhes pa yon tan yin la ta dang ra phral bas tara zhes pa sgrol ba ste gu ṇa (text: na) ta ra zhes pa / yon tan sgrol zhing 'byung bas na rigs so /.*

581 Skt. *uttaranti;* the reading "[the qualities] liberate" would require the causative form *uttārayanti.*

582 MSABh, 11.11–12: *guṇottāraṇārthena gotraṁ veditavyaṁ guṇā uttaranty asmād udbhavantīti kṛtvā.*

583 In fact, something similar can be observed with regard to the works of Gser mdog paṇ chen Śākya mchog ldan, who seems to fully endorse the *gzhan stong* view only in works written after his first meeting with the Seventh Karmapa in 1484 (see Dreyfus 1997:29). For a short description of Śākya mchog ldan's position, see also Tillemans and Tomabechi 1995:891–96: "Le *dbu ma'i byung tshul* de Śākya mchog ldan."

584 For a translation of RGV I.152–55 (J I.149–52), see the third section of my introduction.

585 Tib. *'char gzhi*. "In *rdzogs chen* it has the technical sense of the ground's virtual dynamics, which remain nonmanifest internal radiance but are the energetic and intelligent source of everything that exists in manifest actuality" (see Germano 1992:924).

586 Klong chen pa: *Grub mtha' mdzod*, 171.3–172.1: *de'ang rang bzhin du gnas pa'i rigs dang / yang dag par blang ba'i rigs la gzhi dang lam gyi dbye bas rnam pa gnyis su dbye ste / dbyings kyi rang bzhin gzhi kun la khyab par gnas dus na / 'char gzhi dbyings kyi cha ni nor bu rin po che'i gter dang 'dra ste / gang 'dod 'byung ba'i gzhir gnas la dngos su gang du'ang ma chad pa bzhin du / chos sku ngo bo nyid sku'i dbyings te sku dang ye shes 'char ba'i go 'byed pas bzhag la / shar ba'i ye shes snang ba'i cha rig pa dang sku ni rkyen sgrib pa bral stobs kyis rang la yod pa'i yon tan mngon par 'gyur nges kyi cha tsam nas 'bras bu can gyi ljon shing gong du 'phel ba'i dpes gsungs te / dag rgyu la dag 'bras kyi ming gis btags pa'o / mdo sde rgyan las / gser gyi rigs dang rin chen mchog gi dper bzhag pa yin /.*

587 Ibid., 172.1–4: *zhar la lam la slob dus ltar bshad na / dbyings kyi rigs de gnyis ka rang bzhin lhun grub tu yod pas rang bzhin gyi rigs zer te rten du gnas la / de'i steng du sems dang po bskyed pa nas bzung ste sa bcu rgyun mtha'i bar gyi dge rtsa bsod nams dang ye shes kyi tshogs gnyis kyis bsdus pa thams cad la yang dag par blangs pa'am rgyas 'gyur gyi rigs zhes bya ste / dge ba de yang gnyen po gsar du blangs pa can rang bzhin rigs kyi dri ma bsal stobs kyis rang la yod pa'i yon tan gsar du skye ba ltar ston pa'i phyir ro / ding sang ni gzhi la rigs de gnyis mi brtsi bar / gzhi'i de bzhin dang / lam ni rgyas (text: rgya la) 'gyur du 'jog pa ni dbyings ma go ba'i rnam 'gyur du snang ste / gzhi la snang stong lhun grub tu yod pa dang 'gal ba'i phyir te /....*

588 Ibid., 183.4–5: *lam sbyangs nas dri ma bud stobs kyis sku gsum bskyed pa ltar snang ba'i cha nas rigs kyi rang bzhin zhes bya ste / gter dang shing dang / rin po che'i sku dang / 'khor los sgyur ba dang / gser gyi gzugs kyi dpe lngas bstan to /.*

589 See Ibid., 170.5–6.

590 According to Germano (1992:77–78), Klong chen pa says in the seventh chapter of the *Tshig don mdzod* that the teaching of the second dharmacakra, i.e., the *prajñāpāramitā* and so on, have provisional meaning *(neyārtha)* and are surpassed by the *nītārtha* teachings of the third dharmacakra.

591 'Ba' ra ba Rgyal mtshan dpal bzang: "Chos rje rnam gnyis kyi dgongs bshad nyi ma'i 'od zer," in *Collected Writings*, 496–557.

592 Ibid., 496.4–6: */ chos rje bu ston pa / sems can la bde gshegs snying po med par 'dod do zhes pa dang / kun mkhyen pa sems can la / dag pa ye shes kyi kun gzhi dang / ma dag pa rnam shes kyi kun gzhi gnyis yod par 'dod cing / de gnyis rang bzhin mi gcig par 'dod pa dang / stong gzugs bde gshegs [snying] po yid brtan (text: bstan) du rung par 'dod do zer ba gsan pas /.*

593 See Mathes 2000:319.

594 Lit., the "intentional ground."

595 See Seyfort Ruegg 1985:309–11 and 1988b:1–4; and Cabezón 1992:226–27.

596 See Seyfort Ruegg 1973:40.

597 Ibid., 29–30.

598 Sgra tshad pa: *Yang rgyan*, 34b3: *'di'i sangs rgyas kyi rang bzhin de gang yin / sangs rgyas kyi de bzhin nyid la zer na / sems can la yod par kho bo yang 'dod do / / sangs rgyas kyi chos sku la zer na / de sems can la yod par ma grub par sngar bshad /.* For a French translation see Seyfort Ruegg 1973:31.

599 Seyfort Ruegg 1973:32.

600 'Ba' ra ba: "Chos rje rnam gnyis kyi dgongs bshad nyi ma'i 'od zer," 497.4–498.4.

601 RGVV, 12.14: *ayam eva ca bhagavaṁs tathāgatadharmakāyo 'vinirmuktakleśakośas*

tathāgatagarbha ity ucyate.[a] (*de bzhin gshegs pa'i chos kyi sku 'di nyid nyon mongs pa'i sbubs las ma grol ba 'di ni de bzhin gshegs pa'i snying po'o //*, 'Ba' ra ba: *op. cit.*, 498.4–5.)

a Schmithausen (1971:137) proposes reading *ity ucyate* instead of *sūcyate* (B (8a3) is not clear, A not available).

602 See Seyfort Ruegg 1973:37–38.

603 Ibid., 38ff.

604 'Ba' ra ba: "Chos rje rnam gnyis kyi dgongs bshad nyi ma'i 'od zer," 512.3–5: *...thams cad mkhyen pa bu ston rin po che / sems can la bde gshegs snying po med par gsungs pa ni / sangs rgyas kyi bde gshegs snying po glo (text: blo) bur dri ma'i sbubs las grol ba stobs bcu dang / mi 'jigs pa bzhi dang / sangs rgyas kyi chos ma 'dres pa bco brgyad la sogs pa dang ldan pa'i dag pa gnyis ldan gyi bde gshegs snying po chos kyi sku de sems can la med par bzhed la /.*

605 In order to reinforce this point 'Ba' ra ba refers to RGV III.4a: "The [Buddha's] state of [the ten] strengths is like a vajra [acting] on those who are hindered by ignorance." (RGVV, 91.15: *balatvam ajñānavṛteṣu vajravad.*)

606 'Ba' ra ba: "Chos rje rnam gnyis kyi dgongs bshad nyi ma'i 'od zer," 515.4 and 516.6.

607 Ibid., 518.2: *chos nyid 'od gsal yod pa la dgongs nas yod par gsungs / dbyibs kha dog med pa la dgongs nas stong par gsungs /.*

608 In this regard Sgra tshad pa refers to Sa skya Paṇḍita, who never accepted the truth of any dharma that is established on an ultimate level, however subtle it may be (see Seyfort Ruegg 1973:31). In other words, if 'Ba' ra ba's existence of luminosity that is empty of shapes and colors entails that anything luminous whatsoever is left over in emptiness, it would not be accepted by Sa paṇ, Sgra tshad, or probably even Bu ston.

609 'Ba' ra ba: "Chos rje rnam gnyis kyi dgongs bshad nyi ma'i 'od zer," 501.1–3: *kun gzhi byang chub kyi sems 'di dngos por grub pa'i sgrib byed kyi dri mas ma gos par dvangs (text: dangs) pa ni gsal ba / bem por ma song bas skyid sdug gong bzhin shes pas rig pa / dbyibs kha dog med pas stong pa / de gsum dbyer med pa'o // de la dbye na glo (text: blo) bur dri ma dang bcas pa ni sems can bde gshegs snying po'o /.*

610 According to an explanation of Thrangu Rinpoche.

611 'Ba' ra ba: "Chos rje rnam gnyis kyi dgongs bshad nyi ma'i 'od zer," 501.3–502.2: *de'ang sems can la yod pa'i bde gshegs snying po de nyon mongs pa'i dri ma dang bcas pa / de nyid rang gis gnas lugs ma rtogs par 'khrul pa de ma rig pa yin la / ma rig pa la nyon mongs pa dang / glo (text: blo) bur gyi dri mar gsungs pas / nyon mongs pa'i sbubs na chos nyid 'od gsal gnas pa de la bde gshegs snying po // glo (text: blo) bur dri mas sgribs zer ba yin la / de las gzhan pa'i dbyibs kha dog gi dngos por grub pa mi gtsang ba lta bu / gang gis kyang sgrib pa med pa'i gsal la dangs pa de la 'od gsal dang / rang bzhin rnam dag zer la / de nyid kyis rang nyid ngo ma shes pa ma rig pa de rkyen gyi dbang gis gzung (text: bzung) 'dzin sna tshogs su shar ba 'khor bar 'khyams pas / 'khor ba'i chos kyi sa bon nam / sems can gyi bde gshegs snying po de / ...chos nyid nyams su blangs pas / las dang nyon mongs pa'i sbubs na gnas pa de'i las dang nyon mongs pa bag chags dang bcas pa dag pas / chos nyid 'od gsal ba de mngon du gyur pa ste / sangs rgyas kyi sa yi chos sku'am / bde gshegs snying po ste /.*

612 Basing himself on the *Laṅkāvatārasūtra* (LAS, 220.9–16; see p. 18 in the introduction of this work) 'Ba' ra ba explains (*op. cit.*, 509.2–3: "An *ālaya[vijñāna]*[a] that is different from buddha nature does not exist. That which is one in essence has thus been given two different names" *(bde gshegs snying po las tha dad pa'i kun gzhi med par grub pas / ngo bo gcig la ming tha dad pa gnyis btags).* 'Ba' ra ba also refers to the *Ghanavyūhasūtra,* which says (see Peking Kangyur no. 778, *mdo sna tshogs,* vol. *cu,* 62b1): "The Tathāgata taught buddha nature with recourse to the term *ālaya[vijñāna?]" (bde gshegs snying po dge'ang // snying po la kun gzhi sgras / de bzhin*

gshegs pa ston pa mdzad). For the unusual form …*snying po dge'ang* see Ibid., 49a8: *de bzhin kun gzhi rnam shes pa / de bzhin gshegs pa'i dge snying po.*

a It should be noted that 'Ba' ra ba explicitly equates *kun gzhi* and *kun gzhi'i rnam shes* in his "Chos rje rnam gnyis kyi dgongs bshad nyi ma'i 'od zer," 499.3–4.

613 It should be noted in this regard that neither the *Laṅkāvatārasūtra* nor the *Ghanavyūha* is quoted in the *Ratnagotravibhāgavyākhyā.*

614 'Ba' ra ba: "Kun gzhi'i rnam shes dang ye shes kyi rnam bzhag," 620.1–4. In his "Chos rje rnam gnyis kyi dgongs bshad nyi ma'i 'od zer" (527.6) 'Ba' ra ba explains that it is by virtue of its awareness that the buddha nature experiences suffering. This is said to be like the experience of suffering in a dream *(rig pa'i cha des du kha myong ba ste / rmi lam gyi du kha myong ba bzhin no).*

615 RGVV, 35.18–19 and 36.7–9: *buddhadhātuḥ sa cen na syān nirvid duḥkhe 'pi no bhavet / necchā na prārthanā nāpi praṇidhir nirvṛtau bhavet // bhavanirvāṇatadduḥkhasukhadoṣaguṇekṣaṇam gotre sati bhavaty etad agotrāṇāṁ na tad yataḥ*[a] *//* .

a Johnston reads *vidyate* in place of *tad yataḥ* (I here follow Schmithausen 1971:145).

616 See 'Ba' ra ba ("Chos rje rnam gnyis kyi dgongs bshad nyi ma'i 'od zer," 503.4), where the attainment of the dharmakāya is called the "buddha nature of a buddha."

617 Ibid., 502.2–3: *gdul bya'i rkyen gyis chos nyid 'od gsal de la / bral ba'i 'bras bu stobs bcu dang / mi 'jigs pa bzhi dang / sangs rgyas kyi chos ma 'dres pa bco brgyad la sogs pa 'char bas / snying po dang rnam smin gyi 'bras bu gzugs sku gnyis la sogs pa 'char bas snying po'i sa bon no //.*

618 Ibid., 502.4–6: *'o ma srubs pas mar 'dus te / dar dang bral ba'i mar gyi gong bu de gzhu nas / dar ba dang spu la sogs pa med pa de la mar gyi snying po zer ba ste (text: bas te) / snying po de mngon du gyur pa na / kha dog legs pa / ro zhim pa / bcud che ba / sgron me 'bar ba'i rkyen byed pa lhun grub du 'byung ba bzhin / chos nyid 'od gsal ba ji lta ba mngon du gyur te / spang bya thams cad dang bral bas / sangs rgyas kyi sa'i yon tan thams cad 'byung ba'i snying po'o //.*

619 Ibid., 504.2. See also Ibid., 513.2–4, where 'Ba' ra ba quotes the *Ratnagotravibhāgavyākhyā* (I.155 (J I.152)) to make his point: "…tathāgatahood is the state of being constituted by the threefold buddha kāya. Therefore, since the element of a tathāgata is a cause leading to its being obtained, the meaning of element is here *cause* (RGVV, 72.9–10: …*trividhabuddhakāyaprabhāvitatvaṁ hi tathāgatatvam / atas tatprāptaye hetus tathāgatadhātur iti / hetvartho 'tra dhātvarthaḥ /*).

620 'Ba' ra ba: "Chos rje rnam gnyis kyi dgongs bshad nyi ma'i 'od zer," 519.4–6: *chos rje rin po che kun mkhyen pa / sems can gyi bde gshegs snying po sangs rgyas yin pa dang / sangs rgyas kyi yon tan yod par bzhed (text: gzhed) ces pa 'di ni / bde gshegs snying po chos nyid 'od gsal yin pa ni / de sems can la yod pa dang sangs rgyas la yod pa'i ngo bo la khyad med pa la dgongs nas / sems can la yod pa'i bde gshegs snying po sangs rgyas yin par gsungs te / rgyu la 'bras bus rgyas gdab pa la dgongs pa dang / rgyu la 'bras bu'i ming btags so // sems can gyi bde gshegs snying po la sangs rgyas kyi sa'i yon tan 'byung ba'i nus pa yod pa dang /….*

621 RGVV, 26.3: *bauddhe gotre tatphalasyopacārād.*

622 'Ba' ra ba: "Chos rje rnam gnyis kyi dgongs bshad nyi ma'i 'od zer," 519.6–520.3.

623 Ibid., 522.1–4: …*stobs sogs 'bras bur mi 'gyur te / rgyu rkyen las byung ba'i 'bras bu min pas so / / stobs sogs gdod nas med la / rgyu bde gshegs snying po la rkyen lam bsgoms pas / glo bur dri ma dang bral ba na stobs sogs phyis 'byung bas bral 'bras so / / de ltar na bde gshegs snying po sangs rgyas dngos ma yin cing / sangs rgyas kyi rgyu'am sa bon du gsungs te / …dohā las / sems nyid gcig pu kun gyi sa bon….*

624 "Because [the buddha element] is endowed with faults in [only] an adventitious way, but naturally endowed with qualities, it is of an unchangeable nature: as it

was before so it is after." (RGVV, 41.20–21: *doṣāgantukatāyogād guṇaprakṛtiyogataḥ / yathā pūrvaṁ tathā paścād avikāritvadharmatā //.*)

625 'Ba' ra ba: "Chos rje rnam gnyis kyi dgongs bshad nyi ma'i 'od zer," 545.1: *yon tan rang bzhin nyid ldan phyir gsungs kyi / stobs sogs yon tan nyid ldan phyir / ma gsungs pas so //.*

626 RGVV, 84.3–4: *yad uktam ākāśalakṣaṇo buddha iti tat pāramārthikam āveṇikaṁ tathāgatānāṁ buddhalakṣaṇam abhisaṁdhāyoktam /.* The quotation is an introduction to stanzas RGV II.29–37.

627 'Ba' ra ba: "Kun mkhyen dol bu'i bu chen brgyad la lan phyogs cig tu btab pa nyi ma'i 'od zer," 651.5–6: *bde gshegs snying po sangs rgyas su grub bo zhes ma yin te / don dam pa'i mtshan nyid dam chos sku'i mtshan nyid la bde gshegs snying po'i mtshan dper gsungs par snang ste / rgyud bla ma'i 'grel (text: 'brel) pa las / sangs rgyas nam mkha'i mtshan nyid do // zhes bshad pa ni / de bzhin gshegs pa rnams kyi ma 'dres pa'i [don dam pa'i] mtshan [nyid] la (text: las) dgongs nas gsungs pa yin no /* (The additions in brackets are according Nakamura's edition (1967:163)).

628 Buddhahood is (1) inconceivable, (2) eternal, (3) everlasting, (4) quiescent, (5) constant, (6) perfectly pacified, (7) all pervading, (8) nondiscriminative, (9) without attachment, (10) without hindrance, (11) devoid of gross sensation, (12) imperceptible, (13) incognizable, (14) pure, and (15) immaculate (see Takasaki 1966:323–24).

629 It is not clear what *ces so* refers to.

630 'Ba' ra ba: "Kun mkhyen dol bu'i bu chen brgyad la lan phyogs cig tu btab pa nyi ma'i 'od zer," 652.4–6: *don dam pa'i mtshan nyid ni so so skye bo dang / de bzhin gshegs pa'i don dam pa'i mtshan nyid la khyad par ci yang med la / don dam pa'i mtshan dpe'i mtshan la khyad par yod pas / de bzhin gshegs pa'i ma 'dres pa'i don dam pa'i mtshan nyid la dgongs nas gsungs pa yin no // ces so // des na don dam pa'i mtshan nyid de / bde gshegs snying po la cha mthun nus mthu'i tshul du yod la / sangs rgyas kyi chos sku la yongs su rdzogs par yod pa'o //.*

631 RGVV, 26.14: *abhede jñeyo 'rthasaṁdhiḥ paramārthadhātoḥ /.*

632 'Ba' ra ba: "Chos rje rnam gnyis kyi dgongs bshad nyi ma'i 'od zer," 543.3: "Buddha nature possesses the five qualities of the svābhāvikakāya in actuality" *(ngo bo nyid sku'i yon tan lnga ni / bde gshegs snying po dngos su yod de /).*

633 The translation according to the Sanskrit is as follows: "Since its nature is the dharmadhātu, [the svābhāvikakāya] is luminous and pure."

634 RGVV, 87.2–4: *prabhāsvaraṁ viśuddhaṁ ca dharmadhātu*[a] *svabhāvataḥ / aprameyair asaṁkhyeyair acintyair asamair guṇaiḥ / viśuddhipārami*[b] *prāptair yuktaṁ svābhāvikaṁ vapuḥ /.*

a Schmithausen (1971:164) proposes reading *dharmadhātu* in composition against B (44a5).

b B (44a5) reads *-mī-*.

635 'Ba' ra ba: "Chos rje rnam gnyis kyi dgongs bshad nyi ma'i 'od zer," 523.3–4.

636 Ibid., 523.5–6: *chos dbyings rnam par dag pa la chos sku'i yon tan du gsungs te / dbyibs kha dog dang grangs dang dbyer med pa'o // mtshan dpe la dbyibs kha dog yod / stobs sogs kyi grangs yod pas dbyer yod de /.*

637 'Ba' ra ba: "Kun gzhi'i rnam shes dang ye shes kyi rnam bzhag," 623.4–6: *rnam pa'i khyad par dbyibs sna tshogs pa dang / kha dog sna tshogs par bstan du yod pa / snang ba ltar ma grub pas / stong pa ni glo bur ba kun rdzob kyi chos dang / bde gshegs snying po ni rnam pa'i khyad par dbyibs sna tshogs pa dang / kha dog sna tshogs par dbyer med pa'i mtshan nyid can / mtshan ma med pa / rang (text: ring) rig pa'i ye shes spros pa thams cad dang bral ba / bla na med pa'i chos nyid ni med pa ma yin par gsungs pa la /.*

638 'Ba' ra ba: "Chos rje rnam gnyis kyi dgongs bshad nyi ma'i 'od zer," 530.1–532.4.

639 Ibid., 541.5–6: *nyi ma'i 'od nyi ma'i dkyil 'khor dngos ma yin kyang / nyi ma'i dkyil 'khor gyi gdangs ma 'gags 'od du shar bas / nyi ma'i dkyil 'khor las 'od tha dad pa ma yin pas / nyi ma'i 'od mthong ba la nyi ma mthong zer ba bzhin / stong gzugs bde gshegs snying po dngos ma yin kyang bde gshegs snying po'i gdangs ma 'gags pas du ba la sogs pa'i rtags bcur shar bas / bde gshegs snying po las tha dad pa ma yin pa dgongs pa yin te / stong gzugs la bde gshegs snying por gsungs pa'o //.*

640 This is made clear in 'Ba' ra ba's reply (*op. cit.*, 531.4–6) to an opponent who insists that, according to the *Aṅgulimālīyasūtra*, buddha nature is adorned with the major and minor marks.

641 It should be noted that 'Ba' ra ba does not adopt Dol po pa's controversial Dharma term *kun gzhi ye shes*.

642 'Ba' ra ba: "Chos rje rnam gnyis kyi dgongs bshad nyi ma'i 'od zer," 499.3–4.

643 Ibid., 532.4–6: *ma dag pa'i kun gzhi'i bde gshegs snying po'i rig pa ste rang ngo ma shes par 'khrul pas / kha phyir ltas kyi rnam rtog sna tshogs par shar bas / . . . 'khor ba'i chos rnams kyi gzhi byed pas / ma dag pa'i kun gzhi'i rnam shes te / stobs sogs kyi yon tan med pas sems can no /.*

644 Ibid., 533.2–3: *bde gshegs snying po rang gis rang ngo shes te 'khrul med rang so tshugs pa na sangs rgyas kyi chos sku ste / sangs rgyas kyi sa'i sku dang ye shes mdzad pa dang 'phrin las la sogs pa'i rten byed pas dag pa ye shes kyi kun gzhi ste sangs rgyas so /.*

645 Ibid., 533.3–5: *ma dag pa rnam shes kyi kun gzhi ni / sangs rgyas kyi sa'i chos rnams kyi gzhi mi byed do / stobs sogs kyi yon tan med pas so / dag pa ye shes kyi kun gzhis 'khor ba'i gzhi mi byed do / glo bur dri ma med pas 'khor ba'i bde sdug la sogs pa mi myong bas so / / des na ldog cha la dbye na rgyal khams cho nges gnyis su bzhed pa yin la / kun gzhi gnyis po de'i rang bzhin bde gshegs snying po yin pas ngo bo gcig yin no /.*

646 See Tauscher 1995:188ff.

647 Dharmas and dharmatā are defined in the *Dharmadharmatāvibhāga* as being neither different nor identical. They are not identical because the ultimate *(dharmatā)* exists and the apparent *(dharmas)* not (negation of identity). On the other hand, dharmatā is defined as the absence of duality (equated with dharmas) and as such also in a sense not different from the nonexistent dharmas (negation of difference) (See Mathes 1996:122–23).

648 See Dol po pa: "Bden gnyis gsal ba'i nyi ma," 24ff.

649 'Ba'ra ba: "Dus 'khor ba rdo rje snying po la dri ba yi ger bskur," 587.6–588.1: *ji ltar khyad par med ces na chos nyid ni chos med pa tsam gyis rab tu phye ba yin te / gzugs la sogs pa'i khyad par med pa'i phyir ro // ces pas / dag pa chos nyid / ma dag pa rnam shes sam chos ni rang bzhin dbyer med yin la chos nyid ngo shes ma shes kyi ldog chos ma dag gnyis su byung bas tha dad pa'o / snyam du kho bo ni sems zhing /.*

650 See my translation of Gzhon nu dpal's *Ratnagotravibhāga* commentary (DRSM, 43.2–4).

651 See Stearns 1999:162.

652 For the translation and explanation of these experiential mahāmudrā terms see Callahan 2001:389–91.

653 'Ba' ra ba: "Chos rje rnam gnyis kyi dgongs bshad nyi ma'i 'od zer," 550.4–5: *de lta bu'i gsal rig stong gsum dbyer med de don dam pa'i bden pa ste / gzhi lam 'bras bu thams cad du 'gyur ba med pa'o / / de'i 'char sgo ma 'gags pa ste bag chags kyi dbang bzhin du gzung 'dzin sna tshogs su shar ba ni kun rdzob kyi bden pa'o / / lam bsgom pa'i dus su sems gsal rig stong gsum ston nam dangs pa bzhin du / sal le / sing nge / hrig ge nyams su myong ba de don dam pa'i bden pa /.*

654 'Ba' ra ba: "Dus 'khor ba rdo rje snying po la dri ba yi ge bskur," 585.2–3: *chos nyid rang ngo ma shes pa las tha dad pa'i spang bya med pas / chos nyid rang ngo shes pa na / spang gnyen ye shes skyes pa ste / chos nyid rang ngo ma shes pas med par song bas*

/ spang bya med par song yang / rang ngo shes pa med par ma song bas / gnyen po med par mi 'gro ba'o /.

655 Ibid., 574.1–2: *chu nyid rlung la sogs pa grang ba'i rkyen gyis 'khyags te / rdo bzhin du song kyang khyag pa dang chu gnyis rang bzhin cig tu (text: du) gnas cing / me la sogs pa'i rkyen gyis khyag pa bzhu ste / khyag pa med par song yang / chu med par mi 'gro ba bzhin nam /.*

656 See van der Kuijp 1983:41.

657 "Being empty in essence" could refer to *gzhan stong* emptiness, of course.

658 Blo gros mtshungs med: "Nges don gsal byed sgron me," 257.5–6 and 277.5.

659 See above in the section on Dol po pa's view.

660 Kong sprul Blo gros mtha' yas: *Shes bya kun khyab mdzod*, vol. 3, 34.10–12: ... *ma dpyad pa'i ngor tha snyad tsam du bden pa gnyis rang bzhin gcig la ldog pa tha dad dang / don dam par ngo bo gcig pa dang tha dad gang du'ang brjod du med pa....*

661 Tib. *rnam par grol ba.*

662 Kong sprul Blo gros mtha' yas: *Shes bya kun khyab mdzod*, vol. 3, 34.7–9: ... *bden pa gnyis po 'di'ang chos rnams dang chos nyid ji lta ba bzhin du de nyid dang gzhan las rnam par grol ba yin pas gcig pa dang tha dad pa gang du'ang brjod du med do.*

663 I am indebted to Karl Brunnhölzl for drawing my attention to this passage.

664 Based on the common Madhyamaka reasoning that anything can be conceived of as a member of a pair of opposites, from which it follows that something only exists in view of its respective opposite (cold is only possible in dependence on hot and vice versa): "...because the [two truths] are mutually determined, with falseness being [defined] in view of truth, and truth in view of falseness." (Mi bskyod rdo rje: *Dbu ma la 'jug pa'i rnam bshad*, 147a4: *'di dag phan tshun bden pa la ltos nas brdzun pa dang / brdzun pa la ltos nas bden par rnam par bzhag pa'i phyir te....*)

665 Ibid., 147b5–6: "Thinking that the two truths are in reality not different, Bka' brgyud Rin po ches teach that thoughts are the dharmakāya, that saṁsāra is nirvāṇa, and that defilements are wisdom. Nevertheless it has not been established that [pairs of categories] with the meaning of the two truths, such as thought and dharmakāya, and saṁsāra and nirvāṇa, are one in essence." *(...bden pa gnyis ni don la tha dad du yod pa min pa la dgongs nas / bka' brgyud rin po ches rnam rtog chos sku dang 'khor ba myang 'das dang nyon mongs ye shes su gsung gi / de ltar gsung na'ang bden gnyis gyi don can gyi rnam rtog chos sku 'khor 'das sogs ngo bo gcig yin par bsgrub pa ni ma yin te /.)*

666 Ibid., 149a2–3: "[These mahāmudrā teachings] do not say that saṁsāra and nirvāṇa, taken as actual things, are one in essence. Phrases [like] 'one in being equal in terms of lacking an own-being' are found among the words of all the discourses that teach the profound definitive meaning, such as the *prajñāpāramitā* (lit. 'the mother of the victorious ones') of the illustrious one" *(... 'khor 'das sogs kyi dngos don ngo bo gcig tu gsungs pa ma yin te / rang bzhin med pa'i tshul la mnyam pa nyid du gcig pa'i sgra sbyor ba 'di ni bcom ldan 'das kyi rgyal ba'i yum sogs nges don zab mo ston pa'i gsung rabs thams cad kyi tshig zin la...).*

667 Ibid., 149a3f.

668 According to the colophon (Zhva dmar Chos grags ye shes: *Gzhon nu dpal gyi rnam thar*, 74a2–6), Zhva dmar Chos grags ye shes requested one of Gzhon nu dpal's closest disciples, Slob dpon Smon lam grags pa, to compose a biography, which Chos grags ye shes expanded upon and completed in Yang pa can in a fire ox year (1517). I am indebted to Leonard van der Kuijp, Harvard University, for providing me with a copy of this biography.

I cross-checked this work with the short biographies contained in Situ's and 'Be lo's *Kaṁ tshang brgyud pa rin po che'i rnam thar* (vol. 1, 636.4–637.2), the *Gangs can mkhas grub rim byon ming mdzod* (348.8–349.21), Khetsun Sangpo's *Bibliographical Dictionary* (vol. 3, 568–70), the *Dka' gdams chos 'byung* (vol. 2, 1–10) of Las chen Kun dga' rgyal mtshan, and Zhva dmar Chos grags ye shes's biography of Lo tsā ba chen po Bsod nams rgya mtsho.

For a description of Zhva dmar Chos grags ye shes's biographies of Gzhon nu dpal and Bsod nams rgya mtsho, see Ehrhard 2002:11–13.

669 Occasionally the variant readings Rtse and Rtsed occur.

670 See also Ehrhard 2002:13.

671 Zhva dmar Chos grags ye shes: *Gzhon nu dpal gyi rnam thar*, 12b1–3: "[Gzhon nu dpal] told [me: Once] I was followed by a drunken horseman from Khams Mi nyag. I told [myself it would be better] to leave the way. He also left [the way], trailed [me], drew his sword and came after me. He hit the bag on my back, but I was not hurt. When he made to strike again, [his] sword fell to the ground, and I plucked up courage and jumped from behind on the horse. I thought of stabbing [him with] a small knife I had with me, but controlling myself with a [Buddhist] remedy, only threw him off the horse on the ground and did not harm him otherwise." *(khams pa mi nyag rta pa chang gis myos pa zhig rting la byung / lam zur zer bas bzur byon yang / des ral gri bton nas ded cing rgyab pa / sku rgyab kyi 'bog khres la phog kyang rma ma byung / slar brdeg par brtsams pas ral gri sa la lhung / der thugs ngar langs te / rta rgyab tu rgyangs kyi mchongs / gri chung yod pa bsnun rtsis kyi mod la gnyen pos zin / rta kha nas sa la bskyur ba tsam ma gtogs gnod pa gzhan ci yang ma byas gsung /.)*

672 Ibid., 2b3–4: *sku'i skye ba snga ma mang po rlabs po che'i spyod pa rab tu spyad pa zhes bya ba ni / grub chen o (text: u) rgyan pa'i slob ma go lung pa Gzhon nu dpal du gyur to zhes bya ba dang /.*

For a short biography of O rgyan pa, see the *Blue Annals* (Roerich: 1949–53: 696 and 700–705). Although a disciple of Rgod tshang pa (1189–1258), O rgyan pa received his main practice (namely the *O rgyan bsnyen grub*) from a *ḍākiṇī* in Oḍḍiyāna. It was considered to differ from both the Bka' brgyud practices and the Kālacakra system (see Smith 2001:46).

673 Zhva dmar Chos grags ye shes: *Gzhon nu dpal gyi rnam thar*, 2b4–6: *khyad par du dad 'phel zhing dang po sangs rgyas kyi bstan pa 'dzugs pa'i dus su nges par bya ba rnams la gtogs pa zhig yin bsam pa skye ba zhig yong gi 'dug / su yin ni mi shes bstan pa 'dzugs pa'i dus su nges par bsam yas su skyes pa 'dra gsung zhing / bsam yas bzhengs pa'i lo rgyus dang / rgyal blon rnams kyi bya ba ji ltar mdzad pa dang / mkhan po bo dhi sa tva dang slob dpon padma phebs nas bstan pa btsugs pa dang / lo tsa ba chen po rnams kyis chos ji ltar bsgyur ba gsung dus spyan chab mang du 'byon zhing /....*

674 Ibid., 3a2–3: *bdag gi bla ma mtshungs med nam mkha' blo gros kyi zhal snga nas ni / kho bo bla ma dam pa 'di dpal phag mo gru pa dpon slob kyi skor de na bzhugs pa zhig cis kyang yin bsam pa yod gsung / .*

675 Ibid., 3a3–4: *chos rje rin po che lo chen gyi zhal nas / mdo sngags thams cad la mkhyen pa mtha' yas shing / lo tsā (text: tsa) byang ba dang de'i rtsom pa rnams la'ang dgyes par snang bas / nges par rong zom chos kyi bzang po'i sku skye yin pa 'dra zhes bdag la yang yang gsung ngo /.*

676 Ibid., 3a5–6: *ngas rgyud bla ma 'di dang por blo la bzung ste zin pa dang go ba mnyam du byung nas slob gnyer gsar du byed ma dgos / dus phyis su song nas kyang zhib cha kha yar la blo bskyed ni byung /.*

677 See for example DRSM, 22.23–24 or 94.4–5.

678 Chos grags ye shes's biography of Gzhon nu dpal has only "valley" without specifying whether it was 'Phyong rgyas or Yar klung. According to the *Gangs can*

mkhas grub rim byon ming mdzod (348.10), his birthplace was in the 'Phyong rgyas valley of Lho kha region.

679 Zhva dmar Chos grags ye shes: *Gzhon nu dpal gyi rnam thar,* 4a1: */ rgya sman lha khang gi mda' grong nag mo / de'i nang nas kyang dbus khyim zhes bya bar chu pho spre'u'i lo la sku bltam pa /.*

680 Ibid., 3a7: *...bod rgyal po'i blon po 'gos rgan gyi rgyud pa yin / 'gos yul 'bring mtshams nas...yab mes snga mo'i dus su dbus su lhags nas / rgya sman yang po sar phebs te....*

681 Ibid., 4a2–3: *...yab kyis khams bsang ba thugs kyis dran /...yab snga mo nas mi lag tu song bas yum gyis legs par bskyangs /.*

It is not clear when this happened, but the event must have occured before Gzhon nu dpal completed his ninth year (4a6).

682 The monastery at that time followed the teaching tradition of Bya yul ba Gzhon nu 'od (1075–1138), who was one of Sgam po pa's Bka' gdams pa teachers (see Ehrhard 2002:13).

683 Las chen Kun dga' rgyal mtshan: *Bka' gdams kyi rnam par thar pa bka' gdams chos 'byung gsal ba'i sgron me,* 1.4–5: *lo dgu bzhes pa na spyan g.yas su mkhan chen rin po che sangs rgyas bstan pa'i drung du rab tu byung / mtshan Gzhon nu dpal zhes bya bar btang /.*

684 Zhva dmar Chos grags ye shes: *Gzhon nu dpal gyi rnam thar,* 4b2–3: *slob dpon bsam bzang pa dang dpon slob gnyis kyis bsnyen par rdzogs pa mdzad de /.*

685 Ibid., 4b3: *chos rje de bzhin gshegs pa karmapa...paṇ chen vanaratna'i drung du byang chub mchog tu thugs bskyed cing /.*

686 Ibid., 4b4: *chos rje gung snang ba la bde mchog dril bu lus dkyil gyi dbang bskur....*

687 Ibid., 4b6–7: *sngon gyi dge ba'i bag chags bzang pos rigs sad pa'i skye bu chen po...nges don gyi chos skad thams cad kyi klong rdol / mdo sde zab mo rnams kyi drang ba dang nges pa'i don rnam par 'byed pa la thogs pa med par gyur pa yin....*

688 Ibid., 5a4: *mkhas shing grub pa'i skyes bu drug bcu rtsa drug la brten nas thos bsam phyogs med du mdzad pa ni /.*

689 Ibid., 5a4–6: *rab tu byung nas lo gsum gyi bar du dbyar yum kyi las grogs re tsam mdzad pa ma gtogs spyan g.yas su khu bo slob dpon sangs (text: sang) grags pa'i sar bzhugs te / byang chub sems dpa'i spyod pa la 'jug pa la thugs legs par byangs / slob dpon shes rab dar ba...de la'ang spyod 'jug gsan / de dus dbang grags pa rgyal mtshan bsnyel ba'i sku rim la spyan g.yas pa rnams kyi phyogs (text: phogs) blangs nas sman bla mang du gtong dgos byung bas dang por tshar kha yar cig deb thog nas btang pas thugs la zin nas....*

690 Ibid., 5b1–3: *dgung lo bcu gnyis bzhes pa chu mo lug gi lo'i dgun chos kyi dus su rtses thang du slob gnyer la phebs /...slob dpon bsam grub bzang po ba'i sar bzhugs / tshad ma rnam 'grel la thugs sbyangs /...slob dpon yang spyan rtsa dmar shig ge ba zhal ngom kyang nag pa / non shin du che bar 'dug pas 'dis cig brdung du 'ong dgongs pa byung /.*

In his *Blue Annals* (Roerich 1949–53:324–27) Gzhon nu dpal mentions Bsam grub bzang po ba as the last member of the lineage of the *Pramāṇavārttika.*

691 I.e., So ston Śākya dpal.

692 Zhva dmar Chos grags ye shes: *Gzhon nu dpal gyi rnam thar,* 5b3–6: *de nas shing pho spre'u'i dpyid kyi dus / mdo lung pa'i phu'i chos sdings dgon par chos bar la thegs de...bya lo la...slob dpon ston śāk pa la phar phyin gsan / phag lo'i bar du tshad ma'i gzhung dang nor bzang ṭīkā (text: ṭika) la thugs legs par sbyangs pas...re'i bar la slob dpon pa'i phyag 'jug kyang mang du khur / lan cig sa rub gdong cig tu phyag bcug pas bros thar te / chos ldings kyi ri'i mthur la bros pas ma zin par....*

693 Ibid., 5b7: *khyi lo'i dgun rtses thang gzhung sgyur dang bshad ston mdzad /.*

694 Ibid., 6b1–2: *slob dpon bsam bzang pa de slob dpon bsam yas pa'i grva (text: gra) pa yin pa la dus phyis slob dpon ston śāk pa'i grva (text: gra) tshang du 'phos nas so sor*

song ba la grva (text: gra) pa rnying pa kha cig gis phyogs gcig tu sdeb par zhus nas slob dpon pa dang / bla ma rkyang chen pa grva (text: gra) pa bsre bar byas te / nged gsum rkyang chen pa la sprad pa yin /.

695 I.e., the examinations called "round of monastic colleges" *(grva skor).*

696 Zhva dmar Chos grags ye shes: *Gzhon nu dpal gyi rnam thar,* 6a5–6: *grva (text: gra) skor tshar nas spyan g.yas su thegs pas slob dpon shes rab dar bas gsol ja legs par gnang / 'jam dbyangs kyi gser sku gcig phul nas / 'o khyed kyis slob gnyer legs par mdzad nas grva (text: gra) skor yang 'khor bde legs /.*

697 Ibid., 6b6–7*(gong ma)*a1: *glang lo'i ston jo stan ston śāk pa dpon slob bcu gnyis tsam mdzad nas snye mor chos bar la thegs pa'i phyags phyir ru mtshams su thegs / de'i dgun de slob dpon bsam bzang pas bka' bkyon mang du byon nas spyan g.yas su thegs pas....*

698 Ibid., 7*(gong ma)*a4–b2: *de nas thang sag tu phebs... dmar ston gzhon rgyal ba bzhugs 'dug pas chos gsan / khyad par 'jug pa 'grel dang bcas pa / thang sag pa'i lugs kyi gsung sgros rnams la legs par sbyangs / 'jug pa rang 'grel dang bcas pa thugs la btsud pas legs par zin / rtsa she tshig gsal dang bcas pa yang gsan / khyad par bzhi brgya ba rje btsun red mda' pa'i ṭīkā(text: ṭīka)'i stengs nas gsan te /....*

699 Ibid., 7*(gong ma)*b3–5: *lan cig sras kyi ri sna gcig na chos khri gcig gi steng na gzhan stong ba rtogs ldan blos btang nyag po de skya ser mang pos bskor nas chos gsung gi 'dug pas nged gnyis pa cig gis ci zer blta zhing bgam du 'gro bar byas nas khong la gtad phyin pas mi gcig tshur rgyug bcug byung nas de na tshur mi phebs pa zhu / phebs rin chog pa med zer khong la mngon par shes pa yod pa 'dra gsung.*

700 Ibid., 7*(gong ma)*b7: *slob dpon ston śāk pa la rgyud bla'i thogs med 'grel pa dang bcas pa'i bshad pa dang / de'i zhor la jo nang kun mkhyen chen po'i ṭīkā (text: ṭīka)'i lung yang gsan /.*

701 Ibid., 7*(gong ma)*b6: *de nas slob dpon bsam bzang pa'i sar thegs pas khyed 'phan yul du gros med du 'gro ba ci yin gsung /.*

702 Ibid., 7b1–3: *lan cig spyan g.yas nas / ston pa dge legs phyags phyir khrid nas bros thabs su yol rin chen gling du / mkhan chen sangs blo ba'i sar thegs bla ma'i rnal 'byor zhus / sbyor drug gsan par brtsom pa'i tshe / ston pa 'od dang brtan pa 'bum gnyis rjes su bsnyag tu slebs nas / phyir ldog dgos pa byung bas / slar yang spyan g.yas su bzhugs te /.*

703 Ibid., 7b3–4: *mkhan chen sangs rgyas brtan pa'i drung du dmigs skor gsum / blo sbyong don bdun ma / rma bya dug 'joms / mtshon cha 'khor lo / lhan thabs bzhi pa / byams pa'i rnal 'byor pa'i glu / rtog pa 'bur 'joms thun brgyad ma / sem pa'i rim pa / rten 'brel snying po'i khrid / rgyal sras pas mdzad pa / ku su lu'i tshogs sogs (text: sog) / sgrol dkar gyi tshe sgrub / skyid sdug lam khyer / bla ma'i rnal 'byor sogs gsan /.*

704 Ibid., 8a2–3: *de nas rtses thang du phar phyin / dbu ma 'jug pa / spyod 'jug / rgyud bla rnams kyi gzhung skyur grva (text: gra) skor mdzad pas / slob dpon bsam bzang pa ni / grva (text: gra) skor la phyis pa yin zhes bka' bkyon /.*

705 Ibid., 8a5–6: *dgung lo nyi shu rtsa gnyis bzhes pa sprul kyi dbyar sos de skyi shod du grva (text: gra) skor la thegs / de'i mdo la skyor mo lung du slob dpon bsam gtan don grub pa'i drung du... 'dul ba mdo rtsa ba dang mngon pa mdzod tshar re gsan /.*

706 Ibid., 8a7–b1: *de dus stod lung rnam par du chos rje de bzhin gshegs pa bzhugs pa'i sar / slob dpon chos dbang dang lhan du mjal bar thegs / byin brlabs zhus /.*

707 Ibid., 8b1–2: *der mtshal min rin po che bsod bzang pa phebs 'dug pa la / sum pa lo tsā (text: tsa) ba'i blo sbyong dang sems (text: sem) pa'i rim pa gnyis gsan / khong la lhag par dad pa byung /.*

708 See Ehrhard 2002:78, fn. 43.

709 Zhva dmar Chos grags ye shes: *Gzhon nu dpal gyi rnam thar,* 8b7: *slob dpon pa yab pa chos rje'i drung du zhi byed kyi gdams pa'i 'phro gsan....*

710 Ibid., 9a1: *chos rje śākya bzang po ba la skyes mchog pa'i ka dag gsal ba dang bcom ldan rig (text: rigs) ral gyis mdzad pa'i skye rabs gsan /.*

711 Ibid., 9a6: *de res chos rje de bzhin gshegs pa rtses thang du phebs nas tshogs su byang chub mchog tu thugs bskyed pa dang / nāro chos drug bsdus pa dang / 'jam dbyangs kyi sgrub thabs dang / tshe dpag tu med pa'i mdo rnams gsan /.*

712 Ibid., 9b4–5: *rta lo'i dgun de rtses thang du bla ma rkyang chen pa la rtsis zhus nas...lug gi dpyid de thang po cher chos bar mdzad nas gser khang du bzhugs / de dus kyang rtsis la legs par bsams pa yin gsung /.*

713 Ibid., 13b7: *me pho byi'i lo'i dpyid snar thang du sgra slob tu thegs te chen po saṅgha śrī pa la gtugs / slob (one syllable unclear) gyi stengs nas kalāpa'i sgra'i sa ris tshang mar btang /.*

714 Ibid., 46b1–3: *kar rtsis la dus 'khor rgyud 'grel gyi dgongs pa ji ba bzhin ma longs te / bod kyi mkhas pa snga phyi mang po yang nyung ngu'i byed rtsis sangs rgyas pa rang lugs su 'khrul pa'i dbang gis grub mtha'i rtsis ngos ma zin par / 'das lo'i grangs dang nyi ldog ma dag cing / bod kyi rgyal khrims zhig rjes zla ba'i ngos 'dzin 'chugs pa sogs ma 'khrul ba dgongs nas rtsis la 'khrul sel brtsams pas...la las bzhed pa de 'gog pa'i lugs dang gzhan dag de'i lugs 'thad par bzung ste / gtam chen por gyur zhing /....*

715 Ibid., 9b6–10a2: *de'i ston khar song ba na dbang grags pa rgyal mtshan gyis / rje rin po che blo bzang grags pa...spyan drangs nas chos kyi 'khor lo rgya chen po bskor bar 'dug pa'i drung du thegs / bla ma'i rnal 'byor / byang chub lam gyi rim pa / ...nāro chos drug ji ltar gnang ba'i gsungs la zin bris kyang mdzad / ...gsan /.*

716 Ibid., 10a2: *'dul ba 'dzin pa grags pa rgyal mtshan pa yang phyag phyir phebs pa lags....*

717 Ibid., 10b1: *...'dir bshad pa dang 'gal ba min pa'i drang nges kyi 'byed lugs shig theg pa chen po rgyud bla ma nas bshad 'dug....*

718 Ibid., 29a2: *khyed dga' ldan pa 'di rnams byang chub lam gyi rim pa de la shin tu mkhas te / de gang la brten pa'i lam sgron mi mkhas /.*

719 Ibid., 10b7–11a3: *sngar chos rje rgyal tshab rin po che gsang sngags bla med kyi bde chen gyi ngos 'dzin gyi brtsom pa gzigs pas / de la thugs 'gro ba byung nas / skabs shig tu / de legs par 'dug ste der bde chen de bde ba gzhan 'di yang min 'di yang min zhes mtha' bcad nas / rang lugs zhu ba de la ngos bzung 'dug tshul zhus pas / des mi 'ong chags pa dkar po'i phyogs kyang ma yin / chags bral nag po'i phyogs kyang ma yin pa'i bcu drug pa zer ba gcig yod pa yin gsung ba de la thugs ches lhag par 'khrungs nas / de gcig pus chog par yong / de res zhabs tog che bar ma grub / chos rje thugs spros pa chung bas /....*

720 Ibid., 6b2: *nged gsum rkyang chen pa la spras pa yin / de phyis nga la dus 'khor yong ba de'i rten 'brel du song 'dug /.*

721 Ibid., 10b2–5: *lug gi dgun de dus 'khor la thugs sbyong bar bzhed nas bla ma rkyang chen pa'i drung du gsol ba btab pas / de la sbyor drug gi khrid thob dgos gsung / ...khrid gnang bar zhus pas nga khrid byed gyi med gsung / 'o na su la zhu zhus pas 'ju lha khang stengs su zhus gsung / ...de nas chas kha bsnams nas thegs te dus kyi 'khor lo'i mchog dbang / sbyor drug...gnang /.*

See also Ehrhard 2002:41, fn. 9 and 78, fn. 43.

722 See Ehrhard 2002:78, fn. 43.

723 Zhva dmar Chos grags ye shes: *Gzhon nu dpal gyi rnam thar*, 11a4: *de'i dbyar rkyang chen pa dang dpon slob gnyis kyis lha khang stengs su thegs nas / dpal dus kyi 'khor lo'i rdul tshon gyi dkyil 'khor du dbang bdun / gong ma chen po / rdo rje slob dpon bdag po'i dbang yongs su rdzogs pa dang /....*

724 Ibid., 11a5: *jo nang kun mkhyen chen pos mdzad pa'i nges don rgya mtsho'i lung gsan /.*

725 I.e., the schools of the second diffusion of the Dharma in Tibet.

726 Ibid., 18a3–6: *chos rje lha khang stengs pa rang bzhin (?) du thugs rjes 'dzin pa'i stobs kyis / ...thams cad thugs dgyes par byung ba yin / spyir bla ma thams cad sku drin che / khyad par chos rje 'di shin tu sku drin che ba yin / da ltar tshe ring po yod pa*

'di yang khong gi tshe sgrub gcig gnang ba de'i yon tan yin pa 'dra / ... chos rje rin po che... rnying ma'i bka' gter gnyis ka'i mkhyen pa rgya che / gsar ma'i dus 'khor la sogs pa'i rgyud dang sgrub thabs la sogs pa du ma mkhyen / kun mkhyen chen po jo mo nang pa dang / chos rje bla ma dam pa dang / ... skyes bu dam pa mang du bsten /.

727 Las chen Kun dga' rgyal mtshan: *Bka' gdams kyi rnam par thar pa bka' gdams chos 'byung gsal ba'i sgron me*, 4.5: *chos rje lha khang stengs pa la Jo nang sbyor drug.*

728 Zhva dmar Chos grags ye shes: *Gzhon nu dpal gyi rnam thar*, 12a4–5: *spre'u lo'i ston 'jug tu song ba na lha khang steng su thegs nas / gsum ldan gyi bla ma zhu ba yin zhes sems 'grel skor gsum rnams tshang mar gsan /.*

729 The trilogy of texts known as the *Sems 'grel skor gsum* comprises the *Vimalaprabhā* (Peking Tengyur no. 2064), the *Hevajrapiṇḍārthaṭīkā* (Peking Tengyur no. 2310), and a *Cakrasaṁvara* commentary (Peking Tengyur no. 2117) (see Stearns 1999:178).

730 Zhva dmar Chos grags ye shes: *Gzhon nu dpal gyi rnam thar*, 12b3–7: *kun mkhyen shangs pa'i drung du thegs pas... dus 'khor rgyud 'grel la 'dod pa yod pa de [la] legs gsung nas zhal gyis bzhes byung gsung / der zla ba lnga'i bar du bzhugs nas rgyud 'grel gyi bshad pa legs par gsan / ... bu ston thams cad mkhyen pa'i sa bcad dang mchan bu la brten nas / gsung ba'i bshad pa grol khar / da nyid kyis dus 'khor legs par shod cig /.*

731 Ibid., 13a3–4: *kun mkhyen pa'i drung du... bu rin po che'i mngon dkyil gyi steng nas dus 'khor gyi dbang yongs su rdzogs pa /.*

732 Ibid., 27b2–3: *paṇ chen rin po che'i drung du... dpal dus 'khor lo'i dbang... gsan /.*

733 Zhva dmar Chos grags ye shes: *Lo chen gyi rnam thar*, 14b7–15a2: *me mo yos kyi lo la slar yang rje 'gos kyi drung du rgyud thams cad kyi bla ma dpal dus kyi 'khor lo rgyud 'grel pa dang bcas pa gsan... khyed nges par sbyor drug don du gnyer na / paṇ chen rin po che la bsnyen pa las gzhan pa'i gnas gang yang med /.*

734 See Ehrhard 2002:48, fn. 17.

735 Zhva dmar Chos grags ye shes: *Gzhon nu dpal gyi rnam thar*, 18a1–2: *lan cig lha khang stengs pa'i gsung nas gdan sa pa la khyed kyis gar phyin gsung / ngas drung pa dang 'bel gtam byas pa lags zhus pas / khong gi dus 'khor chos rje phyogs pa dang 'thun par 'dug gam gsung / mi mthun par 'dug lags zhus pas de ci yin nam ma 'thun pa cig 'ong thang ba la / khong skye ba snga ma dus 'khor mkhyen pa cig yin par 'dug gsung skad / de thugs bden par 'dug / ... de dang 'dra bar gsang 'dus 'di yang skye ba snga ma slob myong 'dug /.*

736 Ibid., 19a1–2: *de nas rtses thang gi snang ba khra mor bzhugs nas dus 'khor le'u dang po'i mjug gi go sla'i ṭīkā (text: ṭika) dang mo rnam rtsen yang brtsams /.*

737 Ibid., 56b3–57a1: *lcags pho byi ba'i lo yan du... lo de'i dbyar spyan g.yas su ston pa rin chen dpal bzang zhes bya ba mi phyed pa'i gus pa can gsol ba btab pa ltar / ... dpal dus kyi 'khor lo'i rgyud 'grel chen dri ma med pa'i 'od dang bcas pa'i bshad pa rdzogs par gnang /.*

738 Las chen Kun dga' rgyal mtshan: *Bka' gdams kyi rnam par thar pa bka' gdams chos 'byung gsal ba'i sgron me*, 8.3–5: *rgyud thams cad kyi rtse mo dpal ba 'dus pa dang dus kyi 'khor lo gnyis kyi ṭīkā... poti bcu tsam brtsom snang go.*

739 Ehrhard 2002:41, fn. 9.

740 See Khetsun Sangpo 1973, vol. 3, 568.

741 Zhva dmar Chos grags ye shes: *Gzhon nu dpal gyi rnam thar*, 15a6–b2: *... dgung lo nyi shu rtsa brgyad bzhes pa phag lo'i dpyid de rta nag tu sgrol mar thegs / ... chos rje sgrol ma'i drung du... rnying ma'i skor gyi poti mi gcig pa lnga bcur nye gcig la thugs sbyong chen po mdzad pas....*

742 Ehrhard 2002:55, fn. 24.

743 Khetsun Sangpo 1973, vol. 3, 569.

744 Ehrhard 2002:37.

745 Zhva dmar Chos grags ye shes: *Gzhon nu dpal gyi rnam thar*, 28a7–b1: *...chos sdings su rgod phrug chos rje'i sku mdun du chos gsan du thegs nas...chos rje dang sngar yang mang du mjal / khyad par rgyal bzangs su mjal nas bka' lung mang po gnang mdzad de / ...de res tshe rings mched lnga'i rjes gnang dang phag mo gzhung drug gi skor mkhan chen rin rgyal ba'i yig cha'i stengs nas gnang ba gsan /.*

746 Las chen Kun dga' rgyal mtshan: *Bka' gdams kyi rnam par thar pa bka' gdams chos 'byung gsal ba'i sgron me*, 4.4: *rgod phrug grags pa 'byung gnas pa'i drung du bsnyen sgrub sogs 'brug pa'i chos skor....*

747 Zhva dmar Chos grags ye shes: *Gzhon nu dpal gyi rnam thar*, 52b5–6: *sgrib pa med pa'i chos kyi sgo phul du byung ba mngon du brnyed pa zhes pa ni / sngar zur tsam smos pa bzhin / rong ston smra ba'i seng ge chen po snye phu na chos gsung pa'i sar byon nas /....*

748 Ibid., 52b7–53a2: *phyi'i skyed tshal du gungs sangs la phebs te / kham bu'i sdong po'i bsil grib la bzhugs pa'i tshe / de bzhin gshegs pa'i snying po sems kyi rang bzhin 'od gsal ba'i don la thugs kyi nges shes yang dag pa skyes nas / de'i chos skad phra zhib rnams skad cig la mkhyen / ...bden gnyis ldog thub bshad pa la thugs ma mgu yang / de nas bzung ste de la thugs dgyes par byung /.*

749 Ibid., 19a4–5: *glang lo'i dbyar chos rje rong chen pa dpon slob thang po cher chos bar la phebs pas der thegs nas dpon slob rnams la bsnyen bkur zhig kyang zhus / rgyud bla ma gzhung rkyang gi bshad pa dang rnam nges kyi bshad pa gsan zhing / ...gsang 'dus rim lnga'i bshad pa cig zhus pas...gsungs nas gnang /.*

750 Ibid., 20a7: *...chos rje rong chen pa...sku mdun du thegs / spyi chos gang gsung rnams dang / khyad par...dbu ma 'jug pa gsan....*

751 Las chen Kun dga' rgyal mtshan: *Bka' gdams kyi rnam par thar pa bka' gdams chos 'byung gsal ba'i sgron me*, 3.3: *rong ston smra ba'i seng ge la phar phyin dang spyod 'jug sogs gsan /.*

752 For an account of the lamas of the Rngog familial lineage of Spre'u zhing, see Roerich 1949–53:406–14.

753 Zhva dmar Chos grags ye shes: *Gzhon nu dpal gyi rnam thar*, 21b3–22b1: *spre'u zhing du thegs nas rin po che byang chub dpal pa'i zhabs la gtugs te dbu mdzad bkra shis dpal zhes bya ba'i sar bzhugs nas / dge 'dun sgang pa'i mkhan chen seng ge dpal ba dang lhan du gsan pa la /....*

754 Roerich 1949–53:589–94.

755 Zhva dmar Chos grags ye shes: *Gzhon nu dpal gyi rnam thar*, 22b1–2: *chos rje nyer gnyis rin po che'i sku mdun du phal cher thegs / sku mdun der dge ba'i bshes gnyen mang du tshogs nas 'bel gtam kho nas dus 'da' ba yin pa la / spyan snga rin po che yang dge bshes gzhan rnams kyi chos skad las ches lhag pa'i thugs mthong chen po yang gnang /.*

756 Ibid., 23a5–6: *shing sbrul de nas lo ngo drug gi bar gdan sar bzhugs / phar phyin ṭīkā (text: ṭīka)'i brtsom pa skabs gsum pa yan mdzad / rab brtan gling du'ang thogs re bzhugs / der chu mig dgon gsar nas bla ma tshul rgyal ba phebs byon pa la / thugs rje chen po'i bsgom bzlas gsan /.*

757 Ibid., 23b4–5: *mkhan chen seng ge dpal ba la sgrub thabs rgya mtsho'i rjes gnang / brtag gnyis kyi nāro 'grel chen / mkha' 'gro rgya mtsho'i rgyud / rje mar pa'i shog dril bzhi rnams gsan / spre'u zhing nas / rkyang chen du phyag 'bul du thegs pas....*

758 Ibid., 24b2–25a4: *lcags pho khyi'i so ka chu bo ri na bdag nyid chen po blo gros rgya mtsho ba bzhugs pa'i drung du thegs nas / ...rgya dur gyi mkhan sa sprad pa len ma btub pa...rgya dur nas spyan dren gyis sleb...de'i dbyar de rgya dur gyi mkhan po gtang / de nas nga skyid pa yin / ...slob dpon gzhan gyi thad du bros pa'ang byung / nga rgya bo 'di'i dur yin pas rgya dur zer bar 'dug gsung /.*

759 Ibid., 25a4–5: *lcags mo phag gi lo la chos rje sems dpa' chen po gra na bzhugs pa'i sku*

mdun du thegs te gsang 'dus sgron gsal rje'i mchan mtha' gcọd dang bcas pa'i steng nas bshad pa legs par gsan /.

760 Ibid., 25a7–b3: *de nas spre'u zhing du rin po che'i drung du thegs nas / mtshan brjod phan yon dang bcạs pa / rnam snang sgyu dra / bshad rgyud rdor phreng / rtog bdun / rtog gsum / dam rdzas kyi rtog pa / gdong drug / gshed dmar rim par phye ba bcu dgu pa / rdo rje snying po rgyan gyi rgyud / phyag chen thig le / ye shes thig le / de kho na nyid kyi sgron ma / . . . 'thus nas gsan /.*

761 Ibid., 26a2–3: *chu pho byi ba'i lo la rtses thang du bzhugs nas chos mang du gsungs /.*

762 And the rise of the Rin spungs family. These events marked also the beginning of a century-long power struggle between the provinces of Dbus and Tsang (see Ehrhard 2004:249–50).

763 Zhva dmar Chos grags ye shes: *Gzhon nu dpal gyi rnam thar*, 27b5–6: *byi ba'i lo nas sbrul lo'i bar du gong gi thugs kyis legs par bzung bas sne'u gdong rtser sku mdun du bzhugs nas / dge ba'i bshes gnyen rnams dang / 'bel gtam kho nas dus 'da' bar mdzad / res rtses thang du bzhugs nas chos mang du gsungs kyang phal cher sne'u gdong du thegs dgos pas dang po rgya dur du tshud nas ci thon byas pas thon byung te / 'dir rgyun tu sku mdun kho nar sdod dgos pa 'di yang mdun ma'i phugs bzang po cig mi 'dug bsam nas mdun ma bsgyur 'dod chen po byung ba yin gsung /.*

764 For the rise of the Phag gru dynasty see Petech 1990:85–137.

765 The foundation of Rtses thang is described by van der Kuijp (1991:315–21).

766 The title *spyan snga* points to his religious function as the successor of Spyan snga Rin po che Grags pa 'byung gnas (1175–1255), the spiritual forefather of the family (see Ehrhard 2002:20 and 54–55).

767 See Mathes 2003:xiii.

768 I.e., the Tshal pa Kangyur (see Imaeda 1982:13).

769 Zhva dmar Chos grags ye shes: *Gzhon nu dpal gyi rnam thar*, 26b3: *de'i ston ma dbyar rgyal bzangs su gong ma chen po'i dgongs rdzogs la bka' 'gyur bzhengs pa'i zhu dag gi dpon la thegs /.*

770 Ibid., 26a4–b3: *glang lo'i dpyid grub pa'i dbang phyug nags kyi rin po che. . . rtses thang du phebs pa'i tshe sku mdun du thegs nas dri ba mang du zhus / . . . slob dpon klu sgrub kyis mdzad pa'i sbyor drug gi rgya dpe gcig phyag na 'dug pas de legs par gsan / de sgron gsal gyi sbyor drug logs su phyung ba lta bur 'dug gsung / de rjes su'ang brgyad stong pa / rdo rje phreng ba / rdo rje gur / mtshan brjod kyi 'grel pa nyi ma dpal ye shes kyis mdzad pa / vibhūtis mdzad pa'i de'i 'grel bshad / don yod lha'i 'grel pa / dbang mdor bstan gyi 'grel pa / nāropa / sādhuputra / byang chub rdo rje gsum gyis mdzad pa / chos 'byung zhi ba'i mchod chog / mngon rtogs rgyan / mdo sde rgyan / dbu mtha' rtsa 'grel / nyi khri rnam 'grel / rnam 'grel le'u dang po'i 'grel bshad / slob dpon kalukas mdzad pa / dbu ma tshig gsal rnams kyi rgya dpe gzigs nas skabs 'gar dri ba dang bshad pa mang du gsan /. . . . do hala sogs pa'i rgya dpe rnams kyang gzigs nas dri ba mang du zhus pas. . . bde mchog lū'i pa'i dbang yang gsan / zhabs teg kyang mang du mdzad thub gsung /.*

771 For a description of this visit see 'Gos Lo tsā ba Gzhon nu dpal: *Mkhas pa chen po dpal nags kyi rin chen gyi rnam par thar pa*, 42.6–43.6: *. . . spa gror byon te /. . . . de nas spa gro nas yos lo (=1435) la nyangs stod du phebs / de nas rin spungs su phebs nas. . . .*

772 Zhva dmar Chos grags ye shes: *Gzhon nu dpal gyi rnam thar*, 27a1–2: *de rjes paṇ chen nags kyi rin po che slar yang bod du phebs te rtses thang du dge ba'i bshes gnyen mang po la rnal 'byor yan lag drug pa'i khrid gnang ba gsan zhing / mi g.yo bla med kyi dbang yang zhus /.*

773 Ibid., 27a2–6: *'brug lo'i dbyar paṇ chen rin po che bsam yas mchims phur bzhud pa'i phyag phyir thegs nas bzhugs te. . . der yang dri ba dang 'bel gtam mang du zhus /.*

... de rjes chos rje paṇ chen rin po che sne'u gdong du bzhugs pa'i zhabs phyir yang yun ring bar bzhugs nas 'gyur mang du mdzad /.

774 Ibid., 27b4: *paṇ chen rin po che'i zhal nas ngas dzambu'i gling gi sum gnyis tsam du phyin pa la paṇḍita chen po mi'i nyi ma shes rab che bar mthong / de'i 'og na kumāraśrī las shes rab che ba ma mthong zhes gsungs ba yin yang zer /.*

775 For a description of this third visit see Ehrhard 2004:253–56.

776 Lo tsā ba Mañjuśrī was assigned the task of interpreting by his own master Seng ge rgyal mtshan (from Stag tshang Chos 'khor sgang) during Vanaratna's first visit to Tibet (see Ehrhard 2004:248).

777 Zhva dmar Chos grags ye shes: *Gzhon nu dpal gyi rnam thar*, 36a1: *paṇ chen gyis mdzad pa'i sha ba ra'i bstod pa yang bsgyur / de nas la stod byang du lo tsa ba mañjuśrī ma phebs kyi bar du paṇ chen chos gsung ba dang dbang bskur ba la sogs pa'i lo tsa yang mdzad /.*

778 Ibid., 37a3–4: *de nas rim gyis paṇ chen rin po che sne'u gdong rtser spyan drangs... de nas zla gcig tsam song ba'i tshe gong ma chen po thugs rang bzhin du mi gnas pa'i rnam par 'gyur ba la rten / skyam 'chad pa stengs su dben par bzhugs /.*

779 Ibid., 44a1–3: *gzhan yang phag lo zla ba bcu gnyis pa'i tshes bcu'i srong / dpon sa kun dga' legs pas rgyu med par thugs khrel mdzad de / nga'i lung 'gro sar ma sdod / sang nam seng tshun la skyas tshar bar gyis / de ltar mi byed na dpung khrid 'ong zer ba'i bka' lung drag po bsgyur byung bas / ... ngas dkon mchog la gsol ba btab pas gnod pa ma byung zhes gsung te / ting nge 'dzin gyi mthus gong ma'i thugs rgyal zhi bar gyur pa dang / ...*44b6: *dgung lo don bdun bzhes pa phag lo'i dgun /....*

780 Ibid., 27b7–28a1: *de nas dvags (text: dags) po phyogs su thegs par bzhed nas dvags (text: dags) po 'bru mda' ba la sbyin bdag yong mi yong dris pas / 'ong ba'i zhu ba byung nas pho rta'i lo gsar 'phral de nas / tsa ri phyogs la thegs chog pa'i zhu ba nyin re bzhin du phul bas / gong nas mi 'thad gsung nas mi gnang ba'i ngang la zla ba bdun pa'i tshes nyi shu bdun gyi bar lus gsung /.*

781 Dmar ston Rgyal mtshan 'od zer seems to have been a descendant of Dmar ston Chos kyi rgyal po (eleventh / twelfth century). See Ehrhard 2002:36–37.

782 Zhva dmar Chos grags ye shes: *Gzhon nu dpal gyi rnam thar*, 58a2: *sa pho rta'i lo'i dpyid sos btsan thang gi chos 'khor grol nas bsam gtan gling du dmar ston rgyal mtshan 'od zer ba'i gsungs....*

783 Ibid., 28a2–3: *... rgyal po grags pa 'byung gnas pa'i bka'i lung gis dmar ston rgyal mtshan 'od zer ba la / dge ba'i bshes gnyen mang po dbang gsan du bcug pa'i dus su krīyasamuccaya'i (text: krīyasamuccha'i) dbang yongs su rdzogs pa dang / sgos bka' dang rjes gnang shin du mang bar gsan zhing /....*

784 Zhva dmar Chos grags ye shes: *Lo chen gyi rnam thar*, 8b1–2: *chos rje dmar ston rgyal mtshan 'od zer ba btsan thang na dge ba'i gshes gnyen mang po la dbang rab 'byam gnang ba'i skabs su kye rdor man ngag lugs kyi dbang dang / 'jigs byed ro langs brgyad skor sogs 'ga' shas kyi dbang gsan /.*

785 Zhva dmar Chos grags ye shes: *Gzhon nu dpal gyi rnam thar*, 28a7–b1: *de'i ston dbyar gyi dus su dmar ston pas 'on gyi chos sdings su rgod phrug chos rje'i sku mdun chos gsan du thegs nas / chos rje grags 'byung ba'i zhabs la gtugs / chos rje dang sngar yang mang du mjal / khyad par rgyal bzangs su mjal nas bka' lung mang po gnang mdzad de /.*

786 Las chen Kun dga' rgyal mtshan: *Bka' gdams kyi rnam par thar pa bka' gdams chos 'byung gsal ba'i sgron me*, 4.4: *rgod phrug grags pa 'byung gnas pa'i drung du bsnyen sgrub sogs 'brug pa'i chos skor /....*

787 Zhva dmar Chos grags ye shes: *Gzhon nu dpal gyi rnam thar*, 28b3–5: *zla ba bdun pa'i nang du kong por 'gro ba'i 'grul pa mang du 'dug pas de'i zla la thegs par thag bcad yod pa'i zhu ba btang bas... de nas sne'u gdong rtser sku mdun du thegs pas da khong gi bya bral byed pa la dra ba cig dang gtor cha cig la sogs pa'i gnang byin gyis*

gsung nas de rnams gnang bas thugs dgyes te / dra ba de yang dus phyi mo'i bar du nga'i bya bral gyi bla yin gsung nas....

788 Ibid., 29a2–3: *khyed dga' ldan pa 'di rnams byang chub lam gyi rim pa de la shin tu mkhas te / de gang la brten pa'i lam sgron mi mkhas /.*

789 Ibid., 28b7: *...mkhan chen bkra shis byang bas thugs dgyes dgyes (sic!) kyi 'phros gtam mang du byung /.*

790 Ibid., 29b1–2: *rta lo'i dgun de sku rab tu sku rab khri dpon dpal 'byor bzang po bas spyan drangs nas chos gsungs /.*

791 Ibid., 30a6–b2: *lug lo'i ston mjug kong po nas chos rje chos dpal ye shes pa dpon slob rnams 'bru mdar phebs nas / zhag bcu bzhi'i bar du bzhugs pa'i sku mdun du dpal mkha' spyod dbang po'i chos drug chen mo / karma pakṣi (text: pag shi)'i dam tshig gi bshad pa dpal rang byung rdo rjes mdzad pa dam tshig rgya mtsho zhes bya ba'i lung gsan /.*

792 Situ and 'Be lo: *Kaṁ tshang brgyud pa rin po che'i rnam thar*, 637.1: *zhva dmar chos dpal ye shes las chos drug zhus /.*

793 Zhva dmar Chos grags ye shes: *Gzhon nu dpal gyi rnam thar*, 30a3: *spre'u lo'i dpyid sgam po skor du thegs....*

794 Ibid., 30b5–31a3: *de nas spre'u'i lo'i ston dvags (text: dags) po la bar du thegs nas chos rje ri mi 'babs pa bsod nams rin chen pa'i drung du dpal mkha' spyod dbang po'i skyes sbyor / ngo sprod gnad kyi me long / gsal ba'i me long / ...ri chos gcig shes kun grol / ...chos rje rang byung rdo rjes mdzad pa'i gcod khrid dang / zab don nang don rtsa 'grel / chos dbyings bstod pa'i 'grel pa / de bzhin gshegs pa'i snying po ston pa'i bstan bcos / sku gsum ngo sprod kyi khrid rnams / mi nyag shes rab bzang pos mdzad pa'i do ha'i khrid yig do ha skor gsum / rmangs do ha'i rnam bshad / ...gsan /.*

795 Ibid., 31a5–6: *lar gyi ngo mtshar che khong phyag rgya chen po'i lta ba 'di ngas kyang blos mi gtong / khos kyang blos gtong mi 'ong / dge ldan pa'i rang (text: ngang) tshugs 'di ngas kyang kho blos mi gtong / khos kyang gtong mi 'ong gsung nas rang (text: dang) tshugs shin tu dam par mdzad gsung nas shin tu gus pa gnang /.*

796 According to the 'Bras spungs dkar chag (vol. 1, p. 3, *phyi ka*, no. 000012) the full title is: *Dpal dus kyi 'khor lo'i rgyud bshad pa la 'jug pa rgyud gsum gyi gsang ba rnam par phye ba.*

797 Zhva dmar Chos grags ye shes: *Gzhon nu dpal gyi rnam thar*, 33a3: *de'i zhar la rgyud gsum gyi gsang ba rnam par phye ba'i brtsom pa....*

798 Mi bskyod rdo rje: "Rje yid bzang rtse ba'i Rgyud gsum gsang ba...," 989.2–3: *yang bla ma rin po che blo bzang grags pa'i lta grub tshad mar yang khas blangs nas / mnyam med dvags po bka' brgyud kyi srol 'dzin du bzhed pa dpon slob yid (text: yig) bzang rtse pa dag /.*

799 Zhva dmar Chos grags ye shes: *Gzhon nu dpal gyi rnam thar*, 31a6–b2: *spre'u lo'i dbyar kong por chos rje chos dpal ye shes pa'i drung du chos mang du bsan pa'i phyir thegs par brtsams pa na / sbyin bdag gi gsung nas de mdzad na 'khor 'di rnams la nor nyan pa cig mi 'ong gsung nas shol bsam thon pa yin gsung / 'bru mdar gshed dmar gyi dbang yang legs par gnang / de nas yar phebs par bzhed pa na sbyin bdag sku mched thams cad kyis gzhi phab nas bzhugs par zhus na'ang ma bzhugs /. ...spre'u'i lo'i dgun yar klungs su phebs /.*

800 Ibid., 31b5–7: *bya lo'i dpyid gong ma grags pa 'byung gnas pa'i bka' lung gis gdan sa thel du dge ba'i bshes gnyen chen po du ma bsdus nas smon lam mdzad pa'i grar thegs nas rgod phrug chos rje 'jag spyil na bzhugs pa'i drung du nyin bzhin du bzhugs / de thon rting sna mo rdzong du bzhugs nas / chos rje rin po che nam mkha' blo gros / chos rje rin po che lo chen / ...mang po la phar phyin la sogs pa'i gzhung chos dang 'bel gtam gyis chos kyi sgo mtha' dag la snang ba chen po rgyas par mdzad /.*

801 Zhva dmar Chos grags ye shes: *Lo chen gyi rnam thar*, 15b5–16a1: *dgung lo nyi shu rtsa lnga bzhes pa 'brug gi lo (=1448) la / rje 'gos ljang pho brang du bzhugs pa'i drung*

du thegs nas...chos rje nam pa dang rnam gnyis lhan du gsan zhing / ...de dus rje 'gos kyi zhal las kyang / khong rnam gnyis la rin po che lta bu'i slob mar gzung nas / nges don gyi bshad pa bya rgyu 'dug tshang byas pa yin / de dus nges don bshad pa tsam gzhan gang du'ang byas pa med gsung /.

The same quotation is also found in Zhva dmar Chos grags ye shes: *Gzhon nu dpal gyi rnam thar,* 60a3.

802 Zhva dmar Chos grags ye shes: *Gzhon nu dpal gyi rnam thar,* 31b7–32a1: *de'i dbyar 'on chos sdings su rgod phrug chos rje'i sku mdun du thegs nas / grub chen u rgyan pa'i rdo rje gsum gyi bsnyen sgrub kyi nyams khrid legs par gsan pas....*

803 Ibid., 33a3: *...slar yang rgod phrug chos rje'i sku mdun du rgod tshang brag tu thegs pa na /....*

804 See Ehrhard 2002:39.

805 Zhva dmar Chos grags ye shes: *Gzhon nu dpal gyi rnam thar,* 58a7: *drung rgyal mtshan pa sne'u gdong gyi gnyer son bzhugs pa la phur pa man ngag drug pa lo sogs pa'i dbang gnang /.*

806 Ibid., 32b4–7: *de'i ston mjug kun bzang rtse ba drung bsod nams rgyal mtshan pas sbyin bdag mdzad cing sne'u gdong rtse'i snang bzhugs nas / bzhed pa dang 'thun pa'i dbang mang du gnang / ...yid bzang rtse rnying par phyags phab cing slob dpon nam mkha' dpal 'byor pas nye gnas kyi khur blangs te bya lo'i dgun bzhugs /.*

807 Ibid., 58b1: *yid bzang rtser drung nas kyis gsol ba btab pas rnal 'byor yan lag drug pa'i khrid gnang....*

808 Zhva dmar Chos grags ye shes: *Lo chen gyi rnam thar,* 14b3: *...yid bzang rtser rje 'gos kyi drung du doha skor gsum dang / sgom rim...gsan zhing / khyad par du me pho stag gi lo la brtag gnyis kyi bshad pa gsan te /.*

809 Zhva dmar Chos grags ye shes: *Gzhon nu dpal gyi rnam thar,* 33b6: *dgung lo lnga bcu rtsa gcig pa chu pho khyi'i dgun nas drug bcu rtsa gcig bzhes pa chu pho spre'u'i bar du chos ji ltar gsungs / tshul rgyas par 'og tu 'chad par 'gyur ro /.*

810 Ibid., 37b6–38a1: *dgung lo drug bcu rtsa lnga bzhes pa me pho byi ba'i dgun stod gra'i sman gcig tu thegs nas chos rje sman gcig pa shes rab bzang po'i drung du zhi byed...gsan nas sgrub pa'i dam bca' zla ba drug phul /.*

811 Ibid., 38a1–4: *gzhan yang...shin tu mang bar gsan / ...yar klungs su phebs /.*

812 Ibid., 38b2: *de nas chu pho rta'i bar du zla ba gcig ma gtogs sku mtshams la bzhugs nas dge ba'i bshes gnyen gsung gi bdud rtsi bzhes par bzhed pa rnams dang mjal ba zhig mdzad pa yin no /.*

813 Ibid., 38b5–6: *dgung lo brgyad bcu rtsa bzhi bzhes pa shing mo lug gi lo'i sos bdag mdo khams sogs bskor te /.*

814 Ibid., 39a4–7: *de nas me pho spre'u'i lo zla ba gnyis pa'i tshes bdun gyi nyin / sku mdun bdag gis sleb pa la bkur sti rgya chen po dang / gser zho brgya la sogs pa'i gnang...chos 'bul dgos pa'i bka' lung phebs pas...dpal mkha' spyod dbang po'i yig cha'i stengs nas gsang 'dus rim lnga dang / ...chos rje rang byung rdo rje'i bka' 'bum nas 'brel pa bzhi ldan sogs kyi lung / chos skyong ber nag can gyi dbang bzhi rdzogs phul zhing / me mo bya'i ston mjug phag mo lha lnga'i dbang / ...sa pho khyi'i ston bde mchog mkha' 'gro rgya mtsho'i rgyud 'grel...phul lo / .*

815 Ibid., 55b4–5: *zhi bar gshegs khar yang / rgyud bla ma'i 'grel bshad brtsom pa'i skabs las don gyi go ba ngan du ma song bar 'dug....*

816 Ibid., 56b1–2: *...rgyud bla ma'i 'grel bshad rtsom pa'i skabs su tshig bzhi pa'i tshigs su bcad pa gcig bskal par gsungs kyang de'i don zad par mi 'gyur ba'i spobs pa mnga' bar / slob dpon smon lam grags pa yi ge pa yin pas / de ltar go ba ni rje nyid kyi byin brlabs su nges so zhes /.*

817 Ibid., 69b5–70a1: *sprul lo'i sos ka rgyud bla'i 'grel bshad chen po brtsom par gsol ba btab pas zhal gyis bzhes te rtsom pa la zug pa'i nyin / gzims khang nang na dpon slob gnyis las mi bzhugs pa la sa g.yo ba'i cho 'phrul chen po byung / gzhan sus kyang*

ma tshor bar 'dug / zla ba bzhi pa la zug nas brgyad pa'i tshes bcva lnga la legs par grub / spyan gyis nyin nub dgongs pa tsam las med kyang bshad pa dang lung 'dren la sogs pa thams cad sngar spyan gyis gzigs pas (text: pa bas) tshegs chung zhing rgyas pas / thams cad ngo mtshar du gyur pas mtshon te / rtsom pa gang gnang na'ang / snga gzigs zhib mo dang ṭīkā (text: ṭīka) sogs ji ltar mdzad pa'i don thugs bsam gyis gtan la phab rjes / lung 'dren gyi skabs so so khol 'don gnang rting / yi ge ci tsam zin pa ltar zhal nas sprod (text: spod) pa ma gtogs / rtsom stan gyi thon du bsgyur 'god snon 'bring mang po mi dgos pa la zhal nas / ngas brtsom stan gyi snon 'bring bsam mno kho nas byed pa yin pas / mang du bcos (text: bco) mi dgos pa yin zhes gsung ngo /.

818 Ibid., 71b6: *sa pho khyi lo la deb ther (text: ter) sngon po che ba'i brtsom pa gnang zhing /....*

819 Ibid., 53a6–7: *'dir dpal phag mo gru pas bden pa gzigs pa yin dgongs pa'i thugs kyi dad pa'i stobs lhag par rgyas bzhin pas thegs te / re zhig gi bar du bzhugs nas dgongs pa legs par btang bas /....*

820 Ibid., 53a7–b1: *de bzhin gshegs pa'i snying po sems rang bzhin gyis 'od gsal ba 'khor 'das thams cad kyi gzhi po gang yin pa de'i gnas tshul thugs su ji lta bar byon te / sangs rgyas nas sems can gyi bar gyi gnas tshul 'di lta bu shig 'dug / brjod par bya ba ldog pa ste / sems kyi spyod yul la ldog pas so / zhes bya ba la sogs pa dbu ma las 'byung ba'i bshad pa thams cad kyang 'dir 'jug cing /....*

821 Ibid., 53b2–6: *...gsang ba bla na med pa'i tshul las 'byung ba'i zung du 'jug pa zhes bya ba'i sgra bo che gang yin pa de yang da gzod 'bras bu'i dbang du byas pa min par chos thams cad kyi gnas lugs su gtan la phab nas / byis pa so so'i skye bo tha mal pa dag gis kyang nyams su blang du yod par rgya cher gsung rab kyi sgo nas ston cing / nyams myong cung cad tsam dang ldan pa dag la'ang de nyid kyi steng nas yang dag par ngo sprod par mdzad de / de yang tshig skam po bzung nas gsung ba ne tso'i 'don pa lta bu mdzad pa ma yin / rang nyid kyis thugs su legs par chud de... legs par gsung shing / ...thugs su byon pa'i yon tan gyi khyad par thams cad kyang zung 'jug gi lta ba mthar thug pa rtogs pa de'i dbang las byung zhing /....*

822 Ibid., 54a5–6: *kun mkhyen jo mo nang pas las snang dang ye shes kyi snang pa zhes so so ba rigs mi gcig pa'i chos gnyis bsres nas bzhag pa skad du gsung ste / las snang 'di nyid ye shes kyi snang ba'i khyag par tha snyad btags te ye shes kyi snang ba ngo sprod / ...chu dang khyag pa'i dpe ston par mdzad cing / ji srid rang dang gzhan / snod dang bcud zer ba de srid du de'i tha snyad bzhag ste de nas ni ye shes kyi snang bar ro gcig gsung /.*

823 Ibid., 54a3–4: *yang kha cig gsang sngags bla na med pa'i skabs su'ang stong pa nyid kyi gzugs brnyan chos can / bden par med de / zhes bya ba'i tshul du dpyad par 'dod mod kyi / stong gzugs mthong ba de nyid sems kyi gnas lugs mthong ba yin par bzhed /.*

824 Stearns (1999:44) points out that Yu mo ba's understanding of the Kālacakra concept "reflections of emptiness" found its way into Dol po pa's work.

825 I.e., the translator of Vanaratna (Zhva dmar Chos grags ye shes: *Gzhon nu dpal gyi rnam thar*, 36a1–2: *de nas stod byang du lo tsa ba mañjuśrī ma phebs kyi bar du paṇ chen chos gsung ba dang dbang bskur ba la sogs pa'i lo tsa yang mdzad /*).

826 Ibid., 54a6–b1: *sngon byon pa'i dge ba'i bshes gnyen rnams las grub chen yu mo'i gsung rab rnams dang / dpal sgam po pa slob ma dang bcas pa'i gsung rnams dang / grub pa'i dbang phyug nags kyi rin chen gyi gsung rnams dang / byang chub sems dpa'i 'grel pa rnams dang / 'dus pa sgron ma gsal ba la sogs pa dang / 'jam dpal zhal gyi lung la sogs pa dang / zab mo'i mdo sde du ma rnams dang / gsang sngags snga 'gyur gyi skor mang po la sogs pa 'gal med du yang dag par bstan mdzad pas /....*

827 I would like to thank here again His Holiness the Drikung Kyabgon Trinley Lhundrup (Chetsang Rinpoche) for providing a copy of the handwritten *dbu med*

text of Gzhon nu dpal's *Ratnagotravibhāgavyākhyā* commentary, and Ven. Dzogchen Ponlop Rinpoche for an old block print of the same text.

828 According to a cover page, the first chapter has 550 folios, the second 68 folios, the third 23 folios, the fourth 36 folios, and the fifth 21 folios.

829 This is according to a 34-page-long list of 430 photocopied texts that the Seventeenth Karmapa Drodul Ugyen Trinley Dorje received from the Potala Palace when he was still at Tshur phu (Gzhon nu dpal's *Ratnagotravibhāgavyākhyā* commentary is the first entry).

830 See Lokesh Chandra 1963: vol. 1, 523, no. 11341.

831 Such as *chu 'thungs pas* instead of *mthu chung bas* on p. 3.23, or *snyon mongs* instead of *nyon mongs* on p. 142.17.

832 A reads *...gcig yin pa'i phyir / dper na phung po bzhin / yang na phung po rtag pa dag tu 'gyur te / bdag dang (gcig yin pa'i phyir / dper na phung po bzhin yang na phung po rtag pa dag tu 'gyur te / bdag dang) gcig yin pa'i phyir /*, as opposed to B: *gcig yin pa'i phyir / dper na phung po bzhin / yang na phung po rtag pa dag du 'gyur te / bdag dang gcig yin pa'i phyir /.* The portion in parentheses is wrongly inserted by A.

833 DRSM, 575.7.

834 Zhva dmar Chos grags ye shes: *Lo chen gyi rnam thar*, 92a7–b1: *zla ba bcu gnyis pa'i nang du smon sdang mkhar du rje 'gos kyi drung du phyag phul la thegs / der bzhugs ring zhabs tog bzang po 'bul ba gnang / phar phyin gyi khrid gsan /.*

This visit is recorded in the biography of Gzhon nu dpal as falling in the winter of the year 1472 (Zhva dmar Chos grags ye shes: *Gzhon nu dpal gyi rnam thar*, 69b1–3: *'brug gi dpyid...de'i dgun chos rje rin po che lo chen pa'i zhal snga nas phyag 'bul phebs pa la shes rab kyi pha rol tu phyin pa sgom pa'i rim pa gsungs*).

835 Zhva dmar Chos grags ye shes: *Gzhon nu dpal gyi rnam thar*, 68b5–6: *de rjes smon ldang mkhar du bzhugs nas sgron gsal ṭīkā (text: ṭika) le'u bcu pa yan mdzad /.*

An ox year (=1469) is mentioned on fol. 68a5.

836 Ibid., 69b5–70a1 (see above in p. 145).

837 At the end of his biography of Lo chen Bsod nams rgya mtsho, in the section that covers the years 1479–81, Zhva dmar Chos grags ye shes informs us that the king of the "southern region" (Lho rgyud) was a certain Bkra shis dar rgyas legs pa (Zhva dmar Chos grags ye shes: *Lo chen gyi rnam thar*, 121a6: *skabs der lho rgyud yangs pa'i rgyal khams la dbang sgyur ba bkra shis dar rgyas legs pa'i rgyal po...)*.

838 Lit., "in one step."

839 According to Ehrhard 2002:20.

840 The term *chos kyi spyan snga* is of course descriptive of religious duties as the successor of Spyan snga Rin po che Grags pa 'byung gnas (1175–1255).

841 Lit., "the one who is free from ignorance."

842 Lit., "[the period of] the very clear springing up."

843 DRSM, 575.23–576.8.

844 See Ehrhard 2002:23.

845 See Mathes 2003.

846 Tibetan translations from the Sanskrit are extremely technical, and in many cases a comparison with the Sanskrit ensures a more accurate rendering of the Tibetan. Still, it is my policy to follow the Tibetan wherever possible; the Sanskrit is only given as a reference in the endnotes.

847 See Johnston 1950:vi.

848 See Bandurski et al. 1994:12–13.

849 For a description of the concerned photographs, see Ibid., 31–33.

850 LAS, 40.14; the six manuscripts are: NGMPP reel nos. B 88/2, 23b5; C 13/7, 19a3; D 55/3, 16b2; E 446/15, 19a3; E 625/14, 26b2; and E 712/4, 14b8.

851 See C 13/7, 150a4: ...*nepārābde vahni-muni-mātṛke*... (N.S. 873l; 1753 A.D.).
852 None of the six is dated, but the use of a character symbol on top of the usual pagination—an old custom of marking a text as a copy—suggests an older age than the other five (this is according to the judgment of Diwakar Acharya).
853 See Slusser 1998: vol. 1, 401.
854 Reel nos. A 112/10, 25a4–5; D 58/6, 24a3; and E 1200/8, 17a7 read *traidhātukasvacittamāyādhimuktitaḥ* instead of *traidhātukasvacittatayādhimuktitaḥ* in the remaining mss. (LAS, 42.12–13).
855 A 112/10, 24a3 reads *-satvā-* against all other mss. (LAS, 40.14: *-śraddhā-*).
856 Reel nos. D 58/6, 63b1 and E 1200/8, 44b6 read *padāḥ pṛthivīgāminaḥ* instead of *padavīthīgāmino* in the remaining mss. (LAS, 113.6–7).
857 See E 1200/8, 133b7: ...*samvat* 818... (= 1698 A.D.).
858 Reel nos. D 52/5, 30a3 and D 55/3, 33b7 read *māyādimanomayakāyaṁ* instead of *māyādidharmasvabhāvānugamād anutpattikadharmakṣāntiṁ* in the remaining mss. (LAS, 81.2–3).
859 Reel nos. A 917/6, 54b6 and C 13/7, 52a7 read *yāvaṁ lakṣās* instead of *yāvad dhakāraḥ* in the remaining mss. (LAS, 113.5).
860 This is a deft allusion to the particular mahāmudrā tradition within which Gzhon nu dpal expounds the *Ratnagotravibhāga*. In his *Deb ther sngon po* Gzhon nu dpal characterizes Sgam po pa's *pāramitā*-mahāmudrā as being the *pāramitās* in essence and also in accordance with the secret *mantra[yāna]*. From his reading of Maitrīpa's *Tattvadaśaka* and Sahajavajra's *Tattvadaśakaṭīkā*, he follows Rgod tshang pa in claiming that Rje Sgam po pa's *pāramitā*-based mahāmudrā is grounded in Maitrīpa. ('Gos Lo tsā ba Gzhon nu dpal: *Deb ther sngon po*, 632.6–633.4.)
861 According to RGV I.30–31, water or moisture exemplifies the undefiled nature of the buddha element, an aspect of *tathāgatagarbha*, and in the corresponding *vyākhyā* water stands for the buddha element's moist nature of compassion toward sentient beings (see Takasaki 1966:200–201). This quality is symbolized by the rain-bringing clouds of Maitreya, described here as the most excellent among the sons of the victorious one.
862 Corresponding to the buddha element of sentient beings.
863 A disciple of Maitrīpa who was known for spreading the tradition of *pāramitā*-based mahāmudrā in Tibet under the name of *Sdug bsngal zhi byed*. See DRSM, 5.18–19 and Seyfort Ruegg 1988a:13.
864 His full name is: Sgam po pa Dvags po Lha rje Bsod nams rin chen (see Guenther 1989:9–11).
865 The identification of Lama Rin chen with Sgam po pa is suggested by the poetic figure of the "youthful moonlight," the same name as the ever young Bodhisattva Candraprabha. According to Rgyal ba Yang dgon pa (1213–58), Sgam po pa had once been Candraprabha, who requested from the Munīndra the teaching of the *Samādhirājasūtra* in Rājagṛha. Candraprabha promised to remain faithful to this sūtra and its teacher in order that they might help him in the future. Thus the Muni became Sgam po pa's disciple Phag mo gru pa (see Roerich 1949–53: 451–52). In "Sgam po pa's Song of Response to the Three Men of Khams," which is contained in the *Bka' brgyud mgur mstho*, Sgam po pa himself claims that he is the reincarnation of Candraprabha prophesied in the *Samādhirājasūtra* (Trungpa 1989:277–78).
866 Tib. *snying po*, otherwise translated as "nature" in the the compound *de bzhin gshegs pa'i snying po*.
867 One way to define buddha nature is to follow the *Pradīpoddyotana* (a commentary

on the *Guhyasamājatantra*) and simply equate it with sentient beings (see DRSM, 7.21–22).

868 For Gzhon nu dpal's use of *de la*, see DRSM, 20.22.

869 In the Peking Kangyur (no. 126) the Tibetan title is: *Rnam par snang mdzad chen po mngon par rdzogs par byang chub pa rnam par sprul ba byin gyis rlob pa shin tu rgyas pa mdo sde'i dbang po rgyal po zhes bya ba'i chos kyi rnam grangs*, while the Sanskrit title is given as: *Mahāvairocanābhisambodhivikurvitādhiṣṭhānavaipulyasūtrendrarājanāmadharmaparyāya* (according to the Tōhoku Catalogue). In the Peking Kangyur, the quoted passage is in section *rgyud*, vol. *tha*, fols. 119a7–120a3.

870 Tib. *gsang ba'i bdag po*; see LC, s.v.

871 The Peking Kangyur reads *mtshungs pa rnams las* instead of *mtshungs pa rnams la*.

872 Tib. *res 'ga' zhig la la dag la*. In the Peking Kangyur *la la dag la* is omitted.

873 The Peking Kangyur reads *de'i rgyu nyid kyi* instead of *de'i rgyu nyid kyis*. The instrumental is, however, confirmed by the *vṛtti* (see next footnote): *smyung bar byed pa de nyid la goms par byed pa'i rgyus* (*rgyud 'grel*, vol. *cu*, fol. 25a3).

874 Buddhaguhya explains in his commentary the *Vairocanābhisambodhivikurvitādhiṣṭhānamahātantravṛtti* (Peking Tengyur 3490), which was translated by Gzhon nu dpal (*rgyud 'grel*, vol. *cu*, fol. 25a1–2): "After fasting, one has a mind to offer and give. [Thus] it is not a fault to take fasting as an immediately preceding condition of virtue—generosity and the like" *(smyung bar byas pa'i 'og tu mchod pa dang sbyin pa'i sems 'byung ba ste smyung ba de ni sbyin pa la sogs pa'i dge ba'i de ma thag pa'i rkyen byed pas nyes pa med do).*

875 The commentary (Ibid., fol. 25a3) glosses *mtshan ma dang bcas pa'i nyi ma* as …*zla ba dang skar ma dang nyi ma la sogs pa bzang po'i nyin bar* ("during a day marked by a good [configuration of] the moon, stars, sun, and so forth…").

876 The Peking Kangyur reads *thams cad 'byor pa* instead of *thams cad grub pa*.

877 See Schneider 1993:313.

878 Śaṁkara and Rudra are both an epithet of Mahādeva (Schneider 1993:311).

879 The god of war (Schneider 1993:308).

880 An epithet of Kubera (MW, s.v.).

881 The Peking Kangyur reads *dus mtshan* instead of *dus mtshams*. The *Bod skad dang legs sbyar gyi tshig mdzod chen mo* (s.v.) gives *Kālarātrī* for *dus mtshan ma*, a goddess who is not unexpected in the company of Yama and Nirṛti.

882 Tib. *mya ngan 'das*. Personification of the goddess of death (see MW, s.v.).

883 Lit., "Chief of the World" (Tib. *'jig rten gtso*). Some of the preceding eight gods correspond to a list of the "Chiefs of the Eight Directions" (lit., …of the east, etc.) given in *Amarakośa* I.3.2cd–3ab, for example: *indro vahniḥ pitṛpatir*[a] *nairṛto varuṇo marut / kubera iśaḥ patayaḥ pūrvādīnāṁ diśāṁ kramāt //* (See Pant 2000, vol. 2:60).

a Another name for Yama.

884 I.e., Suparṇa, Aruṇa, and Garuḍa (MW, s.v.).

885 An epithet of Umā (Schneider 1993:315).

886 From *tapas (dka' thub)* and *takṣa (zlog)* (MW, s.v.).

887 *Padma* starts a list of Nāgarājas that correspond (unsequentially) to the eight Nāgarājas given in Mahāvyutpatti § CLXVIII, nos. 3227–34: Śaṅkha, Karkoṭaka, Kulika, Padma, Mahāpadma, Vāsuki, Ananta, Takṣaka.

888 Tib. *nor ldan*. According to MVY no. 3232: *nor rgyas*.

889 Tib. *gdengs ka mang*, "having many *nāga* heads." Śeṣa is, among other things, called the "thousand-headed" (see MW, s.v.). The MVY (no. 3337) has listed Mahāphaṇaka (Tib. *gdengs ka chen po*) as the name of an ordinary *nāga*. Together

with the following *rtag tu*, Skt. Sadā (?), it has been inserted between the seventh and eighth Nāgarāja.

890 The Nāgarāja Ananta (see MVY no. 3233).

891 Ādideva can refer to any of the main Hindu gods.

892 Tib. *rig byed* means Veda only. According to Diwakar Acharya (personal communication) the personification of the Veda is either *Vedapuruṣa* or *Brahmaṇaspati.*

893 I.e., the five Paṇḍava brothers (MW, s.v.).

894 The Peking Kangyur reads *de 'dra'i tshig* instead of *de'i tshig.*

895 See Schneider 1993:52–53.

896 Tib. *bsam pa brlag pa rnams* is glossed as *byis pa* in the *Viśeṣastavaṭīkā.* In order to avoid a clumsy repetition, I follow Schneider (1993:264) and translate it as "fools."

897 The counting of chapters and stanzas follows Steinkellner's (1977) *Verse-Index* (i.e., the chapter on *svārthānumāna* is taken as the first one).

898 The compound *durbodhā* refers to both *nirdoṣatā* and *anyadoṣā[ḥ].*

899 PV I.219 (ed. Gnoli 1960:110.9–10): *ayam evaṁ na vety anyadoṣā*[a] *nirdoṣatāpi vā / durlabhatvāt pramāṇānāṁ durbodhety apare viduḥ /.* In the first *pāda* of Gzhon nu dpal's quotation *('di ni 'di lta min no zhes)* the *'am* after *lta,* which translates the first *vā* (in *vety*), is missing. The version in the Peking Tengyur, however, confirms the reading *lta'am.* (Peking Tengyur (no. 5709), *gtan tshigs rig pa,* vol. *ce,* fol. 198b4.)

a Gnoli reads *anyadoṣā* in compound with *nirdoṣatāpi* which does not make sense here.

The Tibetan has: */ gzhan la skyon ldan skyon med pa'ang /* (DRSM, 3.17). The *Svavṛtti* (Gnoli 1960:110.12–13) explains: "And the [qualities and defects] that are beyond the reach of the senses must be inferred from the manner of the autonomous body and speech" *(te cātīndriyāḥ svaprabhavakāyavāgvyavahārānumeyāḥ syuḥ /).*

900 Peking Tengyur (no. 2004), *bstod tshogs,* vol. *ka,* fol. 50b6–7.

901 Tib. *phyogs [su] 'dzin pa,* which is glossed by the *Devātiśāyastotraṭīkā* as *phyogs su lhung ba* (Peking Tengyur (no. 2005), *bstod tshogs,* vol. *ka,* fols. 67b8–68a1). The commentary on stanza 17 is introduced in the following way: "You [may] think that he (i.e., the author of the *stotra*) said this because he is partial. Therefore he said: 'I [have not taken the side], etc.'" (*khyed ni phyogs su lhung bas de skad smra ba yin no snyam pa la / de'i phyir bdag ni zhes bya ba la sogs pa smras pa yin te,* Ibid., *ka,* 67b8–68a1).

902 Cf. the explanation of the commentary (Ibid., *ka,* 60a3): *gang dag gi tshig rigs pa dang ldan zhing / tshad mas gzhal bar bzod pa de nyid la ston pa nyid du yongs su bzung bar bya zhing...,* "One must hold as [one's] teachers all those whose words are suitable and [able to] stand up to the demands of valid cognition...."

903 See *dpyad pa gsum gyi dag pa'i lung* (*Tshig mdzod chen mo,* s.v.).

904 See Schneider 1993:56–57.

905 Lit., "taught without a measure."

906 Tib. *mdo sde.*

907 The context clearly requires a past participle with the meaning of "taught" or "expounded." Skt. *nīta* (translated as *bzhag* in Tib.) does not exactly have this meaning (Skt. *uktam* would be better in fact), but does it allude to the adjective *nītārtham* depending on *sūtram.* By means of this stylistic device (known as *tantra* in Sanskrit grammar) the hermeneutic term *definitive meaning* can be hinted at. See also de Jong (1979:579) who translates "taught as definitive."

908 RGVV, 118.3–6: *yasmān neha jināt supaṇḍitatamo loke 'sti kaścit kvacit sarvajñaḥ sakalaṁ sa veda vidhivat tattvaṁ paraṁ nāparaḥ / tasmād yat svayam eva nītam*

ṛṣiṇā sūtraṁ vicālyaṁ na tat saddharmapratibādhanaṁ hi tad api syān nītibhedān muneḥ //.

909 Lit., "with a measure."

910 What Gzhon nu dpal has in mind, of course, is the distinction between the provisional and definitive meaning *(neyārtha* and *nītārtha)* according to the *Saṁdhinirmocanasūtra.* This is clear from his commentary on RGV V.5, which says that hearing a word of these teachings on the buddha element yields much more merit than anything else could. Gzhon nu dpal explains that this stanza should be read according to the teaching in the *Saṁdhinirmocanasūtra* on the difference of merit resulting from the devotion to sūtras of provisional and definitive meaning (DRSM, 561.22–23).

911 The translators Dpal brtsegs and Ye shes sde are listed in a transmission lineage of the *Abhidharmasamuccaya,* which goes back to Maitreya (see the *Blue Annals* (Roerich 1949–53:344–45)).

912 See Seyfort Ruegg 1969:38ff.

913 Lit., "wrote the texts." In the *Deb ther sngon po* (308.6) it is said that "he also wrote down [each page of the] texts one by one and gave it to the scholar Jñānaśrī and others" *(dpe yang kha yar bris nas mkhas pa jñānaśrī la sogs pa la phul).*

914 Lit., "with regard to those [texts]."

915 Probably the *Theg chen rgyud bla'i don bsdus pa.*

916 Lit., "to place in [his] mind." Cf. the corresponding sentence in the *Deb ther sngon po* (423.1–2): *...byams pa'i chos la 'chi chos byed pas de'i bshad pa yang dag pa zhig gnang bar zhu zhes zhus /.*

917 Cf. *Deb ther sngon po,* 309.3: *gnas tha dad pa rnams su ji ltar rigs par dge ba'i bshes gnyen don du gnyer ba rnams la byams chos kyi bshad pa mdzad.*

918 Cf. Lokesh Chandra 1963, vol. 3, no. 11338: "An explanation of the *Uttaratantra,* recorded (in the form of notes) by the translator Gzu Dga' [ba] rdo [rje] on the basis of teachings given by the Paṇḍita Sajjana" *(paṇḍitas sajjana'i gsung la lo tsā ba gzu dga' rdor gyi zin bris byas pa'i rgyud bla ma'i rnam bshad).*

919 Tib. *Brgyad stong 'grel chen.* See Lokesh Chandra: *Tibetan-Sanskrit Dictionary,* s.v.

920 See Roerich 1949–53:328 and 404.

921 Ibid., 350.

922 See Khetsun Sangpo 1973 (vol. 5):45–47. Sha ra ba pa was a disciple of the Bka' gdams master Po to ba (1031–1105).

923 Cf. Ibid.:45.11–13.

924 See Ibid., 14–16: Gro lung pa Blo gros 'byung gnas was the chief disciple of Rngog Blo ldan shes rab (see also Roerich 1949–53:331).

925 That is, Zhang tshes Spong ba Chos kyi bla ma, one of whose disciples was Nyang bran pa Chos kyi ye shes (Ibid., 332).

926 Phya pa's main teacher was Gro lung pa Blo gros 'byung gnas. Phya pa himself held the office of abbot at Gsang phu Sne'u thog and was, according to Tauscher, a strict follower of Rngog Blo ldan shes rab's Svātantrika tradition (Tauscher 1999:vii–viii). Gzhon nu dpal informs us in his *Blue Annals* that there is a difference, however, in the two masters' presentation of the ultimate truth (see *Deb ther sngon po,* 309.5–7). According to van der Kuijp (1978:357), Phya pa Chos kyi seng ge was nonsectarian, although in fact he is frequently mentioned in Bka' gdams pa biographies.

927 Gtsang nag pa and Dan bag pa are two of the "eight mighty lions" who stand out as disciples of Phya pa Chos kyi seng ge (Tauscher 1999:vii).

928 Gzhon nu dpal (*Deb ther sngon po,* 309.6–7) informs us that Blo ldan shes rab and Gtsang nag pa equated buddha nature with ultimate truth, whereas Phya pa took the latter (and thus buddha nature) as corresponding to a nonaffirming

negation (see paragraph I.1.1., "The *Ratnagotravibhāga* Commentary of Rngog Blo ldan shes rab" in that work).

929 In different parts of his commentary Gzhon nu dpal explains that "endowed" (Tib. *ldan pa*) should be understood in the sense of "being connected" *('brel pa)*. To support his interpretation, he quotes Vinayadeva's *Hevajravajrapadoddharaṇanāmapañjikā*, and notes that defining the relation between buddha nature and the qualities in terms of *'brel pa* underscores both that the qualities have arisen from buddha nature and that the two have an identical nature (see DRSM, 29.18–21 and DRSM, 323.19–23).

930 This needs to be taken as implying that one focuses on emptiness as the cause of the qualities.

931 Skt. *vyavadānanimitta* (RGVV, 76.7) is the term used in the *Ratnagotravibhāgavyākhyā* for that which does not need to be added. It is the ever-present suchness or emptiness. The root text (RGV I.157–58 (J I.154–55)) suggests that the phrase "nothing needs to be added" refers to the qualities, i.e., that of which the buddha element is not empty.

932 Gzhon nu dpal must follow Rngog Blo ldan shes rab's view, since he maintains that ordinary persons only possess subtle qualities, which must grow naturally. Thus it can be only their emptiness to which nothing is added.

933 The "Three Khampas" were Rje Khams pa Rdor rgyal (see Roerich 1949–53:188), or Phag mo gru pa, together with Khams pa Dbu se (i.e., the First Karmapa), and Khams pa Gsal sto[a] sho sgom (1116–69). Chogyam Trungpa (1989:333) informs us in his *Rain of Wisdom* that Gsal sto sho sgom was the founder of the Sgra legs skyabs mgon line. The Three Khampas were not only Sgam po pa's closest disciples, but also disciples of the Gsang phu Ne'u thog abbot Phya pa Chos kyi seng ge (van der Kuijp 1978:356–57).

a For the spelling "Gsal sto" instead of "Gsal stong" see van der Kuijp 1978:356.

934 Tib. *bzhogs*. According to Thrangu Rinpoche *bzhogs* does not make any sense here, and is probably corrupt.

935 The eight stages refer to the four stages that Gzhon nu dpal identified in Buddhist literature in general: (1) emptiness of a nonaffirming negation, (2) natural luminosity of mind, (3) basic consciousness, (4) all living beings; and the four stages found in this treatise in particular: (1) dharmakāya, (2) suchness, (3) buddha potential, (4) the nonconceptual (see DRSM, 5.1–4). On the basis of the *Ldog pa bsdus pa* and the *Tarkajvālā* he introduces the first point (emptiness) by explaining the distinction between nonaffirming negations and affirming negations, and then discusses the problem of how the ultimate can be grasped by an intellectual act of negation. The understanding of buddha nature as nonaffirming negation is then contrasted with its meaning of "element of awareness" in the third turning of the dharmacakra.

936 Peking Tengyur (no. 5782), *sgra rig pa*, vol. *le*, fol. 246a5.

937 Ibid., fol. 246a7.

938 Ibid.

939 Peking Tengyur (no. 5783), *sgra rig pa*, vol. *le*, fol. 253a5–6.

940 Cf. MAVBh, 22.23–23.5 where the existence or state (Skt. *bhāva*, Tib. *dngos po*) of the nonexistence of duality is taken as a defining characteristic of emptiness: "The nonexistence of duality, which is the state *(bhāva)* of [duality's] nonexistence, is the defining characteristic of empti[ness]. The nonexistence of duality, that is, of a perceived object and a perceiving subject, and the state of its (i.e., duality's) nonexistence are the defining characteristics of emptiness. Thus the defining characteristics of emptiness have been taught in terms of the own-being of nonexistence. Moreover, this own-being of its nonexistence neither exists nor does not

exist. Why is it nonexistent? Because of the nonexistence of duality. How so is it not nonexistent? Because of the state *(bhāva)* of the nonexistence of duality. These are the defining characteristics of emptiness." *(dvayābhāvo hy abhāvasya bhāvaḥ śūnyasya lakṣaṇaṁ / dvayagrāhyagrāhakasyābhāvaḥ / tasya cābhāvasya bhāvaḥ śūnyatāyā lakṣaṇam ity abhāvasvabhāvalakṣaṇatvaṁ śūnyatāyāḥ paridīpitam bhavati / yaś cāsau tadabhāvasvabhāvaḥ sa / na bhāvo nāpi cābhāvaḥ / katham na bhāvo yasmāt dvayasyābhāvaḥ/ kathaṁ nābhāvo yasmāt dvayābhāvasya bhāvaḥ / etac ca śūnyatāyā lakṣaṇaṁ /.)*

941 Peking Tengyur (no. 5783), *sgra rig pa*, vol. *le*, fol. 253a7. The two *pāda*s are quoted as a *pratīka* in the commentary, but I could not find them in the root text itself.

942 Ibid., *sgra rig pa*, vol. *le*, fol. 253a7–b1.

943 According to Lindtner (1995:37–39) the form "Bhavyaviveka" is also correct, whereas the usual one, Bhāvaviveka, is corrupt and should not be used.

944 Approximate dates according to Ejima 1979:496.

945 MH, 10.3: *tatra bhūtasvabhāvaṁ hi norvyādi paramārthataḥ /.*

946 Peking Tengyur (no. 5256), *dbu ma*, vol. *dza*, fol. 63a4–b1.

947 Tib. *min*, Skt. *na.*

948 The object or qualification of a thesis in a nonaffirming negation, such as "do not ultimately exist as their own-being," is said to be ultimately existent. This is an insight attainable by hearing and thinking, and accords with the direct realization of suchness. In this case, both *artha* and *parama* of *paramārtha (ultimate)* are taken to refer to the subject (the consciousness that understands emptiness). See Lopez 1987:314–16.

949 Peking Tengyur (no. 5256), *dbu ma*, vol. *dza*, fol. 64a6–b1.

950 Read *gang ngag blo* instead of *gang dag blo.*

951 If one maintains that the ultimate, which is beyond the intellect, boils down to a nonaffirming negation, it cannot be the negation proper, inasmuch as it would then be the content or object of words.

952 The term *abhisaṁskāra* is normally used in the context of mental fabrication *(prapañca)* and mental effort *(ābhoga)* (see Schmithausen 1969:138–42). *Anabhisaṁskāra* can thus be compared to *niṣprapañca* and *anābhoga.*

953 In the context of the *Madhyamakahṛdaya* (see Lopez 1987:315).

954 In the Svātantrika-Madhyamaka there are two types of ultimate, an inexpressible ultimate *(aparyāyaparamārtha)* and an expressible ultimate *(paryāyaparamārtha).* The expressible ultimate can manifest, among other things, as an understanding that has arisen through a logical proof that establishes emptiness. Cf. Jñānagarbha's *Satyadvayavibhāgavṛtti* 4ab (Eckel 1987:71 and 114–15).

955 Peking Tengyur (no. 5266): *dbu ma*, vol. *ya*, fols. 267b8–268a3. For the Sanskrit title see Seyfort Ruegg 1981:52.

956 Stanza XVI.13 of Āryadeva's *Catuḥśataka* is contained as a *pratīka* in Candrakīrti's commentary (the numbering is according to Vaidya 1923:125).

957 Tib. *mtshan gzhi* is defined as: "that which is the basis for defining the definiendum by means of a definiens. For example, this [particular] golden vase is the basis for defining a vase." (*Bod rgya tshig mdzod chen mo*, s.v.)

958 Peking Tengyur (5256), *dbu ma*, vol. *dza*, fol. 183a2–4. The quotation is from the fourteenth *bam po.*

959 Lit., "a person active internally" (Tib. *nang gi byed pa'i skyes bu*, Skt. *antarvyāpārapuruṣa* (see Hirakawa 1978, s.v.)).

960 MA, 131.17–19.

961 Hopkins (1983:617) translates: "because it abides as the nature of all the phenomena [that makes full enlightenment possible]." For La Vallée Poussin (1910:321) *phyir* functions here as a *dativus finalis* expressing purpose[a] and so he

translates: "in order to introduce to [the knowledge of] the own-being of all things" *(en vue d'introduire dans [la connaissance de] l'être propre de toutes les choses).* In this case, Candrakīrti would have been employing the hermeneutical principle described as *avatāraṇābhisandhi* (Tib. *gzhug pa la ldem por dgongs pa*),[b] which states that the Buddha taught the *ālayavijñāna* with the hidden intention of bringing into Buddhism those who would otherwise be afraid of the teaching of emptiness. In such a construction, however, one would expect a future form such as *gzhug* (see MA VI.43: *gzhug par bya ba'i phyir dang por kun gzhi'i rnam par shes pa la sogs pa bstan pa...*, "In order to motivate [people] to enter the [path], *ālayavijñāna* and the like were taught...." (MA, 133.8)). Jayānanda explains in his *Madhyamakāvatāraṭīkā:* "'Because it follows the nature of all phenomena' means: because of [*ālayavijñāna*'s] conformity to the emptiness of phenomena—in view of [the fact that *ālayavijñāna*, likewise,] does 'not [arise] from self, other, and so forth.' [For this reason] only emptiness is the *ālaya;* and this *ālaya* is [also] *vijñāna.* One should know that emptiness was taught in terms of *ālayavijñāna*, for one thereby thoroughly comes to know [reality] from the practice of not apprehending any phenomena." (Peking Tengyur no. 5271, *dbu ma*, vol. *ra*, fols. 200b8–201a2: *dngos po thams cad kyi ran bzhin rjes su zhugs pa'i phyir zhes bya ba ni gang gi phyir / bdag las ma yin gzhan las min / / zhes bya ba la sogs pas dngos po stong pa nyid kyi rjes su 'jug pa'i phyir stong pa nyid kho na kun gzhi yin la de nyid rnam par shes pa ste / chos thams cad mi dmigs pa'i sbyor bas yongs su shes pa'i phyir des na stong pa nyid la kun gzhi rnam par shes pa'i sgras bstan par rig par bya'o.*)

a See Hahn 1994:121.

b For a list of the four hermeneutic principles termed *abhisandhi*s, see Broido 1984:6–7 and 24.

962 Since Candrakīrti explicitly refers to the *Laṅkāvatārasūtra* when he makes the statement that the term *ālayavijñāna* conveys the notion of emptiness (MA, 131.12), it may be assumed that he was aware of the fact that the *Laṅkāvatārasūtra* equated the *ālayavijñāna* with buddha nature, and implicitly accepted that buddha nature is emptiness as well.

963 See LAS, 78.5–11 and Candrakīrti's autocommentary on MA VI.95 (see paragraph 4 of my introduction, pp. 17–18).

964 The explanations in brackets are according to Khenpo Lobsang (Namo Buddha, Nepal). In fact, Candrakīrti could have distinguished an aspect of the *tathāgatagarbha* teaching that has definitive meaning (inasmuch as it teaches the emptiness of mind and the notion that all sentient beings will become buddhas) from one with provisional meaning (namely that all sentient beings are already buddhas with all major and minor marks). Cf. also Seyfort Ruegg 1973:13 and 27–28.

965 RGVV, 43.9–10: *cittasya yāsau prakṛtiḥ prabhāsvarā na jātu*[a] *sā dyaur iva yāti vikriyām /.* The Tibetan does not render *jātu* (see DRSM, 7.15–16).

a B (24b5) reads *yātu;* A is not available.

966 My translation follows the Tibetan here. Cf. also 'Ju Mi pham's commentary: "Any other mind—[that is,] thoughts or false imagining—different from the mind of dharmatā-luminosity, which cannot be sullied by stains, is not luminosity. The stainless dharmatā-mind, or the wisdom of luminosity, is taught as being the nature of mind, or basic clarity and emptiness united into a pair." (*dri mas gos par byar med pa'i chos nyid 'od gsal ba'i sems las gzhan pa'i sems gzhan rnam rtog gam yang dag min pa'i rtog pa ni 'od gsal ma yin la / dri ma med pa chos nyid kyi sems sam 'od gsal ba'i ye shes ni sems kyi rang bzhin nam gzhis gsal stong zung 'jug la brjod*

do / "Theg pa chen po mdo sde'i rgyan gyi dgongs don theg mchog bdud rtsi'i dga' ston ldeb," 356.4–5.)

The corresponding Skt. of MSA XIII.19a–d is, according to Lévi (MSABh, 88.9–10): [*mataṁ ca cittaṁ prakṛtiprabhāsvaraṁ sadā tad āgantukadośadūṣitaṁ* /] *na dharmatācittam ṛte 'nyacetasaḥ prabhāsvaratvaṁ prakṛtyā (text: prakṛtau) vidhīyate* //. "[The mind is taken to be luminous by nature; it is [only] tainted by adventitious faults.] A natural luminosity of (i.e., consisting of) another [dependent] mind *(cetas),*[a] different from the mind as true nature *(dharmatā)* is not taught."

a Vasubandhu explains (MSABh, 88.17): "of another mind whose defining characteristic is the dependent [nature]" *('nyasya cetasaḥ paratantralakṣaṇasya).*

967 Lit., **Śrīmālāparipṛcchā.*

968 A commentary on the *Guhyasamājatantra* with this name (Peking Tengyur no. 2650) is ascribed to Candrakīrti (Nakamura 1987:334); there is also a *Praddīpoddyotananāmaṭīkā* ascribed to Āryadeva and Bhavyakīrti (Peking Tengyur no. 2659). The quotation has not been identified.

969 RGVV, 40.11: *dhātus tisṛsv avasthāsu vidito nāmabhis tribhiḥ* //. The three states are: the impure state of ordinary persons, the partly pure and partly impure state of bodhisattvas, and the perfectly pure state of a tathāgata (see Takasaki 1966:231).

970 The four aspects are the dharmakāya, suchness, the buddha potential and the nonconceptual (see DRSM, 5.3–4).

971 That is, the terms *mahāyāna, uttara, tantra,* and *śāstra* (DRSM, 8.3–13.2).

972 That is, Gzhon nu dpal's explanation of the first three stanzas of the first chapter (DRSM, 13.2.–80.11), which are a summary of the *Ratnagotravibhāga.*

973 DRSM, 80.11–576.19.

974 The Sanskrit has *Ratnagotravibhāgo Mahāyānottaratantraśāstram* (RGVV, 1.1).

975 Technically, the explanations for those with sharp and average faculties are the commentary on the first two stanzas and the first part of the commentary on the third stanza of the root text. The root text is quoted (as in the entire commentary of Gzhon nu dpal), true to the Indian commentarial tradition, in sequential parts *(pratīkas),* and then commented upon. Since the commentary between two neighboring *pratīkas* can be very long, and even contain numerous quotations from later parts of the *Ratnagotravibhāga,* the quotations that are the next portion of root text or *vyākhyā* (i.e., the ones that constitute stanzas I.1–3 and their corresponding *vyākhyā*) are put in bold letters.

976 Skt. *vijñapti* has the original meaning of "making known" or "act of perception / cognition."

977 According to the Yogācāra ontology of the *Madhyāntavibhāga,* there are no physical sounds outside of the teacher's and the disciples' consciousness that carry audible sense data from ear to ear. Rather, the mental forms of sound that arise in the teacher when composing and explaining a treatise directly create a corresponding mental form of sound in the mindstream of the disciple.

978 NGMPP reel no. A 38/10, fol. 1b6–7 (cf. MAVṬ, 2.16–3.12): (line 6): *[i]dam idānī[ṁ...śās]trarūpam / śāstraṁ ki[ṁ...]* (line 7): *jñaptīnāṁ nā...sya śāsanāc chāstra....*

979 NGMPP reel no. A 38/10, fols. 1b8–2a1: (line 8): ...*śaprahāṇā*[a]*ya bhaved iti*[a] *nirantaradīrghavi...* (fol. 2a, line 1:) ...*stralakṣaṇam / etac ca dvayam api sarvasmin mahāyāne sarvasmiṁś ca tadvyākhyāne vidyate nānyatreti [/] ata etac chāstram / āha ca / yac chāsti ca kleśaripūn aśeṣān saṁtrāyate durgatito bhavāc ca / tac chāsano....*

a MAVṬ, 3.4 might tempt us to read *-yāpadyate* instead of *-ya bhavet iti,* but the manuscript is clear here.

980 Otherwise translated as "vajra point."

981 RGVV, 1.6: *vajropamasyādhigamārthasya padaṁ sthānam iti [vajrapadam /]*. Cf. Gzhon nu dpal's commentary on this passage (DRSM, 20.20–21).

982 I.e., the first of the ten strengths (lit. "...of what abides and what not," Skt. *sthānāsthānajñānabala*). See Rigzin 1993:134.

983 See Nakamura 1987:137.

984 The *'dul ba lung sde bzhi* and the *mdo sde lung sde bzhi*, according to the *Bod rgya tshig mdzod chen mo* (s.v.), are respectively: (1) *lung rnam 'byed*, (2) *lung gzhi*, (3) *lung zhu ba*, (4) *lung phran tshegs*, and: (1) *lung bar ma*, (2) *lung ring po*, (3) *lung dag ldan*, (4) *lung gcig las 'phros pa*.

985 According to the *Bod rgya tshig mdzod chen mo* (s.v.), the correct name of this confession ritual is *rgyun chags gsum pa*.

986 Lit., "the Self-arisen One," Skt. *svayaṁbhū*. The Tibetans read a genitive plural. Cf. DRSM, 507.6–7, who glosses *rang byung* as *sangs rgyas*.

987 RGVV, 90.12–13: *ataḥ kramo 'ntyo 'yam api svayaṁbhuvo 'bhiṣekalabdhā na maharṣayo vidur iti*. According to Takasaki (1966:335) the final *iti* shows that this stanza was quoted from some older material. It *(iti)* was not translated into Tibetan.

988 MSABh, 4.6–7: *vaikalyato virodhād anupāyatvāt tathāpy anupadeśāt / na śrāvakayānam idaṁ bhavati mahāyānadharmākhyaṁ //*.

989 The Sanskrit reads *parinirvāṇa*.

990 Tib. *sgrub pa'i thabs min no* has no equivalent in the Sanskrit.

991 Tib. *thabs ma yin par* would be syntactically better, and also supported by Skt. *anupāyena*.

992 According to the Sanskrit: "One cannot get milk from a horn into a vessel."

993 MSABh, 4.8–18: *vaikalyāt parārthopadeśasya na hi śrāvakayāne kaścit parārthaṁ upadiṣṭaḥ śrāvakānām ātmano nirvidvirāgavimuktimātropāyopadeśāt / na ca svārtha eva pareṣūpadiśyamānaḥ parārtho bhavitum arhati / virodhāt / svārthe hi paro niyujyamānaḥ svārtha eva prayujyate sa ātmana eva parinirvāṇārthaprayukto 'nuttarāṁ samyaksaṁbodhim abhisaṁbhotsyata iti viruddham etat / na ca śrāvakayānenaiva cirakālaṁ bodhau ghaṭamāno buddho bhavitum arhati / anupāyatvāt / anupāyo hi śrāvakayānaṁ buddhatvasya na cānupāyena ciram api prayujyamānaḥ prārthitam arthaṁ prāpnoti / śṛṅgād iva dugdhaṁ na bhastrāyāḥ*[a] */ athānyathāpy atropadiṣṭaṁ yathā bodhisattvena prayoktavyaṁ / tathāpy anupadeśān na śrāvakayānam eva*[b] *mahāyānaṁ bhavitum arhati / na hi sa tādṛśa upadeśa etasminn upalabhyate / viruddham eva cānyonyaṁ śrāvakayānaṁ mahāyānaṁ cety anyonyavirodhe ślokaḥ /*.

a Lévi reads *bhastrayā*.

b See Bhattacharya 2001:7.

994 MSABh, 4.19–20: *āśayasyopadeśasya prayogasya virodhataḥ / upastambhasya kālasya yat hīnaṁ hīnam eva tat //*.

995 The Sanskrit has *parinirvāṇa*.

996 Tib. *chung ba*, Skt. *parītta*.

997 According to the Sanskrit: "In a shorter time..."

998 MSABh, 4.21–25: *kathaṁ viruddhaṁ / pañcabhir virodhaiḥ / āśayopadeśaprayoga upastambhakālavirodhaiḥ / śrāvakayāne hy ātmaparinirvāṇāyaivāśayas tadartham evopadeśas tadartham eva prayogaḥ parīttaś ca puṇyajñānasaṁbhārasaṁgṛhīta upastambhaḥ kālena cālpena tadarthaprāptir yāvat tribhir api janmabhiḥ / mahāyāne tu sarvaṁ viparyayeṇa / tasmād anyonyavirodhād yad yānaṁ hīnaṁ hīnam eva tat / na tan mahāyānaṁ bhavitum arhati /*.

999 See MSA I.10. Gzhon nu dpal forgot to enumerate the second point, *bstan pa*. But in the quotation of MSA I.10 above the list of five points is given correctly.

1000 Construed with the instrumental in Sanskrit and Tibetan.

1001 I.e., the path of accumulation.

1002 That is, the entire path, starting from the path of accumulation up to the end of the path of meditation.

1003 Lit., "...and so forth," which seems to be stylistically acceptable in Tibetan.

1004 PRGSG, 14.3–6: *kiṁ kāraṇaṁ ayu pravucyate bodhiyāno yatrāruhitva sa nivāpayi sarvasattvān / ākāśatulya ayu yānu mahāvimāno sukhasaukhyakṣemam abhiprāpuṇi yānaśreṣṭḥo //.*

1005 Skt. Madhyamaka, Tib. *dbu ma.* But three lines below, the Tibetan reads *dbu ma pa,* which fits the context better.

1006 The Tibetan does not have an equivalent for *vyākhyāyate.*

1007 According to the Sanskrit: "In this regard, the three[fold] way of *pāramitā* is explained...."

1008 TRĀ, 14.5–8 (NGMPP reel no. B 22/24, fol. 9a1–3): *tatra trīṇi yānāni / śrāvakayānaṁ / pratyekayānaṁ mahāyānaṁ ceti // sthitayaś catasraḥ / vaibhāṣikasau* [a]*trāntikayogācāramadhyamakabhedena // tatra vaibhāṣikasthityā śrāvakayānaṁ / pratyekayānañ ca vyākhyāyate // mahāyānañ ca dvividham / pāramitānayo mantranayaś ceti / tatra yaḥ*[b] *pāramitanayaḥ sau*[c]*trāntikayogācāramadhymakasthityā vyākhyāyate //.*

a The manuscript reads *-śrau-* instead of *-sau-.*

b The manuscript reads *yā* instead of *yaḥ.* The Tibetan transliteration suggests *trayaḥ.*

c The manuscript reads *śru-* instead of *sau-.*

1009 Skt. *caiko 'py* has no equivalent in the Tibetan.

1010 RĀ, 160.17–20: *yāvac caiko 'py amuktaḥ syāt sattvaḥ kaścid iha kvacid / tāvat tadartham tiṣṭheyaṁ bodhiṁ prāpyāpi anuttarām //.*

1011 RĀ, 162.1–4: *yad evaṁ vadataḥ puṇyaṁ yadi tan mūrtimad bhavet / gaṅgāyāḥ sikatākhyeṣu na māyāı lokadhātuṣu //.*

1012 The Tibetans did not translate *saṁjñeyaṁ;* in addition, they inserted *'dod* (demanded by the sense?).

1013 RĀ, 162.5–8: *uktam etad bhagavatā hetur apy atra dṛśyate / sattvadhātor ameyasya hitā saṁjñeyam īdṛśī //.*

1014 Skt. *udāgama-* for *samudāgama-* (cf. Tib. *yang dag 'grub*).

1015 MSABh, 171.10–13: *ālambanamahatvaṁ ca pratipatter dvayos tathā / jñānasya vīryārambhasya upāye kauśalasya ca // udāgamamahatvaṁ ca mahatvaṁ buddhakarmaṇaḥ / etan mahatvayogād dhi mahāyānaṁ nirucyate //.*

1016 The obstacles to the first five *pāramitās* can only be removed by *prajñā,* whose focus is the emptiness of everything. It is the importance and greatness of this focus that Gzhon nu dpal is referring to.

1017 RGVV, 117.4: [a]*prajñā śreṣṭhā*[a] *śrutaṁ cāsyā*[b] *mūlaṁ tasmāc chrutaṁ param.*

a According to A (26a6); B (54b2) is not clear. Johnston reads *śreṣṭhā prajñā* (see also Schmithausen 1971:175).

b According to A (26a6) and B (54b2).

1018 According to the Sanskrit: "does not approach."

1019 RGVV, 35.13–14: *chittvā snehaṁ prajñayātmany aśeṣaṁ sattvasnehān naiti śāntiṁ kṛpāvān /.*

1020 RGVV, 14.1: *[ye samyak pratividhya] sarvajagato nairātmyakoṭiṁ śivāṁ....*

1021 In the context of the *Ratnāvalī,* translated as "realm of sentient beings" (see above).

1022 RGVV, 88.16–17: *hetvanantyāt*[a] *sattvadhātvakṣayatvāt / kāruṇyarddhi*[b]*jñānasampattiyogāt /.*

a B (44b6) reads *hetvātyantyāt;* A is not available.

b B (44b6) reads *kāruṇyar(?)di-;* A is not available.

1023 This means seeing in all sentient beings the supreme qualities of their buddha potential.

1024 AA, 8.16: *sarvasattvāgratā cittaprahāṇādhigamatraye....*
1025 RGVV, 98.10: *buddhatvaṁ sarvasattve vimalaguṇanidhau*[a] *nirviśiṣṭaṁ vilokya.*
a B (49b6) reads *-nidhi* against the meter. The commentary (RGV IV.10cd) has *vimalaguṇanidhi-* qualifying *"sentient beings"* and probably read *-nidhau* (see Schmithausen 1971:170).
1026 RGVV, 98.11: *kleśajñeyābhrajālaṁ vidhamati karuṇā vāyubhūtā jinānām.*
1027 RGVV, 25.4: *bodhyaṁ bodhis....*
1028 RGVV, 66.16–17 (RGV I.129): *sattvadhātor asaṁbaddha*[a] *kleśakośeṣv anādiṣu / cittaprakṛtivaimalyam anādimad*[b] *udāhṛtam //.*
a According to A (16b6) and B (23a4); Johnston wrongly reads *asaṁbaddhaṁ* (see also Schmithausen 1971:155).
b A (16b6) reads *-mahad* instead of *-mad.*
1029 RGVV, 53.11: *jagaccharaṇyo 'naparāntakoṭitaḥ.*
1030 The last chapter (18) is listed separately in the Derge Kangyur as an appendix to the *Guhyasamājatantra* (see Tohōku 442 and 443). In the edition prepared by Bhattacharya (1967), the eighteenth chapter (from which the quoted *pāda*s are taken) is part of the tantra itself.
1031 In the Sanskrit, *pāda*s 34b and 34c are in reverse order, probably in order to better convey the sense: "the skillful means of [attaining] it (i.e., the fruit)." *(tadupāya-).* The Tibetan has no equivalent for *tad-*.
1032 GST, 153.6–9: *prabandhaṁ tantram ākhyātaṁ tat prabandhaṁ tridhā bhavet / ādhāraḥ prakṛtiś caiva asaṁhāryaprabhedataḥ // prakṛtiś cākṛter hetur asaṁhāryaṁ phalaṁ tathā / ādhāras tadupāyaś ca tribhis tantrārthasaṁgrahaḥ //.*
1033 RGVV, 40.11: *dhātus tisṛṣv avasthāsu nirdiṣṭo*[a] *nāmabhis tribhiḥ.*
a According to B (23a4); A is not available. Johnston wrongly reads *vidito.* See also Schmithausen 1971:148.
1034 Peking Kangyur (no. 113), *rgyud, nya,* fol. 169a7–b1.
1035 Tib. *zhes pa'o* could indicate the end of a quotation. See DRSM, 80.8–11, however, where a summary of a passage from RGVV I.2 (but not the passage itself) is marked by *zhes bya ba.*
1036 Both texts read *uta* (DRSM, 12.18).
1037 So translated above in the context of breaking out of the prison of saṁsāra.
1038 The Sanskrit has instead the invocation "Oṁ, homage to the venerable Vajrasattva" (RGVV, 1.2: *oṁ namaḥ śrī*[a] *vajrasattvāya*).
a According to B (1b1); Johnston reads *śro-* instead of *śrī-*.
1039 The commentary for those with average faculties is based on the first three stanzas of the root text and the *Ratnagotravibhāgavyākhyā* on the first two stanzas of the treatise. The *vyākhyā* on the third stanza is the beginning of the extensive commentary for those with dull faculties.
1040 The three introductory stanzas of the *Ratnagotravibhāga* show the influence of the five rules laid out in Maitreya's *upadeśa.* The first stanza introduces the seven main topics (vajra points) of the *Ratnagotravibhāga.* The second stanza justifies them doctrinally on the basis of the *Dhāraṇīśvararājasūtra* (in the Tibetan tradition, the *'Phags pa de bzhin gshegs pa'i snying rje chen po nges par bstan pa zhes bya ba theg pa chen po'i mdo,* Peking Kangyur no. 814). The third stanza explains their sequence.
1041 Tib. *Rje btsun gyi man ngag thob pa.*
1042 These first three lines are nearly identical with the opening stanza of the *Vyākhyāyukti*, which is as follows: */ gang dag bdag pas blo chung ba / / mdo rnams 'chad 'dod de dag la / / de la phan par bya ba'i phyir / / man ngag cung zad bstan par bya /* (Peking Tengyur 5562, *sems tsam,* vol. *si,* fol. 32a2). Apart from a few minor

variant readings, Gzhon nu dpal's quote differs from this only in that it lacks the third line *(de la phan par bya ba'i phyir)*.

1043 The last three *pādas* of this quotation are identical with the last three *pādas* of the stanza quoted at the beginning of the *Vyākhyāyukti* (Peking Tengyur 5562, *sems tsam*, vol. *si*, fol. 33b5–6). The corresponding Sanskrit is quoted in Haribhadra's *Abhisamayālaṁkārāloka* (15.24–25): *prayojanaṁ sapiṇḍārthaṁ padārthaḥ sānusaṁdhikaḥ / sacodyaparihāraś ca vācyaḥ sūtrārthavādibhiḥ //.*

1044 I.e., the four *anubandhas* (Tib. *dgos 'brel*, lit. "aim and [its] connection [with the text]") which are discussed at the beginning of Haribhadra's *Abhisamayālaṁkārāloka* (2.3–5): (1) *sambandha* (connection); (2) *abhidheya* (subject matter); (3) *prayojana* (aim); (4) *prayojanaprayojana* (aim of the aim, or ultimate aim).

1045 RGVV, 1.2–3: *buddhaś ca dharmaś ca gaṇaś ca dhātur bodhir guṇāḥ karma ca [bau]*[a] *ddham antyam*[b] */.*

a In B (1b1) one *akṣara* has broken away; A is not available. The gap is filled in accordance with Johnston.

b B (1b1) reads *acintyam* instead of *antyam* (correction according to Johnston); A is not available.

1046 In other words, the aim of the teaching of a buddha nature does not refer to the explanation of the motive of such a teaching, but rather to the realization of one's buddha nature.

1047 RGV I.1cd: "The body of this entire [treatise] is, in short, [all] seven vajra points."

1048 The Tibetan word *dbye ba* can also mean "to divide" or "open," so that it is possible to compare the meaning of buddha nature to a vajra.

1049 Cf. the explanation of the buddha element further down (DRSM, 23.16–24.5).

1050 See Schmithausen 1971:133–34.

1051 RGVV, 7.1–4: *buddhād dharmo dharmataś cāryasaṁghaḥ / saṁghe garbho jñānadhātvāptiniṣṭhaḥ / tajjñānāptiś cāgrabodhir balādyair dharmair yuktā sarvasattvārthakṛdbhiḥ //.*

1052 Only the prostitute's direct speech announcing her commitment is a direct quote from the sūtra, the rest being a short summary.

1053 Cf. the *Mañjuśrīvikrīḍitasūtra* in the Peking Kangyur (no. 764, *mdo sna tshogs*, vol. *ku*, fol. 247b6) for more details.

1054 Tib. Gser mchog 'od dpal. At the beginning of the sūtra (Ibid., fol. 246b7–8) it is said that she went to a grove with the son of a merchant on a beautifully ornamented chariot pulled by four horses. Mañjuśrī saw them, and wishing to convert them, waited along the way for the chariot (Ibid., fol. 247a5–b2).

1055 Cf. the sūtra in the Peking Kangyur (Ibid., vol. *ku*, fol. 248b6) "Sister, generate *bodhicitta*, and I will give you these clothes" *(srin mo khyod byang chub tu sems bskyed cig dang / ngas khyed la gos 'di sbyin no).*

1056 Tib. *chos la snang ba*, Skt. **dharmāloka* (LC s.v.); *āloka* connotes "readiness to meditate on the doctrine" (BHSD, s.v.).

1057 Tib. *bslab pa'i gzhi*, Skt. *śikṣāpada* (see BHSD, s.v.).

1058 The Tibetan has only *sems can* for Skt. *sattvadhātu.*

1059 RGVV, 40.7–8: *aśuddho 'śuddhaśuddho 'tha*[a] *suviśuddho yathākramam / sattvadhātur iti prokto bodhisattvas tathāgataḥ //.*

a B (23a4) omits *'tha.*

My translation follows Schmithausen (1971:148).

1060 RGVV, 20.4–5: *jagaccharaṇam ekāntaṁ (?)*[a] *buddhatvaṁ pāramārthikam / muner dharmaśarīratvāt tanniṣṭhatvād gaṇasya ca //.*

a Johnston reads *ekatra*, which does not make sense. Folio 11b of manuscript B is barely readable, while manuscript A is not available, so that the correct reading could well have been *ekāntaṁ* (see also Schmithausen 1971:140).

1061 Lit., "has settled in it" *(tanniṣṭhatvād…)*.

1062 RGVV, 18.12–13: *tyājyatvān moṣadharmatvād abhāvāt sabhayatvataḥ / dharmo dvi*[a]*dhārya*[b] *saṅghaś ca nātyantaṁ śaraṇaṁ param //.*

a B (11a3) reads *vi;* A is not available.

b B (11a4) reads *yā;* A is not available.

1063 RGVV, 35.18: *buddhadhātuḥ sa cen na syān nirvid duḥkhe 'pi no bhavet / .*

1064 Eckel (1987:71) translates Tib. *rtogs* here as "cognition." He refers to the subcommentary *(Satyadvayavibhāgapañjikā)*, which declares that no inferential valid cognition, such as fire deduced from smoke, is considered to be ultimate; what is meant here, rather, are arguments that prove the nonexistence of such things as fire (Eckel 1987:114).

1065 The quote is from Jñānagarbha's commentary on the first one and a half *pāda*s of the fourth stanza of the *Satyadvayavibhāga:* "Since it cannot be contradicted, reason is ultimate." This is the beginning of the paragraph on the expressible ultimate *(paryāyaparamārtha)*. The example "just as a direct perception" is extremely cryptic. Eckel (1987:115) notes, on the basis of the *Satyadvayavibhāgapañjikā*, that the term *pratyakṣa*, like the term *measure*, can refer both to the cognition that directly perceives an object and to the object itself. See also Schmithausen (1972:160), who observes that the definition of *pratyakṣa* given in AS, 105.8f *(pratyakṣaṁ svasatprakāśābhrānto 'rthaḥ)* requires that the latter be translated as an "object that is 'before the eyes' or directly perceived."

1066 MMK XV.2ab.

1067 Skt. *-bhāvaś…*

1068 According to the Tibetan: "That which is an own-being is not created."

1069 PP, 260.3–8: *svabhāvaḥ kṛtako nāma bhaviṣyati punaḥ kathaṁ /* (XV.2ab) *kṛtakaś ca svabhāvaś ceti parasparaviruddhatvād asaṁgatārtham eva tat // iha hi svo bhāvaḥ svabhāva iti vyutpatter yaḥ kṛtakaḥ padārthaḥ sa loke naiva svabhāva iti vyapadiśyate tad yathā apām auṣṇyaṁ dhātuvādi*[a]*prayatnaniṣpāditaḥ karketanādīnāṁ padmarāgādibhāvaś ca / yas tv akṛtakaḥ sa svabhāvas tad yathā agner auṣṇyaṁ jātānāṁ padmarāgādīnāṁ padmarāgādisvabhāvaś ca / sa hi teṣāṁ padārthāntarasaṁparkājanitatvāt svabhāva ity ucyate //.*

a La Vallée Poussin reads *dhātupiśāca-*, which I have corrected to *dhātuvādi-* in accordance with the Tibetan (see MVY 3754).

It is a clever move to end the discourse on an intellectually realized emptiness with a quote from Candrakīrti's commentary on MMK XV.2ab, since this passage leaves open the possibility of an own-being, as long as the own-being is not created. And this is what Gzhon nu dpal claims the buddha element to be: not created in the sense of having arisen through artificial causes and conditions. Thus the Madhyamaka reasonings of the second dharmacakra are restricted to what is created, namely the outer adventitious stains, and so do not apply to the buddha element. The fact that a little further down even the "hotness of fire" is not accepted as an own-being is not further discussed. That no such own-being is accepted by Candrakīrti can, however, be indirectly explained by the limited scope of the second dharmacakra (see the following paragraph).

1070 Tib. *snying po'i stong pa nyid.* As will become clear in the remaining part of this paragraph, this compound here cannot mean "emptiness of buddha nature," as if buddha nature were simply empty.

1071 This *pāda* is taken from the second of the nine illustrations of how the buddha element is covered with defilements. In the second example, the buddha element is compared to honey, and the defilements with bees surrounding the honey

(RGV I.105 (J I.103)). The Sanskrit has no equivalent for *rig* in I.106b (J I.104b). Gzhon nu dpal is supported by the Derge edition, which stands over against *rigs* in Narthang and Peking (see Nakamura 1967:119).

1072 See PP, 3.11–12 for a similar definition of the subject matter: …*[a]nirodhādyaṣṭaviśeṣaṇaviśiṣṭaḥ pratītyasamutpādaḥ śāstrābhidheyārthaḥ /.*

1073 The quoted passage is part of a final summary in the colophon of the *Prajñāpradīpa* (Peking Tengyur no. 5253, *dbu ma*, vol. *tsha*, fol. 325a7–b2).

1074 Cf. Lindtner (1987:202–3), who edited and translated the *Bodhicittavivaraṇa*. He identified the Sanskrit of this stanza in Maitrīpa's *Pañcākāra* (see PĀ, 132.4–5 and NGMPP reel no. B 22/24, fol. 28a1: *guḍe madhuratā cāgner uṣṇatvaṁ prakṛtir*[a] *yathā / śūnyatā sarvadharmāṇāṁ tathā prakṛtir iṣyate //).*

a The ms. reads *prati* instead of *prakṛtir*, which does not make any sense.

1075 Of particular interest is Zhva dmar Chos grags ye shes's (1453–1524) commentary on the *Bodhicittavivaraṇa*, which he composed on the basis of Gzhon nu dpal's explanations of Smṛtijñānakīrti's *Bodhicittavivaraṇaṭīkā*.[a] The commentary on stanza 57 is as follows: "In the same way as truly all sugar[-based] substances are equivalent in view of their sweetness and the nature/own-being of [all] fire is in partial concordance because of its hotness, the nature/own-being of all phenomena (or entities) is emptiness. It is but proper that all Buddhist tenets should claim this." (*bu ram gyi rdzas mtha' dag kyang mngar bar mtshungs pa dang / me'i rang bzhin tsha bar cha mthun pa yin pa bzhin / de bzhin du dngos po'i chos rnams thams cad kyi rang bzhin stong pa nyid du sangs rgyas pa'i grub mtha' smra ba thams cad kyis 'dod par rigs so.* See "Byang chub sems 'grel gyi rnam par bshad pa tshig don gsal ba zhes bya ba bzhugs so," 99.7–10.)

a See Chos grags ye shes's colophon on p. 123.17–21.

1076 Read *yul gyi rnam pa* instead of *yul gyis rnam pa*?

1077 Tib. *zad par* is short for *zad par gyi skye mched*, Skt. *kṛtsnāyatana* (see LC, s.v.). For the meaning of *kṛtsnāyatana*, see BHSD, s.v.

1078 See Lindtner 1987:198–99.

1079 Lindtner (Ibid.) translates: "In brief: buddhas do not see [what cannot] be seen *(adṛṣṭa)*…"

1080 That this is the way Gzhon nu dpal understands the stanza is clear from Zhva dmar Chos grags ye shes's commentary (*op. cit.*, 123.17–21): "In short, in terms of recognition *(vijñapti)*, buddhas have seen neither past nor present, and in the future they will not see either. If one thinks: 'How is it that the omniscient does not see?,' [the answer is as follows:] Since ultimately [reality] has the own-being of being without an own-being, there is no object to be seen; how [can such an object then] be seen [by the Buddha]? This is the way the teacher himself spoke of *nonseeing.*" (*mdor na / sangs rgyas rnams kyis ni rnam rig gi ngo bor 'das pa dang da lta ba [na?] gzigs par ma gyur la / ma 'ongs pa na gzigs par mi 'gyur ba nyid do / thams cad mkhyen pas ci ste ma gzigs snyam na / don dam par rang bzhin med pa'i ngo bo'i rang bzhin can yin pas / gzigs pa'i yul med pa de ji lta bur na gzigs par 'gyur zhes ston pa nyid kyis ma gzigs par bka' stsal to /*, Zhva dmar Chos grags ye shes: *op. cit.*, 92.15–19.)

1081 Zhva dmar Chos grags ye shes (*op. cit.*, 92.19–93.5) explains: "If somebody says: 'As for not contradicting such canonical scriptures [on not seeing], we explain that [when the Buddha taught this he] was thinking of the perfect [nature], the ultimate absence of an own-being *(paramārthaniḥsvabhāvatā)*[a]'; [we reply]: You followers of *cittamātra* take an entity to be what is called perfect [nature] [or] self-realization, for you claim [this entity] to be, in view of its existence, the defining characteristic of the ultimate. This [is the same as] clinging to the extreme of [taking] the nonconceptual [state] to be something possessing mental fabrications.

Where a fabricated concept has appeared, how can there be a realization of ultimate nonconceptual emptiness, when such a nonconceptual [state] is the emptiness free of mental fabrication?" *(de 'dra ba'i lung dang mi 'gal ba ni nged cag yongs su grub pa don dam ngo bo nyid med pa la dgongs par 'chad do / zhe na / sems tsam pa khyed kyis yongs grub dang so so rang gi rig pa zhes brjod pa de nyid dngos po zhes bya ste / yod pas don dam pa'i mtshan nyid du 'dod pas so / / de ni rnam par mi rtog pa spros pa dang bcas pa'i mthar 'dzin pa yin la / de 'dra'i rnam rtog med pa spros bral stong pa nyid yin pa'i tshe / gang du spros pa'i rnam rtog snang bar gyur pa der ni don dam pa rnam par mi rtog pa'i stong nyid rtogs pa ga la yod /.)*

a In the *Saṁdhinirmocanasūtra* the ultimate absence of an own-being is taken to derive from the fact that everything lacks a true self, which is considered to be an all-pervasive positive quality. A similar notion is associated with the natural emptiness *(prakṛtiśūnyatā)* propounded by the Yogācāra (see Mathes 2000:215–17).

1082 Lindtner (1987:198) identified the Sanskrit of stanza 45: *na bodhyabodhakākāraṁ cittaṁ dṛṣṭaṁ tathāgataiḥ / yatra boddhā ca bodhyaṁ ca tatra bodhir na vidyate //* (BV 45).

Zhva dmar Chos grags ye shes (*op. cit.*, 93.5–11) explains: "One may ask: 'If this is the case, does the fruit of enlightenment itself not exist then?' A mind that manifests the aspects of clinging to the characteristic signs of an enlightenment to be realized, and [to the characteristic signs] of a [subject] seeking to realize [it], is not seen by the tathāgatas and the great bodhisattvas, as they are called on the basis of this term (i.e. enlightenment). Thus they find an enlightenment that has the defining characteristics of space; otherwise—wherever there is an obstinate clinging to characteristic signs such that a bodhisattva [wrongly conceptualizes] realization and object of realization, there is no attainment of enlightenment, because nonconceptual wisdom [and] equanimity are not realized." *(de lta na byang chub kyi 'bras bu yang med dam zhe na / rtogs bya byang chub dang / rtogs byed de don du gnyer ba'i mtshan 'dzin gyi rnam pa'i sems / de bzhin gzhegs pa dang de'i sgras brjod pa'i byang chub sems dpa' chen po rnams kyis ma gzigs pas / nam mkha'i mtshan nyid can gyi byang chub brnyes kyi / gang na byang chub sems dpa' rtogs bya rtogs byed la mtshan 'dzin mngon zhen du byed pa yod pa der ni / byang chub 'thob pa yod pa ma yin te / rnam par mi rtog pa'i ye shes mnyam pa nyid ma rtogs pa'i phyir ro //.)*

1083 Lindtner (1987:198) identified the Sanskrit of stanza 46: *alakṣaṇam anutpādam asaṁsthitam avāṅmayam / ākāśaṁ bodhicittaṁ ca bodhir advayalakṣaṇā //* (BV 46).

Zhva dmar Chos grags ye shes (*op. cit.*, 94.5–14) explains: "[In the *Guhyasamājatantra* it has been said:] 'One's own mind has never arisen since the beginning, [and] it has the nature/own-being of emptiness.' Even though the meaning of our own Madhyamaka tradition, which teaches this, has been taught in detail, [it is repeated here]. There are no defining characteristics that define reality. Since [reality] neither exists nor does not exist, it does not arise. It does not [arise], for [in the case of] existence it would have arisen already; and [in the case of] nonexistence it could not in a proper sense arise. Even though it is expressed in words on the path of speech, it is free from [any] defining traits (Lat. *definiens*). Suitable examples are space, the *bodhicitta* of nonconceptual wisdom, and enlightenment that perfectly realizes in a nonmistaken way all phenomena. [These three] possess the defining characteristic of nonduality. This means that even though space exists conventionally, it is not apprehended ultimately. Likewise, enlightenment exists on the level of apparent [truth], but it does not do so on the ultimate [level]. Non-conceptual *bodhicitta*, too, is talked about on a conventional [level of truth], but if analyzed, [it is found to be] without an own-being. Therefore, their defining characteristics are not different." *(rang sems gdod nas ma skyes pa / stong pa nyid kyi rang bzhin no / / zhes gsungs pa'i rang lugs kyi dbu ma'i don rgya cher bstan pa yang / de kho na nyid mtshon par byed pa'i mtshan nyid med cing / yod pa dang med pa ma yin pa'i phyir skye ba med de / yod gyur skyes zin pa dang / med pa skyer mi rung bas ma yin la ngagi lam nas tshig brjod kyang mtshon pa dang bral ba de ni / dper 'os pa nam mkha' dang / rnam mi rtog pa'i ye shes byang chub kyi sems dang ni / chos thams cad phyin ci ma log par mngon par rtogs pa'i byang chub rnams gnyis su med pa'i mtshan nyid can te / de'i don ni / nam mkha' ni tha snyad du yod kyang / don du mi dmigs pa ltar / byang chub kyang kun rdzob tu yod kyi don dam par med la / rnam par mi rtog pa'i byang chub kyi sems kyang tha snyad du brjod kyi dpyad na rang bzhin med pas / de'i phyir de dag gi mtshan nyid tha dad pa ma yin no //.)*

1084 Cf. Vasubandhu's commentary (MAVBh, 23.23–24.2): "Because it is the cause of the qualities of the noble ones, it is the dharmadhātu (lit. 'sphere of qualities'). Because[, that is,] the qualities of the noble ones arise having it as their focus. Cause has here the meaning of sphere." *āryadharmahetutvād dharmdhātuḥ / āryadharmāṇāṁ*[a] *tadālambanaprabhavatvāt / hetvartho hy atra dhātvarthaḥ /*.

a Nagao reads *-ān*.

1085 MAVBh, 23.14–15 and 18–19: *tathatā bhūtakoṭiś cānimittaṁ paramārthatā / dharmadhātuś ca paryāyāḥ śūnyatāyāḥ samāsataḥ //* (I.14) *ananyathāviparyāsatannirodhāryagocaraiḥ / hetutvāc cāryadharmāṇāṁ paryāyārtho yathākramam //* (I.15).

1086 Tib. *yid la byed pa* may, in mahāmudrā instructions, have the negative connotation of too much thinking, worrying, or a too intellectual approach to reality (Thrangu Rinpoche).

1087 The use of the imperative is justified by the imperative *ltos shig* at the end of the pith-instruction.

1088 RGV I.13: "I bow before those who see that, in view of the natural luminosity of this mind, defilements lack an own-being, and, as a consequence, have completely realized the extreme limit of the selflessness of all sentient beings and the world as quiescent, who see that buddhahood is all pervading, whose intellect is unobstructed, and whose vision of wisdom embraces the purity and infinitude of sentient beings." (See DRSM, 141.10–14. The Sanskrit in Johnston's edition (RGVV, 14.1–4) is as follows: *ye samyak pratividhya sarvajagato nairātmyakoṭiṁ śivāṁ taccittaprakṛtiprabhāsvaratayā kleśāsvabhāvekṣaṇāt / sarvatrānugatām anāvṛtadhiyaḥ paśyanti saṁbu*[a]*ddhatāṁ tebhyaḥ sattvaviśuddhyanantaviṣayajñānekṣaṇebhyo namaḥ //*.)

a B (9a4) reads *ba*.

1089 Cf. *Tattvāvatārākhyasakalasugatavācasaṁkṣiptavyākhyāprakaraṇa* (Peking Tengyur no. 4532).

1090 In the Bka' brgyud traditions the mahāmudrā teachings are called the "path of liberation" *(grol lam)*, and the Six Dharma [Practices] of Naropa the "path of skillful means" *(thabs lam)*.

1091 Tib. *blo byas stong pa bskal par bsgoms gyur kyang* (translation according to Thrangu Rinpoche).

1092 This quotation has not been identified.

1093 The translation of this quotation is according to the explanations of Thrangu Rinpoche. The quoted passage has not been identified.

1094 This passage is from the paragraph on the *tathāgatagarbha* in the third chapter (see Wayman 1974:96). It is also contained in RGVV II.1 (see RGVV, 79.11–13: *yo bhagavan sarvakleśakośakoṭigūḍhe tathāgatagarbhe niṣkāṅkṣaḥ sarvakleśakośavi*[a]*-nirmukte*[b] *tathāgatadharmakāye 'pi sa*[c] *niṣkāṅkṣa[ḥ]*).

a B (41a5) omits *-vi-*.

b Johnston reads *-muktes*.

c B (41a5) omits *sa*.

1095 Gzhon nu dpal reads *pramarta*, which could have been, as a wrong spelling of *pramarda* or *pramardana*, translated as *sangs pas na (awaking from sleep* in the sense of crushing it *(pra-mṛd))*. In this case the second *gnyid sangs* would stand for *prabuddha-* (see the *Bod skad dang legs sbyar gi tshig mdzod chen mo*, s.v., which has for *gnyid sad pa* Skt. *prabuddha*). Ishikawa (1990:5–6) proposes *pramattabuddhapuruṣavat* and inserts *buddha* after *mohanidrā*.

1096 See Mishra (1987:200), who reads *buddhaḥ, vibuddhapadmavat*.

1097 Tib. *kha bye zhing rgyas pa*.

1098 Peking Kangyur no. 904, *mdo sde, vu*, fols. 10b5–12a1.

1099 The Peking Kangyur reads *spyod lam* instead of *smon lam*.

1100 See previous footnote.

1101 I.e., the svābhāvikakāya (see below).

1102 Tib. *kun tu spyod pa*, Skt. *samudācara*? (See BHSD s.v.)

1103 Tib. *cho ga*.

1104 A construction parallel with the explanation of the metaphorical Buddha. In the same way as a buddha propounds the Dharma without effort, the statue of the Buddha necessarily conveys some portion of the teaching to the worshipper.

1105 Ārya Vimuktisena explains in his commentary *(Abhisamayālaṁkāravṛtti)* on AA VII.1: "Because the *pāramitā* of giving and so forth are possessed by the *prajñāpāramitā*, [and all undefiled dharmas] all the way up to the eighty excellent signs are possessed by it, this nondual wisdom, the one-moment comprehension *(ekakṣaṇikābhisamaya)* itself includes in its comprehension all virtuous qualities" (see Makransky 1997:189). For Ārya Vimuktisena *ekakṣaṇikābhisamaya* means that the Buddha comprehends in every moment all phenomena. Haribhadra understood it to refer also to the moment prior to enlightenment (*op. cit.*, 188).

1106 Which happens, according to RGVV I.2, on the eighth level: "...while staying on the eighth bodhisattva level, [the future Buddha] gained control over all phenomena." (RGVV, 3.21–4.1: ... *'ṣṭamyāṁ bodhisattvabhūmau vartamānaḥ sarvadharmavaśitāprāpto bhavati /*[a].)

a According to B 2b6; Johnston omits the *daṇḍa*.

1107 I.e., the *dharmāyatana*.

1108 Tib. *tshe*, Skt. *janman* (Negi: *Bod skad dang legs sbyar gyi tshig mdzod chen mo*, vol. 3, s.v.), that is, the circumstances of existence or life (see BHSD, s.v.).

1109 Tib. *'byung 'gyur*.

1110 See VY, 21.5–8. *Chos lugs* is explained in VY, 22.3 as: "laws of the country and the law of the family" *(yul chos dang rigs chos)*.

1111 This is a further attempt to prepare the reader for the hermeneutic strategy of explaining why the potential of ordinary persons is only metaphorically called a buddha.

1112 RGVV, 1.4–5: *kṛtsnasya śāstrasya śārīram etat / samāsato vajrapadāni sapta //*.

1113 Tib. *'di dag* translates Skt. *eṣāṁ*. The entire stanza is as follows: "These [seven vajra points] should be understood, each together with its own defining characteristics, [as explained] in sequential order in the *Dhāraṇīśvararājasūtra*—The [first] three in the introductory chapter and the [remaining] four in the [chapters on] the 'Distinguishing the Qualities of a Bodhisattva' and on the '[Distinguishing the Qualities of a] Buddha.'" (RGVV, 3.11–14: *svalakṣaṇenānugatāni caiṣāṁ yathākramaṁ dhāraṇirājasūtre / nidānata*[a]*s trīṇi padāni vidyāc catvāri dhīmajji*[b]*-nadharmabhedāt //*).

a B (2b3) omits *ta*; A is not available.

b The syllable *-jji-* is illegible in B (2b4); A is not available.

1114 This portion of the *Ratnagotravibhāgavyākhyā* is not quoted by Gzhon nu dpal in the usual way, but only partly woven into his running commentary.

1115 Otherwise translated as "vajra point."

1116 RGVV, 1.6–2.3: *vajropamasyādhigamārthasya padaṁ sthānam iti vajrapadam / tatra śruta*[a] *cintāmayajñānaduṣprative[dhatvād ana]*[b] *bhilāpyasvabhāvaḥ pratyātmavedanīyo 'rtho vajravad veditavyaḥ / yāny akṣarāṇi tam artham anu*[c] *vadanti tatprāptyanukūlamārgābhidyotanatas tāni tatpratiṣṭhābhūtatvāt padam ity ucyante /] iti duṣprativedhārthena pratiṣṭhārthena ca vajrapadatvam arthavyañjanayor anugantavyam / tatra katamo 'rthaḥ katamad vyañjanam / artha ucyate /* [d] *saptaprakāro 'dhigamārtho yad uta buddhārthaḥ dharmārthaḥ*[e] *saṅghārtho dhātvartho bodhyartho guṇārthaḥ karmārthaś ca / ayam ucyate 'rthaḥ / yair akṣarair eṣa saptaprakāro 'dhigamārthaḥ*[f] *sūcyate prakāśyate /* [g] *idam ucyate vyañjanam / sa caiva*[h] *vajrapadanirdeśo vistareṇa yathāsūtram anugantavyaḥ.* This part of the *vyākhyā* is explained in DRSM, 20.19–23.4.

a Johnston wrongly reads *śruti-* (cf. B1b2); A is not available.

b In B (1b2) four *akṣaras* are missing; A is not available. The gap is therefore filled in with the grammatically more correct *-dhatvād ana-* (Johnston proposes: *-dhād ana-*). Cf. also Schmithausen 1971:131.

c Johnston wrongly reads *abhi-* instead of *anu-* (cf. B1b2). Indeed, *anu-vad*, "to tell," "to say," or "to narrate," fits the context much better here.

d Johnston deletes the *daṇḍa* that is clearly visible in B (1b4).

e B (1b5) has *dharmārthas* instead of *dharmārthaḥ.*

f The *visarga* is missing in B (1b5).

g Johnston omits the *daṇḍa* and reads *prakāśyata.*

h The conjecture is according to Kano; B (1b5) is not clear; Johnston reads, against the Tibetan, *eṣa.*

1117 In the beginning of the next sentence of the *vyākhyā.*

1118 RGVV, 117.5–8: *itīdam āptāgamayuktisaṁśrayād udāhṛtaṁ kevalam ātmaśuddhaye / dhiyādhimuktyā kuśalopasaṁpadā samanvitā ye tadanugrahāya ca //.*

1119 The Tibetan has *tshig* for Skt. *vāg-.*

1120 The Tibetan has *yi ge* for Skt. *vāk-.*

1121 LAS, 86.14–19: *atha khalu mahāmatir bodhisattvo mahāsattvaḥ punar api bhagavantam etam evārtham adhyeṣate sma / deśayatu me bhagavān punar api vāgvikalpābhivyaktigocaram kutra kasmāt kathaṁ kena bhagavan nṛṇāṁ* [a]*vāgvijñaptivikalpaḥ*[a] *pravartate / bhagavān āha / śira-uronāsākaṇṭhatālvoṣṭhajihvādantasamavāyān mahāmate vākpravartamānā pravartante (-tate?) /.*

a K (32b9) reads *vāgvikalpavijñaptiḥ*, but the Tibetan has *tshig rnam par rig pa rtog pa.* E (48b5) omits *-vijñapti-.*

1122 Peking Tengyur no. 5784, *sgra rig*, vol. *le*, fol. 274a2.

1123 The Sanskrit has *kāyo nāma* over against Tib. *ming gi tshogs* "the accumulation that goes to make up words" in the sense of serving as a basis for words.

1124 Here the Tibetan translates Skt. *kāya* with *mang po* and not with *tshogs.*

1125 LAS, 112.10–113.2: *punar aparaṁ mahāmate nāmapadavyañjanakāyānāṁ lakṣaṇam uddekṣyāmaḥ yair nāmapadavyañjanakāyaiḥ sūpalakṣitair bodhisattvā mahāsattvā arthapadavyañjanānusāriṇaḥ kṣipram anuttarāṁ samyak*[a]*saṁbodhim abhi*[a]*saṁbodhim abhisaṁbudhya tathaiva sarvasattvān avabodhayiṣyanti / tatra mahāmate kāyo nāma yad uta yad vastv āśritya nāma kriyate sa kāyo vastu kāyaḥ śarīram ity anarthāntaram / eṣa mahāmate nāmakāyaḥ / padakāyaḥ punar mahāmate yad uta padārthakāyasadbhāvo niścayo niṣṭhopalabdhir ity anarthāntaram / eṣa mahāmate padakāyopadeśaḥ kṛto mayā / vyañjanakāyaḥ punar mahāmate yad uta yena nāmapadayor abhivyaktir bhavati vyañjanaṁ liṅgaṁ lakṣaṇam upalabdhiḥ prajñaptir ity anarthāntaram //.*

a Nanjio omits *-abhi.* E (63a2–3): *samyaksaṁbudhya* instead of *samyaksaṁbodhim abhisaṁbodhim abhisaṁbudhya.*

1126 The Tibetan does not have an equivalent for *kārya.*
1127 I.e., the subject matter expressed by these phrases.
1128 The Sanskrit has only "syllables."
1129 The Tibetan analysis of the compound *hrasvadīrghaplutavyañjanāni (thung ngu dang 'dren pa dang ring du 'dren pa dang yi ge)* is difficult to follow.
1130 The Tibetan has only *ba lang* for *-paśugo-*, but *phyugs* ("cattle") at the end of the compound.
1131 The Tibetan has no equivalent for *aja* ("goat").
1132 The four formless *skandhas* are usually referred to as "name."
1133 LAS, 113.3–12: *punar aparaṁ mahāmate padakāyo yad uta padakāryaniṣṭhā / nāma punar mahāmate yad uta akṣarāṇāṁ ca nāmasvabhāvabhedo 'kārād*[a]*yāvad dhakāraḥ /*[a] *tatra vyañjanaṁ punar mahāmate yad uta hrasvadīrghaplutavyañjanāni / tatra padakāyāḥ punar mahāmate ye* [b]*padavīthīgāmino*[b] *hastyaśvanaramṛgapaśugomahiṣājaiḍakādyāḥ padakāyasaṁjñāṁ labhante / nāma ca vyañjanaṁ ca punar mahāmate catvāra arūpiṇaḥ skandhā nāmnābhilapyanta iti kṛtvā nāma svalakṣaṇena vyajyate*[c] *iti kṛtvā vyañjanam / etan mahāmate nāmapadavyañjanakāyānāṁ nāmapadābhidhānalakṣaṇam atra te paricayaḥ karaṇīyaḥ //.*
a C (52a7) reads: *yāvaṁ lakṣās.*
b E (63b1) and H (44b6) read *padāḥ pṛthivīgāminaḥ.*
c C (52b2) and D (42a3) read *vyañjanam.*
1134 The Tibetan does not have an equivalent for *kārya.*
1135 Translated according to the Sanskrit of the *Laṅkāvatārasūtra* passage.
1136 *Āryalaṅkāvatāravṛtti*, Peking Tengyur no. 5519.
1137 The Sanskrit according to Lévi's edition (MSABh, 2.22) differs considerably: *dharmadvayavyavasthā vyañjanato 'rtho na ca jñeyaḥ.*
1138 I.e., the seven vajra points of the *Ratnagotravibhāga.*
1139 MMK, 34.19: *dve satye samupāśritya buddhānāṁ dharmadeśanā /.*
1140 In my translation of the *pratīka*, I used "called" for Tib. *brjod pa*, but here I choose a construction with "as" in order to make Gzhon nu dpal's grammatical point understandable.
1141 Tib. *gsal bar byed pa*, which can mean "consonant."
1142 The Manang (2a3) manuscript of the *vyākhyā* glosses *saṅgha* as "wisdom of the tenth bodhisattva-level."
1143 DRSM, 23.14: "It is obvious that here the Three Jewels refer to [that aspect of them—the one relating to] *dharmatā.*"
1144 RGVV, 2.4–7: *anidarśano hy ānanda tathāgataḥ / sa*[a] *na śakyaḥ cakṣuṣā draṣṭum / anabhilāpyo hy ānanda dharmaḥ / sa na śakyaḥ karṇena śrotum / asaṁskṛto hy ānanda saṁghaḥ / sa na śakyaḥ kāyena vā cittena vā paryupāsitum / itīmāni trīṇi vajrapadāni dṛḍhādhyāśayaparivartānusāreṇānugantavyāni /.*
a B (1b6) omits.
1145 This portion of the *Ratnagotravibhāgavyākhyā* (which is a quote from the *Dṛḍhādhyāśayaparivarta*) is not quoted by Gzhon nu dpal in the usual way, but only partly woven into his running commentary.
1146 The Manang manuscript of the *vyākhyā* (fol. 2a4) gives an interesting explanation of "[cognitive] object" (Tib. *yul*, Skt. *viṣaya*) and "range" (Tib. *spyod yul*, Skt. *gocara*): the former is the [cognitive] object of wisdom in meditative equipoise *(mnyam bzhag gi ye shes kyi yul)*, and the latter is the range of wisdom obtained after [meditation] *(rjes thob kyi ye shes kyi spyod yul).*
1147 For the construction of this sentence see de Jong 1979:567.
1148 Gzhon nu dpal views this equation in the context of RGV I.27, where the fruit, or the dharmakāya, is only metaphorically applied to buddha nature (DRSM, 24.2–5). In RGV I.27 the third reason for the presence of a buddha nature in

sentient beings is that "its (i.e., buddha nature's) fruit has been metaphorically applied to the buddha potential" (RGVV, 26.3–4: *bauddhe gotre tatphalasyopacārād-*).

1149 RGVV, 2.8–14: *tathāgataviṣayo hi śāriputra ayam arthas tathāgatagocaraḥ [/] sarvaśrāvakapratyekabuddhair api tāvac chāriputra ayam artho na śakyaḥ samyak svaprajñayā [jñātuṁ vā]*[a] *draṣṭum vā pratyavekṣituṁ vā*[b] *prāg eva bālapṛthagjanair anyatra tathāgataśraddhāgamanataḥ / śraddhāgamanīyo hi śāriputra paramārthaḥ / paramārtha iti śāri[putra] sattvadhātor etad adhivacanam / sattvadhātur iti śāriputra tathāgatagarbhasyaitad adhivacanam / tathāgatagarbha iti śāriputra dharmakāyasyaitad adhivacanam / itīdaṁ caturthaṁ vajrapadam /* [c] *anūnatvāpūrṇatvanirdeśaparivartānusāreṇānugantavyam /.*

a Not readable in B (2a2) (several *akṣaras* are broken away); A is not available. The gap is filled in according to the Tibetan (see also Takasaki 1966:143).

b B (2a2) reads *mvā /;* A is not available. De Jong (1979:567) suggests reading *vā* without a following *daṇḍa.*

c According to B (2a4); Johnston omits the *daṇḍa.*

1150 Again, this portion of the *Ratnagotravibhāgavyākhyā* (which is a quote from the *Anūnatvāpūrṇatvanirdeśa* here) is not quoted by Gzhon nu dpal in the usual way, but only partly woven into his running commentary.

1151 Again, this part of the *Anūnatvāpūrṇatvanirdeśa* is woven into the running commentary.

1152 This *sūtra* passage is again woven into the running commentary.

1153 A Tibetan play on words, *btags* and *dvags* sharing the same etymology.

1154 Gzhon nu dpal's replacement of "is an expression for the buddha element" by "is an expression for the emptiness" looks much less like an alteration of the meaning in the Tibetan: he skillfully splits the Tibetan term *(tshig gi bla dvags)* for expression (Skt. *adhivacana*) into *tshig gi* and *bla dvags* and refers the former to "buddha element" and the latter to "emptiness." In other words, buddha nature and the dharmakāya are only equated in terms of their respective emptiness.

1155 RGVV, 3.1–3: *anuttarā samyaksaṁbodhir iti bhagavan nirvāṇadhātor etad adhivacanam / nirvāṇadhātur iti bhagavaṁs*[a] *tathāgatadharmakāyasyaitad adhivacanam / itīdaṁ*[b] *pañcamaṁ vajrapadam āryaśrīmāī āsūtrānusāreṇānugantavyam /.*

a Corrected according to Takasaki (1966:144).

b B (2a5) has four *akṣaras (jajrapadaṁ?)* between *itīdaṁ* and the following word, which is obviously a scribal error.

1156 RGVV, 56.8–9: *sarvākārābhisaṁbodhiḥ savāsanamaloddhṛtiḥ / buddhatvam atha nirvāṇam advayam paramārthataḥ //.*

1157 Gzhon nu dpal includes the vocative "Illustrious one" in his *pratīka.*

1158 Skt. *bodhi* is rendered in Tibetan by the two terms *byang* ("cleansing") and *chub* ("achievement"); and *buddha* by *sangs* ("awakening") and *rgyas* ("blossoming").

1159 I.e., became manifest.

1160 Seyfort Ruegg (1969:360) regards the compound members *avinirbhāga-* and *avinirmuktajñāna-* as qualifications of the dharmakāya and translates: "…le dharmakāya…a pour qualité d'être inséparable, et il a la propriété du savoir non séparé—[inséparable] des dharma de *tathāgata* dépassant [en leur nombre] les sables de la Gaṅgā." But in the *Śrīmālādevīsūtra* they are used to mark the *buddhaguṇāḥ*, which is grammatically also possible in the passage here (see Schmithausen 1971:131–32).

1161 RGVV, 3.4–6: *yo 'yam śāriputra tathāgatanirdiṣṭo dharmakāyaḥ so 'yam avinirbhāgadharmā*[a] */ avinirmuktajñānaguṇo yad uta gaṅgānadīvālikāvyatikrāntais tathāgatadharmaiḥ / itīdaṁ ṣaṣṭhaṁ vajrapadaṁ /* [b] *anūnatvāpūrṇatvanirdeśānusāreṇā*[c] *nugantavyam /.*

a Or *-mī*? (in B (2a6) the *akṣara* is partly disfigured by a stain). But in RGVV I.44, where the same passage is quoted, the reading is *-mā* (see B 22b4).
b According to B (2b1); Johnston reads *-padam* without the *daṇḍa.*
c B (2b1) reads *-ṇevā-* instead of *-ṇā-*.

1162 The vocative "Śāriputra" is not repeated here.

1163 See Gzhon nu dpal's commentary on this *Anūnatvāpūrṇatvanirdeśa* passage in RGVV I.44 (DRSM, 329.12), where *ma bral ba'i ye shes kyi yon tan can ([dharmakāyo...] avinirmuktajñānaguṇo)* is glossed as *khams dang 'bral mi shes su gnas par bstan pa'i phyir bdag nyid gcig pa'i ldan pa:* "The connection of identity has been taught through this explanation of the connection *(ldan pa)* of the fruit inasmuch as the buddha qualities...were taught as abiding in such a way as not to be recognized as something disconnected from the [buddha] element." See also Schmithausen 1971:132.

1164 In other words, for Gzhon nu dpal the equation of the element or buddha nature with the qualities of the Buddha can be valid only in terms of their true nature or dharmatā. Thus the word *kāya* in *dharmakāya* points to the level of ultimate truth, on which there is of course no difference with regard to the true nature or emptiness of anything.

1165 RGVV, 3.7–10: *na mañjuśrīs tathāgataḥ kalpayati na vikalpayati / atha cā*[a] *syānābhogenākalpayato 'vikalpayata iyam evaṁrūpā kriyā pravartate / itīdaṁ saptamaṁ vajrapadaṁ /*[b] *tathāgataguṇajñānācintyaviṣayāvatāranirdeśānusāreṇānugantavyam / itīmāni samāsataḥ sapta vajrapadāni sakalasyāsya śāstrasyo*[c]*ddeśamukhasaṁgrahārthena śarīram iti veditavyaṁ /.*
a Johnston wrongly reads *vā* (cf. B (2b1)), which has no satisfying meaning here (see also Schmithausen 1971:132–33).
b According to B (2b2); Johnston omits the *daṇḍa.*
c B (2b3) reads *śāstrasya / u-*.

1166 Again, this portion of the *Ratnagotravibhāgavyākhyā* (which is a quote from the *Tathāgataguṇajñānācintyaviṣayāvatāranirdeśa* here) is not quoted by Gzhon nu dpal in the usual way, but only partly woven into his running commentary.

1167 According to the Sanskrit: "It should be known that the [first] three of these [seven vajra points]..."

1168 RGVV, 3.11–14: *svalakṣaṇenānugatāni caiṣāṁ yathākramaṁ dhāraṇirājasūtre / nidānata*[a]*s trīṇi padāni vidyāc catvāri dhīmajji*[b]*nadharmabhedāt //.*
a B (2b3) omits *ta;* A is not available.
b The syllable *-jji-* is illegible in B (2b4); (A is not available).

1169 Tib. *rjes su 'gro ba* can have these two meanings (see *Bod rgya tshig mdzod chen mo*, s.v.).

1170 RGVV, 3.15–16: *eṣāṁ ca saptānāṁ vajrapadānāṁ svalakṣaṇanirdeśena yathākramam āryadhā[raṇī]*[a]*śvararājasūtranidānaparivartānu*[b]*gatāni trīṇi padāni veditavyāni /.*
a B (2b4) is broken; A not available.
b Takasaki (1966:146) wants to read on the basis of the Chinese *-vartād anu-* instead of *-vartānu-* on the grounds that the reading is obscure. Manuscript B (2b4) is clear, however, and grammatically there is no reason either.

Did Rngog Blo ldan shes rab read: *eṣāṁ ca saptānāṁ vajrapdānāṁ svalakṣaṇanirdeśenānugatāni yathākramam āryadhāraṇīśvararājasūtranidānaparivartāt trīṇi padāni veditavyāni?*

1171 RGVV, 3.16–17: *tata ūrdhvam avaśiṣṭāni catvāri bodhisattvatathāgatadharmanirdeśabhedād.*[a]
a The syllable *-dād* is illegable in B (2b5).

1172 The translation of the *Ratnagotravibhāgavyākhyā* is in bold letters (this portion of the *vyākhyā* is not quoted by Gzhon nu dpal in the usual way, but only partly woven into his running commentary).

1173 Translated according to the Tibetan. The Sanskrit compound *anantaśiṣyagaṇasuvinītaḥ* must be taken as a *bahuvrīhi* (even though a past participle is not common as a final member): *-gaṇaḥ suvinītaḥ yena sa bhagavān*, "The illustrious one, by whom the...crowd was perfectly led."

1174 I.e., the disciple's enlightenment and so forth.

1175 RGVV, 3.17–21: *i[ti / tatra]*[a] *yad uktam / bhagavān sarvadharmasamatābhisaṁbuddhaḥ su*[b]*pravartitadharmacakro 'nantaśiṣyagaṇasuvinīta iti / ebhis tribhir mūlapadair yathākramaṁ*[c] *trayāṇāṁ ratnānāṁ anupūrvasamutpādasamudāgamavyavasthānaṁ veditavyam / avaśiṣṭāni catvāri padāni triratnotpattyanurūpahetusamudāgamanirdeśo veditavyaḥ /*

a B (2b5) is broken; A not available. Johnston suggests reading *tasmād*, but the following *ya* is clear; i.e., it is not a *dya*. See also Schmithausen 1971:133.

b B (2b6) reads *sa-;* A is not available.

c B (2b6) reads: *yathākramaṁ /.*

1176 RGVV, 3.21–4.2: *tatra yato 'ṣṭamyāṁ bodhisattvabhūmau vartamānaḥ sarvadharmavaśitāprāpto bhavati /*[a] *tasmāt sa bodhimaṇḍavaragataḥ sarvadharmasamatābhisaṁbuddha ity ucyate /.*

a According to B (3a1); Johnston omits the *daṇḍa*.

1177 The part in brackets is missing in Gzhon nu dpal's quotation.

1178 Skt. *pramāṇa* has no equivalent in the Tibetan.

1179 DBhS (ed. Rahder), 46.6–7: *sa evaṁ kāyajñānābhinirhāraprāpto vaśavartī (text: -vatīṁ) bhavati sarvasattveṣu / āyurvaśitāṁ ca pratilabhate 'nabhilāpyānabhilāpyakalpāyuḥpramāṇādhiṣṭhānatayā /.*

1180 Gzhon nu dpal does not quote this last sentence, probably because he has already introduced a slight reformulation of this passage.

1181 RGVV, 4.2–4: *yato navamyāṁ bodhisattvabhūmau vartamāno ['nuttaradharmabhāṇakatvasaṁpannaḥ]*[a] *sarvasattvāśayasuvidhijña indriyaparamapāramitāprāptaḥ sarvasattvakleśavāsanānusaṁdhisamudghātanakuśalo bhavati tasmāt so 'bhisaṁbuddha[bodhi]*[b]*ḥ supravartitadharmacakra ity ucyate....*

a Inserted by Johnston on the basis of the Tibetan and the Chinese. Gzhon nu dpal does not quote any such compound, though, and is thus in accordance with the Sanskrit.

b To be deleted?

1182 RGVV, 4.5–7: */ yato daśamyāṁ bhūmāv anuttaratathāgatadharmayauvarājyābhiṣekaprāptyanantaram anābhogabuddhakāryāpratipraśrabdho bhavati tasmāt sa supravartitadharmacakro 'nantaśiṣyagaṇasuvinīta ity ucyate /.*

1183 DhĪRS, 102a6–7.

1184 Ibid., 102b1–2.

1185 "and to those [disciples]..." is supplied according to the Tibetan in the Tengyur (Nakamura 1967:5, ll. 18–19).

1186 Skt. *suvinītatvād* must be taken as containing a *bahuvrīhi* compound: *suṣṭhu vinītāḥ śiṣyāḥ yena sa suvinīto bhagavān* / "He by whom disciples have been properly led is the illustrious one who has properly led."

1187 RGVV, 4.7–9: *tāṁ punar anantaśiṣyagaṇasuvinītatāṁ tadanantaram anena granthena darśayati mahatā bhikṣusaṁghena sārdhaṁ yāvad aprameyeṇa ca bodhisattvagaṇena sārdham iti / yathākramaṁ śrāvakabodhau buddhabodhau ca suvinītatvād evaṁguṇasamanvāgatair iti.*

1188 Tib. *'grub pa* does not make any sense here. The Sanskrit equivalent *samudāgama-* can mean according to MW (s.v.) "to arrive at full knowledge."

1189 DhĪRS, 102a7–b1.

1190 The Peking Kangyur (Ibid., 102b2) has an instrumental instead of a genitive.

1191 Lit., "conduct."

1192 Ibid., 102b2–103a1.

1193 Skt. *samādhivṛṣabhitā* lit. means "the state of somebody possessing supreme samādhi."

1194 Skt. *samāvartana* can have also the causative meaning *samāvartayati* (see BHSD, s.v.).

1195 RGVV, 4.10–12: *tataḥ śrāvakabodhisattvaguṇavarṇa*[a] *nirdeśānantaram*[b] *acintyabuddhasamādhivṛṣabhi*[c] *tāṁ pratītya vipularatnavyūhamaṇḍalamāḍa*[d] *nirvṛttitathāgatapariṣatsamāvartanavividhadivyadravya*[e] *pūjāvidhānastutimeghābhisaṁpravarṣaṇato buddharatnaguṇavibhāgavyavasthānaṁ veditavyaṁ /.*

a B (3a5–6) has after *-varṇa-* a cancelled letter and a *jra*, an *akṣara* used in B to fill blanks.

b B (3a6) reads *-rām.*

c Johnston would have us read *-bha-* instead of *-bhi-*, for no apparent reason. See also Takasaki 1966:148.

d Emended according to the Tibetan, the *Mahāyānottaratantraśāstraṭippaṇī* (Xc 14/34, fol. 9b5) and Schmithausen 1971:133. But based on the way *vyūha* is written in the same (B3a6) and the next (B3b1) lines, it can be ruled out that B (3a6) reads *-māḍa-* or *-māla-*.

e *-dravya-* is inserted by Johnston on the basis of the Tibetan.

The corresponding portion of the *Dhāraṇīśvararājasūtra* is on fol. 103a5–107a1.

1196 The second part of the sentence starting with "the illustrious one" is taken literally from DhĪRS 103b2–3.

1197 DhĪRS, 103b3–5.

1198 Lit., "the Huge Thousand with one thousand [to the faculty of] three [worlds]."

1199 Ibid., 104a6–7.

1200 That is, on seats in accordance with their status as bodhisattvas and great śrāvakas (DhĪRS, 106b4–5).

1201 Ibid., 107a3.

1202 Ibid., 107a8–b1. The Peking Kangyur reads *dad pa dad pa ched* instead of *dad pa dang ba che* (DRSM, 27.16).

1203 I.e., monks, nuns, and male and female lay practitioners (DhĪRS, 112a7).

1204 RGVV, 4.13–14: *tadanantaram udāradharmāsanavyūhaprabhādharmaparyāyanāmaguṇaparikīrtanato dharmaratnaguṇavibhāgavyavasthānaṁ veditavyam /.*

The corresponding portion of the *Dhāraṇīśvararājasūtra* is on fols. 107a1–113b4.

1205 I have problems figuring out the exact number. The Tibetan number compound consists of (1) *bye ba,* "a crore" (10 million); (2) *khrag khrig,* "one million" or "a hundred thousand millions"; and (3) *brgya stong phrag brgyad cu,* "eighty lakh" (eight million). The obviously high number is followed by *tsam* ("only").

1206 DhĪRS, 112b8: … *'phang du shing ta la bye ba….*

1207 I could not locate the words *rgyan thams cad dang ldan pa byung* in the sūtra. These are thus Gzhon nu dpal's own abbreviated formulation of the sūtra's description of the throne (see Ibid., 112b7–113a2).

1208 Ibid., 113a4.

1209 Ibid., 113b4: *seng ge'i khri la bzhugs te chos kyang bshad du gsol /.* The phrase *'od bsngags zhing* is not found in the sūtra.

1210 Gzhon nu dpal thus reads *'od kyi bsngags pa* in the *Ratnagotravibhāgavyākhyā* (DRSM, 28.5) instead of the mere *'od* in the versions of the Tengyur (see Nakamura 1967:7, l. 3).

1211 DhĪRS, 113b5–6.

1212 Ibid., 114b2–115a7.

1213 Ibid., 116a1–2.
1214 Ibid., 118a3.
1215 RGVV, 4.14–15: *tadanantaram anyonyaṁ bodhisattvasamādhigocaraviṣayaprabhāvasaṁdarśanatadvicitraguṇavarṇanirdeśataḥ saṁgharatnaguṇavibhāgavyavasthānaṁ veditavyam /.*

The corresponding portion of the *Dhāraṇīśvararājasūtra* is on fols. 113b4–118a3.

1216 RGVV, 4.15–5.4: *tadanantaraṁ punar api buddharaśmyabhiṣekair anuttaradharmarājajyeṣṭhaputraparamavaiśāradyaprati[bhānopaha]*[a] *raṇatāṁ pratītya tathāgatabhūtaguṇaparamārthastutinirdeśataś ca mahāyānaparamadharmakathāvastūpanyasanataś ca tatpratipatteḥ paramadharmaiśvaryaphalaprāptisaṁdarśanataś ca yathāsaṁkhyam eṣām eva trayāṇāṁ ratnānām anuttaraguṇavibhāgavyavasthānaṁ nidānaparivartāvasānagatam eva draṣṭavyam /.*

a The reading is uncertain in B (3b3), but the last of the uncertain *akṣara*s looks like a *ha* (see also Johnston 1950:5, fn. 1).

1217 DhĪRS, 118a8–b1: *de nas byang chub sems dpa' gzungs gyi dbang phyug gi rgyal pos be bzhin gshegs pa'i byin gyis brlabs rig nas stan las langs te /.*
1218 Ibid., 118b6–8.
1219 Ibid., 118b8–119a1.
1220 Ibid., 119a5.
1221 Ibid., 119a5–6.
1222 Ibid., 119b3.
1223 Ibid., 119b4.
1224 Ibid., 120a2.
1225 Ibid., 120a2–3.
1226 RGVV, 5.5–6: *tataḥ sūtranidānaparivartānantaraṁ buddhadhātuḥ ṣaṣṭyākāratadviśuddhiguṇaparikarmanirdeśena paridīpitaḥ / viśodhye 'rthe guṇavati tadviśuddhiparikarmayogāt /.*
1227 Tib. *mtshur nag.* Goldstein (2001, s.v.) gives the Latin equivalent "black fibroferitum" (sic). This is also the term (with the same wrong spelling) for *nag tshur ser tshur* in Dga' ba'i rdo rje's *'Khrungs dpe dri med shel gyi me long* (p. 89). However, the correct form, *fibroferritum,* is listed in the Latin glossary (Ibid., 444). The chemical formula of fibroferrite is given as Fe2O3SO3.10H2O (Ibid., 89), but the correct form is Fe+++(SO4)(OH).5H2O (cf. www.webmineral.com). In the DBhS (ed. Rahder), 30.8–10 gold is purified with what is called *kāsīsa* in Sanskrit ("green sulphate of iron" (MW s.v.)). This latter is rendered as *nag tshur* in Tibetan (DRSM, 30.15).
1228 Fibroferrite has the ability to make pure gold manifest, if placed in contact with gold ore. Cf. Gzhon nu dpal's example of a mixture of turmeric powder and lime (to illustrate the sixty cleansing factors applied to the buddha element of sentient beings), which manifests the quality of redness.
1229 The numbering follows Steinkellner's (1977) *Verse-Index.*
1230 The Tibetan has an ablative; according to the Sanskrit the meaning is "through [its] complete cause."
1231 For Dharmakīrti there is no *svabhāva* of a cause as such, the term only denoting an "accumulation of causes" (Steinkellner has an *Ursachenkomplex*). Thus the term *svabhāva* is only used metaphorically, to designate such a set of causes (caused themselves by their own causes), which jointly bring forth the effect (see Steinkellner 1971:185–86).
1232 PV I.7 (ed. Gnoli 1960:6.24–25): *hetunā yaḥ samagreṇa kāryotpādo 'numīyate / arthāntarānapekṣatvāt sa svabhāvo 'nuvarṇitaḥ //.* For a German translation, see Steinkellner 1971:185.
1233 That is, the *Śrīhevajravajrapadoddharaṇanāmapañjikā* (Tōhoku 1192).

1234 The sixtyfold factors of the purifying process (i.e., the four ornaments, the eight lamps, the sixteenfold compassion, and the thirty-two acts) are listed in DhĪRS 5b–11b (see Takasaki 1966:152–53).

1235 Gzhon nu dpal inserts *brjod byar* into the *pratīka.*

1236 Skt. *[viśuddhi]parikarman* (see further down).

1237 RGVV, 5.6–7: *imaṁ cārthavaśam upādāya daśasu bodhisattvabhūmiṣu punar jātarūpaparikarmaviśeṣodāharaṇam udāhṛtam /.*

1238 Gzhon nu dpal inserts into his quotation of the *vyākhyā* two passages from the *Daśabhūmikasūtra* in which the purification of gold by different means is compared to the bodhisattva levels.

1239 According to the Skt.: " ...gold has been cast into fire...."

1240 Tib. *rab tu byang ba* has no equivalent in the Sanskrit.

1241 The Tibetan translation does not render the compound *vibhūṣaṇālaṁkāravidhiṣu.*

1242 Plural in the Tibetan.

1243 Tib. *yang dag par blangs te gnas pa.*

1244 Neither the edition of Kondō nor the Tibetan has Skt. *daśa*/ Tib. *bcu.*

1245 I.e., the mind purifies itself *(ātmanepada).*

1246 Skt. *bhūyasyā mātrayā*, which has no equivalent in the Tibetan.

1247 NGMPP reel no. A 38/5 and A 39/13 (the old Nepalese manuscript in Gupta script was in disorder and not identified as one text during the microfilm work (see Matsuda 1996:xv-xvi)), fol. 11a4–6: *tad yathāpi nāma bhavanto jinaputrā* [a]*tad evañ*[a] *jātarūpaṁ kuśalena karmāreṇa yathā yathāgnau prakṣipyate* [b]*kālena ca kālaṁ samaparipākaṁ gacchati*[b] *tathā tathottapyate*[c] *pariśuddhyate*[d] *karmaṇyaṁ ca bhavati vibhūṣaṇālaṁkāravidhiṣu yathākāmatayā*[e] */ evam eva bhavanto jinaputrā yathā yathā bodhisattvo buddhāṁś ca bhagavataḥ pūjayati sattvaparipākāya ca* [f]*prayujyate / imāṁś ca*[f] *daśa*[g]*bhūmipariśodhakān dharmān samādāya vartate / tathā tathāsya tāni kuśalamūlā*[h]*ni sarvajñatāpariṇāmitāni bhūyasyā mātrayottapyante*[h] *pariśudhyanti karmaṇyāni ca bhavanti yathākāmatayā*[i] */.*

The passage is missing in manuscript B of Matsuda's facsimile edition (NGMPP A 38/7). In Rahder's (1926) edition the passage is on p. 20, ll. 14–18 (1st *bhūmi*, VV) and in Kondō's (1936) on p. 27, ll. 2–6.

a Rahder and Kondō omit *tad evañ.* The Nepalese manuscript (A) is supported by the Tibetan translation, however.

b Rahder and Kondō omit *kālena ca kālaṁ samaparipākaṁ gacchati* ("and after some time it reaches [a state of] ripeness in being in accordance [with its real nature]"). The phrase is also missing in the Tibetan.

c Rahder and Kondō read *tathā* instead of *tathottapyate.* The Nepalese manuscript is supported by the Tibetan translation, however.

d Rahder and Kondō read *-ti.* Like the passive *prakṣipyate*, the passive is here called for, since it is still the example of gold being purified, whereas the mind purifies itself *(ātmanepada).*

e The Nepalese manuscript (A) does not have *yathākāmatayā.* Rahder and Kondō are supported by the Tibetan.

f Rahder: *-prayujyata imān.*

g Kondō omits *daśa-*.

h Kondō: *-nyuttapyaṁte* (omits *sarvajñatāpariṇāmitāni bhūyasyā mātrayo-*).

i In the Nepalese manuscript (A) *yathākāmatayā* belongs to the following sentence. It reads after *bhavanti*: *-anantarāyāṁ samyaksaṁbodhau / yathākāmatayā yena....*

1248 NGMPP reel nos. A 38/5 and A 39/13 (see note 1247 above), fol. 16a1: *tad yathāpi nāma bhavanto jinaputrās tad eva [jātarūpaṁ kāsīsaprakṣi]*[a]*ptaṁ [bhūyasyā]*[a] *mātrayā [sarvama]*[a]*lāpagataṁ bhavati /.*

a The portions in brackets are not readable (the upper part of the folio has broken away with parts of the first line). The missing parts are inserted according to Rahder 1926:30, ll. 8–10 (2nd *bhūmi*, EE) and Kondō 1936:46, ll. 1–2.

The passage is missing in manuscript B of Matsuda's facsimile edition (NGMPP A 38/7).

1249 RGVV, 5.8 *asminn eva sūtre tathāgatakarmanirdeśānantaram aviśuddhavaiḍūryamaṇidṛṣṭāntaḥ kṛtaḥ /*. Gzhon nu dpal inserted some glosses into his quote.

1250 Tib. *khams*, but *vaiḍūrya* is not really one of the four (or six) classical elements. In the Sanskrit it is called a *maṇi*.

1251 "With regard to that, Mañjuśrī, the great compassion called 'playful' arises [in the tathāgata] for sentient beings (Tib. *sems can rnams la*), after the tathāgata has fully awakened to all phenomena that have such a nature, and seen the impure, not stainless or blemished dharmadhātu in sentient beings." (RGVV, 9.17–10.1: *tatra mañjuśrīs tathāgatasyaivaṁrūpān sarvadharmān abhisaṁbudhya sattvānāṁ ca dharmadhātuṁ vyavalokyāśuddham avimalaṁ sāṅgaṇaṁ*[a] *vikrīḍitā nāma*[b] *sattveṣu mahākaruṇā pravartata ity-*[c]....)

a Conjecture according to Kano; Johnston wrongly reads *-naṁ* (cf. B 6a6).

b B (6b1) omits *ma*.

c Johnston reads *iti /*.

1252 RGVV, 10.3–4: *sattvānām iti niyatāniyatamithyāniyatarāśivyavasthitānām /*. This explanation is part of a commentary on a passage quoted from the *Jñānālokālaṁkārasūtra*.

1253 In Tatia's edition of the *Abhidharmasamuccayabhāṣya* the quoted passage is explained in §§ 82–88 (Tatia 1976:76–84).

1254 Tib. *rnam par dgod pa*, Skt. **vyavasthā(na)*? (see LAS, 65.4). Further down Gzhon nu dpal glosses *rnam par dgod pa* as *rnam par bzhag pa*, which must be understood in this context as a "state" or "condition" in which one becomes established. The term is used in the same way as *bhūmi* ("level").

1255 The quoted passage is in section *phal chen*, vol. *ri*, fols. 2b3–3a3 (Peking Kangyur No. 761).

1256 In the context of the *Ratnagotravibhāga* otherwise translated as "potential."

1257 This is what is normally the first bodhisattva-level (see DRSM, 36.16–17).

1258 Youthful because free from mistakes; it is the eighth bodhisattva level (DRSM, 36.18–20).

1259 The Peking Kangyur reads *rgyal mtshan* instead of *rgyal tshab*. Gzhon nu dpal (DRSM, 36.20–22) explains that this is the ninth level and that the bodhisattva knows how to perform the deeds of a buddha, namely the preaching of the Dharma, in the same way as a regent knows how to perform the deeds of a king.

1260 This corresponds to the tenth level (DRSM, 36.22–23).

1261 According to Suzuki (1932:56–58), the following quotation is § XX in the second chapter.

1262 Tib. *mngon par rtogs par 'gyur ba'i rigs*. In fact, according to Gzhon nu dpal, there are only three realizations. The last two potentials lead to either one of the first three, and ultimately to the realization of a tathāgata.

1263 LAS, 63.2–5: *punar aparaṁ mahāmate pañcābhisamayagotrāṇi katamāni pañca yad uta śrāvakayānābhisamayagotraṁ pratyekabuddhayānābhisamayagotraṁ tathāgatayānābhisamayagotram aniyataikataragotram agotraṁ ca pañcamam /*.

1264 Tib.: *bsam gyis mi khyab pa'i 'chi 'pho dang ldan pa*. Further down, Gzhon nu dpal explains this passage as meaning that arhats have abandoned transmigration and rebirth following an ordinary death, but are still subject to inconceivable transmigration within a mind-body (DRSM, 34.6–8). If the long *ā* in *'cintyācyutigataḥ* is correct (all Nepalese manuscripts have this reading), the Sanskrit would be: "somebody who has reached the inconceivable [state] beyond transmigration."

This expression may, however, be intended to exclude only a transmigration within saṁsāra, and thus have the same meaning as the Tibetan. Moreover, it is explained further down in the same chapter of the *Laṅkāvatārasūtra:* "Since neither [pratyekabuddhas nor śrāvakas] have obtained the transmigration of inconceivable transformation...." (*acintyapariṇāmacyuter aprāptitvāc ca....* Cf. LAS, 134.9–10.)

1265 This last sentence is missing in the Sanskrit.

1266 LAS, 63.5–14: *kathaṁ punar mahāmate śrāvakayānābhisamayagotraṁ pratyetavyam / yaḥ skandhadhātvāyatanasvasāmānyalakṣaṇaparijñānādhigame deśyamāne romāñcitatanur bhavati / lakṣaṇaparicayajñāne cāsya buddhiḥ praskandati na pratītyasamutpādāvinirbhāgalakṣaṇaparicaye / idaṁ mahāmate śrāvakayānābhisamayagotram / yaḥ śrāvakayānābhisamayadṛṣṭyā*[a] *ṣaṭpañcamyāṁ bhūmau paryutthānakleśaprahīṇo vāsanakleśāprahīṇo 'cintyācyutigataḥ samyaksiṁhanādaṁ nadati / kṣīṇā me jātir uṣitaṁ brahmacaryam ity evam ādi nigadya pudgalanairātmyaparicayād yāvan nirvāṇabuddhir bhavati //.*

a Emended according to the Tibetan. Nanjio and all Nepalese manuscripts read *-samayaṁ dṛṣṭvā.*

1267 Lit., "do not have."

1268 The Tibetan *(blo can te)* takes *-buddhiḥ* as a *bahuvrīhi* compound. The demonstrative pronoun *eṣā* has no equivalent in the Tibetan, which has a personal pronoun instead *('di ni).* This must be understood with a plural meaning, since it refers to the preceding subject, which is in the plural. The corresponding Sanskrit would be: *ete... -buddhayaḥ:* "Mahāmati, these are people whose mind (lit. 'intellect') entertains the idea of emancipation with regard to nonemancipation[a] of those with a potential...."

a This would require breaking the compound and reading *-aniryāṇe niryāṇa-*, which is supported (with regard to the case ending) by one Nepalese manuscript (NGMPP reel no. A 112/8, fol. 39b2: *-nirvvāṇe nirvvāṇa-*).

1269 Tib. *mu stegs can* has no equivalent in the Sanskrit.

1270 Tib. *khyod kyis.* In the Skt. the personal pronoun is in the dative *(te):* "For you, Mahāmati, work remains to be done in order to [help] overcome [their] unsound views."

1271 LAS, 63.15–64.3: *anye punar mahāmate ātmasattvajīvapoṣapuruṣapudgalasattvāvabodhān nirvāṇam anveṣante / anye punar mahāmate kāraṇādhīnāṁ sarvadharmān dṛṣṭvā nirvāṇagatibuddhayo bhavanti / dharmanairātmyadarśanābhāvān nāsti mokṣo mahāmate / eṣā mahāmate śrāvakayānābhisamayagotrakasyāniryāṇaniryāṇabuddhiḥ / atra te mahāmate kudṛṣṭivyāvṛttyarthaṁ yogaḥ karaṇīyaḥ //.*

1272 Lit., "who is satisfied" (Skt. *-hṛṣṭa-*).

1273 LAS, 64.4–10: *tatra mahāmate pratyekabuddhayānābhisamayagotrako yaḥ pratyekābhisamaye deśyamāne aśruhṛṣṭaromāñcitatanur bhavati / asaṁsargapratyayād bhāvābhiniveśa*[a] *vividhasvakāyavaicitryarddhivyastayamakaprātihāryadarśane nirdiśyamāne 'nunīyate sa pratyekabuddhayānābhisamayagotraka iti viditvā pratyekabuddhayānābhisamayānurūpā kathā karaṇīyā / etan mahāmate pratyekabuddhayānābhisamayagotrakasya lakṣaṇam //.*

a Nanjio inserts against B (36b1), C (29a3), D (23b2), E (36a3), G (42b3), H (25b2), I (30a5), and K (23b4) *-bahu-*. To judge by the Tibetan, *bahuvidha* would indeed be possible instead of *vividha.*

1274 The Tibetan renders the noun *audārya* with the adjective *yangs pa:* "the vast [buddhafields]."

1275 LAS, 64.11–65.1: *tatra mahāmate tathāgatayānābhisamayagotraṁ trividham yad uta svabhāvaniḥsvabhāvadharmābhisamayagotram adhigamasvapratyātmāryābhisamayagotraṁ bāhyabuddhakṣetraudāryābhisamayagotraṁ ca / yadā punar mahāmate trayāṇām apy eṣām anyatame deśyamāne svacittadṛśyadehālaya-bhogapratiṣṭhācintyaviṣaye*[a] *deśyamāne nottrasati na saṁtrasati na saṁtrāsam āpadyate veditavyam ayaṁ tathāgatayānābhisamayagotraka iti / etan mahāmate tathāgatayānābhisamayagotrakasya lakṣaṇam //.*

a According to B (36b4), E (36a5) and G (43a2). Nanjio has, together with A (23b7), C (29a6), D (23b4), F (11b12), H (25b5), I (30b1), K (23b7–24a1), *viṣaya-*.

1276 Tib. *di ltar* has no equivalent in the Sanskrit.

1277 LAS, 65.2–7: *aniyatagotrakaḥ punar mahāmate triṣv apy eteṣu deśyamāneṣu yatrānunīyate tatrānuyojyaḥ syāt / parikarmabhūmir iyaṁ mahāmate gotra-vyavasthā / nirābhāsabhūmy avakramaṇatayā vyavasthā kriyate / pratyātmālaye tu svakleśavāsanāśuddhasya dharmanairātmyadarśanāt samādhisukhavihāraṁ prāpya śrāvako jinakāyatāṁ pratilapsyate //.*

1278 This is part of a quote from the *Avataṁsakasūtra* (see DRSM, 31.8).

1279 MA, 1.13.

1280 Based on a similar stanza in the *Abhidharmasūtra*, Seyfort Ruegg (1971:165) translates *chos* here as "choses" ("things"), which is obviously not Gzhon nu dpal's understanding of it.

1281 The next portion of the quote from the *Avataṁsakasūtra* (see DRSM, 31.8).

1282 The Tibetan version of RGV I.16a is not quoted by Gzhon nu dpal.

1283 RGVV, 15.9–10: *yāvadbhāvikatā jñeyaparyantagatayā dhiyā / sarvasattveṣu sarva-jñadharmatāstitvadarśanāt // .*

1284 See Seyfort Ruegg 1971:469.

1285 I.e., becomes the fortified potential *(paripuṣṭagotra)*. For an explanation of this potential, see MSA III.3 and 12 (cf. Seyfort Ruegg 1969:78ff.).

1286 Chapter II, § XLIII (see Suzuki 1932:93).

1287 LAS, 107.10–11: *āryagotraṁ punar mahāmate triprakāram upayāti yad uta śrāvakapratyekabuddhabuddhaprabhedataḥ /.*

1288 Tib. *mgo reg:* somebody whose entire head is shaven (*Bod rgya tshig mdzod chen mo*, s.v.).

1289 That is, somebody engaged in the practice of the *pāramitās*.

1290 Tib. *'dra bar byas pa*, Skt. **sādṛśyakṛta.*

1291 BBh, 4.16–18: *tatredaṁ bodhisattvasya dānapāramitāyā gotraliṅgaṁ iha bodhi-sattvaḥ prakṛtyaiva dānarucir bhavati.*

1292 See DRSM, 31.25–26.

1293 That is, of the two Hīnayāna potentials of the śrāvakas and pratyekabuddhas.

1294 For the theory of liberation in the Vaiśeṣika school see Frauwallner 1973: vol. 2, 170.

1295 The quoted passage is part of the commentary on AA II.8: AAV Sphuṭārtha, 54.15–17 in the Tibetan text. In the Sanskrit (reconstructed) it is on p. 29, ll. 21–22.

1296 Tib. *bam brgyad ma.* Chos grub's Tibetan translation (Peking Kangyur No. 776) is from Guṇabhadra's Chinese translation (see Suzuki 1930:12–14).

1297 In the Sanskrit version of the *Laṅkāvatārasūtra,* the first potential is defined as the compound *svabhāvaniḥsvabhāvadharmābhisamayagotraṁ* "the potential leading to the realization of phenomena that naturally lack an own-being" (see note 1275 above). The Tibetan translation from the Chinese reads: (*de bzhin gshegs pa'i... rigs de ni rnam pa bzhi yod de 'di lta ste / rang bzhin gyi chos mngon par rtogs par 'gyur ba'i rigs / rang bzhin med pa'i chos mngon par rtogs par' gyur ba'i rigs dang / ...* (Peking Kangyur, *mdo*, vol. *ngu*, fol. 228a8–b1). The Sanskrit original of the Chinese translation by Guṇabhadra must have been: **svabhāvadharmābhisamyagotraṁ ca niḥsvabhāvadharmābhisamayagotraṁ.*

1298 RGVV, 80.13–14: *dvayāvaraṇaviśleṣahetur jñānadvayaṁ punaḥ / nirvikalpaṁ ca tatpṛṣṭhalabdhaṁ taj jñānam iṣyate //.*

1299 The Tibetan has no equivalent for Skt. *sadā.*

1300 In the Tibetan, the equivalent of Skt. *nimittabhūtaṁ* is in RGV II.20b.
1301 Skt. *vibhūti*. Tib. *'byung med* suggests the reading Skt. *vibhūta*. Nakamura (1967:161) emends to *dbang 'byor*. But Gzhon nu dpal explains that *'byung med* has the meaning of not having arisen from elements (DRSM, 478.6). See also Tsultrim Gyamtsho and Fuchs 2000:191.
1302 RGVV, 82.15–18: *vibhūtirūpārthavi*[a]*darśane sadā nimittabhūtaṁ sukathāśuciśrave / tathāgatānāṁ śuciśīlajighraṇe mahāryasaddharmarasāgravindane // samādhisaṁsparśasukhānubhūtiṣu.*
a A (20b3) reads *-ni-*.
1303 MSABh, 69.7: *śrāvako 'niyato dvedhā dṛṣṭādṛṣṭārthayānataḥ /*. The *bhāṣya* (MSABh, 69.9–10) explains: "One should know that there are two types of uncertain śrāvakas: those who go by the Mahāyāna, having seen the meaning of their *yāna* and [its] truth, and those who go by the Mahāyāna without having seen it." *(śrāvako punar aniyato dvidhā veditavyaḥ / dṛṣṭārthayānaś ca yo dṛṣṭasatyo mahāyānena niryāti adṛṣṭārthayānaś ca yo na dṛṣṭasatyo mahāyānena niryāti /.)*
1304 I.e., the bodhisattva levels (see above).
1305 BCA, 76.19–20: *ācāro bodhisattvānām aprameya udāhṛtaḥ / cittaśodhanam ācāraṁ niyataṁ tāvad ācaret.*
1306 The quoted passage is part of the introductive sentence to the second paragraph (called "Avavāda") in the first chapter. It is on p. 17, ll.1–4 in the Tibetan text (Tripathi 1993). In the Sanskrit (reconstructed) it is on p. 10, ll.12–14.
1307 According to the *Avataṁsakasūtra*, the third point is the "bodhisattva level of yoga practice" (see above).
1308 This must refer to the Sanskrit compound that was translated as *'gyur gzhan du skye bar skyes pa* (Skt. **vikṛtijāta?*).
1309 I.e., heat, the first stage of the path of preparation, on which a lesser, medium, and great heat are distinguished.
1310 AAV Sphuṭārthā, 25.19: *ālambanaṁ sarvasattvā ūṣmaṇām iha śasyate /.*
1311 Skt. *nirvedhabhāgīya*, the term used in the *Abhisamayālaṁkāra* for the path of preparation.
1312 AAV Sphuṭārthā, 30.9–10: *trisarvajñatvadharmāṇāṁ paripūrir anuttarā / aparityaktasattvārthā nirūḍhir abhidhīyate //.*
1313 PRGSG, 66.4: *svakabhūmikāṅkṣavigatāḥ sadā (text: sada) merukalpāḥ /.*
1314 A Śrāvaka of lower intellectual capacity who is mainly concerned with *śamatha* meditation and who, upon becoming an Arhat, attains the six extrasensory perceptions of clairvoyance (Rigzin 1993:53).
1315 A Śrāvaka of higher intellectual capacity who is mainly concerned with *vipaśyanā* meditation and who does not attain the six extrasensory perceptions of clairvoyance (Rigzin 1993:54).
1316 The passage with this summary of content is quoted in RGVV II.1 (see Takasaki 1966:312).
1317 RGVV, 5.9–6.1: *tad yathā kulaputra kuśalo maṇikāro maṇiśuddhisuvidhijñaḥ*[a] *sa maṇigotrād aparyavadāpitāni maṇiratnāni gṛhītvā tīkṣṇena khā*[b]*rodakenonmīlya*[c] *kṛṣṇena keśakambalaparyavadāpanena*[d] *paryavadāpayati / na ca tāvanmātreṇa vīryaṁ praśrambhayati / tataḥ paścāt tīkṣṇenāmiṣarasenonmīlya kha*[e]*ṇḍikāparyava*[f]*-dāpanena paryava*[g]*dāpayati / na ca tāvanmātreṇa vīryaṁ praśrambhayati / tataḥ sa paścān mahābhaiṣajyarasenonmīlya sūkṣmavastraparyavadāpanena paryavadāpaya*[h]*-ti / paryavadāpitaṁ cāpagatakācam abhijātavaiḍūryam ity ucyate /.*
a Johnston has a *daṇḍa* after *-jñaḥ*, which is not needed and not in the manuscript (cf. B4a1).
b B (4a2) reads *ṣā* instead of *khā*, which is quite common in Nepalese manuscripts. The quoted passage is not available in A.

c According to B (4a2); Johnston reads *-otkṣālya* instead of *-onmīlya* (et passim).
d B (4a2) reads *-payavadānena.*
e The MUTŚṬ (4.18) reads *ga-.*
f B (4a3) reads *-pa-* or *-ya-* instead of *-va-.*
g B (4a3) reads *-ya-* instead of *-va-.*
h B (4a4) has an extra *-ya-.*
The passage is quoted from DhĪRS, 176b4–7.

1318 The example of the *vaiḍūrya* illustrates that the dharmakāya and buddha nature only differ in one respect: whether one's adventitious stains have been removed or not. But Gzhon nu dpal wants us to restrict this example to the fortified potential, and compares in the following the purification of the naturally present potential to a magical transformation of grass into riches, a process that involves the application of meditative power to the spatial element of grass, etc. In this way buddha nature can skillfully be referred to as emptiness, while equally importantly, a more substantial difference between buddha nature and the dharmakāya is implied. And in the same way as the spatial element of grass allows for a magical transformation into gold, the emptiness of an ordinary mind (i.e., buddha nature) allows for a transformation into enlightenment.

1319 The quoted passage (Peking Tengyur, *dbu ma*, vol. *tsha*, fol. 199a4–7) is part of the commentary on MMK XV.8: "If something exists in terms of its own-being, its [later] nonexistence will not be possible. A real change of nature is logically never possible" (*yady astitvaṁ prakṛtyā syān na bhaved asya nāstitā / prakṛter anyathābhāvo na hi jātūpapadyate*; MMK, 19.20–21). The *Prajñāpradīpa* explains that Nāgārjuna was thinking of the example of the hotness of fire, which by nature can never be coolness. The hotness of hot water, on the contrary, which has been produced by fire, is not the natural property of water. Further down, Bhavyaviveka clarifies, however, that even the hotness of fire, etc., cannot be an own-being *(svabhāva).* The canonical statement adduced by an opponent that wood possesses various elements by no means entails for Bhavyaviveka that these elements are its own-being.

1320 This is the undesired consequence of the assertion that there is an arising from some other entity (see MA, 89.7).

1321 Peking Tengyur, *dbu ma*, vol. *dza*, fol. 43a4. This stanza is missing in the Sanskrit text (see Lindtner 2001:109).

1322 Tib. *dge slong gi dngos po* (see *Bod rgya tshig mdzod chen mo*, s.v.).

1323 RGVV, 6.1–3: *evam eva kulaputra tathāgato 'py apariśuddhaṁ sattvadhātuṁ viditvānityaduḥkhānātmāśubhodvegakathayā saṁsārābhiratān sattvān udvejayati / ārye ca dharmavinaye 'vatārayati* [a].

a B (4a5) does not have a *daṇḍa;* A is not available.

1324 This quotation has not been identified.

1325 This quotation has not been identified.

1326 The repetition of *de'i 'og tu* does not make any sense to me, nor does the reading of the block print *(de'i bog tu).*

1327 I could not locate this passage further down in the *Dhāraṇīśvararājasūtra.*

1328 That is, the teaching of the śrāvakas which are diverted into the single ultimate vehicle, which is the third dharmacakra, according to the *Saṁdhinirmocanasūtra.*

1329 With regard to their future enlightenment (Tsultrim Gyamtsho and Fuchs 2000:202).

1330 I.e., the nature of the dharmadhātu.

1331 RGVV, 86.7–10: *lokeṣu yac chāntipathāvatāraprapācanāvyākaraṇe nidānam / bimbaṁ tad apy atra sadāvaruddham [ākāśadhātāv iva rūpadhātuḥ]* (the last *pāda* has not been quoted by Gzhon nu dpal).

1332 RGVV, 88.8–10: *saddharmapuṇḍarīkādidharmatattvaprakāśanaiḥ // pūrvagrahān nivartyaitān prajñopāyaparigrahāt / paripācyottame yāne vyākaroty agrabodhaye //.*

1333 In a state without *nimittas* one does not have any expectations with regard to anything.

1334 RGVV, 6.3–4: *na ca tāvanmātreṇa tathāgato vīryaṁ praśrambhayati / tataḥ paścāc chūnyānimittāpraṇihitakathayā tathāgatanetrīm avabodhayati.* With regard to this second stage, Gzhon nu dpal makes the interesting remark: "But the highest fruit *('bras bu'i mtha')* of the levels proper to this [second] dharmacakra is obtained by a bodhisattva [only] on the seventh level" (DRSM, 40.4–5).

1335 AA, 3.12: *sarvākārajñatāmārgaḥ [śāsitrā yo 'tra deśitaḥ /].* The part of the sentence in brackets is not quoted by DRSM.

1336 The quoted passage has not been identified. In the *Aṣṭasāhasrikā Prajñāpāramitā,* the three doors are explained in paragraph 3, chapter 20 (see Conze 1958:146–48).

1337 Tib. *mngon par 'du bya ba med pa.* The corresponding term *abhisaṁskāra* is normally used in the context of mental fabrication *(prapañca)* and mental effort *(ābhoga)* (see Schmithausen 1969:138–42). *Anabhisaṁskāra* can thus be compared to *niṣprapañca* and *anābhoga.*

1338 Tib. *'bras bu'i mtha'.*

1339 Skt. *samānās* has no equivalent in the Tibetan. See DhĪRS, 177a3, however: "These sentient beings who have various origins and natures, have entered together...." *(sems can rgyu dang rang bzhin sna tshogs pa de dag mnyam du zhugs nas....)*

1340 RGVV, 6.4–8: *na ca tāvanmātreṇa tathāgato vīryaṁ praśrambhayati / tataḥ paścād avivartyadharmacakrakathayā trimaṇḍalapariśuddhikathayā ca*[a] *tathāgataviṣaye tān sattvān avatārayati*[b] *nānāprakṛtihetukān / avatīrṇāś ca samānās tathāgatadharmatām adhigamyānuttarā dakṣiṇīyā*[c] *ity ucyanta....*

a B (4a6) omits *ca;* A is not available.

b B (4a6) has a *daṇḍa* after *avatārayati.*

c *-yā* is missing in B (4b1).

1341 The DRSM reads *nyan thos theg pa las* and *theg pa chen po las* instead of *nyan thos theg pa la* and *theg pa chen po la* (see Hahn 1982:146).

1342 RĀ, 146.17–20: *yathā śrāvakayāne 'ṣṭāv uktāḥ śrāvakabhūmayaḥ / mahāyāne daśa tathā bodhisattvasya bhūmayaḥ //.*

1343 The quoted passage is at the beginning of the fourth chapter (LAS, 211.11–13): *ṣaṣṭiṁ mahāmate bhūmim upādāya bodhisattvā mahāsattvāḥ sarvaśrāvakapratyekabuddhāś ca nirodhaṁ samāpadyante.*

1344 The Sanskrit is slightly different from the Tibetan here: "A bodhisattva who has obtained this state, becomes equal to a tathāgata on account of having liberated sentient beings in [various] worlds." (RGVV, 52.9–10: *etāṁ gatim anuprāpto bodhisattvas tathāgataiḥ [/] samatām eti lokeṣu sattvasaṁ*[a] *tāraṇaṁ prati //.*)

a According to Johnston. B (29a4) reads *-sāṁ-*. A is not available.

1345 Kong sprul Blo gros mtha' yas understands *rjes thob* in the sense of *pṛṣṭhalabdha,* the technical term for the state obtained after meditation (see Tsultrim Gyamtsho and Fuchs 2000:140). The literal Sanskrit equivalent is the past participle *anuprāpto,* which is subordinate to *bodhisattvaḥ:* "a bodhisattva who has obtained this state *(gati),*" in an allusion to a bodhisattva's true engagement in working for the benefit of others in the preceding stanza.

1346 In the Tibetan translation *tāṁ* was taken as a demonstrative pronoun modifying *tathatām*: "Bodhisattva[s] fully realize this suchness...." See, however, Haribhadra's commentary in the next footnote.

1347 The position of Tib. *zhes* is problematic. Haribhadra comments (quoted according to Yuyama 1976:50): "Therefore, having thoroughly internalized it (i.e., the dharmatā) as the suchness of everything, they are given the names tathāgata, buddha, son of the victorious one, and so forth." *(de lta bas na de yang thams cad kyi de bzhin nyid du thugs su chud pas de'i phyir de bzhin gshegs zhes sangs rgyas dang rgyal ba'i sras zhes bya ba la sogs par mtshan gsol to.)* Tib. *zhes* could be a misspelling for the instrumental *kyis.* In the Sanskrit, tathāgata is in the instrumental, and this, according to Yuyama, is supported by the Chinese. The entire stanza XII.4 reads according to Yuyama (1976:50.3–6): *tiṣṭhanta loka vidunāṁ parinirvṛtānāṁ sthita eṣa dharmata niyāmata śūnya dharmāḥ / tāṁ bodhisattva tathatām anubuddhayanti*[a] */ tasmā hu buddha* [b]*kṛtu nāma*[b] *tathāgatebhiḥ //.*

a I prefer the 3rd person plural ending attested in Yuyama's edition. The subject can be *bodhisattva,* the nominative plural ending *-a* being possible, particularly in stanzas (see Edgerton BHSG § 8.79).

b Obermiller (1937:49) reads: *kṛtanāma.*

1348 The Tibetan has no equivalent for *-pramukhaṁ.*

1349 NGMPP reel nos. A 38/5 and A 39/13 (the old Nepalese manuscript in Gupta script was in disorder and not identified as one text during the microfilm work (see Matsuda 1996:xv-xvi)), fol. 32b1–2: *asyāṁ khalu*[a] *punar bho jinaputra saptamyāṁ bodhisattvabhūmau sthito*[b] *bodhisattvo bhūyastvena rāgādipramukhaṁ sarvakleśagaṇaṁ*[c] *samatikrānto bhavati / so 'syāṁ saptamyāṁ*[d] *[dūraṅgamāyāṁ bodhisattvabhūmau caran bodhisattvo 'saṁkleśāniṣkleśa iti vaktavyaḥ // tat* [e]*kasmāt // a*[e]*samudācāratvāt*[f] *sarvakleśānāṁ]*[g] *na saṁkleśa iti vaktavyaḥ / tathāgatajñānābhilāṣād aparipūrṇābhiprāyatvāc ca na niṣkleśa iti vaktavyaḥ //.*

The passage is missing in the manuscript labeled B by Matsuda (NGMPP A 38/7). In Rahder's (1926) edition the passage is on p. 59, ll.3–8 (7th *bhūmi,* F) and in Kondō's (1936) on p. 119, l.15–p. 120, l.4.

a Rahder and Kondō omit *khalu.*

b Rahder and Kondō read *sthito* (not readable in the Nepalese manuscript).

c Kondō: *-ṇa.*

d Rahder and Kondō omit *saptamyāṁ.* In the Nepalese manuscript the *akṣara* after *sapta-* is not readable.

e Kondō: *kasmāda-* instead of *kasmāt // a-.*

f Rahder: *-cārāt.*

g The passage in brackets has broken away from the palm-leaf. It has been inserted according to the editions of Rahder and Kondō.

1350 Lit., "purity in terms of three circles."

1351 MSABh, 81.9–12: *śuddhā trimaṇḍalena hi [seyaṁ]*[a] *deśanā hi buddhānāṁ / doṣair vivarjitā punar aṣṭabhir eṣaiva vijñeyā //* [XII.]11 *// śuddhā trimaṇḍaleneti / yena ca deśayati vācā padaiś ca / yathā coddeśādiprakāraiḥ / yeṣu codghaṭitavipañcitajñeṣu /.*

a A gap of two syllables was filled by Lévi with *teyaṁ.*

1352 The whole sentence from which this short passage is taken is as follows (translation by Powers 1994:141): "Then the Bhagavan turned a third wheel of doctrine, possessing good differentiations, and exceedingly wonderous, for those genuinely engaged in all vehicles, beginning with the lack of own-being of phenomena, and beginning with their absence of production, absence of cessation, quiescence from the start, and being naturally in a state of nirvāṇa."

1353 I.e., the previous defining characteristic of omniscience (the fourteenth of altogether sixteen), abbreviated as *unmiñjādisaṁjñakaṁ* in the root text (AA, 23.15 (verse IV.16b)). According to the *Sphuṭārtha* (41.5–6) this is the "knowledge of minds that are active and so forth" *(cittonmiñjitādijñāna)* and the fifteenth the "knowledge of [minds that are] active and so forth in their aspects of suchness" *(unmiñjitāditathatākārajñāna).*

The Eighth Karmapa Mi bskyod rdo rje glosses in his *Abhisamayālaṁkāra* commentary (part 2, 161.5) "active and so forth" as "active, withdrawn, scattered, and contracted" *(...g.yo ba dang / la sogs pas 'du ba dang / bkram pa dang bcum pa....)* These four mental states are connected with the fourteen issues (whether the Tathāgata exists after death, etc.) that were not determined by the Buddha when he was asked about them (see Mi bskyod rdo rje: *Dbu ma la 'jug pa'i rnam bshad*, part 2, 161.5–164.6).

1354 AA, 23.17: *punas tathatākāreṇa teṣāṁ jñānam ataḥ paraṁ //.* These two *pādas* are devoted to the fifteenth of sixteen aspects or defining characteristics of omniscience.

1355 AA, 23.18: *tathatāyāṁ muner bodhi [tatparākhyānam]....* (the part in brackets is not quoted in the DRSM). This is the last of an enumeration of sixteen aspects or defining characteristics of omniscience.

1356 DBhS (ed. Rahder), 71.4–5: *[bodhisattvo] ...śakrabrahmalokapālapratyudgataś....*

1357 The Sanskrit has the locative *pṛthivyāṁ* ("on the earth").

1358 In the Sanskrit "music" *(-vāditra-*, Tib. *rol mo)* and "singing" *(-gīta-*, Tib. *glu)* are in the reverse order. The Skt. compound also has one word less then the Tibetan. Possibly there was a word for music such as *saṁgīta* in front of *gīta* that was dropped. The compound member *-vāditra-* would then not be "music" but also like *-vīṇā-*, a "stringed instrument," of which there are two kinds in Tibetan. The problem is, however, that *pi vang* (which is the equivalent for *-vīṇā-*) and *sil snyan* are also in reverse order.

1359 Tib. *sil snyan.*

1360 LAS, 55.3–17: *kathaṁ bhagavan svacittadṛśyadhārā viśudhyati yugapat kramavṛttyā vā / bhagavān āha / kramavṛttyā mahāmate svacittadṛśyadhārā viśudhyati na yugapat / tad yathā mahāmate āmraphalāni kramaśaḥ pacyante na yugapat / evam eva mahāmate svacittadṛśyadhārā sattvānāṁ kramaśo viśudhyati na yugapat / tad yathā mahāmate kumbhakāraḥ kramaśo bhāṇḍāni kurute na yugapat / evam eva mahāmate tathāgataḥ sattvānāṁ svacittadṛśyadhārāṁ kramaśo viśodhayati na yugapat / tad yathā mahāmate pṛthivyāṁ tṛṇagulmauṣadhivanaspatayaḥ kramavṛttyā virohanti na yugapat / evam eva mahāmate sattvānāṁ tathāgataḥ kramaśaḥ svacittadṛśyadhārāṁ viśodhayati na yugapat / tad yathā mahāmate hāsyalāsyagītavāditravīṇālekhyayogyāḥ kramaśaḥ pravartante na yugapat [/] evam eva mahāmate tathāgataḥ sarvasattvānāṁ kramaśaḥ svacittadṛśyadhārāṁ viśodhayati na yugapat.*

1361 Lit., "as something without concepts," i.e., without the usual mental activity that produces appearances.

1362 The syntactic position of *sems can* in the Tibetan translation of the *Laṅkāvatārasūtra* from the Sanskrit (DRSM, 42.14) makes it difficult to construe. The Tibetan translation from the Chinese (Peking Kangyur no. 776, *mdo*, vol. *ngu*, fol. 224a4) reads in accordance with the Sanskrit.: *...bag chags dang bral ba'i sems can rnams la....*

1363 LAS, 55.17–56.6: *tad yathā mahāmate darpaṇāntargatāḥ sarvarūpāvabhāsāḥ saṁdṛśyante nirvikalpā yugapat / evam eva mahāmate svacittadṛśyadhārāṁ yugapat tathāgataḥ sarvasattvānāṁ viśodhayati nirvikalpāṁ nirābhāsagocarām / tad yathā mahāmate somādityamaṇḍalaṁ yugapat sarvarūpāvabhāsān kiraṇaiḥ prakāśayati / evam eva mahāmate tathāgataḥ svacittadṛśyadauṣṭhulyavāsanāvigatānāṁ sattvānāṁ yugapad acintyajñānajinagocaraviṣayaṁ saṁdarśayati /.*

1364 I have found this passage neither in the *Āryalaṅkāvatāravṛtti* (Peking Tengyur no. 5519) nor in the *Āryalaṅkāvatāranāmamahāyānasūtravṛttitathāgatahṛdayālaṁkāranāma* (Peking Tengyur no. 5520). Tib. *zhes pa'o*, however, does not necessarily mark a direct quotation. Cf. DRSM, 80.8–11, where a summary of a passage from RGVV on I.2 (but not the passage itself) is marked by *zhes bya ba*. It is also possible that 'Bri gung 'Jig rten gsum mgon's explanations of the three dharmacakras are being referred to here (Gzhon nu dpal (574.9–10) mentions in his colophon that he based himself on such explanations as well as on 'Jig rten gsum mgon's notes on the *Ratnagotravibhāga*).

1365 According to the Sanskrit, the subject is still the stream, which arises in various forms of consciousness.

1366 LAS, 46.3–6: *taraṅgā hy udadher yadvat pavanapratyayeritāḥ / nṛtyamānāḥ pravartante vyucchedaś ca na vidyate // ālayaughas tathā nityaṁ viṣayapavaneritaḥ / citrais taraṅgavijñānair nṛtyamānaḥ pravartate //.*

1367 In the Sanskrit, the enumerated objects are in the plural: "Blue phenomena."

1368 According to the Sanskrit: "neither different nor not different."

1369 According to the Sanskrit: "waves from the ocean." That means, taking *udadheḥ* as an ablative: "the waves are neither different nor not different from the ocean." According to Tibetan the rays of the sun and the moon are not the end of the enumeration, but one of the examples, rays being neither different nor not different from the sun and the moon. But Gzhon nu dpal, in accordance with the Sanskrit, takes the sun's rays as being the last member of the enumeration (DRSM, 43.11).

1370 LAS, 46.7–10: *nīle rakte 'tha lavaṇe śaṅkhe kṣīre ca śārkare / kaṣāyaiḥ (?) phalapuṣpādyaiḥ (?) kiraṇā yatha*[a] *bhāskare //* [b] *na cānanye na cānye ca*[b] *taraṅgā hy udadher matāḥ*[c] */ vijñānāni tathā sapta cittena saha saṁyutāḥ //.*

a *-tha* is short for metrical reasons.

b According to the emendation Nanjio proposes in a footnote. The reading of A (17a6), C (20b5), D (17a1) and F (8b9): *na cānyena ca nānanyena* is not possible for metrical reasons. G (30b3–4) and K (16b8) read *na cānye na ca nānanye* (which does not make any sense); B (27b3), E (26a5–b1) *na cānye na ca nānātve,* and H (18b7) *na cānya na ca nānātve,* which would mean having the abstract suffix *tva* in the hybrid nominative plural ending. I (21b6) has *na cānyena cānanyena.*

c Nanjio reads *matā.*

1371 Lit., "on account of the sun's rays."

1372 TŚK, 34.13–14: *manovijñānasambhūtiḥ sarvadāsaṁjñikād ṛte / samāpattidvayān middhān mūrchanād apy acittakāt //.* My translation follows Gzhon nu dpal's quote, in which one *pāda* with the "two attainments [of cessation]" *(snyoms par 'jug pa rnam gnyis dang)* is missing.

1373 I.e., eye consciousness, etc.

1374 I could not identify this quotation either in the *Triṁśikābhāṣya* or in the *Triṁśikāṭīkā.* In both the *bhāṣya* and the *ṭīkā* five states void of active consciousness are explained, not only the three of Gzhon nu dpal's quotation.

1375 LAS, 46.11–14: *udadheḥ pariṇāmo 'sau taraṅgāṇāṁ vicitratā / ālayaṁ hi tathā citraṁ vijñānākhyaṁ pravartate // cittaṁ manaś ca vijñānaṁ lakṣaṇārthaṁ prakalpyate / abhinnalakṣaṇā hy aṣṭau na lakṣyā na ca lakṣaṇāḥ*[a] *//.*

a According to G (30b5) and I (22a1). The manuscripts in the Royal Asiatic Society (London), the University Library of Cambridge, the one formerly in the possession of Kawaguchi (according to the Nanjio's edition) and the remaining Nepalese manuscripts read *-ṇāṁ;* Nanjio proposes *-ṇam.* It is, like *lakṣyāḥ,* an adjective depending on *aṣṭau [vijñānāni],* so that the correct reading should be: *na lakṣyāni na ca lakṣaṇāni,* in the same way as the correct form of the preceding *bahuvrīhi* compound is *abhinnalakṣaṇāni.* But so many long endings in the nominative neuter plural *(-āni)* would have been insoluble problems for the meter.

1376 For a discussion of *pariṇāmayati,* etc., see Schmithausen 1969:165f.

1377 LAS, 46.15–16: *udadheś ca taraṅgāṇāṁ yathā nāsti viśeṣaṇam / vijñānānāṁ tathā citte* [a] *pariṇāmo na labhyate //.* My construction of the sentence follows the Sanskrit.

a According to B (27b5), C (21a1), E (26b2), G (31a1) and I (22a2). The locative must be used in its ablative function.

1378 The quoted stanza is from the "Dohās for the People" ("Do ha mdzod kyi glu bzhugs so," fol. 148a3).

1379 That is, coemergent wisdom.

1380 The Apabhraṁsa version of this stanza is as follows: *jatta bi cittaha bipphuraï tatta bi ṇāha sarūba / aṇṇa taraṅga ki aṇṇa jalu bhabasama khasama sarūa //* (Shahidullah 1928:152, stanza 74). Shahidullah (1928:177) translates: "Dans ce qui sort de la pensée, il ya là la nature du maître. La vague et la mer sont-elles choses différentes? L'égalité de l'existance est de la nature de l'égalité du ciel."

Karma Phrin las pa explains in his *Do ha skor gsum gyi ṭīkā 'bring po bzhugs so* (103.5–104.3): "Whatever grasping there is, [namely] all the thoughts of mental factors, which emanate from the mind, and however long [these thoughts] move and emanate, their nature will be that of the protector of all sentient beings, [namely] the [original] mind, the coemergent wisdom. Are waves and water different or not? Just as water waves are water, so too the emanation as multiplicity from the true nature of mind *(sems nyid)* arises from the fundamental state of the mind, [namely] the dharmakāya, which is without origination, and dissolves back [into it]. Therefore it is not different from the dharmakāya.... Moreover, since its own manifold energy of unhindered brightness shines forth from the fundamental state, [namely] the sphere of the unborn dharmakāya, both saṁsāra and nirvāṇa are inseparable in reality, even though they appear as two. Since one understands the identity of worldly existence (saṁsāra) and nirvāṇa, [one knows that] both are of one taste within the sphere of the true nature of mind *(sems nyid)*, even though they are labeled as [if they were] different—in the same way as space has neither middle nor extreme, having the nature of empti[ness]." *(de yang 'dzin pa gang zhig sems las rnam par 'phros pa'i sems byung gi rnam par rtog pa mtha' dag ji srid du 'gyu zhing 'phro (text: 'phre) ba de srid du / skye dgu'i mgon po gyur pa sems lhan cig skyes pa'i ye shes kyi rang bzhin yin te dper na chu dang rlabs dag gzhan yin nam ste chu rlabs chu yin pa bzhin du sems nyid las sna tshogs su 'phro ba de yang sems kyi gzhis skye ba med pa'i chos sku las byung zhing der thim pas na / chos sku dang tha mi dad pa yin no / ...de yang gzhis skye med chos sku'i ngang las mdangs 'gags med pa'i rang rtsal sna tshogs shar bas 'khor 'das gnyis su snang yang de gnyis po ni don la dbyer med de / srid pa 'khor ba dang mnyam pa nyid myang 'das shes rtog pas tha dad du btags kyang / de gnyis ka sems nyid kyi ngang du ro gcig pa ni dper na nam mkha' la mtha' dbus med pa stong pa'i rang bzhin can yin pa bzhin no).*

1381 This quotation has not been identified.

1382 This refers not only to the fact that the perceiving subject and the perceived object are the same in reality, but also that the subject-object duality is in reality not different from the true nature of mind.

1383 This quotation has not been identified.

1384 The translation of the Sanskrit would be: "Thinking of this element of a tathāgata, which has the potential of purity...."

1385 RGVV, 6.8–10: *etat eva viśuddhi*[a]*gotraṁ tathāgatadhātum abhisaṁdhāyoktam / yathā pattha*[b]*racuṇṇamhi jātarūpaṁ na dissati / parikammeṇa tad diṭṭhaṁ evaṁ loke tathāgatā iti //*. Here the portion of the *vyākhyā* commented is not quoted *en bloc*, as is usually done, but embedded in Gzhon nu dpal's glosses. The translation of it is in bold letters.

a According to B (4b1); A is not available. Johnston reads *viśuddha-*.

b In B (4b1) *-ttha-* is not readable (there is an empty space between *-pa-* and *-ra-*).

1386 Tib. *'gyur.*

1387 RGVV, 71.5–6: *prakṛter avikāritvāt kalyāṇatvād viśuddhitaḥ / hemamaṇḍalakau-*

pamyaṁ tathatāyām udāhṛtam //. Cf. Takasaki 1966:287. This refers to the fourth example of the *Tathāgatagarbhasūtra,* in which a traveler loses a piece of gold in some mud.

1388 See MSA XII.11, which is quoted and commented upon above (DRSM, 41.7–10).

1389 The DRSM reads *mos pas sa yang dag par* as against *mos pa las yang dag par* in the Kangyur. This reading serves well to make his point that one realizes the pure bodhisattva levels only with the teaching of the third dharmacakra.

1390 See also Powers 1994:141–43; and Lamotte 1935:207–8. My translation follows Lamotte.

1391 Tib. *glo bur du,* otherwise translated as "adventitious," refers to the fact that the hindrances of defilements are not an indivisible part of the true nature.

1392 The plural particle *rnams* after *btang snyoms* marks the end of the enumeration of the four immeasurable qualities, the first three, *rnying rje, byams pa,* and *dga' ba,* having been described in the lines before (DRSM, 46.1–2).

1393 The last eight stanzas of the first chapter (RGV I.163–70) explain the five reasons why the existence of the buddha element must be taught after the previous presentations of emptiness in the second dharmacakra: If one does not know that all sentient beings possess buddha nature, (1) one may become discouraged about the possibility of attaining buddhahood, (2) one may feel contempt for persons who have a lesser understanding, (3) one may have misconceptions of the true nature and believe that appearances are real, (4) one may think that sentient beings are simply void and ridicule their nature, and (5) one may think more highly of oneself than others (See Takasaki 1966:306–9; and Tsultrim Gyamtsho and Fuchs 2000:177–81).

1394 The quoted passage constitutes the entire introduction of the *Bodhicittavivaraṇa* (see Lindtner 1987:184–85, whose translation I mainly follow).

1395 The following *pādas* correspond to a nonmetrical passage in the second chapter of the *Guhyasamājatantra* (which is on *bodhicitta*): *sarvabhāvavigataṁ skandhadhātvāyatanagrāhyagrāhakavarjitaṁ dharmanairātmyasamatayā svacittam ādyanutpannaṁ śūnyatā[sva]bhāvam /* (GST, 12.3–5).

1396 In the Sanskrit, the first three lines are two compounds depending on *svacittam* ("your own mind"). According to Zhva dmar Chos grags ye shes (who wrote his commentary on the basis of Gzhon nu dpal's explanations), the first three *pādas* are directed against the views of systems that postulate the existence of external, nonmental entities, so that it would be better to add "reality" in brackets for "your own mind." For a follower of Yogācāra-Madhyamaka, there is in any case no difference.

1397 The DRSM reads... *skye mched dang* (which is also supported by Zhva dmar Chos grags ye shes's commentary) against *skye mched kyi* (see Lindtner 1987:184).

1398 Zhva dmar Chos grags ye shes explains in his *Byang chub sems 'grel gyi rnam par bshad pa tshig don gsal ba* (64.10–4): "The first of [these] six *pādas* (*kārikās*) disproves the bad views put forth by heretics; the second and third *pādas* refute the views of the Vaibhāṣikas and Sautrāntikas [from among] our own Buddhist tradition; and the fourth *pāda* makes one abandon the *cittamātra* view. The fifth and sixth *pādas* present and establish the Madhyamaka view" *(tshigs su bcad pa rkang pa drug gi rkang pa dang pos mu stegs byed kyi lta ba ngan pa sun 'byin la / rkang pa gnyis pa dang gsum pas nang sde bye brag tu smra ba dang mdo sde pa'i lta ba 'gog cing / rkang pa bzhi pas sems tsam gyi lta ba spong bar mdzad nas / rkang pa lnga pa dang drug pas dbu ma'i lta ba bsgrub cing rnam par 'jog go /).*

1399 This second quote follows the first one. The reason for two quotes is to omit the qualified subject "bodhisattvas whose conduct is the way of secret mantras" (*byang chub sems dpa' gsang sngags kyi sgor spyad pa spyod pa rnams kyis;* see Lindtner

1987:184). Thus Gzhon nu dpal creates the impression that ultimate *bodhicitta* is also generated by Mahāyāna practitioners in general and not only by followers of Vajrayāna.

1400 Zhva dmar Chos grags ye shes (*op. cit.*, 68.10–6) explains: "Having generated [bodhi]citta as someone possessing the nature of boundless great compassion, [bodhisattvas] must generate in [their own mind]-stream the supramundane ultimate *bodhicitta* that is the object of the wisdom of the noble ones—in the same way as [this ultimate] is realized through the accumulation of wisdom, [that is, by] the power of meditation in which one familiarizes oneself with a mind in equipose [resting] in dharmatā." *(de yang mi dmigs pa'i snying rje chen po'i rang bzhin can du sems bskyed nas / 'phags pa'i ye shes kyi yul du 'gyur ba'i don dam pa'i byang chub kyi sems 'jig rten las 'das pa de ni / chos nyid la mnyam par bzhag pa la sems goms par byed pa'i bsgom pa'i stobs ye shes kyi tshogs kyis rtogs pa ji lta bzhin rgyud la bskyed par bya ba yin te.)*

1401 Zhva dmar Chos grags ye shes (*op. cit.*, 105.1–8) remarks: "Whoever has attained certainty with respect to the nature of ultimate *bodhicitta* should also know that it has been taught by [the use of] synonyms. [Ultimate *bodhicitta*] is suchness, which is nothing other than the true nature of all phenomena. In view of its unmistaken meaning, [ultimate *bodhicitta*] is [also] the limit of reality. In view of being free from all characteristic signs of apprehension, it is signlessness. In view of its being the object of the wisdom of the noble ones, it is ultimate. Since *bodhicitta* with the previously mentioned defining characteristics is the nature of excellent wisdom, it is supreme. [Ultimate *bodhicitta*] is reality, the dharmatā of all phenomena, and [finally] it is emptiness, the pacification of all mental fabrication. In many sūtras and tantras, too, it has been explained as having these defining characteristics." *(gang yang don dam byang chub sems kyi rang bzhin nges par gyur nas / de ming gi rnam grangs kyis bstan pa yang shes par bya ste / chos thams cad kyi gnas lugs las gzhan du ma yin pa'i de bzhin nyid dang / phyin ci ma log pa'i don dang ldan pas yang dag pa'i mtha' dang / dmigs pa'i mtshan ma kun dang bral bas mtshan ma med pa dang / 'phags pa ye shes kyi yul du gyur pas don dam pa nyid dang / sngar smos pa'i mtshan nyid dang ldan pa'i byang chub kyi sems ye shes phul du byung ba'i ngo bo yin pas mchog dang / chos thams cad kyi chos nyid de kho na nyid dang / spros pa thams cad zhi ba stong pa nyid ces bya ba'i mtshan nyid du'ang mdo rgyud mang po las bshad pa yin no //.)*

1402 The corresponding passage in the Peking Tengyur (no. 2010, *bstod tshogs*, vol. *ka*, 74b8–75a4) differs considerably from Gzhon nu dpal's version.

1403 Karma pa Rang byung rdo rje (*Dbu ma chos dbyings bstod pa'i rnam par bshad pa*, 22a8–b1 and 22b5–6 and 22b7–8) explains that this refers to the recognition of the first nonconceptual moment of the eye consciousness that resembles a yogic direct valid cognition: "That which has not entered the conceptual realm of super-imposition with regard to any appearance of form is, by its very nature, appearance as well as empti[ness]. In this [state, appearances] neither arise nor cease as [something possessing] an own-being, they are mere perceptions. This is also called direct valid cognition of the eye-faculties.... Those who follow the [noble ones] have correct perceptions focused on appearances that seem to be outside [of consciousness]. These are valid cognitions, since they resemble yogic direct [cognitions] ...Given that outside objects made up of subtle atoms and so forth, and which are different from that which merely appears outside, do not truly exist, you realize that self-luminous appearances neither arise nor cease, and ascertain that they are the dharmadhātu itself." *(gang gzugs snang la sgro btags pa'i rtog pa ma zhugs pa ni / rang gi ngo bos snang ba yin / stong pa yang yin / de la ni rang gi ngo bos skye ba med cing 'gag pa med pa rnam par rig pa tsam ste / 'di ni mig gi dbang po'i mngon sum tshad ma zhes kyang bya ste / ...de'i rjes su 'breng ba rnams ni / phyi rol ltar snang ba dmigs pa'i rnam rig ma 'khrul ba ni tshad ma yin te / rnal 'byor mngon sum dang 'dra ba'i phyir ro...phyi ltar snang ba tsam las gzhan pa'i phyi rol gyi don rdul phra rab la sogs par bden pa med pas / rang gsal bar snang ba la skye 'gag med par rtogs shing chos kyi dbyings nyid du nges par 'gyur ro /.)*

1404 The Peking Tengyur (*op. cit.*, 75a1) reads *rnam par dag pa'i shes pa gsum*, "three [forms of] pure knowledge." Given that the thrust of this passage is that the eighteen *dhātus* are realized as the dharmadhātu, and thus luminosity, "three forms of consciousness" must refer to the mental forms (similar to the *vijñaptis* in the Yogācāra) of sound, ears, and the corresponding consciousness.

1405 Ibid., 75a2: *rtog pa dang bcas pas thos par 'gyur*, "they become hearing when accompanied by thought." Rang byung rdo rje (*Dbu ma chos dbyings bstod pa'i rnam par bshad pa*, 23a2–4) has the reading of the Peking Tengyur but explains: " ...a pure [ear] consciousness free from thoughts and confusion has arisen. It is, by its very nature, without defining characteristics, [and] must be realized as the dharmadhātu itself, free from the three [processes of] arising, ceasing, and abiding. As for [the state] marked by clinging to sound as a characteristic sign, it becomes hearing owing to a state of consciousness marked by confusion and thought." *(...rnam par shes pa dag pa rtog pa dang bral zhing ma 'khrul pa skyes te / de yang rang gi ngo bos mtshan nyid med pa / skye 'gag gnas gsum dang bral ba'i chos kyi dbyings nyid du rtogs par bya'o / sgra la mtshan mar 'dzin pa dang bcas pa ni 'khrul pa rtog pa dang bcas pa'i shes pas thos par 'gyur te /.)*

1406 The Peking Tengyur (*op. cit.*, 75a2) reads: "Based on the nose and odor, one smells. This is an example of formlessness. Similarly, the olfactory consciousness makes one realize the dharmadhātu" *(sna dang dri la brten nas snom / de ni gzugs su med pa'i dpe / de bzhin sna yi rnam shes kyis / chos kyi dbyings la rtog par byed /)*. Here, too, Rang byung rdo rje (*op. cit.*, 23a4–5) follows the reading of the Peking Tengyur.

1407 Tib. *dben pa*, Skt. *vivikta*, a term referring to reality in the sense of the ultimate mode of existence (see Seyfort Ruegg 1971:467).

1408 Gser mdog paṇ chen Śākya mchog ldan ("Chos kyi dbyings su bstod pa zhes bya ba'i bstan bcos kyi rnam par bshad pa," 318.6–7) explains: "Given the dharmadhātu-nature of both, they do not abide as the cause of the consciousness of taste,..." *(gnyis ka chos kyi dbyings kyi ngo bo yis lce'i rnam par shes pa'i rgyur gnas pa med....)*

1409 The Peking Tengyur (*op. cit.*, 75a3–4) reads: *dag pa'i lus kyi ngo bo dang / reg bya'i rkyen gyi mtshan nyid dag / rkyen dag las ni grol gyur pa / chos kyi dbyings zhes brjod par bya /*, "The nature of the pure body, the pure defining characteristics of the conditions of tangible objects, and [their respective consciousness, which is] free from conditions—these must be called dharmadhātu."

1410 Read *brtags* or *btags* instead of *brtag*? (Cf. Rang byung rdo rje: *Dbu ma chos dbyings bstod pa'i rnam par bshad pa*, 25a1–3.)

1411 Śākya mchog ldan (*op. cit.*, 319.1) explains: "On the level of apparent truth it is on the basis of the mental faculty and phenomena, that [mind] has mainly become mental consciousness" *(kun rdzob tu yid dang chos la brten nas yid kyi rnam par shes pa gtso bor gyur pa ste)*.

1412 The Peking Tengyur (Ibid., fol. 75a4) reads *pa nyid* instead of *nyid las*.

1413 Tib. *nye ba rgyu ba*, Skt. *upavicāra* (see Index to the *Abhidharmakośabhāṣya*, s.v.), i.e., the mental movement that occurs when the eighteen *dhātus* interact.

1414 Tib. *gnas rigs*. Further down they are referred to as "worlds" *('jig rten)*.

1415 Strictly speaking, there are no forms in the formless realms, and in this context it is only their luminosity that is seen.

1416 In contrast to the "eyes of flesh" further up, here the Tibetan honorific term for eyes *(spyan)* is used.

1417 See Eimer 1978:122–23 and BPP, 37.

1418 In the Peking Tengyur (no. 2010) the quoted passage is in *bstod tshogs*, vol. *ka*, fol. 74b3–5. There, however, one *pāda* in the last stanza of the quotation is missing.

1419 The Peking Tengyur (*op. cit.*, 74b3) reads *btags* instead of *brtags*.

1420 Ibid., 74b4: *phra rab rdul gyi ngo bo yis / glang gi rva yang rigs ma yin:* "Even the horn of an ox is logically not justified in terms of an own-being of minute atoms."

1421 Rang byung rdo rje (*Dbu ma chos dbyings bstod pa'i rnam par bshad pa*, 19a5–6) explains: "All phenomena that are free from the three [processes of] arising, ceasing, and abiding, remain, by nature, inseparable appearance and empti[ness]. Anything imagined as arising and ceasing does not exist" *(skye 'gag gnas gsum dang bral ba'i chos thams cad / rang gi ngo bos snang ba dang stong pa dbyer med par bzhugs pa la / skye ba dang 'gag par brtags (text: rtag) pa ni 'ga' yang yod par ma yin no).*

1422 Peking Tengyur, *op. cit.*, 74b5 : *gcig kyang yod pa ma yin no*, "a single [independent thing] does not exist."

1423 This *pāda* is missing in the Tengyur editions and the commentaries of Rang byung rdo rje and Śākya mchog ldan.

1424 Ibid., 74b5: *ri bong ba lang rva yi dpes / ji ltar bde gshegs chos rnams nyid / dbu ma nyid du sgrub par byed //.* Cf. Seyfort Ruegg's (1971:467) paraphrase: "Par l'exemple des cornes du lièvre et du bœuf on établit que les qualités du *tathāgata (sugatadharma)* ne sont autres que le Milieu *(madhyama).*" In a footnote he further explains: "Les *buddhadharma*, qui sont *asaṁskṛta* 'incomposées,' ne sont ni inexistants et purement nominaux comme la corne du lièvre, ni des entités existantes et, partant, *saṁskṛta* comme la corne du bœuf."

Śākya mchog ldan (*op. cit.*, 315.1–3) comments: "The Sugata has proven that all phenomena of saṁsāra and nirvāṇa [conform to] the middle way of abandoning duality. If one asks how, it is on the basis of the examples of the horn of a rabbit and an ox. Even the horn of a rabbit can at least be imputed in mind and speech; and even the horn of an ox does not have an own-being" *(bde bar gshegs pas 'khor 'das kyi chos thams cad gnyis spang pa'i dbu ma nyid du sgrub par byed do / ji ltar zhe na / ri bong gi rva dang ba glang gi rva yi dpe las so / / de yang shes brjod kyi btags pa tsam ni ri bong gi rva la yang yod la / rang gi ngo bo ni glang gi rva la yang med pa'o /).*

Rang byung rdo rje (*op. cit.*, 20a3) notes: "Those, who propound in accordance with the Dharma taught by the Sugata, have abandoned the clinging to extremes and proven that [all phenomena conform to] the middle way" *(bde bar gshegs pas (text: pa'i) bstan pa'i chos dang mthun par smra ba rnams ni mthar 'dzin pa dor nas / dbu ma nyid du bgrub par byed /).*

1425 In the Peking Tengyur (no. 2010) the quoted passage is in *bstod tshogs*, vol. *ka*, fol. 74a3–6. As in the preceding quotations from the *Dharmadhātustotra*, the number of differences between the versions in the Derge and the Peking Tengyurs and Gzhon nu dpal is unusually high. But in this case, the Sanskrit original (stanzas 18–22) has survived as a quote in Nāropa's *Sekoddeśaṭīkā* (see Seyfort Ruegg 1971:466), and Gzhon nu dpal's reading is closer to the Sanskrit in all instances. *Pāda* 18b: P: *du ba khug rna*, DRSM: *khug rna du ba*, Skt. *-nīhāradhūmena; pādas* 18d and 19d: DRSM renders the past participles *āvṛtau* and *āvṛtaṁ* with the auxiliary verb *gyur* in the past tense, whereas P has in both cases *'gyur; pāda* 21b: Skt. *malinaṁ rāgajair malaiḥ* is accurately translated in DRSM as: *chags skyes dri mas dri ma can*, over against DP (Derge and Peking Tengyur) *'dod chags la sogs dri ma can; pāda* 21c: DRSM turns the past participle *dagdhaṁ* into the past form *bsregs*, whereas P has *sreg; pāda* 21d: *na dagdhaṁ tat prabhāsvaraṁ* is precisely rendered in DRSM as *'od gsal de ni bsregs ma yin,* while DP have: *de nyid 'od gsal ma yin no.*

1426 Lit., "the mouth of rāhu."

1427 Seyfort Ruegg 1971:466: *nirmalau candrasūryau hy āvṛtau pañcabhir malaiḥ / abhranīhāradhūmena rāhuvaktrarajomalaiḥ //* (18).

1428 Ibid.: *evaṁ prabhāsvaraṁ cittam āvṛtaṁ pañcabhir malaiḥ / kāmavyāpādamiddhena auddhatyavicikitsayā //* (19).

1429 Ibid.: *agniśaucaṁ*[a] *yathā vastraṁ malinaṁ vividhair malaiḥ / agnimadhye yathākṣiptaṁ malaṁ dagdhaṁ na vastratā //* (20).

a Seyfort Ruegg (Ibid.) has *agniḥ śaucaṁ* and translates: "Le feu étant pureté...," which is syntactically problematic.

1430 Ibid.: *evaṁ prabhāsvaraṁ cittaṁ malinaṁ rāgajair malaiḥ / jñānāgninā malaṁ dagdhaṁ na dagdhaṁ tat prabhāsvaraṁ //* (21).

1431 Ibid.: *śūnyatāhārakāḥ sūtrā ye kecid bhāṣitā jinaiḥ / sarvais taiḥ kleśavyāvṛttir naiva dhātuvināśanam //* (22).

1432 Tib. *tha mal gyi shes pa.*

1433 The quoted passage is from the first part of the first chapter on the view in the *Phyag rgya chen po lam zab mthar thug zhang gi man ngag,* 51–55. For another translation of this passage see Martin 1992:255–58.

1434 I follow Jackson (1990:74) and read *na* as against *nas* in both the block print and the manuscript of Gzhon nu dpal's *Ratnagotravibhāga* commentary.

1435 Here, too, Jackson's (1990:74) reading *kun* is to be preferred as against *nyid* in both versions of Gzhon nu dpal's commentary.

1436 The last nine lines have also been translated in Jackson 1990:28.

1437 According to Sorensen 1999:175.

1438 The "Rin chen rgyan 'dra" is contained in the Collected Works of Phag mo gru pa, edited by Kun dga' rin chen chos kyi rgyal mtshan, in vol. II *(kha),* 216b6–225a4. The quoted passage occurs on fol. 217a3f.

1439 The *Rin chen rgyan 'dra* as edited by Kun dga' rin chen chos kyi rgyal mtshan (Ibid.) has *'dod* instead of *'jug:* "As for the way to maintain pure luminosity...."

1440 The manuscript copy produced by Kun dga' rin chen chos gyi rgyal mtshan (Ibid.) has *pa* instead of *pas,* so that no causal relation is indicated between the third and fourth *pāda.*

1441 In his commentary on Saraha's *Dohākośa* Karma Phrin las pa glosses *sems nyid* as *gnas lugs* ("true nature") (*Do ha skor gsum gyi ṭīkā 'bring po bzhugs so,* 64.4).

1442 In the edition of Kun dga' rin chen chos kyi rgyal mtshan in vol. II *(kha),* 220b4f.

1443 See Gzhon nu dpal's commentary below (DRSM, 51.10).

1444 Tib. *'dzin* in the third line and *gzung* in the fourth and fifth lines are technical terms for the "perceiving subject" *('dzin)* and the "perceived object" *(gzung)* (Skt. *grāhaka* and *grāhya*). Here the intention is to equate the misperception of mind's clarity as one's self with the perceiving subject. The perceived objects are thus the misperceptions engendered by self-awareness and object appearances, as respectively the I and other.

1445 The manuscript copy produced by Kun dga' rin chen chos kyi rgyal mtshan has *nyon mongs can gyi yid* instead of *nyon mongs can yid kyis,* so that the third *pāda* loses its relation to the first two.

1446 Tib. *kun gzhi.* If *kun gzhi* is not an abbreviation for "basic consciousness" *(kun gzhi rnam shes),* we have an early occurrence of the *gzhan stong* term *kun gzhi ye shes* here.

1447 According to Thrangu Rinpoche, the two types of ignorance do not arise, strictly speaking, from wisdom, but from accidental stains that are simultaneously present with coemergent wisdom *(lhan cig skyes pa'i ye shes).*

1448 Both the block print and the manuscript of Gzhon nu dpal's *Ratnagotravibhāga* commentary read *kun gzhi nyid yid du gyur pa.* I suggest to read *nyon yid* instead of *nyid yid,* since it has been explained above that the basic consciousness is the defiled mind appearing as a self. Moreover, the basic consciousness in the form of mental consciousness or the mental faculty can hardly be the substantial cause of the consciousness of the five doors and the mental consciousness.

1449 The quoted stanza is from the "Dohās for the People" ("Do ha mdzod kyi glu bzhugs so," *Nges don phyag chen mdzod,* vol. *oṁ,* 301.1–2). It is not found in Shahidullah's edition.

1450 Karma Phrin las pa explains in his *Do ha skor gsum gyi ṭīkā 'bring po bzhugs so,* 154.1–3: "The seed of both saṁsāra and nirvāṇa is the same true nature of mind *(sems nyid).* Even though the two trunks of worldly existence and quiescence [grown] from this true nature of mind *(sems nyid),* appear to be temporarily separate, the two have the same root. For this reason, their ultimate fruit is the same dharmakāya. Whoever thinks of both worldly existence and quiescence as being undivided [and] equal is liberated from the extremes of saṁsāra and nirvāṇa. Since one does not abide [onesidedly] either in worldy existence or in quiescence, all phenomena must be experienced in such a way that [both of their aspects, namely appearance and emptiness] are united into a pair." *('khor 'das gnyis ka'i sa bon ni sems nyid gcig (text: cig) su yin la [/] sems nyid de las gnas skabs su srid pa dang zhi ba'i sdong po gnyis tha dad pa ltar snang yang de gnyis rtsa ba gcig yin pa'i rgyu mtshan de las mthar thug gi 'bras bu ni chos kyi sku gcig pa'o / srid zhi gnyis po de yang dbyer med mnyam pa nyid du gang sems pa de ni 'khor ba dang mya ngan las 'das pa'i mtha' las rnam par grol zhing srid zhi la mi gnas pas na chos thams cad zung 'jug gi tshul du spyad par bya'o.)*

1451 The quoted stanza is from the "Dohās for the People" ("Do ha mdzod kyi glu bzhugs so," *Phyag chen mdzod,* vol. *oṁ,* 289.5).

1452 My translation follows Karma Phrin las pa who explains in his *Do ha skor gsum gyi ṭīkā 'bring po bzhugs so* (64.4–65.2): "This true nature of mind *(sems nyid),*[a] is like the seed of all saṁsāra and nirvāṇa, because all phenomena of saṁsāra and nirvāṇa appear from it. The true nature of mind *(sems nyid),* in which existence [or] saṁsāra evolves in the form of appearances of a perceived object and a perceiving subject, and in which nirvāṇa spreads in the form of the realization that [mind] is without this duality, is like a wish-fulfilling jewel, in that it bestows whatever fruit one desires, such as the fruits of higher existence or the three *yāna*s. Realizing that the mind is the entire origin of qualities, Saraha prostrates [to it]." *(sems nyid dam gnas lugs gcig pu 'di 'khor 'das kun gyi sa bon lta bu yin te / 'khor 'das kyi chos thams cad 'di las snang ba'i phyir ro // sems nyid gang la gzung 'dzin du snang bas srid pa 'khor ba dang gzung 'dzin gnyis med du rtogs pas mya ngan 'das pa 'phro zhing mtho ris dang theg pa gsum gyi 'bras bu la sogs pa gang 'dod pa'i 'bras bu ster bar byed pa'i don gyis na yid bzhin gyi nor bu dang 'dra ba ste...sems yon tan kun 'byung de rtogs nas sa ra has phyag tshal ba'o.)*

a Both *sems nyid* and *sems kyi gnas lugs* are translated as "true nature of mind."

1453 A cycle of teachings transmitted by the Sa skya school and going back to the mahāsiddha Virūpa.

1454 In the context of "inferior" *(tha ma)* and "average" *('bring), bla ma* must be first of all understood as "superior"; it is obvious, however, that Gzhon nu dpal wants us to understand *bla ma* in the sense of *guru.*

1455 I.e., those of Dam pa Sangs rgyas and Rje Sgam po pa (see above).

1456 Peking Kangyur no. 852, *mdo,* vol. *mu,* fol. 139a6–8.

1457 Tib. *Bir va pa;* see Dowman 1985:52.

1458 According to oral information from Lama Sonam Jorphel: "pure aspects of emptiness."

1459 According to Lama Sonam Jorphel *bla ma rin chen* is here a general term for one's own root lama. Thus Nye gnas Grags pa rin chen glossed the term as Dpal ldan Phag mo gru pa (see *Skyob pa'i gsung bstan bcos tsinta ma ṇi rin po che 'bar ba'i phreng ba'i 'grel pa*, 126.9–10).

1460 I.e., their *rtsa ba'i bla ma.*

1461 According to Lama Sonam Jorphel.

1462 See Ibid., 127.6–7. Tib. *rin chen dbang sngon* means *indranīla* (*Tshig mdzod chen mo*, s.v.), "sapphire."

1463 Nye gnas Grags pa rin chen reads *a nga'i rnam par*, and goes on to explain that *a* stands for the Dharma of nonorigination and nirvāṇa, whereas *nga* stands for the clinging to a self of persons and saṁsāra (*op. cit.*, 130.4–5).

1464 I.e., those inside one's body and the outside world (according to Lama Sonam Jorphel).

1465 According to Lama Sonam Jorphel *chos rje mgon po* is a general term for one's root lama, in this case Phag mo gru pa.

1466 My translation of this quotation is based on the commentary by Nye gnas Grags pa rin chen (Ibid., 125.6–130.11).

1467 See Hahn 1982:71.

1468 Lit., "branch."

1469 Tib. *sems dang ba*, *Skt. *cetasaḥ prasādaḥ* (see LC, s.v., and BHSD, s.v.).

1470 See Hopkins 1998:120.

1471 The quotation in Sgam po pa's *Lam rim snying po* (*Nges don phyag chen mdzod*, vol. *ka*, 321.4) reads *'bi 'bi legs kyang* ("even though perfectly round") instead of *'byi 'byi.*

1472 Small images of buddhas or tantric deities, or else conical figures, molded of clay and used at sacrifices. (see Jäschke 1985: s.v.).

1473 Peking Kangyur no. 26, *rgyud*, vol. *ga*, fol. 285b4. The Peking Kangyur reads *slob dpon sems kyi ngo bo nyid* instead of *slob dpon sems kyi rgyal po ste* (DRSM, 53.18–19).

1474 Lit., "[mind]stream."

1475 In the Tibetan *-duḥkhaṁ* is only translated once.

1476 RGVV, 106.12–15: *deveṣu cyutiduḥkham ity avagamāt paryeṣṭiduḥkhaṁ nṛṣu prājñā nābhilaṣanti devamanujeṣv aiśvaryam apy uttamam / prajñāyāś ca tathāgatapravacanaśraddhānusārād*[a] *idaṁ duḥkhaṁ hetur ayaṁ nirodha iti ca jñānena saṁprekṣaṇāt //.*

a According to B (51b1) and also de Jong (1979:578); A is not available. Johnston wrongly reads *-mānyād* instead of *-sārād.*

1477 Tib. *gnas pa'i don*, i.e., the *ālayavijñāna.*

1478 Peking Kangyur (no. 11), *rgyud*, vol. *ka*, fol. 278a2–5. The quoted passage is on fol. 44a4–6. Gzhon nu dpal's quotation differs often from the Peking Kangyur, but this does not affect the overall meaning.

1479 The text in the Peking Tengyur (TDṬ, 188a7) reads *sa phyogs su* instead of *phyogs su.*

1480 Tib. *sems brlan par bya* (TDṬ, 188b1) is missing in DRSM.

1481 Tib. *dpyad nas kyang* is difficult to construe, but in the Peking Tengyur (TDṬ, 188b3) we have the reading *dpyad nas slar.*

1482 The Peking Tengyur (TDṬ, 188b6) reads: "In keeping with the words: Insight in accordance with meditative equipoise" *(ji bzhin mnyam gzhag gyur pa'i shes rab ces bya ba'i tshig gis so).* Sahajavajra's commentary in the Peking Tengyur (TDṬ, 188b4–5) has two more lines before this sentence that are not quoted by Gzhon nu dpal: "In this connection, its hindrances are abandoned, just as [in the example of] darkness and appearance. In virtue of this [fact], right wisdom arises in the same way as appearances with the help of the eyes, since they (i.e., calm abiding and insight) are actual on account of their mutually separate qualities. They do not contradict each other the way darkness and appearance do." *(de la mun pa dang (text: la) snang ba bzhin du ste / de yi sgrib pa rnams spang bar 'gyur ro / / de nyid kyi phyir mig gis snang ba bzhin du [text: no / /] yang dag pa'i ye shes skye ste / phan tshun so so'i yon tan gyis nges par gnas pa'i phyir ro / / snang ba dang mun pa bzhin du phan tshun 'gal ba dag ni ma yin no /.)*

1483 The corresponding passage in the Peking Tengyur (TDṬ, 189a2) reads: "Here one must meditate before nonanalytical [bodhi]citta (?)" *('dir dpyad pa med pa'i sems kyi sngon du bsgom bya ba nyid do);* the version in the *Phyag rgya chen po'i rgya gzhung* (vol. *ā*, fol. 20a1) is as follows: "Here, too, one needs to meditate directly without an analytical mind" *('dir yang dpyad pa med pa'i sems kyis mngon du bsgom par bya ba nyid do).* According to Thrangu Rinpoche it is possible to ascertain phenomena (such as mental events) by investigating their color, shape, etc., with the help of direct cognitions within your introverted mental consciousness during *vipaśyanā.*

1484 Tib. *rgyun chags su 'jug pa* (DRSM, 55.11). The Peking Tengyur (TDṬ, 189a4) reads: *lhun gyis grub pa rgyun (text : rgyan) gyis 'jug pa.*

1485 HT, 95.6: *sarvadharmaparijñānaṁ bhāvanā naiva bhāvanā //.*

1486 MV, 76.11–12: *dharmaskandhasahasreṣu bu*[a]*dhyatāṁ nāma śūnyatā / bu*[b]*ddhā nāsau parāmarśād vināśārthaṁ bhaved guroḥ //.*

a According to the manuscript (NGMPP reel no. B 22/24, fol. 34b5); the Japanese edition has *ba-*.

b The manuscript (NGMPP reel no. B 22/24, fol. 34b5) and the Japanese edition have *bu-*.

1487 DRSM, 55.15: *gang gis bum sogs 'dzin pa na / / rtag tu sbyor bas bsam gtan te /.*

1488 MV, 78.9–10: *ghaṭāder grahaṇe*[a] *yasya dhyānasātatyayogataḥ / bhaved asau mahābuddhaḥ sarvākāraikavigrahaḥ //.*

a The manuscript (NGMPP reel no. B 22/24, fol. 35a2) and the Japanese edition read: *grahaṇair.*

1489 Not quoted by Sahajavajra.

1490 TD, 94.1–2: *yathābhūtasamādhiś ca bhavet prasthānacittataḥ / ajasraṁ jāyate tattvaṁ yasmāt tatpadavedināṁ //.*

1491 In the *Mahāyānasūtrālaṁkāra*, stanza XIX.45, the four *yuktis* respectively correlate to (a) correct mental engagement, (b) the right view accompanied by its fruit, (c) analysis based on valid cognition, and (d) the inconceivable. (See MSA, 167.24–25: *yoniṣaḥ ca manaskāraḥ samyagdṛṣṭi? phalānvitā / pramāṇair vicayo 'cintyam jñeyaṁ yukticatuṣṭayaṁ //.*)

1492 Lamotte (1935:158, l. 30) reads *chos nyid dbyings* instead of *chos dbyings*, but this does not change the meaning.

1493 See Takasaki 1966:294–95.

1494 Tib. *sbyor ba* and *thabs* are here used as synonyms of *rigs* (Skt. *yukti*); see DRSM, 431.23–432.1.

1495 This is the understanding of Gzhon nu dpal (see below).

1496 DRSM *rten*, D *rtogs*, NP *rtog*. Given Skt. *pratisaraṇa*, the reading must be *rton [pa]*, which is, moreover, the *lectio difficilior.*

1497 The quoted passage introduces the explanation of stanzas I.156–58 (J I.153–55), dedicated to the defining characteristcs of buddha nature. The corresponding Sanskrit is as follows (RGVV, 73.9–16): *sa khalv eṣa tathāgatagarbho dharmakāyavi*[a]*pulas ta*[a]*thatāsaṁbhinnalakṣaṇo niyatagotrasvabhāvaḥ sarvadā ca sarvatra ca niravaśeṣayogena* [b]*saṁvidyata iti*[b] *draṣṭavyaṁ dharmatāṁ pramāṇīkṛtya / yathoktam / eṣā kulaputra dharmāṇāṁ dharmatā / utpādād vā tathāgatānām anutpādād vā sadaivaite sattvās tathāgatagarbhā iti / yaiva cāsau dharmatā saivātra yuktir yoga upāyaḥ*[c] */ yayaivam*[d] *evaitat*[e] *syāt / anyathā naivaitat*[e] *syād iti / sarvatra dharmataiva pratisa(text:śa)raṇam / dharmataiva yuktiś cittanidhyāpanāya cittasaṁjñāpanāya / sā na cintayitavyā na vikalpayitavyā [/ a]*[f]*dhimoktavyeti /.*

a B (38a2) probably reads *-pulastastata-* (*stata* being a case of haplography); the quoted passage is not available in A. See also Schmithausen (1971:158). Johnston reads *-pralambhas ta-*.

b De Jong (1979:575) rejects Johnston's conjecture emending *saṁrvadyatananatija* to *sattvadhātāv iti* and proposes, based on the Tibetan *(yod do // zhes bya ba'i bar ni)* reading *saṁvidyata iti yāvat*. Gzhon nu dpal, however, has simply *zhes bya ba ni*, so that I do not translate the *yāvat* here.

c Johnston inserts after *upāyaḥ*, against B (38a3), *paryāyaḥ* (A is not available), but neither the Tibetan nor the Chinese has an equivalent for *paryāyaḥ* (see Takasaki 1966:295, fn. 8).

d According to de Jong (1979:575).

e According to B (38a3); Johnston reads in both cases *eva tat*.

f Takasaki (1966:296, fn. 14) inserts *kevalaṁ tv*, but the unemended phrase (that is, without Takasaki's insertion, but an additional *daṇḍa*) is also found in ŚrBh, 377.6.

1498 The quotation could not be identified.

1499 MA, 408.12–17.

1500 HT, 91.3–4: *nānyena kathyate sahajaṁ na kasminn api labhyate / ātmanā jñāyate puṇyād guruparvop[āy]a* [a]*sevayā //.*

a The *pañjikā* and Gzhon nu dpal must have read a variant reading containing *-opāya-*.

The additions to my translation of the root stanza are in accordance with the *Hevajratantrapañjikā:* (HTP, 92.12–14): "Time to be obtained from the master *(guru)* is time with the master. What is duly given by the master to the proper disciple is instructions. These instructions are [his] speech, which needs to be understood. To be understood [means] to be realized. [His] speech is pith instructions [obtained] while passing time with the master. Taking recourse to skillful means is to take recourse to the skillful means of [pith instructions obtained] through passing time with the master. Thus [the coemergent] is known from having [accumulated] merit." *(gurulabhyaṁ parva guruparva / yad yogyāya śiṣyāya guruṇā vidhivat dīyate avavāda ity arthaḥ / avagamāya vādo 'vavādaḥ / avagamo 'bhigamaḥ / vāda upadeśaḥ guruparvaṇā / upāyasevā guruparvopāyasevā / tathā jñāyate puṇyāt /.)*

1501 Mi pham explains in his *Dbu ma rgyan rtsa 'grel*, 383: *dngos rnams kyi dngos po* as: *dngos po rnams kyi dngos po'am ngo bo yin lugs.*

1502 MAL, 244.10–13. Ichigō (1985:244) introduces this and the following two stanzas (MAL 73–75) in the following way: "By whom and how is the absence of intrinsic nature in all dharmas understood?" MAL 73–74 are given the subtitle: "Emptiness *(śūnyatā)* and unwise people."

1503 MAL, 246.9–12.

1504 The numbering follows Steinkellner's (1977) *Verse-Index*.

1505 The text in the Tengyur reads *sgrib byed des* instead of *kun rdzob des.*

1506 Even though concrete entities are completely different from each other, certain entities can cause a perception whose image is the same. Such an image is usually mistaken for the concrete entity itself (see Frauwallner (1932:264–65) for a discussion of these stanzas).

1507 PV I.68–70 (ed. Gnoli 1960:38.11–16): *pararūpaṁ svarūpeṇa yayā saṁvriyate dhiyā / ekārthapratibhāsinyā bhāvān āśritya bhedinaḥ // tayā saṁvṛtanānārthāḥ*[a] *saṁvṛtyā bhedinaḥ svayam / abhedina ivābhānti bhāvā rūpeṇa kenacit // tasyā abhiprāyavaśāt sāmānyaṁ sat prakīrtitam / tad asat paramārthena yathā saṁkalpitaṁ tayā //.*

a Manorathanandin reads *-nānātvāḥ*, which is supported by the Tibetan *tha dad pa nyid* (see Miyasaka 1972:124–25 and DRSM, 57.18). My translation is based on Gnoli's edition.

1508 Tib. *dngos po 'dzin pa.*

1509 The quotation could not be identified.

1510 Peking Tengyur (no. 5245), *dbu ma*, vol. *tsha*, fols. 24b8–25a5.

1511 The Peking Tengyur reads *rtag pa yod ces byar 'gyur pa* instead of *rtag pa yod ces bya 'gyur na* (DRSM, 58.13–14).

1512 The Peking Tengyur omits the negation particle in front of *'phrigs* (DRSM, 58.18).

1513 Peking Tengyur (no. 5266), *dbu ma*, vol. *ya*, fols. 249b7–250a4.

1514 Ibid., fol. 250a7–b1.

1515 I.e., the objects of direct valid cognition in the *pramāṇa* tradition.

1516 It seems that Gzhon nu dpal still accepts *svalakṣaṇa*s, like Śāntarakṣita or Kamalaśīla, on the level of apparent truth. For a discussion of the synthesis of the logician's Yogācāra ontology with Madhyamaka, see Tillemans 2003:98f.

1517 See BHSD s.v., "mind talk," "imagination."

1518 Peking Tengyur (5324), *dbu ma*, vol. *a*, fols. 105b6–106a6.

1519 In the Tibetan that is followed here, the order of the two immediately preceding points is reversed.

1520 Skt. *anudarśanaṁ*, Tib. *rjes su mthong ba.* The prefix *anu* refers either to a consequent seeing (i.e., the seeing that results from having turned back the conditions of ignorance, etc.) or to a "repeated" and thus thorough seeing.

1521 According to the Tibetan I take *yun du gnas pa (kālāvasthitaṁ)* as referring to the preceding *dngos po (dravyaṁ).* The Sanskrit is difficult to construe here.

1522 According to the Tibetan, Skt. *bhūtvā ca vyayam* ought to be included in the preceding construction.

1523 Not in the Tibetan.

1524 LAS, 40.11–41.2: *punar aparaṁ mahāmate vikalpabhavatrayaduḥkhavinivartanam ajñānatṛṣṇākarmapratyayavinivṛttiṁ svacittadṛśyamāyāviṣayānudarśanaṁ bhāṣiṣye / ye kecin mahāmate śramaṇā vā brāhmaṇā vābhūtvā sattvaṁ*[a] *hetuphalābhivyakti[ṁ] dravyaṁ ca kāı āvasthitaṁ pratyayeṣu ca skandhadhātvāyatanānām utpāda[ṁ] sthitiṁ cecchanti [/] bhūtvā ca vyayam / te mahāmate saṁtatikriyotpādabhaṅgabhavanirvāṇamārgakarmaphalasatyavināśocchedavādino bhavanti / tat kasya hetor yad idaṁ pratyakṣānupalabdher ādyadarśanābhāvāt /.*

a Nanjio reads *śraddhā* against *saddhā* in his mss., and is thus in accordance with C (19a3) and G (26b2). Mss. H (16b4), I (18b7), and K (14b7) read *sarvva-*, and B (24a3): *satvā-*. Since *sattva* and *sarvva* look very similar in the older Newari script, I propose reading *sattvaṁ,* which is also supported by the Tibetan.

1525 LAS, 42.6–8: *na cirāt te mahāmate bodhisattvā mahāsattvāḥ saṁsāranirvāṇasamatāprāptā bhaviṣyanti /.*

1526 A stage in highest yoga tantra on which the yogin is isolated (i.e., protected) from ordinary appearances.

1527 According to Tibetan "all the [buddha] elements of the sentient beings," but in the Skt. the corresponding word *dhātu* is missing.

1528 LAS, 42.8–10: *mahākaruṇopāyakauśalyānābhogagatena mahāmate prayogena sarvasattvamāyāpratibimbasamatayā-.*

1529 The repetition of the abstract suffix in the instrumental in the Skt. (which is not rendered by the Tibetan) suggests that this and all following compounds depend on *prayogena,* i.e., the practice by which one gains conviction of the fact that the triple world is one's own mind (see below).

1530 My translation follows the Tibetan. The Skt. reads: "through [the practice of seeing the] state in which conditions have not started," which rather refers to a mindstream in time.

1531 LAS, 42.10: *-anārabdhapratyayatayādhyātmabāhyaviṣayavimuktatayā.*

1532 LAS, 42.10–13: *cittabāhyādarśanatayānimittādhiṣṭhānānugatā anupūrveṇa bhūmikramasamādhiviṣayānugamanatayā traidhātukasvacittamāyā*[a]*dhimuktitaḥ prativibhāvayamānā māyopamasamādhiṁ pratilabhante.*

a According to B (25a4–5), E (24a3), H (17a7), and the Tibetan. Nanjio and the remaining Nepalese manuscripts read *-tayā* instead of *-māyā-*.

1533 LAS, 42.14–15: *svacittanirābhāsamātrāvatāreṇa prajñāpāramitāvihārānuprāptā.*

1534 The Tibetan does not render *-yoga-*, which could have been inserted in the Skt. later to exclude the understanding "action of origination."

1535 The Tib. connects the two compounds with a genitive.

1536 My translation follows the Tib. *(rim gyis gnas 'phos pa'i)* here. Skt. *parāvṛttyāśrayānupūrvakaṁ* could be tentatively rendered as "for whom the sequence [of the levels of realization is determined through] the basis in as much as [it has undergone a] transformation."

1537 LAS, 42.15–43.2: *utpādakriyāyogavirahitāḥ samādhivajrabimbopamaṁ tathāgatakāyānugataṁ tathatānirmāṇānugataṁ balābhijñāvaśitākṛpākaruṇopāyamaṇḍitaṁ sarvabuddhakṣetratīrthyāyatanopagataṁ cittamanomanovijñānarahitaṁ parāvṛttyā*[a]*-śrayānupūrvakaṁ tathāgatakāyaṁ mahāmate te bodhisattvāḥ pratilapsyante /.*

a Nanjio and all Nepalese manuscripts read *-vṛttyānu-*, which is probably a reading mistake caused by the following *-yānu-*.

1538 I could not find this sentence in the *Laṅkāvatārasūtra.*

1539 The image is used in RGV IV.45a (J IV.43a).

1540 This *Laṅkāvatārasūtra* quote is interpreted as teaching the stage *isolation of body:* "...the effortless [accomplishment] of great compassion and skillful means...." (DRSM, 60.9).

1541 The *gdul bya'i* in the quoted *pāda (gdul bya'i thabs mang gang gis)* has no equivilent in the Sanskrit. Obviously the translators wanted *vineyasya* to refer not only to the preceding *yasya dhātor,* but also to the following *yenopāyena bhūriṇā.* The stanzas RGV IV.3–4 read as follows:

The wise one[s] are always without effort,
Since thoughts about what guidance [should be undertaken],
[And] for whom, by which [means], where
And when, do not arise [in them]. (IV.3)
For whom, [that is,] for [which] element (i.e., type of) [of sentient being] guidance is required,
By which, [that is,] by [which of the] numerous skillful means,
What, [that is, what] guidance,
Where and when, [that is, in this or] that place and at [this or that] time. (IV.4)

(RGVV, 98.13–17: *yasya yena ca* [a]*yā yatra*[a] *yadā ca vinayakriyā / tadvikalpodayābhāvād anābhogaḥ sadā muneḥ // yasya dhātor vineyasya yenopāyena bhūriṇā / yā vinītikriyā yatra yadā taddeśakālayoḥ //.*)

a According to B (50a1); A is not available. See also Schmithausen (1971:170). Johnston reads *yāvac ca.*

1542 See DRSM, 60.8–9.

1543 Skt. *bhūtabhautika* (see Hirakawa 1978, s.v.).

1544 I.e., the fourth *dhyāna.*

1545 Gzhon nu dpal reads *khams gsum dag gi sems* for *khams gsum bdag gi sems* in the *Laṅkāvatārasūtra*, which means "the three worlds, [that is,] your own mind."

1546 I.e., similar to those of a tathāgata.

1547 Tib.: *la la'i slob ma dang la la'i slob dpon lta bur.*

1548 The quoted passage is from the eighth chapter of the *Phyag rgya chen po lam zab mthar thug zhang gi man ngag*, 89–92. See Martin 1992:278–80.

1549 According to Callahan (2001:390) *sing ge* "conveys the sense of waking up, feeling invigorated, as when feeling drowsy, one throws ice water on oneself. [It is] synonymous with "lucidity" *(dvang ba).*

1550 According to Callahan (2001:389) *ye re* also means "vivid" and "sharp," and is sometimes translated as "lucid openness."

1551 In the "Phyag chen lam zab mthar thug" (p. 91) and in Gzhon nu dpal's second quote of the same passage (DRSM, 65.22) we have the reading *lam rgya* instead of *sgyu lus* (see Jackson 1990:76 and Martin 1992:278). With the reading *sgyu lus* the sentence would mean: "From a single illusory body arises [what it needed] to benefit others." (*sgyu lus żhig nas gzhan don 'char* (DRSM, 62.14–15).) This is very unlikely, because the following *zhig* would have to be understood as an indefinite particle and thus emended to *shig* after final *s.*

1552 According to Thrangu Rinpoche, the qualites of the kāyas would normally unfold within the body during this same final stage. But since the mahāmudrā path is comparatively fast, the body still has traces of defilements from earlier parts of its life (a good example being that of Milarepa), so that the full Buddha activity unfolds only after the constraining "seal of the body" has been left behind. See also Sgam po pa's "Zhal gyi bdud rtsi thun mong ma yin pa," 132.5–133.1, in which he quotes the following instruction: "Although one [may] have realized gradually, [along the stages] of the fourfold yoga, that one's own mind is the coemergent dharmakāya, sickness and suffering [still] occur. They are experienced because one is not [yet] free from the constraining seal of one's ordinary body. It is like the cubs of lions and *garuḍas*...Even though the young *garuḍa* has already fully grown wings, they are still covered by the eggshell. Likewise, even though one has realized that one's mind is the dharmakāya, the conditions of undesired suffering [still] occur, because one is not [yet] free from the constraining seal of the body, which was set by former deeds. So there is no contradiction. So it was said." *(de yang rnal 'byor rnam pa bzhi'i rim gyis rang gi sems lhan cig skyes pa'i chos skur rtogs kyang / na tsha dang sdug bsngal 'ong ba ni tha mal pa'i lus rgya dang ma bral bas len pa yin te / seng ge dang khyung gi(s) phru gu lta bu / ...khyung phru gu gshog phrugs rgyas kyang sgo nga lpags kyis 'thums pa dang 'dra ste / nang du sems chos skur rtogs kyang sngar gyi las kyis bskyed pa'i lus rgya dang ma bral bas / bde sdug dang mi 'dod pa'i rkyen byung ba la 'gal ba med pa yin gsungs.)*

See also Jackson 1992:95–114.

1553 In the sense of yogas. Two of the Nepalese manuscripts (B 36a6; and G 32a1) read *kāraṇaiḥ* instead of *dharmaiḥ:* the four dharmas as "causes" of yogic realization.

1554 Skt. *vibhāvana;* the Tibetan translation from the Chinese has *rnam par 'byed pa.*

1555 Tib. *rab tu rtog pa;* Skt. *upalakṣaṇa* "the act of observing."

1556 The Tibetan supports the reading *abhilaṣaṇa* (cf. also LAS, 82.4–5, where *abhilaṣ* is again used in connection with the wisdom of the noble ones).

1557 My translation of *'phags pa so so rang gi ye shes* is based on the explanation of the Sanskrit equivalent *svapratyātmāryajñāna* in LAS II.202 and Gzhon nu dpal's explanation of it (see DRSM, 66.2–4).

1558 According to the Sanskrit *(pratyavekṣate).* The Tibetan has *rab tu rtog pa*, which is the translation of Skt. *-upalakṣaṇa-* in the paragraph above.

1559 It is somewhat difficult to understand how you can adhere to mere mental imprints. But further down Gzhon nu dpal explains that the *vāsanas* in *dauṣṭhulyavāsanābhiniveśa* also refer to the appearances caused by them: "And also the appearances in their various forms, such as mountains and houses, are called—using the name of the cause for the fruit—imprints. It is like saying 'this is poison' when seeing the [already manifest] disease [caused by it]" (DRSM, 65.3–7). The translation from the Chinese (Peking Kangyur no. 776, *mdo*, vol. *ngu*, fol. 236a6) does not have the problematic *mngon par zhen pa* and reads: *bag chags kyis yongs su bsgos pa.*

1560 Skt. *-upanibaddhaṁ.*

1561 Tib. *snang ba*, rendering Skt. *khyāyate* (see also *Bod skad dang legs sbyar gyi tshig mdzod chen mo*, vol. 7, s.v.). Indeed, Skt. *khyāti* has the old meaning of "appearance." The preceding Sanskrit *vikalpyate* was probably first a gloss but included later when copying the text. It has no equivalent in the Tibetan. It explains the way phenomena of saṁsāra appear; they are imagined or mentally fabricated.

1562 Skt. *gati* at the end of the enumeration *dehabhogapratiṣṭhā* is rendered as *dang 'gro ba.* It is thus understood in the sense of a "state of existence into which rebirth is possible" (see BHSD s.v.). *Gati ('gro ba)* is missing in some of the Sanskrit manuscripts (A 30a2, D 29b7, H 32a4) and has no equivalent in the Tibetan translation of the *Laṅkāvatārasūtra* from the Chinese.

1563 LAS, 79.16–80.11: *bhagavān āha / caturbhir mahāmate dharmaiḥ samanvāgatā bodhisattvā mahāsattvā*[a] *mahāyogayogino bhavanti / katamaiś caturbhiḥ yad uta svacittadṛśyavibhāvanatayā cotpādasthitibhaṅgadṛṣṭivivarjanatayā ca bāhyabhāvābhāvopalakṣaṇatayā ca svapratyātmāryajñānādhigamābhilaṣaṇa*[b]*tayā ca / ebhir mahāmate caturbhir dharmaiḥ samanvāgatā bodhisattvā mahāsattvā mahāyogayogino bhavanti // tatra kathaṁ mahāmate bodhisattvo mahāsattvaḥ svacittadṛśyavibhāvanākuśalo bhavati / yad uta sa evaṁ pratyavekṣate svacittamātram idaṁ traidhātukam ātmātmīyarahitaṁ nirīham āyūhanir*[c]*yūhavigatam anādikālaprapañcadauṣṭhulyavāsanābhiniveśavāsitaṁ traidhātukavicitrarūpopacāropanibaddhaṁ dehabhogapratiṣṭhāgativikalpānugataṁ vikalpyate khyāyate ca / evaṁ hi mahāmate bodhisattvo mahāsattvaḥ svacittadṛśyavibhāvanākuśalo bhavati /.* The corresponding passage of the Tibetan translation from the Chinese is on fol. 236a2–8 (Peking Kangyur no. 776, *mdo*, vol. *ngu*).

a According to G (53b1–2); Nanjio omits.

b According to H (32a2), which drops the following *ṇa*, however. B (46a2) reads *-lāṣa-*, and E (45a3) *-lāṣaṇa-*. Nanjio reads with most of the Nepalese manuscripts *-lakṣaṇa-* (A 29b7, D 29b5, I 37b4). The latter, however, have *-abhinna-* before *lakṣaṇa.*

c A 30a1–2 and I 37b6 read *āyūhānir-*, and B (46a4) *-āyuhāni-;* see BHSD under *āyūhati.*

1564 My numbering is in accordance with Steinkellner's (1977) *Verse-Index*, and in the latter the third chapter is on *pratyakṣapramāṇa.*

1565 PV III.287 (Miyasaka II.287) (ed. Miyasaka 1972:80.5–6): *śabdārthagrāhi yad yatra taj jñānaṁ*[a] *tatra kalpanā / svarūpañ ca na śabdārthas tatrādhyakṣam ato 'khilam //;* (ed. Miyasaka 1972:81.5–6): *shes gang gang la sgra don 'dzin // de ni de la rtog pa yin // rang gi ngo bo'ang sgra don min // de phyir de la kun mngon sum.*

a Miyasaka reads *tajjñānaṁ* (in compound).

1566 Lit., "How does a bodhisattva become somebody who has abandoned...."

1567 The Sanskrit differs a little: "Because they see the nonexistence of external phenomena—in accordance [with the fact that they are] only appearances of their own mind...."

1568 The final sentence of the second explanation is missing in the Sanskrit and the Tibetan translation from the Sanskrit (Peking Kangyur 775). A similar sentence (with the same meaning but different wording) is found in the Tibetan translation from the Chinese (Peking Kangyur 776). Based on the latter, Gzhon nu dpal probably restored the sentence in the wording of the translation from the Sanskrit.

1569 LAS, 80.13–81.5: *kathaṁ punar mahāmate bodhisattvo mahāsattva utpādasthitibhaṅgadṛṣṭivivarjito bhavati / yad uta māyāsvapnarūpajanmasadṛśāḥ sarvabhāvāḥ svaparobhayābhāvān notpadyante / svacittadṛśya*[a] *mātrānusāritvād bāhyabhāvābhāvadarśanād vijñānānām apravṛttiṁ dṛṣṭvā pratyayānām akūṭarāśitvaṁ ca vikalpapratyayodbhavaṁ traidhātukaṁ paśyanto 'dhyātmabāhyasarvadharmānupalabdhibhir niḥsvabhāvadarśanād utpādadṛṣṭivinivṛttau māyādi*[b] *dharmasvabhāvānu*[c]*gamād anut*[c]*pattikadharmakṣāntiṁ*[b] *pratilabhante /*; ...LAS, 81.15–16: *evaṁ hi mahāmate bodhisattvo mahāsattva utpādasthitibhaṅgadṛṣṭivivarjito bhavati //.*

a *Dṛśya* inserted according to E (45b2), K (30b2), and in view of Tib. *snang ba.*

b D (30a3) reads *manomayakāya[ṁ]* instead of *dharmasvabhāvānugamād anutpattikadharmakṣāntiṁ.*

Gzhon nu dpal follows the Tibetan translation from the Chinese, which does not include what corresponds to lines 3–15 in Nanjio's (1923:81) edition (i.e., the passage from *aṣṭamyāṁ bhūmau* to *sattvaparipākārtham*). The first part (Peking Kangyur no. 775, *mdo*, vol. *ngu*, fol. 96a2–6) of this excluded passage (what corresponds to the text from *aṣṭamyāṁ bhūmau* to *manomayakāyaṁ pratilabhante*) contains the explanation of the fourth dharma in the Tibetan translation from the Chinese. This fourth explanation is missing in the available Nepalese manuscripts and the Tibetan translation from the Sanskrit. It is thus reasonable to assume that it was wrongly inserted in the explanation of the second dharma. On the other hand, Gzhon nu dpal does not follow the different sequence of the second and third dharmas in the Tibetan translation from the Chinese (Peking Kangyur 776, *mdo*, vol. *ngu*, fol. 236a8–b7). The second insertion on the "mental body" is not quoted by Gzhon nu dpal in any of the four explanations.

c Nanjio reads against all manuscripts *-gamānut-*, which is probably a reading mistake.

1570 Gzhon nu dpal here quotes again some of Zhang's stanzas on the yoga freedom from mental fabrication (DRSM, 63.24–26 [61.26–62.2]).

1571 Tib. *rtog* in the sense of *kun rtog.*

1572 Not identified.

1573 Skt. *ghoṣānugatā kṣānti.*

1574 The last sentence of the explanation of the second *yoga* in the *Laṅkāvatārasūtra* is repeated here.

1575 Further down (66.7ff.) Gzhon nu dpal explains that the fact that phenomena do not arise can begin to be endured well below the eighth bodhisattva level. Thinking that this endurance applies only to the eighth level, though, could have been the reason that the sequence of the second and third dharmas in the Tibetan translation of the *Laṅkāvatāra* from the Chinese was changed, especially since the explanation of the fourth dharma starts: "Having obtained the [ability to] endure the fact that phenomena do not arise, one abides on the eighth level."

1576 The first *dngos po thams cad* has no correspondence in the Sanskrit.

1577 The corresponding Sanskrit (i.e., the compound ending in *-prakhyā[ḥ]*) is an *upamāsamāsa* compound depending on *sarvabhāvāḥ*, and thus the comparative term *lta bu* is used in the Tibetan translation.

1578 The compound *sarvabhāvasvabhāvā[ḥ]* is problematic (the "own-being of all phenomena" cannot be in the plural, and as an adjectival compound it would have to depend on a noun in the nominative plural, which in this case could only be "entities," but this would not make sense). The Tibetan translators must have read *sarvabhāvāsvabhāvā iti*, which is, in fact, supported by one Nepalese manuscript (F 15a2–3), and assumed that a double *sandhi* was applied. In other words they must have read (*sandhi* rules not applied): *sarvabhāvāḥ asvabhāvā*. The Tibetan translation from the Chinese (Peking Kangyur no. 776, *mdo*, vol. *ngu*, fol. 236b1–2), however, supports a reading with a short *a: ... bag chags kyi rgyu las byung ba'o zhes dngos po thams cad kyi rang bzhin la rab rtog pa ste.*

1579 Strictly speaking, the adhering is to what is produced by the mental imprints. Further down, Gzhon nu dpal explains that the term *vāsana* in *dauṣṭhulya-vāsanābhiniveśa* also refers to the appearances caused by them: "Also the appearances in various forms, such as mountains and houses, are called, using the name of the cause for the fruit, imprints. It is like saying 'This is poison' when seeing the [already manifest] disease [caused by it]" (DRSM, 65.3–7). The Sanskrit compound *-vāsanābhiniveśa-*, for its part, can be analyzed as a genitive *tatpuruṣa:* "adhering of the imprints" in the sense of adhering caused by the imprints.

1580 The Tibetan does not render the compound member *-vipāka-*.

1581 In the Tibetan it is *bag chags* that is qualified by *rnam pa sna tshogs*, not *gnas ngan len*.

1582 The remaining two sentences of the third explanation are missing in the Sanskrit and the Tibetan translation from the Sanskrit, *saṁpaśyan* being followed by the final part of the fourth explanation, *pratyātmāryajñānagativiṣayam abhilaṣate* (LAS, 82.4–5). Gzhon nu dpal's wording of these last two sentences follows exactly the Tibetan translation from the Chinese (*op. cit.*, 236b2–3), which is remarkable, since Gzhon nu dpal otherwise strictly follows the direct translation from the Sanskrit.

1583 LAS, 81.17–82.4: *tatra kathaṁ mahāmate bodhisattvo mahāsattvo bāhyabhāvābhāvopalakṣaṇakuśalo bhavati / yad uta marīcisvapnakeśoṇḍukaprakhyā mahāmate sarvabhāvā anādikālaprapañcadauṣṭhulyavicitravipākavikalpavāsanābhiniveśahetukāḥ* [a]*sarvabhāvasva*[a]*bhāvā iti saṁpaśyan.* The remaining part of Gzhon nu dpal's quote is missing in the Sanskrit. The immediately following sentence *pratyātmāryajñānagativiṣayam abhilaṣate* already belongs to the end of the explanation of the fourth dharma, so that the end of the third and the main part of the fourth explanations are missing. According to the Tibetan translation of the *Laṅkāvatārasūtra* from the Chinese the fourth explanation has been wrongly inserted into the second explanation (Peking Kangyur 776, *mdo*, vol. *ngu*, 236a8–b3).

a According to F (15a2–3): *sarvabhāvāsva-*.

1584 Gzhon nu dpal repeats Zhang's stanzas on the yoga of one taste (see DRSM, 62.3–7).

1585 The following *pāda*s are quoted three times in Gzhon nu dpal's running commentary (DRSM, 119.20–21, 208.26, 453.13–14), and one time in the form of a *pratīka* of the *Ratnagotravibhāgavyākhyā* on I.155 (J I.152). In the Tibetan translation of the *vyākhyā* quotation, however, *khams* is used instead of *dbyings* (which presents no problem since both *dbyings* and *khams* are translations of Skt. *dhātu*).

1586 Cf. RGVV, 72.13: *anādikāliko dhātuḥ sarvadharmasamāśrayaḥ /*. Even though the *Mahāyānābhidharmasūtra* is not available, this stanza from it has been quoted in the *Mahāyānasaṁgrahabhāṣya* and the *Triṁśikābhāṣya*. In the latter, *dhātu* is translated as *dbyings* (cf. Takasaki 1966:290).

1587 Skt. *pāravṛtti*. Together with *parivṛtti* it is the common term for "transformation." But the Tibetan translation has *rab tu gyur ba* instead of *yongs su gyur pa*.

1588 Skt. *gati*, Tib. *rtogs pa*.

1589 Cf. LAS VI.5, where these topics are taught as the general points of the entire

Mahāyāna. The five categories are listed in the following stanza: "Names, characteristic signs, and thoughts are the defining characteristics of the [first] two natures; right wisdom and suchness those of the perfect [nature]." (*nāmanimittasaṁkalpāḥ svabhāvadvayalakṣaṇam / samyagjñānaṁ tathātvaṁ ca pariniṣpannalakṣaṇam*, LAS, 229.8–9.)

The fourth explanation is missing in the Sanskrit and the direct Tibetan translation from the Sanskrit (Peking Kangyur no. 775). The quoted passage is contained in the explanation of the second dharma (the realization that phenomena do not arise, abide, and pass out of existence). The lengthy paragraph on the mental body (starting with *mahāmatir āha* in line 6 and ending with *sattvaparipākārtham* in line 15 (LAS, 81)), which is part of the explanation of the second dharma in Nanjio's edition, and the explanation of the fourth dharma in the Tibetan translation of the *Laṅkāvatārasūtra* from the Chinese, is not quoted by Gzhon nu dpal at all. The Sanskrit corresponding to what is, according to Gzhon nu dpal, the explanation of the fourth dharma is as follows (LAS, 81.3–5): *[anutpattikadharmakṣāntiṁ pratilabhya]*[a] *aṣṭamyāṁ bhūmau sthitāḥ cittamanomanovijñānapañcadharmasvabhāvanairātmyadvayagatiparāvṛttyadhigamānmanomayakāyaṁ pratilabhante //*. In the translation from the Chinese, the fourth explanation starts with this sentence, and is followed by a long passage on the mental body, and then the long passage is repeated in what seems to be a dittography (Peking Kangyur no. 776, *mdo*, vol. *ngu*, fols. 236b8–237b1).

a Restored from the Tibetan.

1590 See DRSM, 62.9–17.

1591 The Sanskrit has a causative form.

1592 LAS, 133.9–13: *pramāṇāptopadeśavikalpābhāvān mahāmate bodhisattvo mahāsattva ekākī rahogataḥ svapratyātmabuddhyā vicārayaty aparapratyayo dṛṣṭivikalpavivarjita uttarottaratathāgatabhūmipraveśanatayā vyāyamate / etan mahāmate svapratyātmāryajñānagatilakṣaṇam /.*

1593 The terms used in the explanation of the fourth yoga in the *Laṅkāvatārasūtra* do not match. A translation of a commentary with the same words as in the quote would be: [The expression] "[acquire] the strong wish" in [the phrase] "[acquire] the strong wish to internalize the wisdom of the noble ones by himself" (Skt. *pratyātmāryajñāna;* see the explanation of LAS II.202 above).

1594 In other words, the ability to endure the nonorigination of phenomena was already cultivated on lower levels, and does not ripen from the realization of nonorigination on the eighth level alone.

1595 See the last quotation from the *Laṅkāvatārasūtra* (DRSM, 65.15–16).

1596 The mental body is explained in RGVV I.36 and I.134 (J I.131), but in neither case is the *Laṅkāvatārasūtra* directly referred to.

1597 The shorter translation is the one by Chos grub from the Chinese translation of the *Laṅkāvatārasūtra* by Guṇabhadra (see Suzuki 1930:13–14), in which the first chapter, featuring the lord of Laṅka, is missing (Peking Kangyur no. 776). The larger version is the direct translation from the Sanskrit (Peking Kangyur no. 775).

1598 See Peking Kangyur no. 776, *mdo*, vol. *ngu*, fols. 236a2–237b1.

1599 *Āryalaṅkāvatāravṛtti*, Peking Tengyur no. 5519, *mdo tshogs 'grel pa*, vol. *ni*, fols. 131b6–132b2.

1600 I.e., the branches of the ten levels of the fruit.

1601 In the Peking Tengyur (no. 3486) the quoted passage is in *rgyud 'grel*, vol. *ngu*, fols. 7b6–8b6.

1602 Tib. *'jug pa*.

1603 The Peking Tengyur (*op. cit.*, 7b7) reads *'jig rten pa'i lam 'ba' zhig pa'i lam* instead of *'jig rten pa'i 'ba' zhig pa'i lam* (DRSM, 67.13).

1604 The Peking Tengyur (*op. cit.*, 8a6) reads *'du shes* instead of *sems* (DRSM, 67.24).

1605 A circle of light produced by whirling a firebrand.

1606 I.e., a selflessness that implies the ultimate existence of a mind empty of duality (the Cittamātra view).

1607 The Peking Tengyur (*op. cit.*) reads *spangs la* instead of *spangs pa* (DRSM, 68.7).

1608 Skt. *upapatti.* For a list of the sixty kinds of mind see Wayman 1992:42–43.

1609 Taking each of the sixty kinds of mind alone makes sixty; taking the same sixty in pairs makes thirty; taking them in groups of three makes twenty; in groups of four makes fifteen; in groups of five makes twelve; in groups of six makes ten; in groups of eight makes seven;[a] and finally in groups of ten makes six. Thus there are altogether one hundred sixty sets with either one, two, three, four, five, six, eight, or ten kinds of mind. For a slightly different calculation see Wayman 1992:42.

a With a remainder of four, which obviously must be neglected in this calculation.

1610 DRSM, 67.25–68.8.

1611 On each of the four levels *stream-entered, once-to-come, not-to-come,* and *arhatship*, there is an enterer and an abider (see Rigzin 1993:230).

1612 Each of the four noble truths has four attributes, those of the first one being "impermanence, suffering, empti[ness], and selflessness."

1613 LAS, 65.9–10: *srotāpattiphalaṁ caiva sakṛdāgāminas tathā / anāgāmiphalaṁ caiva arhattvaṁ cittavibhramaḥ*[a] *//.*

a According to Nanjio *-mam.*

1614 In the Peking Tengyur (no. 3486) the quoted passage is in *rgyud 'grel*, vol. *ngu*, fols. 11b5–13b6.

1615 These are the three stages of mind explained in the *krīyayogatantra:* (1) "To enter" means "to realize that no phenomena arise"; (2) "To abide" means "to actualize nonconceptuality"; (3) "To awaken" means "to enter into great compassion toward sentient beings" (see Tsepak Rigzin 1993:88).

1616 The Peking Tengyur (Ibid., fol. 11a8) reads *rjes su 'dzin pas* instead of *rjes su 'dzin pa na* (DRSM, 69.19).

1617 In other words, even though they have not yet attained the qualities of the actual bodhisattva levels.

1618 This means that the preliminary levels they enter upon appear to them as if they were the actual levels.

1619 The Peking Tengyur (Ibid., fol. 12a5) reads *mkhyen pa yis* instead of *mkhyen pa'i sa,* which would mean: "through omniscience, they are explained as [levels of conviction]."

1620 Chap. 13 is: "Gsang ba'i dkyil 'khor rim par phye ba rgyas pa"; chap. 14: "Gsang ba'i dkyil 'khor du 'jug pa rim par phye ba"; chap. 15: "Gsang ba'i phyag rgya brgyad rim par phye ba"; chap. 16: "Gsang ba'i dkyil 'khor du gzud pa la 'jug rim par phye rgyas pa" (see Wayman 1992:242). The final chapter of the "attached tantra" (chap. 36) on the empowerment of the *maṇḍala* can be seen as a continuation of chapters 13–16 on the secret *maṇḍala* (Wayman 1992:24).

1621 The Tibetan version of the *Vairocanābhisambodhitantra* has an appendix of seven chapters called the "attached tantra" (see Wayman 1992:22).

1622 According to Wayman, the three kinds of mind correspond to the three *manomayakāyas* of the *Laṅkāvatārasūtra.* The first of the three minds (i.e., the unequalled one) would then be the means of the first five perfections; the second mind (i.e., the immeasurable one) would be the sixth and the seventh perfections, i.e., *prajñāpāramitā* and *upāyapāramitā;* and the third mind (i.e., the inconceivable one) would correspond to the last three bodhisattva levels (Wayman 1992:75).

1623 According to the Peking Tengyur (*op. cit.*, fol. 12b6) there is no *sems* before *'od gsal.*
1624 It is not clear whether the plural particle *dag* after *yan lag* is a mere scribal error.
1625 The exact meaning of *nges par sems* here is obscure.
1626 The Peking Tengyur (*op. cit.*, 13a5) has *rnam par spyod par byed pa* instead of *rnam par dpyod par byed pa* (DRSM, 70.26).
1627 In DRSM, 70.16–24 the words *'byor ba* and *'grub pa* are in reverse order.
1628 At the end of the quoted passage the *piṇḍārtha* explains that "the detailed explanation according to the 'attached tantra' will be analyzed in the chapters on the secret [*maṇḍalas*]" (Peking Tengyur, *op. cit.*, 13b6).
1629 The passage referred to is DRSM, 69.15.
1630 Not identified.
1631 I.e., the path of preparation.
1632 The passage referred to is DRSM, 70.6.
1633 RGVV, 14.3: *sarvatrānugatām anāvṛtadhiyaḥ paśyanti saṁbuddhatāṁ.*
1634 The four *dhyānas* are described in II.159 and the preceding prose (LAS, 96–98).
1635 I.e., all ten perfections and levels of engagement based on conviction.
1636 The following ten stanzas from the *Dharmadhātustotra* in the Peking Tengyur (no. 2010) are on fols. 76b5–77a5 (*bstod tshogs*, vol. *ka*).
1637 Rang byung rdo rje (*Dbu ma chos dbyings bstod pa'i rnam par bshad pa*, 38a8) reads *dri ma med par* instead of *dri ma med pas.*
1638 The Derge and Peking Tengyur read *ni* instead of *byar* (DRSM, 72.6).
1639 Rang byung rdo rje (*op. cit.*, 38b2) has *dang* instead of the plural particle (?) *dag* and explains (Ibid., 38b3): "since the wisdom light of not grasping dispels the darkness of the mind of countless sentient beings...." *(yongs su 'dzin pa med pa'i ye shes kyi 'od kyis sems can dpag tu med pa'i blo'i mun pa sel bar byed pas....)*
1640 Lit., "taken to be" *(et passim).*
1641 The Derge and Peking Tengyur read *nyid* instead of *kun* (DRSM, 72.13).
1642 The Derge and Peking Tengyur read *gsum po dang* instead of *gsum po yi* (DRSM, 72.14).
1643 Rang byung rdo rje (*op. cit.*, 39a8) reads *las* in place of *la.*
1644 Rang byung rdo rje (*op. cit.*, fol. 39a8) explains: "After it has become directly manifest that worldly existence and nirvāṇa are not different, one realizes the extremely profound arising and passing out of existence." *(srid zhi ba khyad med du mngon du gyur nas / skye ba dang 'gag pa rab tu zab pa rtogs pa ste.)*
1645 Rang byung rdo rje explains (*op. cit.*, 39b4–5): " ...here it is the design of a wheel, as a sign of having entered the secret place of the Buddha.[a] A web of light like the *maṇḍala* of the Buddha plays about [everywhere], and since one also enters, in a single moment the state of cessation, one realizes equanimity and has gone far. Therefore one has crossed the swamp [of saṁsāra]" *(... 'di la sangs rgyas kyi gsang ba'i gnas la shugs pa'i rtags su 'khor lo'i bkod pa ste / sangs rgyas kyi dkyil 'khor dang 'dra ba'i 'od kyi dra bas rtse zhing skad cig la 'gogs pa la yang snyoms par 'jug pas mnyam pa nyid rtogs nas ring du song ba'i phyir na 'dam las rgal ba yin no).*
a The secret place of the Buddha does not refer to a part of the body, but to the activity of the Buddha's body, speech, and mind (oral explanation of Thrangu Rinpoche).
1646 Lit., "in all aspects."
1647 The Derge and Peking Tengyur read *'bad med lhun gyis grub gyur pas / bdud kyi 'khor gyis mi g.yo pa'o* instead of *lhun gyis grub par dbang thob pas / bdud kyi pho nyas mi g.yos pa'o* (DRSM, 72.19).
1648 Lit., "the limit."
1649 The Derge and Peking Tengyurs read *sangs rgyas rnams kyi* instead of *sangs rgyas rnams kyis* (DRSM, 72.23).

1650 I could not identify this stanza.

1651 My translation of this quote follows Martin (1992:287); see also Jackson 1990:52–53.

1652 The usage of "extremely joyful" instead of the usual "joyful" reflects the distinction between the "real" first bodhisattva level and the preliminary one on the path of preparation (i.e., of engagement based on conviction).

1653 This sentence differs in the edition of La Vallée Poussin (MA 12.7–8): *'di la rang gi ngo bo'i khyad par gyis byas pa'i dbye ba ni yod pa ma yin no / / ji skad du /.* The subsequent quotation of a stanza is identical with Gzhon nu dpal's reading, though.

1654 MA 12.7–12. The two stanzas are in the first chapter of the *Daśabhūmikasūtra;* see NGMPP reel nos. A 38/5 and A 39/13 (the 49 folios of the old Nepalese manuscript in Gupta script were in disorder and not identified as one text during the microfilm work (see Matsuda 1996:xv-xvi)), fol. 6b3–4: *yathāntarīkṣe śakuneḥ padaṁ budhair / vaktuṁ na śakyaṁ na ca darśanopagam // tathaiva sarvā jinaputrabhūmayo / vaktuṁ na śakyāḥ [kuta eva]*[a] *śrotum //.*

a The *akṣara*s in brackets are not readable, and given according to Rahder 1926:10.17–20.

1655 See above.

1656 DRSM, 73.18 *...dang po de las dang por...* must be corrected to *...dang po de la sa dang por....*

1657 This reasoning is not conclusive, given that 112 qualities, as shown in the following quotation from the *Daśabhūmikasūtra*, are attained only after the first real bodhisattva level. In other words, an instantaneous experience of mahāmudrā when the mind is for the first time free from mental fabrication on the level of conviction through engagement does not entail that the buddha qualities have matured on this early level.

1658 Gzhon nu dpal marks the ellipsis within his quote with *zhes bya ba nas.*

1659 The Sanskrit repeats the phrase *tathārūpam vīryam...* in the instrumental, while the Tibetan puts the correlative construction at the end of the sentence.

1660 Skt. *ekakṣaṇalavamuhūrtena.* Technically speaking, *ekakṣaṇa* is the shortest possible moment; *lava*, too, is a term for a short moment, while *muhūrta* designates a period of time that can last a little longer. Given the nonphilosophical context, the compound simply stands for a short period of time.

1661 Matsuda 1996: ms. A, fol. 12a3–4 and 12b1–2: *[yo]*[a] *'syāṁ pratiṣṭhito bodhisattvo*[b] *bhūyastvena jambūdvīpeśvaro bhavati /*[c] *mahai*[d]*śvaryādhipatyapratilabdho...ākāṅkṣaṁś ca tathārūpaṁ vīryam ārabhate /*[c] *yathārūpeṇa vīryārambheṇa*[e] *sarvagṛha*[f]*kalatrabhogān utsṛjya tathāgataśāsane pravrajati / pravrajitaś ca sann ekakṣaṇalavamuhūrtena samādhiśataṁ ca pratilabhate* [g]*samāpadyate ca /*[g] *buddhaśataṁ ca paśyati /*[c] *teṣāñ cādhiṣṭhānaṁ saṁjānīte / lokadhātuśataṁ ca ka[mpayati / kṣetraśatañ]*[a] *cākramati / lokadhātuśatañ cāvabhāsayati / sattvaśatañ ca paripācayati / kalpaśatañ ca tiṣṭhati / kalpaśatañ ca pūrvāntāparāntataḥ praviśati / dharmamukhaśatañ ca pravicinoti / kāyaśatañ cādarśayati*[h] */ kāyaṁ kāyañ ca bodhisattvaśataparivāram ādarśayati /.*

The passage is missing in mansucript B of Matsuda's facsimile edition (NGMPP A 38/7). In Rahder's (1926) edition the passage is on p. 21.31–p. 22.19 (1st *bhūmi*, XX), and in Kondō's (1936) edition it is on p. 29.10–p. 30.7.

a The *akṣara*s in brackets are not readable in the old Nepalese manuscript. The gaps have been filled in with the help of Rahder and Kondō.

b Rahder: *-satvo* (et passim).

c Rahder: omits the *daṇḍa.*

d Kondō: *-he-.*

e Kondō: *-na.*
f Kondō: *-parigraha.*
g Kondō: omits.
h Kondō: *ca darśayati.*
1662 This last sentence is missing in the Sanskrit.
1663 I have problems construing *gsungs pa de.* The demonstrative pronoun probably refers to the qualities taught, and is thus taken up again by *yon tan de dag* in line 4.
1664 Lit., "wife."
1665 In other words, the instantaneous realization of mahāmudrā does not entail that all the qualities are complete from the first moment.
1666 The founder of the Lha pa Bka' brgyud pas (see Smith 2001:43).
1667 RGVV, 6.11: *tatra katame te buddhadhātoḥ ṣaṣṭyākāraviśuddhiparikarmaguṇāḥ.* This sentence of the *vyākhyā* is not quoted in the form of a *pratīka* here.
1668 The causative *[yongs su] sbyong byed,* Skt. *paryavadāpayati* is used in the description of the threefold process of polishing the *vaiḍūrya* gem (see RGVV, 5.9–14), which illustrates the spiritual purification by means of the three dharmacakras.
1669 This clause is a paraphrase of *buddhadhātoḥ* and *-viśuddhiparikarmaguṇāḥ.*
1670 RGVV, 6.11–13: *tad yathā caturākāro bodhisattvālaṁkāraḥ / aṣṭākāro bodhisattvāvabhāsaḥ / ṣoḍaśākārā*[a] *bodhisattvamahākaruṇā / dvatriṁśadākāraṁ bodhisattvakarma /.*
a According to B (4b4); A is missing. Johnston reads *-rī.*
1671 Tib. *de nyid* has no equivalent in the Sanskrit.
1672 MSABh, 119.21–22: *mitraṁ śrayed dāntaśamopaśāntaṁ guṇādhikaṁ sodyamam āgamāḍhyaṁ / prabuddhatvaṁ vacasābhyupetaṁ kṛpātmakaṁ khedavivarjitaṁ ca //.*
1673 The Sanskrit equivalents of the sixty factors within the cleansing process are taken from Vairocanarakṣita's *Mahāyānottaratantraśāstraṭippaṇī* (MUTŚṬ) (Nakamura 1985:4–6).
1674 MUTŚṬ, 4.26–27.
1675 Tib. *rtogs.* The *tippaṇī* (MUTŚṬ, 5.2) has *gati,* which is glossed: "[the bodhisattva] understands all dharmas and intentions of sentient beings" *(gacchati sarvadharmeṣu sattvāśayeṣu).*
1676 Tib. *shes pa;* the *tippaṇī* (MUTŚṬ, 5.3) has *ājñānāvabhāsa,* qualified by the compound *śrotāpannādijinaparyantajñānalakṣaṇaḥ:* "whose defining characteristic is the knowledge of a stream-enterer and so forth (up to the victorious one)."
1677 The four *pratisaraṇas* are (1) relying on the teaching, not the teacher, (2) relying on the meaning, not the letter, (3) relying on the definitive meaning, not the provisional meaning, and (4) relying on wisdom, not on normal consciousness (see Lamotte 1949:341–61).
1678 Read *zhes pa'o* instead of *shes pa'o.*
1679 Vairocanarakṣita's *ṭippaṇī* (MUTŚṬ, 5.10) has *ahaṁkāramamakāra-,* "the notion of an I and my."
1680 The *ṭippaṇī* (MUTŚṬ, 5.14) lists "the demon of thirst" *(tṛṣṇādāsa-)* instead.
1681 MUTŚṬ, 5.16: "overcome by greed" *(lobhābhibhūta-).*
1682 Ibid.: "having ineffective views" *(akarmadarśi-).*
1683 Ibid., 5.17: "rejoicing in saṁsāra" *(saṁsārābhirata-).*
1684 I could not locate this precise sentence in the *Dhāraṇīśvararājasūtra,* but a similar sentence occurs at the end of the presentation of sixteenfold compassion: *khams gsum thams cad las 'byung ba'i phyir de dag la chos bstan par bya snyam du....* (Peking Kangyur 813, *mdo,* vol. *nu,* fol. 132b6).
1685 The paragraph on the thirty-twofold activity in the *ṭippaṇī* (MUTŚṬ, 5.20) is

introduced in the following way: "The special thirty-twofold activity of a bodhisattva" *(bodhisattvasyāveṇikaṁ dvātriṁśadākāraṁ karma).*

1686 MUTŚṬ, 5.20–21: *mohaprasuptān sattvān prajñayā prabodhayati.* The remaining thirty-one points are each introduced by a compound referring to *sattvān*, whose case ending (acc., pl., masc.) they share.

1687 Tib. *yongs su 'dzin pa;* I follow the Sanskrit *samādāpayati* here.

1688 The Tibetan *(theg pa dman pa las)* has probably mistaken *hīnādhimuktikān* (MUTŚṬ, 5.21) for an ablative.

1689 Lit., "connects."

1690 MUTŚṬ, 5.23: *kudṛṣṭipravṛttān samyagdṛṣṭau.* The previous verb *yojayati* refers to this point as well, but the Tibetan has *'god pa.*

1691 Cf. the *ṭippaṇī* (MUTŚṬ, 25–26): *vyāpādabahulān kṣāntimaitrīvihāritāyāṁ.*

1692 MUTŚṬ, 5.26: *kusīdān vīryārambhe.*

1693 The *ṭippaṇī* (MUTŚṬ, 5.27) has *smṛtisaṁprajñāne* ("...in recollection and all-inclusive knowledge") against Tib. *bsam gtan.*

1694 Lit., "connects."

1695 Blo ldan shes rab has *chu bo bzhir* in his *Theg chen rgyud bla'i don bsdus pa,* 17b6. The *Bod rgya tshig mdzod chen mo* (s.v.) explains these four currents as being ignorance, [wrong] view, existence, and thirst; or, alternatively, birth, old age, sickness, and death.

1696 Lit., "connects."

1697 Lit., "connects."

1698 Lit., "connects."

1699 Tib. *rjes su dran pa drug,* i.e., the recollection of the teacher, the Buddha, the Dharma, the Saṅgha, discipline, abandoning, and the deity (see MVY § 1149–54).

1700 The *ṭippaṇī* (MUTŚṬ, 6.11) has *śāstṛratnadūrasthitān* ("...those who are far from the teacher and the jewels") against Tib. *rjes dran drug dang ba.*

1701 The *ṭippaṇī* (MUTŚṬ, 6.12) has *tatprahāṇe* ("...in [the practice of] abandoning those") against Tib. *dge ba'i chos yongs su rdzogs pa.*

1702 RGVV, 6.14: *tannirdeśānantaraṁ buddhabodhiḥ ṣoḍaśākārā*[a] *mahābodhikaruṇānirdeśena paridīpitā /.*

a According to B (4b3); A is not available. Johnston reads *-ākāra-* (in compound). This sentence from the *vyākhyā* is not quoted in the form of a *pratīka* here.

1703 Peking Kangyur 813, *mdo,* vol. *nu,* fol. 135b6.

1704 Ibid., fol. 136a2–3.

1705 In this enumeration the Tibetan text has numbers after each point.

1706 See Schmithausen 1987: vol. 2, 407, fn. 724.

1707 Takasaki (1966:153) lists these sixteen points on the basis of the Chinese translation of the *Dhāraṇīśvararājasūtra.*

1708 RGVV, 6.15–16: *tannirdeśānantaraṁ buddhaguṇā daśabalacaturvaiśāradyāṣṭādaśāveṇikabuddhadharmanirdeśena paridīpitāḥ /.*

1709 Peking Kangyur 813, *mdo,* vol. *nu,* fol. 145a7–8. This is the beginning of the first of the ten strengths, i.e., the strength of knowing right from wrong (lit. "...of what abides and what not," Skt. *sthānāsthānajñānabala*). See MVY § 120–29.

1710 RGVV, 6.16–17: *tannirdeśānantaraṁ buddhakarma dvātriṁśadākāraṁ*[a] *niruttaratathāgatakarmanirdeśena paridīpitam /.* This sentence of the *vyākhyā* is not quoted in the form of a *pratīka* here.

a According to B (4b4); A is not available. Johnston reads *-ākāra-* (in compound). See also Schmithausen 1971:133.

1711 RGVV, 6.17–18: *evam imāni sapta vajrapadāni svalakṣaṇanirdeśato vistareṇa yathāsūtram anugantavyāni / .*

1712 RGVV, 6.18: *kaḥ punar eṣām anuśleṣaḥ /.*

1713 This sentence of the *vyākhyā* is not quoted in the form of a *pratīka* here.
1714 RGVV, 7.1–4: *buddhād dharmo dharmataś cāryasaṁghaḥ / saṁghe garbho jñānadhātvāptiniṣṭhaḥ / tajjñānāptiś cāgrabodhir balādyair dharmair yuktā sarvasattvārthakṛdbhiḥ //.*
1715 In accordance with the Sanskrit *(saṅghe)* the ablative *las* (DRSM 79.2) should be changed into a locative.
1716 Tib. *mthar*, which is a technical translation of *niṣṭaḥ*, is difficult to construe and thus taken over to the next sentence.
1717 See VY, 21.8.
1718 I could locate this quote neither in the *Āryasubāhuparipṛcchānāmatantrapiṇḍārtha* nor its *vṛtti*.
1719 See Rngog Blo ldan shes rab: *Theg chen rgyud bla ma'i bsdus don*, 2b2.
1720 RGVV, 21.6–7: *gotraṁ ratnatrayasyāsya viṣayaḥ sarvadarśinām /.*
1721 See Takasaki 1966:336.
1722 In terms of enlightenment, Gzhon nu dpal (DRSM, 14.19–20) accepts only the svābhāvikakāya as a fit candidate for the ultimate truth, but here the dharmakāya, too, is taken as the support of the qualities (DRSM, 508.12).
1723 For a translation of RGV III.1–3 see above, section 3 in the introduction of this work.
1724 The *pratīka* of the Tibetan *Ratnagotravibhāgavyākhyā* on p. 508, l.12 *de la brten pa* refers to the preceding *pratīka* in line 6 on the same page *(dri ma med pa'i de bzhin nyid bshad zin nas)*, but is glossed as *chos sku* (DRSM, 508.12). To go by RGVV I.24, where stainless suchness is explained as dharmakāya, and suchness with stains as buddha nature, this is not impossible, but it gives RGV III.1 a different connotation (in that the dharmakāya and buddha nature do not only differ in terms of the presence or absence of adventitious stains).
1725 In the sense of being provided with a place to exist.
1726 DRSM, 508.21–22.
1727 The simile of the painters is explained in RGV I.88–92 (see Takasaki 1966: 263–64).
1728 In a base the ochre of a turmeric plant turns red.
1729 DRSM, 98.7–9 and 75.2–4.
1730 The Sanskrit equivalent *yoga* does not rule out such an understanding. The term *yoga* is used in RGV I.42–44 to define the relation between buddha nature and the cause and result of its purification (see Takasaki 1966:225–29).
1731 DRSM, 29.18–21 and 323.19–23.
1732 This is the way Rngog Blo ldan shes rab explains it in his *Theg chen rgyud bla ma'i don bsdus pa* (see fol. 33b1–3 and also DRSM, 5.4–10).
1733 Not identified.
1734 DRSM, 239.17–21.
1735 Ibid., 119.26–120.10.
1736 Ibid., 448.25–449.1.
1737 Ibid., 33.21–24.
1738 Mi bskyod rdo rje: "Rje Yid bzang rtse ba'i Rgyud gsum gsang ba...," 1003.3–5: *khyod kyi sems can thams cad la sangs rgyas kyi snying po gnas pa'i tshe / sangs rgyas de gnas pa min / sangs rgyas de'i rigs dang 'dra ba zhig gnas pa yin / 'dra ba de la skye mched drug gi khyad par ba yin pas 'di lta bu zhig sems can la yod pa yin zer nas / dpal karmapa rang byung rdo rje gi lung drangs mod / 'di mi 'thad pa la /....*
1739 DRSM, 239.15–17.
1740 RGVV, 5.5–6: *tataḥ sūtranidānaparivartānantaraṁ buddhadhātuḥ ṣaṣṭyākaratadviśuddhiguṇaparikarmanirdeśena paridīpitaḥ / viśodhye 'rthe guṇavati tadviśuddhiparikarmayogāt /.*
1741 Fibroferrite has the ability to make pure gold manifest, if placed in contact with gold ore. Cf. Gzhon nu dpal's example of a mixture of turmeric powder and lime

(to illustrate the sixty cleansing factors applied to the buddha element of sentient beings), which manifests the quality "redness."

1742 The numbering follows Steinkellner's (1977) *Verse-Index*.

1743 The Tibetan has an ablative; according to the Sanskrit the meaning is "through [its] complete cause."

1744 For Dharmakīrti the *svabhāva* of the cause does not really exist as such, the term only referring to an "accumulation of causes" (Steinkellner has *Ursachenkomplex*). Thus the term *svabhāva* is only used metaphorically to designate a set of causes (caused themselves by their own respective causes) which jointly bring forth the effect (see Steinkellner 1971:185–86).

1745 PV I.7 (Ed. Gnoli 1960:6.24–25): *hetunā yaḥ samagreṇa kāryotpādo 'numīyate / arthāntarānapekṣatvāt sa svabhāvo 'nuvarṇitaḥ //*. For a German translation see Steinkellner 1971:185.

1746 See DRSM, 37.13–23.

1747 Tib. *ye shes de dag*.

1748 This is probably the example of a huge painting of the universe inside an atom quoted from the *Avataṁsakasūtra* in RGVV I.25 to illustrate the third inconceivable point that buddha qualities are contained in ordinary people (see Takasaki 1966:189–92).

1749 RGV I.137–146b (J I.134–143b). See Takasaki 1966:281–83.

1750 The Tibetan translation *rnam par smin pa bzhin* would then be a misunderstanding of the Sanskrit construction. See de Jong 1979:574.

1751 RGVV, 69.11–12: *garbhakośamalaprakhyāḥ saptabhūmigatā malāḥ*[a] */ vikośagarbhavaj jñānam avikalpaṁ vipākavat //* .

a According to B (36a4); fol. 27b of A is not readable. Johnston reads *malā*. See also Schmithausen 1971:156.

1752 That is, the sixth example, that of a seed inside bark that develops into a tree (see Takasaki 1966:273–75).

1753 Cf. the explanations of the buddha qualities nos. 1, 4, 5, 6, 7 and 8 above.

1754 Cf. the explanations of the buddha qualities nos. 2, 3 and 10.

1755 In a recent study of the *Tathāgatagarbhasūtra*, Zimmermann (2002:63–64) argues that the main focus of the example of the tree lies not on the growing tree, but on the imperishability of its seed and the fact that the result *(kārya)*, namely the tree, is already contained in the seed; while in the eighth example the fact that the *cakravartin* is still an embryo does not seem to be crucial for an understanding of it. His *cakravartin*-like nature will not change, inasmuch as his future role is already preprogrammed, and his poor mother already protected.

1756 The dharmakāya is the nature of the qualities constituting a buddha. It thus stands for fully developed qualities.

1757 Cf. Gzhon nu dpal's explanation of the illustration based on the *vaiḍūrya* stone and the mud in the *Sāgaramatiparipṛcchā*, which is quoted in RGVV I.68: "Since here in this example it was taught that a polished and stainless jewel was thrown into the mud, the example of the jewel illustrated the dharmakāya of the buddhas. Here it was taught as something illustrable by the example of the *vaiḍūrya*, sentient beings' nature of mind and the dharmakāya being so similar in type." (DRSM, 362.18–20)

1758 Commenting on a passage of the *Anūnatvāpurṇatvanirdeśasūtra* in RGVV I.48, which states that the dharmakāya is called the buddha element when covered with stains (see Takasaki 1966:231–32), Gzhon nu dpal says: "Here, as to [the expression] 'the very *(eva)* dharmakāya' as [used] in the context of an impure state, the element of the state of sentient beings has in turn been given the name of the fruit, [namely] the level of a buddha, it having been said: 'Because its (i.e., buddha nature's) fruit has been metaphorically applied to the buddha potential.' And precisely such a dharmakāya is called saṁsāra, the inner essence having been given the name of that which covers [it].” (DRSM, 335.17–20.)

1759 There is no doubt, however, that RGV I.27 belongs to the root text, since it is also contained in the Chinese *kārikā* version.

1760 In fact, the stanza belongs to one of the oldest building blocks of the *Ratnagotravibhāga*. See Takasaki 1966:14 and Schmithausen 1971:126–29.

1761 Skt. *upacāra*. Gzhon nu dpal explains this term by use of the example of a Brahmin boy who is called a lion because he is a hero and fearless (DRSM, 150.10–12). Whereas a real lion is an animal, here the word *lion* is only metaphorically applied to the brave boy.

1762 RGVV, 26.1–4: *buddhajñānā[ntargam]*[a] *āt sattvarāśes tannairmalyasyādvayatvāt prakṛtyā / bauddhe gotre tatphalasyopacārād uktāḥ sarve dehino buddhagarbhāḥ //.*

a Not readable in B (15a4); A is not available.

1763 This is in keeping with explanation no. 11 (see above).

1764 Rngog Blo ldan shes rab: *Theg chen rgyud bla'i don bsdus pa*, 29b1–2.

1765 DRSM, 268.2–3.

1766 RGVV, 76.1–2: *nāpaneyam ataḥ kiṁcid upaneyaṁ na kiṁcana / draṣṭavyaṁ bhūtato bhūtaṁ bhūtadarśī vimucyate //.*

1767 RGVV, 76.3–4: *śūnya āgantukair dhātuḥ savinirbhāgalakṣaṇaiḥ / aśūnyo 'nuttaraiḥ dharmair avinirbhāgalakṣaṇaiḥ //.*

1768 For a list of texts in which it occurs, see Takasaki 1966:300.

1769 In DRSM's quote the equivalent for *evaṁ* is missing.

1770 According to the Sanskrit: “Somebody possessing a vision of reality....”

1771 AAV Sphuṭārthā, 72.1–4: *yasmād evaṁ bhāvābhiniveśena mukter anupapattir ato apavādasamāroparūpam apanayanaprakṣepaṁ kasyacid dharmasyākṛtvā idam eva pratītyasamutpannaṁ saṁvṛtyā tathyarūpaṁ rūpādi niḥsvabhāvādirūpato nirūpaṇīyam evañ ca māyāgajena aparamāyāgajaparājayavad viparyāsanivṛttyā tattvadarśī vimucyata iti /.*

1772 See DRSM, 441.1–3.

1773 See my translation of DRSM, 5.4–10.

1774 One could argue in favor of Gzhon nu dpal, though, that “door of wisdom” can also mean “cause of wisdom.”

1775 RGVV, 77.2: ...*ekanayadharmadhātvasaṁbhedajñānamukham āgamya*....

1776 Skt. *nimitta* can mean both; the Tibetan translation *rgyu mtshan* suggests the meaning “cause.”

1777 RGVV, 76.5–6: *kim anena paridīpitam / yato na kiṁcid apaneyam asty ataḥ prakṛtipariśuddhāt tathāgatadhātoḥ saṁkleśanimittam āgantukamalaśūnyatāprakṛtitvād asya /.*

1778 See RGV I.154 (J I.151). For a translation of this stanza see above, p. 12.

1779 RGVV, 76.6–7: *nāpy atra kiṁcid upaneyam asti vyavadānanimittam avinirbhāgaśuddhadharmatā*[a] *prakṛtitvāt /.*

a See A 19a4 and B 39b3. Johnston omits for no reason *tā;* probably this is only an oversight.

1780 In view of the following quotation of the *Śrīmālādevīsūtra*, the reading of the Narthang and Peking editions *(chos dag nyid)* is preferred, with the compound *avinirbhāgaśuddhadharmatā* taken as the abstract of a *bahuvrīhi*.

1781 This reading is also recorded in the Derge Tengyur (Nakamura 1967:149, l.7).

1782 Rngog Blo ldan shes rab: *Theg chen rgyud bla'i don bsdus pa*, 33a6–b3.

1783 Lit., “properties.”

1784 RGVV, 76.8–9: *śūnyas tathāgatagarbho vinirbhāgair muktajñaiḥ sarvakleśakośaiḥ / aśūnyo gaṅgānadīvālikāvyativṛttair avinirbhāgair amuktajñair acintyair buddha-*

dharmair /. The quoted passage is partially unreadable in B (39b3–4); but available from A (19a4–5).

1785 There are ten aspects of wisdom, which differ only with regard to various objects.

1786 This involves denying the *dharmatā* or suchness the status of a substantial cause, the qualities being merely produced by the fortified potential. For a presentation of such an interpretation, see Seyfort Ruegg 1969:293–96.

1787 See DRSM, 446.5–17.

1788 Cf. RGVV, 8.1: *anādimadhyanidhanaprakṛti*[a] *tvād asaṁskṛtam* (RGV I.6ab).

a According to B (5a4). See also Schmithausen 1971:134. Johnston wrongly reads *-prakṛta-*.

1789 See DRSM, 83.16–21.

1790 MSABh, 46.3*: tribhiḥ kāyais tu vijñeyo buddhānāṁ kāyasaṁgrahaḥ* /.

1791 Cf. Makransky (1997:289ff) who discusses Tsong kha pa's and Go ram pa's views on the distinction between three and four kāyas. According to Tsong kha pa, Haribhadra accepts three kāyas when the first kāya is dharmakāya and *jñāna* is included. But when the first is svābhāvikakāya, the second must be the *jñānātmiko dharmakāyaḥ*.

1792 DRSM, 84.16.

1793 Ibid., 84.21–85.1.

1794 Ibid., 85.1–86.11.

1795 RGVV, 8.7–8: *saṁskṛtaviparyayeṇāsaṁskṛtaṁ veditavyam / tatra saṁskṛtam ucyate yasyotpādo 'pi prajñāyate sthitir api bhaṅgo 'pi prajñāyate / tadabhāvād buddhatvam anādimadhyanidhanam asaṁskṛtadharmakāyaprabhāvitaṁ draṣṭavyam /.*

1796 Not considered as a stanza of the root text by Johnston. See Nakamura 1967:107.4–5 and DRSM, 380.3 and 380.6.

1797 DRSM, 380.12–17.

1798 RGVV, 13.15–20: *ya evam asataś ca nimittārambaṇasyādarśanāt sataś ca yathā-bhūtasya paramārthasatyasya darśanāt tadubhayor anutkṣepāprakṣepasamatājñānena sarvadharmasamatābhisaṁbodhaḥ so 'sya sarvākārasya tattvadarśanavibandhasya pratipakṣo veditavyo yasyodayād itarasyātyantam asaṁgatir asamavadhānaṁ prajñāyate*[a] */ sa khalv eṣa dharmakāyaprāptihetur avikalpajñānadarśanabhāvanāmārgo vistareṇa yathāsūtraṁ prajñāpāramitānusāreṇānugantavyaḥ /*

a According to B (9a2); A is not available. Johnston wrongly reads *pravartate*. See also Schmithausen 1971:137.

1799 DRSM, 111.8.

1800 Ibid., 119.23–24.

1801 A problem that leads Rgyal tshab rje to take merely the fortified potential as the substantial cause of the qualities (see Seyfort Ruegg 1969:295).

1802 Space being compared to buddha nature.

1803 CŚ, 86.13–14: *yathā bījasya dṛṣṭo 'nto na cādis tasya vidyate / tathā kāraṇavaikalyāj janmano 'pi na sambhavaḥ //*. For the Tibetan, Sanskrit, and English see Lang 1986:86–87.

1804 BYCŚṬ, 154.17–18: *yathā nāma cirakālapravṛttasyāsya*[a] *hetuphalaparamparayā pravartamānasya bījasantānasyānādimato 'nto dṛṣto....*

a Skt. *asya* has no equivalent in the Tibetan.

1805 Lit., "looked after."

1806 See BHSD under *āyatanika*.

1807 DRSM, 120.15–121.5.

1808 DhDhVV, 707–8. See Mathes 1996:154.

1809 DhDhVV, 706–7 (Ibid.:154). That this sentence of the *vṛtti* posed a problem is reflected in its deviant transmission in Gzhon nu dpal's commentary. Against the readings of all Tengyur editions *(...gnas yongs su gyur pa rtag pa yin no)* the handwritten commentary (text A) reads *gnas yongs su rtag pa yin no* and the block print (text B) *gnas yongs su brtag pa yin no*, a mistake that conveniently gets rid of the (for Gzhon nu dpal) problematic "permanent." (See DRSM, 121.3.)

1810 RGVV, 41.15–17: *tasmāc chāriputra nānyaḥ sattvadhātur nānyo dharmakāyaḥ / sattvadhātur eva dharmakāyaḥ / dharmakāya eva sattvadhātuḥ / advayam etad arthena / vyañjana*[a] *mātrabheda iti*[a] */.*

a B (24a2) reads *-mātran nāneti;* emended according to Johnston.

1811 RGVV, 41.20–21: *doṣāgantukatāyogād guṇaprakṛtiyogataḥ / yathā pūrvaṁ tathā paścād avikāritvadharmatā //.*

1812 In other words, former and later moments of buddha nature are connected in terms of having an identical nature. The blossoming of buddha nature into buddhahood does not involve a change in quality but only in quantity.

1813 Tib. *tha mal gyi shes pa*. Gzhon nu dpal explains that the word *tha mal* does not mean "ordinary" here, but "unfabricated" (DRSM, 340.2).

1814 See also Mi bskyod rdo rje ("Rje Yid bzang rtse ba'i Rgyud gsum gsang ba...," 1003.3–5), who criticizes Gzhon nu dpal for first distinguishing a buddha nature that abides as the six *āyatana*s from an actual Buddha, and then citing Rang byung rdo rje as a support for such a stance.

1815 Tib. *rnam par rig pa mi rig pa*, Skt. *asaṁviditavijñapti* (see Schmithausen 1987: vol. 1, 89 and vol. 2, 385–86).

1816 The example is quoted in the *Ratnagotravibhāgavākhyā*'s explanation of the third inconceivable point (the buddha qualities also exist inside ordinary people) in RGV I.25 (see DRSM, 239.13–14).

1817 DRSM, 122.2–3.

1818 Ibid., 236.6–8.

1819 Ibid., 121.22–25.

1820 Ibid., 74.26–75.3.

1821 In support, Gzhon nu dpal adduces PV I.7 (see above).

1822 In RGVV I.1.

1823 RGVV, 2.10–13: *śraddhāgamanīyo hi śāriputra paramārthaḥ / paramārtha iti śāriputra sattvadhātor etad adhivacanam / sattvadhātur iti śāri[putra]*[a] *tathāgatagarbhasyaitad adhivacanam / tathāgatagarbha iti śāriputra dharmakāyasyaitad adhivacanam.*

a Missing in B (2a3); A is not available.

1824 RGVV, 20.4–5: *jagaccharaṇam ekāntaṁ (?)*[a] *buddhatvaṁ pāramārthikam / muner dharmaśarīratvāt tanniṣṭhatvād gaṇasya ca //.*

a Johnston reads *ekatra*, which does not fit the context. Folio 11b of manuscript B is hardly readable and manuscript A is not available, so that the correct reading could well have been *ekāntaṁ* (see also Schmithausen 1971:140).

1825 RGVV, 84.3–4: *yad uktam ākāśalakṣaṇo buddha iti tat pāramārthikam āveṇikaṁ tathāgatānāṁ buddhalakṣaṇam abhisaṁdhāyoktam /.*

1826 DRSM, 24.4–5.

1827 Ibid., 14.20–21.

1828 Ibid., 14.19–20.

1829 Tib. *ldan pa*, Skt. *yoga.*

1830 Ibid., 509.9–12.

1831 Ibid., 84.23.

1832 Ibid., 338.23–339.1.

1833 Ibid., 16.14–17.

1834 Ibid., 16.17–18.

1835 In a way it would be better to translate "awareness and emptiness," but "awareness-emptiness" does have this meaning also.

1836 Ibid., 400.23–24.

1837 Ibid., 101.18–24. See also below, "Two Types of Emptiness" (chapter 6).

1838 According to Thrangu Rinpoche one has to distinguish two types of "self-awareness." One is the epistemological self-awareness of the Yogācāras, and the other one the realization of one's own true nature of mind, or soteriological "self-awareness," or rather "self-realization" (for a recent discussion of a similar distinction see also Yao 2005:126–27). In the context of the *Ratnagotravibhāga*, "self-awareness" must be taken in its soteriological sense, namely as described by the term *so so rang gis rig par bya ba* (Skt. *pratyātmavedanīya*) in RGVV, 1.7. In the *vyākhyā* on RGV I.1 the content of self-realization is taken to be the seven vajra points. These seven are further explained by Gzhon nu dpal as "the meaning and object of comprehension that have the nature of self-realization *(so so rang gis rig pa),* [that is,] a direct [perception] arisen from meditation" (see DRSM, 20.26–21.1). In other words, self-awareness does not refer to a mental factor of a perceiving consciousness, but to an experience beyond the ordinary duality of a perceiving subject and perceived object. It is a realization that is not different from its realized object anymore.

1839 DRSM, 481.23–24.

1840 TD, 92.10–11: "Thus [all] phenomena that are of one taste are unobstructed and without an abode. They are all luminous—as [experienced] in the *samādhi* [of realizing] reality as it is" *(evam ekarasā dharmā nirāsaṅgā nirāspadāḥ / prabhāsvarā amī sarve yathābhūtasamādhinā //).*

1841 TDṬ, 186b7–8: *ro gcig pa ni de bzhin nyid du ro gcig pa'o / … / thogs pa med cing zhes bya ba ni rang bzhin sgro btags med pa'o / / gnas med par zhes bya ba ni ma skyes pa ste /.*

1842 See TDṬ, 187a1–2: "Luminosity refers to self-awareness (i.e., self-realization), in view of its being naturally free from stains…. One may ask, How does one see the phenomena of reality, whose nature is such a suchness? Therefore [Maitrīpa] said, '…as [experienced] in the *samādhi* [of realizing] reality as it is.' The latter is a path that is endowed with *śamatha* and *vipaśyanā* united into a pair" *('od gsal zhes bya ba ni rang bzhin gyis (text: gyi) dri ma spangs pas rang rig pa ste / … / de ltar gyur pa'i de bzhin nyid kyi bdag nyid kyi de kho na nyid kyi chos rnams ji ltar mthong zhe na / de'i phyir ji ltar 'byung ba'i ting nge 'dzin gyis zhes bya smras te / zhi gnas dang lhag mthong zung du 'jug pa dan ldan pa'i lam ni ji ltar 'byung ba'i ting nge 'dzin no).*

1843 JNĀ, 478.10–13: "In the *Uttaratantra* (i.e., *Ratnagotravibhāga*) [we find] the words that the Dharma must be realized by oneself. Since it has been stated that false imagining exists, there is no other refuge apart from [this] self-awareness." *(uttaratantre ca/ pratyātmavedyo dharmaḥ / ity evākṣaraṁ / na cābhūtaparikalpo 'stīti bruvataḥ svasaṁvedanād anyac charaṇam /.)*

1844 In the process of self-awareness, or self-realization, I take it that the experience of luminosity is nothing else than a luminous experience.

1845 See also my translation of DRSM, 102.4–9 on p. 356.

1846 See DRSM, 14.22–15.8.

1847 Lit., "an essential nature that is not mixed with other own-beings" (DRSM, 14.25).

1848 Gzhon nu dpal only quotes Candrakīrti's examples of an own-being (see my translation of DRSM, 15.2–8), which could give the impression that Candrakīrti accepts the hotness of fire as being the fire's own-being. In his *Prasannapadā*, however, Candrakīrti continues: "Even though the worldly convention has been established that it is an uncreated own-being, we claim in this case, too, that this heat must not be understood to be the own-being of fire, given that it is created. In this case the dependence of fire on causes and conditions is perceived when a lens, kindling, and the sun conjoin or when sticks are rubbed together or the like, heat not occurring separately from fire. Therefore heat, too, is born of causes and conditions" (PP, 260.9–12: *tad evam akṛtakaḥ svabhāva iti lokavyavahāre vyavasthite vayam idānīṁ brūmo yad etad auṣṇyaṁ tad apy agneḥ svabhāvo na bhavatīti gṛhyatāṁ kṛtakatvāt / iha maṇīndhanādityasamāgamād araṇinirgharṣaṇādeś cāgner hetupratyayasāpekṣataivopalabhyate / na cāgnivyatiriktam auṣṇyaṁ sambhavati / tasmād auṣṇyam api hetupratyayajanitaṁ /*).

1849 In his commentary on MMK V.1 Candrakīrti explains: "In this respect six elements have been taught: they are known as earth, water, fire, wind, space, and consciousness" (PP, 129.8: *tatra ṣaḍ dhātava uktāḥ pṛthivyaptejovāyvākāśavijñānākhyāḥ /*).

1850 In his commentary on MMK V.7ab Candrakīrti explains: "The five remaining elements—earth and the others—should be known, like space, to be, in terms of their own nature, free from the concepts of entity, nonentity, object to be characterized, and defining characteristic." (PP, 134.10–11: *pṛthivyādidhātavo ye pañcāpare 'vaśiṣyante*[a] */ te 'py ākāśavad bhāvābhāvalakṣyalakṣaṇaparikalpasvarūparahitāḥ parijñeyā....*)

a Corrected according to de Jong 1978:42.

1851 This is particularly clear in MMK XVIII.7, which says: "When the realm of mind has ceased, that which is to be expressed also ceases. This is because the true nature of phenomena is, like nirvāṇa, without production and destruction." (MMK, 25.1–2: *nivṛttam abhidhātavyaṁ nivṛtte cittagocare* (de Jong reads *nivṛttaś cittagocaraḥ*) */ anutpannāniruddhā hi nirvāṇam iva dharmatā //.*) Candrakīrti explains: "If there was some realm of the mind, then speech would function after some characteristic sign has been imputed. When, however, an object has not occurred to the mind, where is then the characteristic sign by which speech would function?" (PP, 364.8–10: *yadi cittasya kaścid gocaraḥ syāt tatra kiṁcin nimittam adhyāropya syād vācāṁ pravṛttiḥ / yadā tu cittasya viṣaya evānupapannas tadā kva nimittādhyāropo yena vācāṁ pravṛttiḥ syāt // ....*) This means that the imputation of characteristic signs is necessary for something to be expressible in the concepts of language. But once reality is no longer subjected to one's false imagining, nothing remains to be expressed by speech.

1852 Perception *(upalabdha)* is here explained from the side of the object.

1853 PP, 265.3–5: *avidyātimiraprabhāvopalabdhaṁ bhāvajātaṁ yenātmanā vigatāvidyātimirāṇām āryāṇām adarśanayogena viṣayatvam upayāti tad eva svarūpam eṣāṁ svabhāva iti vyavasthāpyate / tasya cedaṁ lakṣaṇaṁ /.*

1854 "If it is indeed claimed by you that it [only] exists in dependence on labelling, what kind of thing is it, [then, in reality]? It is the true nature of phenomena; it is their true form. And what is the true nature of phenomena? It is the own-being of phenomena. And what is the own-being? It is the natural state. And what is the natural state? It is emptiness. And what is emptiness? It is lack of essence. And what is this lack of essence? Suchness. And what is suchness? It is existence as it is, a state without change, and permanent abiding. The continuous nonarising of fire, etc., is called own-being because it does not depend on anything else and is nonartificial." (PP, 264.11ff.: *yadi khalu tad adhyāropād bhavadbhir astīty ucyate kīdṛśaṁ tat / yā sā dharmāṇāṁ dharmatā nāma saiva tatsvarūpaṁ / atha keyaṁ dharmāṇāṁ dharmatā / dharmāṇāṁ svabhāvaḥ / ko 'yaṁ svabhāvaḥ / prakṛtiḥ / kā ceyaṁ prakṛtiḥ / yeyaṁ śūnyatā / keyaṁ śūnyatā / naiḥsvābhāvyaṁ / kim idaṁ naiḥsvābhāvyaṁ / tathatā / keyaṁ tathatā / tathābhāvo 'vikāritvaṁ sadaiva sthāyitā / sarvadānutpāda eva hy agnyādīnāṁ paranirapekṣatvād akṛtrimatvāt svabhāva ity ucyate //.*)

1855 PP, 265.7–8: *sa caiṣa bhāvānām anutpādātmakaḥ svabhāvo 'kiṁcittvenābhāvamātratvād asvabhāva eveti kṛtvā nāsti bhāvasvabhāva iti vijñeyaṁ //.*

1856 Even though there are a number of differences between the two, they agree that the second dharmacakra is surpassed by the third, and that the reasoning of the analytical Madhyamaka works only apply to what is defined as adventitious stains in the *Ratnagotravibhāga.*

1857 I.e., to the process of labeling, which involves the alteration of one's subjective reality by mental fabrications.

1858 Cf. MMK XVIII.9: "Not dependent on other, peaceful, not artificially created by thoughts, nonconceptual, without many—these are the defining characteristics of reality" (MMK, 25.5–6 : *aparapratyayaṁ śāntaṁ prapañcair aprapañcitam / nirvikalpam anānārtham etat tattvasya lakṣaṇam //.*)

1859 DRSM, 15.16–17.

1860 Gzhon nu dpal quotes BV 57 in order to reinforce his point (DRSM, 15.18–20).

1861 I.e., in being neither artificially created nor dependent on anything else (see above).

1862 DRSM, 15.8–20.

1863 Ibid., 84.23.

1864 Ibid., 239.18–20.

1865 See Ibid., 449.1. In other words, when Gzhon nu dpal speaks of subtle qualities he is thinking of qualities such as the five qualities of the svābhāvikakāya explained in RGV II.47: "The svābhāvikakāya is endowed with qualities that are immeasurable, innumerable, inconceivable, incomparable, and that have reached the [state of] final purity" (RGVV, 87.2–4: *aprameyair asaṁkhyeyair acintyair asamair guṇaiḥ / viśuddhipārami*[a]*prāptair yuktaṁ svābhāvikaṁ vapuḥ /*).

a B (44a5) and Johnston read *-mī.*

1866 See above, in chapter 5 in the section "The Blossoming of Subtle Qualities."

1867 See DRSM, 83.11, for example.

1868 Ibid., 340.19–24.

1869 See Ibid., 340.24–25.

1870 See the following chapter on mahāmudrā (chapter 7).

1871 The first of the four inconceivable points explained in RGV I.25.

1872 See DRSM, 216.12–15.

1873 Lit., "mother" (Tib. *yum*).

1874 Gzhon nu dpal does not distinguish, as his commentary on the four inconceivable points shows, between an own-being and a substantial own-being: "The mere [fact that the buddha] nature is not artificial, implies that it is not something that possesses an own-being. Even the final buddha wisdom lacks a substantial own-being." (DRSM, 226.10–11.)

1875 I.e., generate *bodhicitta.*

1876 Tib. *cung zad.*

1877 MMK XIII.7cd: *na kiṁcid asty aśūnyaṁ ca kutaḥ śūnyaṁ bhaviṣyati //* (MMK, 18.6).

1878 Candrakīrti explains: "If there was any kind of emptiness, then it would be, as the own-being of entities, their basis. But this is not the case. Since one realizes here that emptiness is the general characteristic of all phenomena, and since phenomena that are not empty do not exist, emptiness itself does not exist [either]." (PP, 246.1–3: *yadi śūnyatā nāma kā cit syāt tad āśrayo bhāvasvabhāvaḥ syāt / na tv evaṁ / iha hi śūnyatā nāmeti sarvadharmāṇāṁ sāmānyalakṣaṇam ity abhyupagamād aśūnyadharmābhāvād śūnyataiva nāsti /.*) In other words, Candrakīrti does not say directly that, starting from the premise of emptiness, no support of phenomena can be established in terms of specific characteristics. This follows, however, from the fact that emptiness is taken to be the general characteristic of phenomena.

1879 Sthiramati explains: "Now is the truth of the path conditioned or unconditioned? It is conditioned, since it has to be brought forth. It would not be a fault[, however,] if one said that it is unconditioned, in that it is not being fabricated by *karmakleśa* [defilements] and is constituted by the unconditioned" (MAVṬ on

III.22b-d (MAVṬ, 163.7–9): *mārgasatyaṁ punaḥ kiṁ saṁskṛtam asaṁskṛtam / saṁskṛtam*[a] *utpādyatvāt / yadi [karmakleśābhyām anabhisaṁskṛtād asaṁskṛtena ca prabhāvitatvād* (Yamaguchi: *prabhāvitād*) *a]*[b]*saṁskṛtam iti bruyān na doṣaḥ syād...*).

a The manuscript (NGMPP reel no. A 38/10, 50a7) repeats *saṁskṛtam*, but this is not supported by the Tibetan (see also Yamaguchi 1934:163, fn. 2).

b Cf. Tib. *gal te las dang nyon mongs pas mngon par 'dus ma byas pa dang / 'dus ma byas kyis rab tu phye ba'i phyir 'dus ma byas zhes brjod na nyes pa med do.* Peking Tengyur, sems tsam, *tshi*, 113b4–5.

1880 Tib. *tha mal shes pa*, see DRSM, 339.26–340.1.

1881 Read *brtags* instead of *btags* (DRSM, 441.15). It should be noted that investigations can be carried out on the basis of direct cognition.

1882 See DRSM, 44.5–13.

1883 It is inconceivable that buddha nature is pure and defiled at one and the same time (see RGV I.25).

1884 See the section "The Blossoming of Subtle Qualities" in chapter 5.

1885 See Suzuki 1932:68 (§ XXVIII).

1886 DRSM, 264ff.

1887 Ibid., 135.6.

1888 See p. 17 in the introduction of this work.

1889 See Mathes 1996:122.

1890 See Mathes 1998:465–66.

1891 Cf. MSA XIII.19: "The mind is taken to be natural luminosity at any time; it is [only] tainted by adventitious faults. A natural luminosity of (i.e., consisting of) another, [dependent] mind *(cetas)*,[a] different from the mind as true nature *(dharmatā)*, is not taught." (MSABh, 88.9–10: *mataṁ ca cittaṁ prakṛtiprabhāsvaraṁ sadā tadāgantukadośadūśitaṁ / na dharmatācittam ṛte 'nyacetasaḥ prabhāsvaratvaṁ prakṛtau*[b] *vidhīyate //.*)

a Vasubandhu explains (MSABh, 88.17): "of another mind whose defining characteristic is the dependent [nature]" *('nyasya cetasaḥ paratantralakṣaṇasya).*

b According to Bagchi (1970:86.8). Lévi reads: *prabhāsvaraṁ prakṛtam* ("the [natural] luminosity under discussion here"). This reading not only violates the meter but is also against the Tibetan, which has *rang bzhin* (and thus supports *prakṛtau*).

1892 DRSM, 456.18–23.

1893 What Gzhon nu dpal had in mind here were probably Yogācāra works such as Asaṅga's *Mahāyānasaṁgraha*, where a clear line is drawn between an impure *ālayavijñāna* and a pure supramundane mind, or pure dharmadhātu (see Lamotte 1938: vol. 1, 19–20).

1894 This can also be said of the other two Yogācāra works ascribed to Maitreya.

1895 See Mathes 1996:99: *svabhāvapraveśas tathatāvaimalyam āgantukamalatathatāprakhyānaprakhyānāya /.*

1896 RGVV, 79.10–11: *yo 'sau dhātur avinirmuktakleśakośas tathāgatagarbha*[a] *ity ukto bhagavatā tadviśuddhir āśrayaparivṛtteḥ svabhāvo veditavyaḥ.* For a discussion of the parallels between the *Ratnagotravibhāga* and the *Dharmadharmatāvibhāga*, see Mathes 1996:19–23.

a In B (41a3) *-rbha* is missing. A is not available.

1897 Dam pa sangs rgyas transmitted the mahāmudrā teachings called "The Right Dharma That Calms Suffering" *(dam chos sdug bsngal zhi byed).* See also Karmapa Mi bskyod rdo rje's introduction to his commentary on the *Madhyamakāvatāra*, paraphrased by Seyfort Ruegg (1988a:1,261–62).

1898 See DRSM, 2.7–10.

1899 See Ibid., 5.10–11.

1900 For a detailed analysis of these works see chapter 1 above.

1901 See DRSM, 5.17–20.

1902 I do not take *dag* in *'di dag* as a plural particle, but as a marker denoting the entire corpus of this tradition. See Hahn 1978:137–47.

1903 For Hookham (1991:271) *lugs 'di* refers to Dol po pa's *gzhan stong* tradition: "Shonupal...made a commentary...in accordance with this extraordinary system introduced by...Dol po pa; he also commented on it." This is not only grammatically impossible, but also historically so: in his *Ri chos nges don rgya mtsho* (340–43), Dol po pa distinguishes an ordinary presentation of the contents of the *Ratnagotravibhāga* from his own extraordinary Vajrayāna explanation, which nevertheless accords with the ordinary explanation (it is this ordinary explanation that would then correspond to the meditation school and Gzhon nu dpal, according to Kong sprul).

1904 Kong sprul Blo gros mtha' yas: *Rgyud bla ma'i bshad srol*, fol. 9b1–10a1: *gzu (text: gzus) dga' ba'i rdo rje rgyud bla ma la sajja na'i gsung dang mthun par brgyun ṭīkā (text: ṭika) mdzad cing chos nyid rnam 'byed rtsa 'grel yang bsgyur / 'di la byams chos sgom lugs pa'ang grags shing thun mong ma yin pa'i bshad pa dang nyams len gyi khyad par 'phags pa yin la / / lugs srol de dag las byung yang ye shes kyi gzigs pas ma pham pa'i dgongs pa ji bzhin du (text: tu) rtogs pa thams cad mkhyen pa rang byung rdo rjes rgyud bla ma'i sa bcad bsdus don mdzad pa la / Karma dkon gzhon sogs kyis rgyas par bkral zhing / Karma Phrin las pa chen pos sbyor dag bkod pa'i 'grel ba mdzad / 'gos lo chen po gzhon nu dpal gyis kyang thogs med zhabs kyis 'grel pa la 'grel bshad shin tu rgyas par mdzad pa lugs 'di dang mthun pa / kun mkhyen dol po pa chen pos thun mong ma yin pa'i srol phye (text: phyes) te 'grel pa'i rjes 'brangs nas slob brgyud spyi dang bye brag thams cad mkhyen pa tāranātha sogs gyis bshad pa dang nyams len gyis gzhung btsugs pa'i 'grel pa'i lung rgyun da ltar bar bzhugs pa dang /.*

1905 'Jig rten gsum mgon: "Chos 'khor 'ong ges zhus pa'i gzhung gi rtsa ba," 15.12–14 and "Chos 'khor 'ong ges zhus pa'i gzhung gi 'grel pa," 317.9–11. See "The Mahāmudrā Interpretation of the *Ratnagotravibhāga*" in chapter 1.

1906 Ibid., 14.17–15.2.

1907 Ibid., 10.17.

1908 'Jig rten gsum mgon: "Dam chos dgongs pa gcig pa'i gzhung," 11.11–13 and Rig 'dzin Chos kyi grags pa: "Dam pa'i chos dgongs pa gcig pa'i rnam bshad lung don gsal byed nyi ma'i snang ba," 43.8–52.14. See "The Mahāmudrā Interpretation of the *Ratnagotravibhāga*" in chapter 1.

1909 'Jig rten gsum mgon: "Chos 'khor 'ong ges zhus pa'i gzhung gi 'grel pa," 347.1–6.

1910 See my translation of DRSM, 37.8–40.8.

1911 See Lamotte 1935:85; and Powers 1994:138–41.

1912 As explained in SNS VII.31–32 (see Lamotte 1935:86–87; Powers 1994:141–45).

1913 See Mathes 2007:326–27.

1914 DRSM, 44.20–74.26.

1915 Ibid., 38.19–26.

1916 Gzhon nu dpal quotes MSA XII.11 to elucidate the threefold purity of the irreversible dharmacakra.

1917 DRSM, 40.5–41.10.

1918 See Tsultrim Gyamtsho and Fuchs 2000:283–85.

1919 DRSM, 45.7–22.

1920 Gzhon nu dpal justifies this with reference RGV I.163–70, the last eight stanzas of the first chapter, which give five reasons why the existence of the buddha element must be taught after the previous presentations of emptiness in the second dharmacakra (see my translation of DRSM, 45.22–46.5).

1921 DRSM, 46.5–17.

1922 DRSM, 47.12–19.
1923 DRSM, 48.4–10.
1924 DRSM, 447.14–17.
1925 Ibid., 74.25–26.
1926 'Jig rten gsum mgon: "Chos 'khor 'ong ges zhus pa'i gzhung gi 'grel pa," 338.12–17: *bdag cag gi ston pa sangs rgyas bcom ldan 'das 'di nyid kyang / . . . dang po bla na med pa'i byang chub tu sems bskyed nas / sa dang po man chad bskal pa grangs med gcig 'khor lo dang po'i tshul gyis lam bgrod / sa bdun man chad du grangs med gcig 'khor lo gnyis pa'i tshul gyis lam bgrod / dag pa'i sa gsum gyi grangs med gcig 'khor lo gsum pa'i tshul gyis lam bgrod pa yin. . . .*
1927 DRSM, 41.24–42.25.
1928 Ibid., 74.18–25.
1929 'Jig rten gsum mgon: "Dam chos dgongs pa gcig pa'i gzhung," 15.4. See "The Mahāmudrā Interpretation of the *Ratnagotravibhāga*" in chapter 1.
1930 Ibid., 17.1–4. See "The Mahāmudrā Interpretation of the *Ratnagotravibhāga*" in chapter 1.
1931 According to oral explanations of Lama Jorphel.
1932 DRSM, 74.14–18.
1933 Ibid., 73.3–5. See also Martin 1992:287; and Jackson 1990:52–53.
1934 DRSM, 41.24–43.2.
1935 See DRSM, 339.26–340.2; the lines quoted by Gzhon nu dpal are from Rang byung rdo rje's *Snying po bstan pa:* "The [unfabricated] natural mind is called dharmadhātu [or] buddha nature. It is neither improved by the noble ones nor demolished by sentient beings" (Rang byung rdo rje: *Snying po bstan pa*, fol. 36a4–5).
1936 According to Gzhon nu dpal's reading, awareness, or the element of awareness, is compared in RGV I.106b to honey in the simile of the honey and the bees, and thus to buddha nature (J I.104b).
1937 See DRSM, 15.8–12.
1938 See DRSM, 6.16–23.
1939 See DRSM, 15.8–10.
1940 RGV I.151 (J I.148).
1941 According to an oral explanation by Thrangu Rinpoche.
1942 See my translation of DRSM, 59.7–9.
1943 Technically speaking, this nonconceptual observation of or gazing at one's mind is a yogic direct valid cognition (Tib. *rnal 'byor gyi mngon sum tshad ma*). It is like the mind directed outside, which simply watches, for example, a bird leaving its nest looking for a worm, eating it, and so forth (according to oral explanations by Thrangu Rinpoche).
1944 See DRSM, 16.18–17.4.
1945 See also Pettit 1999:180–81.
1946 See DRSM, 58.26–59.4.
1947 See DRSM, 61.26–62.3 and DRSM, 63.24–64.2.
1948 Otherwise translated as "mental engagement."
1949 See DRSM, 59.12–22.
1950 According to oral explanations by Thrangu Rinpoche.
1951 DRSM, 40.5–8.
1952 Ibid., 40.11–19.
1953 Ibid., 43.2–44.5
1954 See the section "The Blossoming of Subtle Qualities" in chapter 5.
1955 DRSM, 135.6.
1956 See p. 17 in the introduction of this work.
1957 That is, coemergent wisdom.

1958 See DRSM, 44.5–7.
1959 See "The *Ratnagotravibhāga* and Its *Vyākhyā*" in my introduction.
1960 For Gzhon nu dpal's description of these five stages on the basis of the *Laṅkāvatārasūtra*, see DRSM, 59.24–61.18.
1961 See Cozort 1986:69–70.
1962 LAS, 42.8–10: *mahākaruṇopāyakauśalyānābhogagatena mahāmate prayogena sarvasattvamāyāpratibimbasamatayā-*.
1963 PK III, introduction (31.3–7): *utpattikramānusāreṇa prāptābhiṣekhaḥ...vajraguruṁ samyag ārādhya / ...tadanantaraṁ guruvaktrād āptasvādhiṣṭhānakramopadeśaḥ /.*
1964 PK III.14: *svādhiṣṭhānānupūrveṇa prāpyate hi prabhāsvaram / tasmād vajraguruḥ pūrvaṁ svādhiṣṭhānaṁ pradarśayet //.*
1965 LAS, 42.10–13: *cittabāhyādarśanatayānimittādhiṣṭhānānugatā anupūrveṇa bhūmikramasamādhiviṣayānugamanatayā traidhātukasvacittamāyā*[a]*dhimuktitaḥ pratvibhāvayamānā māyopamasamādhiṁ pratilabhante.*
a According to E (24a3), H (17a7), and the Tibetan. Nanjio and the remaining Nepalese manuscripts read *-tayā* instead of *-māyā-*.
1966 TDṬ, 194a3–4: *rang byin brlabs pas rnam brgyan pa'o zhes bya ba ni rang nyid gnyug ma'i de kho na nyid kyi bdag nyid du 'byor pa'i sems kyi rgyun de'i bdag nyid du byin gyis brlabs pa'o / / de bzhin nyid kyi rang bzhin las 'phro ba rang bzhin gyis rgyan pa.*
1967 See "The Mahāmudrā Interpretation of the *Ratnagotravibhāga*" in chapter 1.
1968 RGVV, 98.13–17: *yasya yena ca* [a]*yā yatra*[a] *yadā ca vinayakriyā / tadvikalpodayābhāvād anābhogaḥ sadā muneḥ // yasya dhātor vineyasya yenopāyena bhūriṇā / yā vinītikriyā yatra yadā taddeśakālayoḥ //.*
a According to B (50a1); A is not available. See also Schmithausen (1971:170). Johnston reads *yāvac ca.*
1969 DRSM, 60.20–25.
1970 Ibid., 61.18–22.
1971 LAS, 298.18: *nirābhāsasthito yogī mahāyānaṁ sa paśyati //.* These *pāda*s mark the end of a traditional description of the fourfold Mahāyāna meditation in the *Laṅkāvatārasūtra.*
1972 Cf. TA, 71b8–72a1: *...theg pa chen po zhes bya ba la / mtshan gyi rnam pa gzhan du na phyag rgya chen po zhes bya ba ste / de mthong bar 'gyur ro zhes gsungs pa ni / snang med gnas pa'i rnal 'byor pa / de yis (text: yi) theg pa chen po mthong.*
1973 See my translation of the passage in which Gzhon nu dpal quotes and explains LAS, 79.16–82.4 (DRSM, 62.17–65.25).
1974 Quoted in my translation (DRSM, 61.22–62.17); see also Martin 1992:278–80.
1975 See Mathes 2005:16–19.
1976 Gzhon nu dpal's commentary on the second chapter of the *Ratnagotravibhāgavyākhyā* begins with a detailed explanation of the dharmatā chapter in the *Dharmadharmatāvibhāgakārikās*. For a detailed analysis of Gzhon nu dpal's *Dharmadharmatāvibhāga* commentary, see Mathes 2005:3–39.
1977 See DRSM, 468.18–21: "Second, as to such an apprehension, one apprehends that false imagining lacks an own-being, even though it appears. Thus it is called the apprehension that [everything] is only an image *(vijñapti)*. From this results a consciousness that does not apprehend outer objects, [that is, that apprends them] as lacking an own-being. From such a consciousness results the knowledge that even the perceiving subject called 'only images' lacks an own-being."
1978 DRSM, 63.17–24.
1979 Ibid., 64.2–9.
1980 Ibid., 66.19–26.

1981 Even though the second dharma explains that the world arises through thought, mind-only is established by a kind of Madhyamaka reasoning to the effect that entities neither exist in terms of self, nor other, nor a combination of the two (see DRSM, 64.15–21).

1982 Cf. RGVV, 72.13: *anādikāliko dhātuḥ sarvadharmasamāśrayaḥ /.*

1983 DRSM, 17.4–6 and 142.23–24.

1984 RGVV, 14.1–4: *ye samyak pratividhya sarvajagato nairātmyakoṭiṁ śivāṁ taccittaprakṛtiprabhāsvaratayā kleśāsvabhāvekṣaṇāt / sarvatrānugatām anāvṛtadhiyaḥ paśyanti saṁbuddhatāṁ tebhyaḥ sattvaviśuddhyanantaviṣayajñānekṣaṇebhyo namaḥ //.*

1985 RGVV, 14.6–7: *yathāvadyāvadadhyātmajñānadarśanaśuddhitaḥ / dhīmatām avivartyānām anuttaraguṇo*[a] *gaṇaḥ //.*

a B has something unreadable after *ṇa* (A is not available). Johnston has *-ṇaiḥ*, which cannot be construed in a meaningful way (see also Schmithausen 1971:137).

1986 RGVV, 14.11–12: *yathāvattvaṁ*[a] *jagacchāntadharmatāvagamāt sa ca / prakṛteḥ pariśuddhatvāt kleśasyādi[kṣaye]*[b] *kṣaṇāt //.*

a According to B (9a6); A is not available. Johnston reads *taj-* instead of *-tvam*. But as in the similar construction of stanza RGV I.16, the Tib. *ji lta ba nyid* requires the abstract suffix (see also Schmithausen 1971:137).

b Missing in B (9a6); A is not available.

1987 RGVV, 14.13–14: *tatra yathāvadbhāvikatā kṛtsnasya pudgaladharmākhyasya*[a] *jagato yathāvan nairātmyakoṭer ava*[b]*gamād veditavyā /.*

a Johnston read *-kṣasya* and emended into *-khyasya*, but B (9b1) may well have read *-khyasya* (A is not available).

b B (9b1) has *-koṭer arava-*, and not *-koṭer anava-* (as Johnston remarks in a footnote). It is thus only a case of haplography and not a negation.

1988 RGVV, 14.14–16: *sa cāyam avagamo 'tyantādiśāntasvabhāvatayā pudgaladharmāvināśayogena samāsato dvābhyāṁ kāraṇābhyām utpadyate / pra[kṛ]*[a]*tiprabhāsvaratā*[b] *darśanāc ca citta*[b]*syādikṣayaniro[dha]*[a] *darśanāc ca tadupakleṣasya /.*

a B omits, A is not available.

b B reads *-darśanacitta-* (in compound). The context requires, however, following Johnston's conjecture (which he did not report at such); A is not available.

1989 RGVV, 14.16–15.7: *tatra yā cittasya prakṛtiprabhāsvaratā yaś ca tadupakleśa*[a] *ity etad dvayam anāsrave dhātau kuśalākuśalayoś cittayor ekacaratvād dvitīyacittānabhisaṁdhānayogena paramaduṣprativedhyam / ata āha / kṣaṇikaṁ bhagavan kuśalaṁ cittam / na kleśaiḥ saṁkliśyate*[b] */ kṣaṇikam akuśalaṁ cittam / asaṁkliṣṭam eva tac cittaṁ kleśaiḥ / na bhagavan kleśās tac cittaṁ spṛṣanti /* [c]*nāpi cittaṁ kleśān /*[c] *katham atra bhagavann asparṣanadharmi cittaṁ tamaḥkliṣṭaṁ bhavati / asti ca bhagavann upakleśaḥ / asty upakliṣṭaṁ cittam evaṁ*[d] *ca punar bhagavan prakṛtipariśuddhasya cittasyopakleśārtho duṣprativedhyaḥ /.*

a B (9b2) reads *-kleśā;* A is not available (not reported by Johnston).

b B (9b3) reads *-klinte* instead of *-kliśyate;* A is not available.

c Johnston omitted the sentence *nāpi cittaṁ kleśān /,* which is in B (9b4). A is not available.

d According to B (9b5); A is not available. Johnston has *atha* instead of *evaṁ.*

1990 Oral explanation from Thrangu Rinpoche.

1991 DRSM, 144.15–18.

1992 In other words, if a thought of viewing a self arises during the yoga of one-pointedness, a second thought is not needed to analyze and give up this thought of viewing a self. One-pointed gazing at one's mind ensures that the fact that one's mind lacks a self will directly be perceived again, once the thought of a self has dissolved by itself (oral explanation by Thrangu Rinpoche).

1993 See DRSM, 59.23ff., where the five stages of the *Pañcakrama* are identified in LAS II.98.

1994 See Mathes 1996:142–44.

1995 In the colophon of the prose version, the *Dharmadharmatāvibhāga* is called a sūtra (see Mathes 1996:67).

1996 I.e., the *yathābhūtasamādhi* (see TD, 94.1).

1997 The text in the Peking Tengyur (TDṬ, 190a5) has *gnyen po'i phyogs*, not *snying po*, and Gzhon nu dpal, too, has in his commentary on this quotation (DRSM, 464.1) the syllable *gnyen*.

1998 See my translation of DRSM, 57.1–59.22.

1999 DRSM *rten*, D *rtogs*, NP *rtog*. In accordance with Skt. *pratisaraṇa* the reading must be *rton [pa]*, which is also the *lectio difficilior*.

2000 The quoted passage introduces the explanation of stanzas I.156–58 (J I.153–55), dedicated to the defining characteristics of buddha nature. The corresponding Sanskrit is as follows (RGVV, 73.14–16): */ sarvatra dharmataiva pratiśaraṇam / dharmataiva yuktiś cittanidhyāpanāya cittasaṁjñāpanāya / sā na cintayitavyā na vikalpayitavyā / adhimoktavyeti /.*

2001 See DRSM, 56.5ff.

2002 RGVV, 27.2–3: *prabhāvānanyathābhāva*[a]*snigdhabhāvasvabhāvataḥ / cintāmaṇinabhovāriguṇasādha*[b]*rmyam eṣu hi //.*

a B (15b4) has a space between *-va* and the following *akṣara*. At one point there probably had been a *visarga* that was later omited. A is not available. Here one may follow Johnston (who did not report the gap), since *svabhāvataḥ* must govern all three nouns preceding it.

b B (15b4) omits *-dha-*.

2003 RGVV, 73.2–3: *tasmād bhagavaṁs tathāgatagarbho niśraya ādhāraḥ pratiṣṭhā saṁbaddhānām avinirbhāgānām amuktajñānānām asaṁskṛtānāṁ dharmāṇām /.*

2004 DRSM, 430.4–5.

2005 RGVV, 73.9–11: *sa khalv eṣa tathāgatagarbho dharmakāyavi*[a]*pulas ta*[a]*thatāsaṁbhinnalakṣaṇo niyatagotrasvabhāvaḥ sarvadā ca sarvatra ca niravaśeṣayogena* [b]*saṁvidyata iti*[b] *draṣṭavyaṁ dharmatāṁ pramāṇīkṛtya.* "Now, this buddha nature, which is as extensive as the dharmakāya, whose defining characteristics are not different from [those of] suchness and which has the nature of a definite potential, exists always and everywhere without difference. And this has to be seen in the light of having taking the true nature as a measure."

a B (38a2) probably reads *-pulastastata-* (containing as case of dittography); the quoted passage is not available in A. See also Schmithausen (1971:158). Johnston reads *-pralambhas ta-*.

b De Jong (1979:575) rejects Johnston's conjecture emending *saṁrvadyatananatija* into *sattvadhātāv iti* and proposes, based on the Tibetan *(yod do // zhes bya ba'i bar ni)*, reading *saṁvidyata iti yāvat*. Gzhon nu dpal, however, has *zhes bya ba ni* instead of *zhes bya ba'i bar ni*, so that I do not translate the *yāvat* here.

2006 Lit., "extensively."

2007 See DRSM, 73.3–8.

2008 This is also in line with 'Bri gung 'Jig rten gsum mgon, who says in *Dgongs gcig* VI.10 that meditation is the cultivation of realization, the possession of the latter being the supreme view (VI.7) (see above).

2009 See DRSM, 73.8–14.

2010 See DRSM, 67.8–72.4.

2011 See DRSM, 73.14–19.

2012 The yoga of one-pointedness is equivalent to the penetration of "heat," the yoga of freedom from mental fabrication to "peak," one taste to "forbearance," and nonmeditation to "supreme mundane qualities" (DRSM, 74.5–14).

2013 DRSM, 74.19–22.

2014 Buddhaguhya wrote two works on the *Mahāvairocanasūtra;* see Nakamura 1987:337.

2015 See my translation of DRSM, 61.22–62.17, in which LAS, 55.3–56.6 is quoted.

2016 This is related to the question whether the buddha qualities are already fully ripe before the actual path of seeing. Gzhon nu dpal compares the stains of the impure levels to the womb's confine, and nonconceptual wisdom experienced on these levels to the not yet activated sense faculties of the embryo. In the same way as these sense faculties are activated after birth, nonconceptual wisdom ripens upon one's going beyond the seventh level, when the buddha bodies fully ripen and become perfect. (DRSM, 418.18–22).

2017 DRSM, 73.7–8.

2018 Ibid., 446.5–21.

2019 Ibid., 430.25–26.

2020 Cf. DRSM, 222.12–14, where Gzhon nu dpal remarks that "the direct [perception] of realizing the lack of an own-being by looking is conventionally designated as 'to look at one's own nature' by the followers of mahāmudrā."

2021 See also the abovequoted argument that it takes a bodhisattva much longer to reach the actual eighth level than it takes a follower of the Śrāvakayāna to attain arhatship, and that as a consequence, an arhat does not enter the Mahāyāna on the actual eighth level (DRSM, 500.8–11).

2022 DRSM, 73.8–14.

2023 Ibid., 74.5–7.

2024 Ibid., 73.19–74.2.

2025 A polemic in which one accuses an opponent of neglecting the first *pāramitās* and thus the gradual character of the path.

2026 BCA, 199.9–10: *kleśajñeyāvṛtitamaḥpratipakṣo hi śūnyatā / śīghraṁ sarvajñatākāmo na bhāvayati tāṁ katham //.*

2027 Gzhon nu dpal's reading of this stanza *(/ de ltar rnal 'byor pa rnams kyis / / stong pa nyid ni bsgoms byas na / / blo ni gzhan don la dga' bar / / 'gyur ba 'di la the tshom med /)* differs from Lindtner's edition (1987:206.7–8): */ de ltar stong pa nyid 'di ni / / rnal 'byor pa yis bsgom byas na / gzhan gyi don la chags pa'i blo / / 'byung bar 'gyur ba the tshom med /.*

2028 BCA, 160.15: *mayānyaduḥkhaṁ hantavyaṁ duḥkhatvād ātmaduḥkhavat /.*

2029 See DRSM, 222.12–14.

2030 Zhva dmar Chos grags ye shes: *Byang chub sems 'grel gyi rnam par bshad pa tshig don gsal ba,* 96.19–97.1: *de ltar 'phags pa klu grub kyis bsngags pa'i bsgom 'di / bod snga phyi kha cig rgya nag hva shang gi sgom yin par sgrog kyang / bstan bcos 'dir byang chub sems chen po rnams kyi lugs su mdzad do /.*

2031 Here it is important to remember that for Gzhon nu dpal qualities exist only in a subtle form in sentient being. Otherwise one would attain the complete enlightenment of a buddha in one instant.

2032 RGVV, 30.4–8: *śubhātmasukhanityatvaguṇapāramitāphalaḥ*[a] */ duḥkhanirviccha-maprāpticchandapraṇidhikarmakaḥ // tatra pūrveṇa ślokārdhena kiṁ darśitam / phalam eṣāṁ samāsena dharmakāye viparyayāt / caturvidhaviparyāsapratipakṣa-prabhāvitam //.*

a Johnston reads *-phalam;* B (17b1) *phala;* A is not available.

2033 RGVV, 69.3–4: *pratikūlaṁ yathāmedhyam evaṁ kāmāvirāgiṇām / kāmasevānimit-tatvāt paryutthānāny amedhyavat //.* The additions to my translation are in accordance with Gzhon nu dpal's commentary on p. 418.6–10. The stanza describes the defilements in the fourth example from the *Tathāgatagarbhasūtra* (that is, a piece of gold fallen in mud).

2034 This occurs in some mahāmudrā explanations on the *Ratnagotravibhāga* Gzhon nu dpal used, such as the "notes" *(zur)* of Chos rje 'Bri gung pa (see DRSM, 574.9–10).

2035 Dol po pa criticizes this view as being at odds with the *Ratnagotravibhāga;* the two truths are rather "different in that their identity is negated" *(ngo bo gcig pa bkag pa'i tha dad).* See Stearns 1999:162 and Mathes 2002:91.

2036 See DRSM, 51.16–17 and 122.8–9.

2037 Seyfort Ruegg 1989:8 and Schaeffer 1995.

2038 See DRSM, 340.18–25.

2039 RGVV, 21.3–4: *samalā tathatātha nirmalā vimalā buddhaguṇā jinakriyā / viṣayaḥ paramārthadarśināṁ śubharatnatrayasambhavo*[a] *yataḥ //.*

a According to B (12a6), A is not available. Johnston reads *-sargako* instead of *-sambhavo* without giving any reason.

2040 RGVV, 21.6–7: *gotraṁ ratnatrayasyāsya viṣayaḥ sarvadarśinām / caturvidhaḥ sa cācintyaś caturbhiḥ kāraṇaiḥ kramāt //.*

2041 RGVV, 21.15–16: *śuddhyupakliṣṭatāyogāt niḥsaṁkleśaviśuddhitaḥ / avinirbhāgadharmatvād anābhogāvikalpataḥ //.*

2042 RGVV, 21.17–18: *tatra samalā tathatā yugapad ekakālaṁ viśuddhā ca saṁkliṣṭā cety acintyam etat sthānaṁ gambhīradharmanayādhimuktānām api pratyekabuddhānām agocaraviṣayatvāt /.*

2043 RGVV, 22.5: *tatra nirmalā tathatā pūrvaṁ*[a] *malāsaṁkliṣṭā paścād viśuddhety acintyam etat sthānam /.*

a Johnston and B (13a1) read *-pūrva-;* A is not available. The conjecture is according to Schmithausen 1971:140–41.

2044 RGVV, 22.8–10: *tatra vimalā buddhaguṇāḥ paurvāparyeṇaikāntasaṁkliṣṭāyām api pṛthagjanabhūmāvavinirbhāgadharmatayā nirviśiṣṭā vidyanta ity acintyam etat sthānam /.*

2045 RGVV, 24.9–10: *tatra jinakriyā yugapat sarvatra sarvakālam anābhogenāvikalpato yathāśayeṣu yathāvaineyikeṣu*[a] *sattveṣv akṣūnam*[b] *anuguṇaṁ pravartata ity acintyam etat sthānam /.*

a A (7a3) reads *yathāvainaiyikeṣu;* B (14a6) *yathāvainai(*or *-ne-)keṣu.* The conjecture is according to Takasaki 1966:192 and Schmithausen 1971:141.

b B (14a6) reads *akṣūṇṇam* or *akṣūṇatvam.*

2046 Cf. Gzhon nu dpal's commentary on the first inconceivable point: "Likewise, the mind too is turned into defilements by the fire of [mental] imprints. When the imprints are reversed, there are no [more] defilements. Thus, even though the mind is thereby known to be associated with defilements, it is not the case that at the time of defilement both the pure mind and the defiled one mix as two separate substances; rather, they are simply not differentiated by the mind." (DRSM, 218.10–12.)

2047 See for example Lama Zhang's *Phyag rgya chen po lam zab mthar thug zhang gi man ngag,* quoted by DRSM, 48.24–25.

2048 See DRSM, 430.25–26.

2049 See DRSM, 241.12–14.

2050 Cf. the discussion of the four perfections of qualities in the preceding section.

2051 'Ba' ra ba: "Chos rje rnam gnyis kyi dgongs bshad nyi ma'i 'od zer," 523.3–4.

2052 See DRSM, 443.18–20.

2053 DRSM, 509.7–12.

2054 Zhva dmar Chos grags ye shes: *Gzhon nu dpal gyi rnam thar,* 10b1–2.

2055 Mi bskyod rdo rje: "Rje Yid bzang rtse ba'i Rgyud gsum gsang ba...," 1007.6–1008.2.

2056 Ibid., 1003.3–5.

2057 DRSM, 239.15–17.

2058 Seyfort Ruegg 1969:294–96.

2059 Zhva dmar Chos grags ye shes: *Gzhon nu dpal gyi rnam thar*, 30b5–31a5.

2060 Dreyfus (2003:27) observes that in the second half of the fifteenth century the sectarian rift between the Dga' ldan pas (i.e., Dge lugs pas) and other schools gained particular force after Mkhas grub rje, who was preoccupied with a pure interpretation of Tsong kha pa, became the leader of the Dga' ldan pas.

2061 Klong chen pa: *Grub mtha' mdzod*, 170.5–6.

2062 DRSM, 238.5–8.

2063 Ibid., 239.12–14.

2064 Ibid., 362.18–20.

2065 In support Gzhon nu dpal (DRSM, 80.1–8) adduces RGV I.24ab: "The potential of [these] Three Jewels is an experiential object of those who see everything" (RGVV, 21.6: *gotraṁ ratnatrayasyāsya viṣayaḥ sarvadarśinām /*).

2066 For a translation of this passage see above, Introduction, p 17.

2067 See Schmithausen 1973:131.

2068 Mi bskyod rdo rje: "Rje yid bzang rtse ba'i Rgyud gsum gsang ba...," 976.3–6.

2069 Rngog Blo ldan shes rab: *Theg chen rgyud bla'i don bsdus pa*, 41a6–b1.

2070 It is not clear, though, if Rngog Blo ldan shes rab's above-mentioned explanation of wisdom excludes the possibility that the emptiness of one's mind includes some aspect of clarity that is not the enlightened mind of a buddha.

2071 In reaction with a base, the ochre of turmeric powder turns red.

2072 DRSM, 339.26–340.5.

2073 Zhva dmar Chos grags ye shes: *Gzhon nu dpal gyi rnam thar*, 54a3–4 (see chapter 3).

2074 Stearns 1999:44.

2075 Mi bskyod rdo rje: "Rje Yid bzang rtse ba'i Rgyud gsum gsang ba...," 1003.3–5: *khyod kyi sems can thams cad la sangs rgyas kyi snying po gnas pa'i tshe / sangs rgyas de gnas pa min / sangs rgyas de'i rigs dang 'dra ba zhig gnas pa yin / 'dra ba de la skye mched drug gi khyad par ba yin pas 'di lta bu zhig sems can la yod pa yin zer nas / dpal karmapa rang byung rdo rje gi lung drangs mod / 'di mi 'thad pa la /....*

2076 Ibid., 984.2–3: *'on kyang sangs rgyas kyi snying po la rigs su btags pa'i don ni / dhātu (text: dhatu)'i skad las drangs pas shes bya ches mang ba la 'jug rung bas / 'dir rigs su bsgyur ba ste / don ni / chos kyi dbyings la 'chad dgos pa yin te / chos kyi dbyings kyi ye shes de ni /....*

2077 Ibid., 984.5–6; see above, chapter 2.

2078 Ibid., 978.1–3: *khyed kyis sems can la bde gshegs snying po yod tshul sems can shun pa med la / ... 'o na ri bong gi rva'i snying por bum pa 'jog rigs te /.*

2079 'Ba' ra ba: "Chos rje rnam gnyis kyi dgongs bshad nyi ma'i 'od zer," 509.2–3.

2080 'Ba' ra ba: "Kun gzhi'i rnam shes dang ye shes kyi rnam bzhag," 620.1–4.

2081 Mi bskyod rdo rje: "Rje Yid bzang rtse ba'i Rgyud gsum gsang ba...," 999.2–1000.1: *sangs rgyas kyi snying po chos can / sems can yin te / des sdug bsngal myong ba'i phyir zhes bkod na ma grub cing...sangs rgyas kyi snying po bde ba dam par bshad pa ma gtogs / sdug bsngal tha shal du grub na / spyir sdug bsngal dang bde ba myong ba'i bdag khas len bzhin du / chos thams cad bdag med do ces smra ba zu zhig gis dbang med du bslabs /...bcom ldan 'das kyis sems tsam pa dag rjes su bzung ba'i phyir / kun gzhi rnam shes la snying po'i sgras bstan pa zhig yod pa la dgongs pa yin gyi / de ltar gyi tshe sdug bsngal myong ba'i kun gzhi'i rnam shes ni / / rnam smin gyi cha dgongs pa yin gyi / sa bon sogs kyi cha la dgongs pa min pas / khyod kyi log bshad la ni kho bo cag mgo bo 'khor ba'i skabs mi srid do /.*

2082 DRSM, 178.2–3.

2083 Rngog Blo ldan shes rab: *Theg chen rgyud bla'i don bsdus pa,* 42a4–6.

2084 See DRSM, 44.5–13.

2085 See Zhva dmar Chos grags ye shes: *Gzhon nu dpal gyi rnam thar,* 54a5–6 (see chapter 3).

2086 DRSM, 471.24–472.2.

2087 Ibid., 470.15–16.

2088 Ibid., 456.13–18.

2089 Ibid., 470.12–15.

2090 Lamotte 1938: vol. 1, 19–20.

2091 See above, chapter 3.

2092 Khetsun Sangpo 1973:569.13f.

2093 Klong chen pa: *Grub mtha' mdzod,* 170.5–6.

2094 Ibid., 327.2. Tib. *lhun grub* (Skt. *anābhoga,* "without effort") is translated as "spontaneously present" in a rdzogs chen context.

2095 DRSM, 509.7–9.

2096 Ibid., 83.11–16.

2097 Ibid., 509.9–12.

2098 Ibid., 16.2–12.

2099 I.e., as propounded by Rang byung rdo rje (if one chooses to follow Kong sgrul and see in him a proponent of gzhan stong).

2100 Zhva dmar Chos grags ye shes: *Gzhon nu dpal gyi rnam thar,* 54a5–6 (see chapter 3).

2101 Seyfort Ruegg (1989:119–20) notes that also Mo ho yen often used the *Laṅkāvatārasūtra* in support of Ch'an.

Table of Tibetan Transliteration

Akhu Ching Sherab Gyatso	A khu ching Shes rab rgya mtsho
Barawa Gyaltsen Palzang	'Ba' ra ba Rgyal mtshan dpal bzang
Belo	'Be lo
Bernagchen	Ber nag can
Chapa Chökyi Sengé	Phya pa Chos kyi Seng ge
Chegom Sherab Dorjé	Lce sgom Shes rab rdo rje
Chennga Jungné	Spyan snga Shes rab 'byung gnas
Chennga Ngagi Wangpo	Spyan snga Ngagi dbang po
Chenpo Saṅghaśrī	Chen po Saṅghaśrī
Chenyé	Spyan g.yas
Chimpu	Mchims phu
Chöding	Chos sdings
Choglé Namgyal	Phyogs las rnam rgyal
Chöjé Drigungpa Jigten Sumgön	Chos rje 'Bri gung pa 'Jig rten gsum mgon
Chöjé Rinpoché	Chos rje Rin po che
Chomden Rigpai Raldri	Bcom ldan Rig pa'i ral gri
Chongyé	'Phyong rgyas
Dagpo Rinpoché	Dvags po Rin po che
Dagpo Tashi Namgyal	Dvags po Bkra shis rnam rgyal
Dampa Sangyé	Dam pa sangs rgyas
Denbagpa Mawai Sengé	Dan bag pa Smra ba'i seng ge
Densapa Sangyé Gyaltsen	Gdan sa pa Sangs rgyas rgyal mtshan

Densatel Chöjé Nyernyi Rinpoché Sönam Gyaltsen Palzang	Gdan sa thel Chos rje Nyer gnyis rin po che Bsod nams rgyal mtshan dpal bzang
Dezhin Shegpa	De bzhin gshegs pa
Dingri	Ding ri
Dölpopa Sherab Gyaltsen	Dol po pa Shes rab rgyal mtshan
Dorjé Pagmo	rdo rje phag mo
Dragpa Gyaltsen	Grags pa rgyal mtshan
Dragpa Jungné	Grags pa 'byung gnas
Dragpa Sengé	Grags pa seng ge
Drapa Ngönshé	Grva pa Mngon shes
Dratsepa Rinchen Namgyal	Sgra tshad pa Rin chen rnam rgyal
Dreuzhing	Spre'u zhing
Drigungpa Jigten Sumgön	'Bri gung pa 'Jig rten gsum mgon
Drölmawa Sangyé Rinchen Palzang	Sgrol ma ba Sangs rgyas rin chen dpal bzang po
Drolungpa	Gro lung pa
Druda	'Bru mda'
Drudar	'Bru mdar
Drugpa	'Brug pa
Drung Sönam Gyaltsen	Drung Bsod nams rgyal mtshan
Dükhorwa Dorjé Nyingpo	Dus 'khor ba Rdo rje snying po
dzogchen	rdzogs chen
Gampo	Sgam po
Gampopa	Sgam po pa
Ganden	Dga' ldan
Gedenpa	Dge ldan pa
Gelugpa	Dge lugs pa
Geshé Sherab Gyatso	Dge bshes Shes rab rgya mtsho
Gö Lotsāwa Zhönu Pal	'Gos Lo tsā ba Gzhon nu dpal

Gönpo Pal	Mgon po dpal
Götrugpa	Rgod phrug pa
Götsangpa	Rgod tshang pa
Gungnang Chöjé Dzepa Pal	Gung snang Chos rje Mdzes pa dpal
Gyadur	Rgya dur
Gyaltsab Jé	Rgyal tshab rje
Gyalwai Trinlé Lhündrub Namrin	Rgyal ba'i phrin las lhun grub nam rin
Gyalzang	Rgyal bzangs
Gyamen Yangpo	Rgya sman yang po
Jamyang Shākzhön	'Jam dbyangs Shāk gzhon
Jangpo Drang	Ljang pho brang
Jé Drigungpa	Rje 'Bri gung pa
Jigten [Sum]gön	'Jig rten [gsum] mgon
Jigten Gönpo	'Jig rten mgon po
Jomonang	Jo mo nang
Jonang Künga Drölchog	Jo nang Kun dga' grol mchog
Jonangpa	Jo nang pa
Jowo	Jo bo
Ju Lhakhang Teng	'Ju Lha khang stengs
Kadampa	Bka' gdams pa
Kagyüpa	Bka' brgyud pa
kama	bka' ma
Kamtsang	Kaṁ tshang
Kangyur	Bka' 'gyur
Karma Könzhön	Karma Dkon gzhon
Karma Trinlepa	Karma Phrin las pa
Khachö Wangpo	Mkha' spyod dbang po
Kham	Khams
Khenchen Rinpoché Sangyé Tenpa	Mkhan chen Rin po che Sangs rgyas bstan pa

Khenchen Sanglowa	Mkhan chen Sangs blo ba
Khenchen Sangyé Tenpa	Mkhan chen Sangs rgyas brtan pa
Khenchen Sengé Pal	Mkhan chen Seng ge dpal
Khenchen Tamché Khyenpa Butön Rinpoché	Mkhan chen thams cad mkhyen pa Bu ston Rin po che
Khenchen Tashi Jangwa	Mkhan chen Bkra shis byang ba
Khenpo	Mkhan po
Kodragpa Sönam Gyaltsen	Ko brag pa Bsod nams rgyal mtshan
Kongpo	Kong po
Kongtrül	Kong sprul
Kongtrül Lodrö Tayé	Kong sprul Blo gros mtha' yas
Künga Drölchog	Kun dga' grol mchog
Künga Gyaltsen	Kun dga' rgyal mtshan
Künga Legpa	Kun dga' legs pa
Künkhyen Shangpa	Kun mkhyen Shangs pa
Künkhyen Sherab Gyaltsen	Kun mkhyen Shes rab rgyal mtshan
Künpang Chödrag Palzang	Kun spangs Chos grags dpal bzang
künzhi	kun gzhi
künzhi nampar shepa	kun gzhi rnam par shes pa
künzhi yeshé	kun gzhi ye shes
Kurab	Sku rab
Kyangchenpa Śākya Śrī	Rkyang chen pa Śākya Śrī
Kyishö	Skyid shod
Kyormolung	Skyor mo lung
Lama Dampa Sönam Gyaltsen	Bla ma Dam pa Bsod nams rgyal mtshan
Lama Dawa Gyaltsen	Bla ma Zla ba rgyal mtshan
Lechen	Las chen
Lhai Gyaltsen	Lha'i rgyal mtshan

Lhakhang Tengpa Sangyé Rinchen	Lha khang steng pa Sangs rgyas rin chen
Lhazig Lang	Lha gzigs rlangs
Lobpön Sherab	Slob dpon Shes rab
Lobpön Yabpa Chöjé	Slob dpon Yab pa Chos rje
Lochen Sönam Gyatso Gyaltsen Özer	Lo chen Bsod nams rgya mtsho rgyal mtshan 'od zer
Loden Sherab	Blo ldan shes rab
Lodrö Tsungmé	Blo gros mtshungs med
Longchen Rabjampa	Klong chen rab 'byams pa
Longchenpa	Klong chen pa
Lötang Nyagpo	Blos btang nyag po
Lotsāwa Zu Gawa Dorjé	Lo tsā ba Gzu Dga' ba rdo rje
Martön Gyaltsen Özer	Dmar ston Rgyal mtshan 'od zer
Martön Zhöngyalwa	Dmar ston Gzhon rgyal ba
Mikyö Dorjé	Mi bskyod rdo rje
Minyag Sherab Zangpo	Mi nyag Shes rab bzang po
Möndang	Smon ldang
Mönlam Dragpa	Smon lam grags pa
Nagtso	Nag tsho
Namkha Lodrö	Nam mkha' blo gros
Namkha Paljor	Nam mkha' dpal 'byor
Nartang	Snar thang
Nedrug	Gnas drug
Neudong	Sne'u gdong
Ngagi Wangchug Dragpa	Ngagi dbang phyug grags pa
Ngagi Wangpo	Ngagi dbang po
Ngog Jangchub Pal	Rngog Byang chub dpal
Ngog Loden Sherab	Rngog Blo ldan shes rab
Norzang	Nor bzang
Nub Sangyé Yeshé	Gnubs Sangs rgyas ye shes

Nyangdren	Nyang bran
Nyal	Gnyal
Nyemo	Snye mo
Nyingma	Rnying ma
Nyö Gyalwa Lhanangpa	Gnyos Rgyal ba Lha nang pa
Ön	'On
Orgyen Nyendrub	O rgyan bsnyen grub
Orgyenpa Sengé Pal	O rgyan pa Seng ge dpal
Pagdru	Phag gru
Pagmo Drupa	Phag mo gru pa
Palden Zangpo Ngödrub	Dpal ldan bzang po dngos grub
Paljor Zangpo	Dpal 'byor bzang po
Paltseg	Dpal brtsegs
Penyül	'Phan yul
Rabtenling	Rab brtan gling
Rangjung Dorjé	Rang byung rdo rje
Rendawa	Red mda' ba
Rigdzin Chökyi Dragpa	Rig 'dzin Chos kyi grags pa
Rimi Babpa Sönam Rinchen	Ri mi 'babs pa Bsod nams rin chen
Rinchen	Rin chen
Riwo Gepel	Ri bo dge 'phel
Rongtön Sheja Künrig	Rong ston Shes bya kun rig
Rongzom Chökyi Zangpo	Rong zom Chos kyi bzang po
Rutsam	Ru mtshams
Sabzang Mati Panchen Jamyang Lodrö Gyaltsen	Sa bzang Mati paṇ chen 'Jam dbyangs Blo gros rgyal mtshan
Sakya	Sa skya
Śākya Chogden	Śākya mchog ldan
Sakya Khön	Sa skya 'khon
Sakya Paṇḍita	Sa skya Paṇḍita
Śākya Zangpo	Śākya bzang po

Sakyapa	Sa skya pa
Samdrub Dragpa	Bsam 'grub grags pa
Samdrub Zangpo	Bsam grub bzang po
Samten Döndrub	Bsam gtan don grub
Samyé	Bsam yas
Sangpu	Gsang phu
Sangpupa Lodrö Tsungmé	Gsang phu pa Blo gros mtshungs med
Sangyé Dragpa	Sangs rgyas grags pa
Sangyé Rinchen	Sangs rgyas rin chen
Sarma	gsar ma
Sé	Sras
Sempa Chenpo	Sems dpa' chen po
Serdog Panchen	Gser mdog Paṇ chen
Shangpa Künkhyen Sherab Palzang	Shangs pa Kun mkhyen Shes rab dpal bzang
Sharawapa	Sha ra ba pa
Shelri Trülku	Shel ri sprul skus
Sherab Darwa	Shes rab dar ba
Situ	Si tu
Sönam Zangpo	Bsod nams bzang po
Śrī Tarkyi	Sri thar skyid
Sumpa Lotsāwa	Sum pa Lo tsā ba
Tai Situ Jangchub Gyaltsen	Ta'i Situ Byang chub rgyal mtshan
Tanag	Rta nag
Tangpoché	Thang po che
Tangsag	Thang sag
Tengyur	Bstan 'gyur
Tenpa Bum	Brtan pa 'bum
terma	gter ma
Tingnamo Dzong	Rting sna mo rdzong

Tölung	Stod lung
Tön Śākpa	Ston Śāk pa
Tönpa Jungné Dorjé	Ston pa 'Byung gnas rdo rje
Tönpa Rinchen Palzang	Ston pa Rin chen dpal bzang
Tönpa Wangö	Ston pa dbang 'od
tsatsa	tsha tsha
Tsalmin	Mtshal min
Tsalminpa Sönam Zangpo	Mtshal min pa Bsod nams bzang po
Tsang	Gtsang
Tsangnagpa	Gtsang nag pa
Tsen	Btsan
Tsen Kawoché	Btsan Kha bo che
Tsentang	Btsan thang
Tsering Chenga	Tshe rings mched lnga
Tsetang Khenpo Samten Zangpo	Rtses thang mkhan po Bsam btan bzang po
Tsetang Khenpo Samzangpa	Rtses thang mkhan po Bsam bzang pa
Tsöndrü Sengé	Brtson 'grus seng ge
Tsongkhapa	Tsong kha pa
Tsültrim Gyaltsen	Tshul khrims rgyal mtshan
Tsurpu	Tshur phu
Tuken Lozang Chökyi Nyima	Thu'u bkvan Blo bzang chos kyi nyi ma
Ü	Dbus
vajra	vajra
Wangchug Dorjé	Dbang phyug rdo rje
Yagdé Panchen	G.yag sde paṇ chen
Yangpachen	Yangs pa can
Yarlung	Yar klung
Yeshé Dé	Ye shes sde
Yeshé Dorjé	Ye shes rdo rje

Yizangtsé	Yid bzang rtse
Yöl Rinchen Ling	Yol Rin chen gling
Yön	Yon
Yumowa Mikyö Dorjé	Yu mo ba Mi bskyod ro rje
Zhamarpa	Zhva dmar pa
Zhamar Chödrag Yeshé	Zhva dmar Chos grags ye shes
Zhamarpa Chöpal Yeshé	Zhva dmar pa Chos dpal ye shes
Zhamarpa Khachöd Wangpo	Zhva dmar pa Mkha' spyod dbang po
Zhang Tsalpa Tsöndrü Drag	Zhang Tshal pa Brtson 'grus grags
zhendröl	gzhan grol
zhentong	gzhan stong
Zilung Panchen	Zi lung Paṇ chen
Zuga Do	Gzu Dga' [ba] rdo [rje]

Bibliography

Indian Works

AN: *Aṅguttaranikāya* (part I)
Ed. by Richard Morris. London: Pali Text Society, 1885.

Anūnatvāpūrṇatvanirdeśa
As quoted in the RGVV

AS: *Abhidharmasamuccaya*
Ed. by Pralhad Pradhan. Santiniketan: Visva-Bharati Publishing Press, 1950.

ASBh: *Abhidharmasamuccayabhāṣya*
Ed. by Nathmal Tatia. Patna: K.P. Jayaswal Research Institute, 1976.

AA: *Abhisamayālaṁkāra*
Ed. by Ramshankar Tripathi (together with the *Abhisamayālaṁkāravṛttiḥ Sphuṭārthā*) (Bibliotheca Indo-Tibetica Series 2). Sarnath: Central Institute of Higher Tibetan Studies, 1993.

AAŚV: *Abhisamayālaṁkārakārikāśāstravivṛti*
Ed. by Koei H. Amano. Kyoto: Heirakuji-Shoten, 2000.

AAV Sphuṭārthā: *Abhisamayālaṁkāravṛttiḥ Sphuṭārthā*
See AA

AAA: *Abhisamayālaṁkārāloka*
Ed. by Unrai Wogihara, part I. Tokyo: The Toyo Bunko, 1932–35.

Avataṁsakasūtra (Tibetan translation)
Peking Kangyur no. 761

Kālacakratantra
See VPṬ

KDN: *Kudṛṣṭinirghātana*
Ed. by the "Studying Group of Sacred Tantric Texts" (Mikkyō-seiten kenkyūkai): "The Results of a Joint Study on the Buddhist Tantric Texts: Advayavajrasaṁgraha—New Critical Edition with Japanese Translation." *Annual of the Institute for Comprehensive Studies of Buddhism Taisho University* 10 (March 1988), 225–198 (=10–37).

GST: *Guhyasamājatantra*
Ed. by Benoytosh Bhattacharya (Gaekwad's Oriental Series 53). Baroda: University of Baroda Press, 1967.

Ghanavyūhasūtra (Tibetan translation)
Peking Kangyur no. 778

CŚ: *Catuḥśataka*
Ed. by P.L. Vaidya. Paris: Librairie Orientaliste Paul Guenther, 1923.

CS: *Cūḷasuññatasutta*
Ed. by R. Chalmers. *Majjhimanikāya*, vol. 3 (Text Series 62), 104–9. London: Pali Text Society, 1899.

JNĀ: *Jñānaśrīmitranibandhāvali*
Ed. by Anantalal Thakur (Tibetan Sanskrit Series 5). Patna: Kashi Prasad Jayaswal Research Institute, 1987.

Ḍākinīvajrapañjarātantra (Tibetan translation)
Peking Kangyur no. 11

TD: *Tattvadaśaka*
—In: *Advayavajrasaṁgraha.* Ed. by Haraprasad Shastri (Gaekwad's Oriental Series 40), 59. Baroda: Oriental Institute, 1927.
—Ed. by the "Studying Group of Sacred Tantric Texts" (Mikkyō-seiten kenkyūkai): "The Results of a Joint Study on the Buddhist Tantric Texts: Advayavajrasaṁgraha—New Critical Edition with Japanese Translation." *Annual of the Institute for Comprehensive Studies of Buddhism Taisho University* 13 (March 1991), (92)–(94) (=pp. 245–43).
—See also NGMPP reel no. B 22/24

TDṬ: *Tattvadaśakaṭīkā* (Tibetan translation)
—Peking Tengyur no. 3099
—See also *Phyag rgya chen po'i rgya gzhung*, vol. *ā*, fols. 1a1–27a6. Ed. by Phun tshogs rgyal mtshan (end of 19th century). Dpal dpungs block print. No date.

TRĀ: *Tattvaratnāvalī*
—In: *Advayavajrasaṁgraha.* Ed. by Haraprasad Shastri (Gaekwad's Oriental Series 40), 14–22. Baroda: Oriental Institute, 1927.
—See also NGMPP reel no. B 22/24

TA: *Tattvāvatāra* (Tibetan translation)
Peking Tengyur no. 4532

Tathāgatagarbhasūtra
—As quoted in the RGVV
—See also Zimmermann 2002

Tathāgataguṇajñānācintyaviṣayāvatāranirdeśa (Tibetan translation)
Peking Kangyur no. 852

TŚK: *Triṁśikākārikā*
See VMS

DBhS: *Daśabhūmikasūtra*
— Reproduced in facsimile by K. Matsuda. Tokyo: The Toyo Bunko, 1996.

— Ed. by Johannes Rahder. Leuven: J.-B. Istas, 1926.
— Ed. by Ryūkō Kondō. Tokyo: The Daijyō Bukkyō Kenyō-Kai, 1936.

Dṛḍhādhyāśayaparivarta
As quoted in the RGVV

Devātiśāyastotra (Tibetan translation)
Peking Tengyur no. 2004

Devātiśāyastotraṭīkā (Tibetan translation)
Peking Tengyur no. 2005

DKG: *Dohākośagīti*
See Saraha and Shahidullah

DhDhVK: *Dharmadharmatāvibhāgakārikā* (Tibetan translation)
Ed. by Klaus-Dieter Mathes. See Mathes 1996:104–14.

DhDhVV: *Dharmadharmatāvibhāgavṛtti* (Tibetan translation)
Ed. by Klaus-Dieter Mathes. See Mathes 1996:69–98.

DhS: *Dharmadhātustotra* (Tibetan translation)
Peking Tengyur no. 2010

Dharmasaṁgītisūtra (Tibetan translation)
Peking Kangyur no. 904

DhĪRS: *Dhāraṇīśvararājasūtra* (Tibetan translation)
Peking Kangyur no. 814 (listed under **Āryatathāgatamahākaruṇānirdeśanāma-mahāyānasūtra,* the title given in the beginning of the Tibetan translation).

PK: *Pañcakrama*
Ed. by Katsumi Mimaki and Tōru Tomabechi (Bibliotheca Codicum Asiaticorum 8). Tokyo: The Centre for East Asian Cultural Studies for Unesco, 1994.

PĀ: *Pañcākāra*
—Ed. by the "Studying Group of Sacred Tantric Texts" (Mikkyō-seiten kenkyūkai): "The Results of a Joint Study on the Buddhist Tantric Texts: Advayavajrasaṁgraha—New Critical Edition with Japanese Translation." *Annual of the Institute for Comprehensive Studies of Buddhism Taisho University* 10 (March 1988), (122)–(134) (=pp. 223–211).
—In: *Advayavajrasaṁgraha.* Ed. by Haraprasad Shastri (Gaekwad's Oriental Series 40), 40–43. Baroda: Oriental Institute, 1927.
—See also NGMPP reel no. B 22/24

PRGSG: *Prajñāpāramitāratnaguṇasaṁcayagāthā*
Ed. by A. Yuyama. London: Cambridge University Press, 1976.

Prajñāpradīpa (Tibetan translation)
Peking Tengyur no. 5253

PV: *Pramāṇavārttika*
—Ed. by Yūsho Miyasaka (Sanskrit and Tibetan), in *Acta Indologica* 2 (1972), 2–206.

—(First chapter:) Ed. by Raniero Gnoli (together with the *Svavṛtti*). Rome: Istituto Italiano per il Medio ed Estremo Oriente: 1960.

PVSV: *Pramāṇavārttikasvavṛtti* (on the first chapter)
See Gnoli's edition of the first chapter of the PV

PP: *Prasannapadā*
Ed. by Louis de la Vallée Poussin (Bibliotheca Buddhica 4). Reprint (first published in 1903–13). Delhi: Motilal Banarsidass, 1992.

BCA: *Bodhicaryāvatāra*
Ed. by Vidhushekhara Bhattacharya (Bibliotheca Indica 280). Kalkota: Asiatic Society Calcutta, 1960.

BV: *Bodhicittavivaraṇa* (Tibetan translation)
Ed. by Christian Lindtner. See Lindtner 1987:184–216.

BPP: *Bodhipathapradīpa*
—Ed. by Losang Norbu Shastri (Bibliotheca Indo-Tibetica 7). Sarnath: Central Institute of Higher Tibetan Studies, 1984.
—See Eimer 1978

BBh: *Bodhisattvabhūmi*
Ed. by Unrai Wogihara. Tokyo: 1930–36.

BYCŚṬ: *Bodhisattvayogācāracatuḥśatakaṭīkā*
—Ed. by Kōshin Suzuki in *Sanskrit Fragments and Tibetan Translation of Candrakīrti's* Bodhisattvayogācāracatuḥśatakaṭīkā. Tokyo: Sankibo Press, 1994.
—See also Peking Tengyur no. 5266

Mañjuśrīvikrīḍitasūtra (Tibetan translation)
Peking Kangyur no. 764

MŚ: *Madhyamakaśāstra*
Ed. by Raghunath Pandeya. 2 vols. Delhi: Motilal Banarsidass, 1988–89.

MH: *Madhyamakahṛdaya*
Edited by Christian Lindtner (The Adyar Library Series 123). Chennai: The Adyar Library and Research Centre, 2001.

Madhyamakahṛdayavṛtti Tarkajvālā (Tibetan translation)
Peking Tengyur no. 5256

MAL: *Madhyamakālaṁkāra*
Edited by Masamichi Ichigō. Kyoto: Kyoto Sangyo University, 1985.

MA: *Madhyamakāvatāra* (Tibetan translation)
Ed. by Louis de la Vallée Poussin (Bibliotheca Buddhica 9). Reprint (first published in 1907–12). Delhi: Motilal Banarsidass, 1992.

MAṬ: *Madhyamakāvatāraṭīkā* (Tibetan translation)
Peking Tengyur no. 5271

Madhyamakopadeśa (Tibetan translation)
Peking Tengyur no. 5324

MAV: *Madhyāntavibhāga*
Ed. by Gadjin M. Nagao. Tokyo: Suzuki Research Foundation, 1964.

MAVṬ: *Madhyāntavibhāgaṭīkā*
—Ed. by S. Yamaguchi. Nagoya: Librairie Hajinkaku, 1934.
—See also NGMPP reel no. A 38/10

MAVBh: *Madhyāntavibhāgabhāṣya*
See MAV

Mahāparinirvāṇasūtra (Tibetan translation)
As quoted in Mati paṇ chen: "Nges don rab gsal"

MV: *Mahāyānaviṁśikā*
Ed. by the "Studying Group of Sacred Tantric Texts" (Mikkyō-seiten kenkyūkai): "The Results of a Joint Study on the Buddhist Tantric Texts: Advayavajrasaṁgraha—New Critical Edition with Japanese Translation." *Annual of the Institute for Comprehensive Studies of Buddhism Taisho University* 12 (March 1990), (74)–(79) (=pp. 291–86).

MS: *Mahāyānasaṁgraha*
Ed. by Étienne Lamotte. Vol. 1: the Tibetan and Chinese versions. Louvain (Belgium): Bureaux du Muséon, 1938.

MSA: *Mahāyānasūtrālaṁkāra*
—Ed. by S. Bagchi (Buddhist Sanskrit Texts 13). Darbhanga: The Mithila Institute, 1970.
—Ed. by Sylvain Lévi (Bibliothèque de l'École des Hautes Études, Sciences historiques et philologiques 159). Paris: Librairie Honoré Champion, 1907.

MSABh : *Mahāyānasūtrālaṁkārabhāṣya*
See MSA

Mahāyānābhidharmasūtra
As quoted in the RGVV

MUTŚṬ: *Mahāyānottaraśāstraṭippaṇī*
Ed. by Zuiryū Nakamura in: *Various Problems in Buddhist Thought: A Collection of Articles in Honor of Professor Akira Hirakawa's Seventieth Birthday.* Tokyo: Shunjūsha, 1985, (1)–(16) (=pp. 246–31).

MMK: *Mūlamadhyamakakārikā*
Ed. by J.W. de Jong (The Adyar Library Series 109). Madras: The Adyar Library and Research Centre, 1977.

RGV: *Ratnagotravibhāga Mahāyānottaratantraśāstra*
Ed. by Edward H. Johnston. Patna: The Bihar Research Society, 1950. (Includes the *Ratnagotravibhāgavyākhyā.*)

RGVV: *Ratnagotravibhāgavyākhyā*

—See RGV
[The manuscripts A and B on which Johnston's edition is based are described in Johnston 1950:vi–vii. See also Bandurski et al. 1994:12–13.] For an edition of the Tibetan translations of the Tengyur see Nakamura, Zuiho 1967
—*Theg pa chen po rgyud bla ma'i bstan bcos [rnam par bshad pa]:* (unpublished manuscript from Nawal (Manang), with glosses)

RĀ: *Ratnāvalī*
Ed. by Michael Hahn (Indica et Tibetica 1). Vol. 1: the basic texts (Sanskrit, Tibetan, Chinese). Bonn: Indica et Tibetica Verlag, 1982.

Laṅkāvatāravṛtti (Tibetan translation)
Peking Tengyur no. 5519

LAS: *Laṅkāvatārasūtra*
—Ed. by Bunyiu Nanjio (Bibliotheca Otaniensis 1). Kyoto: Otani University Press, 1923.
—See also NGMPP reel nos. A 112/9, A 112/10, C 13/7, D 52/5, D 58/6, D 73/8, E 625/14, E 1200/8, E 1725/5, and H 45/6.
—See also Peking Kangyur nos. 775 and 776

Vacanamukhāyudhopama (Tibetan translation)
Peking Tengyur no. 5784

Vajraśikharamahāguhyatantra (Tibetan translation)
Peking Kangyur no. 113

VMS: *Vijñaptimātratāsiddhi*
Ed. by Sylvain Lévi (Bibliothèque de l'École des Hautes Études, Sciences historiques et philologiques 245). Vol. 1 : The text. Paris: 1925.

VŚ: *Viṁśatikā*
See VMS

VPṬ: *Vimalaprabhāṭīkā*
Ed. by Jagannatha Upadhyaya (Bibliotheca Indo-Tibetica 11). Vol. 1. Sarnath: Central Institute of Higher Tibetan Studies, 1986.

Viśeṣastava (Tibetan translation)
Ed. by Johannes Schneider. See Schneider 1993:52–72.

Viśeṣastavaṭīkā (Tibetan translation)
Ed. by Johannes Schneider. See Schneider 1993:74–270.

Vairocanābhisambodhitantra (Tibetan translation)
Peking Kangyur no. 126

Vairocanābhisambodhitantrapiṇḍārtha (Tibetan translation)
Peking Tengyur no. 3486

Vairocanābhisambodhivikurvitādhiṣṭhānamahātantravṛtti (Tibetan translation)
Peking Tengyur no. 3490

VY: *Vyākhyāyukti* (Tibetan translation)
Ed. by Jong Cheol Lee in *A Study of Vasubandhu: With Special Reference to the* Vyākhyāyukti (in Japanese). Vol. 2: *The Tibetan Text of the* Vyākhyāyukti *of Vasubandhu.* Tokyo: Sankibo Press, 2001.

Vyākhyāyuktiṭīkā (Tibetan translation)
Peking Tengyur no. 5570

ŚBh: *Śrāvakabhūmi*
Ed. by Karunesha Shukla (Tibetan Sanskrit Works 14). Patna: K.P. Jayaswal Research Institute 1973.

Śrīmālādevīsūtra
As quoted in the RGVV.
See also Peking Kangyur no. 24

Śrīlaghukālacakratantrarāja
See VPṬ.

Satyadvayavibhāgavṛtti (Tibetan translation)
Ed. by Malcolm David Eckel. See Eckel 1987:155–190.

SNS: *Saṁdhinirmocanasūtra* (Tibetan translation from the Kangyur)
Ed. by Étienne Lamotte. Louvain (Belgium): Bureaux du Recueil, 1935.

Saṁpuṭitantra (Tibetan translation)
Peking Kangyur no. 26

Sākārasaṁgraha
See JNĀ

Sākārasiddhiśāstra
See JNĀ

SS: *Sūtrasamuccaya* (Tibetan translation)
Ed. by Bhikkhu Pāsādika. Copenhagen: Akademisk Forlag i Kommission, 1989.

SN: *Sekanirdeśa*
Ed. by the "Studying Group of Sacred Tantric Texts" (Mikkyō-seiten kenkyūkai): "The Results of a Joint Study on the Buddhist Tantric Texts: Advayavajrasaṁgraha—New Critical Edition with Japanese Translation." *Annual of the Institute for Comprehensive Studies of Buddhism Taisho University* 13 (March 1991), (48)–(60) (=pp. 289–77).

Hastavālavṛtti (Tibetan translation)
Peking Tengyur no. 5245

HT: *Hevajratantra*
Ed. (together with the *Hevajrapañjikā Muktāvalī*) by Ram Shankar Tripathi and Thakur Sain Negi (Bibliotheca Indo-Tibetica 48). Sarnath: Central Institute of Higher Tibetan Studies, 2001.

HP: *Hevajrapañjikā*
See HT

Ldog pa bsdus pa (Sanskrit title uncertain)
Peking Tengyur no. 5782

Ldog pa bsdus pa bstan pa'i rnam 'grel (Sanskrit title uncertain)
Peking Tengyur no. 5783

Tibetan Works

Karma pa Mi bskyod rdo rje (the Eighth Karmapa)

—"Rje yid bzang rtse ba'i rgyud gsum gsang ba dang paṇ chen shākya mchog ldan gyi bde mchog rnam bshad gnyis kyi mthar thug gi 'bras bu gzhi dus kyi gnas lugs / lam dus kyi rnal 'byor rnams la dpyad pa bdud rtsi'i dri mchog zhes bya ba bzhugs so." *Dpal rgyal ba karma pa sku phreng brgyad pa mi bskyod rdo rje'i gsung 'bum*, vol. *ba*, 975–1024. Lhasa: Dpal brtsegs bod yig dpe rnying zhib 'jug khang, 2003.

—*dBu ma la 'jug pa'i rnam bshad dpal ldan dus gsum mkhyen pa'i zhal lung dvags brgyud grub pa'i shing rta zhes bya ba bzhugs so.* A reproduction of the Dpal spungs block prints by Zhva dmar Chos kyi blo gros. Rumtek Monastery: 1974.

—*Shes rab kyi pha rol tu phyin pa'i lung chos mtha' dag gi bdud rtsi'i snying por gyur pa gang la ldan pa'i gzhi rje btsun mchog ti dgyes par ngal gso ba'i yongs 'dus brtol gyi ljon pa rgyas pa zhes bya ba bzhugs so.* A reproduction of the Dpal spungs (?) block prints by Zhva dmar Chos kyi blo gros. Rumtek Monastery: no date.

Karma pa Rang byung rdo rje (the Third Karmapa)

—*Snying po bstan pa: Bde bzhin bshegs pa'i snying po bstan pa.* See Karma pa Rang byung rdo rje: *Zab mo nang gi don zhes bya ba'i gzhung bzhugs*, fols. 35a5–39a3.

—*Dbu ma chos dbyings bstod pa'i rnam par bshad pa bzhugs so.* 52 fols., *dbu med*, unpublished.

—*Zab mo nang gi don zhes bya ba'i gzhung bzhugs* (block print). Published together with the *Rnam shes ye shes 'byed pa* and the *bDe bar bshegs pa'i snying po bstan pa.* Rumtek Monastery: 1970.

—*Rang 'grel: Zab mo nang gi don gsal bar byed pa'i 'grel pa bzhugs so* (block print). No place, no date. (The work was composed at the O rgyan kyi mkhan po padma 'byung gnas kyi sgrub gnas in 1325 (fol. 92b6).)

—*Rang byung rdo rje'i mgur rnams.* Tashigang (Bhutan): Bidung Kunchhap, 1983.

Karma 'Phrin las pa

—*Do ha skor gsum gyi ṭīkā 'bring po bzhugs so* (*dbu med* text). No place, no date.

—"Dris lan yid kyi mun sel zhes bya ba lcags mo'i dris lan bzhugs." *The Songs of Esoteric Practice (mGur) and Replies to Doctrinal Questions (Dris lan) of Karma 'Phrin las pa*, 88–92. Reproduced from prints of the 1539 Rin chen ri bo blocks. New Delhi: Ngawang Topgay, 1975.

Kun dga' grol mchog
—"Khrid brgya'i brgyud pa'i lo rgyus bzhugs so." *Gdams ngag rin po che'i mdzod*, vol. 18, 67–98. Kathmandu: Shechen Publications, 1998.
—Also in: *Jo nang kun dga' grol mchog gi khrid brgya'i skor*, 81–125. Dehra Dun: Sa skya Centre, 1984.

Ko zhul Grags pa 'byung gnas and Rgyal ba blo bzang mkhas grub
Gangs can mkhas grub rim byon ming mdzod. Koko Nor: Kan su'u mi rigs dpe skrun khang, 1992.

Kong sprul Blo gros mtha' yas
—*Rgyud bla ma'i bshad srol: Theg pa chen po rgyud bla ma'i bstan bcos snying po'i don mngon sum lam gyi bshad srol dang sbyar ba'i rnam par 'grel pa phyir mi ldog pa seng ge'i nga ro zhes bya ba bzhugs so.* Rumtek Monastery: no date.
—*Rnam par shes pa dang ye shes 'byed pa'i bstan bcos kyi tshig don go gsal du 'grel pa rang byung dgongs pa'i rgyan ces bya ba bzhugs so.* Rumtek Monastery: no date.
—*Zab mo nang gi don gyi 'grel pa: Rnal 'byor bla na med pa'i rgyud sde rgya mtsho snying po bsdus pa zab mo nang gi don nyung ngu'i tshig gis rnam par 'grel ba zab don snang byed.* Rumtek Monastery: 1970.
—*Shes bya kun khyab mdzod.* 3 vols. Beijing: Mi rigs dpe skrun khang, 1982.

Klong chen rab 'byams pa
—"Grub mtha' mdzod": "Theg pa mtha' dag gi don gsal bar byed pa grub mtha' rin po che'i mdzod." *Mdzod bdun*, vol. 4. Gangtok: Dodrup Chen Rinpoche, no date.
—"Rdzogs pa chen po sems nyid ngal gso'i 'grel pa." *Ngal gso skor gsum, rang grol skor gsum, sngags kyi spyi don*, vol. 1. Gangtok: Dodrup Chen Rinpoche, 1973.

Bka' 'gyur and Bstan 'gyur
The Tibetan Tripitaka: Peking Edition. Ed. by Daisetz T. Suzuki, 168 vols. Reproduced under the supervision of the Otani University. Tokyo, Kyoto: 1955–61.

Glag bla Chos 'grub and Chos grags bzang po:
Kun mkhyen klong chen rab 'byams kyi rnam thar bzhugs. Chengdu: Si khron mi rigs dpe skrun khang, 1993.

'Gos Lo tsā ba Gzhon nu dpal
—*Mkhas pa chen po dpal nags kyi rin chen gyi rnam par thar pa.* The Biography of the Fifteenth Century Bengali Pandita (sic), Vanaratna. Thimphu: National Library of Bhutan: 1985.
—*Deb ther sngon po.* Reproduced by Lokesh Chandra (Śata-Piṭaka Series 212). New Delhi: International Academy of Indian Culture, 1974.

—DRSM: *Theg pa chen po rgyud bla ma'i bstan bcos kyi 'grel bshad de kho na nyid rab tu gsal ba'i me long.* Ed. by Klaus-Dieter Mathes (Nepal Research Centre Publications 24). Stuttgart: Franz Steiner Verlag, 2003.

Sgam po pa Bsod nams rin chen

—"Tshogs chos bkra shis phun tshogs." *Khams gsum chos kyi rgyal po dpal mnyam med sgam po pa 'gro mgon bsod nams rin chen mchog gi gsung 'bum yid bzhin nor bu,* vol. *ka,* 289–332. Published by Ven. Khenpo Shedrup Tenzin and Lama Thinley Namgyal. Delhi: Sherab Gyaltsen 2000.

—"Tshogs chos yon tan phun tshogs." Ibid., vol. *ka,* 505–75.

—"Zhal gyi bdud rtsi thun mong ma yin pa." *Nges don phyag chen mdzod,* vol. *ka,* 81–141. Ed. by Zhva dmar pa Mi pham chos kyi blo gros. New Delhi: no date.

—"Lam rim snying po." Ibid., 320–27.

Sgra tshad pa Rin chen rnam rgyal

"Yang rgyan": "De bzhin gshegs pa'i snying po gsal zhing mdzes par byed pa'i rgyan gyi rgyan mkhas pa'i yid 'phrog." *The Collected Works of Bu-ston,* vol. 28 *(sa),* 161–284. Ed. by Lokesh Chandra (Śatapiṭaka Series 68). New Delhi: International Academy of Indian Culture, 1971.

Dga' ba'i rdo rje

'Khrungs dpe dri med shel gyi me long. Beijing: Mi rigs dpe skrun khang, 1995.

Ngag dbang blo gros grags pa

Jo nang chos 'byung zla ba'i sgron me. Chengdu: Krung go'i bod kyi shes rig dpe skrun khang, 1992.

Rngog Blo ldan shes rab

Theg pa chen po rgyud bla'i don bsdus pa rngog lo chen pos mdzad pa bzhugs so. NGMPP reel no. L 519/4, 66 fols. See also Jackson 1993

'Jig rten gsum mgon

See 'Bri gung Skyob pa 'Jig rten gsum mgon

'Ju Mi pham rgya mtsho

—"Theg pa chen po mdo sde'i rgyan gyi dgongs don theg mchog bdud rtsi'i dga' ston ldeb." *Sde dge dgon chen Prints of the Writings of 'Jam mgon Mi pham rgya mtsho,* vol. 2. Reprinted by Jamyang Khyentse. Kathmandu: Shechen Publications, 1987.

—*Dbu ma rgyan rtsa 'grel.* Chengdu: Si khron mi rigs dpe skrun khang, 1992.

Nye gnas Grags pa rin chen

See 'Bri gung Skyob pa 'Jig rten gsum mgon: *Bstan bcos tsin dha ma ṇi'i phreng ba zhes bya ba bzhugs so*

Tāranātha

—"Zab don nyer gcig pa bzhugs so." *Rje btsun Tāranātha'i gsung 'bum bzhugs so,* vol. 4, 781–795. Leh: Namgyal and Tsewang Taru, 1982–85.

—"Zab mo gzhan stong dbu ma'i brgyud 'debs." *Ibid.,* 483–490.

—"Gzhan stong snying po ces bya ba bzhugs so." *Ibid.,* 491–514.

Gter bdag gling pa 'Gyur med rdo rje

Dus gsum rgyal ba thams cad kyi mkhyen brtse nus gsum gcig tu bsdus pa'i bdag nyid kun mkhyen chos kyi rgyal po'i mtshan gyi rnam grangs la mchog tu dad pa'i dbyangs kyis bstod pa yon tan rgya mtsho'i rlabs phreng zhes bya ba bzhugs so. No place, no date.

Bstan 'dzin phun tshogs et al.

[Compiled by a group of the Dpal brtsegs bod yig dpe rnying zhib 'jug khang, Lhasa]

'Bras spungs dgon du bzhugs su gsol ba'i dpe rnying dkar chag. 2 vols. Beijing: Mi rigs dpe skrun khang, 2004.

DRSM

See 'Gos Lo tsā ba Gzhon nu dpal, DRSM

Dol po pa Shes rab rgyal mtshan

—*Jo nang ri chos nges don rgya mtsho.* Beijing: Mi rigs dpe skrun khang, 1998.

—"Nyi ma'i 'od zer": "Theg pa chen po rgyud bla ma'i bstan bcos legs bshad nyi ma'i 'od zer." *The 'Dzam-thang Edition of the Collected Works of Kun-mkhyen Dol-po-pa Shes-rab rgyal-mtshan*, vol. 4 *(ma)*, 883–1161. Delhi: Shedrup Books, 1992.

—"Bden gnyis gsal ba'i nyi ma." *Kun mkhyen dol po pa'i gsung 'bum*, vol. 1, 1–45. Published by Jamyang Khyentse. Kathmandu: Shechen Publications, no date.

Phag mo gru pa

"Rin chen rgyan 'dra." *Phag mo gru pa'i bka' 'bum*, vol. 2 *(kha)*, fols. 216 b6–225a4. Edited by Kun dga' rin chen chos kyi rgyal mtshan, NGMPP reel no. E 3169/1 (continued on E 3170 and E 3171).

Bu ston rin chen grub

Bu ston chos 'byung gsung rab rin po che'i mdzod. Chengdu: Krung go'i bod kyi shes rig dpe skrun khang, 1988.

Blo gros mtshungs med

—"Nges don gsal byed sgron me": "Theg pa chen po rgyud bla ma'i bstan bcos kyi nges don gsal bar byed pa'i rin po che'i sgron me bzhugs so." *Sa skya pa'i mkhas pa rnams kyi gsung skor*, vol. 3, 239–565. Kathmandu: Sa skya rgyal yongs gsung rab slob gnyer khang, 1999.

—*Theg pa chen po rgyud bla ma'i bstan bcos kyi nges don gsal bar byed pa'i rin po che'i sgron me bzhugs sho.* Tezu (Arunachal Pradesh): Tibetan Nyingmapa Monastery, 1974.

'Ba' ra ba Rgyal mtshan dpal bzang

—"Kun mkhyen dol bu'i bu chen brgyad la lan phyogs cig tu btab pa nyi ma'i 'od zer." *A Tibetan Encyclopedia of Buddhist Scholasticism. The Collected Writings of 'Ba' ra ba rgyal mtshan dpal bzang*, vol. 11, 637–709. Dehra Dun: Ngawang Gyaltsen and Ngawang Lungtok, 1970.

—"Kun gzhi'i rnam shes dang ye shes kyi rnam bzhag." Ibid., 602–37.

—"Chos rje rnam gnyis kyi dgongs bshad nyi ma'i 'od zer." Ibid., 496–557.
—"Dus 'khor rdo rje snying po la dri ba yi ger bskur." Ibid., 557–602.

'Bri gung Skyob pa 'Jig rten gsum mgon
—"Chos 'khor 'ong ges zhus pa'i gzhung gi rtsa ba." Chos kyi 'khor lo legs par gtan la phab pa theg pa chen po'i tshul 'ong ges zhus pa zhes bya ba bzhugs so ('Bri gung Bka' brgyud 5), 1–24. Dehra Dun: Drikung Kagyu Institute, 1998.
—"Chos 'khor 'ong ges zhus pa'i gzhung gi 'grel pa." Ibid., 1–372 (the commentary has its own page numbering).
—*Bstan bcos tsin dha ma ṇi'i phreng ba zhes bya ba bzhugs so* (together with a commentary by Nye gnas Grags pa rin chen) ('Bri gung Bka' brgyud 4). Dehra Dun: Drikung Kagyu Institute, 1997.
—"Dam chos dgongs pa gcig pa'i gzhung zhes bya ba bzhugs so." *Dgongs gcig 'grel ba nyi ma'i snang ba* (see Rig 'dzin Chos gyi grags pa), 11–22.

Tshal pa Kun dga' rdo rje
Deb ther dmar po. Beijing: Mi rigs dpe skrun khang, 1981.

Zhang Tshal pa Brtson 'grus
"Phyag rgya chen po lam zab mthar thug zhang gi man ngag." *Rtsib ri spar ma*, vol. 4, 49–117. Darjeeling 1978.

Zhva dmar Chos grags ye shes (the Fourth Zhamarpa)
—*Lo chen rnam thar: Rje thams cad mkhyen pa lo tsa ba chen po'i rnam par thar pa ngo mtshar rgya mtsho*, 130 fols., *dbu can*, unpublished.
—"Byang chub sems 'grel gyi rnam par bshad pa tshig don gsal ba zhes bya ba bzhugs so." *Yid bzhin gyi za ma tog* 1, 62–123. Dharamsala: 'Gro mgon gtsug lag dpe skrun khang, 2001.
—*Gzhon nu dpal gyi rnam thar: Dpal ldan bla ma dam pa mkhan chen thams cad mkhyen pa don gyi slad du mtshan nas smos te gzhon nu dpal gyi rnam par thar pa / yon tan rin po che mchog tu rgyas pa'i ljon pa*, 74 fols., *dbu can*, unpublished.

Rig 'dzin Chos kyi grags pa
"Dam pa'i chos dgongs pa gcig pa'i rnam bshad lung don gsal byed nyi ma'i snang ba zhes bya ba bzhugs so." *Dgong gcig 'grel ba nyi ma'i snang ba*, 23–441. Maryland: Drikung Kagyu Meditation Centre, 1995.

Rong ston Shes bya kun rig
"Theg pa chen po rgyud bla ma'i bstan bcos legs par bshad pa bzhugs so." *Theg pa chen po rgyud bla ma'i bstan bcos rtsal 'grel bzhugs so*, 49–264. Chengdu: Si khron mi rigs dpe skrun khang, 1997.

Las chen Kun dga' rgyal mtshan
Bka' gdams kyi rnam par thar pa bka' gdams chos 'byung gsal ba'i sgron me. 2 vols. Ed. by B. Jamyang Norbu. New Delhi: 1972.

Sa skya Paṇḍita
Thub pa dgongs gsal. NGMPP reel no. L 604/3.

Sa bzang Mati paṇ chen 'Jam dbyangs Blo gros rgyal mtshan
"Nges don rab gsal": "Theg pa chen po'i rgyud bla ma'i bstan bcos kyi rnam par bshad pa nges don rab gsal snang ba." *Sa skya pa'i mkhas pa rnams kyi gsung skor*, vol. 4, 1–520. Kathmandu: Sa skya rgyal yongs gsung rab slob gnyer khang, 1999.

Saraha
"Do ha mdzod kyi glu bzhugs so." *Phyag rgya chen po'i rgya gzhung*, vol. *oṁ*, fols. 142b2–151a5. Ed. by Phun tshogs rgyal mtshan (end of 19th century). Dpal dpungs block print. No date.

Situ Paṇ chen Chos kyi 'byung gnas and 'Be lo Tshe dbang kun khyab
Sgrub brgyud karma kaṁ tshang brgyud pa rin po che'i rnam par thar pa rab 'byams nor bu zla ba chu sel gyi phreng ba. 2 vols. Reproduced from a print of the Dpal spungs edition. New Delhi: D. Gyaltsan and Kesang Legshay, 1972.

Gser mdog Paṇ chen Shākya mchog ldan
—"Chos kyi dbyings su bstod pa zhes bya ba'i bstan bcos kyi rnam par bshad pa." *Collected Writings of gSer mdog paṇ chen Shākya mchog ldan*, vol. 7 *(ja)*, 304–91. Delhi: Nagwang Topgyal, 1988.
"Blo mchog pa'i dri lan bzhugs so." Ibid., vol. 17 *(tsa)*, 561–78.
—"Dbu ma'i 'byung tshul rnam par bshad pa'i gtam yid bzhin lhun po zhes bya ba'i bstan bcos bzhugs so." Ibid., vol. 4 *(nga)*, 209–48.

Other Works

Achard, Jean-Luc 1999
L'essence perlée du secret: Recherches philologiques et historiques sur l'origine de la Grande Perfection dans la tradition rNying ma pa (Bibliothèque de l'École des Hautes Études, Section des Sciences Religieuses 107). Turnhout (Belgium): Brepols.

Bandurski, Frank et al. 1994
Untersuchungen zur buddhistischen Literatur. By Frank Bandurski, Bikkhu Pāsādika, Michael Schmidt, and Bangwei Wang. (Sanskrit-Wörterbuch der buddhistischen Texte aus den Turfan-Funden. Beiheft 5.) Göttingen: Vandenhoeck and Ruprecht in Göttingen.

Bentor, Yael 2002
"Fourfold Meditation: Outer, Inner, Secret and Suchness." *Religion and Secular Culture in Tibet: Tibetan Studies II* (Proceedings of the International Association of Tibetan Studies 2000), 41–58. Ed. by H. Blezer with the assistance of A. Zadoks (Brill's Tibetan Studies Library 2/2). Leiden: Brill.

Bhattacharya, Kamaleshwar 2001
"For a New Edition of the *Mahāyānasūtrālaṁkāra*." *Journal of the Nepal Research Centre* 12, 5–16.

Broido, Michael M.
1984 "Abhiprāya and Implication in Tibetan Linguistics." *Journal of Indian Philosophy* 12, 1–33.

1987 "Sa-skya Paṇḍita, the White Panacea and the Hva-shang Doctrine." *The Journal of the International Association of Buddhist Studies* 10 (1), 27–68.
1989 "The Jo-nang-pas on Madhyamaka: A Sketch." *Tibet Journal* 14 (1), 86–91.

Cabezón, José I.
1992 "Vasubandhu's *Vyākhyāyukti* on the Authenticity of the Mahāyāna *Sūtras*." *Text in Context: Traditional Hermeneutics in South Asia*, 221–43. Ed. by Jeffrey R. Timm. Albany, N.Y.: SUNY.
2003 "Two Views on the Svātantrika-Prāsaṅgika Distinction in Fourteenth-Century Tibet." *The Svātantrika-Prāsaṅgika Distinction*, 289–315. Ed. by George B.J. Dreyfus and Sara L. McClintock. Somerville (Massachusetts): Wisdom Publications.

Callahan, Elizabeth M. 2001
Mahāmudrā: The Ocean of Definitive Meaning: The Ninth Gyalwang Karmapa, Wangchuk Dorje. Seattle: Nitartha International.

Chalmers, R. 1899
See CS: *Cūḷasuññatasutta*

Conze, Edward 1958
Aṣṭasāhasrikā Prajñāpāramitā. Translated into English by Dr. Edward Conze (Bibliotheca Indica 284). Kalkota: Asiatic Society of Bengal.

Cozort, Daniel 1986
Highest Yoga Tantra. Ithaca, N.Y.: Snow Lion Publications.

Dowman, Keith 1985
Masters of Mahamudra: Songs and Histories of the Eighty-Four Buddhist Saints (SUNY Series in Buddhist Studies). Albany, N.Y.: SUNY.

Dreyfus, Georges B.J.
1997 *Recognizing Reality: Dharmakīrti's Philosophy and its Tibetan Interpretations* (SUNY Series in Buddhist Studies). Albany, N.Y.: SUNY.
2003 *The Sound of Two Hands Clapping: The Education of a Tibetan Buddhist Monk*. Berkeley and Los Angeles: University of California Press.

Eckel, Malcolm D. 1987
Jñānagarbha on the Two Truths: An Eighth Century Handbook of Madhyamaka Philosophy. Albany, N.Y.: SUNY.

Edgerton, Franklin 1953
Buddhist Hybrid Sanskrit Grammar and Dictionary. 2 vols. (William Dwight Whitney Linguistic Series.) New Haven: Yale University Press.

Ehrhard, Franz-Karl
2002 *Life and Travels of Lo-chen bSod-nams rgya-mtsho* (Lumbini International Research Institute Monograph Series 3). Lumbini: Lumbini International Research Institute.
2004 "Spiritual Relationships between Rulers and Preceptors: The Three Journeys of Vanaratna (1384–1468) to Tibet." *The Relationship Between Religion and State* (chos srid zung 'brel) *in Traditional Tibet* (Proceedings of a sem-

inar held in Lumbini, Nepal, March 2000), 245–66. Ed. by Christoph Cüppers. Lumbini: Lumbini International Research Institute.

Eimer, Helmut 1978
Bodhipathapradīpa: Ein Lehrgedicht des Atiśa (Dīpaṁkaraśrījñāna) in der tibetischen Überlieferung (Asiatische Forschungen 59). Wiesbaden: Otto Harrossowitz.

Ejima, Yasunori 1979
Development of Mādhyamika Philosophy in India: Studies on Bhāvaviveka. Niigata: The Technological University of Nagaoka.

Frauwallner, Erich
1932 "Beiträge zur Apohalehre." *Wiener Zeitschrift für die Kunde des Morgenlandes* 39, 247–85.
1951 "*Amalavijñānam* und *Ālayavijñānam.*" *Beiträge zur indischen Philologie und Altertumskunde, Walther Schubring zum 70. Geburtstag dargebracht* (Alt- und Neu-Indische Studien 7), 148–59. Ed. by Gerhard Oberhammer and Ernst Steinkellner. Hamburg: Franz Steiner Verlag.
1969 *Die Philosophie des Buddhismus.* 3rd revised edition. Berlin: Akademie Verlag.
1973 *History of Indian Philiosophy.* 2 vols. Delhi: Motilal Banarsidass.

Germano, David F. 1992
"Poetic Thought, the Intelligent Universe, and the Mystery of Self: The Tantric Synthesis of rDzogs chen in Fourteenth-Century Tibet." 3 parts. Ph.D. thesis, University of Wisconsin-Madison. Ann Arbor: UMI no. 9231691.

Goldstein, Melvyn 2001
The New Tibetan-English Dictionary of Modern Tibetan. Berkeley: University of California Press.

Guenther, Herbert 1989
Juwelenschmuck der geistigen Befreiung. Munich: Diederichs Verlag.

Hahn, Michael
1978 "On the Function and Origin of the Particle dag." *Tibetan Studies,* 137–47. Ed. by Martin Brauen and Per Kvaerne. Zurich.
1982 See RĀ
1994 *Lehrbuch der klassischen tibetischen Schriftsprache.* 6th revised edition (Indica et Tibetica 10). Swisttal-Odendorf: Indica et Tibetica Verlag.

Hirakawa, Akira 1978
Index to the Abhidharmakośabhāṣya. Part Three: *Tibetan-Sanskrit.* Tokyo: Daizo Shuppan Kabushikikaisha.

Hookham, Susan K. 1991
The Buddha Within (SUNY Series in Buddhist Studies). Albany, N.Y.: SUNY.

Hopkins, Jeffrey
1983 *Meditation on Emptiness.* London: Wisdom Publications.
1998 *Buddhist Advice for Living and Liberation: Nāgārjuna's Precious Garland.* Ithaca, N.Y.: Snow Lion Publications.

Imaeda, Yoshiro 1982
Catalogue du Kanjur Tibetain de l'Edition de 'Jang sa tham. Vol. 1: edition en fac-similé avec introduction (Bibliographia Philologica Buddhica. Series Maior IIa). Tokyo.

Ishikawa, Mie 1990
A Critical Edition of the sGra sbyor bam po gnyis pa: *An Old and Basic Commentary on the Mahāvyutpatti: Materials for Tibetan-Mongolian Dictionaries.* 2 vols. (Studia Tibetica 18). Tokyo: The Toyo Bunko.

Jackson, David
1990 "Sa skya Paṇḍita the 'Polemicist': Ancient Debates and Modern Interpretations." *Journal of the International Association of Buddhist Studies* 13 (2), 17–116.
1992 "Birds in the Egg and Newborn Lion Cubs: Metaphors for the Potentialities and Limitations of 'All-at-once' Enlightenment." *Tibetan Studies* (Proceedings of the 5th Seminar of the International Association for Tibetan Studies, Narita 1989), vol. 1, 95–114. Narita: Naritasan Shinshoji.
1993 *Introduction to Theg chen rgyud bla'i don bsdus pa: Commentary on the Ratnagotravibhāga.* Dharamsala: Library of Tibetan Works and Archives.
1994 *Enlightenment by a Single Means.* Vienna: Verlag der Österreichischen Akademie der Wissenschaften.

Jäschke, Heinrich A. 1985
A Tibetan-English Dictionary. Reprint (first published in 1881). Kyoto: Rinsen Book Company.

Johnston, Edward H. 1950
See RGV

de Jong, Jan W.
1978 "Textcritical Notes on the Prasannapadā." *Indo-Iranian Journal* 20, 25–59.
1979 "Review of Takasaki 1966" (see below). *Buddhist Studies by J. W. de Jong,* 563–82. Ed. by Gregory Schopen. Berkeley: Asian Humanities Press.

Kajiyama, Yuichi 1998
An Introduction to Buddhist Philosophy. An Annotated Translation of the Tārkabhāṣa *of Mokṣākaragupta.* Reprinted by the "Arbeitskreis für tibetische und buddhistische Studien" (first published in Kyoto 1966). (Wiener Studien zur Tibetologie und Buddhismuskunde 42.) Vienna: Arbeitskreis für tibetische und buddhistische Studien.

Kano, Kazuo
2001 "Chibeto ni okeru hōshōron no juyō to tenkai" (On the Acceptance and Development of the *Ratnagotravibhāga* in Tibet). Master's thesis, University of Kyoto.
2003 "Hōshōronchū kenkyū (1)—Phya pa niyoru hōshōron I.26 kaishaku—(Study of Commentaries of the *Ratnagotravibhāga* (1)—Phya pa's Interpretation of the Verse I.26—). *Indogaku Bukkyōgaku Kenkyū* 51 (2), 109–11.

Kapstein, Matthew T.

1992 "Introduction." *The 'Dzam-thang Edition of the Collected Works of Kun-mkhyen Dol-po-pa Shes-rab rgyal-mtshan: Introduction and Catalogue*, 1–43. Delhi: Shedrup Books.

2000 *The Tibetan Assimilation of Buddhism: Conversion, Contestation and Memory.* Oxford: Oxford University Press.

Karma Thinley 1980

The History of the Sixteen Karmapas of Tibet. Boulder: Prajñā Press.

Karmay, Samten G. 1988

The Great Perfection (rDzogs chen): A Philosophical and Meditative Teaching in Tibetan Buddhism. Leiden: Brill.

Keira, Ryusei 2004

Mādhyamika and Epistemology: A Study of Kamalaśīla's Method for Proving the Voidness of All Dharmas (Wiener Studien zur Tibetologie und Buddhismuskunde 59). Vienna: Arbeitskreis für tibetische und buddhistische Studien.

Khetsun Sangpo 1973

Bibliographical Dictionary of Tibet and Tibetan Buddhism. Vols. 3 and 5. Dharamsala: Library of Tibetan Works and Archives.

Kondō, Ryūkō 1936

See DBhS

van der Kuijp, Leonard. W.J.

1978 "Phya-pa Chos-kyi Seng-ge's Impact on Tibetan Epistemological Theory." *Journal of Indian Philosophy* 5, 355–69.

1983 *Contributions to the Development of Tibetan Buddhist Epistemology* (Alt- und Neu-Indische Studien 26). Wiesbaden: Franz Steiner Verlag.

1991 "On the Life and Political Career of Ta'i-si-tu Byang-chub rgyal-mtshan (1302–?64)." *Tibetan History and Language: Studies Dedicated to Uray Géza on His Seventieth Birthday*, 277–327 (Wiener Studien zur Tibetologie und Buddhismuskunde 26). Vienna: Arbeitskreis für tibetische und buddhistische Studien.

1993 "Fourteenth Century Tibetan Cultural History III: The Oeuvre of Bla ma dam pa Bsod nams rgyal mtshan (1312–75), Part One." *Berliner Indologische Studien* 7, 109–47.

La Vallée Poussin, Louis de 1910

"[Madhyamakāvatāra:] La terre Abhimukhī ou sixième production de la pensée d'illumination." *Le Muséon* 11, 272–358.

Lamotte, Étienne 1949

"La critique d'interprétation dans le bouddhism." *Annuaire de l'Institut de Philologie et d'Histoire Orientales et Slaves* 9, 341–61.

Lang, Karen 1986

Āryadeva's Catuḥśataka: On the Bodhisattva's Cultivation of Merit and Knowledge (Indiske Studier 7). Copenhagen: Akademisk Forlag.

Lee, Jong Cheol

2001a *A Study of Vasubandhu: With Special Reference to the* Vyākhyāyukti (in Japanese). Tokyo: Sankibo Press.

2001b See VY

Lhalungpa, Lobsang P. 1993

Mahāmudrā: The Quintessence of Mind and Meditation. Delhi: Motilal Banarsidass.

Lindtner, Christian

1987 *Nagarjuniana: Studies in the Writings and Philosophy of Nāgārjuna.* Reprinted by Motilal Banarsidass (first published 1982) (Buddhist Tradition Series 2). Delhi: Motilal Banarsidass.

1995 "Bhavya's Madhyamakahṛdaya (Pariccheda Five): *Yogācāratattvaviniścayāvatāra.*" *The Adyar Library Bulletin* 59.

1997 "*Cittamātra* in Indian Mahāyāna until Kamalaśīla." *Wiener Zeitschrift für die Kunde Südasiens* 41, 159–206.

Lokesh Chandra

1963 *Materials for a History of Tibetan Literature.* 3 vols. (Śata-Piṭaka Series 28–30). New Delhi: International Academy of Indian Culture.

1971 *Tibetan-Sanskrit Dictionary.* Reprint (first published in 1959–61). Kyoto, Rinsen Book Company.

Lopez, Donald, S., Jr. 1987

A Study of Svātantrika. Ithaca, N.Y.: Snow Lion Publications.

Makransky, John J. 1997

Buddhahood Embodied: Sources of Controversy in India and Tibet (SUNY Series of Buddhist Studies). Albany, N.Y.: SUNY.

Martin, Dan 1992

"A Twelfth-century Tibetan Classic of Mahāmudrā, The Path of Ultimate Profundity: The Great Seal Instructions of Zhang." *Journal of the International Association of Buddhist Studies* 15 (2), 243–319.

Mathes, Klaus-Dieter

1996 *Unterscheidung der Gegebenheiten von ihrem wahren Wesen (Dharmadharmatāvibhāga)* (Indica et Tibetica 26). Swisttal-Odendorf: Indica et Tibetica Verlag.

1998 "Vordergründige und höchste Wahrheit im *gŹan stoṅ*-Madhyamaka." *Annäherung an das Fremde: XXVI. Deutscher Orientalistentag vom 25. bis 29.9.1995 in Leipzig.* Ed. by H. Preissler and H. Stein. *Zeitschrift der Deutschen Morgenländischen Gesellschaft* 11, 457–68.

2000 "Tāranātha's Presentation of *trisvabhāva* in the *gŹan stoṅ sñiṅ po.*" *Journal of the International Association of Buddhist Studies* 23 (2), 195–223.

2001 [Review of:] "Cyrus Stearns: *The Buddha from Dolpo: A Study of the Life and Thought of the Tibetan Master Dolpopa Sherab Gyaltsen.* Albany, N.Y.: SUNY, 1999." *Journal of the Nepal Research Centre* 12, 311–19.

2002 "'Gos Lo tsā ba Gzhon nu dpal's Extensive Commentary on and Study of the *Ratnagotravibhāgavyākhyā*." *Religion and Secular Culture in Tibet: Tibetan Studies II* (Proceedings of the International Association of Tibetan Studies 2000), 79–96. Ed. by H. Blezer with the assistance of A. Zadoks (Brill's Tibetan Studies Library 2/2). Leiden: Brill.

2003 See 'Gos Lo tsā ba Gzhon nu dpal: *Theg pa chen po rgyud bla ma'i bstan bcos kyi 'grel bshad de kho na nyid rab tu gsal ba'i me long*

2004 "Tāranātha's 'Twenty-One Differences with regard to the Profound Meaning'— Comparing the Views of the Two *gŹan stoṅ* Masters Dol po pa and Śākya mchog ldan." *Journal of the International Association of Buddhist Studies* 27 (2), 285–328.

2005 "'Gos Lo tsā ba Gzhon nu dpal's Commentary on the *Dharmatā* Chapter of the *Dharmadharmatāvibhāgakārikās*." *Studies in Indian Philosophy and Buddhism, University of Tokyo* 12, 3–39.

2006 "Blending the Sūtras with the Tantras: The Influence of Maitrīpa and His Circle on the Formation of *Sūtra Mahāmudrā* in the Kagyu Schools." In: *Tibetan Buddhist Literature and Praxis: Studies in its Formative Period 900–1400*. Ed. by Ronald M. Davidson and Christian K. Wedemeyer (Proceedings of the Tenth Seminar of the IATS, Oxford 2003, vol. 10/4). Leiden: Brill, 201–27.

2007 "The Ontological Status of the Dependent *(paratantra)* in the *Saṁdhinirmocanasūtra* and the *Vyākhyāyukti*." In: *Indica et Tibetica. Festschrift für Michael Hahn zum 65. Geburtstag von Freunden und Schülern überreicht*. Ed. by Konrad Klaus and Jens-Uwe Hartmann. (Wiener Studien zur Tibetologie und Buddhismuskunde 66). Vienna: Arbeitskreis für tibetische und buddhistische Studien, 323–39.

Mimaki, Katsumi 1982
Blo gsal grub mtha'. Kyoto: Zinbun Kagaku Kenkyusyo.

Mishra, Kameshwar Nath 1987
"Reflections on the Tibetan Etymologies of the Sanskrit Synonyms of Buddha." *Śramaṇa Vidyā: Studies in Buddhism*, 197–209 (Samyag-Vāk Series 3). Sarnath: Central Institute of Higher Tibetan Studies.

MW: Monier-Williams, Sir Monier 1899
A Sanskrit-English Dictionary. New edition, greatly enlarged and improved with the collaboration of E. Leumann, C. Capeller, and other scholars. Oxford: Clarendon Press.

Nakamura, Hajime 1987
Indian Buddhism: A Survey with Bibliographical Notes. Reprint (first published 1980) (Buddhist Tradition Series 1). Delhi: Motilal Banarsidass.

Nakamura, Zuiho 1967
Zōwa-taiyaku Kukyōichijōhōshōron-kenkyū (The Tibetan Version of the *Mahāyānottaratantraśāstra*, edited and translated into Japanese). Tokyo: Suzuki Gakujutsu Zaidan.

Negi, J.S. 1993–2005
Tibetan-Sanskrit Dictionary. 16 vols. Sarnath: Dictionary Unit. Central Institute of Higher Tibetan Studies.

Newland, Guy 1992
The Two Truths in the Mādhyamika Philosophy of the Ge-luk-ba Order of Tibetan Buddhism (Studies in Indo-Tibetan Buddhism). Ithaca, N.Y.: Snow Lion Publications.

Nishio, Kyōo 1936
A Tibetan Index to the Mahāvyutpatti / Zō-Bon Taisho: Honyaku Myōgi Taishū Chibettogo Sakuin (Butten Kenkyū 1). Kyoto.

Obermiller, Eugène 1931
"The Sublime Science of the Great Vehicle to Salvation Being a Manual of Buddhist Monism." *Acta Orientalia* 9, 81–306.

Pant, Mahes Raj 2000
Jātarūpa's Commentary on the Amarakoṣa. 2 vols. Delhi: Motilal Barnasidass.

Perler, Dominik 2002
Theorien der Intentionalität im Mittelalter (Philosophische Abhandlungen 82). Frankfurt a. M.: Vitttorio Klostermann.

Petech, Luciano 1990
Central Tibet and the Mongols: The Yüan-Sa-skya Period of Tibetan History (Rome Oriental Series 65). Rome: Istituto Italiano per il Medio ed Estremo Oriente.

Pettit, John W. 1999
Mi pham's Beacon of Certainty Illuminating the View of Dzogchen (Studies in Indian and Tibetan Buddhism). Boston: Wisdom Publications.

Powers, John 1994
Wisdom of the Buddha: The Saṁdhinirmocanasūtra. Translated by John Powers (Tibetan Translation Series 16). Berkeley: Dharma Publishing.

Rahder, Johannes 1926
See DBhS

Rhoton, Jared D. 2002
A Clear Differentiation of the Three Codes: Essential Distinctions among the Individual Liberation, Great Vehicle, and Tantric Systems (SUNY series in Buddhist Studies). Albany, N.Y.: SUNY.

Rigzin, Tsepak 1993
Tibetan-English Dictionary of Buddhist Terminology. Second revised edition. Dharamsala: Library of Tibetan Works and Archives.

Roerich, George N. 1949–53
The Blue Annals. 2 vols. (Royal Asiatic Society of Bengal, Monograph Series 7). Kalkota. See also Wylie

Schaeffer, Kurtis 1995
"As It Was Before, So Is It After: A Study of the Third Karma pa Rang byung rdo rje's Treatise on Buddha Nature." Master's thesis, University of Washington.

Schmithausen, Lambert
1969 *Der Nirvāṇa-Abschnitt in der Viniścayasaṁgrahaṇī der Yogācārabhūmiḥ* (Veröffentlichungen der Kommission für Sprachen und Kulturen Süd- und Ostasiens 8, philosophisch-historische Klasse, Sitzungsberichte, 264, vol. 2, Abhandlung). Vienna: Österreichische Akademie der Wissenschaften.
1971 "Philologische Bemerkungen zum Ratnagotravibhāga." *Wiener Zeitschrift für die Kunde Südasiens* 15, 123–77.
1972 "The Definition of Pratyakṣam in the Abhidharmasamuccayaḥ." *Wiener Zeitschrift für die Kunde Südasiens* 16, 153–63.
1973 "Zu D. Seyfort Rueggs Buch 'La Théorie du Tathāgatagarbha et du Gotra' (Besprechungsaufsatz)." *Wiener Zeitschrift für die Kunde Südasiens* 22, 123–60.
1987 *Ālayavijñāna: On the Origin and the Early Development of a Central Concept of the Yogācāra Philosophy.* 2 vols. (Studia Philologica Buddhica, Monograph Series 4). Tokyo: The International Institute for Buddhist Studies.

Schneider, Johannes 1993
Der Lobpreis der Vorzüglichkeit des Buddha: Udbhaṭasiddhasvāmins Viśeṣastava *mit Prajñāvarmans Kommentar* (Indica et Tibetica 23). Bonn: Indica et Tibetica Verlag.

Seyfort Ruegg, David
1963 "The Jo nang pas: A School of Buddhist Ontologists according to the *Grub mtha' shel gyi me long.*" *Journal of African and Oriental Studies* 83, 73–91.
1966 *The Life of Bu ston Rinpoche.* With the Tibetan text of the *Bu ston rnam thar* (Rome Oriental Series 34). Rome: Istituto Italiano per il Medio ed Estremo Oriente.
1969 *La Théorie du Tathāgatagarbha et du Gotra: Études sur la Sotériologie et la Gnoséologie du Bouddhisme* (Publications de l'École française d'Extrême-Orient 70). Paris: École française d'Extrême-Orient.
1971 "Le *Dharmadhātustava* de Nāgārjuna." *Études Tibetaines: Dediées à la Mémoire de Marcelle Lalou (1890–1967),* 448–71. Paris: Librairie d'Amérique et d'Orient.
1973 *Le Traité du Tathāgatagarbha de Bu ston rin chen grub* (Publications de l'École française d'Extrême-Orient 88). Paris : École française d'Extrême-Orient.
1981 *The Literature of the Madhyamaka School of Philosophy in India* (A History of Indian Literature 7, fasc. 1). Wiesbaden: Franz Steiner Verlag.
1985 "Purport, Implicature and Presupposition: Sanskrit *Abhiprāya* and Tibetan *dGongs pa / dGongs gzhi* as Hermeneutical Concepts." *Journal of Indian Philosophy* 13, 309–25.
1988 a"A Kar ma bKa' brgyud Work on the Lineages and Traditions of the Indo-Tibetan dBu ma (Madhyamaka)." *Orientalia Iosephi Tucci Dedicata,*

1249–80 (=[1]–[32]). Edited by G. Gnoli and L. Lanciotti (Rome Oriental Series 56,3). Rome: Istituto Italiano per il Medio ed Estremo Oriente.

1988 b"An Indian Source for the Tibetan Hermeneutical Term *dGongs gzhi* 'Intentional Ground.'" *Journal of Indian Philosophy* 16, 1–4.

1989 *Buddha Nature, Mind and the Problem of Gradualism in a Comparative Perspective: On the Transmission and Reception of Buddhism in India and Tibet* (Jordan Lectures in Comparative Religion 13). London: School of Oriental and African Studies.

2000 *Three Studies in the History of Indian and Tibetan Madhyamaka Philosophy* (Wiener Studien zur Tibetologie und Buddhismuskunde 50). Vienna: Arbeitskreis für tibetische und buddhistische Studien.

Shahidullah, M. 1928

Les chants mystiques de Kāṇha et de Saraha: Les Dohākoṣa (en apabhraṁsa, avec les versions tibétaines) et les Caryā (en vieux-bengali). Paris: Adrien-Maisonneuve.

Slusser, Mary 1998

Nepal Mandala: A Cultural Study of the Kathmandu Valley. 2 vols. Reprint (first published in 1982). Kathmandu: Mandala Book Point.

Smith, E. Gene

1970 "Introduction." *Kongtrul's Encyclopaedia of Indo-Tibetan Culture*, vol. 1, 1–28. Ed. by Lokesh Chandra (Śata-Piṭaka-Series 80). New Delhi: International Academy of Indian Culture.

2001 *Among Tibetan Texts: History and Literature of the Himalayan Plateau.* Boston: Wisdom Publications.

Sorensen, Per K. 1999

"The Prolific Ascetic lCe-sgom Shes rab rdo rje *alias* lCe sgom zhig po: Allusive, but Elusive." *Journal of the Nepal Research Centre* 11, 175–200.

Stearns, Cyrus

1995 "Dol-po-pa Shes-rab rgyal-mtshan and the Genesis of the *Gzhan stong* Position in Tibet." *Asiatische Studien* 49 (4), 829–52.

1999 *The Buddha from Dolpo: A Study of the Life and Thought of the Tibetan Master Dolpopa Sherab Gyaltsen* (SUNY series in Buddhist Studies). Albany, N.Y.: SUNY.

Steinkellner, Ernst

1971 "Wirklichkeit und Begriff bei Dharmakīrti." *Wiener Zeitschrift für die Kunde Südasiens* 15, 179–211.

1977 *Verse-Index of Dharmakīrti's Works (Tibetan Version)* (Wiener Studien zur Tibetologie und Buddhismuskunde 1). Vienna: Arbeitskreis für tibetische und buddhistische Studien.

Suzuki, Teitaro Daisetz

1930 *Studies in the Laṅkāvatāra Sūtra.* London: Routledge and Kegan Paul.

1932 *The Laṅkāvatāra Sūtra: A Mahāyāna Text.* London: Routledge and Kegan Paul.

Takasaki, Jikido 1966

A Study on the Ratnagotravibhāga (Uttaratantra) Being a Treatise on the Tathāgatagarbha Theory of Mahāyāna Buddhism (Rome Oriental Series 33). Rome: Istituto Italiano per il Medio ed Estremo Oriente.

Tatz, Mark

1987 "The Life of the Siddha-Philosopher Maitrīgupta." *Journal of the American Oriental Society*, vol. 107, 695–711.

1994 "Philosophic Systems according to Advayavajra and Vajrapāṇi." *The Journal of Buddhist and Tibetan Studies* 1, 65–120.

Tauscher, Helmut

1995 *Die Lehre von den zwei Wirklichkeiten in Tsong kha pas Madhyamaka-Werken* (Wiener Studien zur Tibetologie und Buddhismuskunde 36).Vienna: Arbeitskreis für tibetische und buddhistische Studien.

1999 *Phya pa Chos kyi seng ge: dBu ma shar gsum gyi stong thun* (Wiener Sudien zur Tibetologie und Buddhismuskunde 43). Vienna: Arbeitskreis für tibetische und buddhistische Studien.

Tillemans, Tom J. F. 2003

"Metaphysics for Mādhyamikas." *The Svātantrika-Prāsaṅgika Distinction*, 93–123. Ed. by George B.J. Dreyfus and Sara L. McClintock. Boston: Wisdom Publications.

Tillemans, Tom J.F. and Tomabechi, Toru 1995

"Le *dbu ma'i byung tshul* de Śākya mchog ldan." *Asiatische Studien* 49 (4), 891–918.

Trungpa, Chögyam 1989

The Rain of Wisdom. Translated by the Nālandā Translation Committee under the direction of Chögyam Trungpa. Boston: Shambala Publications.

Tsultrim Gyamtsho Rinpoche and Fuchs, Rosemarie 2000

Buddha Nature: The Mahayana Uttaratantra Shastra with Commentary. Ithaca, N.Y.: Snow Lion Publications.

Ui, Hakuju 1959

Hōshōron Kenkyū (Daijō Bukkyō Kenkyū 6). Tokyo: Iwanami Shoten.

Wangchuk, Dorji 2004

"The rÑiṅ-ma Interpretations of the Tathāgatagarbha Theory." *Wiener Zeitschrift für die Kunde Südasiens* 48, 171–213.

Wayman, Alex 1992

The Enlightenment of Vairocana. Book I: study of the *Vairocanābhisaṁbodhi-tantra* (Buddhist Tradition Series 18). Delhi: Motilal Banarsidass.

Wayman, Alex and Wayman, Hideko 1974

The Lion's Roar of Queen Śrīmālā. New York: Columbia University.

Wylie, Turrell V. 1957
A Place Name Index to George N. Roerich's Translation of the Blue Annals (Rome Oriental Series 15). Rome: Istituto Italiano per il Medio ed Estremo Oriente.

Yao, Zhihua 2005
The Buddhist Theory of Self-Cognition. London and New York: Routledge.

Zhāng, Yísūn 1985
Bod rgya tshig mdzod chen mo: Záng-Hàn Dàcídian. 3 vols. Published by Zhāng Yísūn. Beijing: Mi rigs dpe skrun khang.

Zimmermann, Michael 2002
A Buddha Within: The Tathāgatagarbhasūtra. The Earliest Exposition of the Buddha-Nature Teaching in India (Bibliotheca Philologica et Philosophica Buddhica 6). Tokyo: The International Institute for Advanced Buddhology.

Subject Index

The numbers in bold indicate that the term in question occupies a central position or is best explained on these pages.

as the selflessness of phenomena, seen on the first level, 332, 400
as a single path, 27
as support of the Dharma, 268
ultimate, 71
as ultimate buddha, 88–89
as uncontaminated seed, 88–89
as unfabricated natural mind, 340, 360, 414, n. 1935
wisdom of, 101, 328, 415

dharmakāya
activity, endowed with, 346
actual/real, 16, 65, 86, 114–15, 118
arisen from (the accumulation of) wisdom, 52, 221, 335, n. 271
of a buddha/tathāgata, 80, 114, 115, 118, 120, 123, 190, 202, 203, 228, 238, 279, 332, 361, 400
buddha nature/dharmadhātu distinguished from, 11, 325, 334, 338, **343–45**, 347, 400, 413, n. 40, n. 1148, n. 1154, n. 1318, n. 1757, n. 1758
buddha nature/dharmadhātu equated with, 8, 10, 11, 16, 52–54, **70–72**, 80, 90, 93, 95, 114, 115, 168, 201, 202, n. 416, n. 616, n. 935, n. 970
as emptiness, 106, 168, 329, 334, 347
as the essence of the ground (*rig pa),* 99, 100, n. 338
five wisdoms, equated with the, 313
four perfections of, 119, 244, **403–5**, 410
free from mental fabrications, 45, 280, 384, n. 338
as the fruit of dissociation, 77, 81, 318
individual, 16–17, 413
knowledge/mind, equated with, 259, 271, 280, 384, 396, n. 1380
of/as luminosity, 40, 55, 117, 242, 250, 280, 384, n. 290
mind based/grounded in, 280, 284, 383
as the nature of qualities, n. 1756
as (the nature of) thoughts, 47, 48, 56, 65, 128, 129, n. 665
not absolutely unconditioned, 336
as perfect nature, 357
pervasive nature of, 29, 82, 93–94, 97, 163, n. 2005
possessing inseparable qualities, 7, 121, 203, n. 1160
purified, stainless, 95, 96
as purity, 179
seed of, 65, 225
as self-arisen, coemergent wisdom, 85, n. 1552
sentient beings not included in the, 48, 60
as stainless suchness, 317, n. 1724
suchness and potential, 89, 163, 395
as support of purification/qualities, 58, 317
svābhāvikakāya, in relation to the, 11, 97, 109, 111, 259, 333, 346–47, n. 574, n. 1791
tantric, 73, 86
ultimate, equated with the, 8, 120, 126, 183, 255, n. 499
ultimate that is really permanent, 56, 91
unborn, 251, n. 1380
unchangeable, 251, 334
unconditioned, 98, 333, 334, 363, n. 512
in view of not appearing to disciples, 47, 56, 73, 87

Dharmakīrti, 160, 271, 272, 274, n. 1231, n. 1744

dharmatā
as the basis of emptiness, 102, 126, 417
buddha nature, equated with, 115, 119, n. 499
containing form kāyas, qualities, 78, 83, 95, 122, 330, 411
as the continuity of stainless mind, 337ff., 364–65, 417
endowed with both purities, 84
etymology of, 268–69
indivisible, 398
as luminosity, 101, 116–19, 121, 411
meditation on, 117, n. 1400
of the mind, 94, 95, 102, 126, 255

Indian Text Index

When a sūtra or śāstra is quoted, the page number in the index is followed by the stanza numbers or, in case of a prose text, the page and line numbers of this passage in parentheses. As for the content of these parentheses, a combination of a roman and arabic number stands for a stanza of a chapter. "X.3" thus means "stanza no. 3 of chapter no. 10." In case a stanza is quoted from a text without chapter divisions, a simple arabic number is preceded by the word stanza. A passage from a prose text is described by two arabic numbers indicating page and line numbers. "10.3" thus means "page no. 10, line no. 3" of the edition listed in the bibliography. When the Tibetan translation from the Peking Kangyur and Tengyur is referred to, this is indicated by the words Kangyur or Tengyur, followed by the folio number, the letters a or b, which stand for "front" or "back," and the line number.

About Wisdom

Wisdom Publications, a nonprofit publisher, is dedicated to making available authentic works relating to Buddhism for the benefit of all. We publish books by ancient and modern masters in all traditions of Buddhism, translations of important texts, and original scholarship. Additionally, we offer books that explore East-West themes unfolding as traditional Buddhism encounters our modern culture in all its aspects. Our titles are published with the appreciation of Buddhism as a living philosophy, and with the special commitment to preserve and transmit important works from Buddhism's many traditions.

To learn more about Wisdom, or to browse books online, visit our website at www.wisdompubs.org.

You may request a copy of our catalog online or by writing to this address:

Wisdom Publications
199 Elm Street
Somerville, Massachusetts 02144 USA
Telephone: 617-776-7416 • Fax: 617-776-7841
Email: info@wisdompubs.org • www.wisdompubs.org

The Wisdom Trust

As a nonprofit publisher, Wisdom is dedicated to the publication of Dharma books for the benefit of all sentient beings and dependent upon the kindness and generosity of sponsors in order to do so. If you would like to make a donation to Wisdom, you may do so through our website or our Somerville office. If you would like to help sponsor the publication of a book, please write or email us at the address above.

Thank you.

Wisdom is a nonprofit, charitable 501(c)(3) organization affiliated with the Foundation for the Preservation of the Mahayana Tradition (FPMT).

Wisdom's Studies in Indian and Tibetan Buddhism series

Freedom from Extremes
Gorampa's "Distinguishing the Views" and the Polemics of Emptiness
José Ignacio Cabezón and Geshe Lobsang Dargyay
448 pages, paper, ISBN 0-86171-523-3, $32.95

Foundations of Dharmakirti's Philosophy
John D. Dunne
496 pages, paper, ISBN 0-86171-184-X, $39.95

The Svatantrika-Prasangika Distinction
What Difference Does a Difference Make?
Edited by Georges Dreyfus and Sara McClintock
416 pages, paper, ISBN 0-86171-324-9, $34.95

Vajrayogini
Her Visualizations, Rituals, and Forms
Elizabeth English
608 pages, paper, ISBN 0-86171-329-X, $34.95

Reason's Traces
Identity and Interpretation in Indian and Tibetan Buddhist Thought
Matthew T. Kapstein
496 pages, paper, ISBN 0-86171-239-0, $34.95

Mipham's Beacon of Certainty
Illuminating the View of Dzogchen, the Great Perfection
John Whitney Pettit
592 pages, paper, ISBN 0-86171-157-2, $28.95

Among Tibetan Texts
History and Literature of the Himalayan Plateau
E. Gene Smith
384 pages, cloth, ISBN 0-86171-179-3, $39.95

Luminous Lives
The Story of the Early Masters of the Lam 'bras in Tibet
Cyrus Stearns
320 pages, paper, ISBN 0-86171-307-9, $34.95

Scripture, Logic, Language
Essays on Dharmakirti and His Tibetan Successors
Tom J.F. Tillemans
320 pages, paper, ISBN 0-86171-156-4, $32.95

Approaching the Great Perfection
Simultaneous and Gradual Methods of Dzogchen Practice in the Longchen Nyingtig
Sam van Schaik
448 pages, paper, ISBN 0-86171-370-2, $29.95